Upholsterers and Interior Furnishing in England

1530–1840

Upholsterers and Interior Furnishing in England 1530–1840

Geoffrey Beard

CINOA PRIZE 1996

PUBLISHED FOR
THE BARD GRADUATE CENTER FOR STUDIES IN THE DECORATIVE ARTS
BY
YALE UNIVERSITY PRESS NEW HAVEN AND LONDON
1997

Designed by Kate Gallimore
Typeset in Bembo by Best-Set Typesetter Ltd, Hong Kong
Printed in Hong Kong

Library of Congress Cataloging-in-Publication Data
Beard, Geoffrey W.
Upholsterers and interior furnishing in England: 1530–1840 / Geoffrey Beard
p. cm. – (Bard studies in the decorative arts) Includes bibliographical references and index.
ISBN 0-300-07135-3
1. Upholstery-England-History. I. Title. II. Series.
NK3243.B43 1997
749.9 5 0942–dc21   96–39874 CIP

Title page illustration: Hendrick van Steenwijk and others, Charles I as Prince of Wales (detail) *c.* 1620. *Copenhagen, Statens Museum for Kunst.* (See Pl. 26).

Illustration on page vi: Part of a long cushion cover (detail) *c.* 1625. *London, Victoria and Albert Museum.* (See Pl. 33).

Illustration on page x: Tester cloth from the Melville state bed *c.* 1698. *London, Victoria and Albert Museum.* (See Pl. 96).

Endpapers: Silk, damask weave, nineteenth century with an eighteenth century pattern. Selvage width 22 in (56 cm); repeat of 64 in (162.5 cm). *Virginia, Colonial Williamsburg Foundation.*

CINOA
Confédération Internationale des Négociants en Œuvres d'Art
International Confederation of Art and Antiques Dealers
Prix CINOA Prize
This book has received the 1996 international award above.

Previous prize winners were:

1977 Penelope Eames (UK), Furniture in France and England from the 12th to the 15th Century
1978 Claire Lindgren (USA), Classical Art Forms and Celtic Mutations
1979 Bertrand Jaeger (Switzerland), Essai de Classification et Datation des Scarabées Menkhéperre
1980 Norman Bryson (UK), Paintings as signs: Word and Image in French Painting of the Ancien Régime
1982 Marianne Roland-Michel (France), Jacques de Lajoue et l'Art Rocaille
1983 Edson Armi (USA), Masons and Sculptors in Romanesque Burgundy
1984 Nicola Gordon Bowe (Ireland), The Life and Work of Harry Clarke
1985 Johannes R. Ter Molen (Netherlands), Van Vianen, een Utrechtse Familie van Silversmeden
1986 Jörg Martin Merz (Germany), Pietro de Cortonas Entwicklung zum Maler des römischen Hochbarock
1987 Roland Dorn (Germany), Vincent van Goghs Werkreihe für das Gelbe Haus in Arles
1988 Marcelle Baby-Pabion (France), Ludovic Bréa et la Peinture Primitive Niçoise
1989 Walter Liedtke (USA), Royal Horse and Rider
1990 Ulrich Leben (Germany), Bernard Molitor, Ebeniste, 1755–1833
1991 Thomas Crispin (UK), The Windsor Chair
1992 Lucy Wood (UK), The Lady Lever Art Gallery, Catalogue of Commodes
1994 Anne Crookshank and Desmond Fitzgerald (Ireland), The Watercolours of Ireland
1995 Alvar Gonzales Palacios (Italy), II gusto dei Principi

CINOA's Member Associations:

A   Bundesgremium des Handels mit Juwelen, alter & moderner Kunst, Antiquitäten, Briefmarken und Numismatika
AUS   Australian Antique Dealers' Association
B   Chambre Royale des Antiquaires de Belgique
CH   Association des Commerçants d'Art de la Suisse, Zürich
       Verband schweizerischer Antiquare und Kunsthandler, Bern
CZ   Asociace Starozitniku
D   Bundesverband des deutschen Kunst- und Antiquitätenhandels
DK   Dansk Antikvitetshandler Union
E   Asociación de Profesionales en Arte Antiguo y Moderno
F   Chambre Syndicale de l'Estampe, du Dessin et du Tableau
       Syndicat National des Antiquaires, Negociants en Œuvres d'Art, Tableaux Anciens et Modernes
GB   British Antique Dealers' Association
       London and Provincial Art & Antique Dealers' Association
       Society of London Art Dealers
I   Associazione Antiquari d'Italia
IRL   Irish Antique Dealers' Association
NL   Vereeniging van Handelaren in Oude Kunst in Nederland
NZ   New Zealand Antique Dealers' Association
P   Associacao Portuguesa Antiquarios
S   Sveriges Konst- och Antikhandlareförening
USA   Art and Antique Dealers' League of America
       National Art and Antique Dealers' Association of America
       Private Art Dealers' Association, New York
ZA   South African Antique Dealers' Association

For John and Suzy Lewis
and in Memory of L. and R.J. Lewis

CONTENTS

ACKNOWLEDGMENTS

In the writing of this book I have been assisted by many people; by the owners of houses, by librarians, archivists, museum and art gallery staff, by many friends and several former colleagues and students. I am deeply indebted to them, fearing that a general expression of thanks is, at best, inadequate for all their kindnesses. At the same time several friends have rendered especial help over a long period and should be mentioned individually. John Lewis helped with the heavy costs of research and illustration fees. I am also grateful for assistance in this respect to the President and Committee of CINOA (Confédération Internationale des Negociants en Œuvres d'Art), who awarded the book its first prize for 1996; to The Pasold Research Fund and to Humphrey Whitbread. On my frequent visits to London Helena Hayward was an unfailing mentor and generous hostess. She had read the text of this book but died while it was in production. Annabel Westman gave expert advice on historic textiles, and also accompanied me on several research trips.

I have been able to benefit on many occasions from the special knowledge of, or help from: Dr Brian Allen; Janet Arnold; Dr Brian Austen; Bruce Bailey; Robert Bearman (Senior Archivist, The Shakespeare Birthplace Trust) and a team who volunteered to search archives for me; Peter Brown; the late Dr Lindsay Boynton; Sybil Bruel; Charles Cator; John Chesshyre; Frannie Colburn; John Cornforth; Sebastian Edwards; Christopher Gilbert; Sir Nicholas Goodison; John Hardy; Dr Negley Harte; Wendy Hefford; Kathy Hiesinger; John Houston; Gareth Hughes; the late Gervase Jackson-Stops; Susan Jenkins; Joe and Carol Keenan; Michael and Polly Legg; The Hon. Christopher Lennox-Boyd; Florence Montgomery; Henry Neville; Sarah Nichols; Mindy Papp; Bill Rieder; Hugh Roberts; The Hon. Mrs Jane Roberts; Dr John Martin Robinson; Guy Shaw; Sheila Stainton; Dr Simon Thurley; Karin-M. Walton; Robin Harcourt Williams; and Lucy Wood. Peter Thornton, a friend of thirty-five years and an outstanding authority on upholstery, was especially helpful over a long period.

Several more friends at three major collections eased my task. Firstly, Christopher Wilk and his colleagues in the Department of Furniture and Woodwork, Victoria and Albert Museum (Frances Collard, Nicholas Humphrey, Sarah Medlam, Dr Tessa Murdoch, Carolyn Sargentson and James Yorke). In particular Carolyn Sargentson guided my researches in Paris at the Archives Nationales. Secondly, Brock Jobe, Donald Fennimore, Deborah Kraak and Neville Thompson at the Henry Francis Du Pont Museum, Winterthur, and thirdly, Graham Hood, Linda Baumgarten, Wallace and Liza Gusler, Ron Hurst, John and Margaret Pritchard, Jonathan Prown and Laurie Suber at the Department of Collections, Colonial Williamsburg. The use I have made of their generously imparted information is, of course, my responsibility.

A number of other colleagues and friends were invaluable to me in the long quest for suitable illustrations. I am grateful to: Jenny Band; Gwyneth Campling; Dr David Connell; Camilla Costello; Valerie Davies; Martin Drury; Martin Durrant; Maggie Grieve; John Hardy; Jonathan Harris; Peter Holmes; Graham Hood; Angelo Hornak; Christopher Hutchinson; Gordon Kelsey; Anthony Kersting; Edward Lennox-Boyd; Gayle Mault; Lucy Morton; Clare Murphy; James Montrose Sansum; Francesca Scoones; Ken Shelton; Isobel Sinden; Laurie Suber, and Annabel Wylie.

My text was transferred to a word processor with skill and intelligence by Maureen and Reg Barton. What had escaped me did not escape their caring oversight. My wife, Margaret, daughter Helen and son-in-law Mark, busy as they were with two young grandchildren who knew nothing of upholsterers and their work, endured my preoccupied presence and frequent absence with cheerful understanding, backed with much practical help.

Finally, for the care they have shown to this title I am much indebted to two friends: John Nicoll of Yale University Press and Susan Weber Soros, Director of The Bard Graduate Center for Studies in the Decorative Arts in New York. John steered the volume expertly through all its many stages of production and the title is the first in the Bard Center's exciting series of books on the decorative arts. The effective design is by Kate Gallimore who also acted as editor.

Geoffrey Beard
Bath
September 1996

PREFACE

In this prefatory note I want to explain the scheme of the book and the reasons for undertaking this volume. Following a short introduction the text is divided into seven chapters, spanning the years 1530 to 1840. For the most part, these take the unfashionable route of following (1530 and 1840 apart) the dates of the reigning monarchs. This is done deliberately, to give a necessary framework to the lives of the upholsterers, for whom crown and court were very important sources of patronage. I have also thought it necessary to set the activities of upholsterers against the wider panoply of English history, as it affected important stages in life and death. It is, for example, sensible to be reminded that when the Catholic upholsterer, Ralph Grynder, was working in the late 1630s for Queen Henrietta Maria (Appendix A15) England was on the threshold of Civil War and the queen was soon to be exiled and, moreover, widowed.

I have tried to unearth new biographical information, but some problems remain unresolved. Nevertheless, the facts are gathered together to help future appraisal. As for starting the narrative in 1530 I have no reason other than it being a convenient date in the maturing, scheming life of Henry VIII, who was ready to go forward, at Cardinal Wolsey's downfall, in the decoration and furnishing of Hampton Court and Nonsuch Palace.

I have concluded the book in 1840, just a few years into Queen Victoria's reign. Upholstery over the subsequent hundred years or so, mainly factory produced, is a separate subject, to which I (or a younger historian) must return. In any case it has been given authoritative treatment in Edwards (1993) and by Grier (1988); the last was a most comprehensive study to 1930, attracting several awards, and it would have been difficult, if I were concerned solely with techniques, to do other than quote it ceaselessly.

Authors have, I am sure, an obligation to explain why they have written their books at all. Only novels, contrived from the imagination, may be allowed the indulgence of requiring no such explanation. For over forty years, from about 1951, I have researched and then published details of craftsmen of various professions – from my *Georgian Craftsmen and their Work* (1966), to those concerned with plasterwork (1975), modern glass (1976), many forms of interior design (1981), stuccoists in Europe (1982) and furniture makers, edited (with Christopher Gilbert) in 1986. Upholsterers merited attention due to my long interest in furniture makers and because 'detective-work' about their activity (particularly prior to 1660) was in primary sources all too little known.

This had the same heady fascination as that which had preoccupied me over all the previous years, making much use of the palaeography which had been taught to me by the late Harry Sargeant, first County Archivist of Worcestershire. It is a subject too which allows me, here, to draw attention to the pioneering displays and researches which Peter Thornton and his then colleagues at the Department of Furniture and Woodwork in the Victoria and Albert Museum in London, undertook in the 1970s, particularly at Ham House and Osterley Park. Like much that was innovative it was misunderstood and criticized but with the hindsight of time undoubtedly changed perceptions of furniture and the upholstered room. Mr Thornton followed this with his seminal study of seventeenth-century interior design (Thornton, 1978); in addition there was an important conference on upholstery at the Museum of Fine Arts, Boston, the papers of which were published (Cooke, ed. 1987), as were those of the seminar on upholstery conservation at Colonial Williamsburg (Williams et al., 1990).

Apart from the notes to the text (the short titles and abbreviations used therein are expanded fully in a separate list) and my captions to the plates I have felt it useful to provide a selection of extracts from some contemporary documentation (Appendix A). One of the valued features of the excellent studies of Thomas Chippendale (Gilbert, 1978) and of William and John Linnell (Hayward and Kirkham, 1980) was their printing of many documents. Concerned with over 300 years I have had to be more selective, but its chronological arrangement will enable this section, I hope, to have use independent of the main text, although cross-references to it are given there. I have also enjoyed the compilation of an adequate glossary.

Any study of upholstery needs a great number of illustrations, for the most part reproduced in colour. My list of acknowledgments records the indebtedness I have to those who helped provide them. It is a tribute to what survives in England, of so fugitive a subject, that many pieces still retain their original coverings. Finally, I offer to captious critics, one reminder, made memorable by Dr Johnson: 'In this work, when it shall be found that much is omitted, let it not be forgotten that much likewise is performed.'

INTRODUCTION

The trade of upholsterer, much confused before the eighteenth century with that of 'upholder', or a dealer in small wares and secondhand clothing,[1] may be traced back to the late thirteenth century. However, the details of these early manifestations are of little use in establishing what was done. Much was made by coffer-makers but, despite the similarities in technique (padding, shaping and embellishing) I have found no evidence for upholstered work being done by saddlers. They merely occupy adjacent pages in royal accounts. Upholstery, by its fragile nature, has not survived to any degree before the early seventeenth century and even well-fashioned furniture of the high years of eighteenth-century achievement may possibly have its third cover after the original in place. The quest for status and comfort which was early in evidence and pursued earnestly from the middle of the sixteenth century onwards, shows a concern with very rich trappings. The archival evidence (Appendix A) is abundant and suggests interiors more brightly coloured and coordinated from an earlier date than might be expected.

Some of this early upholstery was done on the instructions of the important agency controlling work for the crown, the Great Wardrobe. Studies exist of the Wardrobe's early history,[2] and there is an exemplary examination of the contribution the Wardrobe of Robes played in the commissioning and care of Elizabeth I's clothing and jewels.[3] Some use has been made of the extensive records which survive[4] to chart the role of the upholsterer in supplying royal furnishings, and servicing coronations and funerals, but a greater emphasis is made in this present study.

The seventeenth century divided, neatly enough, into two through the ravages of the Civil War in the 1650s. Prior to the restoration of Charles II in 1660 the upholsterer's work had been grounded in the long and archaic traditions of the London craft guilds. The king's return to England in 1660 saw a need for extensive refurbishing of royal palaces and a growth in the presence here of foreign craftsmen, particularly from France and Holland. I have examined this activity in some detail, through the principal achievements at this time of the upholsterer and his team – state beds and furniture *en suite* – which are of surpassing brilliance and quality. Furthermore, it is suggested that the presence of Protestant monarchs, William III and Queen Mary, did not necessarily imply that all craftsmen needed to follow that religious faith to secure employment. Whilst the much heralded migration of Protestant craftsmen throughout Europe, following the Revocation of the Edict of Nantes (1685), brought many to England,[5] it was their talent which was paramount. The French *tapissier*, Francis Lapiere (1653–1714),[6] followed the Catholic faith, and yet worked in England from about 1683 to his death for Protestant and Catholic patrons alike. A careful examination of the careers of these French craftsmen has also shown, for the first time, the relationship of Jean Poictevin, upholsterer to Charles II, James II, William III and even Queen Anne, to Etienne [Stephen] Penson, whom I have credited with the design of the important state bed (*c.*1702) at Drayton House, Northamptonshire (Pls 115–20). Nevertheless, and unlike members of the Goldsmiths' Company, who were worried constantly by the presence in England of talented foreigners,[7] much work in the late seventeenth century and early years of the eighteenth was done, essentially,

1   The early origins, dictionary definitions etc. are cited by Walton (1973) and Houston (1993).
2   Tout (1920–33).
3   Arnold (1988).
4   Public Record Office (hereafter PRO), AO3 (Exchequer and Audit Accounts); LC5/LC9, Lord Chamberlain's Department, Bill Books.
5   Murdoch (1985).
6   Beard and Westman (1993).
7   J. F. Hayward (1969) p.15.

by English artificers. Yet the achievements of, say, Richard Bealing, Thomas How, Thomas Phill and his partner Jeremiah Fletcher are largely unknown. Their names and a rudimentary outline of their activities have been noted[8] but a fuller befitting treatment is given to them here.

The admiration accorded to much English upholstered furniture is owed, in the main, to the variety of its coverings. In the late seventeenth century in particular there was an extensive use of materials such as silk and velvet, obtained from France and Italy, although commendable imitations soon followed from English looms in Spitalfields and elsewhere. The beginning of the eighteenth century was marked by a sudden rise in the popularity of needleworked upholstery. This coincided with a growing use of the winged easy chair which offered ideal surfaces for covering with biblical or mythological scenes in finely executed needlework. The most durable material for this was wool needlework on canvas. It was fixed to the frame by gilded nails, or, in the case of chairs or settees with movable seats, to the seat itself. Many of the needlework designs can be traced to John Ogilby's *Virgil* (1658), which remained popular for at least a hundred years; some simply followed the pattern of Italian damasks. One partnership which seems to have exploited this was that of William Bradshaw and the painter–designer Tobias Stranover who were part of a small group based around the Soho premises of the Great Wardrobe. Their famous signed suite of *c*.1730 (Pls 176–7) came to light again, after its 'disappearance' in 1929, as a result of the researches made for this book.

The output of several important firms was predominantly in the rococo style from around 1740, their techniques changing from the early 1760s to adopt neoclassicism. There was also the frequent informed intervention from architects of the calibre of Robert Adam (1728–92) or Sir William Chambers (1726–96). In 1773 Chambers reproached his patron, Lord Melbourne, for failing to consult him over the furnishings for Melbourne House in Piccadilly, which were to be provided by Chippendale. He disapproved, among other things, of the method of fitting-up Lady Melbourne's dressing-room and the number of chairs for the great room. Craftsmen obviously had to please both patrons and architects to survive, and could ill afford to be acrimonious, even when payment for work was more than usually tardy. Sir Rowland Winn, displeased, told Chippendale on 17 September 1767[9] that he would 'take care to Acquaint those Gentlemen that I have recommended you to & desire that they will oblige me in employing some other person . . .'.

As the eighteenth century progressed, the involvement of the architect and the ability of craftsmen to provide drawings increased, and pattern books were published freely. Thomas Chippendale also provided small finished coloured sketches for his clients and John Linnell's many drawings (Pls 225, 236–8) display an enviable talent. The late years of the eighteenth century saw the publication of books of designs by George Hepplewhite (1788) and Thomas Sheraton (1791–4). Later, in 1803, Sheraton set out to explain in his *The Cabinet Dictionary* '. . . all the Terms used in the Cabinet, Chair and upholstery Branches . . .'. It has been quoted freely, in the glossary.

At the end of the eighteenth century the Prince of Wales – he became Prince Regent in 1811 and King George IV in 1820 – started extensive works at Carlton House and, a little later, at the Brighton Pavilion. The scholar–architect Thomas Hope was busy in 1807 issuing his book of designs, *Household Furniture and Decoration*, which reflected both his wide travels – in Egypt, Turkey, Syria and Greece – and his extensive collections.

One of the visitors to Thomas Hope's London house may have been the fashionable cabinet-maker and upholsterer, George Smith. With premises off Cavendish Square, Smith described himself as 'Upholder Extraordinary to His Royal Highness the Prince of Wales'. In 1808 he endeavoured to join the ranks of the successful compilers of pattern books and volumes of designs by issuing *A Collection of Designs for Household Furniture and Interior Decoration*. The knowledge of the Egyptian style shown in this collection is less exact than Hope's, and Smith relied heavily on a French publication, Baron Dominique-Vivant Denon's *Voyage dans la Basse et Haute Egypte*. Denon had accompanied Napoleon Bonaparte on his Egyptian campaign at the end of the eighteenth century, and in 1801 he introduced Egyptian motifs into the furniture in the private apartments Napoleon occupied at the Tuileries. In England, Thomas Chippendale junior supplied 'Egyptian' furniture to

8 Beard and Gilbert (1986).   9 Gilbert (1978) I, p.168.

Stourhead in 1804 and Sheraton depicted Egyptian motifs in his *Cabinet Encyclopedia* (1804–6). Smith's plates in *Household Furniture* are dated 1804 to 1807. While Hope's book is mainly concerned with formal settings, Smith's was more practical and suggested articles suitable for the whole of a domestic household. It also had a wider range of styles, showing Gothic designs and designs in the Chinese and French tastes; it showed a weakness for animal forms, console supports, divided columns with lotus-leaf ornament and bold classical adornments.

In 1826 George Smith issued a second volume, *The Cabinet-Maker and Upholsterer's Guide*. The text was 'flamboyant, captious and critical and unctuously self-satisfied'.[10] He started by explaining that he had devoted forty years to the study of furniture, and that his previous book (1808) had become 'wholly obsolete and inapplicable'. He saw the position as desperate – the Egyptian style was now 'anathematized as barbarous' and the 'necessity of economy' was, he thought, but one explanation for the morass into which design had fallen. The survival of the archaeologically based styles had only lingered because of the rare talents possessed by such designers as Thomas Hope.

Changes came, at odds with the moralizing tendencies of the age, and all was overlaid by the ornamental excesses of Gothic, Louis quatorze or one of the fashionable revivals. For all of it there was a suitable upholstered form, capable of keeping the back morally upright or of sensuously enfolding its occupier into near-oblivion.

10   Edwards (1937) p.272.

I

The Arte or Misterie of Upholders

MASTERS AND APPRENTICES

There is an immediate difficulty in recording the early history of the upholstery trade. The Worshipful Company of Upholders did not always represent the trade we now know as upholstery, and on two occasions most of its archives have been destroyed. The ravaging spread of the Great Fire of London in 1666 gutted the company's hall, Wingfield House, near Lambeth Hill, and its boxes of records. Then another fire on 4 July 1812 at the premises of two of the company's important liverymen, Francis Say and his partner, Quentin Kay, also consumed a 'Box of Trophies and chest of writings' belonging to the company.[1] Six volumes only have survived, namely Court Minute and Wardens' Account Books, 1678–1825, lists of presentments of apprentices, 1704–72, and Freedom Admissions, 1698–1747. A list of the Admissions 1698–1803 was published[2] in 1973.

There are often good reasons for listing the names of medieval craftsmen – John Harvey's seminal work on architects and masons down to 1550[3] is an excellent example. Soaring lierne vaults and chiselled buttresses can often be credited to a particular hand. With upholders it is much less useful to do this as the work never survives and can only be visualized at all through archival references. Furthermore, the early and confusing use of the title of 'upholder' implied, usually, a dealer in small wares and second-hand clothing, rather than the work known as 'upholstery'. For my purposes I shall use the term 'upholsterer' throughout, even when the term 'upholder' is used, as it is in the title The Worshipful Company of Upholders of the City of London. As for the phrase incorporating 'misterie', this is taken from the Latin word 'misterium' and implied an occupation or trade with secrecy attached.

What the company did on behalf of the trade or misterie was to act as a regulatory body, if at times imperfectly, over master craftsmen, freemen and liverymen who imparted their skills to a regulated number of apprentices. The company had campaigned in 1585 to be granted a royal charter,[4] but this was not obtained until 1626 in the reign of Charles I. It was confirmed by Charles II in an Inspeximus Charter of 1668,[5] which set out the hierarchy of people common to most livery companies, of a master, two wardens, twelve (or more) assistants who served the master and his wardens, a clerk and the many upholsterers who were admitted as 'freemen'. Many of these were invited subsequently to adopt the company's livery.

From the time of the royal confirmation of the company's constitution it was not:

> lawful to any pson or psons to sett up use or excise the arte or mistery aforesaid, or to worke or make any of the workes or workings in any wise touching or concning the said Arte or mistery unless he or they bee first brought upp in the same Arte as an Apprentice or Apprentices by the space of seaven yeares att the least . . .

1   Houston (1993) p.2.
2   Walton (1973) pp.51–79.
3   Harvey (1984).

4   Unwin (1902) pp.296–7.
5   Houston, pp.16–31 (text of the Charter of 1668).

The London company served only one trade but the company in Newcastle upon Tyne, incorporated on 22 July 1675, was titled 'The Incorporated Company of Upholsterers, Tinplate-Workers and Stationers'.[6] The initial membership was of six upholsterers, three tinplate-workers and two stationers.

The English guilds had been active since the fourteenth century with the goldsmiths, for example, obtaining a charter from Edward III in 1327. Guilds worked on the basic principle of establishing a monopoly within a craft, with firm powers over admittance, regulation and supervision, leading, hopefully, to its economic advancement. If work could be produced within a district or town and sold at a fair price to the local townspeople as well as to foreign consumers, all was well.[7] If competition intervened to take trade away it was usually held to be a cause for appeal, to the crown, parliament, city officials or to anyone who would listen.

As early as 1363, in the reign of Edward III, it had been enacted by parliament that 'no English merchant shall use no ware or merchandise . . . but only one which he shall choose betwixt this and the feast of Candlemas next coming'; and more importantly, for consideration here, 'artificers, handicraft people, hold them every one to one mystery . . . and two of every craft shall be chosen to survey that none use other craft than the same which he has chosen'.[8] Nevertheless, Edward III encouraged the settlement of Flemish weavers in England.

By the opening of the sixteenth century London had become an important centre for furniture making. Over 400 Continental carvers, stool-makers, joiners, upholsterers and men of allied trades recognized this and had set up, mostly at Southwark, from about 1510, alongside the English artisans. They came from Flanders, Brabant, Holland and Germany and were one of the means whereby late Renaissance motifs were grafted slowly into English patterns.[9] The early settlement of weavers in London continued and in 1547 the Privy Council arranged for Bretons skilled in weaving to be brought into England. Whilst the London Weavers' Company regulated in 1551 the pay of journeymen silk-weavers, a steady stream of 'foreigners' was admitted to the Company.[10] Indeed, the Acts of the Weavers' Company from 1547 to 1553 show thirty were so admitted.[11] Perhaps with difficulties arising from similar admissions in mind it was confirmed on three occasions, during the reign of Henry VIII, that a foreign-born craftsman could only employ native-born Englishmen as apprentices – a statute that had been first enacted in 1483.[12] The presence of foreigners, as noted, did see some fresh ideas entering English practice and this was helped by the availability of many Continental engravings of decoration.

The English apprenticeship system, revised and up-dated by the Statute of Artificers of 1563, allowed masters to take apprentices for varying periods of instruction.[13] Usually this was for seven years but could vary upwards. The principal history of apprenticeship, by Dunlop and Denman, published in 1912,[14] told a story which, while in essence true, has now been varied in its detail by modern research.[15] They had concentrated in 1912 on the straightforward elements – the term of the contract between master and apprentice for a fixed number of years, normally seven, with the master subject to the oversight of an urban guild. Further, the apprentice was held to be under 'the authority of the master who stood to him *in loco parentis*'. Apprenticeship was, it was felt, 'a type of family relationship rather than labour relationship, and the apprentice was viewed as a child, rather than a trainee, an assistant in a shop, or a skilled worker'. There was stress on the obligations of obedience to the master, avoiding drinking and refraining from marrying.

This description of a young naïve apprentice does not accord with the maturity and skills many apprentices acquired during their years of training in the larger towns. In mid-sixteenth-century London the mean length of term served in various companies varied between 7.4 and 7.9 years. In a sample of 1,945 Bristol apprenticeships in the first half of the seventeenth century, the mean length was 7.9 years; more than half the

6 Tyne and Wear Archives Service, MS., GU/UP/1/2.
7 Kahl (1960) p.13.
8 Kramer (1927) p.1.
9 Forman (1971) pp.94–120.
10 Pettegree (1986) p.96.
11 Consitt (1933) pp.234–85.
12 *The Statutes of the Realm* (1817) pp.735–6.
13 Derry (1931–2) pp.67–87.
14 Dunlop and Denman (1912).
15 Ben-Amos (1994); Mitchell (1995).

Bristol apprenticeships were for terms varying between eight, nine and more years.[16] Nevertheless, there were many who were quite able to conduct a business in their master's absence after having served only part of their allotted time. Manufacture was becoming more organized and a greater focus on improved techniques of selling meant that capital was acquired and retained at slightly better levels. Innovation and transfer of skill were necessary adjuncts of these essential aspects of the master-apprentice relationship.

Guild regulation within the furniture-making trades was thought by some to be responsible for its slow growth. In 1668 Sir Josiah Child had attacked the whole system because he felt there was obstruction to trade with the reductions it caused in the supply of skilled men. The London companies, mistakenly in his opinion, tried to limit the number of apprentices in the service of a master.[17]

There was always a hope, on the company's part at least, that on penalty of fines (although gathered inadequately), a master would pass on his skills as they had been earlier passed to him. Thomas Spratt referred[18] to this in 1667 in over-gloomy terms: 'The *Tradesmen* themselves, having had their hands directed from their youth in the same *Methods of working*, cannot when they pleas to easily alter their custom and turn themselves into new Rodes of Practice.'

There is, nevertheless, adequate evidence that many masters were innovative beyond the numbing effects of instruction by rote. The ability to draw was always a useful skill although the ways of imparting it in England are obscure, with few 'drawing masters'. Nevertheless to set out a staircase required considerable knowledge of geometry on the part of a joiner. It might be noted that the tombstone of the joiner, John Etty, at All Saints Church, York records that he had 'acquired great knowledge of Mathematics, especially Geometry and Architecture in all its parts far beyond any of his Contemporaries in this City'. A similar need for such knowledge was necessary in most trades but with a slightly older age of entry to an apprenticeship, sixteen to eighteen years or older rather that fourteen years, this was accomplished more effectively.[19]

For a master to be unreceptive to the transference of skills led to the stagnation of his business. The possibility of financial loss always loomed and even, in extreme cases, bankruptcy: an ability to profit from new ideas introduced from whatever source, or to seek out variations to old ones was of vital importance in a changing trade scene. There are many significant entrepreneurial examples, for instance the rapid adaptation in the early 1760s of furniture makers such as the partners William Vile and John Cobb, or Thomas Chippendale, turning from mahogany furniture carved richly in the rococo style to the fine, precise marquetry patterns well suited to the new moods of classicism. It was necessary both in terms of these new feelings and of business survival to sell what was fashionable and they did not fail in seizing their opportunities.

Having sought out a suitable master, the parents of an intending apprentice paid a premium to him and were given an indenture setting out the conditions of training. The premium varied widely in amount but was higher if the business included both upholstery and cabinet-making. William Vile and John Cobb charged £60 and £63 of apprentices in 1752 and 1753 respectively. Their apprentice, William France, who set up as an upholsterer, charged as much as £70 on three occasions. It has been shown[20] that the London rates were ahead of those in the provinces, which averaged £30 to £50 in the years from 1711 to 1808.

The taking of apprentices may have restricted the ability of businesses to grow but, equally, the rigid ordinances acted as some protection against casual instruction. In other words, a master having one apprentice bound to him could not, usually, take another until two years of the first apprentice's term had expired. A third apprentice could not be indentured until the term of the first apprentice was within one year of expiration. Some guilds allowed a variation to this in that their master could take three apprentices, the wardens two and ordinary members one. In Bristol, out of 604 masters active in the early years of the seventeenth century fifty-one took four or more apprentices in a seven year span and 123 took three or more apprentices each.[21] Two masters, as partners, were accounted as one person during the time of their co-partnership. Only in the case of an apprentice dying during his period of training was it lawful for his master to take another in his place.

---

16   Ben-Amos (1994) pp.85, 93.
17   Child (1668) p.12.
18   Spratt (1667) pp.391–2.

19   Ben-Amos (1994) p.92; Mitchell (1995) p.19.
20   Kirkham (1988) p.170.
21   Ben-Amos (1991) p.168.

Contravention of the rules on the number of apprentices incurred a £10 fine and some crude oversight was provided by the yearly 'search' undertaken by the master and wardens. There was a rule about employing 'any fforreigner either Alien or English' – although I have noted exceptions to this above. English 'foreigners' were those from places other than London. They were supposed to be presented to the master and wardens of the company serving their trade within three months of the start of their service.

Most apprentices in the larger towns came from smaller towns and from rural areas. In London in the mid-sixteenth century 90 per cent of the apprentice population was migrant. Even by the late seventeenth century in London they still comprised 'about half of all the youths apprenticed in the towns'. They did not always complete their training.[22]

In the early eighteenth century the number of London apprentices increased, still with local areas paramount in providing the apprentices. From 1730 to 1739 73 per cent of the apprentices indentured at the Grocers' and Goldsmiths' Company Halls were from London. In the years, 1712 to 1745, London apprentice upholsterers, totalling in number fifty-four, produced twenty-seven with an unrecorded address, ten from London and seventeen from outside the city.[23] For those who left to take up a new life in the American colonies it was a London training they claimed, whatever the truth. They did so against a gradual loss of guild control over the London handicraft and retail trades.[24]

It can be seen that apprenticeship was a system with the main purpose of providing steady competence in a trade. It is obvious that some skills[25] were more difficult to acquire than others and that the time taken for an apprentice to be useful in them was likely to vary. If one was observant and diligent progress usually followed. But those with a rarer level of application had an advantage. It has been emphasised[26] that 'differences in individual talents and abilities must have enabled some youths to proceed with greater speed than others . . . the initiative and perhaps even ambition of individual apprentices could have an effect on the length of their training'. Given this, allied to an innate ability, allowed some in the furniture trades such as Thomas Chippendale to attain a very significant advantage over their contemporaries.

The company's rule was meant to be paramount in the closing stages of training, but there was a widespread ignoring of submitting samples of work for examination by the company's officers. It was held that apprentices well trained had proficiency in such things. They did, of course, arrange for the apprentice to be called; if no one objected to the election, the apprentice was sworn in as a freeman of his guild, before the mayor at the borough court in the case of apprentices in the city of Durham.[27]

Any searcher of livery company records soon encounters the details and the difficulties of the methods of entry to the freedom. Writing in 1695 in his *A New Method of Educating Children*, T. Tryon noted: 'of all the youth that yearly come up to London, to be apprentices to mercers, drapers, silk-men, etc., there is not one in twenty that serves his time out, or lives on his trade.' A comparison has been made of the Upholders' Apprentice Bindings and Freedom Admissions and shows some truth in Tryon's somewhat sweeping assertion.[28]

An apprentice having served his time with an upholder appeared before the Court of Assistants and, after the due fees were paid, he (or more rarely, she) was made a freeman of the company 'by servitude'. It was customary to also make a gift of silver, but after 1700 a sum of money in lieu of plate was acceptable. The other usual way of obtaining the freedom was 'by patrimony', it being only necessary to prove that at the time of the apprentice's birth his father had been a freeman of the company. For example, the virtuoso carver Grinling Gibbons (1648–1721) was made free of the Drapers' Company in 1673 and even acted as its Master from 1718 to 1720. His grandfather and father had been freemen of the Drapers' Company, his father, James, from 1638. There is no doubt this brought into a guild members with no knowledge of the trade represented. The London leathersellers, in the second quarter of the seventeenth century, noted: 'as the manner of London

22 Kahl (1957) pp.17–20; S. R. Smith (1973) pp.197–8; Kirkham (1988) p.170; Earle (1989) pp.85–100; Ben-Amos (1991) p.155.
23 Kirkham (1988) pp.174–5.
24 Kellett (1957–8) pp.381–94.
25 Ben-Amos (1994) p.116.
26 Ben-Amos (1994) p.119.
27 Whiting (1945) p.xvii.
28 Walton (1973) p.51; Ben-Amos (1991) p.159.

is the sonne being free by the father's copy the company is long since changed to those that know not leather'. Supervision of guild policy was on a slow decline and after 1711 the right of company officials to search for poor quality goods or evasion of regulations was declared obsolete.[29] A less popular way of entry to the freedom of a company was to become elected 'by Redemption', which involved its purchase. The Upholders' Company made a somewhat desperate bid in 1750 to increase its membership. It obtained approval of a petition to the Lord Mayor and Aldermen which stipulated that those who 'shall use or Exercise the said Art Trade or Mystery of an upholder . . . within the said City and the libertys thereof shall take upon himself the Freedom and shall be made a Freeman of the said Company of Upholders . . .'.[30]

By whatever method of entry a freeman became a member of the Company's 'yeomanry', and was invited in due course to take up the livery. This meant, in the case of upholders, that 'every person so by them elected . . . shall finde and provide himselfe with a Decent Livery Gowne and Hood. And shall also pay to the Upper Warden of the said Company . . . fower pounds and Ten shilings and to the clerke . . . six shillings and Eight pence and to the Beadle . . . Three shillings and fower pence . . .'.[31] The size of the upholders' livery, although unlimited, was returned at 121 in 1699, 144 in 1724, 131 in 1739, rising to 159 in 1829.[32] Only about half of the number were upholsterers by training.

At the end of the years of training some apprentices stayed on in their master's service as journeymen, or were so employed by other masters. Some money was needed to set up one's own business, unless there was a fortunate marriage to a widow who had inherited her former husband's business. Small-scale businesses which had little use for expensive machinery could be set up economically and tools were often obtainable from a former master. R[obert?] Campbell, in his *The London Tradesmen* (1747), listed the sums of money needed to become a master upholsterer and the hours of working required:

To set up as a master	£100–£1,000
Hours of working	6 a.m.–8 p.m.
Apprenticeship Premium	£20–£50

His figure for setting-up accords with that given in 1761 in Joseph Collyer's *The Parent's and Guardian's Directory*. It is wise to regard the figures as approximate, but with some assistance from parents and relatives the capital required was often forthcoming.

Campbell (see Appendix B) has useful points to make about the division of labour among the various categories of furniture-maker, upholsterers, chair makers and carvers, cabinet-makers, turners and gilders of wood. He regarded the upholsterer as being the senior craftsman and in charge, with the cabinet-maker as his right-hand man.

The upholsterer was expected to be able to handle a needle and shears with dexterity. Campbell regarded the 'stuffing and covering a Chair or Settee Bed . . . the nicest part of this Branch', but stated, loftily, that 'the skill may be acquired without any remarkable genius'. Nevertheless this was an activity which was undertaken by apprenticeship trained men who had the responsibility of cutting and fitting expensive materials. The onerous tasks of sewing window curtains, case-covers, bed furniture and carpets were done by women whom Campbell assumed could 'handle the needle so alertly as to sew a plain seam, and sew on lace without puckets'. They were also often required to attend at the site to help with the time-consuming job of fitting it all into place.

Campbell made no reference to the established fact that medieval furniture[33] and much of the furniture made prior to 1660 was constructed or 'joined' by joiners. But both the diarists John Evelyn and Samuel Pepys, writing in the 1660s, recorded a subtle change by their mentions of visits to a 'cabinet-maker'. By the mid-eighteenth century, the cabinet-maker, according to Campbell, was able to furnish the upholsterer with

29   Unwin (1902) p.109; Dunlop and Denman (1912) p.59.

30   Guildhall Library, London MS., 7141/2, ff.132–4.

31   Houston (1993) p.60, citing the Upholders' Company byelaw
     22 of 1679.

32   Kirkham (1988) p.137; Houston (1993) p.35.

33   Eames (1971).

'Mahogany and wallnut-tree Posts for his Beds, Settees of the same Materials, Chairs of all Sorts and Prices, carved, plain and inlaid . . .'

An alternative view of the cabinet-makers' abilities was taken in 1740 by Batty Langley: 'Cabinet Makers were originally no more than spurious Indocible Chips, expelled by Joiners, for the Superfluity of their Sap . . . Tis a very great Difficulty to find one in Fifty of them that can make a Book-Case &c, indispensably true, after any one of the Five Orders . . .'[34] He was, mercifully, quiet about upholsterers, although their work, involved as it was, had little concern with the 'Five Orders'.

In the early nineteenth century apprentices had to come to terms with a more mechanized production. Springs were being introduced from Austria and elsewhere into well-padded upholstery in the 1820s, and more buttoning and tufting required extra attention. Shorter-term apprenticeships were on the increase and, finally, in 1814 the formal requirement of apprenticeship was under severe threat. By 1820 'the London West End cabinet-makers' trade society was urging a closed shop and the maintenance of a five-year apprenticeship' as they worked against the threat of the complete breakdown of the system. Outdoor apprenticeships, where the apprentice did not live with his master, became common; low wages enforced a regimen of cheap labour as opposed to instruction without remuneration. In the upholstery trade matters had been made worse by unapprenticed females doing many of the unskilled tasks. The division of labour came slowly to the upholstery trade and employment was dependent as late as 1870 on 'skill in all the sub-divisions of the craft'.

PLACES TO WORK

The Great Wardrobe

The principal workshops for the Crown were those of the Great Wardrobe. For over 300 years, from 1361 to the Great Fire of London in 1666, these had been housed on a site adjacent to Baynard's Castle in the parish of St Andrew's. The site, which can still be traced, is shown on John Ogilby and William Morgan's post-Great Fire map of London of 1676 (Pl. 53), and is occupied by St Andrew's Rectory, Wardrobe Place and Wardrobe Terrace. On Nos 4 and 5 Wardrobe Place there is a modern Corporation of London plaque which states: 'Site of / the King's / Wardrobe / Destroyed in the / Great Fire, 1666.'[35]

There is no site plan to indicate the exact areas of the Wardrobe's workshops but a small colony of artificers lived in the precincts, carrying out many functions such as upholstery, bed-making, knitting, weaving, embroidering, lace and button-making and silver-wire winding. The complex intermesh with divisions of the Wardrobe in other premises has been examined in detail for the robes provided and maintained for Queen Elizabeth.[36]

The names of several artificers are known. For example, the 'upholsterer' Edward Baker,[37] whose heirs were active in the trade and in royal service in the reign of James I, provided materials at the queen's coronation, and 'our maker of beds' Nicholas Horton, was active there in the 1560s, making and filling cushions with down or feathers. He appears in a list of artificers of 15 January 1559[38] along with Mary Wilkinson, silk-woman; Guillam Brallot and David Smythe, embroiderers; John Grene, coffer-maker; and James Byttamye, feathermaker. Some further indication of the nature of the workforce is given by the wages of arras makers and cutters, which rose from £189 in 1562 to £756 in 1602.[39] This accorded with an overall concern with rising costs. Despite the comparative frugality of the Elizabethan court – better a nobleman part-beggared by gifts to the queen than a bankrupt state – wardrobe officials were considering 'causes why charges in the wardrobe increase',[40] and during the last fifteen years of the queen's reign the charge of the wardrobe increased by a fifth. Nevertheless only some £13,000 a year, or even less was disbursed, and during the last four years of the queen's life only £9,500 or so.

34   Langley (1740) p.iii.
35   Ellis (1947) pp.246–61.
36   Arnold (1988) chapters VII and VIII.
37   P.R.O., LC4/3.
38   P.R.O., LC5/31; LC9/54; AO.1/2339,1.
39   F. Dietz (1932) p.400.
40   B. L., Lansdowne MS., 46, f.195.

During the first six months of James I's reign the purchases for the wardrobe by its master, Sir John Fortescue, created a debt of £29,000. By 1606, when George, Earl of Dunbar succeeded Fortescue as master, a debt of £50,567 had been incurred. Some of this was accounted for by the £17,647 spent on the funeral of Queen Elizabeth (of which some £11,198 remained unpaid for several years) and by the expensive entry to London and coronation of James I.[41] Annual expenditure was at about £36,300 a year, a four-fold increase over the last years of the queen's reign. Matters did not improve overmuch. Admittedly, Sir Roger Aston, master from 1606 to 1612, tried to reduce expenditure and succeeded to the annual extent of £14,000 less. However, when Lord Hay became master graft extravagant spending typified his tenure. The profit to the occupant was about £4,000 a year, arising mainly from orders and payment for excessive purchases of cloth not undertaken and other loop-holes arising in a department awash with large stocks, arrears and slow payment.

The most successful master at controlling stocks and expenditure was Lionel Cranfield, first Earl of Middlesex. He promised to run the office at £20,000 a year by cutting down on purchases and personnel. This was resented bitterly and Cranfield's enemies were delighted when in 1624 he was impeached. He had halved crown expenditure but the savings were overlooked, with most being regarded as Cranfield's gains. There were always ample reasons to suspect bribery. For example, Cranfield's friend, the lawyer John Hoskyns, had asked him in 1618 to extend a part of the contract for mourning cloth at Queen Anne's death to his brother, a London draper. No matter if Cranfield refused – the slow time-fuse to his fall was alight. As for his successor, Viscount Feilding, expenditure was again in fashion, with him asking for £13,000 in 1625 for 'extraordinary expenses'.[42]

During the reign of Charles I the establishment of the Wardrobe has been given as comprising a total of about sixty persons,[43] that is: the master; comptroller; clerk; two under clerks; yeoman cutter; carrier; robe cutter; fifteen to twenty cutters; thirteen to fifteen arras makers; around ten artificers; nine to ten keepers of standing wardrobes and a porter. There was obviously recourse to many more on a commission basis.

The official residence of the Keeper or Master of the Wardrobe until the Great Fire of 1666 was in a house adjacent to Baynard's Castle, built there in the 1350s by Sir John Beauchamp, later Steward of the Household to Richard II. It was purchased by the crown from his executors after his death for treason in 1388 and became crown property. When Sir Edward Montagu, first Earl of Sandwich (1625–72) became master in 1660 he found his official residence on St Andrew's Hill ruinous and unfit for use. He spent some £1,200 over the next three years making it more habitable, but to little avail.[44] However, one of the master's perquisites was a house with its grounds, granted to him for life. When the Wardrobe moved after the fire to premises in Buckingham Street in the Savoy, on the banks of the river and near to Somerset House, there was no suitable residence available. Sir Edward was given compensation of £2,200 a year in lieu of a property.[45] With much of the Wardrobe's daily business supervised by its comptroller and a surveyor, Sir Edward, who, as a diplomat and naval commander was often away, soon tired of his office. In 1671, a year before his death, he sold the Mastership on to his cousin, Sir Ralph Montagu, later first Duke of Montagu.[46] He acted as master until 1685 and again from 1689 to his death in 1709. During his term of office the wardrobe moved to Great Queen Street, in the parish of St Giles-in-the-Fields. Here, the tapestry workshop became celebrated for the wonderful Indo-Chinese hangings issued by the yeoman arras-worker, John Vanderbank. He was in charge from 1689 to his death in 1717.[47] The Duke of Montagu was succeeded as master by the reversion of the post to his son John, the second Duke. This continued to 1750, and then another seven masters succeeded in turn, until the wardrobe was abolished in 1782.[48] Such departmental affairs then became the responsibility of the Lord Chamberlain's Office.

41 F. Dietz (1932) pp.401–2.
42 Prestwich (1966) pp.100–3.
43 Aylmer (1961) p.475, table 63.
44 Harris (1912) II, p.187.

45 Bodleian Library, Oxford, Carte (Sandwich) MS., 74, f.249.
46 *Cal.S.P.Dom.*, 13 February, 6 August 1671.
47 *Survey of London*, 34 (1966) p.515.
48 Haydn (1851) p.213.

Places to Work

Individual Shops

The setting-up of a place of business, to receive customers, store materials, part-finished and finished upholstered furniture, with adequate room to construct it and sub-divide activities was a craftsman's primary consideration at the end of his training. Any space that was available was better than none, but those intent on advancement, rather than a placid role, looked constantly to improvement of location and layout. Location needed to take account of not being too distant from suppliers of textiles, feathers, hair and other essentials, and with access to furniture makers, embroiderers, dyers, ironmongers and other specialists for the necessary support to assembly. Whilst a certain amount is known about, for example, training in an artist's or sculptor's studio in Renaissance and Baroque Rome, there is little evidence for the plan and effectiveness of Tudor and later workshops for any trade in England. Even for the eighteenth century information is sparse and representations of interiors largely misleading. The layout of a famous furniture maker's London premises such as those of Thomas Chippendale is known only from a plan annexed to his son's fire insurance policy of 1803, twenty-five years after his death.[49]

There is, however, a certain amount of evidence, particularly in probate inventories, that the upholsterer's place of work in the seventeenth and eighteenth centuries centred around his shop. This was usually a part of his living premises, although the court books of the Upholders' Company mention, frequently, 'shopsellers', implying a place at which ready-made goods were available for sale (Pl. 355) but were made by others, elsewhere. The shop was obviously the appropriate place from which to sell goods although some of the upholsterer's work needed to be finished *in situ* at the customer's house – the laying of carpets, cleaning and remodelling of furniture and hanging fabric on walls.

It may well be that the figures standing in the interior of Christopher Gibson's London upholstery shop (Pl. 195) would never be engaged in their respective tasks together, or in that location. Gibson was at The King's Arms in St Paul's Churchyard from about 1730 to 1747.[50] The engraving shows two ware-rooms overlooking a courtyard and a wide flight of steps leading up to the first floor. The stock included cane chairs, chairs and a stool with upholstered seats, an angel bed, a mirror, funeral hatchments and numerous bales of cloth. Two Hampshire upholsterers' inventories of 1605 and 1638 and one of an Oxford upholsterer (1626),[51] chosen at random, show this provision of a shop. In 1605 the goods and chattels of Nicholas Webster, a Southampton upholsterer, show that he had in his house a back and a fore chamber, a hall, kitchen, stable, stable-loft and a shop. In the last he had stock of several sorts of beds, crimson cloth, valances, blankets, pillows, cushions and rugs. It amounted in value to £24 19s 7d by contrast to the £11 14s 4d for the contents of the back and fore chambers.

John Stretton, the Oxford upholsterer, had a respectable stock, including Turkey work and kersey cushions, 8 yards of darnix, $9\frac{1}{2}$ yards of sackcloth, Spanish leather, bed tickings, mostly from Flanders, '19 Bushill of Skinnes', and, in tools, two shears, two hammers, pincers and brushes, 100 curtain rings, tacks and small yellow nails, tape, girth webbing, great chair, back stool and low stool frames, curled hair, crewel fringe, gilded balls (as finials?), two backs and seats of gilded red leather for two chairs, and an array of his clothes. He was obviously in a modest manufacturing way for everyday furniture, covered in leather or a woollen cloth.

The third inventory, of 1638, relates to the possessions of James King the elder of Odiham. He had a somewhat larger house than that of either Webster or King, with a hall, kitchen, brewhouse, chambers over the hall and the buttery, an apple loft, bakehouse, milk buttery, chamber over the shop, a malt loft, a feather loft and a yard. In the 'chamber over the shoppe' he had bedsteads and valances, court cupboards, wainscot tables, small stools, with green cloth covers, pillows, blankets, cushions, table cloths and napkins. In his feather

49 Gilbert (1978) I, pp.22–3.
50 Beard and Gilbert (1986) p.337.

51 Hampshire C. R. O., MS., 1605 A 86/2 (Webster); 1639 A 137/2 (James King the elder); Oxford C. R. O., 173/3/16.

loft there was five hundredweight of feathers, lead weights, a beam and scales, together with various rugs, remnants of valances, curtains and cushions, amounting in both places to some £56 15s 0d out of a total inventory of £151 12s 4d. From such premises Webster, Stretton and King could ply their trade.

An analysis made of a sample of London upholsterers' inventories, 1667 to 1721, in the records of the Orphans' Court, has also shown a shop as part of the overall premises. All the stocks contained a substantial yardage of about fifty different sorts of furnishing textiles overall, as well as finished or ready-made goods. The average value of stock was about £600 but one shop in Cornhill, that of William Ridges, housed in 1670 an extensive stock worth about £7,000, in a total inventory of £17,567. There were at least five rooms for display and six for storage and production.[52] Ridges was obviously trading in a large way and I refer to his activities elsewhere (p.16). The change from apprenticeship to independent shopkeeping was likely to have been swift and, in this case, very successful.

For the eighteenth century the evidence about premises is supported by many mentions in fire insurance records, by a wide array of newspaper advertisements, and, from about 1760, by the issue of town directories listing trades. The London furniture trade, 1700 to 1870, has been looked at in detail[53] and due attention given to the size and stock of many workshops. A good upholsterer's workshop in the eighteenth century would include garrets for storing feathers, flock and fustian as well as rooms for cutting, sewing and starching and carpet and chair rooms. On 19 April 1723 John Bevis of Northampton took out a Sun Insurance fire policy on his dwelling house for £500 and on 13 September 1725 a second policy for £500. His house accounted for £300 of this and there were kitchens, with a wool chamber above. The stable, wool house and feather chamber were valued at £200.[54] It is unwise, usually, to assume a total number for the workforce when only the number of tool chests or benches is mentioned. A fire in 1755 destroyed the tool chests of twenty-two men at Thomas Chippendale's St Martin's Lane, London premises but his workforce has been assessed for this time as at least forty.[55]

Chippendale had fire insurance cover with the Sun office and claimed in May 1755 for compensation for the fire damage. At the renewal of the policy in 1757 his 'Household Goods, Utensils and Stock in Trade therein under the said warehouse, on the roof thereof, and in an Upholsterer's Shop adjoining and Communicating' did not exceed £2,600. By 1767 this was at £1,200 with the insured totals at £5,100 and £3,100 respectively.[56] In the same year, 1755, fire was again the destroyer of the tool chests of thirty-seven journeymen at the London workshops of Bradshaw, Saunders and Smith. It is thought, however, that on this occasion this is an accurate assessment of the size of the workforce, as the fire consumed the whole premises.[57]

Upholsterers tended to congregate in Cornhill and Long Acre, with many furniture makers at St Paul's Churchyard and Clerkenwell. Two who elected to be out of the centre were Giles Grendey (1693–1780), who is reputed to have had one of the larger London workshops in the reign of George I, taking eleven apprentices in a little over twenty years, 1731 to 1754. The second was William Gomm (c.1698–1780) who built large double-storeyed workshops, with nine windows to each storey on the main façade, as well as using his adjacent house as a showroom.[58] Francis Peter Mallet operated from the 1760s at Newcastle House, the Close in Clerkenwell. His insurance cover in 1776 indicated extensive premises. Newcastle House had six warehouses and workshops, a shed and a saw-pit. This was covered by insurance of £9,100 of which £6,000 was for goods and stock.[59]

The fortunate circumstance of the London carver and gilder, Samuel Norman, wanting to take over new premises in 1760 because a fire had destroyed his old shops has given a useful stock list, one of only two known. That of William Linnell in 1763 is noted below. He began negotiations in May 1760 to take over the royal tapestry factory in Sutton Street from Paul Saunders, a leading upholsterer and yeoman arras-worker to the Great Wardrobe. The premises comprised a dwelling house, with an apprentices' room, together with

52   Grassby (1980); Rogers (1994).
53   Kirkham (1988).
54   G.L., Sun registers 115, No.28227; 21, No.36689.
55   Gilbert (1978) I. p.13.
56   Gilbert (1978) I, pp.22, 295–6.
57   Kirkham (1988) p.74.
58   Boynton (1980) p.395; Kirkham (1988) p.73.
59   G.L., Sun registers, 245, p.580.

several workshops for gilding and silvering, tapestries, feathers, upholstery, carpets and for cabinet work. There was also a counting house, a drying yard and a timber drying yard. Norman also agreed to purchase the unwrought stock-in-trade and to help in fulfilling orders from Saunders's clients. He could take all the profits made on jobs undertaken after June 1761 and allow Saunders 5 per cent of the annual total.[60]

The stock included a considerable amount of timber, including '11,986 Feet and half of Inch Mahogany' valued at £599 6s. In respect of upholsterer's work there were '61 sides for beds, 102 Ends for Do, 5 Pair of Head Posts . . .' and a separate Schedule 2 of 1764 took 'Inventory of Stock of Upholstery Branch'. This included many blankets of different weights, brass nails, baize (29 yds), buckram, braids, check, carpets, cloak pins, 31 yards of crimson mixed damask in four remnants, $9\frac{1}{2}$ yards of blue worsted damask, 9 ounces of floss silk, 46 lbs of 'Seasoned Down', 480 lbs of feathers, feather bags, webbing, leather in skins, lace, moreen, 'O's or rings for curtains, thread and tape.

Many of the tools noted in the Saunders and Norman documents were useful to both the cabinet-maker and the upholsterer, such as glue kettles and work benches with trestles, but others were exclusive. There was a beating frame and poles for feathers, a large drying stove for them, twelve old chairs and stools in the shop, a four post bedstead of 'Yellow Arateene Furniture', drying racks, iron, lead and brass weights, many kinds of castors, pulleys, handles, hinges and sacking-bottoms for beds.

A detailed inventory[61] was taken in 1763 of the 'Household Goods, Stock in Trade, Working Tools etc of Mr Wm. Linnell of Berkely Square, Deceased, Carver, Cabinett-maker & Upholsterer'. The extensive work-premises comprised a counting-house, feather garret, a large garret joining to the carving shop, a gilding shop, cabinet shop, a closet, a chair room, fore and back ware rooms, a back store room, glass room, an upholsterer's shop with 'middle' and 'back' upholsterers' shops, a joiners' shop, saw-pit, stables and a yard. It supported an active and successful trading position.

Trade cards often give a useful idea of activities and the extent of premises and stock. That of Ann Buck (Pl. 207), the mother of the successful topographical artists, Samuel and Nathaniel, working from the 'Queen's-head, near Hatton Garden in Holborn' (and so bearing a likeness of Queen Anne) suggests that she stocked items rather than making them – 'Buys and Sells Bed, Bedding . . . and all Sorts of Household Furniture New & Old' as well as selling, wholesale and retail, 'Quilts, Blankets, Tickens, Harrateens & Cheneys'. Francis Pyner became free of the Upholders' Company in 1764 and then traded from 'The Tent' in Lombard Street, London, both as an upholsterer and cabinet-maker, in company with his son, Francis junior. The Pyner trade-card[62] listed the items they claimed to make and had for sale, including: 'bedsteads & Furnitures, Window Curtains, Goose & other Feather Beds, Quilts, Blankets, Counterpanes & Coverlids, Damasks, Harrateens, Cheneys & Bed Tickings, Easy Chairs, Wilton, Turkey & other Carpets . . . Spring Blinds and all Sorts of Window Blinds.'

They also bought and appraised household goods and performed funerals 'in any Part of Town or Country'. Jonathan Fall issued a trade card about 1765[63] on which he indicated he was at the Blue Curtain in St Paul's Churchyard, London. He made and sold: 'all sorts of Beds and Beding, Mohair Silk worsted and mix'd Damask. And all kind of Upholder's goods, Great Choice of English French and Turkey Carpets, Screens of every kind . . .'

In the later eighteenth century upholstery warehouses became a usual means of supplying goods wholesale to the trade and, to a lesser degree, at retail prices to customers. William Gilbert issued a trade card[64] about 1780, stating he was 'at the Blanket, Carpet and Upholstery Warehouse, Three Doors below Fetter Lane in Fleet Street, London'. He sold 'Stuff & Washing Furniture of all Sorts, with Bedsteads, Compleat Feathers, Down & Featherbeds, Bed ticks, Matrasses, Blankets, Quilts, Cotton Counterpanes, Rugs, Coverlids & Floor and Bedside Carpets of every kind. N.B. Upholstery work done in ye Compleatest manner, Sea-Bedding'.

In 1786 Sophie von La Roche was a traveller to London. She visited the very large furniture workshops of George Seddon, situated on a two-acre site in Aldersgate Street. She recorded[65] that he employed a large

60 Kirkham (1969) pp.501–13.
61 Hayward and Kirkham (1980) pp.168–80.
62 Heal (1953) p.144.
63 *Ibid.*, p.52.
64 *Ibid.*, p.65.
65 *Sophie in London* (1933) pp.173–6.

number of tradesmen – some three hundred – housed in a building with six wings. Some departments housed only chairs, sofas and stools. There were also chintz, silk and wool materials for curtains and bed-covers; hangings in every possible material and carpets and stair-carpets to order. Support for the number of 300 men being employed was given in a newspaper account[66] of a fire at Seddon's three years earlier, in November 1783: 'among the unfortunate sufferers are Mr Seddon's journeymen, near 300 in number, each of whom, according to the custom of the trade found his own tools, and all those belonging to Mr Seddon's workmen are destroyed. A chest of cabinet tools is worth from five to fifty pounds . . . the loss in tools only is very great'. Despite the vast scale of the business Seddon's two sons brought it only, in 1804, to bankruptcy. The firm's creditors included horsehair manufacturers, carpet manufacturers and warehousemen, dyers, linen and blanket suppliers.

Some firms stayed successful, and one of these was Morgan and Sanders (a partnership of Thomas Morgan and Joseph Sanders). They opened a fashionable London shop. Much is known about their business in the first quarter of the nineteenth century because of their involvement with Rudolph Ackermann, a successful print seller, art dealer and publisher. For his monthly periodical *The Repository of Arts . . .*, they supplied a succession of furniture designs, which were published between 1809 and 1815, and they also took advertising space. In August 1809 a coloured illustration of their upstairs warerooms was published in the *Repository* (Pl. 355). They stocked the 'best & most approved Sofa Beds, Chair Beds, patent Brass Screw Bedsteads' and many other examples of 'Patent Furniture', popularized by their neighbour, Thomas Butler.[67]

In 1818 Thomas Wilson of Cathedral Yard, Exeter advertised his business[68] as a 'Fashionable Upholstery, Chair and Cabinet Ware-Rooms'. He stocked 'Kidderminster, Brussels, Venetian and East India Hemp carpeting, paper hangings obtained from London sources, feathers and mahogany and fancy woods'. The rooms he had for storing and cleaning feathers were said to have been 'lately completed . . . on the same construction as the principal houses in London'. Henry Goff, a Brighton upholsterer, advertised in 1828[69] that his business was an 'Upholstery, Featherbed, Mattress, Carpet and Hearth Rug warehouse'. He aimed his trade at 'Hotel, Tavern, Lodging House keepers and families' and stated that his stock featured bedding, drawing, dining and sitting room chairs and sofas, carpeting and paper hangings.

In 1843 George Dodd described the furniture trade as still being largely in the hands of the smaller manufacturers: 'The tables, the chairs [etc] all are made to a vast extent in London, but not generally in large factories: they are the production of tradesmen, each of whom can carry on a tolerably extensive business without great extent of room, or a large number of workmen.'[70] Indeed, the 1851 Census confirms that most of the London furniture making firms employed fewer than fifty people.[71]

THE SOURCES OF SUPPLY

One of the main needs of an upholsterer's business was a ready supply of a wide range of textiles.* Whilst a considerable yardage of the items used most frequently could be held in stock the better system was to rely on their availability from mercers and, to a lesser extent, weavers. The mercers imported cloth, especially in the early sixteenth century, from Antwerp, which acted as both an *entrepôt* and a distributor of items manufactured locally. But by the 1580s Antwerp's commercial greatness had declined, perhaps helped by the entrepreneurial activity of English merchants who had expanded their trade to Italy and the Levant, and who, by 1600, had established the East India Company to trade further afield, in India and south-east Asia.[72]

A surviving London port book of 1567/8 shows that ships out of Antwerp carried an astonishing array of commodities. Among the textiles carried by the *Edward* were Oudenarde thread, 40 pieces of mockado, 2 bales of Ulm fustian, 6 cwt. flax, 25 pieces of Genoa fustian, 5 dozen crewel pieces, 150 yards of taffeta, 60

*   The main types are noted in the glossary but are described in greater detail in Thornton (1978) and Montgomery (1984).

66   *Norfolk Chronicle*, November 8 1783.
67   Beard and Gilbert (1986) p.712.

68   *Exeter Flying Post*, April 16 1818.
69   *Brighton Herald*, May 17 1828.
70   Dodd (1843), cited by Edwards (1993) p.18.
71   Kirkham (1988) pp.78–9.
72   H. van der Wee (1963).

yards of velvet, 6 dozen Ghentish carpets, 27 ells of silk tapestry, 150 ells of caddis tapestry, 900 ells of hair tapestry[73] – one ship's cargo amongst many that served the London mercers. The port books charting this trade do not survive in sufficient quantity[74] to record all the varied activity, but it was obviously a significant enterprise.

From at least the early fifteenth century many English towns had guilds of special merchants such as mercers who had then amalgamated with other merchant companies. Only in active trading centres such as London and Bristol were there guilds devoted to one trade. They made available a wide variety of furnishing textiles. In London there were also a number of leading cloth merchants who were active in promoting trade, such as Sir Thomas Gresham (1519?–79), the royal agent or king's merchant at Antwerp from 1551. The government-backed body of cloth exporters, the Merchant Adventurers, concentrated their activities at Antwerp, and the Tudor governments of Henry VIII, Edward VI, Mary I (and for the first decade of Elizabeth's reign) were also dependent on loans arranged on the money market there, though at high rates of interest. Gresham sorted out the tangled financial situation by persuading the government to delay the cloth fleet of the Merchant Adventurers until they lent money from Antwerp, to be repaid at a fixed exchange rate in London. He was also much involved in the reform of the currency in 1560 which even netted the queen a profit of £45,000.[75]

With some financial stability established trade, and especially the import and export of cloth, could flourish, even if set against a background of intense claim and counter-claim by various sections of the English textile trade. London became an important cloth finishing centre, whilst Norwich had some 4,000 alien weavers,[76] and there was a Huguenot community of silk-weavers at Canterbury.[77] The Russia Company, founded in 1553, traded in and out of Archangel and had a monopoly of imports and exports, with furs[78] and Russia leather among the many commodities. Contacts were made with Turkey by the Levant Company[79] to open up the trade routes. A great deal about the dyeing of cloth was known there and an English factor in Turkey in 1582 was urged 'to know all the materials and substances that the Turks use in dyeing' and to send home samples of cloth.[80] Sir Francis Willoughby of Wollaton Hall, near Nottingham had hoped to make a fortune at this time from growing woad, which was used in producing blue dye.[81] The scheme's failure, leading to prolonged litigation, threw reliance back to foreign woad, grown by the French and Portugese. There were many plants besides woad, and insects that gave other colours. Some, such as cochineal and kermes, animal in origin, gave mordant dyes. These needed to be applied to the fabric after it had been treated with a metallic salt. Four other widely used red dyestuffs of the medieval period were vegetable in origin: madder, Brazil-wood, orchil and henna. The most widely-used was madder, but a variety of shades could be obtained by mixing woad with red or weld yellow.[82]

The stock of fabrics held in the sixteenth century by the Great Wardrobe and used extensively by the Wardrobe of Robes for the clothes of Queen Elizabeth has been well researched. For example, in 1578 a mercer delivered there a typical sample of its continuing stock, black, tawny and russet velvet, black, white, yellow, green and crimson satin, together with 'ashe-colour', 'murry' and 'strawcolour' satin, black taffeta and white and black sarcenet.[83] Tudor and Stuart inventories listing the furnishings of rooms show, in addition to these textiles, a considerable use of richly coloured damask, grandly, at Oatlands Palace in 1618,[84] a mixing of pale pink and yellow in 'a Canopy & Curtaines of Carnaton & Yellow damaske'. There were gilt-leather hangings, mostly from Holland. Turkey-work carpets, bales of silk, silver and gold lace, cloth of silver and of gold, often embroidered with 'Venice gold' or 'Venice silver', thread of those precious materials imported from Venice. The linen and woollen mix of 'darnex' (there are many variant spellings) came from Dornick, the

73   B. Dietz (1972) p.21.
74   Stephens (1969).
75   Burgon (1839) p.234; Read (1955) ch.IX, 'The Restoration of the Coinage'.
76   Unwin (1902); Lipson (1921) pp.23, 224; Ramsay (1982); Clay (1984).
77   Cunningham (1897) p.150; Rothstein (1989).

78   Veale (1966).
79   Wood (1935) p.7.
80   Lipson (1921) p.85; Walton (1977) pp.319–54.
81   R. S. Smith (1961) pp.24–34; Bettey (1977).
82   De-Graaf (1983) pp.71–9.
83   Arnold (1988) p.172.
84   East Sussex Record Office, MS., GLY 319.

Flemish name of Tournai, whilst the linen fabric 'holland', first made there, was soon available widely throughout Europe for sheets and linings.

Pride of place in the upholsterer's repertory must, however, go to velvet, damask and silk. All the supplying mercers stocked it in sumptuous colours and patterns. Velvet, either with a woollen or silk pile (cotton velvet is mentioned in archives from the early eighteenth century), damasks and silks came into England from various parts of Europe, but particularly Italy and France. Their importance to the upholsterer's trade merits a brief introduction to their characteristics.

The production of silk and velvet had been established in Italy by the twelfth century at Lucca, and soon spread to Venice, Genoa, Florence and Milan. As a heavy fabric velvet could take metal thread embroidery well and was often used for canopies and ceremonial robes. It was also a trade prestigious enough for painters such as Crivelli, Bellini and Pollaiuolo to produce cartoons for velvet and silk weavers. The Genoese velvets, best-known in England, owed their 'chased' pattern effects to a 'contrast of seemingly dark cut pile with uncut pile which appears lighter and glossier'. They were unsurpassed in quality.

With the close of the seventeenth century the creative period in Italian velvet weaving came to an end. There had been a surge in French production towards 1650 with Lyon continuing to imitate Genoese velvets, in great favour as a wall covering. Next to Lyon the Paris manufactories produced costly silks and velvets. There had always been a concern to make France independent of Italian imports. Weaving was also active at Zurich and Basle and was introduced to Antwerp towards the end of the sixteenth century, and also to Hamburg.[85]

England owed its introduction to the weaving of silk fabrics and velvets, as noted, to immigrant Flemish weavers. The entry of skilled Huguenots in the late seventeenth century enabled the country to lead in velvet and silk production.[86] Important centres were at Spitalfields in London, Norwich and Canterbury. Velvet-like fabrics from cotton yarn, or 'velveteens', were produced in Manchester in the latter half of the eighteenth century. This was appropriate as Manchester had produced 'fustians', a class of raised velvety cotton fabrics, since the Middle Ages. As pile fabrics, plushes and moquettes are velvets in a technical sense, differentiated by a longer pile and stouter material. Foremost among the upholstery plushes was Utrecht velvet with an all-cut pile of resistant mohair, patterned by pressing between engraved blocks or rollers. By means of this pressing process an effect similar to Genoese velvet was obtained, although it was in no way comparable to the true silk velvets. Whilst some writers have said this velvet was made at Utrecht the current theory is that this is a misnomer; the term may derive from the fact that the figured versions were woven on a draw-loom and were thus *velours de trek* (i.e. *à la tire*, drawn).[87]

The name of damask derives from Damascus in Syria but this does not imply that the fabrics were made in that town.[88] It could be of silk, a combination of silk and worsted, or entirely worsted. Again, as with its velvets, Genoa was an important manufacturing centre for silk damasks and maintained its high reputation for their supply well into the second half of the eighteenth century. An extensive list of citations of its use in English room and furnishing schemes can be made and this has been done for one important group of houses.[89] The names and main activities of the leading London mercers who handled damasks and silks in the eighteenth century have also been established.[90] Even so, house archives contain details, of other names and many patrons, referred to in later chapters, who also supplied damask of their own purchase to their upholsterers.

Finally, there needs to be a consideration of Turkeywork and cotton. Turkeywork, also called Norwich work, is a woollen pile fabric made to imitate Turkish carpets. It was worked on a loom but with coloured yarns tied by hand to a strong warp thread. It was well suited to seating furniture. In the 1670 inventory compiled at the death of William Ridges,[91] he had '10 doz of Turkywork back seats for chayres', made to a standard size and '1 doz & $\frac{1}{2}$ of fine Turkywork chayres' in his shop stock.

85 Latour (1953) pp.3441–63; De' Marinis (1994).
86 Thornton (1965); Rothstein (1990).
87 Thornton (1978) p.112.
88 Schreus and Braun-Ronsdorf (1955) pp.3966–94.
89 Cornforth (1989) pp.155–74.
90 Rothstein (1990) pp.300–44.
91 C.L.R.O. Orphans' Invs. 1670 No.692.

Cotton was imported in large quantities by the East India Company, with calico, the particular kind of cotton brought from Calicut, much in use for clothing. The London weavers struggled against the competition, mainly by petitioning Parliament. By the turn of the eighteenth century they had achieved some measure of success. Parliament, in 1680, did reject the petition against the wearing of East India fabrics, but added an additional 10 per cent duty in 1685, doubled this in 1690 and made it permanent in 1711. However, action against the importing of large numbers of calicoes and pieces of Bengal wrought silks rumbled on throughout this period with rioting English weavers attacking East India House, entering the House of Commons and tearing up shop stock.[92]

TRIMMINGS (*Passementerie*)

Elizabethan inventories show the use of trimmings such as fringe and bone lace to further embellish what was already grand. The Earl of Leicester's inventory of 1588[93] shows most of the bed valances 'fringed with deepe fringe of crimson silk and silver' and the 'fyne curteines of crimson sattin' were 'striped downe with a bone lace of silver' or of 'golde and silver'. Chairs were embroidered with 'clothe of goulde fringe, with black silck and goulde' or with 'silck of their own collour'. Even chosen at random few inventories disappoint in their descriptions. That of Edward Sackville, fourth Earl of Dorset,[94] taken in 1645 notes the use of silk lace 'with copper ffringe', or in the Rich Gallery with six elbow chairs and six backstools of crimson satin 'embroydred with twisted silver & gold ffringe'.

The silk-making manufactories in Italy and France were also able, in a supplementary sense, to provide a wide variety of fringes and by the late seventeenth century both the London mercers and itinerant fringemakers active in England could supply all that was needed. The French fringemaker, Peter Dufresnoy,[95] who had been in England from before 1670, worked at Burghley House, Cambridgeshire and at Drayton House, Northamptonshire in the 1690s. The fringe on the state bed at Burghley (Pl. 82) is presumably of his working, incorporating exquisite needlework cyphers (Pl. 80) of John, fifth Earl of Exeter and his wife Anne Cavendish. There are also several heavy patterns of silver 'galloon' of the late seventeenth century which survive (Pl. 109).

Tassels to finish the lines which held back curtains, made of silk thread wound round a wooden core, are shown frequently in paintings, and survive in some small measure in various eighteenth century interiors (Pl. 59). They are also well represented in the French national collections at the Musée des Arts Decoratifs.[96] Whilst never easy to date, there is a plate of six kinds of fringe, not unlike tassels as they are made of spools covered with silk thread, in James Barron's *Modern and Elegant Designs of Cabinet and Upholstery Furniture*, issued at London in 1814.[97]

BEDDING

The blankets, bolsters, pillows, mattresses, coverpoints, quilts and sheets that made up bedclothes was a frequent and bulky stock item for upholsterers and upholstery warehouses. Since medieval days England had experienced a dependence on large sheep flocks for food and for wool. The returns therefrom in a time of rising wool prices had shored up incomes of both monastic communities and private landlords.[98] It also led to thriving manufacture of wool blankets in such towns as Witney, relying on the Cotswold sheep flocks for raw materials. Even so, 'Spanish blankets' were what Elizabeth I and Elizabeth, 'Bess of Hardwick' pulled around themselves – the 1601 Hardwick inventory included for Bess's bedchamber 'Six spanish blanketes' and the adjoining room of Lady Arabella Stuart had three. They were held to be thicker and better than ordinary wool blankets.

92   Plummer (1972) pp.292–311.
93   Halliwell (1854) pp.121–3, 137.
94   Phillips (1929) II, p.358.
95   Beard and Westman (1993) pp.523–4, citing entries in Exeter bank account, Child's Bank ledgers (Royal Bank of Scotland, London).
96   Paris (1973); Thornton (1978) pp.127–8; Donzel and Marchal (1992).
97   Montgomery (1984) p.65.
98   Bowden (1962) pp.5–12.

The late seventeenth-century records of the Worshipful Company of Upholders contain many citations of fining members for filling bolsters, pillows and cushions with 'trash' rather than selected swan or eider down or feathers. In the early seventeenth century James I's bed mattress was canvas-covered and filled with straw. By contrast that of George II was of white leather filled with fine curled hair.[99] Horsehair began to be used for mattresses during the 1660s, as also for padding seat-furniture. In consequence a feather-room, as noted, was a frequent provision in upholsterers' premises, and was used additionally for storing related materials.

In John Strype's 'Survey' of the Cities of London and Westminster,[100] an updating in 1720 of John Stow's Elizabethan 'Survey', there is sharp comment about upholsterers: 'great was the Deceit by these Tradesmen used in their Feathers, in their Quilts and Coverlids, in their Quishions for Chairs and Stools'. He stated that from 1578 'most Feathers that were in Sacks came out of the Low Countries', so packed up out 'of the spoil of Houses' that they had lime, dust, stones and 'heavy Rubbish' to make their weight. The Court Books of the Worshipful Company of Upholders contain many examples of the finding of poor, inadequate fillings and support Stow's original observation. The account continued: 'a better sort of sacks of Feathers came out of Eastland, but near as faulty'. The Eastland Company was founded in 1579 'to take advantage of the trading privileges granted by the small port of Elbing'.[101] Their ships carried out cloth and returned with cargoes, principally of corn, but there was much else, including feathers. They were trade rivals of the more successful Merchant Adventurers.

Strype's *Stow* was equally condemnatory of 'stuff' that came out of France or Flanders 'filled with Thistle-Down, naughty Flocks & all baggage in them that would breed worms'. Good feathers were available from Danzig, the most important port for English traders and a main outlet for the products of Poland and the western Ukraine. It acted as the principal grain port of Europe.[102] Strype also mentions 'down', gathered by the poor people of Ely, and 'Ticks which came out of Flanders'. They are mentioned frequently in inventories and filled with good feathers or down provided a superior, closely woven under-covering of pillows, bolsters, coverlids and cushions. The feathers, down beds, pillows and bolsters are usually listed by their weight.

Webbing

This essential upholsterer's aid as a bottom for seating and beds has only, alas, merited one detailed examination.[103] Its origins lie in the use of 'girth webbing' as an encircling or binding medium, whether of oaken girths for binding casks, or leather ones as a part of horse harness. In relation to furniture it is 'a narrow fabric of varying width, usually from about $1\frac{1}{2}$ inches (38 mm) up to about 4 inches (102 mm), and until modern times was made by weaving together yarns spun usually from vegetable fibres into a single yarn'. Flax fulfilled this requirement until the end of the nineteenth century, although hemp and jute were in use too. Most were then replaced by a use of cotton. The material was produced from the early seventeenth century by girth weavers (Campbell in 1747 wrote 'the whole Tribe of Narrow Weavers make but poor Bread . . .').[104] About 1698 it was stated that seated furniture was using 'great quantities' of girth web 'all of our own Growth and Manufacture'.[105] It is assumed that by this time the upholsterer had established trade contacts with the narrow-loom weavers of webbing, ribbons and tapes, centred on London and later Manchester. There was, however, an active trade in such small wares in Holland with the Dutch loom able to weave from six to twenty-four narrow fabrics at once. One important conclusion of the webbing study needs restating: 'If an upholstered item is truly of the date it appears to be, then the webbing should be of that period. If the webbing is of a later period, then the item cannot be completely original, and has an original frame which has been reupholstered or it is a reproduction.'[106]

99   P.R.O., LC.
100   Strype, *Survey* (1720) pp.229–30.
101   Friis (1927); Hinton (1959); Davis (1962) p.212.
102   Davis (1962) p.219.

103   Milnes (1983).
104   Campbell (1747) p.259. (See Appendix B.)
105   Symonds (1934) pp.221–2.
106   Milnes (1983).

Iron and Brass Wares

Each upholsterer had great need for large and small headed nails and tacks. Those with brass or gilded heads, to be seen in particular in early seventeenth-century portraits (Pl. 35), must have been made in London. All too little is known about the provision of such items, but the concentration of small iron manufacturing, and so of nails and tacks, was in the area fifteen miles round Birmingham.[107] The brass industry there was mostly of the later eighteenth century and this gave London an early supplying monopoly. Besides supplies from Midland smiths its merchants could also draw on iron manufacture in many other areas such as the Weald of Kent and the Forest of Dean.[108] During the fifteenth century the classification of iron nails according to their price per hundred came increasingly into fashion. Nails with tinned heads were often used for fixing the rails bearing tapestry or for positions where fabric needed to be pierced. Additionally the black nails used in tacking up black cloth for funerals were varnished. It would seem that such insignificant things as nails were graded and labelled, but archives often use many terms for an identical article. What is clear is that during the eighteenth century the close nailing of upholstery (Pl. 294) had become an art.

As well as the provision of many sizes of nails and tacks, the same centres of the iron industry provided chains, spikes, nuts and bolts. The sharp spikes and chains were used in two ways. Driven into a wall the spike could hold a chain to support a bed tester of the 'angel' kind, cantilevered and without foot posts, or, as spikes only, driven down into the tops of all the bed posts to accept a tester pierced with holes at each corner. Such spikes are mentioned in the accounts of Francis Lapiere (1653–1714), a French upholsterer active in England in the late seventeenth century in the provision of grand and imposing beds.[109] Nuts and bolts were used to tension bed-frames when these were not 'joined' with wooden pegs.

To protect the hangings of a bed case curtains were provided to draw round them. These were suspended on a bright polished iron or brass rod fixed by brackets to the front and two sides of the tester. Inventories usually include mention of both case and window curtain rods to support the draw curtains. Brass curtain rings and small rings to guide draw-lines (Pl. 299) were available from London and Birmingham brass-founders. The silk draw-lines were wound around cloak pins (Pl. 344) to maintain the curtain height. These pins were screwed to the window frame jambs. The number of cloak pins noted in accounts is a useful guide to the number of windows in the room, usually two pins to each.[110]

The upholsterer's trade made an important contribution to commerical life as practised in many cities and smaller English towns. The supplies needed to keep such businesses going were available through mercers and upholstery warehouses. Patrons extracted a hard bargain from merchants often suffering from considerable trading difficulties. Payment by them was always tardy but as those well used to virtuosity this did not stop them expecting near-perfection in the decoration of their houses.

---

107   Court (1938).
108   Straker (1931); Johnson (1952).
109   Beard and Westman (1993) pp.523–4.
110   Westman (1990) p.1411.

II

Tudor Opulence

On 21 April 1509 King Henry VII, revered for many years as victor over Richard III at the field of Bosworth, died at his palace of Richmond. He left to his tall, handsome heir Henry, then almost eighteen years old, a quiet peaceful kingdom, and one economically secure. He had, however, given his son little instruction in the awesome responsibilities of kingship. As a second son Henry VIII had led a restricted bookish life,[1] being tutored by the poet laureate, John Skelton (1460?–1529). But he learned and acted quickly, as he assumed his great responsibilities.

Henry VIII was crowned in June 1509, the month he married Catherine of Aragon. As soon as the lavish ceremony was an immediate memory (there are no detailed accounts), Henry turned his thoughts to commissioning an imposing monument to the memory of his father and his mother, Elizabeth of York. The Florentine sculptor, Pietro Torrigiano, had been in England from about 1511 and between the years 1512 and 1518 he created, to the king's order, a major Renaissance tomb to enrich the Henry VII Chapel in Westminster Abbey. The black marble tomb-chest with its white marble top bears gilt-bronze effigies of Henry and his wife, in flowing robes, their hands raised in silent prayer. In his will Henry VII had directed that the decoration of the chapel bearing his name should be magnificent enough 'as to a king's work appertaineth'.[2] The obsequies leading to this final commemoration had been within the control of the Master of the Great Wardrobe, with the imperious oversight of the Lord Great Chamberlain, the Lord Chamberlain, the Treasurer of the Household, with heraldic propriety observed by Garter, King of Arms and his heralds.

The Great Wardrobe's daily activity across the reigns of Henry VII and Henry VIII, that is from 1485 to 1547, was concerned basically with the furnishing needs of sixty-eight houses. These ranged from the small manor of Collyweston in Northamptonshire, which had been granted to Henry VII by his mother, Lady Margaret Beaufort, to the imposing residences within Whitehall, Greenwich, Hampton Court and Westminster, as well as Henry VIII's great palace of Nonsuch, started in about 1537, but regrettably demolished in the late seventeenth century.[3]

The artificers of the Great Wardrobe included in their number what we now call 'upholsterers', but in the Tudor period the description did not appear in wardrobe, or indeed other, accounts, although there were many bed-makers, coffer-makers and embroiderers. For example, the privy purse expenses of Elizabeth of York included in 1502: 'To John Warreyns [of London] bedmaker for making of a trussing bedde, seler, testere . . .'[4]

Furthermore, from an early period those who pretended to the trade of upholsterer had also concerned themselves with the undertaking of funerals. The requirements for velvet-clad coffins with elaborate gilded nailing, and the provision and setting-up of much black cloth of various qualities needed their special skills and sources of supply.

As the monarch had moved in earlier years about the country 'on progress' (the later journeys of Elizabeth I and James I are noted below, pp.24, 52), it was convenient that the more important royal palaces

1   Williams (1971) p.13.
2   H.K.W., IV, Pt II (1982) p.22; Whinney (1988) pp.31–2; Thurley (1993) p.12.
3   Dent (1962) pp.210 ff.
4   Nicholas (1830) p.65.

had a 'Standing Wardrobe'. This obviated the need to move many essentials from the Great Wardrobe or its palace location in London. At Nonsuch Palace the duty of keeper was undertaken from the start of building by Sir Ralph Sadler (1507–87), a gentleman of the privy chamber who went on to many greater things. He became master of the Great Wardrobe in 1543, was one of the council of twelve to assist in the guardianship of the boy king, Edward VI, and, late in his life, became guardian of Mary, Queen of Scots.[5] His duties as keeper at Nonsuch from 1537 ended on September 29 1543 and Letters Patent of 2 March 1544 confirmed the appointment to the post of another gentleman of the privy chamber, Sir Thomas Cawarden, who also succeeded in 1545 to the remunerative and important office of Master of the Revels.[6] But soon Sadler and Cawarden and all the officers of the royal household would need to come to terms with the demands of a new sovereign.

Death of Henry VIII

On 28 January 1547, Henry VIII, 'that serene and invincible prince', died in his palace at Westminster. Since midnight, amid the stench of the sickroom, he had been sinking towards death, and had been attended by the cleric he knew and revered the most, Thomas Cranmer, Archbishop of Canterbury. Monarchs, above all mortals, could still command such single attention even as eternity enfolded them. The new king, Edward VI, assumed his father to be 'now in heaven', and 'that he hath gone out of this miserable world into happy and everlasting blessedness'.[7] Whilst many were ready to dispute that exalted state the earthly rituals would be unaffected. A mixture of solemnity, ceremonial and grand theatre, these were bound by precedents known to the officers of the household and especially, in the details, to those serving within the Great Wardrobe.

With measured and precise deliberation the Great Wardrobe had dealt since the fourteenth century with the complex problems attendant on royal coronations, marriages and deaths, as well as the refurbishment of the many royal palaces. In addition to its main functions of furnishing and of storing cloth of all kinds the Great Wardrobe also kept the tents and pavilions which were used on special occasions such as masques, pageants, and entry to London. It had become, across the years, supportive to the sovereign's household but detached from it. In January 1554 the then keeper or master, Sir Edward Waldegrave (?1517–61) – he had succeeded Sir Ralph Sadler in 1553, the year of his knighthood – received, on behalf of the wardrobe, grant of the status of a 'body corporate and politic'. As master he became responsible for all the 'mansions, tenements and other properties' administered by the wardrobe and he was required to present annual accounts to the exchequer.[8] Each yard of velvet, cloth of gold or black cloth had a reckoning, a price to be engrossed in the vellum-bound books of expenditure; each royal occasion or need had an assertive, though, if at death, unplanned, place in the year's accounting. There was also separation in 1544 of the Great Wardrobe from the subdivisions of the Privy Wardrobes of Beds and of Robes. Sir Edward's finest moment was to be in charge, in 1559, of the Great Wardrobe's contributions to the coronation of Elizabeth I.

John Strype (1643–1737) the ecclesiastical historian and biographer has given a careful account[9] of the attentions needing to be given to the corpse of the dead king, Henry VIII. They have been set out in some detail[10] and the processes of 'spurging, cleansing, bowelling, searing, embalming, furnishing and dressing with spices the said corpse', as Strype has it, need not concern us here. The detailed expenses[11] incurred show the vital roles played by the artificers of the Great Wardrobe. After a blue velvet robe, doublet and jerkin of blue satin, and a nightgown had been provided for the king's corpse by the tailor, John Bruges, attention was turned to 'the charyott wherin the Corpse of the Kinge Matie was carried unto Windsor'. William Locke provided fourteen yards of purple velvet to garnish the inner part of the chariot, under the coffin hood and the pillows therein, together with blue velvet for the canopy of the great many-storeyed hearse. At the instructions of the

5   D.N.B., vol. L. p.169.
6   Dent (1962) pp.143–4.
7   Halliwell (1846–8) II, pp.75–6.
8   *Cal. Pat. Rol.*, Mary I, 1554, p.47.

9   Strype (1721) II, pt ii, pp.289–311.
10 Litten (1991) pp.39–40.
11 P.R.O., LC2/2.

wardrobe master, Sir Ralph Sadler, black cloth hangings for mourning were set up in the queen's great chamber at St James's Palace.

The blue velvet-covered chest containing his late majesty had lain in state, under a gold pall, in the privy chamber. A wax effigy had been fashioned, so like the king in life that it was as if he had robbed the grave of its victory. On 8 February 1547 the bells were tolled in all the English churches and almost a week later, on 14 February as though in slow response to their urgent stridency, the great hearse set off for Syon House, by the Thames, on the way to Windsor. Letters Patent of 15 February 1547[12] set out the 'Order of Ceremonies to be observed at the funeral of Henry VIII in conveying the body from Westminster Palace to Windsor'.

The order is a long and detailed one and must be quoted selectively. Attention was to be given that there were no broken bridges or overhanging branches to hinder the trundling progress. The Dean of the King's Chapel was to find priests and clerks to follow the high-held cross. Carts were to carry torches that were lighted as the cortège came through towns and villages, and 250 poor men in black gowns and hoods would lead, ahead of the carried cross, the priests and clerks. The king's sword and embroidered banner of the royal arms bobbed in front of those banners which commemorated earlier rulers such as Edward IV and Henry VII.

All the noblemen bearing banners and all the varied retinue of the great and good are then named. The officers of the Great Wardrobe were accompanied by the parson of the church of St Andrew by the Wardrobe, together with the king's embroiderer, Guillam Brallot, and three men each from the wardrobes of the beds and of the robes. Prelates were to meet the procession at Syon and Windsor. The bishops of London, Durham, Ely, Worcester, Bangor, Bristol and Gloucester were allotted tasks. The funeral sermon was entrusted not to Cranmer but to the Bishop of Winchester, Stephen Gardiner. At all relevant stages a canopy denoting royal status was borne aloft by the Lords Abergavenny, Conyers, Latimer, Fitzwalter, Bray and Cromwell.

The Master of the Great Wardrobe had early requisitioned all the 'cloth of gold, satin, velvet, banners and other furnishings'[13] as well as the thousands of yards of black cloth which were needed. The black-covered ropes that slid the chest to its appointed place returned finally to a shelf in the Great Wardrobe.[14] Perhaps the unkindest epitaph to it all was that of Daniel Barbaro, reporting in 1551 to the Venetian Senate that the 'many acts of disobedience perpetrated' were the result of the king's placing himself in a sinful position to the church of Rome.[15]

It was not the Great Wardrobe's task to agree or disagree and there was, in any case, the greater need to assess the merits and foibles of a new ruler.

THE REIGN OF ELIZABETH I

The last years of Henry VIII's reign, as the Venetian envoy had noted, had foreboding of the divisive factions of his son's reign, in his minority, and the regrettable folly of his daughter Mary's Catholic tenure, with its burning of heretics and religious repression. This had undermined the structure and authority of English government, and events had been further dominated by the complications of Mary's marriage, in July 1554, with Philip II of Spain. Anthonis Mor's portrait of the queen (Pl. 4) shows her seated in a richly embroidered crimson chair: that used, allegedly, at her marriage to Philip in Winchester Cathedral survives there and is one of the earliest survivals of a royal chair of estate (Pl. 3). But within four years the Catholic queen lay dead at St James's Palace. It was the morning of Thursday 17 November 1558 and on that afternoon her young, twenty-five year old sister, Elizabeth, was declared, inexorably, as queen in her stead.

On succeeding to the two kingdoms of England and Ireland Elizabeth realized at once that she was head of an exhausted realm, with the nobility 'poor and decayed'. She herself had suffered the intractabilities of her sister's will by a sojourn in the Tower, with ample time to think and reflect. There was need to proceed with

12   *Cal. S.P. Dom.*, Edward VI, 1547, pp.5–7.
13   *Ibid.*, p.7 No.17.
14   Thomas (1861) p.79.
15   *Cal. S.P. Venetian*, 1534–54, p.346.

caution. Sir Nicholas Throckmorton (1515–71), who had been sent also to the Tower in 1554, on a charge of complicity in the Wyatt rebellion to prevent the marriage of Queen Mary with Philip of Spain, had finally been acquitted. Elizabeth appointed him as Chief Butler at her accession. He soon gave her valuable advice: 'succeed happily through a discreet beginning . . . have a good eye that there be no innovations, no tumults, or breach of orders'.[16] It was advice, repeated by others, which accorded with the queen's own viewpoint. A vital aspect of public relations was the funeral of her sister and then her own coronation. The Great Wardrobe waited in patience for its instructions.

In simple, precise words the *Calendar of State Papers* recorded, for 13 December 1558: 'The corps of Queen Marie was right honourably conveyed from her Manor of St James unto the Abbey of Westminster. Her picture [? effigy] was laid on the coffin, apparelled in her royal robes, with a crowne of gold set on the head thereof . . .'

As with Edward VI the precedent-bound Great Wardrobe acted with decorum and precision. Its embroiderers, tailors and upholsterers (although the term is nowhere used) had worked to a long-established set of precedents, which, with only subtle variations, suited joyous occasions as well.

Up to the reign of Queen Elizabeth the coronation of the monarch consisted of four essential parts. There was need to take 'possession' of the Tower, to signify control of London. It was then necessary for the sovereign to progress in state through the city to Westminster on the eve of the coronation. The third event was the impressive staging of the coronation itself and on the same afternoon the fourth and final occasion, a banquet in Westminster Hall, the most ancient part of the Palace of Westminster.

Elizabeth had made her way in her state barge to the Tower on 12 January 1559. The richest trappings of state barges in later years were entrusted to joiners and upholsterers from the Great Wardrobe: the same jobs were now performed by the queen's artificers. On 14 January, the day before the coronation, there was the long procession through the city. Richly furnished timber stagings had been set up at various points; firstly, at Fenchurch, 'whereon stood a noise of instruments, and a child in costly apparel, which was appointed to welcome the Queen's majesty in the whole city's behalf'. At Gracechurch Street there was an edifice with gates and battlements, decked with the figures of Henry VII and his queen, Elizabeth of York, and Henry VIII and Anne Boleyn. The houses of York and Lancaster were commemorated by white and red roses. In Cornhill amid many banners and along the streets stood members of the city companies, including the upholders, in their liveries and thick furs. The wooden rails enclosing the streets were hung with tapestry and with velvet, damask, silk and satin. On, to St Paul's Churchyard, to hear Latin orations composed by the boys of St Paul's School, through Ludgate to Temple Bar, and then to rest overnight at Westminster.[17]

Setting out on her coronation morning the queen was carried in a white and gold litter with high scroll ends, with her back resting against cushions of cloth of gold (Pl. 5). A quilt of white damask was set about her feet. The materials used for this litter were of the 'richest sort' from the queen's wardrobe stores, namely cloth of gold tissue at £4 a yard, trimmed with real gold and silver fringes (which cost £138 6s) and with gold 'Passamain' lace, all garnished with gilt nails. Its making was a combined effort by six artificers, the chariot-maker Anthony Silver, the silk-woman Mary Wilkinson, Thomas Cure, a sadler, David Smith, embroiderer, Nicholas Lysarde, painter and Thomas Doughtie, bitmaker. Lysarde, as serjeant-painter, was responsible for the 'iiij greate Knoppes gilt with fyne gold with Kerved Lyons' which were set at the corners of the scroll ends of the litter. The carved lions were the masks on the sides. They cost 7s 6d each.

The inside of the litter was lined with a flesh-coloured satin and round the outside edge were four skirts of cloth of gold, fringed and lined with yellow buckram. The canopy over the litter was held aloft by four corner posts. It was made by the bed-maker, Nicholas Horton, with Mary Wilkinson providing the silk. It was of 'Clothe of Tisshewe of the Richest sorte the ground Silver and Tisshewe gold' and 'Satten crimsin Caffa makinge striped with golde for Lynynge'. The staves, or posts, were gilded by Lysarde. The queen, in a

16 Neale (1950) pp.91–8.   17 Williams (1953) pp.397–411; Rowse (1953) pp.301–10.

wonderful robe and a gold cap which have been described expertly elsewhere,[18] sat alone in the high-held litter, which was borne by two richly caparisoned mules; The chariot-maker, Anthony Silver (with two of his journeymen), the sadler (Cure), bitmaker (Doughtie) and Lysarde, serjeant-painter, were in their liveries of red cloth embroidered with the letters 'E' and 'R'. They were part of the one thousand strong procession in their roles as royal artificers. They were, providing a 'chariot' little different in materials used to furnish the palaces. Ahead of them as far as the eye could see was the whole body of the officers of state and of the queen's household. A fine folio volume of pen and ink drawings survives to document the ritual of the grand occasion.[19]

The streets of Westminster had been new-laid with small gravel and fine blue cloth and railed in timber at each side, the queen proceeded through it all headed by a mighty procession, led by trumpets and the heralds at arms. She was met, formally, by Nicholas Heath, Archbishop of York, but he represented the group of bishops who fancied a Catholic course. Archbishop Cranmer had been burned at the stake by Queen Mary and was therefore not available to crown her as he had her mother. The task fell to the only bishop willing to do so, Owen Oglethorpe, Bishop of Carlisle, in robes he borrowed from the hated persecutor, Edmund Bonner, Bishop of London. The coronation chair dating from about 1300 had been decked by the upholsterers of the Great Wardrobe with cloth of silver. Inside the abbey the walls had been covered with the great tapestries[20] Henry VIII had commissioned after designs by Raphael. Before the peers of her realm Elizabeth was anointed and crowned.

At an early meeting in her first year the queen signed the Patent Roll of 22 July 1559 of the 'Grant for life for his service to John Fortescue, the Queen's Servant of the Office of Keeper of the Great Wardrobe, as formerly held by Ralph Sadler and Edward Waldegrave, Knights, from Lady Day last'.[21] Waldegrave's services in charge of the furnishings for the coronation were over and Fortescue held the post for the remainder of the queen's reign.

QUEEN ELIZABETH'S PROGRESSES

The event beyond all others which led to the owner of a great house inspecting the quality of his furnishings, and particularly that of the beds, was an intended visit by the queen. Of all monarchs hitherto, Queen Elizabeth travelled the most, usually with a great entourage accompanying her. The precise details of the journeyings have been set out magisterially in three volumes.[22] The itineraries, for mid-July until the end of September, were worked out by the Vice-Chamberlain, in consultation with the queen. For the active years of her reign this post was held, firstly, 1559–70, by Sir Francis Knollys (?1514–96), who then became Treasurer of the Household, and secondly, and more importantly, until 1587, by Sir Christopher Hatton (1540–91). Sir Christopher had built his fine, great house of Holdenby in Northamptonshire in the late 1570s.

The sovereign's stays cost an owner a great deal of money. An early biographer of William Cecil, Lord Burghley stated[23] that it cost £2,000–£3,000 each time Elizabeth visited his house, Theobalds, in Hertfordshire. This was, however, untrue, as the Burghley accounts show,[24] with the amount averaging £300–£400; a stay by the queen at Sir Nicholas Bacon's Gorhambury in 1577 cost him £577 6s 7½ d.[25] Lord Burghley noted, wryly, to Hatton that both Theobalds and Holdenby had been built to honour the queen, 'for whom we both meant to exceed our purses'. Hatton further described Holdenby, to Sir Thomas Heneage, as his 'other shrine' and hoped, blasphemously, 'that holy saint' Queen Elizabeth 'might sit in it'.[26] Both houses were destroyed during the Commonwealth (1648–1660), with only fragments remaining.

18   Arnold (1978) pp.727–41.
19   B. L., Egerton MS., 3320.
20   Campbell (1994) pp.22–31.
21   *Cal. Pat. Rol.*, Elizabeth, 1558–60, p.90.
22   Nichols, *Progresses* (1823) 3 vols.

23   Peck (1779 ed.) p.15.
24   Read (1960) p.556, n.10.
25   Rogers (1933) pp.35–112; Mercer (1962) p.14.
26   Brooks (1943) pp.17, 155, 158; Summerson (1959) pp.107–26.

William Harrison touched in 1577 on the economics of the Queen's travels: '. . . whereby it cometh to pass that when the Queen's Majesty doth remove from any one place to another, there are usually four hundred cartwares [teams], which amount to the sum of 2,400 horses, appointed out of the countries adjoining, whereby her carriage is conveyed safely unto the appointed place'.[27] But no one complained openly of the inconvenience or expense; for the most part the queen was a welcome visitor[28] and the various Standing and Removing Wardrobes were compliant and active.

The most outstanding visit was the one the queen paid in 1575 to Robert Dudley, Earl of Leicester at Kenilworth Castle in Warwickshire. The detail of the festivities is known, lasting over seventeen days and set out by the upholsterer, Robert Laneham, who extended his skills to providing elaborate *son et lumière* set-pieces.[29]

TUDOR INVENTORIES

The Greater Houses

The richness of decoration and contents of Tudor palaces and houses is well shown by contemporary inventories, although the work itself has long disappeared. At the same time some caution has to be observed in their use. Few inventories list the full contents of both fixed and movable items and the purposes for which they were compiled, usually financial or legal, often carry their own distortions.[30] Inventories do, however, note furnishings, allow reconstruction of the physical layout of a house, as well as indicating an owner's wealth and status and his interest (even if well-intentioned) in conspicuous consumption.

In 1509 Edmund Dudley (1462–1509), Speaker of the House of Commons in 1504, but suspected of corruption, had his goods seized by the crown and an inventory was taken at his London house in Candlewick Street.[31] This had both a Great Wardrobe for storing carpets, tapestries, cushions, beds and blankets and a Little Wardrobe mostly for clothes. The great chamber was furnished (Appendix A1) with green curtains at the windows, a bed with hangings formed from an embroidered silk fabric interlaced with metal threads, a featherbed to it, three quilts, a bolster, a selection from six pairs of sheets, a counterpoint with representations of 'forest work', cushions of various colours of velvet, a long carpet, two short carpets, a great coffer filled with clothes made from luxurious fabrics, and several sparvers, or conical hangings suspended by cords from the ceiling, 'the commonest form of canopy for the hung bed in the later Middle Ages'. The grant-of-arms to the Upholsterers' Company in 1465 incorporated three such pavilions or sparvers.[32] The reign of Edmund Dudley's sovereign had already endured many dire problems. There were more in plenty.

Henry VIII's burning concern to have a male heir had meant that Catherine of Aragon's long record of miscarriages and still-births caused her to be ousted in 1533 in favour of Anne Boleyn. She settled at Baynard's Castle, adjacent to St Paul's Cathedral, and near to the place from the 1360s onwards in which the Great Wardrobe also functioned. The castle ranked in importance next to the Tower of London and a grant of it had been made to Henry VIII's illegitimate son, Henry Fitzroy, Duke of Richmond. He died, tragically young, at the age of seventeen, in 1536, the same year as Catherine of Aragon. Inventories were therefore taken of both of their possessions.[33] These are replete with beds, sparvers, ceilers and testers, cloths of estate, counterpoints, long and square cushions, fustian pillows filled with down, sheets, chairs and little stools. I can but sample the riches listed (Appendix A2): a square bed of blue velvet embroidered with roses and crowned initials, lined with blue buckram and fringed with red silk and gold. The counterpoint was of the same stuff, likewise embroidered and lined. The resplendent hanging sparvers could be of yellow cloth of gold, cloth of silver with 'work', and russet velvet lined with blue buckram, having a single valance, fringed as well with white silk, yellow and russet colouring, as also with Venice gold, with a mantle and curtains of russet sarcenet.

27 Harrison (1968 ed.) pp.227, 307.
28 Johnson (1974) p.229.
29 Nichols, *Progresses* (1823) I, p.472; Furnivall (1890) p.12.
30 Eames (1973) pp.33–40.

31 Dudley Inv. pp.39–41.
32 D.E.F., (1954) I, p.69, Eames (1977) p.83.
33 *Camden Misc.*, III, (1855).

There were five iron-framed chairs, four of them covered with crimson cloth of tissue, fringed with red silk and Venice gold with gilt pommels (see Pl. 4). Protective cases to them were provided, of leather lined with yellow cotton. All the long and square cushions were paned with cloth of tissue, crimson velvet or green damask, all having red silk or Venice gold tassels. The Duke of Richmond's rooms had mostly velvet cushions, in russet, crimson and purple, set on chairs of crimson and black velvet, fringed with green silk and having pommels of either silver or gilt.

Henry VIII's visits to his new Nonsuch Palace were rare enough, but that was no excuse for the household to be ill-prepared. The king paid a visit there in July 1545. The palace was in readiness and, indeed, was kept more or less furnished at all times. An inventory of Nonsuch, compiled at the king's death in 1547,[34] shows the kind of items the king found ready for his use. The beds, as usual, were the most impressive of the many possessions, with one having a ceiler measuring 14 ft 3 in by 12 ft fashioned of dark crimson velvet, with one half having double valances and the other half single. It was 'embroidered with flowers of gold and the crowned head of a woman and wings'. The tester, also in crimson velvet, measured 9 ft 9 in with a width of 13 ft 6 in.

The king's bed had a gilded frame in gold and silver, painted also in light blue, measuring 9 ft in length and 8 ft 7½ in breadth. The ceiler, tester, six valances and bases were made of panels of crimson gold tissue. The purple velvet and crimson velvet areas were embroidered with the King's arms and crowned badges. Comfort was assured amid the bolster, two fustian pillows filled with down, four linen quilts filled with wool and a large counterpoint (10 ft wide by 13 ft 6 in long) made of russet and yellow quilted silk, lozenged with cords of Venice gold, embroidery of white cloth of silver fringed with Venice gold and silver, lined with white fustian.

Other ceilers and testers were of white Turkey silk, of blue and crimson satin, or striped russet and red velvet. Some of the valances, enveloping curtains and counterpoints were of matching colours, but many were of white sarcenet, embroidered with birds, of velvet lined with black buckram, or, sumptuously, quilted yellow silk lined with green linen.

The hangings in many of the rooms at Nonsuch were supplemented by the addition of French tapestries, silk and satin carpets, tapestry table carpets bearing the king's arms, painted carpets and plain ones having self-coloured embroidery or gold and silk thread embellishments. Set on them in various rooms were eighteen chairs covered in white cloth of silver, black velvet with raised flowers of cloth of silver and crimson velvet, or purple ones fringed with purple silk. When not in use they were protected by buckram case-covers in various colours.

The chairs were made more comfortable by a lavish use of cushions. The covers of these were fashioned from purple and green velvet, purple tinsel, cloth of gold, crimson silk bearing gold embroidered lions and silk and damask of various bright colours. Those of lesser status who were in attendance sat on folding or square stools covered with velvet.[35]

As well as these grand requirements the upholsterer needed to cater for the king when he was infirm. Late in life, Henry, ill with his ulcerous leg, apart from his inordinate weight, needed, in 1546, at Whitehall, a special chair, or 'tram'. This had shafts, back and front, rather like the later sedan chair. Two of these are recorded: 'two chairs called trams for the King's Majesty to sit in, to be carried to and fro in his galleries and chambers, covered with tawny velvet, all over quilted . . .'[36]

In the first (1577) edition of his *An Historical Description of the Island of Britain*, William Harrison intended a full portrayal of Elizabethan England.[37] In this aim he succeeded well and his words on furniture and furnishings are relevant to our study. At the same time they can be fleshed out, effectively, with details from many surviving inventories.

At the accession of Queen Mary, Thomas Howard, third Duke of Norfolk (1473–1554) who had been in prison in the Tower was released, the attainder against him reversed and his title and most of his estates

34   B. L., Harleian MS., 1419A; Dent (1962) p.137.   36   Williams (1971) p.249.
35   Dent (1962) p.139.   37   Harrison (1968 ed.) p.xv.

restored to him.[38] However, when he was imprisoned in 1546 his vast estates in Sussex and other counties had fallen into the king's hands, and, after the accession of Edward VI they had been granted, in August 1547, to Sir Thomas Seymour. Little more than sixteen months elapsed before Seymour himself was in custody, with all property seized. An inventory of his goods was taken in 1549 by Sir Thomas Cawarden, in particular of those at Seymour's house at Cheseworth in West Sussex.[39] A fragmentary brick range is all that now survives of this property, which had been acquired by the Dukes of Norfolk about 1506.[40] There were many similarities to the third Duke of Norfolk's own house at Kenninghall in Norfolk, built in the 1520s and having an inventory dating to the mid-sixteenth century.[41] The duke's lodgings were on the second floor, adjacent to those of his mistress. A crimson and white canopy stood over the bed which was hung with curtains of yellow sarcenet. Chairs were covered with Bruges satin and the cushions were of white and yellow damask. Tapestries incorporated 'imagery' in their pattern and the carpets were strips of Turkey work.

At Cheseworth, as could be expected, there were many tapestry hangings too: in the hall, great chamber, dining chamber, 'my Lord's Bed Chamber', and Chapel. The carpets and cupboard cloths were, as at Kenninghall, mostly of Turkey work, with cushions in red damask, with green damask ones for the chapel. There were several truss, or travelling beds, and a number of testers of tissue and red velvet, paned or embroidered 'with droppys of golde, with curtins of sarsenet, paned blewe and yellow'. There were curtains made mostly of green velvet or sarcenet, some embroidered with baskets and letters of gold. Of bedding there were both 'good and bad' feather beds, bolsters, down pillows, blankets, coverlets and quilts. A painting such as Holbein's *The Ambassadors* (Pl. 1) shows not only hangings of rich green figured damask but a cupboard carpet and joined furniture common to the greater houses in early Tudor England.

The inventory of household goods, plate and farm stock attached to the will of Sir John Gage of Firle Place in East Sussex[42] is an interesting and valuable confirmation of this. It gives a complete insight into what may be considered to have been the necessary appointments of a large country residence of an influential nobleman in the middle of the sixteenth century. At the fall of Thomas Cromwell Sir John Gage had been appointed Comptroller of the Household, Chancellor of the Duchy of Lancaster, and Constable of the Tower of London. In this last respect he received in 1555 the young Lady Elizabeth, detained at the pleasure of her sister, Queen Mary. A year later, at the age of seventy-seven, John Gage died. His long will, proved on 10 June 1556, directed his son Edward, one of the executors, to sell 'my coll[or] [collection] of golde and th ordre of the Gartier' and to employ the money raised to help 'poor folkes'. The inventory of household goods, appended as a codicil to his will, covered some three and a half closely written pages in the folio register book. Again, the plate apart, it is the beds and their appurtenances that impress (Appendix A3). There were at least twelve wondrous testers, of crimson velvet and cloth of gold, paned, with fringes of crimson silk and gold, with three curtains to the same of sarcenet, of 'murrey velvet' or a dark purple–red velvet, again paned with cloth of gold and set to a standing bedstead made of walnut. Perhaps the most dramatic testers were the black velvet and yellow satin paned ones, with fringes of black and yellow silk and black and yellow sarcenet curtains. Even the trussing or camp beds had testers of blue and yellow satin with matching curtains, or fashioned from darnex, a coarse sort of damask. The wall hangings were of tapestry, or, as in the little parlour, paned green and red saye, or serge – some forty-three panes, with a further four pieces for over the chimney and under the windows. There were forty feather beds, many coverlets, blankets, pillows and wool quilts. Some mattresses 'of a wourser sorte' were laid under feather beds, presumably helping to soften the tautness of the rope webbing. The use of carpets as table and cupboard coverings was well established and 'two new Turkey carpetes' were provided for the great table in the Great Parlour, as well as several, both old and new, for cupboards, including 'one other cupbourd carpet of Inglishe makinge', and many of Turkey work and crewel embroidery. The long cushions were of tawny, green, purple and crimson velvet, of black damask, of silk 'wrought with the nedle',

38 Robinson (1983) pp.34–5.
39 Ellis (1861) p.118.
40 Howard (1987) p.216.

41 P.R.O., LR 2/115 f. 47d; Williams (1964) pp.3–4.
42 Firle Inv. 1556 (1902) pp.114–27.

with six great and six small cushions of 'carpet worke'. Some of these were used in the house chapel and some in the church.

Greater comfort had been established in houses by excluding the sight of a dreary, cold winter landscape by hanging curtains. The entry 'iiij Curtens for wyndoes, of grene and red saye, payned' evokes a certain rich effect. They were lined with a linen material called 'soultwich'. The chairs at Firle Place were well described too, including five of Spanish making, garnished with inlays of coloured bone. There was also a wainscot chair of 'the Frenche makinge'. Sir John had accompanied Henry VIII on his French expedition in 1513; he was appointed captain of the castle of Guisnes and later, in the early 1520s, became comptroller of Calais. So there had been ample opportunity to acquire French objects. Gage was affluent and in royal favour to the extent that Henry VIII had appointed him as one of his executors.

Inventories indicate an owner's main considerations: the comfort and warmth which came with good beds and the necessary supplies of blankets, sheets, and pillows. The hangings of the bed served also to exclude draughts and additionally were a source for the display of embroidered arms and initials. The family had need too of provision for sanitation, however crude and noisome. It was the upholsterer's task to provide close stools, often inappropriately covered in nail-studded velvet. Daily life can be invoked further by studying the contents of the living rooms and by observing the setting-up of rooms which gave greater privacy to the occupants of the house.

Eight inventories show the nature of these provisions. Firstly, in 1565 an inventory of the Earl of Lennox's house at Temple Newsam, Leeds was prepared. This was a forerunner of the present house, remodelled for the financier, Sir Arthur Ingram, 1622–30. Sir Henry Sharington entertained Queen Elizabeth in 1574 at his Lacock Abbey in Wiltshire. She was on progress to Bristol and spent a short time at the house, conferring a knighthood on Sir Henry. The following year, for attachment to his will, he had an inventory prepared; this was six years before his death. Dame Elizabeth Blount's will in 1581 listed items at Mapledurham, Oxfordshire, and inventories were prepared in 1590 of the possessions of John, Lord Lumley; in about 1591 of the contents of Browsholme Hall, Lancashire, home of the squire Robert Parker, and in 1599 of Sir Charles Morison, of Cassiobury in Hertfordshire. Finally, there is the celebrated inventory prepared in 1601 for Elizabeth, Countess of Shrewsbury, 'Bess of Hardwick'.

At Temple Newsam House[43] the great chamber contained (Appendix A5) a bewildering variety of goods from nine portraits, 'one olde cloke and hoode lined with sarcenett' to 'a tester of clothe of gold and silver with the armes of Therle [the Earl] & his wife imbrodered & curtens of yellow and white sarcenett'. There was an additional red damask tester with curtains of crimson taffeta; a coverlet for each of the two beds, of down, with two bolsters and five pillows. Five chairs, one specified as of 'wallenuttree & wroughte', were covered, respectively, in red damask, green taffeta, old cloth of gold, old cloth of silver and satin, and russet satin. They were made comfortable by an ample provision of cushions, twenty in all, some paned with velvet and satin, others of crewel work or made from plain coloured satins, damasks and velvet.

In the earl's bedchamber a splendid tester of cloth of gold and purple velvet had the arms of England embroidered thereon. The bed-curtains were of crimson damask and the tapestry hangings on the walls of the room incorporated 'huntynge and hawkinge' scenes. Unusually, there was a parcel-gilt 'barge bedstead', perhaps a four-post boat-shaped one. In the 'Chambre called the Ladies Chambre' there were ten pieces of old tapestry with cascades or fountains ('cunductes') worked on them, with various bed-coverings, blankets, coffers, a close stool and a little table and cupboard.

In 1540 Sir William Sharington purchased from the crown the dissolved Convent of St Mary and St Bernard at Lacock in Wiltshire. At Lacock Abbey (as it has been called since the late eighteenth century) there is still evidence of Sir William's rebuilding and there is a fine carved stone table of c.1550 bearing his cypher and that of his third wife. The ladies of the household had provided the soft furnishings and the 1575 Lacock inventory[44] lists a profusion of cushions in the wardrobe chamber. The many stools were covered with

43 Temple Newsam Inv. 1565 (1920) pp.91–103.   44 Lacock Abbey Inv. 1575 (1968) pp.72–80.

needlework, velvet or Turkey work, standing on Turkey carpets, one of which was 'large' and valued at the high price of £20. The close stool was covered with black damask; in a corner there was a field bedstead with canopy curtains and a covering of green cloth.

Inventories exist usually as separate documents, or, as with the Lacock one, are appended to a will. Dame Elizabeth Blount's is an example in this latter category, in that the inventory was incorporated in 1581 in the text of her will.[45] It referred to her property of Mapledurham House, Oxfordshire, but it is presumed that Dame Elizabeth's possessions (Appendix A6) were in an earlier house as she bequeathed items to Sir Richard Blount, who only started to build the present house in about 1585.[46] In the middle chamber of Mapledurham there were five pieces of tapestry 'wherewithe the chamber is hanged', the standing bedstead, the bolster, featherbed, two pillows and two blankets, a coverlet, 'the tester and the corteynes therto belonginge'. There was an inner chamber to this room containing another bedstead and its coverings. In a chamber above, Dame Elizabeth's son could gaze at 'paynted hanginges of blewe and yellow'. Again, there was a bedstead and clothes, with an inner chamber having red and yellow hangings, as well as a further bed. Furniture to sit on seemed to consist of joined stools, benches and settles, a provision in slight contrast to William Harrison's words of 1577:

> The furniture of our houses also exceedeth and is grown in manner even to passing delicacy; and herein I do not speak of the nobility and gentry only but likewise of the lowest sort in most places of our South Country that have anything at all to take to. Certes in noblemen's houses it is not rare to see abundance of arras, rich hangings of tapestry, silver vessel, and so much other plate as may furnish sundry cupboards, to the sum of ten times of £1,000 or £2,000 at the least, whereby the value of this and the rest of their stuff doth grow to be almost inestimable. Likewise in the houses of knights, gentlemen, merchantmen and some other wealthy citizens, it is not geason [uncommon] to behold generally their great provision of tapesty, Turkey work, pewter, brass, fine linen, and thereto costly cupboards of plate . . . the costly furniture . . . descended yet lower, even unto the inferior artificers and many farmers, [who] . . . for the most part [have] learned to garnish their cupboards with plate, their joint beds with tapestry and silk hangings, and their tables with carpets and fine napery whereby the wealth of our country . . . doth infinitely appear.[47]

The truth of Harrison's words may be observed, however, in the 1588 inventory[48] of the possessions of Robert Dudley, Earl of Leicester. As a favourite courtier of the queen's (he had had marriage in mind), he had entertained the queen on occasions at Kenilworth Castle. He had bedsteads of walnut with rich hangings of 'clothe of gould tysshue' (Appendix A9) and others of satin, silk and velvet. The embroidery included depiction of his arms and of his supporters, of the 'bear and ragged staff'. One bed had red painted posts with 'five plumes of coloured feathers, garnished with bone lace and spangells of gould and silver standings in cupps knitt all over with goulde, silver and crymson silke'. It was a lavish setting and one rivalled only rarely. A contender might have been any of the houses of John, Lord Lumley.

One of the most famous collections of paintings, sculptures, stone tables and fountains in the late sixteenth century was that owned by John, Lord Lumley at his various residences, Lumley Castle, near Durham, his London house on Tower Hill and possibly also at Nonsuch Palace. The Lumley inventory of 1590 was printed in 1904, and again in 1918[49] and I have looked also at the original copy.[50] Regrettably none of its wonderful coloured drawings represent upholstered items, but stone tables, fountains, obelisks and columns abound. Nevertheless, what is relevant to this study is 'A Sumarye of certayne stuffe within your Lo: houses, the XXIIth of May Anno 1590' taken by John Lambton, gentleman, and steward of Lord Lumley's household.

45   P.R.O., Probate 11/proved 1582.
46   Pevsner, *Oxfordshire* (1974) p.695.
47   Harrison, (1968 ed.) p.200.
48   Halliwell (1854) pp.212–14; Clark (1981).

49   Milner and Benham (1904); Lumley Inv. 1590 (1918).
50   I am indebted to the Earl of Scarbrough, Lumley's descendant, for showing it to me.

As for Lumley himself, he was a member of the Elizabethan Society of Antiquaries, a former high steward of Oxford University, and someone who tried to forget, presumably, that he had been implicated, as a Catholic sympathizer, in the Ridolfi Plot (1571) to overthrow Queen Elizabeth and replace her with Mary, Queen of Scots.

Under the hands of those in charge of his house wardrobes he had fifty-seven suites of hangings, 'of arras, sylke and tapistre', eleven 'Turkey carpettes of sylke', carpets of velvet for tables and windows, ninety-five 'other Turkey carpettes', twelve testers, three sparvers, three pavilions, six canopies and four field beds, wrought with gold, silver and silk. The coverings and quilts were of silk and both the chairs and stools were covered with cloth of gold, velvet and silk, the material used for some 109 cushions. The frames of the chairs, bedsteads and stools were of walnut, some inlaid with marquetry, and there were others covered in red Spanish leather. There were seventy-six chairs in all, and enough pallet beds, bolsters, sheets, woollen coverlets and blankets to cover a large retinue. The cold darkness was banished further by damask curtains and the velvet window carpets. To reduce bright light on summer days, traverses, or as the inventory has it, 'Travyses of sylke for wyndowes', were fitted. These may well have been placed across the inside of a bay window.

A later Lumley inventory of Lumley Castle[51] for 1609 shows that of this large number of items twelve suites of hangings were at the castle with five Turkey silk carpets, twenty other Turkey carpets, twenty-five chairs and thirty-eight cushions. Lumley also had an extensive library rivalled only by that of his celebrated contemporary, the mathematician and astrologer Dr John Dee. Many of Lord Lumley's books passed to Henry, Prince of Wales, James I's son, and subsequently, through George III to the King's Library. This was presented to the British Museum in 1823 by George IV. This rich Lumley collection was surrounded by 233 paintings from a total of 255.[52]

It is useful, for comparison, to look at the contents of a house owned by a member of the squirearchy, Robert Parker of Browsholme Hall in Lancashire. He was descended from a family settled there, or nearby, from the early fourteenth century. The editor of five of its inventories,[53] of which comment is included here on two of about 1591, indicated both sharp differences as well as similarities (for example, common furniture types and use of textiles) with items listed in the 1601 inventory[54] of the great Derbyshire house, Hardwick Hall. This was prepared for the redoubtable Elizabeth, Countess of Shrewsbury, 'Bess of Hardwick' (1520–1608). It stands, among many available inventories,[55] as a fitting finalist in the listings of the contents of a greater house.

The two 1591 inventories for Browsholme list twenty-two and twenty-eight rooms or locations respectively. Standing beds, some with testers, are listed together with chairs, both 'great' and 'wicker', forms, stools, chests, cupboards and tables. The three great chairs had 'three great sett quissions in them' – the ever-present cushions; (there were five more green ones), and, additionally, the upper parlour cupboards had cupboard cloths and one long table had a 'dornix' covering, a large-patterned upholstery material akin to tapestry.[56] With many other items at Browsholme these gave a modest lustre to lives lived in an agricultural community in which little change took place. The contents listed in the 1634 inventory are little different from those listed in the two Tudor ones.

After the dissolution of the monasteries Henry VIII granted in 1541 the estate of Cassiobury in Hertfordshire, which had belonged to the Abbot of St Albans, to Sir Richard Morison. Fifty years later in 1590 when Sir Richard's grandson, Sir Charles Morison, died, an inventory was taken. The estate passed eventually to Sir Charles's only child, Elizabeth, and so to her husband, Arthur Capel, later Earl of Essex. The house was, alas, demolished in 1922.

The inventory[57] is eleven yards long, so, obviously, I must be very selective. The Great Chamber was hung with tapestry and had six stools embroidered with black velvet upon green satin, three low stools of black

51 Lumley Inv. 1609 (1918) pp.36–45.

52 Piper (1957); many of the Lumley paintings were dispersed at sales in 1785 and 1807 (Lumley Inv. 1918 pp.31–4).

53 Browsholme Inv. *c.*1591 (1986) p.4.

54 Hardwick Inv. 1601 (1971).

55 Overton (1983).

56 Thornton (1978) pp.108–9.

57 Roethlisberger (1972).

and green figured satin, long needlework silk cushions, a livery cupboard and two great window curtains with rods to them. There were two short and three longer (three yards each) Turkey carpets, one Turkey carpet five yards long, more stools having tapestry or Turkey work covers, two green chairs embroidered with crewel, eight tapestry cushions and four window curtains with their rods.

In 'Sir Charles, his Chamber' there was an old suite of tapestry hangings, a yellow silk embroidered canopy, a yellow rug and a canopy bedstead. This had a feather bed, bolster, two pillows and two blankets. There was also a chair and two yellow embroidered stools, a livery cupboard and a small table, with cloths to cover them, a window cloth and a window curtain of blue saye, with its rod. Sir Charles had a closet within his chamber where he kept papers and other effects. There was a great press, a leather chest, a cupboard with boxes, all for storing 'writinges', a case of Scottish pistols and an old lute.

Lady Morison's chamber was adjacent. The walls were hung with 100 ells of old tapestry hangings. I assume the Flemish ell of 27 inches was intended rather than the English ell of 45 inches, as Flanders was a more likely source for tapestry. It surrounded a standing bedstead with tester, curtains and valances of green caffoy (or woollen velvet), fringed with green silk. This had the usual complement of bedding but with four pillows to Sir Charles's two. Three chairs were covered in another form of wool velvet, 'mockado', with a high cushioned stool, a green carpet, three green curtains, cushions bearing embroidered arms, two perfuming pans and wainscot and leather-covered chests.

Cassiobury had many rooms, each filled with furniture suitable to the status of the occupant. The porter's lodge, for example, had a bedstead, a featherbed, two bolsters, a blanket and a coverlet. Unusually there was an armory with swords, rapiers, pistols, even a bow and case with arrows. All the gilt plate, clothes, linen and livestock was listed, as well as the contents of the London house near to Fleet Street.

At the London house there is the same preoccupation with a yellow and black colour scheme. The great chamber was equipped with two chairs, four stools, one footstool and six joined stools all covered with black and yellow taffeta. Two further chairs were embroidered with black velvet upon yellow satin, perhaps part of the set at Cassiobury. Whilst, overall, an *en suite* look was not yet common in interiors, Cassiobury and the London house did have many matching elements. For example, the little dining chamber had green carpets and green cushions and 'my Ladyes Chamber' had a green carpet, green chair and green stool too.

Sir Charles Morison also had a house in Cambridgeshire at Shingay on the site of a preceptory of the Knights Hospitallers. It was demolished in 1697. The usual preoccupation with green furnishings is apparent in the inventory but a more exotic note was created in the great chamber with the use of murrey velvet and cloth of silver. This was used for the bed tester 'with sarcenet curtyns suitable to yt', as well as for chair and stool coverings. In the chapel chamber the bedstead had a tester of black velvet and yellow satin curtains, matched by chairs and stools in a black and yellow chequered pattern.[58]

The 1601 Hardwick inventory listed the contents of sixty-four locations spread across three floors of the great Derbyshire house of Bess of Hardwick. It is not now easy to identify all these rooms for, contrary to popular legend, Hardwick underwent 'a substantial amount of internal restoration in the late eighteenth century' and William George Spencer, sixth Duke of Devonshire (1790–1858), arranged for a great deal more to be done from the late 1820s. Nevertheless, the exterior of Hardwick speaks out for earlier Tudor years. It was a house on which much architectural ingenuity and innovation was lavished. Its great windows dominated and within, the hall was set on a different axis of west to north, rather than at right angles to the entrance. Bess of Hardwick and her surveyor, Robert Smythson, were concerned to lead rather than to follow.

The hall now contains a number of needlework pictures, originally cushion-covers (Pl. 15); there are tapestries up most of the staircase, and the sixteenth-century tapestry suite representing 'The Story of Ulysses' has been in the high great chamber since the 1590s.

The patterns and still bright colouring of Elizabethan embroidery may be seen well at Hardwick, even if in remounted form on 'farthingale' chairs in the high great chamber. The transient nature of upholstery itself

58   Herts. C. R. O., MS., 8870.

can be noted, for in 1794 it was mounted on 'black velvet, nearly concealed by a raised needlework of gold, silver and colours . . . in fresh preservation'; but both the chair frames and velvet were replaced at one or more dates in the nineteenth century. One chair is dated 1845 and a guidebook published (but not necessarily written) in 1885 stated that the stools had been restored 'recently'.[59] Hand work by ladies was always important at Hardwick; the collection forms 'an unrivalled museum of Elizabethan embroidery'[60] (Pls 16, 17).

One of the upholsterer's most important jobs, charted in inventory contents, was the provision and furnishing of beds of various kinds. 'Lady Shrewsbury's Bed Chamber' at Hardwick, which was tapestry-lined, had a bedstead, the posts of which were 'covered with scarlet layd on with silver lace'. The bed-head, tester and single valance were also of scarlet, with the valance 'imbrodered with golde studes and thissells'. Five purple baize curtains enclosed the bed which, apart from the usual bedding, had six Spanish blankets thereon. Curtains of red cloth were at the windows and there were also 'coverletes' to hang before 'a window' and 'a door', and a counterpoint of tapestry before another door. Eight mats or herring-bone weave 'fledges' were set around the bed to cut down any contact of bare feet with the floor. A conscious attempt had been made to render the room as warm and comfortable as possible.

The one chair in the room was also covered lavishly, with russet satin striped with silver and a matching fringe (it had a case-cover of scarlet embroidered in *petit-point* with flowers). This minimum seating provision was supplemented by high stools, stools and footstools, including some listed as 'joined'. The three cushions were, respectively, of cloth of gold (on both sides), crewel needlework in panes and one with 'my Ladies Armes in it', lined with red velvet. Other contents of the room were velvet-covered books, an hour glass, inlaid and carved cupboards, a looking-glass, hair-brushes, three leather-covered desks, a writing-desk, trunks, coffers and boxes, a folding table, a wicker screen and fireside implements. Adjacent was Lady Arabella Stuart's bed and chamber. She was Bess's granddaughter, born in 1575, and her residence came about in a complex way.

Bess of Hardwick had, foolishly, not sought the queen's permission for her daughter's marriage to Lord Charles Stuart. For someone less friendly than Bess with the queen that might have meant time in the Tower. As it was, when Bess's daughter, Elizabeth, died in 1582 (her husband Lord Charles had died six years previously), Arabella came to live with her firstly at old Hardwick Hall. When the new house was ready for occupation by 1597 the old Hall was still used to house visitors and some staff.

At Hardwick, 'My Ladie Arbells bedsted' had a blue and white darnix canopy with gilt knobs and a blue and white fringe. There was 'a Cloth of Checker work of Cruell about the bed', which had a mattress, a feather-bed, a bolster, quilt, four Spanish blankets, and a pair of fustians, or blankets of cotton and linen. In her chamber there were six hangings of yellow, blue and other coloured damask and satin, wrought with gold trees and flowers and lined with canvas. There was a further bed with its bedding, and a canopy of taffeta, laced and fringed with red and white silk, with three curtains 'of the same stuffe to it'. A cupboard was covered with a needlework carpet and a square table, also had a russet velvet 'carpet' for it, paned with gold and silver lace and laid with gold and silver lace. There were several silk and needlework cushions. All of it made a comfortable room for a young woman. In contrast, and as a prelude to inventories describing the Lesser House, 'Mr Reason's Chamber', also in the Old Hardwick Hall, had: 'a bedsted seeled with tester of wood and turned postes, too blanketes, too coverletes, a square table, a carpet of grene cloth, a chare, a joyned stool'. The essentials, with few concessions to comfort.

As the inventories of some larger houses have demonstrated, during the Tudor period medieval constraints had been gradually cast aside in favour of a more comfortable way of life. This had involved changes in the uses of rooms, with less concentration on the hall as the hub of daily activity. Another area for dining was created and withdrawing after dinner was not to the 'solar' but to living areas which were smaller and warmer. A considerable use was made of many rich textiles, although it is perhaps surprising to encounter such

59 Hardwick Inv. 1601, introduction, pp.10–11.

60 Wingfield-Digby (1963) p.53; Nevinson (1973); Nevinson (1975–6).

a wide range of colours and materials. Nothing could be more striking as at Firle Place, East Sussex than the bed testers of black velvet paned with yellow satin. In addition, there is little mention of simple joined oak furniture (although that is understood for many bedsteads, stools and forms), but there are several instances too of walnut and inlaid beds and cupboards. There was a great provision of cushions to lean on in chairs and thick Spanish blankets to pull around one in bed. Whilst bed curtains might match in colour other parts of the bed, such as the valances, the total *en suite* look had yet to appear in a room. Nevertheless the start of the concept can be observed in the remarkable colour schemes which Sir Charles and Lady Morison had co-ordinated for Cassiobury in the 1590s. Finally, much of what was provided had the careful involvement of someone skilled in the arts of upholstery, but such a trade description is not found in Tudor house archives, although the inventories of many Tudor upholsterers' possessions do survive.

TUDOR INVENTORIES

The Lesser Houses

There are many Tudor inventories of the lesser house, and several record societies have issued a relevant volume. I have based my few comments here on those which have been edited for Nottinghamshire,[61] Yorkshire,[62] Coventry[63] and, based on similar sources, for Essex.[64] It might be expected in most houses that the basic requirements for sleeping were there. The will of William Richardes of Cropwell Bishop, Nottingham-shire dated 15 August 1558,[65] shows this typical provision, if a trifle more lavishly than some:

Item	2 fether beddes & 5 bolstares	£3
	6 matteris, 3 coverings, 15 coverlettes,	
	2 blanketes, 9 pillows	£10
	9 paire of lynen sheetes & one shete	£3
	4 payre of hempten shettes & 15	
	paire of hardin shettes	£2.6.8
	. . . one trusse bedde & 4 othere	
	bedde stockes	£0.13.4

The 'hardin' sheets were those made of coarse flax or hemp ('hards'). Again in the 1555 inventory[66] of Robert Clawghton of Coventry, a tanner, there is a bed, but it is described tersely:

In the Chambare	
A bed & all that longys to yt	£0.13.4
A torl [tall] bed	0.5.0
viii per a shettys	0.16.0

But, when an inventory was taken in April 1580 of the effects of a Coventry haberdasher, Richard Fitzherbert,[67] there is a greater degree of furnishings apparent when compared to the contents of the other two inventories. In Fitzherbert's parlour there was a bedstead and a tall bed (£1), two chests, two coffers (3s 4d), three stools (2s 8d), a close chair (2s), six cushions (5s), a carpet (3s 4d), two featherbeds (£1 10s 0d), two blankets (3s 4d), two bolsters (6s 0d), three pillows (3s), curtains, on an iron rod (4s), a table and two formes (10s) and paintings (5s). The house also had a hall, buttery, uppermost chamber, a chamber and a kitchen.

Inventories, carefully examined, tell a great deal about beds and bedding and other domestic furnishings. The term 'furniture' itself is often used to describe the bed-clothes; William Shakespeare refers, in his will, to 'my second best bed with the furniture'. This provision was usually for the wife; the best bed was for an eldest

61   Notts. Inv. 1516-62.
62   Yorks. Inv. 1542-1689.
63   Coventry Inv. (1987).
64   Emmison (1976).

65   Notts. Inv. 1516-62, p.57.
66   Coventry Inv. (1987) pp.39-41.
67   *Ibid.*, pp.55-60.

son. The bed and the table in whatever provision were, however, important basic requirements in the yeoman's house. The bed rarely had a ceiling, or tester, although in the Elizabethan period the terms are not synonymous, with the tester denoting what was called, at a later date, the vertical headboard. Many rooms were furnished both with a bed and a low trundle bed, frequently on wheels, which was pushed underneath the higher bed in daytime. Such beds were provided for children or maidservants.[68] As for bed-clothes – whilst William Harrison in his *Description* (1577)[69] implied that pillows were only for 'women in childbed' and that under-sheets were not given to servants, 'to keep them from the pricking straw that ran oft through the canvas of the pallet and rased their hardened hides', others fared better. Mattresses and pillows were often filled with feathers, down or flock and there were many quality sheets – 'fine holland with a bone lace set on' (1597) and coverlets, 'my best coverlet of tapestry work'.[70]

Floor carpets in the lesser house were rare, although 'carpets' were often provided to cover tables and cupboards. Elizabeth Harwoode of St Nicholas, Colchester, left in 1594 'My greatest Turkey carpet lying on the table in the hall'. Cushions, so much a feature of more lavish interiors, were rare; indeed seating itself was not common. The head of the household might have a 'joined chair', although sitting on stools or forms was more common: 'my long joined table with the stools thereunto belonging'. More comfortable seating was scarce in ordinary houses so that when, say, 'my embroidered chair and three embroidered stools' are mentioned in a will (1598) we can assume rare, treasured possessions.[71] Coffers to store clothing were listed frequently in a selection of Tudor Oxfordshire inventories,[72] some 168 of them over a forty year period. There is little doubt that in the skilled deployment of coverings of leather, fabric and often nail-patterned, some coffer-makers challenged and often usurped the upholsterer's trade. As the seventeenth century came into being this last calling, long in use, if unheralded, came to its true recognition.

68   Emmison (1976) pp.12–14.
69   Harrison (1968 ed.) p.204.
70   Emmison (1976) p.15.

71   *Ibid.*, p.18.
72   Oxfords. Inv. 1550–90, p.322.

1.   Cupboard cloth seen in *The Ambassadors* by Hans Holbein the Younger (1533) *London, National Gallery.*

A double portrait of Jean de Dinteville and Georges de Selve (right). Jean de Dinteville was French ambassador to the court of Henry VIII in 1533; in that year he was visited by Georges de Selve, later Bishop of Lavaur. They stand before a green figured damask curtain and are leaning on the cupboard cloth.

References: Rowlands (1985) No.47.

BEATVS vir qui non abiit
in confilio impiorum, & in via
peccatorum non ftetit, & in cathedra pe=
ftilentiæ non fedit.

2.   X-frame chair seen in the *Psalter of Henry VIII*, f.3 (1540) *London, British Museum*, (MS, Royal 2A, XVI).

Henry VIII is shown as 'Beatus Vir' reading the Psalms in his bedchamber. He is seated in a blue velvet upholstered X-frame chair, with a gold fringe at the arms, *en suite* with the bed valance and curtains.

3. (*opposite*)   'Queen Mary's Chair' (*c.*1554) $37\frac{1}{2} \times 24 \times 16\frac{1}{2}$ in (93.8 × 60 × 41.3 cm) *Winchester Cathedral.*

An oak X-frame chair covered with purple velvet held by gilt-headed nails. The X-frames have bronze *repousse* medallions at the intersections. The seat and arms are cushioned with hessian stuffed with horse-hair. Despite alterations and additions the chair is traditionally held to be that used by Queen Mary at her marriage in 1554 to Philip II of Spain in Winchester Cathedral. It is first mentioned in a cathedral inventory of 1633.

The Quieres and footemen nepte about her highnes litter barehed

The Auenes maiestie In her litter vnder the canapie borne by

The lord Robert Dudley mr of the horses leading the palfrey of honor

The lorde ambroye Dudley leading the second litter horse

The lord giles paulet leading the firste litter horse

4.   Armchair seen in a portrait of *Queen Mary I* by Studio of Anthonis Mor (1554) *Boston, Isabella Stewart Gardner Museum.*

The chair is covered in crimson velvet, embroidered in gold with a gold fringe at the centre back, arms and seat rail.

5.   Canopy and litter shown in *Queen Elizabeth I progressing to her Coronation* (1559) *London, College of Arms* (MS, M6, f.41v).

The litter is borne on posts passing through the harness of a leading and following horse. The canopy is held at the four corners by noblemen.

6. (*opposite*) X-frame chair seen in the portrait of *Mildred, Lady Burghley*, attributed to Hans Eworth (*c*.1563) *Hatfield House, Hertfordshire*.

The chair is covered in green velvet, held at the back with gilt boss nails with copper pommels at the top of the seat rail corners. There is a fringe at the top, lower back, and arms.

References: Auerbach and Adams (1971) No.35.

7. X-frame chair seen in the portrait of *William, first Earl of Pembroke*, attributed to Hans Eworth (*c*.1567) *Wilton House, Wiltshire*.

The chair is covered in brown velvet, held by gilded boss nails with gilded copper pommels at the top of the seat rail and arms. It is fringed at the top, centre back, and arms. Part of a tasselled cushion is also visible.

8.   Long cushion and tasselled sparver or canopy seen in portrait purporting to be of Frances Sidney, Countess of Suffolk (1575) *Sidney Sussex College, Cambridge.*

Research continues into confirming the identity of the sitter. Frances Sidney was the founder of Sidney Sussex College, Cambridge. The long cushion is a particularly fine example of gold thread work on black.

References: exhibited Tate Gallery, London, 'Dynasties' (1995) No.48.

9–10.   Canopy and tester cloth (1578) 108 × 62 in (274 × 157.5 cm) *Glasgow, Burrell Collection,* Inv. 445.

The headcloth, seat and cushions, known as the 'Kimberley Throne', are made of dark red velvet with applied gold and silver tissue tinted with colours and edged with gold bullion thread and embroidered in silks and metal threads. It bears the achievement of Wodehouse, supporters, helm, mantling and crest. On the tester cloth, formed from an extension of the headcloth, is a raised work of the arms of Wodehouse impaling Corbet within a circular embossed wreath. Queen Elizabeth I stayed at the Wodehouse Tower at Kimberley, Norfolk in 1578. Some restoration on the seat, sides and below the headpiece has been carried out.

11.   Table carpet (*c.*1580) 108 × 108 in (274 × 274 cm) *Hatfield House, Hertfordshire.*

Unlike many table carpets, this example, with its stylized Tudor roses in the border, was made in England.

References: M. J. Mayorcas, *English Needlework Carpets, 16th to 19th Centuries*, Leigh-on-Sea (1963) Pl. 4.

12. (*opposite, top*)   Long cushion cover (last quarter of the sixteenth century) *London, Victoria and Albert Museum*, Inv. T79-1946.

Embroidered in coloured silks and silver thread on canvas, applied to white satin.

13. (*opposite, bottom*)   Long cushion cover (*c.*1580) *London, Victoria and Albert Museum*, Inv. T120-1932.

Silk on linen canvas, incorporating the arms of the Warneford family.

possit et valeat possint et valeant perpetuis
alias personas quascunq; in socios et sch
ordinationes et statuta per eundem **Walter**
successoribus nostris per presentes comedi
illius sint unum corpus corporatum et pos

14. (*opposite*) Canopy and dais seen in the initial letter of the Charter of Emmanuel College, Cambridge, with the seated figure of Elizabeth I (1584) *Emmanuel College, Cambridge.*

15. (*above*) Cushion cover (detail) (*c.*1595) *Hardwick Hall, Derbyshire* (The National Trust).

Made of velvet with applied pieces showing the 'Fancie of the Fowler' returning from the chase to his family. Part of 'Winter' from a Four Seasons set, probably based on a Flemish engraving. The lady is Anne Keighley, first wife of William Cavendish, later first Earl of Devonshire. The initials 'AC' attached to the tree to identify her may, however, be a later insertion. Mentioned in the 1601 Hardwick inventory as being in the gallery.

16. (*right*) Braid (late sixteenth century) *Hardwick Hall, Derbyshire* (The National Trust).

17. (*overleaf*) Elizabethan 'Hunt' Embroidery (*c.*1595) chair 42 × 30 in (106.5 × 76.2 cm) *Hardwick Hall, Derbyshire* (The National Trust).

Mounted in the nineteenth century on brown velvet. The chair is signed, in pencil, 'P. Revell, 1845'. There is a footstool *en suite.*

III

For Court and Country 1603–1660

In the Time of King James

When Queen Elizabeth died at her favourite palace of Richmond, early in the morning of 24 March 1603, England was still at war with Spain. Admittedly, the creaking, heavy-laden ships of the Armada had been repulsed some fifteen years before, but England was ill-equipped, economically, for a long war. Therefore, when the new King, James I, arrived in England after a long journey from Scotland in early April via York, Burghley House and Theobalds House, he announced that he wished to end the war and, anxious for the profits of peace, few of his courtiers disagreed. But first there was the queen's funeral and the king's coronation to attend to, both occasions of defined and elaborate ritual.

In the book of accounts for the queen's funeral drawn up by Sir John Fortescue,[1] Master of the Great Wardrobe, there is an important addition to the names and trades of the artificers. In former years the Greene family,[2] succeeding each other with monotonous regularity as royal coffer-makers, had carried out most of the required tasks in upholstery. The list of 1603 now included, alongside details of work by the Greenes, the name of John Baker, Upholsterer. It is the earliest reference I have traced to the trade of upholsterer being mentioned in royal accounts. The full biographical story is difficult to chart, as there may be three John Bakers. A John Baker assisted at the coronation of Queen Elizabeth in 1559,[3] but no trade is given in the Latin text recording expenditure. This is presumably the same John Baker, noted above, who was confirmed again in his appointment in 1603, by James I, with a warrant for his livery.[4] The story might be as follows. By 1624 the elder John Baker was dead and he was succeeded on 29 September in that year by Oliver Browne. The record reads: 'Oliver Browne, whom we have appointed to be ye upholsterer in the roome and place of John Baker, deceased, 3 yds of red cloth, livery, at 12s a yard.'[5]

There is need to reckon too with Anthony Lasingby (there are several variant spellings of his name in use, such as Lacenbury) and with the partnership of Lasingby and Baker.[6] Lasingby was active, as was Baker, at James I's coronation in 1603, a fact noted below. However, on 25 February 1625, together with John Baker, he was granted his livery on then entering the service of Charles I.[7] John Baker, junior, was still alive in 1660 when he allowed his patent of appointment[8] to revert to the French upholsterer, John Casbert. This document stated: 'the said Oliver Browne is long since deceased', but referred to him as being earlier in the king's service, by Letters Patent of 17 November 1624, along with John Baker, holding 'the Office and place of Upholster of his Wardrobe of Bedds and standing Wardrobes . . .'

At the queen's funeral, Baker senior was supportive to the duties carried out by the faithful Greene family. Abraham Greene enclosed the queen's corpse in lead and John Greene covered the coffin with purple

1 P.R.O., LC2, 4/4.
2 Symonds (1943) pp.966 7; 1054–5 See also P.R.O., LC5/31; LC5/33; LC5/49; LC5/50; E101, 427/5 f.12.
3 P.R.O., LC4/3.
4 P.R.O., LC5/50, f.20.

5 P.R.O., LC5/50, f.166.
6 P.R.O. E101/434/9 f.40.
7 P.R.O., LC5/51 f.29, Cal. S.P. Dom, 1625–1626 (p.562).
8 P.R.O., LC5/52, ff.123–30.

velvet, garnished with gilt nails. The chairs, square stools and footstools used by the chief mourner, the Marchioness of Northampton, the senior lady of the nobility, and the two countesses who held her train, were covered by him with some of the many available yards of black velvet, as was also the chariot bearing the coffin as it lay in state.

John Baker had meanwhile been busy in hanging in black the various chambers where the corpse rested, and he also provided cloths of estate for the chapel at Whitehall. There is a majestic cadence about the entry[9] recording his work on the hearse:

> Item: for Covering & garnishinge the same hearse being covered all over with black velvett with
> a deepe vallance of black velvett round about garnished with depe frendge & lace of Venice
> gold; & black silke, the same being twice don, first with broadcloth, & velvett for the vallance
> and posts & after the black cloth taken of and Covered with velvett by command^mt of . . .

Twelve yards of black buckram was used to line a taffeta border. It was all fitting and distinguished in its stark morbidity.

The queen's funeral did not take place until 28 April 1603,[10] five weeks after her death. The procession involved over a thousand persons, each allotted the yardage of black cloth for cloaks or hoods appropriate to their station. Riderless horses, also clad in black, were led; trumpeters blew resounding blasts to keep the processional order demanded by the sergeants-at-arms. The great banner of England was held aloft at the head of so many more flapping pennants, by the Earls of Nottingham and of Pembroke. They preceded the hearse, itself decked in black by John Baker, and with the waxen image of the queen,[11] lying beneath a canopy carried by six earls. At the rear, with the guard, their halberds downwards, was Sir Walter Raleigh, still 'tall, handsome and bold', as John Aubrey had it, and ever the faithful maverick of Elizabeth's court. He had yet to realize that James I would deal with him harshly. At Westminster Abbey the coffin was lowered, creakingly, into its space alongside Mary Tudor; the household officers threw in their broken white staves of office, severing their formal service. At the closing of the tomb Sir John Fortescue's duties as Master of the Great Wardrobe were at an end.

Sir George Hume, later Earl of Dunbar and Lord High Treasurer of Scotland, was soon busy, as a newly created English baron, and the Wardrobe's new Master.[12] The earl had experience, having been Master of King James's Wardrobe in Scotland since 1592, but he needed now to come to terms with the duties of the Great Wardrobe in London. In the forty-five years or so that Sir John Fortescue had been its Master, with the last major event (the funeral apart) long ago in 1559, there had been time for the Wardrobe to become too complacent, for its officers to have witnessed it all before and for them to look only to their own advantage.

The coronation on 25 July 1603 was arranged at a level well below that considered normal because of the plague. Nevertheless, the upholsterer John Baker, senior and his team of Great Wardrobe artisans had, as usual, covered the fronts of the rows of seats and the abbey screen with fabric, laid carpets and put the chairs of estate in their prominent positions. Eight chairs were covered with fifty-four yards of cloth of gold and silver, at a cost of £202 10s, with thirteen yards of crimson damask (18s a yard) to cover the backs. There was provision too for gold and silver lace, and fringe, sewing silk, fustian for the seats, down to stuff them, and various bullion, gilt and black nails. The backs of the chairs were adjustable by means of iron ratchets. Two foot-stools were covered with cloth of gold and silver tissue.[13] Ceremony enough, but that of an even more lavish kind was reserved for the king's triumphal entry into London, in March 1604. This royal progress was made more dramatic for all who took part by the great arches erected along the route, designed by Stephen Harrison, and illustrated by him in his book of 1604, *Arches of Triumph*. Based on those for the entry of the Archduke Albert and the Infanta Isabella into Antwerp in 1599 they represented 'the earliest acknowledged application of the principles of harmonic proportion to architecture in England'.[14] The King of Scotland, and

9   P.R.O., LC2 4/4.
10 Nichols, *Progresses* (1828) III, pp.621–6.
11 Harvey and Mortimer (1994).

12 *Cal. S.P. Dom., 1603–1610*, p.80.
13 B.L., Add. MS., 34, 321.
14 Harris, Orgel and Strong (1973) p.23.

now of England, could ask for nothing more theatrical and they resembled to some degree the magnificent scenery of the imposing masques that were soon to be a regular part of his court's life.

THE KING'S CHIEF SECRETARY

One of the houses of which the king became especially fond was Theobalds in Hertfordshire. He had rested there first when coming from Scotland to London in May 1603, as the guest of Elizabeth's chief minister, William Cecil, Lord Burghley.[15] Cecil had started the building in 1564 and it had taken over twenty years to complete.[16] At Lord Burghley's death in 1598 it passed to his second son, Robert Cecil, soon, like his father, to be a leading member of the ruling administration. In fact, with typically adroit forethought Lord Burghley had obtained, in 1596, the post of Chief Secretary for his son. With careful manœuvres Robert Cecil not only became indispensable to the ageing queen, particularly in the matter of the French and Spanish conflict, but had extended, by secret letters over two years to James VI, the wish to see his safe succession to the English crown. In this he was successful, the culminating point in his long service, pursued despite chronic ill-health and a deformity that had dogged him from childhood.

One of the early diplomatic negotiations which Cecil arranged, to settle the war with Spain, was the conference at Somerset House on 16 August 1604. The king had assigned the house to his queen, Anne of Denmark, but she was rarely there, even after it was reconstructed (1609–12) on a lavish scale. The well-known painting of the conference in session (Pl. 18) shows Cecil on the right, at the head of the English negotiators, facing the delegation of six representing Spain and the Catholic Netherlands. The upholsterer, John Baker senior, had hung tapestries on the walls[17] and on the table there was a splendid carpet, a Turkish import of the small-pattern 'Holbein' kind. The eleven delegates sat in red or black fabric-covered X-frame chairs. These were meant to fold, in the way they had since early Egyptian times,[18] but those fashioned from the late Tudor period onwards rarely did, being covered with fabric, fringe and a near immovable superstructure. They are the type of chairs which appear regularly in the canvases of Hans Eworth, Marcus Gheeraerts the Younger and William Larkin (Pls 6, 24), replete with fringed and tasselled cushions. Studio props they may well have been, but of a kind well known and mentioned frequently in inventories.

At Theobalds Lord Burghley and his son 'had let the Renaissance strain in their imagination have full rein there'.[19] The king was both dazzled by its splendour and appreciative of the opportunities its estate gave him to hunt. Hunting was his major preoccupation and he entered into it with relish, oblivious of danger or of time needed for other more pressing matters, and being alternately depressed or elated by the success of his day's sport.[20] So Theobalds had to be his possession and he offered Cecil several properties in exchange for it, including the palace of Hatfield, where the young Elizabeth had first appointed William Cecil to be her minister. On 27 May 1607 James I was invited by Cecil for a visit to Theobalds before the formal handing-over to him took place. The visit was commemorated by a lavish entertainment in the long gallery in which Mercury 'descended in a flying posture to tell the mourning Genius of the house of her new master'.[21]

Despite his illnesses Robert Cecil's great extravagance was on building. He had begun in 1602 a London mansion, Salisbury House, just south of the Strand, and his exchange of Theobalds for Hatfield led to further building there on a grand scale. Additionally, there was the New Exchange in the Strand or 'Britain's Burse' as John Donne called it, built for Cecil by the royal surveyor, Simon Basil (although there is an unexecuted design for it by Inigo Jones at Worcester College, Oxford), and a fine hunting-lodge at Cranborne in Dorset.

The upholsterers hovered ready to attend to their part of these commissions. Unfortunately, only one important bill, tendered to Lord Salisbury (as Robert Cecil had been since 1605) in 1611 from the upholsterer,

15   Read (1955) and (1960).
16   Summerson (1959) pp.107–26.
17   *Cal. S.P. Venetian, 1602–7*, pp.143, 155, 175.
18   Eames (1977) pp.182–7.

19   Cecil (1973) p.129.
20   Willson (1956) pp.179–81.
21   Harris, Orgel and Strong (1973) p.32.

Robert Singleton, survives, together with an inventory of Hatfield for the same year.[22] The 1611 bill, of 31 December, paid in 1614, was addressed to Cecil as Lord Treasurer of England, a post he had held since 1607 alongside that of Chief Secretary. It is mostly concerned with work (Appendix A10) at Salisbury House – the first page has the heading 'in the new Rome at London' – but Hatfield work is perhaps also listed. One of the most poignant aspects is the provision of a number of items, including a wheelchair, to ease Lord Salisbury's growing incapacity:

> . . . for altaring & macking the turky bolster to lay under my Lords back.   0.3.0.

The wheelchair had a jointed frame with iron work, 'to rise & fall at plesure, with wheales & macking it fit for iron worke £2.5.0'. The sack cloth and girth web for the back and seat of the chair supported flock or down-filled bags; there were 'dubell elbowes' and a lavish use of black tacks, great and small (1s 6d), 'half a thousand of gilt nails' (5s), and eight great gilt nails (1s 4d). The frame was painted, as were the wheels and stay for the back. It went with Lord Salisbury to Bath in 1612 where he had gone to take the waters in a desperate attempt to stave off his serious illness. But the hot sulphurous vapours did him little good. On the way back to Hatfield the slow cavalcade got as far as Marlborough; he died there on 24 May, clasping the hand of his chaplain. Tidily, he had approved, three years earlier, the design, by Maximilian Colt, for his tomb. This, 'a simple contrast of black and white marble',[23] with the effigy in the robes of Lord Treasurer, and the actual staff of office in his hand, was erected in 1612 in Hatfield Church, within site of his greatest building enterprise.

The 1611 Hatfield inventory (there are eight others for later dates in the seventeenth century) lists the contents of over fifty rooms. These were ranged around the north, east and west sides of the site, with, at first floor level, a long gallery connecting the east and west projecting wings, and adjacent to a great chamber. The recessed south front formed a grand entrance, flanked by an open loggia (filled in during the nineteenth century). The east wing contained the private apartments, the chapel having been resited to enable this to be done.[24] I have noted the inventory text concerning the great parlour, 'Your Lo. bedchamber', the great chamber, and 'the King's bed chamber' (Appendix A11).

Queen Elizabeth visited many courtiers' houses – Theobalds, Holdenby and Audley End among them – but she had not engaged herself as her father Henry VIII had done, in major palace building. At eight houses a standing 'wardrobe' of furniture was maintained, which did not need to be moved to another place when the sovereign left. This useful facility applied at Whitehall, St James's, Somerset House, Hampton Court, Richmond, Greenwich, Eltham and Oatlands. In the essentials the functions which took place in the royal palaces had not changed to any extent since the early sixteenth century. However, within the reign of James I there was more building activity at royal palaces. The king had both a wife and heir who needed separate households, and I have noted his great interest in acquiring or setting up many lodges from which to hunt.[25]

THE KING'S SON

One of the important factions which Lord Salisbury had kept a secret eye on was that of the court of his monarch, James I and that of the king's son and heir, Henry, Prince of Wales. Life at both courts had been rendered more ill-at-ease in the last two years of Salisbury's life by the rising influence, since 1607, of the king's favourite, Robert Carr, later Earl of Somerset.[26] Henry's mother, Anne of Denmark, had kept the officers of the Works and of the Great Wardrobe (as well as the Standing Wardrobes) busy, as she altered, or moved to, the various palaces assigned to her: to Somerset House, to Greenwich, to Oatlands and to Byfleet Lodge, Surrey, hitherto a house granted to her son, Prince Henry. Her extravagances and interests had rubbed off on him but little is known of the precise details, as expenditure was from her privy purse.

---

22   Hatfield MSS., Bills 67b; Inventory.
23   Whinney (1988) pp.60–1.
24   Stone (1955) p.113.
25   H.K.W., IV. PtII, pp.29 fn.1, 31.
26   Seddon (1970) pp.48–68; Williams (1970) pp.133–7.

The prince had been allotted the palaces at Richmond and at St James's to his own use. At the latter he created a court filled with what have been termed 'young and Sprightly Blossoms';[27] gentlemen, for the most part, of the bed and privy chamber, some of them already receiving the king's favour. They had travelled abroad, seen much in the way of architecture and luxuriant stretching gardens, acquired Italian and Netherlandish paintings and formed many ideas on 'religion, learning and courteous behaviour'. As foreign travel was not in the prince's early curriculum they could bring their wider observation to his service, albeit only for a few short years. There can only be speculation at what might have been achieved at the prince's sparkling court had he not died, at the age of eighteen years, on 6 November 1612.[28]

At the end of his *History of the World* Sir Walter Raleigh, confined within the Tower, lamented the death 'of the most noble and most hopefull Prince Henry'. This took place on the November evening, leaving the king, his queen and the two remaining children (Elizabeth and Charles, now the heir to the kingdom) distraught, and with the knowledge, as the Earl of Dorset had it, 'that our Rising Sun is set ere scarce he had shone'.[29] The king withdrew, grieving, to Theobalds. The news of the calamitous loss travelled swiftly enough to the Master of the Great Wardrobe, James Hay, later the first Earl of Carlisle. He had come south from Scotland with James I, and had had a barony conferred by him in 1606. His six principal artisans in the Great Wardrobe set to work with their men in the certainty that the precedents were known well to the many who would take part in the sad ceremony.

The funeral expenses of Henry, prince of Wales are set out in a folio volume,[30] sombre and precise, with each yard of black cloth accounted for. The open chariot, drawn by six horses, on which the coffin and a 'goodly image' of the prince lay, had had its pillars covered in black velvet by the coffer-maker, John Lewgar, and armorials and banners had been painted by the king's serjeant-painter, John de Critz. Richard Norris had provided an elm coffin and the upholsterer, John Baker, senior, covered this with 'purple velvet garnished with silke lace, guilt nailes & other necessaries'. The procession,[31] over a mile long, and with two thousand mourners dressed in black, wound its way, on 7 December, to Westminster Abbey, where the coffin, with its effigy, was placed on 'a great stately hearse'. The chief mourners were the twelve year old Charles, Prince of Wales, a slight weakly child bowed at the loss of his brother, and Frederick V, Elector Palatine, later King of Bohemia and soon to be married to Henry's sister, Elizabeth.

Within the abbey, John Baker and his men had been busy throughout the latter half of November and early days of December. The hearse, supported on six Ionic columns (Pl. 22), with its woodwork by William Portington, was enriched with one of the few splashes of colour amidst the black, the banners, arms and mottoes embroidered by the king's embroider, William Broderick (1558–1621). Baker had provided a cloth of estate, black hangings for various rooms and chairs and cushions for the two chief mourners. He covered the choir, the pews and pulpit with fabric or with cloths, set curtains of black cloth, lined with taffeta, to all the windows and erected two 'Paules of black velvet, and the Rich banner of England' in blue and crimson satin and cloth of gold. He also supplied banners of black taffeta to hang, mute enough, below the upheld, sounding trumpets. For his attendance Baker was attired in the four yards of black cloth allowed for his cloak. He knew that the four suppliers of the hundreds of yards used would wait as long as he would for any payment – his £158 8s was carried forward in the account book – but at least his job as upholsterer had not depended on the Prince's patronage.

The Earl of Northampton's House

The marriage of Frederick, the Elector Palatine of the Rhine, to the Princess Elizabeth took place on 14 February 1613, at the decent interval of three months after Prince Henry's death. One who abhorred the expense of this St Valentine's Day match was Henry Howard, Earl of Northampton, one of the king's

27 Strong (1986) pp.220–1.
28 Wilson (1653) p.52.
29 Strong (1986) p.221.
30 P.R.O., LC2, 4/6.
31 Set out in P.R.O., S.P., 14/71, ff.104.

courtiers, whose life had been one long, intricate and ill-tempered affair.[32] He knew, as a Commissioner for the Treasury, that the King's Exchequer was under severe strain. Northampton had hated Lord Salisbury and after the earl's death had gathered the great Howard family to his side, and was mainly responsible for ensuring its future secure position. Parliament was proving difficult to manage, and was seriously at odds over the king's mounting debts. On 4 May 1614 the king took the extreme measure of addressing the Commons, but they still refused him supply, and determined to conduct no useful business. But by 15 June the arch-conspirator in all these intrigues, the Earl of Northampton, was also dead. When the inventory of his effects was published in 1869[33] the editor, E. P. Shirley, noted that the earl would always be connected to the 'still existing Northampton, or as it is now called Northumberland House, built by this same earl, with Spanish gold . . .'. He also stated that all previous inventories needed to yield in importance to the Northampton one, 'in the enumeration of plates and jewels'. The inventory does list a vast number of such precious metals, totalling 2820 ounces. It is, however, the upholstered household goods in London, and at Greenwich, which are of concern here. Some of them were exotic. Quotation about them at some length could be justified (Appendix A12), but only one example must suffice:

> a field bedstead of *China* worke, blacke and silver, branched with silver, with the Armes of the Earle of Northampton upon the head peece, the toppe and valance of purple velvett, striped downe with silver laces and knottes of silver, with 8 cuppes and plumes spangled suteable, the 5 curtanes of purple taffata with buttones and lace of silver, the counterpoint of purple damaske suteable laced, with two featherbeds and one fustian downe bed, a wool bed, a French quilte, one fustian blankett, and another blanckett, one bowlster and two pillowes.   xxx li [£]

The bedstead was presumably an early lacquer import to England by the East India Company. Northampton House was furnished, in short terms, with a great deal of tapestry, with the bed chamber, containing the 'China' field bedstead, hung with 'fowre pieces of hanginges of Bruxels worke garnished in the border with Cardinall Wolsey his armes . . .'; there were also leather hangings 'ten foot deep', in azure and gold, Persian and Turkish carpets, velvet chairs and pillows, long tables and inlaid cabinets.

In addition over one hundred paintings hung on the gallery walls; there was also a considerable library and a fine collection of plate and jewels. An analysis of what chairs were available is instructive. The great chamber had six green stools, 'embrodered with velvett and greene twist upon clothe', a green velvet chair with a large cushion and four further green velvet stools. In the dining chamber, set out over a long 'Turkie carpett of Englishe worke', there was a high chair, a low chair, a short and a long cushion, two high stools, one low stool of cloth of gold, 'the ground maidenheare with frindge and tarsels of golde lined with damaske watchett and maidenheare', and six high stools of fringed russet velvet. There are too many rooms listed in the Northampton inventory to extract such details for each one, but one or two items do tempt mention. The long wardrobe had, besides a great chair of embroidered purple satin, a scroll chair, one high stool, a low stool and a footstool, *en suite* to the purple chair, 'one faire crimson velvett chaire richlie imbosted with copper and spread eagles, and blewe and white flowers, China worke, the frame painted with gold, and my Lord's crest upon the same'.

At Lord Northampton's Greenwich house, within the royal park, there is only a single mention in the inventory of red cotton covers. These were to protect a large chair, two stools and one long cushion 'laced with redd taffata of crimson damaske frindged with silke and golde'. The inventory makes clear, by its listing of a lavish provision of tapestry and gilt–leather hangings, chairs, stools, beds, cushions, tables (mostly of walnut) and carpets that it was all calculated to show the status and comfort needed by the earl's affluent position. He owed this to the king and had garnered it in the time of an expanding European market, as an assiduous Catholic bachelor, but with friends as hard an unscrupulous in the trading field as Lionel Cranfield, Earl of

---

32 Peck (1982).   33 Howard Inv. (1869) p.347.

Middlesex and Sir Arthur Ingram.[34] All three of them had put making large profits at the head of their considerable enterprises, and Cranfield and Ingram remained active at it all for many years after Lord Northampton's death.

QUEEN ANNE OF DENMARK

Festivities such as masques were numerous at the Jacobean court. Both the king and his queen delighted in them and they had been revitalized from their Elizabethan form by the combined talents of Inigo Jones and Ben Jonson. Strong beliefs 'about the nature of kingship, the obligations and perquisites of royalty' could be expressed in them. Queen Anne was an early patron of Jones in this respect, and she and her ladies danced in many of the masques he devised. The court, wrote Arthur Wilson in 1653,[35] was 'a continued masquerado, where the Queen and her ladies, like so many sea-nymphs, or Nerieds, appeared often in various dresses to the ravishment of the beholders, the King himself being not a little delighted with such fluent elegancies as made the night more glorious than the day'. In addition, Jones had created many masques for Prince Henry and one for his sister Elizabeth's wedding, but he was most active from 1615 in building for the queen at Greenwich, Oatlands and Byfleet. Principally, this included work at the Queen's House at Greenwich, 'the fount of the classical tradition in Britain', which had been started under Simon Basil, 1607 to 1609, and continued by Jones from 1616.[36]

Oatlands Palace in Surrey had been granted to Queen Anne by the king in August 1611. It was a large house, due to the extensions to it Henry VIII had made in 1544, seven years after he had acquired it, by exchange. Queen Elizabeth made few amendments there and, apart from some gateways and various minor works designed by Inigo Jones, Queen Anne left the structure alone too. But the furnishings she inherited or acquired for the house were most lavish. Some of these were tapestries and carpets left from Henry VIII's huge collections. Others, more recent, were put into position for the great reception and banquet she gave there on 30 September 1617, for Pietro Contarini, the Venetian ambassador in England.

The ambassador reported back[37] to his masters that the queen had sent him, prior to his visit, gifts of two bucks and a stag, dressed ready to eat. His visit to Oatlands was conducted in pouring rain which ruined the intended hunt. After his reception Contarini's secretary noted that all had remained standing during the first ceremonies, 'which were most stately and grave'. He continued:

> . . . Then the Queen seated herself on the dais, making His Excellency sit likewise and cover himself. A circle of cavaliers and ladies was formed round them at some distance . . .
>
> The dinner was prepared in a large and comely place for about 20 persons, as a mark of honour to his Excellency, who was to sit alone in a high elbow chair of crimson velvet, whereas all the other cavaliers and ladies were on stools without any support, though covered with silk.

After retiring, at its conclusion, the ambassador was brought finally to the king, with whom he had 'a pleasant discourse'.

Knowledge of the furnishings at Oatlands comes from three inventories; one of October 1616 endorsed 'her ma^t stuff in Otelands left in Ober 1616', and two others of October 1618, which are almost identical except that one is arranged by rooms and the other, mostly, by type of content.[38] The categories listed were: hangings; carpets; suites of canopies, couches, chairs, stools, cushions, beds, window curtains; screens; looking-glasses; tables, forms and cupboards; brass handirons; pictures '& postures'; 'Stuffe said to bee the kings not belonging to his Mats wardrobe at Oatlands but to other wardrobes'; and 'stuff missing that were in last Survey, 1617'. I have listed the hangings and other furnishings at some length because of the opulent setting they portray (Appendix A13).

34 Peck (1982) p.122ff.
35 Wilson (1653) pp.53–4.
36 Harris, Orgel and Strong (1973) pp.35–6, 95–9; Harris and Higgott (1989) p.13ff., p.64.

37 *Cal. S.P. Venetian, 1617–19* (1909) p.314.
38 Oatlands Inv. (1618).

The furnishings at Oatlands described in the inventories were those spread through fourteen of the most important rooms. The arrangement of separate apartments for the king and queen had been determined in the extensive rebuilding on the moated site, carried out for Henry VIII from 1537 to 1545. Queen Anne's apartments were in one of the cross-wings on either side of an inner courtyard at the north-west end of the building. But, lavishly as the palace was equipped, the queen's residence there was short. Since about 1606 she had lived apart from the king, at Greenwich or at Denmark House.[39] The queen, moreover, was an ardent Catholic and as her health and spirits declined she had become more dependent on the compelling advice of her priests. They refused her the sacrament unless she ceased to attend the Church of England. Ill from dropsy, she moved in 1618 back to Hampton Court which necessitated the taking of the Oatlands inventories. Being nearer to London (Oatlands was twenty miles away) made it easier for the king to visit her, twice a week. Yet he was far away, at Newmarket, when she died on 2 March 1619. He fell into a dangerous sickness, encouraged by melancholy, and did not even attend the queen's funeral. This was arranged by the new master of the Great Wardrobe, Lionel Cranfield, Earl of Middlesex, who had been in office for six months. He had been active in promising to rid the office of graft and extravagance. The funeral was estimated to cost not less than £24,000, but Cranfield offered to arrange it for £20,000; in fact he cleared it all at £15,000.[40]

Some of this was achieved by his cutting down on personnel, bringing in his own personal servants and introducing a new accounting system. Cranfield held that a principal source of profit to the Wardrobe arose from a long extension of credit. To withstand this merchants charged a third or double above market rates and were ready to share the surplus with the master, his deputy and the tradesmen. Payment to them was slow and there were large arrears which absorbed any provision of funds.

Cranfield's system of reorganization involved cancelling all existing contracts and negotiating new ones. In the defence of April 1632 which he made, following his unfortunate (and, perhaps, unfair) impeachment in 1624, the master explained:

> I bought my cloth of gold, silver and tissues, my velvets, satins, damasks and taffetas, and my hangings, carpets and all other things of value of the merchants at the first and best hand with ready money and charged his Majesty with no other prices than I paid them. And by that course damned the detestable names of Wardrobe prices.

As part of this process Cranfield had arranged an early meeting with the suffering merchants and told them 'that I would have his Majesty's money as good and valuable as other men's', to which, if they would conform and provide their usual services, he would arrange prompt payment. The threat of otherwise going 'where I could have the best and best cheap' led to acceptance of the offer.[41] I shall refer to Cranfield again because in a private capacity the early and important upholstered seat furniture from Copt Hall, Essex, acquired by Cranfield in 1624,[42] and now at Knole in Kent, came there through his daughter, Frances after her marriage to Richard Sackville.

THE DUKE OF BUCKINGHAM

In King James's last remaining years, moving in and out of bouts of illness, he still had enough charismatic presence to overshadow his young son, Prince Charles, who had been born in 1600. The Venetian ambassador described him, in 1617:[43] 'The Prince is a youth of about sixteen, very grave and polite, of good constitution so far as can be judged from his appearance. His hair is light and he closely resembles his royal mother. He was dressed in scarlet and gold lace, with a gilt sword and white boots, with gold spurs according to the fashion of the country'.

39 Williams (1970).
40 Prestwich (1966) p.231.
41 *Ibid.*, pp.229–31.

42 *Ibid.*, p.412.
43 *Cal. S.P. Venetian, 1617–19*, p.241.

One of the things the rather dull, shy young man had to contend with was the king's love for the handsome George Villiers, Duke of Buckingham. 'No one', wrote Arthur Wilson in 1653, 'dances better, no man runs or jumps better. Indeed he jumped higher than ever Englishman did in so short a time, from a private gentleman to a dukedom'. By 1617 he was Master of the Horse, a Knight of the Garter, a member of the Privy Council and had been given large gifts of land. He was also soon possessed of New Hall, Essex and York House, in the Strand, London, arranged with the advice of Balthazar Gerbier, a talented young diplomat then in the service of the Dutch ambassador. Gerbier was soon to serve the prince when he became king and survived adroitly into the age of Charles II, designing the triumphal arches for the king's coronation in 1661.

The young Prince of Wales (Pl. 26) found that the upholsterers Anthony Lasingby and John Baker could make his residences more comfortable with their large X-framed chairs, high stools and footstools. All these were covered with crimson velvet, garnished with lace and fringe of silk and gold; the lavish chair and stool cushions were filled with down. Gilt copper nails were used to garnish the same chairs and stools and the backs were enhanced with 'great Bullion nails of Copper guilt'. The crimson velvet and damask they used had been provided by Thomas Woodrove and the broad gold lace and deep gold fringe from Samuel Paskefor. Woodrove charged 30s a yard for the velvet and 18s for the damask. This was used to line the cushions and chair backs. Paskefor charged 7s 6d an ounce for the gold laces and fringes, supplying in all some 270 yards of various kinds.[44]

In 1620 the favoured Duke of Buckingham had married Lady Catherine Manners, the only daughter of Francis Manners, sixth Earl of Rutland. She had grown up in the hill-top castle of Belvoir in Leicestershire, built by the first Earl about 1528, but demolished in 1649 after a prolonged siege during the Civil War; the present castle is the fourth on the site, created between 1800 and 1830. Catherine's grandfather, Roger Manners, the fourth earl, had welcomed James VI to Belvoir on 22–3 April, 1603 on his journey south from Scotland. He had been pardoned for his share in the Essex plot against Queen Elizabeth and released from the Tower a year or so before the new king's visit. The earl was also honoured by being chosen to carry the Kirtle and Mantle of the Order of the Garter from James I to his brother-in-law, Christian IV, King of Denmark and Norway.[45]

King James approved of Buckingham's marriage but disapproved of the quarrels the duke had frequently with Prince Charles. He finally reconciled their several peevish differences and there were rumbustious parties at Belvoir, at Wanstead (which the duke had acquired in 1619) and at Whitehall. In all of these locations help was given by John Baker, senior, as the 'King's Upholster'.[46] He was presumably ready to recall that many years before, in 1603, he had provided five purple and crimson velvet cushions and two long cushions of purple velvet, tasselled with Venice gold and purple silk, for use in displaying the Order of the Garter, including that carried by the Earl of Rutland to Denmark.[47]

As is often the way, the Duke of Buckingham and the Prince became very good friends. They travelled together to Spain, in March 1623, on an impetuous mission in which Charles sought the hand of the Spanish Infanta. This approach greatly embarrassed the Spanish king, who had no wish to allow the marriage. He instituted delays and tests of good faith, which led to an angry Charles and his friend the duke returning to England in October, eager only for a declaration of war on Spain.

PRIVATE PALACES IN LONDON AND THE COUNTRY

Near to the Duke of Buckingham's house in the Strand was the imposing late Elizabethan Bedford House, built for the third Earl of Bedford. Its family apartments, numbered among some forty-five rooms, were hung with splendid tapestries and the long gallery, overlooking the Strand, had gilt leather and green cloth on its walls. The furniture, set over many Turkey carpets (as at Oatlands) was upholstered in red velvet, or Spanish leather.

44 P.R.O., E101/434, ff.9–13.

45 Arnold (1992).

46 *Cal. S.P. Dom. 1619–23*, pp.502–3.

47 P.R.O., LC5/37, f.321.

It was a fitting setting for housing the Russells who, as a family, were regularly in London for the London season, before returning to their Tudor house, Chenies in Buckinghamshire.[48]

A considerable increase in refinement and luxury in England had taken place during the latter part of the sixteenth and early years of the seventeenth century. This is borne out by many inventories, including that taken on 30 April 1622 at the death of Sir George Shirley 'of Nether Etindon in the County of Warwick and of Shirley in the County of Derby'. It can be compared with that taken in 1517 at the death of Sir Ralph Shirley.[49] Sir George had a more elaborately decorated bed in the best chamber, with red taffeta curtains, gilt cups with feathers, an embroidered tester head and valance, as well as more furniture, with two low stools 'sutable to the bed', an embroidered chair, a turkey work stool and carpet, a square table, a court cupboard, velvet cushions with gold lace, five pieces of 'arras worke', one window curtain (to draw on a single rod to cover all the opening), bedding with a silk quilt and fire-irons of silver.

There was also ample provision, in the house's great parlour, of floor carpets, cupboard and table carpets, sixteen turkey-work and wrought velvet stools, window cushions of black velvet with yellow silk lace, and a pair of tables in a French 'du Cerceau style' having supports of carved 'men'. Sir Ralph had no musical instruments in his 1517 house but Sir George, in 1622, had a harpsichord in the gallery, surrounded by several sumptuous chairs and couches, covered in red leather, turkey-work, tawny velvet and cloth of silver. Further, in Sir Thomas Fairfax's chamber at Walton in Yorkshire, there was, in April 1624, an 'orpharion', a musical instrument shaped like a lute, but strung with wire.[50] Again, there was the provision of a bed 'with tester and head peece wrought with black velvet & yellow silk', which, with a white damask chair and a little red chair, must have presented a comfortable opulent setting.

THE KING'S DEATH

James I was free from his painful arthritis in the warm, dry summer of 1624. By the autumn he had succumbed to severe attacks, and his hands became too swollen and crippled for him to sign his name. Whilst Christmas was celebrated at the royal palace of Whitehall, the king kept to his room, journeying away, early in the New Year, to Royston and to Newmarket. By the beginning of March he was at Theobalds, but his favourite house could not lift health and spirits already severely weakened. He became ill with an acute fever and, ever a bad patient, disobeyed his physicians constantly, and sought dubious remedies from a doctor recommended by both the Duke of Buckingham and his mother, Mary Beaumont, the Dowager Countess. These potions failed and one of the king's doctors, George Englishman, published a tract accusing Buckingham of poisoning the sovereign. By 24 March, the king's illness, howsoever determined, was severe. He received the final Sacrament and called to his presence the twenty-five year old heir, Prince Charles, 'but nature being exhausted he had no strength to express his intention'. On the morning of Sunday, 27 March 1625, at a little before noon, and 'without pangs or convulsions at all', the king died, 'his lords and servants kneeling on one side, his archbishops, bishops and other of his chaplains on the other side of his bed . . .'[51]

At some point shortly after 1620 the death of John Baker, senior, occurred. He is last mentioned in the Wardrobe archives, for May 1620, with the warrant for his livery.[52] On 29 September 1624, Oliver Browne, 'whom wee have appointed to be ye upholster in the roome and place of John Baker, deceased', received his livery of three yards of red cloth, at 12s a yard.[53] Moreover, Browne had been involved with John Baker, junior, for a few years and they were to act together at the king's funeral in 1625. However, Baker junior's activities were soon to be linked, seemingly as a partner, with those of Anthony Lasingby. Looking ahead a year or so, they are listed together as taking delivery of their new liveries, as 'His Majesty's Upholsters', on 25 February 1626, in the first year of Charles I's reign.[54]

48   Thomson (1937) p.38; Thomson (1949) Ch.II.
49   *Stemmata Shirleiana* (1873) p.92, Appendix, p.cxv.
50   Fairfax Inv. (1624) p.138.
51   Nichols, *Progresses* (1828) IV, pp.1028–52; *Cal. S.P. Venetian, 1623–5*, pp. 625–7.

52   P.R.O., LC5/50, f.20.
53   *Ibid.*, f.166.
54   P.R.O., LC5/51, f.29.

A Funeral and a Marriage

It was expected of royal servants that they showed no approval or disapproval of what their masters wanted or did. Only at death could they permit themselves a private analysis. The Earl of Denbigh, as Master of the Great Wardrobe, oversaw the lavish preparations for the king's funeral. All the artificers are listed in the book of accounts,[55] with work as varied as paying Nicholas Read for the timber work of seven Chairs of State, and the sculptor Maximilian Colt for a wood crown for the effigy and copper plates on the coffin. The coffermaker, John Lewgar, had covered the coffin in purple velvet supplied by Richard Miller, who also provided satin, cloth of gold and taffeta, as well as hanging Denmark House, as Somerset House was renamed when it was the home of Anne of Denmark from 1617–19, with the black cloth of mourning. Oliver Browne and John Baker, junior, as the king's upholsterers, provided cloths of estate at Whitehall, and covered the great hearse designed for Westminster Abbey by the surveyor, Inigo Jones,[56] with black velvet garnished with fringe and lace of black silk. The upholsterer, Ralph Grynder (as he habitually signed, and of whom more presently), assisted with 'divers necessaries', curtains of black taffeta, the making of folding chairs and supplying them with 'long pillows' of black velvet. The winding, hierarchical procession to the abbey, common to all royal funerals, consisted on this occasion of 9,000 persons. Amongst them, Inigo Jones and the sculptor Maximilian Colt had been granted nine and seven yards of black cloth respectively for their mourning robes, and Browne and Baker, the upholsterers, together with John Lewgar (coffer maker), Benjamin Henshaw (silk-man), Peter Bland (skinner) and John Shepley (embroiderer) received seven yards each with two yards each for their servants.

The Prince's Marriage

Despite King James's declining health throughout 1624 negotiations had been in hand for a marriage between Prince Charles and Henrietta Maria, born in 1609 as the daughter of Henri IV of France and his Queen, Marie de' Medici. Henri was assassinated within a few months of Henrietta's birth; her brother eventually became king as Louis XIII. It was necessary that any marriage alliance secured many dispensations for Henrietta, such as demanding Catholic chapels and chaplains in all the royal houses outside London, and that her household retinue should consist of French Catholics. It was decreed, by the complicated arrangements necessary to satisfy the Pope, Louis and his French negotiators, and amongst many other restrictions and diplomatic requirements, that the queen was married at Notre-Dame, on May Day 1625.[57] The Duc de Chevreuse stood as proxy for the absent and Protestant bridegroom, and in lieu also of the Duke of Buckingham. He had intended to come as proxy bridegroom but had been delayed. He arrived finally, with a richly equipped entourage ready, after due dalliance, to escort the new young queen to England. She was fifteen years old and inflexible in her religion. She had been instructed initially at the hands of the Carmelites, and such devotion was to last throughout a further fifty years of her life, causing much unease in an unreservedly Protestant England. But it did not blind her to the secular necessity of a lavish trousseau, as well as the intention to bring a great bed of red velvet, embroidered with silver, a dressing table, silver mirrors, Turkey carpets and four sets of plate for celebrating the Mass.[58] She arrived at Dover on Trinity Sunday, 13 June 1625, and was carried (after an overnight stay at Dover Castle) to Canterbury Cathedral. There, at her second wedding was her husband, and not merely the Duc de Chevreuse. Two days later, on 16 June, the couple were in London and travelling in the royal barge along the Thames to Somerset House which was soon to be in King Charles's gift to his queen. She also had use of several other grand residences, enough to lift the most jaded of situations, such as St James's Palace, the Queen's House at Greenwich, Nonsuch, Oatlands, Richmond, Wimbledon and the sprawling

---

55 P.R.O., LC2/6, ff.16–18.
56 Harris, Orgel and Strong (1973) p.136.
57 Hamilton (1976) p.48.
58 *Ibid.*, p.50.

palace of Whitehall. In most of them, aided by brilliant adaptations by Inigo Jones, she was able to impose 'a lavish new style of interior decoration in the royal apartments of England in the French manner.'[59]

THE QUEEN'S UPHOLSTERER

Mindful of the queen's wishes, expressed previously and in strong terms by her advisers, that her household staff should be, in the main, French and Catholic, the choice of queen's upholsterer was interesting. Ralph Grynder had been involved to some extent, as noted above, in the preparations for James I's funeral. It might be assumed on his entering the queen's service that he was a Catholic, but a further, if slight confirmation of this is provided in the headings of several of his bills, the contents of which are referred to below. He charged, for example, for the period 'from our Lady day 1628 to Midsomer'.[60] Catholics, in my experience, refer to 'Our Lady', and a non-Catholic might have written 'from Lady Day . . .'

The queen had been accompanied on her journey from France to England by the Duc and Duchesse de Chevreuse. In the accounts covering 1623–7[61] Grynder charged for his work in 1624–5, which included:

> for the hire of nine and fifty pieces of Tapestry hangings, 42 standing bedsteads with their furniture, 76 featherbeds and bolsters to them, 79 pair of blankets, 74 rugs and counterptes, 24 down pillows, 36 leather chairs, 84 bed mats and 44 bed cords, all for the service of the Duc and Dutchesse d' Chevereux and their followers at Denmark House in the Strand by the space of five weeks.   £25 5s 5d

The hiring-out of furniture by upholsterers and others in the furniture trades is an interesting subject. It is obvious that in cities such as London or Bath, with defined 'seasons', and, in the case of Bath, residence to take the waters, hiring furniture made for good and sensible business. Grynder had charged previously, in 1623,[62] on 'the Tower charge', 'for the hire of six complete suite of Tapistry hangings cont. thirtie peeces for that time', of sixteen weeks and five days. The comforts which long-held prisoners in the Tower were able to solicit may be relevant here, but equally the bill included making and covering two chairs of state, making and backing cushions 'trimmed with gold and silver fringes and tassels', baize cases to cover them all, and several Persian and 'Turq. making' carpets.

As early as 1623, in anticipation of Charles's marriage with the Catholic Spanish Infanta, Inigo Jones had been busy with chapels at St James's Palace and at Somerset House. When the marriage with Henrietta Maria had gone ahead instead the chapel at the palace was pushed to completion. It survives as one of the least altered of Jones's innovative structures. However, damage to it during the Civil War destroyed Ralph Grynder's upholstered furnishings and the present fittings date from the 1680s. Apart from the chapel providing sustenance for the soul, the queen's bedchamber was adorned in 1629 and 1630, and a sculpture gallery built in the orchard garden.

The years from 1630 to 1640, immediately preceding the Civil War in England, saw a dramatic change in social and political life. In personal terms, for Queen Henrietta, her influence could only be recognized after the death, by assassination on 23 August 1628, of the king's favourite courtier, the Duke of Buckingham. Hurrying to the king's stricken side at Farnham, the queen 'stepped effortlessly into the place which the Duke had occupied so long'.[63]

One of the abiding problems to beset the royal household at the succession of the new king and his queen was finance. In 1626 the Exchequer almost stopped the payment of wages to household officers. Within a couple of years, whilst long-suffering at non-payment, they were threatening to suspend their duties.[64] Additionally, the artificers had suffered the same problem. On 15 November 1626 Oliver Browne, 'one of his

59   Harris and Higgott (1989) p.193.
60   P.R.O., LR5/64.
61   P.R.O., LC5/38, f.31.

62   *Ibid.*, f.17.
63   Hamilton (1976) pp.89–91.
64   F. Dietz (1932) pp.223, 228.

Majesty's upholsterers', was finally able to claim, by warrant, £380 1s 4d for goods supplied over 'eight years since'.[65] Corruption, waste and duplicity were rife and departmental stringency was ordered. Sales of crown lands, the pawning of the crown jewels in Holland, the reining in of household provision added to the coffers but dribbled through as rapidly as spilled grain. It was reported that the queen was so ashamed of her worn-down apartments that she received the Duchess of Tremouille in the dark.[66] Also the costs of the wardrobe had mounted as sharply as they had done at the earlier accession of James I.[67] A detailed set of orders (Appendix A14) for its better conduct was issued in April 1630, following a report to the king and Privy Council. Payment of its wages and debts due to April 1630 were suspended, so that the wardrobe's finances could be set on a more structured base. Little was done, however, that alleviated the problem and wardrobe expenditure for 1630–1 still amounted to over £27,600. Some of this was laid at the door of Sir Bevis Thelwall, the clerk of the Great Wardrobe, who was then charged with irregular conduct over payments.[68] Uneasy attempts at reform followed through the 1630s with little enough success as to allow the queen to spend, lavishly, on her several houses. Lying-in at one of them, St James's Palace, Charles, Prince of Wales, the future Charles II, was born on 29 May 1630. Her First Lady of the Bedchamber, Susan, Countess of Denbigh (the late Duke of Buckingham's sister), had been allowed, by warrant, some £2,000 for the provision of linen for the event, and over £600 was spent on the embroidery of the queen's bed. It was some five years before the bill was paid. The entry reads: 'embroidering a rich bed and canopy of green satin with other furniture for Her Majesty's Bedchamber against her lying in 1630, £675, & similar charges for a bed of tawny velvet in 1631 £771 16s 3d.'[69] This was a considerable amount to spend in a time of financial stringency but was, perhaps, an acceptable deviation from the usual pattern.

When the queen was well again and busy, accompanied on all suitable occasions by the king, her ladies, favourite dwarf, Jeffrey Hudson, and pets, she turned back to her abiding interest with architecture. Funds from her privy purse, and therefore difficult to assess, were directed towards the completion of the Queen's House at Greenwich, begun by Jones in 1616 for Queen Anne of Denmark and remaining still as one of his most influential works.[70] The tasks of decoration went on throughout the 1630s, with a fascinating series of little-known bills[71] documenting much of the activity. The upholsterer, Ralph Grynder, worked faithfully, here and at all the queen's residences but, nevertheless, waited several years for his payment. In his bills he often described following a 'french fashion'. For example, in his bill for 1628 he made two damask carpets in 'french fashion', garnished with gold and silver buttons and gold fringes. In that for 1637 he provided 'french Cupps' to her Majesty's 'Rich Bedd' and made '2 french Chayres, being Courvad all over with figured Velvett & garnisht Round with silver fringes'. One wonders whether, in fact, he was French.

Furniture had to be carried from various houses to Greenwich by water, and some indication of Grynder's workforce is instanced by his charging for himself and for boat or horse hire for up to three men. Grynder's 1637 bill (Appendix A15) is a long and interesting one, again with several mentions of French items. In making a large couch bed covered with figured velvet he used a stuffing of felt with a lining of buckram for the back and elbows. Forty-six pounds of 'fine Burgis feathers' filled the seat and wings and a final, lavish effect was given by the use of five hundred 'silvered Bullen nayles' and one thousand of burnished silver. All the iron stays which allowed the backs of the couches or chairs to be raised or lowered were silvered. Further, he charged in 1637 'ffor 2 days work for 2 men to putt upp her Maties Bedd & hanging up hangings & Takinge downe at Hampton Court'.

The mid-1630s had seen Inigo Jones active on behalf of the queen in preparing the chapel at Somerset House for Catholic worship. The Office of Works was busy there too, under his direction, in installing works of art the king had purchased from the Duke of Mantua and in making and gilding frames for the many

65 *Cal. S.P. Dom., 1625–6*, p.562.
66 Sharpe (1992) p.105.
67 *Cal. S.P. Dom., 1628–9*, p.396.
68 *Cal. S.P. Dom., 1631–3*, p.485.
69 *Cal. S.P. Dom., 1629–31*, p.158; *ibid.*, 1635, pp.456–7.

70 Summerson (1963) pp.68–9, 73–4; H.K.W., IV, Pt.II, pp.118–21. For the controversy surrounding its restoration in 1989 see *Apollo*, vol.132, October 1990, pp.256–60 and a reply in *ibid.*, vol.133, January 1991, pp.64–5.
71 P.R.O., LR5/64–7, first noticed by Hero Granger-Taylor.

paintings acquired. The queen attended the first mass in the chapel on 10 December 1635, sinking to her knees on Ralph Grynder's crimson velvet cushions,[72] and marvelling, surely, at the device the Flemish sculptor, François Dieussart, had installed for exhibiting the holy sacrament. It was a machine worthy of a setting in one of the masques Jones had designed for the queen, and in which she had often danced. In fact, it was decided in the autumn of 1639 by the king and queen that they would take part in a new masque, *Salmacida Spolia*, in which kingship would triumph over rebellion, an optimism soon to be unravelled. The Queen was now resting, in 1640, at Oatlands where her son Henry, Duke of Gloucester was born on 8 July; the king meanwhile was doing what he could to raise an army to be used against the troublous marauding Scots. The queen was apprehensive at the ready anger being directed against Catholics and against their chapels, with images and stained glass windows wantonly destroyed. Leading Catholics at court had been forced to leave London. To criticize the king might be seen as close to blasphemy: to rail against a Catholic queen incurred few strictures, and she became the scapegoat for all disorder.

LITTLE TIME FOR COMFORT

For the duration of the English Civil War work of decoration and the rich trappings of upholstery had to be set, mostly, to one side. There were brief revivals when a more serious kind of life intervened. The trial of Thomas Wentworth, first Earl of Strafford (indicted for treason on the intention of bringing an Irish army to subdue England by force) opened in Westminster Hall on 22 March 1641.[73] The Great Wardrobe provided a curtained box for the royal party to hear the proceedings from. These were conducted with great confidence, not least by the accused: the queen attended each day and watched, with some admiration, as the earl mounted a spirited defence which, for the moment, outwitted his accusers and succeeded in gaining him his freedom.

The years of rebellion saw many bloody battles which had erupted at the rising of solid citizens in arms. The royal family had to flee from London and hurried to Hampton Court, on to Windsor, and then to Dover. Here, a troubled queen embarked for Holland, taking with her the crown jewels. The king's hopes and firm endeavours in the succeeding years were destroyed slowly but surely under the ruthless, brilliant generalship of Oliver Cromwell, whose professional New Model Army had been set to fight the Royalists.

Most of the king's supporters in the field, such as Edward Sackville, fourth Earl of Dorset (?1589–1652), suffered heavy losses of furniture, armour and other goods at the hands of the Parliamentarians. His younger son was also captured and stabbed to death by one of Cromwell's men. How Edward Sackville and his wife Mary, a governess to Charles I's children, reacted to the sale of most of their possessions (Appendix A21) is not known but can be assumed. In battle after battle the royal cause was slowly destroyed. By June 1647 the king was in Parliamentary hands and moved, in custody, to many houses. The insurrections he still tried to stir up led, inexorably, towards his trial. The Great Wardrobe, in early January 1649, hastened forward their preparations for this, in the painted chamber in Westminster Hall. Clement Kynnersley, a gentleman of the wardrobe, had prepared Hampton Court for the royal prisoner. He as hurriedly got together furnishings for a royal bedchamber and dining room at the home of Sir Robert Cotton, adjacent to the Westminster landing stairs. Within Westminster Hall itself the tiered benches had been covered with red baize and a great chair, reading desk and scarlet cushion had been set for John Bradshaw, President of the High Court of Justice, and Chief Commissioner at the trial. The clerks' table was covered with a fine Turkey carpet and the armchair in which the king would sit was covered with red velvet.[74] By 27 January 1649 the long days of accusation and counter-argument were over, with the measured announcement: 'the said Charles Stuart, as a Tyrant, Traitor, Murderer and a public enemy, shall be put to death, by the severing his head from his body'.

The two Dutch ambassadors sent at the urgent instigation of the Prince of Wales had arrived in London on 26 January 1649. They were received correctly, if belatedly, and sat, at their audience, on chairs covered

72 P.R.O., LR5/67.

73 Wedgwood (1935) pp.292–330.

74 P.R.O., Rossetti MSS., 31/9/20, f.79.

in cloth of silver. They visited the House of Lords and an hour or so later were received in the Lower House. Again John Baker, junior had set out two chairs on a Turkey carpet. Their entreaties for the stricken king came to nothing; no one seemed to have any good reason why the erection of the scaffold should not take place. It was set against the wall of the Banqueting House in Whitehall, and covered in black. This fine classical building, redolent of Italy under a bright sun, had been designed by Inigo Jones. It contained (as it still does) ceiling canvases by Rubens, glorifying in their subject matter, both the reign of James I and the triumph of wisdom and justice over rebellion and falsehood. With urgent prescience Parliament was hurrying through a brief emergency bill to prevent the proclamation of a new king. As for Charles I, wearing two shirts to avoid any sign of shivering fear, he passed through the Banqueting Hall and out to the covered platform. After lengthy entreaties, in which the king attested his innocence, the axe was swung and at one blow killed a king and created the myths leading towards martyrdom. It was 30 January 1649, but it was a long five days before the news reached the Prince of Wales at The Hague, and an even lengthier nine days before the queen, in her little court in the Louvre, heard what she had been afraid to hear.

THE WORST OF TIMES

A fortnight before the king was executed the Commons gave readings to an instrument that provided for the 'Discovery, Inventorying and Preserving' of the goods in his 'several Houses'. Most of the king's possessions had survived the Civil War and the new republican government was in possession of vast quantities of goods and valuable works of art. Parliament ordered that the Council of State should take responsibility for these and by an act, published in July 1649, the sale of the goods of the king, queen and prince was authorized. A team of trustees was appointed to locate, list and value the royal goods. In this they were assisted by Clement Kynnersley of the Great Wardrobe (and in charge of the Wardrobe established at Whitehall for the use of the state). He was appointed the wardrobe-keeper to Cromwell and delivered fine quality furnishings to Hampton Court for the Protector's use. He was helped by a London draper and upholsterer, Ralph Grafton, who lived in the parish of St Michael's, Cornhill but died early in his life, in 1659.[75]

The team of appraisers were assiduous in their searches and found items in the houses of the king's embroiderer, Edmund Harrison, the upholsterer Ralph Grynder and the painter Emmanuel de Critz. Grynder had in his possession important royal pictures and de Critz also had the superb marble bust of the king by Bernini. The inventories have been edited meticulously,[76] and the critical commentaries thereto show how the accumulated riches at houses such as Oatlands (the product of much expenditure by the queens, Anne of Denmark and Henrietta Maria) were scattered for dubious ideological reasons and considerable monetary gain.

Some Tudor chairs and stools had survived to the mid-seventeenth-century accounting, but most were of the Stuart period, covered in either Turkey work, embroidery, silk fabrics, China satin, leather, and sometimes with silvered and gilt frames. Surprisingly, the cushions at the Tower in 1649 had been described as there in Henry VIII's inventory, but those at Denmark House and Whitehall again bore the embroidered arms or initials of Anne of Denmark. The most valuable furniture was that relating to court ceremonial. The upholstered furniture, in matching suites of varying size, was matched according to circumstance. John Baker, senior and Anthony Lasingby had supplied three large chairs, six high stools and three footstools, all covered in crimson velvet in the reign of James I. This number of items seemed to be the ideal number for the suites listed in the inventories. Most of the chairs of state were of the X-framed type (Pls 6–7, 21, 24, 29, 30–1), all richly upholstered. The back stools usually had Turkey work, velvet or cotton covers and were present in large numbers in all the palaces; some of these were also of a folding type. All 'high chairs' were complemented by fabric-covered footstools, with little of the frames visible under the coverings of rich fabric (Pl. 40).

It is to be expected that the details of royal beds were the most extensive of the listings. There were a few 'French' beds, of a box-like nature (Pl. 37), with the wooden structure concealed, but many were of

---

75 P.R.O., Prob. 11/287, f.96.   76 Millar, ed. (1972); MacGregor, ed. (1989).

joined construction, made rich-looking solely by hangings, or half-headed bedsteads, field and slope ones.[77] Whilst all were dispersed they bore elaborate testimony to a court style which had owed much in the reign of Charles I to the French decorative style favoured by his French wife.[78]

Finally, there were many close or necessary stools, needed at all times, but often covered, inappropriately perhaps, with coloured velvet. Those covered with gilt Spanish leather were more practical. They were all near in style to the coffers and chests provided by, in particular, the Greene and Lewgar families of coffermakers, serving between them the Tudor and Stuart monarchies. As a type they only became the upholsterers' province after 1660 (Pl. 39).

Between 1649 and 1651 most of the textile furnishings[79] listed in the inventories were sold, ostensibly to help pay the late king's debts. At Oatlands almost everything was sold to Sir Gregory Norton, a former servant of the crown and now execrated by the Royalists. At Hampton Court, much dating from the time of Henry VIII and Cardinal Wolsey was sold to various purchasers. However, much was reserved for the use of the Commonwealth government. Textiles served both decorative and utilitarian purposes and many of the most valuable sets of tapestries, including the Raphael tapestry cartoons and the equipment at the tapestry manufactory at Mortlake, were retained. In contrast the royal cloths of state and canopies, denoting a rank to be despised, all went, together with most of the bed hangings, cushions and table carpets. The king's embroiderer, Edmund Harrison, had purchased, in 1651, two valuable items: Henry VIII's pearl-embroidered table carpet from the paradise chamber at Hampton Court and the principal Stuart cloth of state, at the Tower. In 1660 Harrison returned these two items to the crown's use, as part of a deal by which he received payments outstanding to him.[80] Pre-eminently, the set of tapestries of Henry VIII's time, telling the story of *Abraham*, is still to be seen at Hampton Court.[81]

The carpets were, principally, of Turkish or Persian origin, but two or three were listed as Indian or East Indian. Three carpets at Denmark House had grounds of gold and silver with their patterns woven in silver and coloured silk. Two, at Hampton Court, had been recorded in Henry VIII's inventory, and many more had been used from the Tudor period as table or cupboard carpets (Pls 1, 18). A number of fine needlework carpets, some worked with armorials or monograms, had survived from Henry VIII's time.

The many silk cloths of state, some three dozen, denoted the status and power of the royal personage who sat beneath them – there were a dozen at the palace of Whitehall, one of purple velvet associated with Henry VIII's use of Hampton Court, and two dating from Queen Elizabeth's reign, at Windsor. The round, half-round and square canopies, related in function to the cloths of state were also in ready quantity, fifteen at Denmark House alone. These were of velvet or silk and embroidered either with Anne of Denmark's crowned initials or of woven patterns. The 1649 inventories listed over a hundred sets of bed hangings. At a castle as distant from London as Ludlow the bed hangings were in the lesser materials of darnix and Kidderminster stuff. Those at Windsor were richer, of plain or patterned silk and trimmed, frequently, with gold, silver, silk or even pearls. It was all a poignant reminder of what had been and what had now gone.

DECLINE AND AMBITION

With the king's collections dispersed, his court destroyed and power held by Cromwell and the New Model Army, it might be held that building, decoration and a need for upholstered comfort was at a low point. However, more was done than realized, with some important houses such as Wilton, Wiltshire, seat of the Earls of Pembroke and Montgomery, and Forde Abbey, Dorset, seat of Cromwell's Attorney General, Edmund Prideaux, receiving major rebuildings. The architectural history of these and some nine other major houses belonging to Cromwell's officials and friends (together with several more minor houses) has been examined

77   Thornton (1978) pp.160–6ff.
78   Jervis (1989) pp.277–306.
79   King (1989) pp.307–21.

80   *Cal. S.P. Dom., 1660*, p.191.
81   Campbell (1994) pp.22–31.

recently.[82] Unfortunately no documentation survives about their mid-seventeenth-century furnishings and in consequence the concerns of this study cannot be satisfied.

All that might be assumed is that important personages like the Earl of Pembroke, Edmund Prideaux and the Royalist, William Murray (at Ham House, Surrey) would have known the advanced French-style decorations done for Queen Henrietta Maria at Somerset House and at the Queen's House, Greenwich. Some of these works were carried out under the supervision of Francis Cleyn, who had worked in Denmark and Italy before becoming artistic director of the Mortlake tapestry-weaving workshops. At Ham House it has been assumed that some decoration, limited due to the troubled times, took place when Elizabeth Murray, Countess of Dysart succeeded on the death of her father in 1654. An inventory[83] taken at that time shows, for example, that 'divided' curtains, of red cloth, were already in use in the most important rooms, throwing doubt on their supposed introduction to England from Paris in the 1660s.[84]

A Sale at Montacute

Away in the south-west of England Sir Robert Phelips, an able but impetuous man, found himself frequently in opposition to the king. As a strong anti-Catholic he had opposed the proposed marriage between Prince Charles and the Spanish Infanta. As a result of these protests he was arrested at his house of Montacute in Somerset in January 1622 and imprisoned for eight months in the Tower of London. When released he proceeded to set up in as great a style as conditions allowed at Montacute. A 1638 inventory[85] taken at his death lists expensive and colourful furnishings. Their acquisition had put a great strain on his finances and his stepmother was one of the first of his creditors eager to sue. To clear his debts Sir Robert arranged for his eldest son, Edward, to marry Ann Pye, daughter of the Auditor of the Exchequer, Sir Robert Pye. Sir Robert Pye agreed to pay off Phelips's debts if Montacute was made over at once to Edward. The contents of the house were bequeathed to Lady Phelips and Sir Robert implored his son to behave in such a way that would give her no reason to 'unfurnish the house'.

Daily life at Montacute in the early years of the Civil War was not comfortable, and on a personal level Edward Phelips quarrelled with his mother. But he was soon fighting for the king in the Civil War, and the story is related that he sold the Montacute tapestries to raise funds for the Royalist cause. Certainly many of the textiles recorded in the 1638 inventory – the dining room alone had '8 peice of arras hangings', as well as an arras carpet, two Turkey carpets and many chairs and stools of 'new greene velvet' – do not feature in that of 1651. When events began to look dire for the king, Edward's loyalty waned, and rather than risk forfeiture of his estate he left the Royalist army in 1646 and paid a heavy fine, imposed by Parliament.

Thus impoverished, Edward was in no position to pay the many legacies and annuities specified by his father and, eventually, a commission of sequestration was appointed in 1651 to raise the owed sum of some £1,202. The long list of items sold by the commissioners included most of the furniture from the state rooms. The 1651 inventory listed it all (Appendix A17); the listing, including some fine upholstered pieces, is noted briefly, here. The overall impression the inventory gives is of a considerable use of cloth-covered items with a sparse display of velvet and damask.

In all the contents of thirty-two rooms at Montacute are listed, ranging from gate-house to various larders and lesser rooms. Few contents were listed for the great chamber which seems to have been serving as a simply furnished bedroom. The gallery chamber also had two bedsteads in it, standing on yellow rugs. The bed had white taffeta valances with a white fringe and there were white taffeta curtains at the windows. There was a silk canopy, a cupboard with a green cupboard cloth and '2 greate sikke [silk] chaires'.

The great parlour had three turkey carpets on the floor, with six high red cloth stools, with a black and silver fringe, flanked by two great high chairs in the same coloured material and fringing. There were also four

82   Mowl and Earnshaw (1995).
83   Thornton and Tomlin (1980) pp.4–5.
84   Thornton and Tomlin, II (1980).

85   Somerset C.R.O., MS., DD/PH 226/8. The 1638 inventory is MS., DD/PH 226/3.

low stools 'of ye same'. The furniture was completed by one large red cloth couch and four red cloth curtains. Eating or other activities took place at four 'long table boards'.

The round parlour was furnished in a green colour scheme with high stools, velvet chairs with cushions, and, appropriately, 'a round table board', a cupboard and a green cupboard cloth.

OLIVER CROMWELL'S DEATH

What could have continued as a difficult time, disruptive of normal life, came into its final phase with the death of Cromwell, Lord Protector on 3 September 1658. Whilst he had, by word of mouth, appointed his son, Lord Richard, to succeed him power lay still with the Privy Council and the army. Nevertheless, for the moment, they were loyal adherents to his cause and statesmen in Holland and France were amazed at the seemingly peaceful transition. There was no recall, yet, of the exiled king and there was a funeral to attend to. On the night of 20 September 1658 the Lord Protector's body, embalmed, filled with spices and cased in lead, was conveyed quietly from Whitehall to Somerset House. The officials of his household had worked, with Kynnersley of the Great Wardrobe, to arrange a grand lying-in-state.

Three rooms, which had formerly been the king's presence, privy and withdrawing chambers, were covered from dado to cornice with black cloth and heraldic escutcheons. In a fourth room, a bed of state, raised two steps above the floor, carried a wax effigy of the Protector, clad in a robe of purple velvet, a sceptre and orb in its hands. Behind the head was a chair of state covered with cloth of gold, with 'the imperial crown set with stones' resting on a cushion. Eight wax tapers, in candlesticks five feet high, cast a yellow flickering light over the unreal regality. Clement Kynnersley had made a proposal about cloths of estate:

> If these are wanting the rooms will lack much of what many subjects have, for every Earl may have a cloth of estate. If enough velvet is not to be had, 2 might be of velvet, 1 for the hearse and 1 for her Highness, and the others of cloth. There shd be in Whitehall & Somerset House 7 cloths of estate, 5 of cloth, 2 of velvet.[86]

On 10 November the corpse was moved to Westminster Abbey and buried at dead of night in a vault in Henry VII's chapel. But in obsequies, pursued in some disarray, the funeral service itself took place a fortnight later, on 23 November. Contrary to the ordered provision of black cloth by the Great Wardrobe for any royal funeral all London was searched for enough yardage. The procession was delayed through no controlling Earl Marshal having arranged precedence, no candles were available to guide the mourners to the mortuary chapel, and there were no prayers, sermon or funeral oration. The poet Abraham Cowley commented on the costly scene: 'Much noise, much tumult, much expense, much magnificence, much vain-glory; briefly, a great show, and yet after all this, but an ill sight'.[87] The *Calendars of State Papers* are silent as to any presiding upholsterers but, like the army, some forty weeks in arrears with pay, they waited a long time for even the promise of money. They record in August 1659 'debts due to eleven mercers and drapers for the funeral, totalling £19,303 0s 11d.'[88] Richard Cromwell stayed, nervously, within the Palace of Whitehall, where he was immune from arrest for debt,[89] and a group of army officers caused Parliament to be summoned, the first in a dreary cycle of summonses and dissolutions.

THE KING'S RETURN

In the cool days of late winter news filtered that the thirty year old King Charles had some 2,500 men-at-arms with him in the Low Countries. No one in England had the heart for more fighting and the professional soldier, George Monck, who had marched with his men on London and was now at the head of affairs, was

86 *Cal. S.P. Dom., 1658–9*, p.131.
87 Davies (1955) pp.40–3; Hutton (1985) pp.3–20.
88 *Cal. S.P. Dom., 1659–60*, p.146.
89 Fraser (1979) p.161.

anxious for the return of the monarch. On 4 April 1660 the king wrote formally to the Speaker of the House of Commons from Breda. His Declaration of Breda suggested that he had a role to play – that king and Parliament were 'best preserved by preserving the other', that free pardons were available to all but a few, and their property would remain untouched. On its reading, before the Commons on 1 May, an official resolution was passed asking Charles to resume the governance of his kingdom. It was taken to him at The Hague by a delegation of Parliamentary commissioners.

The king had for some weeks been enjoying himself hugely, wining and dining at many banquets. He was even presented by the States of Holland with a splendid bed made for his sister Mary, the Princess Royal and Princess of Orange, but stored since the death of her husband, William II, in November 1650. The final and grandest banquet, given by the States of Holland, had both his sister Mary and his aunt, Elizabeth of Bohemia, to his left and right. The ship *Royal Charles* lay nearby at anchor, and on the night of 23 May the English king set out for Dover. Samuel Pepys, well entrenched in all matters naval, had been part of the party to Holland. He recorded in his diary of the journey he made on board the king's ship, the presence of the king's two brothers, the royal Dukes of York and Gloucester, and of all of them landing at Dover, on 25 May 1660. On 1 June he wrote: 'Mr Cooke brought us word that the Parliament had ordered the 29 May, the King's birthday, to be kept for ever as a day of thanksgiving for our redemption from tyranny and the King's return to his government, he entering London that day.'[90] Perhaps all things could now flourish again, not least for His Majesty's upholsterers.

90   Latham and Matthews, eds (1970) I, p.32.

18. Table carpet seen in the painting *The Somerset House Conference* by an unknown artist (1604) *London, National Portrait Gallery.*

The delegation representing Spain and the Catholic Netherlands is on the left. The English delegates are headed (first right) by Robert Cecil, later first Earl of Salisbury. The groups are seated on red and black upholstered X-frame chairs. The table carpet is of the 'small-Holbein' pattern and of a type commonly made in Anatolia.

19.   Canopy and dais seen in the engraving of *James I in Parliament* by L. Elstrack (1604) *London, British Museum.*

The headcloth to the canopy is richly embroidered with royal emblems.

20.   Table carpet (detail) (1605–15) 13 ft × 5 ft 9 in (396.3 × 175 cm) *London, Victoria and Albert Museum,* Inv. T134-1928.

The border is silk on linen canvas; there arc 400 stitches per square inch (62 per square cm). It uses stem stitch, long and short stitch. It was probably made by a professional workshop for sale in the open market rather than for a specific commission. Acquired from Castle Bromwich Hall, Warwickshire in 1928.

21. (*left*)   X-frame chair seen in the portrait of *James I* by John de Critz (*c*.1605) *Loseley Park, Surrey*.

A number of different forms of chair appear in other portraits attributed to de Critz. Of the several portraits of James I by de Critz, who was Serjeant Painter from 1605, this one shows the X-frame chair to the best advantage.

References: Strong (1969) pp.259–68.

22. (*below*)   Catafalque of Henry, Prince of Wales, shown in an engraving by 'B.V.' (1612) *London, National Portrait Gallery*.

It was enriched with a fringed valance and embroidered armorials on velvet by John Baker, senior.

23. (*opposite*)   Chair seen in the portrait of *Launcelot Andrewes* attributed to Marcus Gheeraerts the Younger (1615) *Richmond, Virginia, Agecroft Association*.

The chair has a reading table extension to its arms. It is upholstered and has gilt pommels and large bullion nails at the back.

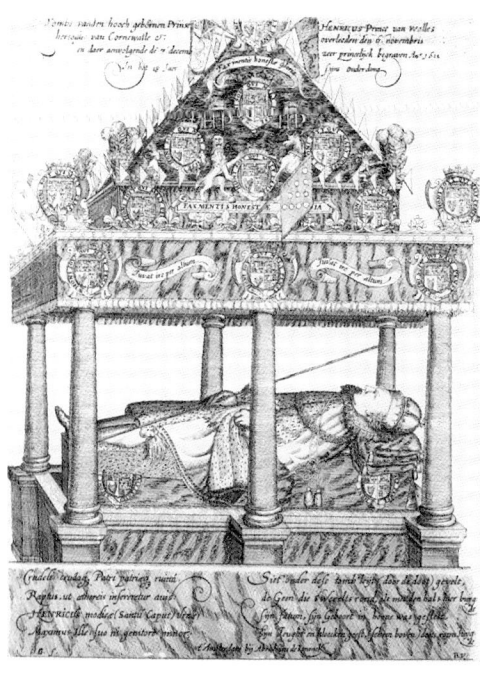

24.   X-frame chair seen in the portrait believed to be of Dorothy St John, Lady Cary, attributed to William Larkin (*c*.1615) *Ranger's House, London* (English Heritage).

Upholstered in red with a gilt fringe on the pommels, arms, seat and stretchers. With a tasselled gold fringed long cushion.

References: Strong (1969) No.354; Bryant (1993) p.20.

25. Table carpet seen in the portrait of *Lady Isabella Rich*, attributed to William Larkin (*c.*1615) *Ranger's House, London* (English Heritage).

Fringed and embroidered in gold and coloured silks. In the background are silk draw-curtains.

References: Strong (1969) No.356; Bryant (1993) p.20.

26. (*opposite*)   Canopy, cloth of estate and table cover seen in the portrait of *Charles I as Prince of Wales* by Hendrick van Steenwijk and others (*c.*1620) *Copenhagen, Statens Museum for Kunst*.

Elements of the royal coat-of-arms appear on the cloth of estate. This portrait is thought to have been a gift to Christian IV of Denmark, the brother of Charles's mother, Queen Anne of Denmark.

References: exhibited Tate Gallery, London 'Dynasties' (1995) No.142.

27–9.   X-frame chair (*c.*1620) *Knole, Kent* (The National Trust).

The chair is similar to that shown in the portrait of James I by Daniel Mytens. The chair is upholstered in red cloth, over which is laid a cover of crimson and silver damask (now faded). The back is divided into panels by a fringe and there is a stuffed cushion. The view and detail of the chair upturned shows the royal inventory mark for Hampton Court – a stamp on the canvas under the seat of a royal crown, the initials H.C., and the date 1661. The stamp which formed this mark remains at Hampton Court.

30–1.   X-frame chair (*c*.1620) 50 × 33 in
(127 × 83 cm) *Knole, Kent* (The National
Trust).

The chair is upholstered in red and buff silk
set with spangles. The back is headed by
egg-shaped finials banded with braid and
studded with large gilt nails. The arms and
seat are trimmed with a deep fringe. It is in
the spangled bedchamber at Knole with
eight stools *en suite*.

32. (*opposite*)   Chair seen in a portrait of an
unknown Jacobean lady (*c*.1620) *Private
Collection, England*.

The chair back is embroidered on white silk
(?) and is fringed at the arms. In the background is a green curtain, edged with gold
fringe and an elaborate green table carpet
with Florentine stitching.

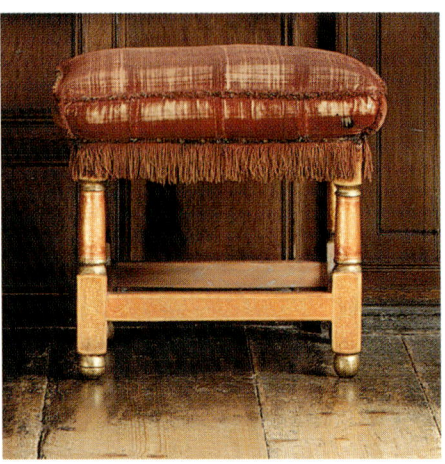

33. (*top left*)   Part of a long cushion cover (*c.*1625) *London, Victoria and Albert Museum*, Inv. T63-1933.

Made of linen embroidered with silk in long and short herringbone and satin stitches, with laid and couched work.

34. (*top right*)   Stuffed seat on a stool (detail) (*c.*1625) 12 × 15½ × 14¾ in (30 × 47 × 37.5 cm) *Knole, Kent* (The National Trust).

Made of red velvet, trimmed with a fringe. The stools, both high and low are in the Leicester gallery at Knole.

35.   Chair seen in a portrait of *Philip Herbert, fourth Earl of Pembroke* by Daniel Mytens (*c.*1628) *Hatfield House, Hertfordshire.*

The chair has a gold fringe at the arms and gilt nails at the back.

References: Auerback and Adams (1971) No.86.

36.   (*opposite, top left*) Armchair (*c.*1630) 40 × 27½ × 19½ in (101.5 × 70 × 50.5 cm) *London, Victoria and Albert Museum*, Inv. W31-1918.

Covered in velvet, originally red, now faded to dull green. Front legs in walnut, back legs in beech with (later) oak stretchers. Originally at Boughton House, Northamptonshire.

37.   (*opposite, top right*) French bed seen in the engraving *An English Lady's Bedchamber* signed 'Edmond Marmion, invent et fecit' (*c.*1640) *Magdalene College, Cambridge.*

The bed has a fringed top valance and draw curtains. There is an upholstered chair and stool and a table with a flounced and fringed cover.

38.   Couch Chair (*c.*1640) 41 × 68 × 22 in (104 × 172.5 × 56 cm) *Knole, Kent* (The National Trust).

Stuffed and covered with crimson velvet. The cushioned headpieces are hinged to the arms, and adjusted by ratchets. The upholstery is fixed with large gilt nails and trimmed with a silk thread fringe, overlaid with silver threads. The dating of this

unique couch has been much disputed. I incline to *c.*1640 on the basis of entries in the 1630s in the furniture bills of items supplied to Queen Henrietta Maria (Apppendix A15). I have not yet established the precise differences between a couch chair and a couch bed. Similar items were supplied by John Casbert, the French upholsterer to Charles II from 1660.

39.   Close stool (*c.*1660) 18 × 23 × 23 in (45 × 59 × 59 cm) *Knole, Kent* (The National Trust).

Upholstered in crimson velvet and nail studded. This stool is likely to have been acquired from one of the royal palaces by the sixth Earl of Dorset who, as Lord Great Chamberlain, was entitled to take perquisites.

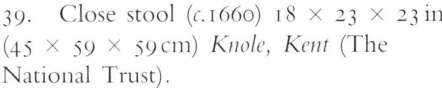

40–2.   Armchair and footstool (*c.*1660)
armchair, 50 × 33 in (125.4 × 84 cm); stool,
$19\frac{3}{4}$ × $21\frac{3}{4}$ in (50 × 55 cm) *London, Victoria
and Albert Museum*, Inv. W12–13, 1928.

Made of beech and upholstered in velvet
which was originally crimson. It is trimmed
with galloon and fringed and studded
with brass-headed nails. Formerly in the
possession of William Juxon, Archbishop of
Canterbury (d.1663). Tradition has it that
the chair was used by Charles I at his
trial in 1649. However, in 1995 it was
established by James Yorke that it had
been made by the French upholsterer John
Casbert for use by the Archbishop at
Charles II's coronation (see p.82). The
details show the front and side of the 'Juxon
Chair', as it is known, showing the velvet,
galloon and nails.

References: Furniture History Society,
Newsletter, November 1995.

IV

'Solidity, Conveniency and Ornament'

When Sir Balthazar Gerbier wrote his book *A Brief Discourse concerning the Three Chief Principles of Magnificent Building* (1663), he categorized them with the words 'Solidity, Conveniency and Ornament'. They describe, accurately, the nature of much interior decoration in the latter half of the seventeenth century. This chapter is concerned with the period from 1660 until William III's death in 1702.

THE KING RESTORED

When King Charles, weary from the noise of welcoming gun salvos, cheering people and the self-important clatter of mounted soldiers, reached London at the end of May, 1660 he went to Whitehall Palace. This had stood empty since Cromwell's death on 3 September 1658 and the architect, John Webb, whilst acting in no established office, had made urgent preparations there for the king's arrival.[1] The king had been in exile for fifteen years and apart from John Webb's immediate activity there was much to do to all the royal palaces. Those not in use by the Cromwell family had become government offices, regalia had been melted down and paintings, sculpture, jewels and plate dispersed by sale, gift or even theft. The king had grown up surrounded by his father's superb art collection, and strenuous effort was being made to recover as much of that as possible. A Convention Parliament had been set up to supervise the restoration of the monarchy. They gave powerful support to Charles's own wishes (sent whilst waiting to return) to retrieve royal goods by appointing a committee to oversee the attempts. In these endeavours they were aided by the bureaucratic efficiency of Thomas Beauchamp, who as Clerk to the Trustees for the Sale of the King's Goods had kept precise records of the Commonwealth dispersals. He was ordered by the House of Lords to hand these valuable records over to John Webb, now confirmed as Surveyor of the King's Works. They were of vital assistance in the tasks of recovery, with such celebrated artists as Sir Peter Lely and Emmanuel de Critz, the son of Charles I's Serjeant Painter, making significant returns of royal possessions. All of these, and more, some made voluntarily and some under threat of 'our high displeasure', were received by the Keeper of the Great Wardrobe, Clement Kynnersley, who had served Commonwealth masters with the same obsequious attention to detail.

One problem which arose is that many creditors of Charles I had been 'paid' by the Commonwealth with goods from the royal collections. They, therefore, found themselves the unwitting owners of goods being sought. For example, an artisan, William Shirley, was in possession of a fine set of cloth-of-gold curtains for which he stated in his petition that he had paid £1,400. He was one of the fortunate ones for whom it was declared that if the curtains were returned he was to be allowed their value. Other wronged petitioners were not so fortunate, but all were harried or allowed as their cases determined. At the conclusion of it all, one of the world's great art collections, swelled by a gift of paintings from the Dutch States as a mark of goodwill, together with 'an extraordinary crimson embroidered velvet Bed, Cloth of State, Chaires and Stooles suitable, worth very many thousands of pounds', had taken on something of the greatness it had known during the reign of Charles I.[2]

---

1 H.K.W., V (1976) p.265.   2 Gleissner (1994) pp.103–15.

The king's restored status was to be confirmed at the great Garter ceremony of 15–18 April 1661, and his coronation, on St George's Day, 23 April.[3] He was to be the last English monarch to progress over the same route, from the Tower of London to Whitehall, as all the medieval kings had taken. Samuel Pepys, ever ready with detail, wrote in his diary: 'And a pleasure it was to see the Abbey raised in the middle, all covered with red and a throne (that is a chaire) and footstoole on the top of it.'[4] He did not mention the false ceiling of red baize for St Edward's Chapel, or the work of the joiner, John Whitby, in providing the canopy frame, chairs, stools and so on for John Casbert's men to cover in fabric. For example Casbert charged £20 for making 'a rich Canopy of State of Crimson velvet rich Embroydered all over . . .', as well as making 'a rich chaire of State, with 3 stooles and two Cushens suitable' (£5) and three other 'Chairs of State', two of dove colour and gold, and one 'of the Skie Collour and gold', all with footstools and long and short cushions (£9; £4 10s). The chair used by Archbishop Juxon (Pls 40–2), long thought to date from Charles I's reign, was established in 1995 as Casbert's work in 1660, by reference to the accounts.[5] Pepys went on from the crowning and enthronement in the abbey, splendidly realized in 1662 in the engravings in John Ogilby's *The Entertainment of His Most Excellent Majestie, Charles II*, to Westminster Hall, over ground covered, less grandly, with blue cloth. Inside the hall, 'very fine with hangings and scaffolds', Pepys described how the king's champion, Sir Edward Dymock, had come on a white horse three times before the royal table and throwing down his gauntlet each time to challenge any who dare 'deny Ch. Steward to be lawful King of England'.

'This happy day', as John Dryden described it, was short of but one important person, a queen. The king's eyes, and those of his Restoration court, had turned, with this in mind, to the Infanta Catherine of Portugal. In international intrigues this was to be a match welcomed by the young Louis XIV, who now saw his favoured ally against Spain, Portugal, supported by England. It was this accord with France, strengthened by Charles's sister Henriette-Anne becoming married shortly before the Coronation to Louis XIV's brother, Philippe, Duc d'Orleans, which helped French ideas to flourish in England, and for some of its talented craftsmen to settle here.

The king, dazzled by the large marriage portion the Infanta had been promised, had to be content for the moment (again, as his father had done with Henrietta Maria) with a proxy courtship. Catherine therefore became Queen of England while in Lisbon and did not reach England until 13 May 1662. As a Catholic queen (and there had been Anne of Denmark and Henrietta Maria before her) Catherine needed access to Catholic chapels, the Mass, priests and confessors. As a twenty-three year old woman she would have to steer a way through the firm doctrines of English Protestantism, and also come to terms with the sharp reality of the king's mistresses, the influential Barbara Villiers, Countess of Castlemaine and later Duchess of Cleveland, first among them. For the moment it was enough for the king to see that orders were made so that the coffers containing objects of devotion Catherine had brought with her were covered by the coffer-maker, John Lewgar, with red velvet, embroidered with the royal arms of England and of Portugal.

THE FRENCH UPHOLSTERERS

One of the significant aspects of decorative work during Charles II's reign and beyond (until about 1710) was the presence in England of several talented and innovative French upholsterers. Extensive details of their varied activity fills many pages below, and the archives[6] relating to, at least, their royal service, are exact in detailing their names, albeit with casual inattention to spellings and variants from the French. Principally, they were John Casbert and his son John, Jean Poictevin (perhaps the most able of them all), Monsieur La Grange, Jean Peyrard, Simon Delobel, Francis Lapiere, Poictevin's nephew (by his sister) Etienne Penson, the fringe-maker Peter Dufresnoy, and Philip Guibert. Only in the cases of Peyrard and Penson is there any manuscript material,

3   Coronation expenditure in P.R.O., LC2/8.
4   Latham and Matthews, eds (1970–6) I, p.12.
5   P.R.O., LC2/8; James Yorke, Furniture History Society *News-letter*, November 1995.

6   Particularly P.R.O., LC5 and LC9 series; specific citations are given below.

preserved at the Archives Nationales in Paris. Simon Delobel, as an upholsterer in the service of Louis XIV, and therefore active at Versailles, is the only one of those known to have come to England to be mentioned in the records of the *Bâtiments du Roi* and the *Meubles de la Couronne*, edited by Jules Guiffrey.[7] Nothing, alas, is known of the birth or training of any of these Frenchmen, but something of their activity is traceable, given a persistence with the archival sources.

There is, however, little doubt that craftsmen such as Casbert and Poictevin, who are noted below, will have been familiar with Parisian interiors furnished in the years 1630 to 1660 when Richelieu and Mazarin were active. It has been said that 'the period of Richelieu and Mazarin saw the rise of French classicism',[8] but it is the engravings of Abraham Bosse, *c.*1640, in particular, which show many beds and chairs whose 'design' spread from France to England.[9]

John Casbert

John Casbert was in the king's service from 1660 until his death in 1677. It is not too profitable to speculate why Casbert and the others were attracted to England and who, if anyone, introduced them. There were of course many opportunities here to display mature skills to a king anxious to repair the years of depredation and material denial, and to serve, too, his courtiers, many of whom had seen something of France, even in dismal exile, or knew of its many riches from the numerous engravings in active circulation.

The formal position of 'Upholsterer' at the time of the king's restoration in 1660 was held by John Baker, junior, his service having lasted for almost forty years. It had been one of his jobs to provide a red canopy, red-covered dais and chairs of estate when Charles II received Claude Lamoral, Prince de Ligne at the Banqueting House, Whitehall on 17 September 1660. His duties were, however, shared, perhaps uneasily, with Casbert, and when the king's brother Henry, Duke of Gloucester died of smallpox in London in September 1660, it was Casbert who was responsible for the funeral furnishings. It was a great ceremony, all clad in black velvet and damask.[10] But in 1663 the professional tension was shed when 'John Carisbert, senior and junior' were made 'Upholsters' to the king, a position left vacant after the death of John Baker.[11]

Whilst almost nothing is known of Robert Moore, who described himself as 'Royal Upholsterer Extraordinary', it is worth recording his petition to the king in 1661. He stated that he had supplied the Great Wardrobe 'with all such provisions as ye Lord Genl. Montague and others the officers thereof, have from time to time desired, amounting to over £9,800'. He had only received £600 or so 'wch was about 14 months since'. He was fearful of losing his credit and bringing ruin to his family. The king, as hard-pressed for ready money as his forebears had been, nevertheless, on 20 January 1661, ordered Edward Montagu, Earl of Sandwich, the Master of the Great Wardrobe, to 'take steps for discharge of the debt'.[12] No more is heard of the matter.

In the first accounts of the king's reign, 1660–61, 'John Casbert, Upholster' was craving allowance 'for worke done and wares by him delivered for his Maties service'. He charged for 'Altering & fitting [a] Crimson damaske bedde, bought by his Matie of a Frenchman' and tackled a large order for eighteen chairs, to be covered in crimson serge, with false cases of crimson damask, trimmed with gold and silver fringes. There was need too of many couches and chairs: one couch for Whitehall was covered in green damask, needing two thousand large gilt bullion nails to fasten it; a crimson velvet 'french Chair' was covered 'all over with gold and silver fringe, with bags filled with down', and the Princess Royal had need of a 'standing French Bedstead'. This was 'apparrelled' with crimson velvet and embroidered with strips of white satin and silver. The four posts were cased in sleeves, and plumes of feathers rose from the cups on top of them; such a bed is shown here (Pl. 49). I have also noted (p.82) that Casbert was active at the king's coronation.

The Crown worked to a system, sponsored by necessity, which rarely paid what was due to its craftsmen. Enough was released to maintain their service, but there were possible advantages to them in

7　Guiffrey (1881–1901); Guiffrey (1886).
8　Blunt (1970) p.195.
9　Thornton (1978) p.29.
10　P.R.O., LC5/39, (8 October 1660).
11　*Cal. S.P. Dom.*, 1663–4, p.397.
12　*Cal. S.P. Dom.*, 1660–1, p.33.

commissions from those anxious to use whoever the king was using. A part of Casbert's long bill of 1677 (Appendix A18), totalling some £1,371 8s 1d, shows the range of his activity. What is apparent is that the French upholsterers, and firstly the Casberts, father and son, were ready with some new fashions. This can be noted in the materials used for certain beds and in providing sleeping chairs. In two cases in his 1677 bill Casbert made for two beds what one might expect of him – valances, curtains, cantoons, a tester, head cloth, cases for the posts, a counterpoint and four carved and gilded feet. However, he then stated: 'to the Bed Sixty Copper Pulleys & Tape, Ribbon and Ringes', and in a second reference: 'Sixty Copper Pulleys, Tape, Ribbon and Ringes'. By reference to a further bill of Jean Poictevin in 1678 it has been proved these pulleys were used for a new style of drawing up the case-curtains all round.[13] A sombre entry in Casbert's bill shows him providing 'Tacks, white nayles, used about the formes and seates, four dayes worke for six men' for the arraignment for manslaughter of Philip Herbert, the seventh Earl of Pembroke. In the same bill, however, Casbert's duties were as varied as to have provided oil-cloth curtains to cover the queen's aviary, and the chapel furnishings for Charles Howard, first Earl of Carlisle, who was governor of Jamaica from 1677–81.

In 1675 Casbert had charged the Great Wardrobe thirteen shillings 'for Covering a Sleeping Chaire for our owne use with four yards and a halfe of dyed Linnen and caseing it with Taffaty . . .'. This entry implies an existing chair. The two examples at Ham House, home of the Duke and Duchess of Lauderdale (Pls 54–6) are not listed in the 1677 inventory but occur in that for 1679 as 'Two sleeping chayres carv'd and guilt frames covered with Crimson and gould stuff with gould fringe, Cases of Crimson sarsnet.' They were probably made by Jean Poictevin, as he had supplied such chairs to the Great Wardrobe in 1675 and 1677. What the king had, the Duke of Lauderdale presumably wanted too. The form (perhaps modified from a French original) by either Casbert or Poictevin was obviously innovatory and the stability of the empty chair, when tilted back to its full extent against the pegs (which are set in holes in a pair of quadrants at the back of the arms) had not been fully worked out – it easily overbalances.

In 1674 the services of 'John Caresbert the elder, and John Caresbert the younger' were recognized by their being appointed to the 'office and place of our Upholster of our Wardrobe of Bedds and of our Standing Wardrobe'.[14] The almost ritualistic set-out of their duties bears giving here:

> . . . the makeing of all our standing bedds, Pallet Bedds, Canopies, Chaires, Stooles, Cushions, quilt Lynings of Counterpoints, Cloathes of Estate, window Curteynes, ffustian Blancketts, Cloth Blancketts, Gilt Sarge Cloathes, necessary Stooles, Straw cases, Downe Pillowes, Cart, Carriages and alsoe all our Bedd Seates and Curteynes for all our Caroches, Litters and Charriotts, together wth the repay ring & mending of all our Wardrobe Stuffe in all our severall wardrobes and to Serve and attend in all our Progresse, Journeyes for repayring and mending of all our Wardrobe stuff from time to time . . .

It was a privilege enjoyed for three years. In 1676 John Casbert, senior, made his will, which came into force at his death in 1677.[15] I have assumed it is Casbert senior's will but there is no mention of a wife or of his son John; equally, but more unlikely, if it is the son's will there is no mention of his father. The will is in any case a simple affair, leaving ten guineas each to his two sisters, Judith and Ann, three guineas each to his seven grandchildren, and the remainder of his estate, goods and money to his three brothers, George, Anthony and William. As with all craftsmen working for the Crown there were arrears of salary, with 'John Casbert, deceased in 1677, upholster' being owed £1,464 01s 07½d.[16]

James Frontin

Casbert's position was taken by James Frontin, of whom little is known, including whether he was English or French. The patent allocating him to his office was dated 23 June 1678[17] and noted, as usual, that he should

13   By Annabel Westman, who is researching the whole subject of case-curtains. The entry in P. R. O., LC9/275 reads: 'for thirty Eight pulleys to drawe up the Case of the Bed and thirty Eight small peices of Lead'.

14   P.R.O., LC5/53, ff.31–2.
15   P.R.O., Prob. 11/354 f.46.
16   P.R.O., LC3/37.
17   P.R.O., LC5/53, ff.110–11.

enjoy the 'profits, Commodityes and advantages' pertaining to his predecessors, 'John Baker, John Casebert the Elder, or John Casebert, the younger, deceased'. Of much more importance than Frontin, however, was the French upholsterer, Jean Poictevin, who, whilst holding no formal office, was to serve the crown for almost forty years. I have kept to the form of his name he used on a 1688 bill, noted below, and on a legal document mentioned in chapter V (p.139). His name was given many variants by others.

Jean Poictevin

The earliest mention I have traced of Poictevin's activity in England is in a treasury order of 1671, when he was paid £14 14s 6d.[18] It seems sensible to depart from my normal pattern of following a strict chronology to pursue his career through to the turn of the eighteenth century. Mentions of him in the reign of Queen Anne are made in chapter V (p.139). I have noted above that we do not know anything about the early life in France of the upholsterers who came to England. There were some *maîtres menuisiers* in Lyon in the late sixteenth century named Denis and David Paudefin,[19] and an important architect in Paris, Nicolas Poictevin (1650–1719),[20] but there is no reason to connect Jean Poictevin to them. There were several Huguenots with variant names of Poictevin in London from the 1660s, but, again, no relevant Jean Poictevin is recorded.[21]

Easing himself into a long number of years of English activity, Poictevin is next encountered on 29 July 1673 as 'Paid Mr Poitavin, £20', in the bank account of the Marquess of Worcester.[22] His service for the Crown was of course the most activity he undertook, and his name appears regularly in accounts of work undertaken for the Great Wardrobe.[23] Poictevin was certainly as inventive as Jean Casbert and in 1677 he also charged for 'Thirty Eight pulleys and thirty small lead weights' in respect of pulling up 'the case of the Bed'.[24] His bills also contain, frequently, mentions such as that of 1678, when 'Jean Paudvine' charged 'ffor altering and Making a Crimson dammaske Bed into a New ffashion'.[25] This new fashion related, undoubtedly, to providing beds with a *lit d'ange*, angel (or flying) tester, where the roof of the bed was suspended by cords or chains, and did not rely on the support of any foot posts. Such beds were known in Europe in the 1630s, and Louis XIV's bed at Versailles was of this type.[26]

All of Poictevin's beds for use by the royal family incorporated fine materials. In 1677 he made 'A flowred velvet bed, chaires, stooles &c for his Mats Bedchamber in the new Lodgings at W[hite] Hall'.[27] The bed was lined with cherry-coloured satin, and had inner and outer valances, cups atop, 'scollops' or raised patterns on the headboard, six enclosing curtains, cases on the posts, two 'cantoon' curtains at the front corners, and seven chairs and stools *en suite*, 'all double fringed with silk fringe'. For making such a bed Poictevin charged £20.

The need to be 'after the Japan fashion' was to satisfy a demand for Oriental-style furniture. For Windsor Castle, in 1677, 'a sky Damaske state' was provided by Poictevin but the stools and forms were varnished, and painted in the Japan fashion (at £5), and for the 'Queene's Great Bed Chamber at Windsor', (but in 1679), two great armchairs were provided at 50s each, 'with fine greene Japan'.[28] I have mentioned above the 'sleeping chayres', c.1679, at Ham House, Surrey (Pls 54–6), and that Poictevin was their probable maker. John Casbert had covered such a chair in 1675 but it is not known who made it. Poictevin charged on 20 December 1677 for use in 'her Mats Bed Chamber' at Whitehall 'for a sleeping Chaire neately Carved and the Irons all gilt with gold, £6' and, on 13 June 1679, he charged further for 'her Mats service at Sommerset house, For an Elbowe Chaire of Wallnuttree to fall in the Back and a table to it, Covered with Crimson velvet and stuffed with downe . . .'.[29] A chair similar to this description is illustrated (Pl. 58).

The business of hiring furniture was a lucrative one and Poictevin was active at this in the 1680s. For example, in October 1682, he charged £36 to hire furniture for the use of the Savoy ambassador: 'For the hire

---

18 P.R.O., LC5/82, f.15, 'John Paudevine'.
19 Havard (1889) III, p.726.
20 Thieme–Becker, XXVII (1941) p.525.
21 International Genealogical Index, microfiche records.
22 Royal Bank of Scotland, Child's Bank ledgers.
23 For example, P.R.O., LC5/41, ff.106, 111–13, 122, 139, 157, 174, 194; LC5/42, ff.43, 183, 227.

24 P.R.O., LC9/275. I am indebted for this reference to Annabel Westman.
25 *Ibid.*
26 Thornton (1978) p.168.
27 P.R.O., LC9/275, 22 December 1677.
28 P.R.O., LC9/275, 22 December 1677; LC9/276, 12 June 1679.
29 P.R.O., LC9/275, 20 December 1677; LC9/276, 13 June 1679.

of a Crimson Damaske Bed, a Feather Bed, Bolster, Quilts and Blankets and Six Caned chaires with Cusheons for 9 monthes.'[30] As he charged but £3 for making a covered easy chair, and £8 for a carved and gilt chair, admittedly without the cost of fabric, the £36 might be reckoned as good income.

Poictevin lived for most of his years in England in Pall Mall, as did his relative Peter Poictevin and his countryman and talented upholsterer Francis Lapiere, of whom more is related below. Poictevin also had a son, named as 'John' in the important document of 1710 (p.139), by which time he was a widower, and another relative, who worked on occasion for the Crown, Nicholas 'Baudovin'. In 1683 this craftsman charged 'for makeing and finishing a bed of Crimson velvet begun by the Aforesaid John Poctovin lined with gold and Silver Tissue', and he also supplied a bed in green silk, with *en suite* armchairs and stools, 'to the Queen Mother' (£70 9s).[31]

THE DEATH AND FUNERAL OF CHARLES II

For a king born to a position of privilege and a life within the rich trappings of the royal palaces his own last illness and death were mortal enough. In early February 1685 the king had collapsed in the palace of Whitehall; attended by several anxious doctors, purging and treating him by various arcane means, he rallied and declined with a wearying rapidity. As the medicine bottles increased in number so did the many curious onlookers. The convulsions of the king became more frequent. There were urgent moves by the Duke of York to introduce a Catholic priest to the royal chamber in the person of Father Huddleston, who had served both the Queens Henrietta Maria and Catherine of Braganza. The king received the Catholic communion from him and at noon on Friday, 6 February 1685 the king died.[32]

The volume which sets out the expenditure on the king's funeral[33] is little different from all those in former years. It is redolent with phrases based on precedent, such as 'Two Palls of Black Velvett to be provided, and a Holland Sheete as att the Duke of Gloucesters Funerall.'

A wax effigy of the king had been prepared, to stand upright over the catafalque. The queen received all the mourning ambassadors and court officials from a great black bed set within a room all hung with black cloth. Finally, and as tradition decreed, at night, on 14 February, the king's body, within a lead coffin which bore inscriptions dating his reign back to 1649, the time of his father's execution, was laid in a vault beneath the Henry VII Chapel in Westminster Abbey. Whilst not as grand as the funeral of Lord Protector Cromwell, the king had been attended in death by the rich panoply monarchy commanded. A velvet canopy had been carried high over the body, which was attended by the Chief Mourner, Prince George of Denmark, by James II, Mary of Modena and a long black-arrayed procession of noblemen and their servants, headed by William Sancroft, Archbishop of Canterbury. For their part the officers of the Great Wardrobe gathered up the hundreds of yards of black cloth and looked on their groaning storeroom shelves for something more suited to a festive occasion.

In contrast to the grand spectacles which had been arranged for earlier coronations, that of James II, whilst dignified, was not expensive. The plates in Francis Sandford's *History of the Coronation of James II* (1687) show the set-out of carpets, tapestry and other hangings, a throne and chairs of estate (Pl. 62), all done under the supervision of Jean Poictevin. All of it cost £1,181, almost £360 less than the cost of the coronation of Charles II (£1,558).[34] The king had entered Westminster Hall grandly enough, under a triumphal arch painted by Robert Streater in *trompe l'oeil*, the personification of regality and splendour. In less than eighteen months he was at odds with his parliament, frequently proroguing it, and was hard into a vigorous campaign to secure the repeal of the penal laws against Catholics.[35]

30   P.R.O., LC9/276, 17 October 1682.
31   P.R.O., LC5/41, ff.196, 205, 216, 225; LC9/277, f.120.
32   Fraser (1979) pp.454–7.
33   P.R.O., LC2/11(1).
34   H.K.W., V (1976) p.454; P.R.O., LC9/121, f.35 (Poictevin).
35   Miller (1989) p.69.

THE DELOBEL BED

In 1685 James II, on a visit to Paris, had bought two expensive items from Louis XIV's upholsterer, Simon Delobel (de Lobell). They were a crimson velvet bed, with the usual two elbow chairs and six stools *en suite*, and a green velvet cloth of estate, with a chair of estate, two cushions, one footstool and two stools, all embroidered 'suitable to the Estate'. The furniture was charged on 6 August 1686 at the high sums of £1,515 for the bed and furnishings *en suite*, and £1,508 for the cloth of estate and its accompanying items.[36] On 7 August Delobel was paid £200 'By his Mats Comand' for his 'Extraordinary Charges in packing up at Paris the furniture of the Rich Embroidered Bed and State bought of him by his Matje' and for its custom and freight charges from Paris through Calais to London, 'and for his attendance here some time before he received his whole money with other small expenses here'.

The crimson velvet bed was, as the account indicates, a grand affair. It was:

> lyned with Crimson Sattin Embroidered with gold and silver, containing a Tester, four Inside Vallance & outside Vallance, one headcloth, four Cantoones (Two of them Embroidered on both sides) Four Curtaines, Three Bases, one Counterpoynt, 4 Cupps, one Bedstead, one Bedd and Bolster, one Fustian quilt, one Holland Quilt, one sett of Feathers with Spriggs, Two Elbow Chaires, six stooles, the Frames carved and gilt, all suitable to the Bedd
>
> The Sume of £1,515.0.0

The green velvet cloth of estate was embroidered with gold and silver too, and had a tester, three outside valances, with four inside, a headcloth, an estate frame, together with the chair of estate, two cushions, a footstool and two stools, again 'embroidered all suitable to the Estate. The sume of £1,508.0.0.'

Within a few months, the bed, at least, was undergoing alteration by 'John Poictevin, Upholsterer'. The accounts record for 23 December 1686:[37]

> . . . for ye Great Bedchamber . . . For raising all the Curtaines of the new Embroydered Bedd bought of Mons. De Lobell, the Cantoones and making a new headboard, lineing ye testor, vallance, Counterpoint and all ye Bases ye sume of . . . £250.0.0
> For 4 Carved feet gilt   004.00.00
> For a false Case Rodd gilt   007.00.00.

All Poictevin could do was to add this to the large sum of money owing to him by the crown. By the end of 1687 this amounted to over £2,461, having been swelled by his work for the king's coronation in 1685 and by the £303 6s he had expended in 1687 for providing and attending on the funeral of the Duchess of Modena, the king's mother-in-law.[38] An important royal bill of 1686 from Poictevin is given in the appendix (A19).

Within the next eighteen months the king's world and that of his queen, Mary of Modena, were to undergo dramatic changes far removed from the domestic ritual of ordering furniture. The king, an ardent Catholic, had always believed himself to be right but he failed, miserably, to understand his English subjects. They assumed, as Protestants, that he would seek to establish Catholicism by force and join forces with the French king against the Protestant states in Europe. They disbelieved the king's stated opinions on avoiding religious persecution, and few thought he would not alter the succession to the throne. Even the birth of his son, James Francis Edward, Prince of Wales, on 10 June 1688 was not believed, as most Protestants did not want to reckon with a Catholic heir; in October the king was forced to make a formal declaration as to the genuine birth of his son.

36 P.R.O., LC9/278, ff.20–1, 40–1.
37 *Ibid.*, f.100.
38 P.R.O., LC9/278, f.28.

Meanwhile, in a rapidly deteriorating situation which involved France and the Dutch States, William, Prince of Orange needed to act decisively, and did. He stated that 'if he was invited by some men of the best interest . . . to come and rescue the nation and the religion' he would, and so invited, he began his preparations for an invasion of England. James II finally escaped to France in December 1688, and his court, helped by Louis XIV, was established at Saint-Germain-en-Laye. His desperate attempt in 1689, landing in Ireland with a French force, was defeated by King William at the Battle of the Boyne.

Two Poictevin Commissions

Two documented private commissions of Poictevin's are known: the provision of furniture to the first Duke of Hamilton, and work for the sixth Duke of Somerset at Petworth, Sussex. Poictevin wrote out his own bill for 'the Duke of Hambillton commansee le 15 May, 1688'.[39] He provided (for £35) a crimson mohair bed lined with green satin. Eighty yards of 'greene morela mohare' were used for the bed and some chairs (5s 6d a yard) and one hundred and twenty-three yards of 'white florance satting for the lynein' (6s a yard). The cups were covered with green mohair but there is no mention of surmounting them with feathers. The text of this bill is given (Appendix A20).

The 'Proud Duke', Charles Seymour, sixth Duke of Somerset, had married the young heiress, Elizabeth Percy, in May 1682; she came into her inheritance three years later, in 1685, at the age of eighteen. It provided the means for the duke to start altering the Elizabethan house at Petworth in Sussex, which itself had been formed from a medieval one, of which the fourteenth-century chapel still survives.

Most of the workmen employed by the sixth duke at Petworth from 1686 to 1692 were also active in the service of the king's works. They have been mentioned elsewhere,[40] and included the upholsterer, Jean Poictevin. He provided spectacular furniture which has, alas, all disappeared, a casualty of decay and decline in fashion. Some of what was supplied is mentioned in the inventory of 1748, made at the time of the duke's death. There was, for example, an 'Indian green and white satten bed, laced with broad and narrow silver lace and 34 silver tassels'. There may have been some involvement in the design of this, as indeed with the house, by the talented designer, Daniel Marot. It could have looked similar to those beds illustrated in his *Seconde Livre d'Appartements* (see also Pl. 95). 'Mr Podvin' and Robert Rhodes between them received £50 in 1687, 'besides £340 already paid',[41] and probably used the various damasks and velvets which had been supplied by the London mercer, Sir William Gostlin, in the previous June (1686), for £71 9s 3d.[42]

As well as Poictevin's attentions to what the sixth Duke of Somerset had ordered, there were other English upholsterers attendant on the imperious patron. The competent London craftsman, Thomas Strawbridge (who was also working at the time for Theophilus Leigh at his great Warwickshire house, Stoneleigh),[43] charged the duke £80 in 1690 for a 'damaske bed and 6 chaires'.[44] Nothing is known of the Robert Rhodes who received money along with 'Mr Podvine', or of the Mr Wiseman who was paid £77 16s in 1690 for 'striped damask for the Dss. Apartment'.[45]

State Beds by Poictevin

It is not profitable to speculate overmuch on surviving furniture which could be attributed to Poictevin. I think the state bed at Belvoir Castle, Leicestershire is by him. It was made, probably, for Catherine, the third wife of the first Duke of Rutland, and her cypher is amid the embroidered acanthus foliage on the headboard. She

39 Scottish Record Office (NRA (S) 2177-F2/501).
40 Jackson-Stops (1977) pp.324–33; Beard (1989) pp.38–41. The mention of Poictevin at Boughton by Jackson-Stops is a mistake; it was in fact Francis Lapiere who was involved there. See Jackson-Stops (1981) p.255 and Beard and Westman (1993) p.520.
41 West Sussex C. R. O., MS., PHA 171.
42 *Ibid.*, MS., 652.
43 Beard and Gilbert (1986) p.861.
44 West Sussex C. R. O., MS., PHA 173.
45 *Ibid.*, MS., 172.

had married John Manners, the ninth Earl of Rutland (as he then was) in 1673. The bed, however, exquisitely embroidered in white silk with birds and emblems and surmounted by a velvet-covered tester, is most likely to date from the late 1680s. For many years the bed was at Haddon Hall, Derbyshire, a property of the Duke of Rutland, before being returned by the ninth Duke (d.1940) to his principal seat at Belvoir Castle.

Poictevin's work for the first Duke of Hamilton, a Scottish peer, may mean he also supplied another state bed (now in the Victoria and Albert Museum, London; see Pls 95–6) to the Scottish peer, George, first Earl of Melville. This fine bed has also been attributed to Francis Lapiere, due to its similarity to a documented fragment of the state bed which Lapiere made, *c.*1697, for William Cavendish, first Duke of Devonshire (Pls 92–4). It is, however, sensible to rehearse a full argument. Both the Duke of Hamilton, Poictevin's patron in 1688, and the Earl of Melville were members of the ruling class in Scotland. They each held office there at about the same time and must have known one another. The Earldom of Melville had not been created until 1690, when George Melville returned from his exile on the Continent following a part in the Monmouth conspiracy. There he had joined the Prince of Orange, and followed him to England, and so eventually was rewarded with office. He had much to do to restore his domestic life and there was now money to help that along. The matter is referred to again below in discussing Lapiere, but attributions, whilst easy to make, do not advance knowledge and should, for the most part, be resisted. As for Poictevin, his career moved inexorably forward but he disappeared from the royal archives for a short time in the 1680s. He was, however, involved in the making of a lavish state bed for James II, now at Knole (discussed below), and was active at the coronation of William and Mary in 1689.

STUART FURNITURE AT KNOLE

The dream-like, quiet country house of Knole, in Kent, has been in continuous habitation since Archbishop Bourchier built the greater part of the existing quadrangles, great hall, chapel and gateways in the mid-fifteenth century. The house was granted by Elizabeth I, in 1566, to her cousin Sir Thomas Sackville, later first Earl of Dorset and he, perhaps with designs from the surveyor, John Thorpe, remodelled it all between 1603 and 1608. The presence of outstanding Stuart furniture at Knole[46] is due, however, to both a fortunate marriage and subsequent inheritance, and to the taking of royal perquisites in the 1690s.

Firstly, Richard Sackville, the fifth Earl of Dorset, had married Frances, the daughter and heiress of Lionel Cranfield, first Earl of Middlesex. Cranfield had gained his fortune and positions in the reign of James I, and I have referred earlier (p.10) to his mastership of the Great Wardrobe (1618–22). Cranfield furnished his principal house of Copt Hall, Essex with a grandeur made possible by his business success. But, when he died in August 1645 it was in the sad knowledge that parliamentary demands and confiscations had eroded his estates, and his other house at Milcote had been set to the torch. Cranfield's son, James, succeeded to the earldom but, like his younger brother, Lionel (who became third Earl of Middlesex in 1651), he had no sons. Therefore at Lionel's death in 1674 his possessions were bequeathed to his nephew, Charles Sackville, who succeeded his father Richard in 1677 as sixth Earl of Dorset. Despite such bequests Charles was in debt. To alleviate this urgent pressing of his problems he sold off the most revenue-demanding of his assets, Copt Hall, and sent off to Knole in 1701 a long procession of waggons carrying furniture, silver and hangings. Much of this was in the form of perquisites which Charles, as Lord Chamberlain to William III and Queen Mary, had obtained, by right of office, at various times from the royal palaces.[47] In particular, some pieces can be traced to those acquired in 1694–5 after the death of Queen Mary. There is, therefore, at Knole, an unrivalled collection of early English furniture.

As Knole, over the years, was only used intermittently, and kept shuttered and dust-sheeted, the furniture has survived with much of its original painted decoration and upholstery. Although somewhat faded,

46   Jourdain (1952).   47   Jackson-Stops (1977).

it is a unique survival. There is also a full archive,[48] but a careful re-examination of all that is relevant, whilst full of interest for the wider study of upholstery, has done little to resolve the many problems of authorship and identity. The documentation includes a series of lists which show movement of furniture and fabrics between various palaces, the Standing Wardrobes and Lord Dorset's own houses. They are, of course, referred to or given as appropriate in the appendix of documents (Appendix A21). As most of the important furniture came, after the Restoration, in one of these two ways to Knole, I am discussing it all in this chapter, despite the fact that some is of early seventeenth-century date.

Furniture from the Spangled Bedroom at Knole

The early Stuart furniture in this room includes a bed, a cross-framed (or X-frame) chair, and eight high stools. It is furniture which is probably royal in provenance, but it is not known whether it was acquired by the sixth Earl as a perquisite or, much earlier, by his grandfather Lionel Cranfield. Whatever the truth is does mean that at Knole there are several examples of chairs of estate, a description so often found in archives, and one of the chairs has its matching two high stools and a footstool. Some of the furniture sent from London can be identified in an inventory taken almost certainly at the sixth earl's death in 1705.[49] Facing page 10, which lists the contents of the Wardrobe at Knole, is a note dated 'October ye 26: 1708 1 Crimson Satin spangled bed with gould and Crimson fring.' It was set in its present position in 1765.

The rich fabric of this bed (Pl. 57) has an *appliqué* pattern, overall, in a strapwork design on white silk bands sewn over a ground of red satin. The bands were oversewn, originally, with small glittering metallic spangles, many of which survive, and these give the room in which the bed is housed its name. The dating of the bed is somewhat problematic. The consensus would seem to be that whilst the fabric may date to somewhere between 1610 and 1620, it was all formed from a canopy suspended over a chair of state. The curtains may have been made out of associated wall hangings and may have been done about 1680.[50] The bed then came, via Copt Hall, to Knole as a perquisite. The counterpoint (counterpane) and pillowcase are in a matching fabric, and gold and silver fringe is sewn to the lower edges of the outer and base valances.

There are five X-frame chairs at Knole, either upholstered completely or with a painted arabesque decoration. Perhaps the most resplendent is that *en suite* to the spangle bed, which is upholstered with *appliqué* of cloth of gold on a red satin ground. Whilst it is illustrated here (Pl. 30), I have chosen to describe it also to stress the considerable importance of the upholsterer's work. His is the achievement which makes this chair such a significant object: the wooden frame is completely hidden beneath the splendid covering. The ground is set with silver spangles whilst the back is topped by two egg-shaped finials, banded vertically with braid held by gilt nails. The fabric on the back is held by five large gilt bullion nails at each side, and is divided by a cut fringe. The arms are covered and hold a tasselled squab cushion, above an upholstered seat. A separate back cushion is fringed all round. The X-frame is also covered with fabric and edged with fringe at the cross-stretchers. The shield-shaped escutcheon at the front intersection of the legs, reversed at some date, has been corrected. It is the kind of chair that the royal upholsterer, John Baker, was providing for James I *c.*1620; similar chairs are shown in the king's portrait by John de Critz (Pl. 21), and in that at Knole itself by Daniel Mytens (Pl. 29).

Two of the other X-framed chairs, obviously brought to Knole as perquisites, have the canvas under the seats stamped (Pls 27–8) with the date 1661, a Royal crown and the initials H.C. (Hampton Court). However, this date probably relates to a stocktaking at the palace after the Restoration as the chairs are of a similar date (*c.*1620) to that in the spangle bedroom. There is a footstool *en suite* to one. A set of furniture in the brown gallery, of purple velvet embroidered in silver thread, is the only chair of estate at Knole that has, as I have mentioned, its two flanking high stools and footstool. The pair of stools have stuffed and upholstered seats embroidered with a design in applied leather, covered with silver thread. One of the other

48 Kent C. R. O., MSS U.269.
49 *Ibid.*, U269, E3.
50 Thornton (1977) p.137.

X-chairs also in the brown gallery has a cross-frame made to fold and its tasselled cushion has been converted into a covering for the seat. However, its green velvet, edged with silver fringe, is an early replacement for upholstery which probably matched the white arabesques on a scarlet ground which are painted on the frame.

THE KING'S BED AT KNOLE

This outstanding royal bed (Pls 49–50), one of the great examples of the upholsterer's skill, was restored meticulously over thirteen years from 1974 to 1987, and gives again a remarkable insight into late seventeenth-century opulence.[51] The conservation has done as much as is possible to stabilize the heavy fabrics, although no attempt has been made, wisely, to try to recapture the original colours. It is believed to have been made in 1673 for the future James II, then Duke of York, for his second marriage, to Mary Beatrice, Duchess of Modena. Early visitors to Knole (such as J. H. Brady in his *Guide* of 1849) assumed that because James I had visited the house in 1608 the bed had been prepared for him. However, its style and construction probably make it French and of a much later date. It was again acquired by the sixth Earl as a perquisite from Whitehall Palace, after the death of Queen Mary in December 1694.

In 1672 and in 1673 Louis XIV's upholsterer, Jean Peyrard, had visited England, bringing as many as six beds to Charles II. The 1672 account[52] shows record of the first four beds:

> John Peyrard for two Rich Beds bought in ffrance and agreed for there by Our Lord Embassador Mountague, one of them of Crimson Damaske Trimd with gold ffringes of Goldsmiths worke with Chaires &c and hangings for the Above all sutable, the other of Yellow Damaske trimd with Silver ffringes of like Goldsmithes worke with chaires &c and Hangings . . . As also for two other Beds of Crimson Damaske trimd with Silke fringes with chaires &c., . . . conveyance of the above named Goods from Paris to Whitehall with allowance to himselfe and Two Servants for that Journey to London . . . and their returne to Paris.
>
> (£1,773 16s 6d)

In 1673 there is further record[53] of 'Monsr Peyrard, a ffrenchman for his time, expens of and charges with one Servant in his Journey from Paris to London with Beds and divers Other Goods' (£2,080). On the second visit the suites were in purple and crimson damask.[54]

The king's bed is most likely to be one of those made in France by Peyrard. It bears the coronet of a royal duke with its cap of red velvet in stumpwork on the headboard, suggesting James, Duke of York. The gold and silver flowers and scrolls are stuffed with horsehair over a leather foundation. The bed furniture is of cloth of gold embroidered in gold and silver thread backed by a now faded cherry coloured satin, and the six curtains, valances and counterpoint are trimmed with a heavy gold and silver metal fringe. The detachable feet of the bed are formed as lions *couchant*, and the posts have ostrich feathers, originally in white and dyed crimson.

Peyrard's accounts show he provided the usual accompanying chairs and stools to the bed. These too have been restored (in 1968)[55] and a layer of gilding and silvering was then found under a coat of black paint; some of the latter can still be seen and may well have been applied as 'mourning' at the death of the sixth Earl in 1705. There are a pair of armchairs, four stools and a pair of squab-frames, with the front stretchers and legs of all carved, variously, as standing classical figures or as *amorini* holding a crown, or bows and quivers, amongst billing doves. The carved toes of the squab-frames are of a characteristic Parisian form.

In the enveloping gloom of the brown gallery, part of Archbishop Bourchier's mid-fifteenth-century house, are a number of late seventeenth-century walnut armchairs. A pair with their feet finishing in dolphin

51 Cornforth (1987) pp.64–5.
52 P.R.O., LC5/41, f.12.
53 *Ibid.*, f.26.
54 Symonds (1942) pp.218–22.
55 Edwards (1968) pp.69–71.

heads and a royal crown on the front stretchers have the canvases under their seats stamped (Pl. 51) with 'W.P.' and a crown (for Whitehall Palace). There is also a set of six stools in the spangled dressing room, some of which are similarly marked on the canvas webbing. These have been attributed[56] to the royal joiner Thomas Roberts (fl.1685–1714), whose collaboration with Poictevin is noted below.

In the Leicester gallery, at the north-east corner of the house (which may have been created, or remodelled, by Robert Dudley, Earl of Leicester), there is more remarkable furniture. Principally, there is the so-called Knole Settee (Pl. 38), which is, more correctly, a couch or couch chair;[57] it would be placed beneath a canopy. The French upholsterer John Casbert was paid in 1660–1 for 'a large Couch of green damaske . . . [with] iron worke double gilt used about the Couche . . .'[58] Whilst the Knole couch has been dated variously to 1610 and 1625, I suggest a date of about 1640 on the basis of entries in Queen Henrietta Maria's accounts (Appendix A15).

There is in the Leicester gallery at Knole a set of five chairs, *c.*1625, each with painted birchwood and gilded frames, the seats and backs of which are covered with crimson velvet trimmed with a red silk netted fringe. Such chairs are shown in French engravings, by Abraham Bosse in particular, and they had a wide European circulation. Nevertheless the Knole examples are particularly fine ones.[59] It has further been suggested that a set of two gilt armchairs and six stools at Knole (now in the ballroom), upholstered in crimson damask and attributed to Francis Lapiere, were acquired by the sixth Earl. The Sackville archive does include two bills from Lapiere but neither of these relates to the ballroom furniture (Appendix A21). The first, of 26 December 1694, totalling £47 10s 0d, is for various fabrics, particularly Scotch plaid, for case-covers, two easy chairs with black japanned frames covered with linen, gilt-nailed and with down-filled cushions, a travelling field bed with two cartons to contain it and a walnut 'Engreaved Teable'. The second, of 5 April 1695, is for 'three Pictures' (£20).

Finally, there is a third sumptuous bed, in the Venetian ambassador's room, the name deriving from a portrait hung there of the ambassador Nicolo Molino, by Mytens (1622). The bed is *en suite* to a pair of armchairs, covered in blue-green Genoa velvet, and a set of six stools (Pls 68–9). Again, restoration of the seat furniture took place in 1959.[60] The head-board of the bed has at its centre two carved and gilt figures supporting a royal crown. At each front angle of the cornice are the carved and gilded royal supporters of lion and unicorn, and at the centre (Pl. 66) is a shield held by *putti* with the letters 'JR' (for Jacobus Rex). The hangings are of green patterned velvet trimmed with a ball fringe, which has faded to shades of pink and russet.

There is a royal warrant of August 1688[61] which required Richard Graham, Viscount Preston, the Master of the Great Wardrobe, to supply 'a bed of green and gold figured velvet with scarlet and white silk fringe', with two armchairs and six stools, all for the king's use at Whitehall Palace. The royal joiner at this period, Thomas Roberts, is likely to have collaborated with the most active of the French upholsterers working for the king, Jean Poictevin. However, the documentation reveals only a payment in November 1689 to Roberts for the frames of two armchairs and six stools 'richly carved with figures and gilt all over with gold'.[62] A month later, on 10 December 1689, James II left England for the last time for an uncertain exile in France.[63] He had perhaps never slept in the bed, or sat on the chairs or stools; they were in the Standing Wardrobe at Whitehall in February 1694,[64] but ever watchful, the perquisites were brought to Copt Hall in 1695 after the death of Queen Mary. It is listed as 'the bedstead, beding and furniture belonging to my Lady Mary's bed'.

56 Beard and Gilbert (1986) p.753.
57 Thornton (1978) p.174.
58 P.R.O., LC5/52.
59 Thornton (1974) Pl. 6.
60 Edwards (1960) pp.164–7.

61 P.R.O., LC9/123, f.27.
62 *Ibid.*, f.42.
63 Miller (1989) p.205.
64 Kent C. R. O., MSS., U269, O69/1 (J) p.3.

The chairs and stools reached Knole in late September 1695,[65] the bed seemingly in 1701, and were stored in the Library at the time of the 1705 Knole inventory.[66] This lists:

    1 Green and Gold Coloured velvet Bed Compleat
    2 Elbow Chairs & 6 Square Stools with Guilt fframes, and 4 Plumes of Feathers
    1 Down Bed Covered with Satin, 1 Quilt and Bolster of the same
    4 Case Curtains and Rods to the bed.

It can be seen that the history of the three state beds at Knole is incomplete and confusing. In summary it might be held that the spangled bed (Pl. 57) dates from the 1680s but incorporates textiles provided for James I. The king's bed (Pl. 49) was probably one of those acquired from Jean Peyrard on one of his two visits to England in 1672 or 1673. The emblems carved on the *en suite* chair frames could celebrate the marriage in 1673 of James, Duke of York (the future James II) to Mary of Modena. The bed in the Venetian ambassador's room (Pls 66–9) was made for James II a little before he was deposed in 1688. The upholstery was by Jean Poictevin on frames (to the bed and *en suite* chairs) made by Thomas Roberts.

A LESSER COMPANY AT KNOLE

Despite the advantages his office as Lord Chamberlain gave to Lord Dorset he still used several craftsmen in a private capacity. The Sackville archive contains an interesting account[67] for fabrics bought from 'Thomas Alchorne & Part[ner]' in April 1687 totalling £339 9s 9d. Alchorne's partner seems to have been Benjamin Raye who signed 'for my Selfe & Compa[ny]'. The earl was charged 28s for each yard of Antwerp woollen velvet, 24s for each yard of Genoa silk velvet; Indian damask was at 12s but leading the list was 'rich sky and silver tishew' at 35s a yard.

In London there was patronage in July 1686 of 'John Reynolds, upholsterer att the fox and Crowne in fleetstreet'. In his bill[68] for a modest £37 6s 11d he provided the services of dyeing white taffata into 'a Sad Cloth Culler', elbow chairs at 12s each, various cushions in blue moreen and serge for lining curtains and lead plummets to weight them. His most expensive charge was £21 17s 4d in repairing twelve green velvet chairs. Two of them may have had damaged frames as he provided 'two new Irons to the frames', gilded the 'fore Rayles and the Carved work', polished the frames, 'new Bottumed them', varnished the old and new nails, and finally packed them up to send to his patron.

FRANCIS LAPIERE, A FRENCH CATHOLIC UPHOLSTERER

Although Francis Lapiere is known as one of the grandest and most accomplished of the French upholsterers working in late seventeenth-century England, a supplier of magnificent state beds such as that now partly surviving at Hardwick Hall, Derbyshire (Pls 92–4), little is known of his career and much of the published information is inaccurate.[69] In the first edition of Macquoid and Edwards, published in 1927,[70] the short entry on 'Francis La Pierre' states that this French upholsterer supplied carpets and beds to the Great Wardrobe (charged with furnishing the royal palaces) between 1690 and 1696, and similar items for William Cavendish, first Duke of Devonshire at Chatsworth, including a bed recorded in an account book entry of September 1697 ('in part of £470 for a Bed payable at £6 a week – 17 paymts, paid £102'). Finally it is stated, on the basis of an entry in the *Calendar of Treasury Papers*,[71] that 'La Pierre' was 'prosecuted as an alien enemy' in 1697. This account was repeated in the second edition of the *Dictionary* (1954), and it has been assumed that Lapiere was

65   Kent C. R. O., *Ibid.*, MSS., U269, E79/2.
66   *Ibid.*, MSS., U269, E3.
67   *Ibid.*, MSS., U269, A194/4.
68   *Ibid.*, MSS., U269, A193/4.

69   Beard and Westman (1993) pp.515–24.
70   D.E.F., (1927) I, p.284.
71   *Cal. S.P. Dom., 1697–1701/2*, p.49.

a Huguenot. In the list of London furniture makers issued the previous year by Sir Ambrose Heal, Lapiere's year of death is given as 1717.[72] All these errors – Lapiere's Huguenot connection, his imprisonment and date of death – reappear in the *Dictionary of English Furniture Makers* published in 1986.[73] It is therefore necessary to reassess his career, and the discovery of Lapiere's will, an inventory of his possessions, and details of his involvement in a Chancery suit, allow much of the record to be put straight.

That Lapiere was a Catholic, not a Huguenot, is immediately apparent from his will, dated 22 August 1714 and filed (after his death on 14 November 1714) in London on 22 January 1715.[74] The opening lines of the English version run as follows: 'In the Name of the most Holy Trinity one only God in three persons the Father, Son and Holy Ghost and in whom I believe, Professing the Holy Catholick Apostolick and Roman Religion I beseech the Holy Virgin and the Saints of Paradise to make intercession for me . . .' One might therefore be tempted to look instead for Catholic connections in his English career but, although the religious beliefs of Lapiere's patrons, where known, are noted in the account of his documented activity that follows, they appear not to have been of great importance in the pursuit of his career. He seems to have been in demand by Catholic and Protestant patrons alike.

The suggestion that Lapiere was imprisoned as an enemy alien also proves to be a misunderstanding. The relevant volume of State Papers matching the treasury document cited by Macquoid and Edwards notes that the 'Francis La Peyre' who came into England without a pass and was put into custody as a spy died in 1696, eighteen years before the date of death now established for the upholsterer.[75] The spy's estate had been reckoned valuable enough for the treasury to have had an interest in appropriating it, which accounts for the frequent mentions of him in treasury and state papers.

The first traced mention of Lapiere's presence in England is in 1683, when he started work for John, fifth Earl of Exeter (1648–1700) at Burghley House, Cambridgeshire. Between then and 1704 he appears frequently in the Exeter bank accounts of the earl, his executors, and of his wife.[76] Unfortunately the goods he provided are not itemized, as there are no bills, and any furniture which may be from his workshop is impossible to identify with certainty among the present contents of Burghley House because of subsequent amendment and re-upholstery. Nevertheless, I think a bed at Burghley, together with the suite of furniture in the Elizabeth room, in which the bed stands, may be by Lapiere. Much of what he received regular payments for has gone, but there are fine embroidered cyphers on the cornice and bed-rail (Pls 80–1) which are, in miniature, like that on the head-board of the documented Hardwick bed. There would appear to have been no religious bias behind Lapiere's employment at Burghley, for the fifth Earl of Exeter was a staunch Protestant.

Something of the busy journeyings of a craftsman in demand may be discerned in Lapiere's subsequent commissions. In October 1685 he was paid £9 10s for unspecified work for Sarah, Duchess of Marlborough, as is recorded in a receipt book for domestic expenses kept by the first Duke and Duchess:

> October 14, '85
>   received then of the Right Honble the Lady Churchill the sum of Nine Pounds Tenn Shill.,
> which is in full of all Debts & demands to this Day. I say Receved £09-10-
>   By mee Francis de Lapiere
>   [Endorsed] the Upholsters[77]

Both Lapiere and his first wife Dorothy, a tailoress, travelled to Drayton House, Northamptonshire, to work for Henry Mordaunt, second Earl of Peterborough. The earl had been adding to the medieval and Elizabethan ranges of the house, and his daughter, a significant patron to both Lapieres, employed William Talman to design a baroque inner courtyard in about 1700. The second Earl was an ardent Catholic, having converted at Rome in March 1687, and at the revolution of 1688 he was captured at Ramsgate while trying

72   Heal (1953) p.102.
73   Beard and Gilbert (1986) p.528.
74   P.R.O., Prob. 11/544, f.11.
75   *Cal. S.P. Dom., 1696*, p.24.

76   Royal Bank of Scotland, Child's Bank Ledger, Exeter account, 20 August 1683.
77   B.L., Add. MS, 61346, f.183.

to flee abroad and imprisoned in the Tower for almost two years. His troubles, which did not diminish, may have contributed to his treatment of Mrs Lapiere who, from some point in 1685, was also serving the earl's daughter, Lady Mary Mordaunt. Lady Mary had married Henry, seventh Duke of Norfolk in 1677, but lived quite openly with a Dutch soldier of fortune, Sir John Germain, who was reputed to be an illegitimate half-brother of William III. The estranged Duke of Norfolk started divorce proceedings in 1691, but the marriage was not dissolved until April 1700. In all that time, and even after her marriage in September 1701 to Sir John, Lady Mary found advantage in retaining the title of Duchess of Norfolk; she was styled 'Duchess, Dowager of Norfolk' when she died in November 1705.

At Drayton there is a bill dated May 1687[78] which shows Francis Lapiere providing, among much else:

for A bedstead a dubbell Riseing teaster & Sacking bottom	03.00.00
for 12 yeards of Lining to Line ye Bed	00.12.0
for tape, Small rings & ye Lead in ye Bottam of ye Curtins & ye Brass Pulleys to draw by ye Curtins	00.15.0
For ye Silke String	00.16.0
For a Box to Pack ye Bead	00.06.0
. . .	
for 14 Ells of Holland for ye Vestements for ye Prieste	02.18.00
for makeing ye Vestments & other things to them	00.07.00

An account of 1700 for work for the duchess also survives (Appendix A24). In 1993 I had assumed this too to be by Lapiere, but a closer inspection suggests it is by Etienne Penson, Poictevin's nephew.

Charles Sackville, sixth Earl of Dorset, whose activity as Lord Chamberlain is noted above, made use of Lapiere's services in the 1690s, and two of Lapiere's bills relating to that work are given (Appendix A21). Lord Dorset would see, frequently, the Lord High Steward of the Household, William Cavendish, first Duke of Devonshire. It may well have been the duke who mentioned Lapiere's name to the Earl of Dorset; and there seems no doubt that it was the Earl of Exeter, the duke's brother-in-law, who recommended both Lapiere and the decorative painter Antonio Verrio for work at Chatsworth after they had finished at Burghley.

The one surviving documented and substantial example of Lapiere's work, the state bed (Pls 92–4) he made for the first Duke of Devonshire in c.1697 for Chatsworth, is now in the long gallery at Hardwick Hall, Derbyshire, having been moved there from Chatsworth in the 1820s by the sixth Duke of Devonshire.[79] It has often been stated[80] that the bed cost the considerable sum of £470 (of which the wood carcase accounted for an insignificant £15) but this is not an exact account. No bills survive, only regular payments to Lapiere in instalments of six pounds a week are listed in John Whildon's account books, amounting to £470.[81] The last entry records that the sum also included 'other things besides', but there is no mention of the bed frame as a separate item. However, in the accounts of 1706 there is note of another bed, with a carved tester, cornices and a large carved wood headboard, the latter costing £15.[82] Examination of the fragment at Hardwick, which consists of the tester, carved cornices and headboard covered with crimson silk damask and trimmed with gold thread lace galloon, shows two holes in the silk-covered lath for foot posts of a four-poster bed. This undermines the claim that it was originally an 'angel' bed (a type with no foot posts), and it is highly probable that the end posts were removed when the sixth Duke displayed the bed as a canopy. It remains today as one

78 Drayton MS., No.2475.
79 It appears in David Cox's view of the Long Gallery at Hardwick in 1827 (National Trust Collection).
80 For example Fowler and Cornforth (1974) p.84.
81 Chatsworth, Building Accounts, vol.1, various dates from September 1697 to September 1699.
82 D.E.F., (1954) vol. 1, p.54.

of the most elaborate pieces of late seventeenth-century upholstery surviving in England, and a fine example of Lapiere's outstanding skills.

It is not easy to assess the extent of Lapiere's involvement with the Great Wardrobe. He appears infrequently in the relevant archives.[83] A first mention of him is for the hire of furniture to furnish the Duke of Schomberg's apartment for twenty months between November 1688 and August 1690 (the duke died in 1690 at the Battle of the Boyne), for which he was paid £230. The bill is signed by Ralph, later Duke of Montagu, who had been reinstated as Master of the Great Wardrobe in 1689 and kept the post until his death in 1709. The list of supplies includes several beds, ranging from the best with hangings of crimson Genoa damask with a suite of six arm chairs with matching damask cases, to three 'half headed' bedsteads for the servants. Various other types of seat furniture are listed: cane chairs with and without cushions; Turkey work chairs; 'a table and stands a looking glass'; 'three large tables to dine on and six ordinary tables'; and a selection of floor coverings from mats to 'a Large Turkey carpett to lay under the (best) bed'. This range of goods suggests that Lapiere was established firmly in London, probably in his house at Pall Mall, and could offer a wide range of furnishing services. In 1691 he supplied 'a large very fine Persian carpett for our Service in our Gallery att Kensington' for £64 10s. Two years later, in 1693–4, he was authorized to provide 'Five French bedsteads . . . for the Gentlemen and Groomes of our Bedchamber att Hampton Court and for our Staff Officers Room there'. These beds with their 'rising testers', 'handsome cornishes' and 'deep headboards' were hung with damask and trimmed with fringe at a total cost of £337 13s 4d. For Windsor Castle, Lapiere supplied two lots of five pieces of 'fine Tapestry Hangings' for Mr Keppell's bedchamber in 1694–5 (£236 5s) and for the Earl of Albemarle's lodgings in 1696 (£150). He also provided a bed for Dr Radcliffe's room at Windsor (£134 7s 6d) and a wainscot bed hung with 'Mazarine' blue Genoa damask with six armchairs 'for the entertainment of foreign Ambassadors at Saint James's Square' (£630 5s 9d). These two beds are priced together in the bill (£764 13s 3d) and a comparison of their descriptions shows vividly that the expense of grand beds lay in the cost of their fabric and trimmings. It is worth noting that this wainscot bed was more expensive than all Lapiere's work for the first Duke of Devonshire (£470), no doubt because of the massive 'thirteene hundred sixty four ounces of gold coloured tufted and twisted fringe' required for the bed and chairs. The seat furniture and bedding listed in the bill might be similar to that referred to as 'other things besides' in the Chatsworth accounts.

A significant aspect of Lapiere's English activity was his involvement with Ralph, Earl and later first Duke of Montagu.[84] Montagu had been ambassador to France until, after complaints by the Duchess of Cleveland, with whom Montagu had an early dalliance, the king struck him out of the Privy Council and replaced him as ambassador with the Earl of Sunderland. One of the Duke's companions was the Duchess of Mazarin and in April 1706 Montagu ordered from Lapiere 'a bed of Striped Tapestry needle work' for her, which had carved cups, draw curtains, and polished case rods for the protective case curtains. The bill includes the entry: 'Paid to Marrot for drawing the cornishes £1 15s 0d'. This need not necessarily refer to Daniel Marot, since an Isaac Marot, perhaps a younger brother, is described as *dessignateur* in the registers for 1707 of the Huguenot church of the Savoy.[85] Finally, Lapiere's name appears in a list at Boughton of the creditors of the Duchess of Mazarin to whom the duke had lent £300.[86] The Boughton archive also provides a mention of Lapiere's only known apprentice, Thomas Elrington, aged '22 years and upwards' in September 1711.[87]

One of the problems facing craftsmen was late payment or indeed no payment at all. As we have seen, Lapiere came up against this at Drayton, and in 1698 he proceeded in a Chancery suit against Barbara, Duchess of Cleveland, Charles II's erstwhile mistress,[88] a Catholic convert who was then living apart (but was not divorced) from her husband, Roger Palmer, Earl of Castlemaine, a prominent Catholic peer. Between 1687 and 1697 Lapiere had supplied her with goods amounting to £41 11s 6d, for which he had submitted a bill.

83   P.R.O., LC5/43, variously; LC5/44, f.28; LC9, 28v.

84   Murdoch, ed. (1992).

85   G. Jackson-Stops in Murdoch, ed. (1992) p.61 fn.36.

86   Murdoch, ed. (1992) p.34, fn.15.

87   Boughton House, MS., BC IV Pt.II, Book 4, ff.97–103.

88   P.R.O., C5/138, No.19, 8 July 1698.

He objected strongly in his legal submission that he had been sent merely 'a damaske bedd with ye furniture things thereunto' worth between £20 to £30 as settlement. Further, he complained that the duchess and Lord Castlemaine were raising a counter-action against him for £200 damages, on grounds which he completely refuted. The list of goods he supplied (Appendix A22) is a useful indicator of the range of activity.

Lapiere married for the second time at a ceremony held in 1701 in Paris. Two documents survive, the marriage certificate and a proxy of power of attorney. The former,[89] dated 9 January 1701, shows that Didier François Lapiere, *marchand tapissier à Londres*, and his intended wife, Marianne Vallance, daughter of Jean Vallance, a French merchant trading also in London, were lodged temporarily in rue de la Sourdière in the parish of Saint-Roche. Lapiere's parents are named as Dominique Lapierre, *marchand tapissier à Paris*, and Reyne Regnaudin, *sa femme*, but they do not appear to have been present. Jean Vallance made over 15,000 *livres* as a settlement on his daughter and, in the second document of 10 February 1701,[90] the newly married couple gave power of attorney to the Paris wine merchant, Jean Binville, to collect for them 350 *livres* of *rente* (annuity) from 7000 invested in the salt tax by the Vallance family. We may assume that a little after this Lapiere and his wife resumed their active life in London. His death, like that of Jean Poictevin, occurred in the early eighteenth century (1714) and is noted in chapter V (p.139).

THE FRINGE-MAKERS

One commodity which an upholsterer needed constantly was braid and fringes in a wide variety of elaborate styles and widths. No one supplied these more consistently than the French fringe-maker resident in London from the late 1660s, Peter Dufresnoy. The first mention I have traced of him is in the list of debts owed at the death in 1670 of the successful and wealthy upholsterer, William Ridges. These are appended to a several yards long inventory[91] of Ridges' effects which show that, whilst he was owed, in 'doubtful' or 'desperate' debts, over £9,000, he himself owed £6,680.

Dufresnoy's name is most often encountered in connection with Francis Lapiere's activities. Particularly in the case of upholstery and fringes, both of them provided for the fifth Earl of Exeter at Burghley House, Cambridgeshire. The earl's bank account[92] for January 8 1687 records, firstly, a payment of £100 on account to 'Mounsr Dufrenoy, fringe maker' towards a bill of £226 6s 10d, with £392 paid on 8 June 1704. The last was a payment of arrears by the trustees of the fifth Earl, who had died in 1700. The fine fringe (Pl. 82) on the Queen Elizabeth bed is worthy of being Dufresnoy's work.

A principal craftsman working for the Crown in the late seventeenth century, providing lace and fringes in large quantities, was 'His Majesty's Laceman' Sir William Gostlin. In May 1686 Jean Poictevin provided a blue, white and gold bed for James II's queen, Mary of Modena (Appendix A19).[93] Sir William had charged for the grandest of *passementerie* for it two months earlier, as follows:

> For ye Queenes new blewe white & gold colour Damask Bedd conteyning 6 Curtaines, 2 Cantoones, headcloth, headboard, Tester, Inner & Outer Vallance, Bases and Surbases, 2 Armchaires & 6 Stooles in Her Mats Bedchamber att Windsor with a Counterpoint to the sd. Bedd.
>
> For 211 yards of rich Gold & Silver tufted Edgeing fringe, $106\frac{1}{2}$ yards of ditto, Inch deep, 10 yards of ditto, small bow fringe, 14 yards of ditto vallance, & 18 yards of Ditto-Seaming, all weighing 128 lb 15 oz silke which is 2,750 oz $\frac{2}{3}$ ven: att 7s p. oz. £962 14s 08d
>
> Cupps of bedd had a further 58 yds of gold & silver purled twisted lace £11 19s 09d

89 Paris. Archives Nationales, Minutier Central. Etude XXXIII, f.398.
90 *Ibid.*
91 C.L.R.O., Orphans' Invs. No.692.
92 Royal Bank of Scotland, Child's Bank Ledgers.
93 P.R.O., LC9/287, f.34.

Gostlin was also involved in the mourning obsequies for the Duchess of Modena, providing lace and fringe in a quantity and a quality[94] befitting the funeral of someone related to the reigning monarch.

On the evening of 18 December 1688 bonfires burned in London and its environs. Bells pealed and as John Evelyn, the diarist, had it: 'All the world go to see the Prince at St James's, where there is a great Court. There I saw him and several of my acquaintance who came over with him'. A day or two earlier James II had escaped to Rochester and on the 26 December he set sail to exile in France. The throne was declared vacant and on 6 February 1689 the crown was offered to William and Mary jointly. Subtly, a Declaration of Rights (which became a Bill eventually) restricted the power of the monarchy to suspend national laws; parliaments must be called frequently and kings must learn to reign with, rather than against.[95]

WILLIAM III AND THE ROYAL PALACES

Within a few months of William and Mary's accession as joint sovereigns war was declared against France. This did not stop the king from ordering his surveyor, Sir Christopher Wren, to prepare schemes to adapt the old Tudor palace at Hampton Court. By June 1689 the foundations were begun and whilst Wren had made his many plans in haste, he was able, eventually, to achieve a grand effect.[96]

With the king absent in Ireland, Queen Mary had been acting as regent. In July 1690 she visited Hampton Court and wrote to the king that things went on very slowly there because of the scarcity of both money and Portland stone. Work was also going on concurrently at Kensington Palace, and at both houses there occurred a disastrous building failure. At Hampton Court part of the great trusses of the roof on the privy garden front fell, carrying away the floor over certain rooms near the cartoon gallery. At Kensington the additional buildings fell down in November 1689. Fortunately for Wren the queen intervened, writing to the king in December[97] that she had often gone over to Kensington to hasten on the workmen. She wanted to take up residence there quickly and all the pressure on them, she insisted, had brought errors in the work but the hand of God had also intervened. One can imagine that this statement, with which few could satisfactorily argue, endeared her to the hard-pressed officers of the King's Works.

At this time, in 1689, William Talman had been appointed Comptroller in the King's Works. He had an uneasy relationship with Wren and both were called to a meeting on 21 December 1689 to explain the building failures. Talman tried to use the opportunity to belittle the Surveyor with an angry Wren countering the accusations. As a compromise the Lords of the Treasury nominated three witnesses to report, but the king, upon hearing Wren's evidence, ordered the works at Hampton Court to proceed unless his officers found material cause why this would be dangerous or ill-advised. No such cause was found.

HAMPTON COURT

As Hampton Court progressed the Master of the Wardrobe was asked in 1693 to begin the provision of tapestry for the new rooms. The queen, with her passion for building, decoration, gardens and arrangements of porcelain and flowers, followed eagerly Wren's work on completing Charles II's Fountain Garden. But at her deeply mourned death on 28 December 1694 the king lost interest and Bishop Burnet recorded[98] that the king's spirits sank so low that it was feared he too would die.

Around Christmas 1693 Wren had estimated that it would take £35,315 to complete the new quadrangle at Hampton Court. By 1697 when, by the Treaty of Ryswick, England found herself no longer at war with France, William, his chief occupation gone, resumed his interest in making improvements to his house and garden. Wren sent the king a letter on 28 April 1699 giving a revised cost for finishing part of the house. He supposed that the king would finish the rooms as decently as their size and position required. In

94 P.R.O., LC9/278, f.11.
95 Van der Zee (1973) p.272.
96 Thurley (1994) pp.10–20.

97 *Wren Soc.*, VII, p.135.
98 Green (1967) p.73.

September Talman had also written to the king, in the belief that he would wish to hear how work progressed – that five rooms were almost finished and the great stone stairs of the king's staircase, with Jean Tijou's iron balustrades and Verrio's wall paintings, complete. With this insistence from his officers the king allowed work to press ahead. The staircase led through to the guard room, and to the five south-facing state rooms. In them is a great variety of wood-carving by Grinling Gibbons. In the chapel Wren designed the reredos, flanked by two groups of Corinthian columns, and carved by Gibbons in superb fashion.

The courtier Robert Jennings wrote on 28 October 1699 'Yesterday I was at Hampton Court. The King's apartment is finished, and I fancy t'will be made the prettiest place in the world . . .'[99] The king was at Hampton Court several times that winter and in late April 1700 moved his court there. The rooms in the Fountain Court not allocated for state purposes were used as domestic offices and apartments and were allocated to royal servants and favourite courtiers. The king had decreed in August 1699, in a message[100] he had sent whilst journeying in his favourite Holland, that 'all foreign ambassadors for the future are to have their audience' at Hampton Court. In consequence of all these requirements of daily occupation and state use the upholsterers were soon busy.

For the many visits of a day or two's duration which the King made to Hampton Court in the winter of 1699/1700 the Lord Chamberlain had arranged that several pieces of furniture were delivered for the use of the few retainers there. These included a damask bed, bedclothes, two Dutch armchairs, a table, looking glass, a 'handsome camlett bed lin'd with silk' and other items. Hangings were carried from Whitehall and three boat loads of royal 'goods' were delivered. The king had his rooms in the south wing at a first floor level, but until these were completed he needed to stay elsewhere in the palace. The grandest of the courtier suites in the court quadrangle was allocated to the Dutchman, Arnold Joost van Keppel, created the first Earl of Albemarle in 1697. This had fifteen rooms and four closets and over £1,200 was to be spent between 1699 and 1702, in decorating them. One of Lord Albemarle's great friends, Edward Villiers, first Earl of Jersey, had been rising fast in the king's favour. By April 1700, as one of the Lords Justices and a former ambassador to France, he had established himself in rooms at Hampton Court. I note below his selling of a state bed to the king which is still at Hampton Court (Pl. 87).

THE KING'S UPHOLSTERER

Whilst Jean Poictevin remained in royal service (as well as serving private patrons) he had never received a warrant confirming him in an official position. It was different for the English upholsterer, Richard Bealing, who served the crown from 1688 to at least 1714.[101] He is first mentioned in 1680 for private work for the fifth Earl of Bedford at Woburn Abbey. His bills[102] show him providing a twelve skin leather carpet bound with gilt leather, scouring tapestry, taking down hangings and beds. It is worth quoting details of his altering a bed for its attention to a new style, with a springing tester, cantilevered and without need of foot posts.

For a springing teaster and cut head band	0.17.00
For dyeing all the Insid lineing of sarsnet & quilt chery culler in graine	2.10.00
For 14 yds of sarsnet to finish the bed and quilt at 3s.4d.	02.04.04
For a french fring and 9 pair of loops	02.05.00
For 71 ounces of silk fring about ye bed at 18d.	05.06.06
For Imbrodering all ye flourishes	02.00.00
For making the bed and sowing silke and thred used about it	01.00.00
For a set of larg guilt cups for ye bed	00.16.00
For a set of feet sutable	00.08.00
For a set of sad culler searg curtains and vallens, teastr and head cloth	05.03.00

99   Cowper (1888) II, p.393.
100   Luttrell (1857) IV, p.35.
101   *Cal. Treasury Books*, 1714, Pt.II, p.107.
102   Woburn Abbey, Bedford MSS., Bills, Nos 28–9, 1680.

It was sensible that officers of the household should also turn to a craftsman whose abilities they knew. Lord Dorset, who had been Lord Chamberlain of the Household 1689–97, turned to Bealing for work at Knole at various times in 1689, 1692 and 1693. Bealing's bills are noted (Appendix A21), and concern themselves with providing elbow and easy chairs, cushions, black japanned chairs, case covers, Barbary mats, fustian quilts, 'a large and very high bedstead' with the scrolls of the tester japanned, and all the bedclothes.

The book of royal bills for 1689 has a brief comment 'Richard Bealing, "Upholster for the Coronacon", April 5, 1689. In the House of Lords, Westr Abbey & Hall, 7 doz. Turkey work chairs at £7.4s p. doz.' There could be no better recommendation. He upholstered all the chairs of state and footstools made by Thomas Roberts for use in the Abbey. The splendid cloth baroque canopy shown in Romeyn de Hooghe's engraving (Pl. 70) of the coronation is his too.

Furniture for all the king's rooms at Hampton Court had begun to arrive there from November 1699 and continued to do so until the king's death in March 1702. The king was concerned that his state rooms be furnished 'as cheap as is possible',[103] but nevertheless, a great deal of new furniture was ordered. Nine estimates totaling £3,386 survive[104] for furniture 'for his Majesties services at Hampton Court'. As well as furniture for the state rooms there was an adequate provision for the apartments of the Groom and Gentleman of the Bedchamber and three rooms for the officers of the Horse Guards. The estimate (Appendix A23) totalled £92. Regrettably little is known of what was provided in the suites allocated to courtiers such as Lord Albemarle. The Lord Chamberlain's bill volume for 1699–1703[105] is, however, full of detail for the state apartments. Across the south front these, for the king, were, in order from west to east, the guard chamber, presence chamber, eating or 'next' room, privy chamber, withdrawing room, great bedchamber, little bedchamber, then a room for the gentlemen of the bedchamber, the closet and two 'backstairs',[106] one for the king's use.

The presence chamber and privy chamber were each provided with a throne canopy of state made from some of the 232 yards of crimson Genoa damask supplied by another Frenchman, Guillaume (William) Portal at 24s a yard. They were each surmounted, originally, by four cups with feathers. The canopies still survive intact, and their importance and prestige has been commented on.[107] Portal may, indeed, have supplied a superior form of damask but it could be obtained at the time for 18s a yard, quite possibly giving him a handsome profit.[108]

The bed in the great bedchamber was sold to the king in 1699 by Lord Jersey. Little is known of the exact transaction but a warrant against its acquisition was issued by the Lord Chamberlain on 6 November 1699 for the upholsterer (Richard Bealing) 'to be sent to Hounslow to take down beds and other furniture and thence to Hampton Court to sett up . . .'[109] The bills for 1698–9 show the continual presence on royal commissions of Bealing as upholsterer, Thomas Roberts (joiner), William Sherrard (mercer), William Elliot (lace maker), Thomas Carr (fringe maker) and Jonathan Chase (feather dresser).

Seemingly, when the bed reached Hampton Court there was work to be done on it. Bealing charged 'for work in altering ye velvet bed, cantoons & head curtains and new making them up againe',[110] also for large polished rings and 'crimson ribbon to ye case curtains', 'making ye taffata case Curtaines to ye Bed, sewing Silk to ye same and using 123 yards of crimson broad fflorence taffata' for a *tour du lict*, the counterpoint, window curtains 'of the same' and to case the *en suite* chairs and stools.

The accounts for 1700–3 (within the same volume as those for 1699) record the use of '26 yards of white satin to cover quilt & bolster of the crimson velvett bed' to which Bealing had also supplied five very large silk blankets.[111] Finally, there were always minor repairs to attend to, and William Portal charged for four yards of crimson Genoa velvet 'to repair Cupps for his State beds at 3s 6d a yard'. The bed itself (Pl. 87) has

103 *Cal. Treasury Books*, 1699–1700, p.42.
104 National Art Library (Victoria and Albert Museum) MS., RCU6.
105 P.R.O., LC9/281.
106 Thurley (1994) p.16.
107 Westman (1994) p.40.

108 National Art Library (Victoria and Albert Museum) MS., L464–1905.
109 P.R.O., LC5/68.
110 P.R.O., LC9/281, f.31.
111 *Ibid.*, LC9/28 ff.31, 78v.

lost much of its original furnishings. The front valance and headboard remain as part of a restrained rectilinear and rather French design. Indeed, might not Lord Jersey have acquired the bed in Paris during his embassy there (1688–9)? It is quite unlike the baroque flourishings of contemporary beds (Pls 92–6) such as those made for the Duke of Devonshire and the Earl of Melville.

The king slept for the most part not in this grand apartment but in the adjacent little bedchamber. At one stage in 1700–2 in the several changes of furnishings the accounts[112] record that this contained a 'yellow (Indian) damask bedd . . . finely laced with silver'. The lace men Thomas Parr, Thomas Plomer and William Elliot were very active, meshing their activities in to those of their friends in the king's service, the upholsterer Richard Bealing and the joiner, Thomas Roberts. It was Bealing who had made the hangings of the yellow damask bed, equipping it also with fine silvered compass rods, curtains and bedding, enclosing it in case curtains and covering three stools with Parr's laced damask. There was a fine walnut firescreen also covered in damask and yellow laced taffeta, and yellow taffeta window curtains, 'laced', hung beneath covered cornices. There was even 'a yellow Spanish skin for the bottom of a large Cushion for the King's feet'. There were also two cushions for this purpose in the great bedchamber. The Mytens portrait of Charles II (Pl. 47) shows the monarch resting his feet on such a cushion. Finally 'a fine barbery matt to lay under the yellow bed, galloon and silver nails to lay the same' were provided. The making of the frame of the bed by Thomas Roberts is listed in exact detail. There is also a reference to his 'laths for Pull up window Curtaines with box holes for ye Strings to play in', his carved *portières* for the doors, carved walnut firescreen 'with a quiet spring', and three square walnut stools. The provision by Roberts of pulley boards for 'Pull up' or festoon curtains shows that this style of curtain was used. It is shown in most of Daniel Marot's engravings (Pl. 98), and was of the 'new fashion', introduced from France.[113] William Elliot, as one of the lacemen, charged for '585 yards $\frac{3}{4}$ of broad, narrow & severall other breadths of fine Silver arras lace, weight Venice, 499 ounces & half, at 1s 6d, [and for] 4 rich silver tassels & strings to hold back the curtains of the bed'. Some of his yardage also trimmed the two window curtains, cornices, an elbow chair, three stools and a firescreen.

The curtains in the rooms used for public occasions, such as the privy and presence chambers, together with those for the eating room, withdrawing room and closet, were made from 530 yards of 'white flowered damask' at a cost of £397 10s. This was also used to cover Thomas Roberts's carved wood cornices. Something of the richness of Bealing's curtains may be appreciated from his £1,700 bill[114] for those in 'his majesties privat gallery at Hampton Court'. This long room lay on the east side of the Fountain Court and had seven windows and the bill mentions 'making 14 green taffata curtains & 7 vallance for the seven windowes very deep, laced with gold five polished rings & tape for said curtains 7 Curtain rods & 14 hooks guilt with gold'. Bealing also supplied '7 large pear mould tassells green, with lead' and 99 yards of large green cord to help close the curtains.

The 1699–1700 bills[115] may be summarized as follows in terms of the provision of fabrics on which Richard Bealing, in particular, could rely. The number within parentheses is that of the relevant bill.

(17)   *Window Curtains: Cornices (Public Rooms)*
530 yards white flowered damask   15s yard
Canopies of State; furniture, en suite
232 yards rich crimson Genoa damask   24s yard

King's Private Gallery: 81 yards green rich Genoa Damask to cover couches and arm chairs   22s yard

King's Private Gallery: Crimson Genoa velvet for two arm chairs and two cushions. $9\frac{5}{8}$ yards at 36s yard

(f20v)   *Presence Chamber, Privy Chamber and Eating Room*
54 yards $\frac{3}{8}$ of crimson Genoa Damask to cover formes & Cups for two States a closet stole & to lengthen ye States by his Majesty's directions . . .   24s yard

112   P.R.O., LC9/281, f.68v.
113   Westman (1990) pp.1406–17.
114   P.R.O., LC9/281, f.78v.
115   P.R.O., LC9/281.

Great Bedchamber
> 123 yards of crimson broad taffata for a tour du lict, window curtains & to case
> chaires and stooles   17s yard
> For 68 yards $\frac{1}{4}$ of Green narrow Mantua for window curtains when the green damask
> bed brought from Windsor was set up   19s yard

King's Private Gallery 110 yards $\frac{3}{4}$ of green $\frac{3}{4}$ wide
> Manta to case Chaires & Couches   14s yard

The bills then list in absorbing detail the various laces and fringes which were used to finish the appearance of the already rich fabrics. That for the Bedchamber window curtains and cornices reads:

> (f21) 27 yards of fine gold broad arras lace & 28 yards of ditto narrow lace weight Venice,
> 40 oz 3 qrs 3 dwts., at 7s 6d oz.
> > For 14 dozen and four yards of gold colour silk and gold purle lace at 4s dozen.

For Hampton Court this period of intense activity came to a rapid end. The titled tenants had departed during the summers of 1700 and 1701. William III issued an 'Especiall Command' in July 1700 ordering that the keys to rooms be returned to the housekeeper. No one was to 'inhabit his own Lodgings' at the palace unless the Lord Chamberlain gave permission: none seems to have been sought or given. The house became for the most part one in the hands of caretakers and building staff. It has been ascertained[116] that Queen Anne spent only three months at Hampton Court, George I less than four and George II, as Prince of Wales and as king, barely nineteen months over a span of forty-five years. For William III and his courtiers to have spent ten months there in residence and for the king to have paid at least twenty other brief or weekend visits to the palace was therefore rewarding. But there were other residences too and consideration needs to be given to Kensington Palace, Queen Mary's favourite residence.

KENSINGTON PALACE

A work which proceeded concurrently with Hampton Court was Kensington Palace. In June 1689 the king bought the Earl of Nottingham's house in Kensington and the work of adding to it began at once. The king did not like living at Whitehall, and work at Hampton Court had only just begun when the building failure occurred. As if this was not enough for the Office of Works to cope with, anxious as it must have been without knowledge of the new king's moods, the additional buildings at Kensington fell down in November 1689. I have noted the queen's letter telling the king that she had put undue pressure on the workmen in her desire to take up residence quickly. In February 1690, John Evelyn records in his diary that he visited Kensington and that, despite the patching and alterations, it made with its gardens, 'a very sweet villa'. It was to be at Kensington that the queen died in 1694. The whole history of building was contained into the previous five years, and the main decorations by William Kent and others came, of course, several years after William's own death, at Hampton Court, in March 1702.

By the late summer of 1689 the king and queen had a good idea of what they needed to do at Kensington in respect of furniture and decorations.[117] The slow processes of ordering and making were in hand, a housekeeper and wardrobe keeper had been appointed, and the use of various apartments reserved for each of the joint sovereigns. These followed the arrangement of baroque apartments – an anteroom to the presence chamber, the king and queen's privy chambers, in which audiences were held, the anteroom to the king's bedchamber, his bedchamber, his new bedchamber (equivalent to the great and little bedchambers at Hampton Court), two closets above stairs, the closets and privy lodgings below stairs, a council chamber, the anteroom to the queen's drawing room, the drawing room itself, her closet, inner closet, dressing room and the anteroom to the dressing room. Some of these rooms were in the process of being fully furnished under the authority

---

116   Gaunt (1987) pp.143–4.   117   Gaunt (1988) Chapter 3.

of a warrant[118] of 30 November 1689. The anteroom to the presence chamber, for example, had in it two armchairs, two cushions, two footstools and two forms, all covered with crimson velvet with silk fringes, two more forms covered with red serge and window curtains 'large and downe to the floor', fashioned from crimson damask lined with crimson serge.

A second warrant, also of 30 November 1689, was concerned with the issue of simpler items for lesser rooms. Its interest, however, lies in its listing of many items needed for the installing or repair of furniture: bedcords, a 'bedwinch' (for use in tightening bed-cords?), 50,000 tacks, 20,000 tenterhooks, 5,000 'crotch hookes', hammers, pins and thread. In December 1689 quantities of English and Dutch matting and leather (used to cover tables and stands and 'to keep rooms clean') were delivered. Furniture was also transferred from other royal palaces. At each window of the presence chamber crimson damask screens were placed, curtain rods were supplied to many other windows and keys giving access to rooms were issued – 'treble', giving entry to most rooms for the king, queen, Prince and Princess of Denmark (the future Queen Anne), the Lord Chamberlain, Vice Chamberlain and Groom of the Stole. The king and queen also ensured privacy in their own bedchambers by each holding the key to them.

It was again the beds which were important and on which skilled attention was lavished. In December 1689 the London mercers, John Martin and Company, rendered a bill of £94 for 61 yards of fine and coloured velvet. This was to finish the bed and hangings in the queen's bedchamber. Also in December the embroiderers John Barber and William West carried out work on the king's orange-coloured damask bed and the Queen's new bed, as well as adding crowns and cyphers to other items of furniture (£428). Most of the walnut carcase furniture came from the over-busy Gerrit Jensen but upholstered items were made by Richard Bealing and William Farnborough.

For the next four years, until Queen Mary's death in 1694, furniture was ordered for Kensington Palace in increasing quantity. Those for the queen's apartments were as varied as a carved 'angel bed', and double seat canopy chairs carved with 'figures, scrowles, leaves and cherubins' heads' for her dressing-room and outer closet. The queen's new 'angel' bed may have been the 'ash and crimson damask bed' embroidered by Barber and West in 1690 (£39) but they were over-busy with working the 'pillars, festoons, borders etc' of twenty-six hangings in the gallery (£600). The fringemaker's bill, concerned for the most part with embellishments to window curtains, also included some crimson edging 'for her Majesty's bird cages at Kensington' (17s). The provision of upholstery for pets, minor, arcane, amusing, is touched on at later points. It occupied the attention of both architects and upholsterers, anxious to please.

During 1690 it had been the queen's apartments that had received attention. The king's requirements surfaced only occasionally. He had a need of cushions to sit on and place his feet on but his officers and servants were attended to lavishly. The queen also had need of a summer bed, items in 'India stuff', curtains of scarlet lustring for her gallery and many black lacquered pieces of furniture – tables and stands, looking glasses and chairs.

In December 1692 it was the turn of the chapel in the hierarchy of ordering and providing. New altar cloths, curtains, chairs, covers to footstools, forms, cushions with the mercer supplying crimson Genoa velvet, crimson Genoa damask and gold flowered tissue (£163) for this decking of the place of quiet worship. The upholsterers and fringemakers transformed the scene with these bright wares in the early months of 1693.[119]

The French Catholic upholsterer, Francis Lapiere, whose activities are noted earlier in this chapter, stayed somewhat remote from royal patronage. However, in 1692 he charged £64 for 'a large very fine Persian carpet for the Gallery', presumably the queen's gallery. It took its place surrounded by carcase items from Jensen, John Fergusson (a large japanned cabinet, £53), and a screen, picture frames, a glass frame and a chimney glass frame from Robert Derignee £52. The merchant, Mark Anthony, sold the queen two large rich 'Indian' or Chinese lacquer screens at £250 the pair.[120]

118 P.R.O. LC5/149, p.319.

119 P.R.O., LC5/151, p.164; LC9/280, ff.103v, 141, 159–72.

120 P.R.O., LC9/280, ff.28–9, 44–5, 100, 103, 111.

During the last two years of the queen's life, 1693–4, the ordering for Kensington declined. A great deal had already been provided. The king's sleeping chair needed re-covering, in yellow Florence taffeta, and in 1693 a new velvet close stool was put in his private closet. This was provided by the coffer maker Richard Pigg in crimson velvet garnished with gold lace and fringe, locks, handles and nails all gilt, a velvet seat and pans (£4 10s). More richly carved picture frames from Derignee, glass sconces from James Catignon, whilst the upholsterer Richard Bealing concentrated mostly on work in the chapel covering the king's sleeping chair and setting-up the staff officer's new bed in crimson morella mohair and crimson sarsenet and equipping, lavishly, the apartment of the king's favourite, the Earl of Albemarle.[121]

With the queen's death the first phase of the history and furnishing of Kensington Palace was at a close. But it opened also the usual grand commemoration. The Master of the Great Wardrobe instructed Bealing to deck out rooms at Kensington with fine purple cloth and made 1,230 yards of it available. A further 2,970 yards of black cloth defined other royal apartments and the king's bedchamber was hung with 156 yards of purple cloth. The exact rituals determined that this full mourning survived until replaced by second mourning of scalloped black cloth hung at the height of the windows in several public rooms, and in purple cloth in the bedchamber. The windows there, however, were to be dressed in white silk.[122] The housekeeper had been directed to return the cloth used for the full mourning and the ever-cautious Treasury decreed that until it was so returned no estimates for further furniture would be approved.[123] They were hangings of a special kind, set up by upholsterers whose main experience was in providing hangings of brighter hue. In 1689 Richard Bealing had hung mohair, blue damask with Indian borders (queen's closets), brocatelle (anteroom to dressing room) and so on.[124] The queen's gallery was hung with silk, of a colour chosen by her (1690), and in 1692 the mercer provided 112 yards of seven-colour figured velvet to alter the hangings and make *portière* curtains for the queen's bedchamber.[125] How splendid and polychromatic it must have looked. The sideboard room was hung with gilt leather, but the tapestries vied with it in colour and subject-matter.

After the queen's funeral the king had, in May 1695, gone abroad, and the palace was left largely to the noisy ministrations of builders, without a kind but inquisitive queen to oversee them. It was also time for the housekeepers, Simon and Mary de Brienne, 'to make a true and exact Inventory of all his Majesty's goods' there. Two copies survive, countersigned by the Lord Chamberlain on 6 April 1697. The first section dealt with the king's rooms, the second with the chapel and rooms of principal servants. The third section, which has been published with a scholarly commentary,[126] concerned the March 1697 survey of the queen's apartments. It endorsed the queen's expensive taste and gives some idea, however imperfectly, of the lavish manner in which her rooms were furnished during her lifetime. Most extensive was the huge collection of porcelain, some 800 items, surveyed room by room.

In the immediate years after the queen's death most of her collections were moved from Kensington. Some of the king's furniture went too, including a white and red damask bed, his sleeping chair, 'Lapiere's' Persian carpet and many chairs, couches and stools. A purple bed of state and purple fringed window curtains went in June 1696 together with a great number of chairs upholstered in many colours of figured velvet – crimson, blue, green, black, orange and purple stripes. The Briennes, as housekeepers, were given an embroidered bed from the king's bedchamber and 'her late Majesty's dressers' also received their beds and the contents of their rooms. A chief beneficiary of the king's generosity in this respect was, however, the Earl of Albemarle. By warrant dated 7 November 1695 he was given 'all the goods and furniture in his lodgings at Kensington . . . all which sayd furniture he is to keep to his own propertie'.[127] But four years later, on 24 November 1699, he was given the greater gift of all Queen Mary's porcelain, together with the contents of two of the king's closets and many hangings, chairs and damask window curtains.[128]

121   P.R.O., LC5/165 pp.1–2; LC9/280 ff.124, 126, 159–72; LC9/280, ff.187, 189v, 192v.

122   P.R.O., LC5/123 (loose warrants); LC5/165, p.5; LC9, 386.

123   Gaunt (1988) p.121.

124   P.R.O., LC5/165, p.5; LC9/279, ff.119–34v.

125   P.R.O., LC9/280, ff.103v, 104v–11.

126   Scheurleer, ed. (1960–2) pp.21–58.

127   P.R.O., LC5/165, p.11.

128   Gaunt (1988) Appendix B.

In seeming confusion much was being given or taken away to other royal palaces at the time that items were being ordered and delivered. By August 1695 the building work had advanced for Bealing's men to enter the new rooms to take measurements for hangings. Warrants were issued regularly over the next six months for fitting up or replenishing rooms. The king's five new closets, above and below stairs, were hung 'with silk proper to hang pictures upon'. Interestingly, for observers of picture hanging schemes, the old hangings had been ruined by nailing pictures into them. Between them Gerrit Jensen and Thomas Roberts supplied the good and the humbler case furniture respectively. The mercers too were active with Mathias Cupper supplying 405 yards of fine white 'Indian' or Chinese damask for window curtains in the new gallery at 10s a yard.[129] There were also large quantities of Genoa damasks and velvets – green and gold, crimson and green, blue and hair colour and olive and crimson Lucca damask to hang the five new closets, costing a little over £350 in total.

The king, whilst in Flanders in July 1696, had issued a list of the furniture which should be in place by the time he reached Kensington again. There were to be chairs of state in the presence and privy chambers, new beds and bedding, dining room furniture, and many items for the grooms' and pages' rooms. During September white damask curtains were ordered for several rooms, including the library and chapel. Sconces, branches and looking glasses were hung on silk line to preserve the hangings. New leather covers were provided for furniture in the king's great and new bedchambers, with a Persian carpet under his chair, and 'one thick square blue figured velvet cushion' in the council chamber 'for the King to kneel on'. As for the king's two new beds the mercers alone charged £800 for the 470 yards of crimson and green flowered India velvet used on one and for the fine cloth used to the other. Proudly, over the work by Bealing and the upholsterers, the feather dresser Jonathan Chase stuffed the 'panaches' or 'plumes' with white bedfeathers which had 'hern' (heron) spriggs to decorate them (£190). His work was foiled against the white and buff striped flowered damask used for the furniture of the crimson and green bed. The window curtains in the room were made from 120 yards of rich white Indian damask supplied by William Portal (15s a yard). His price, admittedly for 'rich' damask, contrasted in price with the white Indian damask Mathias Cupper had supplied for the gallery at 10s a yard.

The new gallery also received the careful attentions of Bealing and his men. He used the 405 yards of fine white India damask which Mathias Cupper had supplied to make the window curtains (£18), '9 large and deep window curtains to draw up, with valence to the same with tassels to each curtain and carved cornice covered with damask.' The rings, nails and thread cost £2 more. The '305½ yards of white tufted silk, lacing and tassels' was provided (£195) to their making, by the fringemaker, Thomas Carr, noted in work at Hampton Court. He was responsible for the fringes, lace, tassels and strings in most of the Kensington rooms. For the king's bedchamber, grandly enough, there was 'scarlet, green, gold and white tufted fringe, edging and lace, and orange, green and ginger line for a State bed of crimson and green velvet, an elbow chair, 6 stools, an easy chair, a cushion, a fire screen, a Tour du Lict, 3 portiere curtains and 4 window curtains (£490).'[130] The effects must have dazzled the eyes, but few were privileged to enter the king's bedchamber to witness the display of such rich fabrics and trimmings.

Richard Bealing's bill of 1697[131] recorded his attention to the gallery wall hangings:

> making all the green velvet hangings for the gallery, containing 16 pieces, 54 yards by 5 yards, all lined with linnen and fringed   £50.00.00
>
> dyed linnen to line all the gallery hangings being 54 yards by 5 yards deep   £25.00.00

The sewing silk used (£5 10s), carriage (10s) and 'work for severall men to fit all the hangings in the gallery and putting up window curtains in the King's closet' (£3 15s), together with his coach hire 'for myself to attend the business there' (15s) added a further ten guineas. Bealing had also bottomed and covered twenty large stools for the gallery, with velvet 'finely fringed and tassells to the same' (£6), and given them all large

129 P.R.O., LC9/280, f.340.
130 P.R.O., LC9/377 (loose bills).
131 *Ibid.*, LC9/380 (loose bills).

down cushions (£15). A novel way of transporting them was charged at 12s: 'sending all the stools on porters' backs'. The stools were complemented by two large couches which had been stuffed with fine curled hair within linen casings, with 'fine seats of down in fine ticken'. These were covered in green velvet, fringed with gold.

When Bealing worked on the hangings to a bed the frame had often been made by Thomas Roberts. The latter's bill for 1699[132] for the king's crimson and gold velvet bed in the great bedchamber indicates what he provided:

a strong wainscot bedstead 7 feet long and 6 feet wide to stand 15 feet high, lath bottom to hang low, with ironwork and large double screws to the bedsides and for the woodwork of the tester, cornices, headboard and bases and for ironwork to support the tester and outside cornices	£30.00.00
carving the tester, headboard, outside cornices and bases	£26.00.00
a set of large bright filed curtain rods and platoons	£01.05.00
helping to set up the bed	£00.15.00
a long pole with a ferril and hook to turn the curtains of the bed by	£00.08.00
4 carved bedfeet	£01.15.00

The bill[133] in 1699 from the mercers, Richard Cooper and partners, listed:

gold and crimson Venetian velvet bed in King's great bedchamber.	
79½ yards of narrow green satin to line the bed	£53.13.03
83 yards of broad green flowered satin to line the bed and for the counterpoint	£72.12.06
23¾ yards of rich green Mantua to case chairs and stools	

The year of 1699 had been busy at Kensington. There was Roberts and Bealing's new crimson Venetian velvet bed lined with green satin, a cedar screen with gilt wire decoration to help guard against draught, a bear skin rug covered with black velvet from Richard Pigg (£6) for the king to put his feet on; it was made with silk strings and tassells to draw over the knees; gilt leather hangings measuring 60 by 25 inches, chairs, stools and screens covered in green taffeta. In fact so much was spent, £990 in the great bedchamber alone, that the treasury was insisting that details be given to them.

A new inventory made by housekeeper Brienne at the very end of the century (November 1699, and complete by January 1700) indicated that all the porcelain and goods allowed to the Earl of Albemarle had been removed. The storerooms presented a morbid picture of past furnishing splendour, mostly filled with items from the king's and queen's apartments. The palace, whilst not neglected, started to take second place to Wren's completed Fountain Court at Hampton Court. Much of the furniture the king needed had been sent there and the warrants issued for work at Kensington related to repairs. But demand on a royal scale was ever changing. Within a year, in September 1701, a new suite of crimson Lucca damask furniture, including a bed, was in preparation. But almost as much attention was given to rooms for two of the king's physicians, Doctors Bidloe and Lawrence. Again Richard Bealing had more work to do at Kensington, including making the upholstery of a crimson velvet arm chair to carry the king up and down stairs. Roberts had provided a walnut frame with ironwork for poles to slide in – a little like an open sedan chair.

Some of the daily work gave Bealing many problems. He damaged a wall trying to set up the screws to hold the bed tester. It needed repair by a bricklayer and a carpenter to provide a timber support 'to hold the iron of the King's bed'. Far less troublesome were making up window and *portière* curtains, and the beds and bedding for the two doctors. As he worked away in 1701, supervising the cutting and mounting of fabric, and attending to the many stages of making the King's new crimson damask and gold lace bed, Bealing could have no idea that it was the one in which the king would die, on 8 March 1702, in his 'new little Bedchamber'.

132   P.R.O., LC9/377 (loose bills).   133   Gaunt (1988) p.130, citing P.R.O., T27/16 p.164.

Within a month he was buried, on 12 April,[134] at night, as was customary, in Westminster Abbey, but a stranger and a Dutchman to the end. Anne was crowned eleven days later;[135] she knew that an excessive display of mourning, such as had attended the late queen, would be out of place. This was left to the Dutch in Holland, where church bells tolled three times a day, with justice done to the reputation of a Stadholder who had led them in war and heightened national pride. Within a month Queen Anne had given the grand bed in which he died, and the bedding which covered his emaciated body, to the Groom of the Stole, Lord Romney.

A LESSER COMPANY

There were of course many upholsterers who did not work for the crown and whose activities are less well recorded. For example, in the late seventeenth century Thomas Arne, father of the more celebrated composer and musician, worked in London from Bedford Court. Whilst much of his activity was within the reign of Queen Anne and George I, he was active in the 1690s at Felbrigg, the Wyndham's house in Norfolk.[136] Arne was also a busy officer within the Worshipful Company of Upholders. He was Assistant in 1687, Under Warden in 1695, Warden in 1696 and Master in 1704.[137] William Allen supplied goods to the Royal Hospital, Chelsea between 1687 and 1692 and also did some work in 1689 in the household staff rooms at Whitehall Palace.[138] A 'Mr Cooper' was active at Chatsworth for the first Duke of Devonshire from September 1699 with £43 14s paid for 'a new bed'.[139] Thomas Strawbridge worked for Theophilus Leigh at his Warwickshire house of Stoneleigh in 1691. Some of his surviving work passed through the London saleroom in 1981.[140]

There were also Frenchmen, less well known than Poictevin or Lapiere. A 'MS Guillotin' was living next to 'The Black Lion' in Pall Mall in 1691 and may be the one of that name active at Drayton, Northamptonshire. A more significant craftsman, however, was Philip Guibert. Whilst he was involved in commissions at both Windsor Castle and Kensington Palace and supplying beds to several royal yachts, he was soon in trouble with court officials. On 1 February 1699 he petitioned, as so many had done before, for £1,695 5s 3d due to him for work in the king's bedchamber and dining room at Windsor. This was sent for verification to the Master of the Great Wardrobe, the Earl of Montagu. There was enough truth for payment of £1,000 to be made on 26 May 1699 and a further payment of £350 came in 1702 after the king's death.[141]

One of Guibert's principal patrons was Thomas Osborne, first Duke of Leeds. It is thought that the day bed and sofa covered with Genoese cut velvet and with the Duke's coronet atop them (now at Temple Newsam House, Leeds, Pls 100–3) may be by this upholsterer. Despite being a foreigner Guibert obviously found it useful to be involved in the activities of the Worshipful Company of Upholders. On 14 October 1702 'Philip Guibert, an Upholder in St German's Street was Admitted into the Freedom of the Company and chosen of the Livery. Paid £4 10s 0d to the Warden'. He rendered a gift to the company of a triangular gilt salt.[142] It is convenient to record here that he was chosen as one of the stewards in 1705 but by 1731 it was ordered that 'Mr Guibart have Ten Shillings given him towards his reliefe out of the Poor Box'.[143]

The peculiarities of the apprenticeship system often meant that upholsterers claimed their freedom through a company such as the Skinners rather than the Upholders. This was the case with the successful London upholsterer John Hibbert who whilst a 'skinner' was admitted eventually into the freedom of the Upholders also, on 1 February 1680.[144] He had been active in royal service since the late 1660s, hiring furniture to the Lord Chamberlain's office. Between 1682 and 1692 he worked for the fifth Earl of Bedford. His three surviving bills[145] show him active in the usual tasks – providing a 'Rich Blue Damask Bed', chairs, tapestry

134 P.R.O., LC2, 14/2.
135 P.R.O., LC2, 15/1.
136 Beard and Gilbert (1986) p.18.
137 Guildhall Library, London, MS., 7141/1, ff.4, 108, 197, 217.
138 *Wren Soc.*, XIX, p.85; P.R.O., LC9/279, ff.512–56.
139 Beard and Gilbert (1986) p.195.
140 Shakespeare Birthplace Trust, Leigh receipts, DR 18/5/1030; Christie's, 15–16 October 1981, lots 100–1.

141 P.R.O., LC5/43, f.245.
142 Guildhall Library, London, MS., 7141/1, ff.4, 311.
143 *Ibid.*, ff.24 (1705), 31 (1731).
144 *Ibid.*, f.37.
145 Woburn Abbey, Bedford MSS., Bills, Nos 30–2.

hangings, bedding, gilt leather, 'Gould Culler printed stufe', crimson paragon, rugs, drugget, hiring furniture and making 'umbrellas' to shield rooms from the sun. During this period Hibbert was in partnership with his first partner, Thomas Dixon. The second, Philip Bodham, outlived him. In 1701 'John Hibbert & Co' also supplied '2 rich pieces of fine Japanese tapestry' at a cost of £69 to the Marquess of Annandale, and in 1702 'Mr Hibbert, £73 10s' appears in the bank account of the first Duke of Leeds.[146] As later with Thomas Arne, Hibbert moved to office in the Worshipful Company, becoming its Under Warden in 1691, its Upper Warden in 1692 and Master in 1698.[147]

An important firm trading from the Great Piazza in Covent Garden was that of Henry Heasman, senior and junior. Heasman lived in a house formerly owned by the painter Sir Godfrey Kneller, and in the late 1680s he was providing furnishings to the Royal Hospital at Chelsea.[148] He had become free of the Worshipful Company in 1689[149] and had trained an apprentice, James Gronous, who became free in 1700[150] and like his teacher became, himself, Master of the Worshipful Company, in 1739.[151] Because the late activity of Jean Poictevin and his nephew Etienne Pinson intermeshed after 1702 I have left consideration of the important state bed and *en suite* furniture at Drayton House, Northamptonshire to the first pages of chapter V.

146   Beard and Gilbert (1986) p.427.
147   Guildhall Library, London, MS., 7141/1, ff.148, 156, 251.
148   *Wren Soc.*, XIX, p.85.
149   Guildhall Library, London, MS., 7141/1, f.121.
150   *Ibid.*, f.276.
151   *Ibid.*, MS., 7141/2, ff.31, 54.

43–4. The red room at Cotehele (*c.*1665) *Cotehele, Cornwall* (The National Trust).

This shows a French bed, of which only the superstructure is original, upholstered in red worsted cloth. The detail (*right*) shows the front corner at which the valances meet, with the buttons and loops of metal thread which joined them later becoming only a decorative feature.

References: Thornton (1974) p.187.

45. (*left*)   Furnishing panel (*c*.1670) 102 × 60 in (259 × 152.4 cm).

A silk damask structure with axially aligned stylized foliate and floral motifs centred on an urn form topped by a coronet. From the large range of Italian fabrics such as this upholsterers could create lavish effects.

46. (*above*)   Furnishing panel (*c*.1670–90) 122 × 104 in (313 × 264.2 cm).

A crimson silk damask structure with an ogival design of stylized sunflowers and other floral forms. Red or scarlet was a difficult (and expensive) colour to achieve.

47.   Long cushion seen in the portrait of *Charles II* by John Michael Wright (1671) *Royal Collection*.

Made of patterned silk damask (?) with tasselled corners. The Great Wardrobe archives frequently include mention of cushions and mats for the king to place his feet on in cold audience and bed chambers.

References: Millar (1963) I, p.129, Pl. 123.

48.   Canopy, headcloth and dais seen in a detail of an engraving of a banquet given by (?) Charles II for the Knights of the Garter from *The Institution, Law and Ceremonies of the Most Noble Order of the Garter* by Elias Ashmole (1672).

The king is separated from the knights by a low curtained balustrade and has his own square table.

49–50. State bed, called 'The King's Bed' (c.1673) *Knole, Kent* (The National Trust).

This bed and its furniture are more likely to be French than English and to be one of those supplied by Louis XIV's upholsterer Jean Peyrard. He visited England, 1672–5, bringing six beds for Charles II. This bed may have been made for the wedding of James, Duke of York to Mary of Modena, also in 1673. A lavish use of gold and silver threads characterizes the bed, which was lined with cherry coloured satin. It was restored in 1987. The detail shows the headboard.

51. (*top left*) Stamp (*c.*1675) *Knole, Kent* (The National Trust).

This stamp can be seen under the seat of those chairs and stools with dolphin head feet. The front stretcher centres on a royal crown. The 'WP' under the crown indicates that the items were once at Whitehall Palace.

References: Jourdain (1952) Pl. 15.

52. (*top right*) Braid of red silk and gold thread (*c.*1675) *London, Victoria and Albert Museum*, Inv. T270-1965.

53. The site of the Great Wardrobe shown in a detail from *A Large and Accurate Map of the City of London* by John Ogilby and William Morgan (1676) *London, Guildhall Library*.

54–6.   Sleeping chair (*c*.1677–9) 55 × 29 × 34½ in (139.7 × 73.5 × 87.5 cm); back panel, 33 × 27 in (84.5 × 69.5 cm); arm length, 24 in (61 cm); seat width, 27 in (84.5 cm) *Ham House, London* (The National Trust).

One of a pair with a frame of carved and gilded wood, upholstered in crimson brocaded silk with a gold fringe and brass-headed nails. Iron ratchets at each side allow adjustment of the back and wings. Made for the Duke and Duchess of Lauderdale for use at Ham House. It does not feature in the 1677 inventory but is noted in that for 1679. It was possibly supplied by Jean Poictevin. Two other chairs of this type are at Grimsthorpe, Lincolnshire and Athelhampton, Dorset. The chair shown here is slightly larger than its pair, suggesting one was for the duke and one for the duchess. The queen's closet in which they stood was hung with gold stuff, bordered with green, 'crimson and gold and silver stuff'. The details show the lower part of the seat, the back, and wings.

57. (*opposite*)   State bed called the 'Spangle Bed' (*c*.1680) *Knole, Kent* (The National Trust).

The bed is hung with crimson satin with an *appliqué* strapwork pattern, originally sewn with small metallic spangles, or sequins. The bed is thought to have been constructed using textiles from the 1620s. It is probably of royal provenance and was acquired as a perquisite by the sixth Earl of Dorset. It was brought to Knole from Copt Hall, Essex in 1701.

58. (*left*) Armchair (*c*.1680) 48 × 27 in (122 × 68.5 cm) *London, Victoria and Albert Museum,* Inv. W40-1927.

Carved in walnut and upholstered in black leather with gilt nails. It has an iron ratchet for adjusting the back and front supports extending from the thickness of the arms for a book table (see Pl. 23).

60. (*right*) Armchair (*c*.1680) *Boughton House, Northamptonshire.*

It has a walnut frame and is upholstered in red velvet with a loose cushion and a fringe at the seat ears and arms.

59. (*left*) Tassels (*c*.1680) *London, Victoria and Albert Museum,* Inv. 150 ZA and Z1-1888.

Made of silk, silver-gilt and thread on a wooden core and parchment strip.

61. (*right*) Turkey work (*c*.1680) 37 × 20 in (94.5 × 50.8 cm) *Leeds, Temple Newsam House.*

On the back and seat of a walnut framed chair formerly at Hampton Court, Herefordshire.

62.   Coronation chairs, covered dais and tapestry covered sanctuary seen in the engraving of the *History of the Coronation of James II and Queen Mary* by Francis Sandford (1685) *London, Victoria and Albert Museum,* Inv. E814-1959.

63–5. *(below)*   Tester of the Glemham state bed *(c.*1685) *Private Collection, USA.*

The bed was made for the London house of Sir Dudley North of Glemham Hall, Suffolk. The bed has a straight moulded cornice covered with crimson velvet, trimmed with a tawny and brown fringe. The ceiling of the tester, headcloth and counterpoint are in cream satin, embroidered with coloured silks. The details show the headboard, tester cloth and the embroidery.

References: *D.E.F.* (1954) I, p.51.

66–7.   State bed, called 'The Venetian Ambassador's Bed' (*c.*1688) *Knole, Kent* (The National Trust).

The bed was made in 1688 for James II whose monogram is incorporated in the carving of the tester with the royal crown, lion and unicorn. The frame is by Thomas Roberts and the hangings in 'green and gold figured velvet with scarlet and white silk fringe' are probably by Jean Poictevin. No wardrobe accounts survive for 1688, when the king fled to France. Acquired as a perquisite at the death of Mary II in 1694 by the sixth Earl of Dorset; taken to Copt Hall , Essex in 1695 and by 1702 to Knole.

68. (*right*)   Armchair (1688) *Knole, Kent* (The National Trust).

One of a pair *en suite* to the Venetian Ambassadors bed at Knole (Pl. 66). Carved and gilded frames by Thomas Roberts with the front legs as standing classical figures and the front stretcher centring on two cherubs blowing trumpets. Upholstered by Jean Poictevin (?) in blue-green Genoa velvet with a ball fringe.

69. (*below*)   Stool (1688) *Knole, Kent* (The National Trust).

One of a set of six *en suite* to the Venetian Ambassador's bed and armchairs at Knole (Pls 66–8). Carved and gilded frames by Thomas Roberts, upholstered by Jean Poictevin (?) in blue-green Genoa velvet.

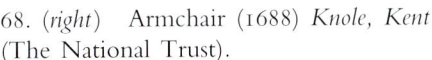

72. (*opposite, top left*)   Chair (*c.*1690) 55 × 18 in (140 × 45.5 cm) *London, Victoria and Albert Museum*, Inv. W31-1925.

Walnut frame with cane back and seat upholstered in green velvet with ball fringe.

73. (*opposite, top centre*)   Chair (*c.*1690) 51½ × 22 × 27 in (130.8 × 55.9 × 68.6 cm) *Philadelphia Museum of Art*, Inv. 36-5-2.

One of a set of four with beech frames stained to resemble walnut, upholstered in green silk velvet, trimmed with a wide woven yellow band; this appears to be original to the chair. The back is covered in a green moreen with a bizarre pattern on it. Probably trimmed originally with a deep fringe.

74. (*opposite, top right*)   Armchair (*c.*1690) 49 × 28½ in (125 × 73 cm) *Port Sunlight, Lady Lever Art Gallery*, Inv. LL4053.

Walnut frame, upholstered in crimson velvet with tasselled fringe. Formerly at Rushbrooke Hall, Suffolk. A similar one, in green velvet is illustrated in *D.E.F.* (1954) I, Pl. XII.

70. (*above*)   Canopies and covered dais in a detail of an engraving by Romeyn de Hooghe (1689) *Amsterdam, Rijksmuseum*.

The canopies were erected by Richard Bealing for the coronation of William III and Mary II in Westminster Abbey in 1689.

71.   Silk damask (*c.*1689) width, 21 in (53.4 cm) *London, Victoria and Albert Museum*, Inv. T43-1937.

Italian (Genoa) silk damask removed from a wall in a presence chamber at Hampton Court, London having been supplied by Guillaume (William) Portal at 24s a yard in 1689.

References: Thornton (1965) Pl. 105A.

75–6. (*opposite, bottom left*)   Chair (*c.*1690) 49 × 28 in (125 × 71.5 cm) *Drumlanrig Castle, Scotland*.

One of a pair. With a walnut frame, upholstered in crimson velvet, presumably Italian, similar to that covering armchairs formerly at Kimbolton, Cambridgeshire. The detail shows the fringe.

References: *D.E.F.* (1954) I, Pl. IX.

77. (*opposite, bottom right*)   Armchair (*c.*1690) 49½ × 29 in (125.75 × 74 cm) *Boughton House, Northamptonshire*.

Walnut frame, upholstered in crimson velvet with tasselled fringe. This chair is similar to those formerly at Kimbolton and Rushbrooke (Pls 74–6).

References: D.E.F. (1954) I, p.252.

78. Settee (c.1690) $54\frac{1}{4} \times 62$ in (138×157 cm) *London, Victoria and Albert Museum*, Inv. W15-1949.

Carved walnut, upholstered in cross-stitch embroidery. Formerly in the possession of Thomas, first Earl of Coningsby at Hampton Court, Herefordshire. Two state beds from the house are at the Metropolitan Museum of Art , New York.

References: White (1982) pp.84–8.

79. Armchair (c.1690) 54×36 in (138×90 cm) *On loan to London, Victoria and Albert Museum.*

Walnut frame with scrolled arms and wings covered in blue and silver damask with a seat cushion.

References: Illustrated in *D.E.F.* (1954) I, p.250.

80–2. State bed, called the 'Queen Elizabeth Bed' (*c.*1695) *Burghley House, Cambridgeshire.*

Due to payments in the Exeter bank account (Royal Bank of Scotland, Child's Bank ledgers) I believe this bed was made for John, fifth Earl of Exeter and his wife Anne Cavendish, by Francis Lapiere, with fringes by Peter Dufresnoy. The detail of the cornice shows the fine embroidered cypher for John and Anne Cecil. The tester-cloth of blue satin backed with linen and worked in silk embroidery has at its centre an oval shape, backed with cream taffeta and paper, representing Apollo and Venus, flying within 'a blue sky, garlanded with flowers'. The head-cloth was made from alternated flat and festooned strips of embroidered satin edged with a fringe. The fringe has a heading of coloured silk with the strands wound around a central linen core, ending in silk bobbles.

The bed was conserved in 1986–7, Landi (1992) pp.237–47 describes all the stages.

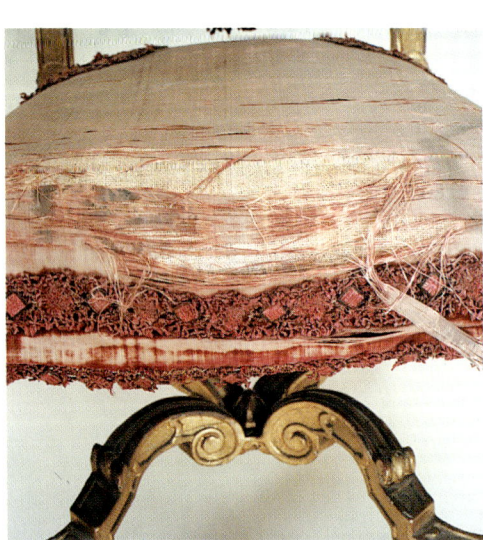

83–4.   Chair (*c*.1695) 48 × 21 in (121 × 53 cm) *Hampton Court, Surrey*.

One of two (possibly originally a set of six), carved and gilded beech, upholstered in crimson velvet trimmed with an elaborate fringe. Formerly at Hampton Court, Herefordshire and probably made for Thomas, first Earl of Coningsby.

References: White (1982); D.E.F. (1954) I, p.253.

85.   Chairs (*c*.1695) 48 × 21 in (121 × 53 cm) *Hampton Court, Surrey*.

A pair of carved and gilded beech chairs. Formerly at Hampton Court, Herefordshire. They are shown stripped to their stuffed state prior to reupholstering following the pattern of the two with original upholstery (see Pl. 83).

86.   Settee (*c*.1695) 52 × 56 × 23 in (132 × 142 × 58 cm) *Lyme Park, Cheshire* (The National Trust).

Walnut frame (overpainted in the nineteenth century) upholstered in worsted material embroidered in coloured silk, edged with openwork gimp with two seat cushions. The designs on the back derive probably from engravings by Jean Baptiste Monnoyer (1635–99) or from Dutch flower paintings.

87–91. State bed of William III (*c.*1696)
Hampton Court, Surrey.

Acquired in 1698 by purchase from the Earl
of Jersey. The French style of the bed may
indicate it was made in Paris (see p.101).
The bed was amended by Thomas Roberts
with reupholstery by Richard Bealing. The
bed has part of its original cornice and
headboard but after the 1993 Hampton
Court fire was newly provided with two
curtains, a counterpoint, case-rod and
case-curtains. The details show the base
planks and headboard; the braid on the right
outer valance; one of the five mattresses and
the stuffing of the arm of a chair *en suite*,
prior to reupholstering.

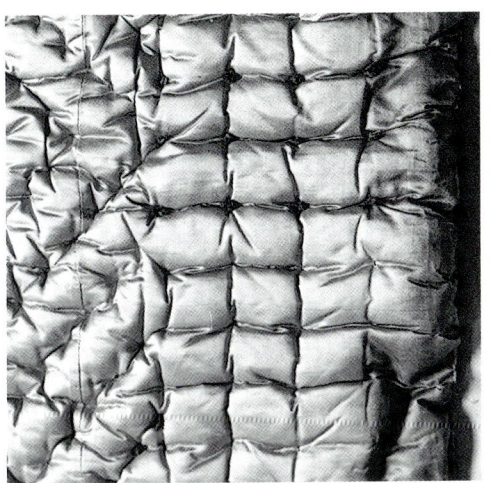

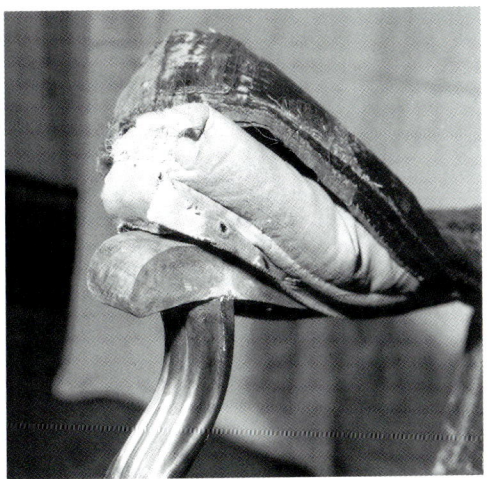

92–4   'Lapiere' state bed (c.1697) *Hardwick Hall, Derbyshire* (The National Trust).

The head-board is upholstered in crimson damask and centres on the cypher of William Cavendish, first Duke of Devonshire. The bed was made for use at Chatsworth and its remaining fragments were moved early in the nineteenth century to the long gallery at Hardwick Hall on the orders of the sixth Duke. Payments to Lapiere occur at regular intervals in the Chatsworth building accounts. The details of the tester and tester cloth show the holes for posts in the front edges of the tester cloth implying that the bed originally had four posts and was not (as at present) an 'angel' tester bed without foot supports.

References: Beard and Westman (1993).

95–6.   Melville state bed (*c*.1698) 15 ft 2 in × 8 ft × 9 ft (4.62 m × 2.44 m × 2.74 m) *London, Victoria and Albert Museum*, Inv. W35-1949.

The headboard and tester cloth centre on the cypher of George, first Earl of Melville and his wife, Catherine Leslie. Lord Melville was one of William III's chief agents in Scotland. He probably ordered the bed about 1697; it was erected at his Scottish house by 1700. It is upholstered with crimson silk Genoa velvet, lined with white Chinese silk damask and embroidered with crimson silk braid. It is attributed to Francis Lapiere (although the claims of Jean Poictevin should not be discounted, see p.89).

References: Clinton (1979).

97. Emboidered panel (c.1700) 84 × 92 in
(213.5 × 232.7 cm).

Probably for a headboard, mounted later on
a blue silk ground. It is made with chenille
yarn, couched stitches and metallic gimp. It
is thought to have been made in Piedmont
but showing the triangular shape and
sophisticated design made popular by the
engravings of Daniel Marot.

98. (bottom left)   Designs for upholstered
furniture (c.1700).

Daniel Marot's treatments for chair
upholstery and valances were seized on
eagerly by upholsterers, who developed
further the festoon form of curtain, drawing
up vertically. The form may also be seen on
elaborate bed testers as in that made by
Francis Lapiere in 1697 (Pl. 93).

99. (bottom right)   Designs for headboards
for state beds (c.1700) New York, Cooper-
Hewitt Museum, Inv. 1988-4-58.

This is plate 29 in Daniel Marot's Nouveaux
Livres d'Apartements (1702). Designs such as
this, incorporating acanthus scrolling, may
have been the inspiration for their use in
the headboard of the Melville bed (Pl. 95).
There is evidence too in the Boughton
archive that Daniel Marot knew the
upholsterer Francis Lapiere, to whom the
Melville bed is attributed.

References: Jackson-Stops (1981) p.255.

100–3. (opposite)   Day-bed and sofa (c.1700)
day-bed, $43\frac{1}{2}$ × 60 × 28 in (110 × 152 ×
71 cm); sofa, $43\frac{1}{2}$ × 82 × 28 in (110 × 208 ×
71 cm) Leeds, Temple Newsam House.

Probably made by Philip Guibert for
Thomas Osborne, first Duke of Leeds.
Beech frames, painted black with gilt
carvings, upholstered in Genoa cut-velvet in
crimson, green and cinnamon on a dark
cream satin ground edged with a tasselled
fringe.

References: Gilbert (1978) II, pp.320–1.

104.   Counterpoint (*c.*1700) *Cotehele, Cornwall* (The National Trust).

Wool embroidery. In the King Charles room at Cotehele.

105.   Armchair (*c.*1700) 48 × 30 in (122 × 76.6 cm) *Castle Howard, Yorkshire.*

Gilded frame, covered with Genoese cut-velvet in red and gold. *En suite* to open armchairs and chairs elsewhere in the house, some of which have been reupholstered.

106.   Chair (*c.*1700) 45 × 26 in (113 × 66 cm) *Private Collection, England.*

Upholstered in Genoese cut velvet (remounted). The gilded frame has a shell motif on the front of the seat and the piercing in the front legs is almost identical to the large suite of chairs, open armchairs and armchairs at Castle Howard, Yorkshire (Pl. 105). The upholstery carried over a gilded top rail ending in a scroll is unusual.

107.   Chair (*c.*1700) 46 × 20 in (117 × 50.8 cm) *Dyrham Park, Avon* (The National Trust).

One of a set of eighteen. Carved walnut, upholstered in red velvet. Designed in the style of Daniel Marot. A set of eighteen similar chairs were supplied for Hampton Court in 1717 by Richard Roberts.

108–9.   Armchair (*c.*1700) $55\frac{1}{2} \times 27\frac{1}{2} \times 21$ in ($141 \times 69.9 \times 53.3$ cm) *Hardwick Hall, Derbyshire* (The National Trust).

From a set of two with eight stools, attributed to Thomas Roberts with upholstery by Francis Lapiere. Walnut frame, red silk velvet with applied central panel of silver embroidery (detail); loose back and seat. Intended to complement the Lapiere state bed (Pls 92–4) for use at Chatsworth. Moved to Hardwick Hall in the early nineteenth century.

110. (*bottom left*)   Chair cover (*c.*1700) *Virginia, Colonial Williamsburg Foundation.*

This cover is made of stamped leather in a pattern derived from damask and often called damask leather. It is for an armchair with openings for the arms and tapes to tie around the chair. Used originally at Ham House, London.

111–12.   Chair (c.1700) 48 × 28 in (122 × 71 cm) *Drayton House, Northamptonshire.*

Carved beechwood frame. Embroidered seat and back. The frame dates from *c.*1685 and the embroidered covers by Elizabeth Rickson and Rebekah Dufee from *c.*1700. The covers have early hook and eye fastenings (detail) with embroidery *en suite*

to the Drayton state bed (Pls 115–20). A chair from the set is now in the Victoria and Albert Museum.

113. (*bottom right*)   Part of a velvet curtain in six widths (*c.*1700) repeat length from cornice pole to floor, 10 ft 4 in (336 cm) *Penrhyn Castle, Wales* (The National Trust).

Voided cut-velvet made at Genoa, Lyon or even Spitalfields. Yellow/cream silk warp, cut and uncut leaves and flowers with 'bizarre' elements. A copy of *c.*1830 also survives (180 cm).

V

The Upholstered Room 1702–1760

THE DRAYTON STATE BED

I have made mention (pp.94–5) of the upholstery and tailoring tasks done by Francis Lapiere and his first wife, Dorothy for Henry, second Earl of Peterborough at Drayton House, Northamptonshire. Part of the commission involved the earl signing an obligation which stated that if £50 owed to Lapiere was paid to him by 11 June 1693 then the obligation, being met, was rendered void; otherwise, it was 'to remaine in full force'. The earl died in 1697 with the debt unpaid and at some point Lapiere proceeded at law against the earl's heir, Lady Mary Mordaunt, and her second husband, Sir John Germain. He was eventually awarded his legal costs and some eleven and a half years' interest.[1]

It might have been expected that Lady Mary would have been content with controlling the daily domesticity of the great houses of Arundel Castle and Worksop Manor. Sir John had lent large sums of money to the king, but received little in return except for the conferring in 1698 of a baronetcy,[2] and there was need for much expensive remodelling of a new home.

The state bedroom at Drayton had been remodelled in 1653 by John Webb, and his great chimneypiece and overmantel are witness to this. However, the principal contents of the room are four rare and celebrated Mortlake tapestries, *c*.1660, and the state bed and *en suite* furniture. The 'duchess' had ordered this in 1700, some months before her liaison with Sir John Germain was regularized in marriage.

The bed has long been credited to 'Elizabeth Vickson and Rebekah Dufee', the embroideresses of the superb hangings which adorn and enclose it. 'Vickson' is a misreading in the relevant documents for 'Rickson'. The signature, badly formed, could be read as either, but at several points it is quite clear, including one mention of 'Rickson' in capital letters. On 24 July 1700 the two ladies entered into an agreement:[3]

> The bargen is made And Agreed upon for ye embroadery of ye bed, she to find Silks and all other things fitting for yt use. Agreed at 22 Shillings a yard they having Receivd six pound in hand
> Sep ye 24 Receivd of ye Dutches of Norfolk ye sum of Aleven poud for finishing ye embroidred curtin. I say Receivd by me
> > Eliz rickson
> > Rebekah Dufee
> Rec fore pound in hands for ye begining of ye other curtin.
> Rec two gunies more
> Nov ye 5 Rec more tow guines
> > Eliz rickson

But who made the bed itself? The Huguenot named Guillotin has been suggested but his undated bills, noted

---

1 Beard and Westman (1993) p.517.
2 Cornforth (1965) III, p.1287.

3 Drayton MS., MM/A/353.

below, are probably of *c*.1696. I subscribe, for the following reasons, to the French upholsterer, Etienne Penson, who signed a number of Drayton receipts and for whom a large bill has survived (Appendix A24). Furthermore, he was the upholsterer charged with the arrangements in 1705 for the duchess's funeral (p.148).

As shown below, Penson, a French upholsterer, was the nephew 'by the sister' of the talented French upholsterer, Jean Poictevin, whose considerable activity in England for the court of William III has been described (p.88). I had assumed, in 1993,[4] that an unsigned bill at Drayton related to Lapiere's work, but a more rigorous examination leads me to think that it was submitted by Penson. Indeed it is endorsed 'pen . . . /now pd 80 in part/more pd. by Joyntell, 10.' Regrettably, the paper is partly decayed by damp at the crucial part of the endorsement, but 'penson' is, I am sure, what was written, about 1701–2.

The bill gives, among many items, details of the making of four beds; a grey cloth one, a yellow damask bed, a white Indian embroidered bed and 'ye wrought [or embroidered] bed lynd wt yeallow'. The Drayton bed is 'lined' with yellow (Pls 115–20) and of the two in that colour in the bill is presumably the one charged for on 22 September 1701:

> for a Ocken bedstead, headboard, taster, Cornishes and base moldings for ye wrought bed lynd wt yeallow   09.00.00
>
> ffor all ye Carv'd worke belonging to ye Sd bed, which is head board & taster,   03.10.00

Significantly, no curtains are charged for, only the polished rod, chains, woodscrews, spikes to hold the tester, the lining materials and the workmanship. The lining consisted of forty-eight yards of material (unspecified) for the headboard, headcloth, tester and the inside and outside valances and bases (12d a yard), and seven yards of buckram to line the outside valances and bases (1s 2d a yard).

Apart from the lining we may assume the yellow watered damask to be that supplied by the duchess, and referred to in Penson's receipt to her of 10 September 1701:

> Je Recu de Madame la Duchesse de Norfolke 8 pies de damas dessin de jaune/conttennan 15 Virge chaque pies qui fais 120 Virge au toutt fait a Londre ce 10 em Septembre, 1701.
>
> Par moi Estienne Penson

There is also an undated bill, seemingly in Penson's hand: 'the yellow Damaske hangs a 11 ffoott and a Halfe Deep, the Cortons 13 ffoot Deep and 4 bredths will Drawe a 11 bredths and a halff will hange ye Roome besides the window Cortons.'[5]

There are, apart from the bill and this receipt, six other references to Penson, namely, one, of no date, for an addition of 44 ells of tapestry work to two 'peices of hangings' (£77); an account book entry of 13 September 1701 'in Partt upon acount of Upostllers worke' (£30) – which is immediately below Rickson's receipt, also of 13 September, in part of a sum of money, 'for sume Imbroidery by mee' (£30) and three receipts in 1702 (26 January, 8 April and 22 May 1702).[6] The last receipt, for 22 May, is pasted above an undated bill, but assumed to be also of 1701 or 1702, signed for by Elizabeth Farmer or Hamer. This could perhaps be Elizabeth Rickson using a new married name. She charged for making the embroidery pieces into curtains:

> Seven yards and a half wrought for the Vallens first and 5 yards and a quarter last at £1.9.4 pr yd.   18.14.0
>
> ffor 15 yards and a half of the Stripes down the middle Curtains at £1.9.4 p yard   22.14.8
>
> Drawing the vallens 12 yards three quarters, the Cornish 4 yards, and 15 yards and three Quarters of the Stripes going down the middle of the great Curtains the Basis 14 yards and a quarter all at 1s p yard   2.6.6

4   Beard and Westman (1993) pp.523–4. I am indebted to Bruce Bailey for his help with the Drayton archives and for his establishing the correct reading of Elizabeth Rickson's name.

5   Drayton MSS., MM/A/409; 187.

6   *Ibid.*, MM/A/451 (account book); receipts, MM/A/438, 448, 450.

ffor 6 yards & a quarter and half quarter of the small Border at 8d p yard	0.4.3
ffor an Ounce of Silk	0.2.3
ffor Cleaning the Curtaines	0.3.0
ffor working the said 6 yard at 18s p yard & a quarter & half quarter	5.8.9
	49.13.5
Rec'd at sevell times	32.13.6
	16.19.11
	3.4.4
	13.15.7

By a calculation, which cannot take account of all the possible variations, it can be reckoned that Rickson and Dufee provided embroidered curtains and valances as follows:

Valances (7 yards; $5\frac{1}{4}$ yards)	$12\frac{1}{4}$ yards
Cornice	4 yards
Bases	$14\frac{1}{4}$ yards
Middle Curtains	$15\frac{1}{2}$ yards
'Great' Curtains	$15\frac{3}{4}$ yards
Small Border	($6\frac{1}{4}$ yards; $\frac{1}{8}$th yard; $6\frac{1}{4}$ yards plus)

This total, of a little over $67\frac{1}{2}$ yards in length, and presumably of varying width to suit its location, is not, of course, related to 48 yards of lining material provided because that was used mostly for the headboard, headcloth and tester. However, if the inner and outer valances are measured they do, as expected, relate to the bill. Rickson and Dufee charged for 21 feet of the outer valance (7 yards). The valance measures 8 feet at each side and 5 feet at the base of the bed. The 15 foot 9 inches of inner valance ($5\frac{1}{4}$ yards) measures 5 foot 9 inches at each side and 4 foot 3 inches at the base.

The Penson, Rickson and Dufee receipts[7] include eighteen mentions. Those for the ladies are:

1700	24 July (Elizabeth Rickson and Rebekah Dufee)	
	'for ye embroadery of ye bed	£6 in hand
	24 Sept. embroidred curtin	£7
	ye beginning of ye other curtin	£4
	5 Nov.	£2
1700	12 December	
	'for the second grate curtane £11,	
	I have two guyness in hand'.	
1701	7 January, receipt for 2 guineas;	
1701	28 January, 5 guineas	
1701	3 January	02.03.00
	16 March	01.01.06
	28 January	05.07.06
	18 March	03.02.00
	4 April	15.19.00
1701	19 July	006.09.00
1701	2 September	
	'sume Imbrodery'	005.00.00
	10 September	08.17.00

7 Drayton MSS., MM/A/347, 353, 361, 364, 365, 367, 373, 380, 386, 387, 388, 389, 404, 417, 438, 448, 450, 451.

1701   10 September
        Mentioned on a bill to James Foard
        'Pd to Mrs Rickson 9.0.0'
        2 other payments to
        [? Rickson] Mrs Richardson   4.17.0
                      Mrs Richison   04.00.00
1701   13 December
        'In Partt for sume Imbrodery'   30.00.00

What therefore seems acceptable in the light of these documents is that Penson was the maker of the bed, using material provided by the duchess for the tester, headcloth, headboard and counterpoint. Rickson and Dufee's curtains were the outstanding addition. As was usual, a settee and six chairs (Pl. 111) were embroidered *en suite*, although the settee has lost its seat covers and only has mounted panels of embroidery. What may well be a small fragment of this wool and silk embroidery which has been protected (through being on a 'hidden' surface) from light survives in all its rich colouring (Pl. 119). The original *en suite* chairs are in the king's dining room at Drayton[8] but the earlier chairs (*c*.1675) are in the state bedroom (one chair from the suite is in the Victoria and Albert Museum, London (W34-1950)). The Rickson–Dufee embroidered covers were loosely mounted, almost as case-covers would be, using hooks and eyes (Pl. 112). The present fastenings are of an early date but may not be the originals. They too may well be related to the Guillotin bill. In 1691 this craftsman was living in London 'next to *The Black Lion*, Pall Mall, near St James's',[9] but by 1701 he was in Air Street, off Castle Street in Soho. It must for the sake of completeness be pointed out that a bill from Guillotin at Drayton[10] relates to his provision of both a bedstead, tester, cornice, base mouldings and headboard with a yellow taffeta lining, and one in yellow damask. However, the bill was originally pasted in a sequence surrounded by dated bills of 1696. It does not seem to relate to the embroidered bed. For completeness in recording the story it reads:

Guillotin Living in Castle Street near to Air Street at ye twisted Posts near to Picadilly.
Lined with blew vizt, and for ye Bedsted, Tester, Cornishes, base moldings, headboard &
Curtain Rods.   10.00.0
ffor making ye Sd Bed   10.00.0
ffor another bedsted, tester, Cornishes Base moldings, headboard & Curtain rods, Colour
yellow Taffeta   10.00.0
ffor making ye sd Bed last mentioned   12.00.0
ffor a yellow damask bed, bedsted tester, Cornishes, Base moldings, headboard & Curtain
rods   16.00.0
ffor making the said Bed   12.00.0

Penson's name occurs in documents preserved in Paris, dated April 1702,[11] in respect of his wife, Catherine Françoise Doumillier, and her sister, Catherine, being declared joint beneficiaries of their grandmother's estate. She was named Françoise Boucher and the benefit in the estate recorded was in transferring it from her son, Louis Doumillier, a 'marchand tapissier', to his two daughters. Penson and his wife, Catherine, were then stated to be living in Pall Mall, where Jean Poictevin, Penson's uncle, as well as Francis Lapiere, had been resident at various dates.

8   Jackson-Stops (1978) p.31.
9   Heal (1953) p.72.
10   Drayton MS., MM/A/188, 191.

11   Paris, Archives Nationales, Minutier Central, Etude XXXVIII, 41 and CXVIII, 316.

POICTEVIN'S DEATH

Jean Poictevin died about 1709, seemingly in France, and as a widower. Penson prepared an inventory in London in 1710 of his uncle's English effects.[12] The document is an interesting one and I give part of it in the appendix (A25). It is made clear that the son of the deceased, John Poictevin, was in a regiment of dragoons and that eight guineas was to be allowed for his discharge. The sum of £119 2s 6d was owed by the deceased to Peter Poictevin, who may have been his brother, but this is not stated. Of more concern to knowledge of Poictevin's career as an upholsterer is the list of credits due. Queen Anne (when Princess of Denmark) owed £70, Lord Ranelagh £72, Mr Poulteney £3 7s, Lady Fretwell £4 3s and 'the late King James the Second' a considerable £2,377 16s. These amounts, particularly the last, were probably never collected.

I have not been able, as yet, to resolve the details behind the statement in the 'inventory' that Penson had paid £17 5s 10d to Mr Dottin, the attorney 'for Law charges of the Suits between the deceased and the Lord Cholmondley and Dutchess of Buckingham and others' as well as £3 18s Penson had lent to his uncle 'at severall times when he was in trouble with my Lord Ranelagh'. Normally, this would relate to actions in the Chancery Court for unsatisfactory work or disputed payment. There seem to be no traces in the surviving records,[13] but the details may be there as many cases went forward or continued in different names from the original plaintiffs, such as those of their notaries. Further, the inventory noted money due or received from these several potential litigants, which complicates the issue. Finally, I may never know whether it is coincidence, or whether there was the connection of a very distant relationship between Poictevin's family and Lapiere's. There is Poictevin's nephew Etienne (Stephen) Penson, whose wife, Catherine, benefited from the estate of her grandmother, Françoise Boucher. This estate was presumably in England as the matter was attested before a French attorney in London. Lapiere's eldest daughter, Frances, married a tailor named John Boucher. Further, both Catherine Penson's father, Louis Doumillier, and Lapiere's father, Dominique, were 'marchand tapissiers' in Paris and probably knew one another. The matter is recorded here, but must wait for further evidence.

LAPIERE'S DEATH

Francis Lapiere made his will in France, on 22 August 1714, before his executors, Andrew Feriere and Didiere Richard. But, as all his estate was in London – apart from the receipt of the equivalent of £1,500 from 'town rents in Paris' – the will was entered in January 1715 in the Prerogative Court of Canterbury, with two male witnesses, Blomore Goodiar and Francis Fox (both upholsterers) attesting that they were familiar with the deceased's handwriting.

Lapiere stated in the will that he was making it 'to prevent the disputes or jealousies that may happen after my death between my two daughters, Frances Lapiere my elder and Marianne Lapiere my younger, and my second wife, her mother'. Lapiere left his wife the rent from the Dover Street house which, like his Pall Mall house, was probably leased from Lady Dover. To his younger daughter, Marianne, who was under age and living in France (he urged his executors to keep her there), he left £1,000 'which I give her as a Marriage Portion or to enjoy the same when she shall come to age'. After her mother's death she was to have the house in Dover Street. To his elder daughter Frances, to whom he had already given £1,000 at her marriage (£500 of which he seems to have received from the Duke of Montagu in settlement of the duke's debt to Frances's husband, the tailor Joseph Boucher),[14] he gave the interest on a further £1,000 during her lifetime. The duke seems to have acted as a trustee. Frances died in 1732, at which point the £1,000 capital, as willed, went to Marianne, presumably still living in France.

---

12 P.R.O., Prob. 30/54, ff.28–35.

13 *Ibid.*, C5–10 *c.*1570–1714. Poictevin does not appear as a plaintiff. He has not yet been traced as a defendant.

14 Boughton House, MS., BC IV Pt.II, No.609 and p.1078.

In addition to the will, a declaration[15] was made by the elder daughter, Frances Boucher, on 3 February 1715, of items held by her and not set down in the inventory – perhaps the kind of situation Lapiere had anticipated. Frances and her husband had already received a quarter's rent on the Dover Street house, which was the jointure Lapiere had left to his wife; they had twenty-two dozen (264) bottles of French wine (84 red and 180 white), four or five pieces of gold in a green purse, several tickets in the Dutch lottery, of which seven had drawn benefits of 45 shillings each, and all Lapiere's wearing apparel, linens and woollens. Frances Lapiere (Boucher) declared finally that she knew of no other estate of the deceased than that mentioned in the inventory, namely the Pall Mall house. As an acquisitive daughter she was no doubt well informed.

A second document forming the full declaration adds to the foregoing list by noting various sums of money due to Lapiere. Most interesting is the information that Mrs Boucher was possessed 'of a Note or Bill of about twenty one pounds which was due and owing to the said deceased from the Lady Brownlow . . .' This provides a possible connection between Lapiere and Belton House, Lincolnshire, built in c.1685–7 by Sir John Brownlow, who had married Alice Sherard in 1676. Unfortunately this payment does not allow the assumption that the state bed in the blue room at Belton is by Lapiere. While several beds are listed in the Belton inventories for 1688, 1698, 1737 and 1754, they are not easily identified. The archives and style of the state bed in the blue bedroom (named in 1830) suggest that it was made at the turn of the eighteenth century, and originally upholstered in crimson damask. It was subsequently altered and completely re-upholstered by William Stephens in 1813 in blue damask at the time of Sir Jeffry Wyatville's changes to the house. He used 123 yards of 'rich made tabouret blue' at 11s a yard which included that for the curtains *en suite*. They are still in the room, but faded to a different colour. Stephens's men spent almost seven weeks on their various upholstery tasks, using 2 lb of glue and 2,000 tacks.[16]

The inventory of Lapiere's household possessions, which has been edited,[17] is a full document detailing the contents of some thirty-three rooms or parts of his Pall Mall house, in addition to his wearing apparel. Included, but in a separate document,[18] is a long list of 'Leases, Bonds, Securities and Credits', showing details of leases for the Pall Mall property, dated to 1704, between Lord and Lady Dover, the Earl of Montagu (a significant name), and Lapiere. These are over various periods of years from 1704, with Lapiere having an interest therein to the value of £1,050. Lapiere sub-let various attached parts of the premises in Pall Mall not in his own use. The list of debts shows he was still due a sum of money from Algernon, sixth Earl of Essex: that is, 'payment of £428 18s with interest at five per cent'. There were eight other notes or bonds – one for jewels as security on £371 owed – from a Lady Charlotte de Roye (whose identity I have not established), and a further note from the sixth Earl of Essex, in March 1713, for payment of £41 6s.

The inventory then provides a fascinating intermesh of items with those listed in the declaration made by Lapiere's daughter, Frances Boucher – the Dutch lottery tickets, the 'Town House Rents in Paris', rent from the Dover Street house, interest on eight Exchequer notes and a further list of 'Debts esteem'd Desperate'. These included a bond of 15 April 1703 for £300 from Anne, Dowager Countess of Exeter, widow of the fifth Earl, and one of 8 November 1688, from the Catholic peer, George, Earl of Dunbarton. When James II had been exiled from Whitehall in December 1688 the earl was one of the four peers who accompanied him to Rochester. Both the earl and his wife had died in 1691–2 at the exiled court at Saint-Germain-en-Laye and were buried in the Abbey there.[19]

The inventory lists other sums of money due, from several unknown gentlemen – Thomas Arnold, Robert Murden, Henry Coape (but involved with a debt of the Duke of Norfolk for £154 18s), William Gould, Richard Robins, Burdyn Anderson, William Lawson and Arthur Winewood, all of them totalling some £2,800. Francis Lapiere had been a leading exponent at creating the effect of an 'upholstered room' and there is no doubt that more will be established about his considerable activities. Nevertheless, some of the details have

15   P.R.O., Prob. 5/5204.

16   I have used the notes on the Belton archives made for the National Trust (Regional Office, Clumber Park, Notts) by Rosalind Westwood.

17   P.R.O., Prob. 5/5204, edited Westman (1994) pp.1–14.

18   P.R.O., Prob. 5/5205, see also Beard and Westman (1993) p.522.

19   G.E.C., *Complete Peerage*, IV (1916) p.515.

been set straight for one who in some thirty years of upholstery work in England rose above mere competence to virtuosity. Poictevin's and Lapiere's activities in England show that they had a wide and varied patronage among court circles. They brought to England a kind of upholstered magnificence which had no contemporary parallel. It brought them wealth and position and allowed their clients to fancy themselves at the forefront of French-inspired taste.

A Throne for Queen Anne

It has been explained that the Lord Great Chamberlain 'was entitled to claim for his benefit old or redundant furniture from within the Palace [of Westminster] as soon as it ceased to have any use'.[20] At the accession of a new king or queen much new furnishing was needed, both in the House of Lords and in Westminster Hall. The last great historic space was used for the reception given to the new monarch and for the banquet which followed. The most advantageous of the Lord Great Chamberlain's rights, or perquisites, was that by which he could claim items used at or after the coronation. This also included 'the bed and all the furnishings of the sovereign's bedroom on the night before the Coronation, the sovereign's night robe; and two basins, a ewer and a cup of assay . . .'.

The exact story of how Queen Anne's coronation chair and footstool came to Hatfield House, the early Jacobean seat of the Cecils, is not known. James, the fifth Earl of Salisbury, who held the title at the time of Anne's accession in 1702, did not hold any office. The family chronicler has noted that if the 'fifth Earl is mentioned at all by his contemporaries, it is disrespectfully as a man with a taste for low company and henpecked by his wife . . . He was the type of English peer who feels happiest residing in his country home and surrounded by his own estates'.[21] The cost of the upholstery of the throne and stool (Pl. 121) at £72 contrasts with the £20 paid for the frames. Thomas Roberts charged (£17 nett) for 'a rich chair of State, the top of the back carved with a Lyon and a Unicorn and Shields, Cypher, Crown and Sceptres, the lower part carved rich, all gilt . . .'. The footstool was provided at £3. Then Anthony Ryland submitted his bill for 'covering a Chair, Footstool and Cushion set on ye Throne in Westminster Abbey – For 8 yds of rich gold and blue brocade at £9–£72.'[22] The throne and footstool were renovated in 1965 under the auspices of the Department of Furniture and Woodwork and that of Textiles at the Victoria and Albert Museum. Small fragments of the original gold and blue brocade were found to be adhering to the frames under their present dark crimson-coloured coverings.

Thomas How at Hatfield House

In 1710 a state bed had been delivered to Hatfield for the green damask room. With its headboard centred on a coronet it was a grand affair, listed in Thomas How's bill[23] for 19 December 1711:

> ffor A very handsom large Teaster richly carve'd & ornementid w moldings very handsom & for A sett of very handsom large carved cornishis & headcloth, carved w pillows & pilastors very handsom & a sett of base Moldings, broke w sweaps & pillows att ye Cornors richly carvd & 2 Cornor peces Dito & A large wainscot bedsted with A Lath bottom & duble screws all Compleat   £38.00 –

As usual, the valances and bases were lined with buckram (16s), lining was provided to the headcloth with hair to stuff the fabric 'pipes' of its decoration (7s 6d). A bright filed compass rod, pulleys and rollers (£1 15s) assisted in drawing the crimson harateen curtains (£3 15s). The case curtains were drawn on a gilded case rod (£4). Two cyphers and a coronet were worked in gold (£4), and 36 yards of crimson and gold line (£9 8s) with ten 'very Large rich gold & Crimson Silke Tassells' (£18), nine lesser ones and 56 smaller added a further

20 Roberts (1989) p.61.
21 Cecil (1973) p.181.
22 P.R.O., LC2/15/1.
23 Hatfield House MSS., Bills 467 (1710–13).

£39 18s. For making the damask bed 'all Carve'd very Rich & glewing on All ye Silke & lase & Imbrodoring of itt all Cumplet' How charged a further £35. The 'upholstered room' effect was further enriched by four large window and door cornices 'broke in Sweaps & Carveid very Rich & Ornemented w Cronitts very handsom' (£18), and four pair of damask window and door curtains, double laced, with the valances (lined with buckram and crimson harateen) embroidered and 'laseid all Cumpleat' (£10).

The Thomas How bed at Hatfield is an example of present-day conservation by the house team, an average of ten a day working for two years, under the overall supervision of the Marchioness of Salisbury.[24] Remains of the original red damask were found glued inside the tester. These were dated by the textile department of the Victoria and Albert Museum to 1710, near enough to locate the 1711 bill in the voluminous house archives. It was not possible to reproduce exactly the original silk damask curtains, of which only one complete pattern repeat remained. Their place has been taken by a plain rose-red woven silk, lined with a copy of the original cloth of gold based on a surviving scrap which had been turned in and remained untouched.

How's 1711 bill also included the provision of '2 very handsom large Easy Chares w Carveid Sides & Cross Stretchers richly Carveid & gilt w gold (£12 10s)'. The 'gilts, bottoming & backing' added 8s and five skins of leather were dressed in oil for the two cushions (5s). This made them very supple, ready to receive a stuffing of fine feathers (15s). Making the chairs with borders, cushions 'ornementid with lase & tassells all Cumpleat' was done for £5.[25]

These two armchairs are still at Hatfield, *en suite* with the bed. One of their distinctive features was red silk squares criss-crossed with gold thread which flanked the arms. The squares survived, lacking their thread which has been replaced with gold lurex.

How's chairs have a slightly *retardataire* look, which is not surprising given that his active years of training would be in the late seventeenth century. He would be typical of the usually unknown upholsterer responsible for chairs with shaped wings, an upward sweeping covered top rail, scrolling arms, a walnut frame with stretchers (or one in simulated ebony) and perhaps covered in cut-velvet (Pl. 105) or damask.

Thomas How acted from the early eighteenth century as the usual upholsterer concerned with work at Hatfield House. He submitted bills (which survive) at regular intervals but the fact that he was employed almost continuously meant he was rarely paid promptly. His bill for 1710 to 1713 amounting to £289 13s 4d was paid on 3 April 1713. His bill for 1713–15 amounting to £711 13s 0d was paid, likewise, almost two years late in relation to its first items.

As with several upholsterers, undertaking was considered a service they could provide. Frances Bennett, fourth Countess of Salisbury, died in 1713. She had spent much time abroad, particularly after the death of her husband in 1694. Frances had been a daughter of a rich city magnate, Sir Simon Bennett. He had decreed in his will that if she should marry before she was of age, all her fortune except for £10,000 should go to her married sister, Grace, 'and that if she married without her mother's consent she should lose that also'.[26] She did, however, marry Lord Salisbury when only thirteen years old; he spent much time and money trying to recover the lost ten thousand pounds. Thomas How charged in 1713 for '8 days work at Hatfield to take down the mourning and put it up again . . . work fixing up the mourning in King Street' and, interestingly, 'the hire of set mourning, £80'.[27]

How's undertaking services were again in demand for the funeral, in January 1721, of the Hon. Bennett Cecil:

> A lead coffin the inside inceared & lined with a sarsnett quilt & ruffle, 2.15 – an elm coffin covered with the best velvet & a silvered plate with inscription, coat of arms, 3 pr of silvered chased handles & set off with 3 rows of the best silvered nails 4.10 – a man & a horse to carry the coffin & attend the funeral 1.10 – the use of a velvet pall, 10s.   Sum £9 5s[28]

24 *World of Interiors* (December 1989) pp.116–21.
25 Hatfield House MSS., Bills 486.
26 Cecil (1973) p.176.

27 Hatfield House MSS., 'Family Papers, Supplement 3', p.188.
28 *Ibid.*, 3, p.232.

Upholstery by Thomas How for a number of other patrons has been attributed or documented. During the early 1720s the Warwick architect, Francis Smith, was working on a rebuilding of his own design at Sutton Scarsdale, Derbyshire. A lead rising-plate, formerly at the house (but since the demolition of Sutton Scarsdale in 1920, now lost) recorded the dates of 1724 and 1728 and How's name, as a 'gentleman upholsterer', along with a named carpenter, joiner, plumber, a locksmith, stone-carver and two Ticino stuccoists. The text of the plate was given in 1919 and again in 1995.[29] A number of chairs with *verre eglomisé* panels in the back splat, bearing the Scarsdale arms, but of indifferent upholstery, have been regarded as How's work.[30] Francis Smith was faithful in employing his reliable team of craftsmen and it is presumed How moved with them to Stoneleigh Abbey, Warwickshire. Smith had been involved there since about 1714, working for Edward, third Lord Leigh. The parish registers at Cubbington, two miles from Stoneleigh, record that the house was finished in May 1726.[31] The Sutton Scarsdale chairs have some similarities to an armchair and a set of six backstools owned now by the Stoneleigh Abbey Preservation Trust. They are veneered in walnut and upholstered with embroidered covers in *gros-* and *petit-point* (Pl. 180). The scenes depicted are taken from Ovid's *Metamorphoses* and are presumably from a professional embroiderer's stock because space is allowed on some of the covers for arms which are not present on the single backstools. Further, an example in the Untermyer Collection (Metropolitan Museum of Art, New York)[32] has a semi-circular notch at the centre of the top rail which only makes sense when incorporating painted coats of arms. The Stoneleigh ones have the coronet and arms (and the armchair also bears the gilded monogram) of Edward, third Lord Leigh.

The Stoneleigh archives[33] have been examined carefully but there are few receipts and vouchers for the 1720s and no documentation has been traced. An inventory of 1738 taken at Lord Leigh's death lists 'seven fine needleworkt chairs in Walnut and Gilt frames and Green cases, in the Drawing Room, valued at £60'.

Nothing is known of How's activity from the late 1720s (if indeed he was the upholsterer at Stoneleigh) until 1733, when he worked in Lincolnshire for Lady Sondes, providing her with a small quantity of bedding, materials and cushions (£13 6s 6½d).[34] The bank account of the second Earl of Lichfield of Ditchley Park, near Oxford – another Francis Smith building, to designs by James Gibbs – does have payments in it from 1727 to 1730 to Thomas How.[35] It is always interesting to speculate what these might have been for, but difficult to be certain. In 1933, at the time of the Ditchley sale, Margaret Jourdain mentioned 'six chairs dating from the early years of George I's reign. The tall-backed armchair and chairs are upholstered, and supported upon 'broken' cabriole legs, of which the straight section is inlaid with arabesque marquetry, a detail resembling a contemporary set of chairs from Streatlam Castle.' A year later, again in *Country Life*, Arthur Oswald described and showed illustrations of the house as it had been prior to the sale and its eventual acquisition by Mr Ronald Tree.[36]

Thomas How died in 1745. In his will he described himself as 'weak in body',[37] and desired to be buried in Kensington churchyard, near to his mother and father. He left a wife, two sons, Robert and an extravagant younger son (to whom he left a shilling only), and two daughters, Elinor and a youngest one, unnamed. One of his executors was the upholsterer Thomas Allam of the parish of St George, Hanover Square. The will was proved on 22 May 1745 with the residue of the estate, after some simple bequests, to his eldest son and eldest daughter.

29   *Country Life*, 15 February 1919, p.171, and by Colvin (1995).

30   The chairs are divided between the Metropolitan Museum of Art, New York (Hackenbroch, 1958, Pls 64–5), Cooper-Hewitt Museum and The Frick Collection, New York, and Temple Newsam House, Leeds.

31   Victoria County History, *Warwickshire*, VI, p.232.

32   Hackenbroch (1958) Pl. 80; Rieder (1977).

33   A team of volunteers at the Shakespeare Birthplace Trust kindly checked these for upholstery details.

34   Beard and Gilbert (1986) p.453.

35   Royal Bank of Scotland, Child's Bank ledgers, 1727, June 15, £35; received £50, 1729, March 4; £25, 1730, July 3 and November 18; £50, 1730, May 19.

36   Jourdain (1933) p.490; see also Oswald (1934) and Cornforth (1988) pp.82–5.

37   P.R.O., Prob. 11/739, f.330.

BEALING AND REEVE

As Richard Bealing's upholstery activities died away towards the end of Queen Anne's reign, they ran, concurrently, for a short time, with those of Hamden Reeve. I have been unable to establish whether it was an estate administration for Richard Bealing which was filed in 1724.[38] It does make mention of 'An Accompt relateing to the Wardrobe, 1697', but so many clothes and vast quantities of silk and calico are listed that there is reason to think it is more the stock of a draper than an upholsterer. No will for the upholsterer has been found in records of the Canterbury or Middlesex probate courts.[39]

Reeve worked from his house at the sign of the Lamb & Lyon in the Strand. He supplied furnishings to the royal household and to the Houses of Parliament from 1704. On Lady Day 1705 he provided 'for Her Majties Bedchamber at Kensington . . . a large fine Dimity Bed tick and Bolster covered with White Satin and filled with Seasoned Swans Downe containing ninety pounds of Down in them, £18.10.0'. In 1704–5 he supplied forty-eight turkeywork chairs to the House of Commons, three large turkeywork arm chairs and a carpet to the House of Lords and twenty-four turkeywork chairs for the Lobby of St James's Palace. In 1709–10 he provided a further twelve for the Court of Wards at Westminster.

At Kensington Palace the longest bills which were submitted were from Reeve. He furnished Prince George's apartments during 1708. Most of the rooms were upholstered in blue, with only the closet and waiting room in green. The frames of all the furniture Reeve covered were provided by Thomas Roberts. Whilst the queen showed little interest in the palace Reeve charged in 1710 'for the queen's service at Kensington', providing eight pairs of 'very large fine blankets' (£12 06s 00), twelve pairs of coarser blankets (£14 08s 00), a feather bed and bolster of fine seasoned feathers (£06 00 00) and a fustian mattress and a chequered mattress (£04 00 00). Finally, in 1713–14 he was the upholsterer of Queen Anne's bed for Windsor (now at Hampton Court, Pls 132–6), although it was not delivered until after the queen's death.

A BED FOR QUEEN ANNE

The bed was shown still at Windsor in the illustration of Charles II's Eating Room in W. H. Pyne's *History of the Royal Residences*, published in 1819. In Pyne's caption he referred to the preservation of the bed in that hallowed setting by George III: 'he would not displace the venerable relic for the most splendid bed in the universe.' The warrant for its making was signed by Lord Shrewsbury on 27 July, 1714: '. . . a Standing bed . . . large armchair and eight square stools, all of crimson gold and white figured velvet . . . case curtains to the bed of gold coloured silk . . . curtains . . . lined with white sattin . . .'[40]

By this date, Richard Roberts had succeeded his father Thomas, who died in 1714. In his will[41] he divided '£1,000, due to me from the Crown' and gave a quarter each to his two sons, Richard (who carried on the joinery business at 'The Royal Chair', Marylebone Street) and a younger son, John. The remainder went to his three daughters, with the rest of his goods to Richard as the sole executor. For making the queen's bed Richard Roberts, as the bills (Appendix A26) show, was helped by Hamden Reeve as upholsterer, with 'John Johnson and Comp' as the supplying mercers of 321⅛ yards of velvet, 81 yards of satin to line the bed and curtains, and 125½ yards of white Mantua silk to line the window curtains. William Weeks, the laceman, made 'several patterns of tassels to shew her Matie'. Minor work was undertaken by Thomas Phill and his partner, Jeremiah Fletcher. Some of this was necessary because Reeve (as well as Thomas Roberts) also died in 1714.[42] Phill and Fletcher succeeded Reeve as the royal upholsterers. The bed had, *en suite*, eight matching

38   P.R.O., Prob. 31/23/f.387, 26 June 1724.
39   P.R.O. (Canterbury); Greater London Record Office (Middlesex).
40   P.R.O., LC5/72; Rutherford (1927) p.80; Thornton (1977) pp.136, 140–1.

41   P.R.O., Prob. 11/540, f.124.
42   Beard and Gilbert (1986) p.735.

stools and an elbow chair with frames by Richard Roberts. The carved woodwork of the armchair does not match exactly any of the eight stools. These indeed appear to belong now to different sets with one stool matching one at Knole.[43]

THE UPHOLSTERER, THOMAS PHILL

Thomas Phill (whose work has occasionally been represented as being by Thomas 'Hill') had been apprenticed at some undetermined point in the late seventeenth century to the 'Merchant Taylor, James Sims'. By 1700 he was ready for admission to the freedom of the Worshipful Company of Upholders: '1700, 23 April. Thomas Phill, Apprentice to James Sims, Merchant Taylor, admitted to freedom, paid IIIs iiijd for his admission.' He was also 'chosen of the livery' and allowed the charge of 'freedome of the City out of his livery money'.[44] As well as dealing with his work for the Crown, there are two other commissions which need description; firstly, his provision of a settee, a set of six chairs and a firescreen in 1714 to Edward Dryden of Canons Ashby, Northamptonshire. These were supplied from Phill's premises at the sign of the Three Golden Chairs in the Strand, and he had been supplying the house with bedding since 1709. The bill for the furniture survives, and has been published.[45] Phill charged £7 10s on 12 February 1715 for '6 wallnuttree back chaires frames of ye newest fashion stufft up in Lynnen & ye slats coverd a 2nd time' with a further £1 13s 'ffor makeing ye needle work covers & fixeing ym on ye Chaires & for sewing silke', and 5s 6d for green serge for the six chair backs. Case-covers in gold colour serge were supplied with a charge of £1 11s 7½d for the serge and 15s for silk, tape and making them.

The low cost for 'makeing' the covers suggests that the needlework had been supplied by the household and was perhaps the work of a team under the direction of Anne Dryden, Edward's wife. The settee and chairs (Pls 141–2) have kept much of their original brilliant colours; having been sold from Canons Ashby between the wars the suite was reacquired in 1983 for the house (which is now administered by The National Trust) via Mallett's of Bond Street.

One of Phill's early tasks for the Crown, along with his partner, Jeremiah Fletcher, was involvement in the coronation of George I.[46] This took place in October 1714, with George wearing the crown made for Queen Anne. The king, with his rudimentary knowledge of spoken English, may not have understood all that was said, but the solemnity and grandeur of the occasion, enhanced in material trappings by the upholsterers, must have impressed him. Taking part in the coronation ceremony was the newly created Prince of Wales, George Augustus, then a young man of thirty-one and, as the king's eldest son, the future George II. He had married Charlotte Caroline of Ansbach in 1705. One of Phill and Fletcher's early tasks in 1715 was to provide them with a State Bed, now at Hampton Court. The bill of 28 March 1715 (Appendix A27) is as interesting as the one recording the making of Queen Anne's Bed, with some of the same craftsmen involved. Again the warrant[47] was signed by Lord Shrewsbury (as Lord Chamberlain) on 18 March 1715: 'a Crimson Damask Bed with Bedding . . . with case curtains for ye Bed of Taffaty . . .'. Richard Roberts provided the oak bedstead and smooth filed curtain rods, Richard Chamberlayne & Co the crimson Genoa damask, crimson taffeta and white florence satin. Then Phill and Fletcher made the hangings and case-curtains (which hung on a double gilt case rod), provided the beddings and embellished it all with the silk arras lace from the laceman, William Weeks (Pls 137–8).

There were of course many less grand tasks, each demanding time and men. In 1717 Phill and Fletcher charged for '9 days work for 6 men to new stuff up and cover with scarlet cloth all the Forms, Woolpacks and Bar of the House . . .'[48] These were trimmed with scarlet silk fringe and over seven thousand gilt nails (at 24s a thousand) were used. The 'private Rooms and Lobbys' were hung with green serge and the Bar of the

43   Information kindly communicated by the then Surveyor to the
      Queen's Works of Art, Sir Geoffrey de Bellaigue.
44   Guildhall Library, London, MS., 7141/1, ff.267–8.
45   Jackson-Stops (1985) pp.217–18.

46   P.R.O., LC2/19.
47   P.R.O., LC5/72, Rutherford (1927) p.83; Thornton (1977)
      p.141.
48   P.R.O., LC5/47, f.7, *et seq.*

Painted Chamber with green baize (at 3s 6d a yard). A very large 'Musketa Carpet' (£19) was laid under the throne, with one, at £10, under the Clerks' Table.

Such large commissions, and they continued year after year (for the House of Lords, for the royal palaces and for the royal yachts) meant large bills, at best paid tardily. In one quarter of 1719 Phill and Fletcher's work totalled £1,233. Phill was also an early provider, in the 1720s, of the new form of festoon curtain, where the fabric was drawn up vertically.[49] It could be held that as his Canons Ashby chairs were described as 'of ye newest fashion', together with a bill for work at Kensington Palace in 1727 (Appendix A28) in which nine wire rods were sewn to the bottoms of the festoon case curtains to make them draw straight, that he was an innovative craftsman.

Like many monarchs before him George I had his share of mistresses. Melusine von der Schulenburg had occupied that position from about 1691. She became successively Duchess of Munster in the Irish peerage (1716) and in 1719, Duchess of Kendal in the English peerage.[50] She had apartments at Hampton Court and received, during the summer of 1717 and 1718, many of Thomas Phill's beds and bedding, and her daughter and servants also received beds, bedding, chairs and other furniture.[51] Phill also supplied the Hampton Court apartment of the king's half-sister, Sophia Charlotte, Frelin von Kielmansegg, who had become a naturalized British subject after her husband, Johann Adolf von Kielmansegg, had died in 1717. She was created Countess of Leinster in the Irish peerage in 1721 and Countess of Darlington in the English peerage in 1722.

The Duchess of Kendal's bedchamber was to be furnished by Phill in blue, with a standing bed, with blue camblet trimmings and counterpoint, two pairs of window curtains, cornices and valances trimmed with blue silk lace, window seats, a quantity of bedding, six back stools and an easy chair, covered in the same blue camblet as the bed. In complete contrast the dressing room was furnished in yellow with curtains and a couch in yellow camblet.

By October 1718 George I and his court had left Hampton Court, and were not to return. The king had been ill and in 1719 set out for Hanover. Nevertheless the palace was maintained in good order, although its place as a royal residence declined further during the long reign (1727–60) of George II.

At some point in 1723 Phill's partner, Jeremiah Fletcher, died and his widow, Rebecca, continued the Sun insurance policy on his Strand premises.[52] Phill carried on alone in his upholstery duties for the Great Wardrobe. He had work enough if only to change draw-back curtains into festoon ones. In June 1727[53] he charged for some at Kensington Palace:

> The altering them from Draw Back Curtains to Festoons And for putting them up again with Sewing Silk & Nails us'd   £1 6s

The last important commission for the Crown in which Phill was involved was his work in 1727 for the coronation of King George II and Queen Caroline in Westminster Abbey. It has been suggested[54] that William Kent, who had been appointed Master Carpenter to the Board of Works in May 1726, may have designed the coronation chairs. He had certainly designed the temporary Triumphal Arch erected at the west end of Westminster Hall, and counted furniture design among his considerable accomplishments. Richard Roberts had been busy supplying the walnut frames of six chairs of state, with their accompanying footstools. The upholstery fabrics for these came from the London shop of David Bosanquet, and Charles Mathews and John Hasell were the two lacemen. The six chairs were made up of 'two Great Chairs, Cushions and Footstools' upholstered in crimson Genoa velvet, with two in green Genoa velvet, and two more in purple velvet, for use by the Archbishop of Canterbury and the Bishop of London. A further dressing chair, for use by Queen Caroline, was upholstered with crimson Genoa velvet, garnished with gilt nails. The two elaborate thrones, and the steps leading to them, were covered with 'rich gold tabby'. The chairs of state were ordered

49   Westman (1990) pp.1406–17.
50   Hatton (1978) p.49 *et seq.*
51   P.R.O., LC5/89, ff.29–29v; LC5/157, ff.16–16v.
52   Guildhall Library, London. Sun policy registers Vol. II, p.37.
53   P.R.O., LC9/287, No.57.
54   By Dr Tessa Murdoch, unpublished notes shared with me.

under a warrant dated 5 October 1727 from the Great Wardrobe's Master, John, second Duke of Montagu, and Roberts provided, under its terms '. . . rich Chairs of State Frames the tops of the Backs richly carved with a Lyon and a unicorn, Shield, Cypher and Scepter, the Lower Parts carved and all gilt and two Footstool frames suitable for the thrones . . .' Phill was then paid for 'girt webb bottoming . . . rolling curled hair, linen and stuffing two large armed chairs and footstools, two large down cushions, making said chairs, cushions and footstools covered with green velvet and trimmed with gold and silver fringe and for gilt nails, tacks and sewing silk used for two green velvet chairs, cushions and foot stools . . .'[55]

This upholstering by Phill of the state chairs was assumed, in error, in 1994 to be for a chair used by Queen Caroline at the coronation (Pl. 171). This was first noted in 1921 when it appeared in a *Country Life* view of a room at Houghton Hall, Norfolk.[56] It cannot be assumed that it is the same chair noted there in 1728 by Sir Matthew Decker, described by him as: 'the costly chair werein the present Queen was crowned'. It was not listed in the Houghton inventories of 1745 or 1792 and was not, seemingly, part of a perquisite acquisition by the leading politician and sometime Prime Minister, Sir Robert Walpole, for whom Houghton was being built. Admittedly, the eagle-headed arms of the chair, symbolic of Jupiter, its scallop-shell headed cabriole legs and hairy paw feet do resemble Kent's design of the chairs (Pl. 174) made for the marble parlour in Walpole's house.[57] The chair may have been reupholstered about 1919, but still has a strong claim to be considered as one of the several chairs in use at the coronation ceremony in 1727.

In 1727 also, and after his considerable work in the abbey, Phill started to reduce his activities. His many duties for the Crown were assumed for a short time by John Gilbert, but he did not have long in office, as he died in 1729. Phill had made his own will,[58] prudently, in 1724, four years before his death in 1728. He described himself as living in the parish of St Mary le Strand, but had property which he left for life to his sister in the parish of Everdon in Northamptonshire. Phill may have originated from that county (possibly explaining the use of his skills, locally, by Edward Dryden at Canons Ashby), but he does not appear in the 1702 or 1705 polls for the county of Northampton, as he does for that of 1710 for the City of London.[59] The remainder of his estate, after bequests to his sister, brother-in-law and '12 poor housekeepers of the parish of St Mary le Strand', he left to the sole executrix, his wife Mary. By 1 May 1728 his goods were for sale in an auction,[60] spread over six days:

> . . . All the Household Goods and Stock in Trade of Mr Thomas Phill, deceased, Upholsterer to her late Majesty, Queen Anne, to his late Majesty, King George I, and to his present Majesty, King George II,
> Consisting of:
> fine damask, Mohair, wrought Camblet and other Beds, window Curtains and Chairs, several Swan's Down Beds, Swan's and other Feather Beds, a right India Cabinet, Chests of Drawers, Scrutores, Desks and Bookcases . . . above 100 Carpets of all Sizes, particularly a most curious Needlework Carpet, four yards long and three yards wide, which was intended for a Foreign Prince. To be viewed.

A considerable career went under the auctioneer's resounding hammer.

55 P.R.O., LC9/287, No.57.
56 *Country Life*, 15 January 1921, p.66, fig.3.
57 I am indebted to Dr Tessa Murdoch for sharing her notes on various chairs at Houghton (some sold, Christie's, 8 December 1994, lots 126–32) and to Mr John Hardy; Furniture History Society, *Newsletter*, February 1995, pp.23–4.
58 P.R.O., Prob. 11/619, f.21.
59 'Copies of the Polls for the County of Northampton, 1702, 1705, 1730 . . .' (1832); 'The Poll of the Livery-Men of the City of London' (1710) pp.160–2. I have used the copies at the Institute of Historical Research, University of London.
60 *Daily Post*, 1 May 1728.

THE COMPANY OF UPHOLSTERERS

In 1714 the glass dealer, John Gumley, had set himself up in the upper part of the New Exchange on the south side of the Strand and opened a warehouse there for sales of his glass and mirrors. He also entered into a partnership with the cabinet-maker, James Moore (infamous as the Duchess of Marlborough's 'Oracle'), and they were soon appointed royal cabinet-makers in succession to the Dutchman, Gerrit Jensen. They were at once busy in providing the royal palaces with gilt furniture and mirrors, as well as walnut tree furniture which was used by, among others, the future George II, then Prince of Wales, and his wife, Caroline. I have noted Thomas Phill and Jeremiah Fletcher's involvement in upholstering a state bed for the royal couple. Researches for a series of articles about Gumley and Moore[61] have, together with my own enquiries, shown that a 'Company of Upholders' was active from the late seventeenth century at the Exeter Change. The newspaper *The Flying Post* announced on 23 November 1699: '. . . At Exeter Change in the Strand and from Upholsters Hall next the East India House in Leadenhall Street at which Places there are extraordinary conveniences for Funerals and Lying State . . .'

As early as 1700 a 'Society of Upholsterers', a similar name to that of the company, had been involved in the funeral of the first Duke of Beaufort, receiving £385 17s 6d when the first Duke's debts were finally accounted for, about 1720. In 1705 Stephen Penson, Poictevin's nephew, and an otherwise unknown William Williams charged Sir John Germain £190 for the burial of his wife, who retained her former title of Duchess of Norfolk (p.95). The money was received 'for the use of the Company or Society of Upholsters Concerned, interested in the undertaking and performing funeralls . . .'[62]

There is some reason to think that Gumley and Moore were involved in continuing this enterprise. In 1722 a bill from the company was submitted in respect of the funeral on 16 June of Queen Anne's redoubtable commander, John Churchill, first Duke of Marlborough. His victories had earned him the nation's gratitude, with the building of Blenheim Palace as his seat.[63] James Moore had been much involved with this as a clerk of works, and was particularly active from 1712 or so when the Duchess of Marlborough had started to quarrel with the architect of Blenheim, Sir John Vanbrugh.

The lying-in-state in 1722 of the Duke of Marlborough took place at Marlborough House, with a temporary burial following in Westminster Abbey. The chapel at Blenheim (with the eventual erection of a fine monument sculpted by Rysbrack) was far from finished. The duke's body was not moved there until 1744. The duchess, observing the etiquette of a widow not attending the funeral, sent her black coach, lined with 48 yards of black cloth and six for harness ('which', she said, 'is enough to cover my Garden'), with her son-in-law, the second Duke of Montagu, as the chief mourner. The bill for the funeral itself came to £5,265, if household mourning is included.[64] It is to be hoped that Gumley and Moore's possible involvement with the 'Society of Upholsterers' will be established eventually. James Moore died in October 1726, and his partner, John Gumley, in December 1728. Elizabeth Gumley, his mother, then entered into partnership with William Turing and they succeeded for a short time as Royal Cabinet-Makers. Accused of overcharging in December 1729 they, in turn, were succeeded by Moore's erstwhile apprentice, Benjamin Goodison (d.1767).

61   Caldwell (1986) and (1987). I am indebted to Ian Caldwell for his help over Gumley and Moore's career, supplementary to the entries in Beard and Gilbert (1986) pp.618–19.

62   Gloucestershire C.R.O. I am indebted to Lucy Abel-Smith for a copy of these accounts. Drayton MS.MM/A/650. I am indebted to Bruce Bailey for this reference.

63   Green (1961).

64   For moving the body from Windsor Lodge to London see British Library, MS., 61410; also Green (1967) pp.227–9. An account of the funeral is in *Applebee's Original Weekly Journal*, 11 August 1722, p.2438.

FURNITURE AT HOUGHTON HALL, NORFOLK

The several large and impressive suites of chairs at Houghton Hall, dispersed through the great house, have patterns and textures in their upholstery which make a major contribution to the overall effect. A careful analysis of the house and the furniture has been published[65] but there is a paucity of exact fact, since Sir Robert Walpole contrived a deliberate erasing of record; it has been stated[66] that 'after 1718 the personal letters almost disappear and they are replaced by the typical correspondence of a successful statesman', and one in which the whole system of contemporary patronage and office-seeking was reflected. The great house gave Walpole a status but, at his fall from power in 1742, it was time to hide expenditure on it from prying eyes. Nevertheless, in addition to the Cambridge deposit of documents there are a number at Houghton itself relating to building and decoration, including a long one of April 1729 for upholstery (seemingly a duplicate of one at Cambridge) totalling £1,420 8s 7½d. This was mostly for work by Thomas Roberts at Walpole's houses.

It is necessary at this point, in respect of the two 1729 bills for furniture for work by Thomas Roberts at Houghton to set out the intricacies of that family's pedigree. Thomas Roberts, 'joyner', whose activities in royal service in the late seventeenth century were, as noted, considerable, died in 1714. In his will Thomas left to his son, Richard, the principal part of his estate, with a share to his other son, John, then a minor. Richard carried on with the business and may have been the one who married Catherine Helsam in October 1691.[67] He died in 1733 and his own will[68] mentioned the still unpaid debt of 'a Thousand Pounds & Upwards due from his late Majesty, King George I'. This had been mentioned in his father's will when he had been left a quarter share of it. Richard had, according to his will, a son William, a wife, Catherine, and two daughters, Nancy and Catherine. So who is the 'Thomas' submitting the 1729 bills at Houghton? There seems need therefore to reckon with an upholsterer, Thomas Roberts, who is not mentioned in the 1714 or 1733 wills of the 'joyners', Thomas and Richard Roberts. As all the bills submitted by them were for making frames for furniture and did not include upholstery, an 'unknown' Thomas is a possibility. He was presumably a nephew or cousin. But unfortunately I have not traced any will and, as stated, he is not mentioned in the wills of Thomas, senior or his eldest son, Richard.

There was no doubt that Roberts was an innovative craftsman if it is assumed that the upholstery on the major sets of green velvet or damask-covered furniture at Houghton is his work. One important set of walnut and parcel-gilt side chairs have unusual drop-in seats (Pls 167–9). This allowed the upholstery to be carried so that the outer cover did not need to be nailed to the gilded and veneered frame. The gap between the upholstery on this inner seat and the outer cover was filled with a roll of hair, grass and wood chips. The principle of fastening such a cover is observed easily on the walnut side chairs with gilded frames and lion-masks (Pls 182–4). The green silk velvet, lined with glazed scrim, has tiny eyelet holes at the back and corners. These are located on small studs or iron pegs in the seat-rail. Each cover has an embroidered numeral (No.13 is shown) to match it to its relevant numbered chair (Pl. 182). The trim was 'plated' originally in gold (silver-gilt) and has now worn to its silver underlay.[69]

It has been stated, percipiently, that after frequent visits to Houghton it becomes possible to 'appreciate the carving and gilding and how pattern and texture play their part in the complete composition of the house'. Some of its decoration – for example, the stucco work in the stone hall – paid tribute to Sir Robert Walpole's election as a Knight of the Most Noble Order of the Garter in June 1726. The expenditure on the celebrations, as the 1726 vouchers show, was extraordinary, even by early eighteenth-century standards. I have traced elsewhere[70] some of the duties of various craftsmen at the house, including the supplying in 1726 of 184 yards of fine Dutch canvas at 9d a yard to line tapestries.

65 Cornforth (1987) II, pp.104–8.
66 Plumb (1965) p.4.
67 International Genealogical Index, microfiche. 27 October 1691, at St James's, Duke's Place.
68 P.R.O., Prob. 11/660, f.228.

69 I am indebted to Peter Holmes of Spink and Son Ltd for facilitating a detailed examination of these chairs.
70 Beard (1981) pp.173–6; also an account in the Castle Museum, Norwich, exhibition catalogue, Moore, ed. (1996).

The engravings of the house in Isaac Ware's *The Plans, Elevations and Sections of Houghton in Norfolk*, published in 1735, show a central hall and saloon with state apartments to the north and family rooms to the south. The 1745 inventory shows as many as twenty-four chairs in the common parlour on the east front. It is not known where all the sets supplied were originally placed because only two bills by Thomas Roberts survive.[71] That of 24 April 1729 shows, for example, the providing of the drawing room chairs:

> . . . 12 fine wallnuttree Chair frames stuff'd back & seats with a Carved Shell on each foot and a small beed round the seat girts, bottoms curl'd hair linnen to line, and work stuffing and covering them with your own Crimson Damask being Corded and Laced at 32s.   £19.4 –

There was also a settee frame covered *en suite*, and a couch frame covered 'with your own Damask'. The damask was edged with 624 yards of:

> fine Crimson silk flower'd Lace used also to the window curtains in three rooms at 8d a yard   £20.16 –

At this stage Roberts's bill amounted to a little over £904, and continued with the provision of case covers for the chairs, lined in linen. The backs of the chairs and settee were covered with 'Crimson Mantua' (6s 6d a yard), with the use of three thousand nails (3s).

One of the principal rooms at Houghton was the saloon (Pl. 187). The walls were lined with crimson caffoy, of which 164 yards were provided by Thomas Roberts at 14s 6d a yard (£118 18s 0d).[72] The bill is undated but seems to refer to items supplied to the end of January 1730. The design has a vertical repeat of 54 inches with three complete repeats being used. Twelve chairs, two settees, and four stools were covered with the rich caffoy, with a stamped harateen for the backs. I noted in 1981[73] that the carver James Richards was busy at Houghton. He was soon also to carve, with extraordinary skill, the sea creatures which adorned the state barge (1732) designed by Kent for Frederick, Prince of Wales.[74] It seems reasonable to assume that he was responsible for the rich carving on the saloon chairs at Houghton (Pl. 185) but attributions are always too hazardous: equally Benjamin Goodison or William Bradshaw could have done the work as effectively.

Towards mid-October 1731, Francis III, Duke of Lorraine, visited England, and, as the husband-presumptive of Maria Theresa of Austria, was courted carefully. He visited Hampton Court and Kensington Palace and was a popular guest at many other dinner tables. Towards the end of 1731 Sir Robert Walpole invited him to Houghton to see his fine great house, then complete in most of its essentials. One that was lacking, however, was the green velvet bed. Sir Robert had already used a plain green silk velvet to hang the drawing room, bedchamber and dressing room. Thomas Roberts's name is endorsed on an undated estimate of the yardage required for this, $521\frac{3}{4}$ yards.[75] Lord Hervey was at Houghton with Stephen Fox in the summer of 1731 as a guest at Sir Robert's house-party, the Norfolk Congress, held twice a year for intimate friends.[76] He indicated that the rooms were not yet finished – 'the furniture is to be green velvet and tapestry'. The duke had to sleep in the embroidered bed (Pl. 150), a fact referred to by Horace Walpole in 1743: 'His Highness, Francis, Duke of Lorraine, afterwards Grand Duke of Tuscany and since Emperor, lay in this Bed, which stood where the velvet one is now when he came to visit Sir Robert Walpole at Houghton.'[77]

It has been assumed that the green velvet bed (Pls 188–94) was upholstered by Roberts at the house. A little confusingly, however, it was announced in *The Daily Post* in November 1732: 'A Crimson Velvet bed with Gold Fringes said to have cost £3,000 finished to be sent . . . to Houghton.'[78] Strangely, so important a bed is not mentioned ten years later by Horace Walpole or, indeed, by anyone else. Crimson and green velvets

71 Cambridge University Library, Cholmondeley (Houghton) MSS.
72 The Saloon caffoy pattern is illustrated by Cornforth (1987) II, p.106. See also the discussion in Moore, ed. (1996).
73 Beard (1981) p.174.
74 Beard (1970) pp.488–94.
75 Cornforth (1987) II, p.106.
76 Halsband (1973) pp.120–1.
77 Horace Walpole, *Aedes Walpolianae*, in Collected Works, 1798, Vol. II, p.257.
78 *The Daily Post*, 16 November 1732.

are not easily confused, but the account of a London making may be true. Unfortunately the only bill[79] to survive is that of 1732 from Walter Turner, Richard Hill and Robert Pitter at the White Hart in the Strand, amounting to £1,219 3s 11d. The principal items, accounting for all the expenditure except for some £21, were:

		£	s	d
266¾	yds dble rich gold clouded lace			
209	″ do			
36¼	cord			
305	″ Gold Vellum Rivicea	584	8	12
8	″ small do			
202	″ small Vellum ornaments do			
8	″ vellum corners do			
16¾	yds Dble rich gold bullion fringe with a vellum head	481	11	12
87	yds Dble rich gold bullion roses			
6	″ gold bullion tassells do			
11	Dble rich gold ornaments with bullion roses and a large vellum bottom for the shell with Flowers do for the Tester and Pedestal and a large vellum Flower for the Counterpain, do	131	12	12

The chairs (Pl. 182) for the velvet Bedchamber were part of a large set of thirty-three *en suite* with settees and stools ordered for three of the state apartments (the velvet drawing room, van Dyck dressing room and the bedchamber). They were intended to complement the green velvet state bed and were probably made towards the end of 1731. Lord Hervey's comment, quoted above, indicated that the state rooms were not finished at his visit in the summer of 1731. By observing recently the slightly different colour in two weavings of the covering green velvet,[80] it has been possible to establish that the sets in light olive green silk were for the velvet drawing room and green velvet bedchamber and those in a blue-green velvet were used in the van Dyck dressing room.

At the north-east corner of the house was the cabinet, hung, as Horace Walpole also noted in 1743 (two years before the important inventory of 1745), with green velvet. It was furnished with a table, two settees and fifteen chairs (some armchairs), covered with green velvet, and including the important parcel gilt walnut chairs with hoof feet (Pls 167–9), of which several remain at the house, trimmed in 'silver' lace; others have been sold across the years.[81] It has been possible to photograph the interesting and rare slip-in seat (Pls 168–9) of one chair sold in 1994[82] when it was stripped down prior to re-upholstery. The slip-in seat would have carried the webbing supporting the upholstery materials within a cover, which was then covered overall with the green velvet. The practical reason for this method of upholstering the chairs (other than the chance it gave to divide tasks within a busy workshop) was, as noted, to avoid nailing into a veneered or a gilded frame. Among so much at Houghton mention should be made of two further sets of furniture, firstly the carved and gilded chairs with eagle head arms covered in green damask of the Amberley pattern (Pl. 173). They were intended for use in the marble parlour, which was in progress for some three years, from 1730. The 1730 vouchers record the cubic capacities of Plymouth, black and gold, purple and white, and veined marbles obtained for this room from Henry Bowman by the London mason, Christopher Cass, in partnership with Andrews Jelfe. Careful study of the two inventories of 1745 and 1792 has shown that the green colour scheme was rigorously followed for this room too. In 1745 the marble parlour contained a settee and twelve armchairs,

79   Cambridge University Library, Cholmondeley (Houghton) MSS., 1732 vouchers.
80   For explanations about the green silk velvets used see Cornforth, quoted Christie's, 8 December 1994, sale catalogue of furniture from Houghton, p.316 and in Moore, ed. (1996).
81   Sotheby's, 29 January 1960, lot 117, six chairs, assumed to have come from Houghton (but I think this is unlikely), now in locations in New York, Melbourne, London and Leeds – the distribution noted in the sale catalogue describing two more chairs, Christie's, 8 December 1994, lot 126.
82   Cornforth (1987) II, p.108.

which by 1792 were described as covered in green silk damask with serge case covers. The chairs are still in the house, some in store, covered in what might be the original damask, with two sold in 1994.[83]

Secondly, there is a splendid series of walnut chairs upholstered in caffoy (Pl. 172), intended for the yellow drawing room on the west front of the house, next to the blue damask bedchamber. It was hung with yellow caffoy and has a plaster ceiling, incorporating at its centre the Garter star. The 1745 inventory includes in its listing for this room a couch and three pillows, twelve chairs and two settees. The chairs in yellow caffoy had, by 1792, pink tammy cases because, by that date, the walls had been rehung with rose coloured silk hangings.[84]

UPHOLSTERERS TO THE PRINCE OF WALES

The antagonism between George II, Queen Caroline and their eldest son is not of concern here. Anyone, however, who reads the letter the king sent in 1736, expelling Frederick from St James's Palace, will recognize the depth of the rift between them.[85] The prince had come from Hanover in December 1728 and the intervening years, family matters apart, were filled with the pleasant task of creating a patronage of art and artists of all kinds.[86] This patronage was to make a significant contribution to the decorative arts in the rococo years. He married Princess Augusta of Saxe-Gotha in April 1736, from which time an annuity of £50,000 was paid. Soon he was busy spending in building at Kew and at Carlton House. Benjamin Goodison's name as cabinet-maker appears consistently in the vouchers of expenditure[87] of both Frederick and his wife, but his upholsterer was George Cure.

George Cure was probably the son and successor of a George Cure who was active as an upholsterer at the end of the seventeenth century. Cure junior's work seems to have been entirely for the Prince of Wales. He was appointed to be the prince's upholsterer in January 1730 and was then living at the sign of the Three Golden Chairs in the Haymarket.

In 1732 William Kent had designed a royal barge for the prince, now at the National Maritime Museum, London. It was carved superbly by James Richards, gilded by Paul Petit (who also made wonderful picture frames to the prince's order), with George Cure doing upholstery to the value of £49 16s 8d. This included providing the chintz curtains and flags, green cloth for the table and laying the armorial decked carpet in the state house, and making the case-covers and awnings to shield items from the sun and spray.[88]

Aside from his almost exclusive service to the prince and his wife Cure had a connection with the Company of Upholders which still continued to function from Exeter Exchange (p.148) in the Strand. On behalf of the company he had furnished mourning in 1732 at Norfolk House for the death of Thomas, eighth Duke of Norfolk. His trustees had acquired the house in 1722 and it was to Norfolk House that Frederick, Prince of Wales went in September 1737 after the estrangement with his father. The Duchy of Cornwall vouchers[89] list a payment of £1,312 to the upholsterer William Bradshaw for working on Norfolk House 'for ye reception of His Royal Highness ye Prince of Wales and his Family', together with £417 to a carpenter and £99 10s to a smith. He leased the house at an annual rent said to be £1,200,[90] and it was there that the future George III was born on 24 May 1738. But the house was really in a dangerous structural condition, and so in 1739 the prince leased Cliveden in Buckinghamshire[91] from Lady Orkney and proceeded to live there in great style until his death in 1751. A typical entry for his work at Cliveden reads:

> 21 May 1743 for a Windsor Chair for Lord Carnarvon   11s
> For a fine large Turkey Carpitt for the Rooms where the young Princes Dine in,
>   by Ordr.   £7 7s

83 Christie's, 8 December 1994, lot 130.
84 Cornforth (1994) pp.iv–x.
85 Smollett (1765) VI, p.281.
86 Rorschach (1991) and (1993).
87 Duchy of Cornwall Office, London.

88 Beard (1970) p.491.
89 Duchy of Cornwall Office, London. Vouchers, Vol. VII (1737) December 31.
90 *Survey of London* XXIX (1960) p.191.
91 Crathorne (1995).

For a fine Large Hanin blankitt bound with white Ribbon for Prince George	£1 7s
For 3 Large Green Sherge coushions fil'd with flox for the Doggs	£1 3s
For Cuttong out and Makeing 2: crimson Lutstring cases for 2: Easy Chairs & Coushions for their	
Royall Highness to Dine on	£1 4s

As well as his upholstery duties, and after the prince's death in 1751, Cure filled the role of Wardrobe Keeper to Princess Augusta. For this he received a salary of £50 a year. As he was friendly with the joiner and chair-maker Henry Williams (and his daughter Katherine Naish) who were active in the service of the Great Wardrobe, he could effect requirements more speedily. As Wardrobe Keeper it was his responsibility to move items about to wherever the princess was staying. It was a duty he had undertaken in her husband's lifetime – to Kew, Norfolk House, Carlton House and to the seventeenth-century Leicester House, built by Robert Sidney, second Earl of Leicester. After almost thirty years in royal service Cure died in 1759 with his goods and chattels being administered for his two children, George and Capel, who were minors at this time.

WILLIAM BRADSHAW AND THE TAPESTRY-MAKERS

As with so many craftsmen, little is known of the first thirty years or so in the life of the cabinet-maker, upholsterer and 'tapissier' William Bradshaw (1700–75). It has been established that he was born in 1700 in Cockerham, probably the son of James Bradshaw and Elizabeth Clark, who were married there in 1696. William acquired Halton Hall, Lancashire in 1743 as a place for semi-retirement. His imposing mausoleum is in the churchyard at Halton.[92] However he comes to notice first in 1727 in a law-suit brought by William Hogarth, as plaintiff, against the Soho tapestry-weaver, Joshua Morris.

The tapestry workshops in Soho derived from those under royal patronage at Mortlake, which were established in 1619. By the late seventeenth century the Great Wardrobe's tapestry workshops had been set up in Great Queen Street, under the patronage of the Wardrobe's Master, Ralph Montagu, later the first Duke of Montagu. There was a talented succession of yeoman arras-workers in John Vanderbank (d.1717) and his younger son Moses, followed by the painter, John Ellys. A worker of great skill who was known for his Soho *Arabesque* tapestries was Joshua Morris, who occupied a house and workshops in Frith Street. It has been suggested that the high quality of his tapestries may be due to their having been designed by Andien de Clermont, a French painter resident in England from about 1716 to 1756. In *The Daily Journal* of 26 November 1726 Morris had advertised 'a large Quantity of Curious Fine New Tapistry Hangings' to be sold by auction. He was in active business and that attracted attention from enemies.

In 1728 the painter and engraver William Hogarth started an action against Morris in the Court of Common Pleas. He accused Morris of failing to pay for a design of a tapestry. Hogarth won his case and was paid £30. In his defence Morris called on both his several workmen (including one of the Danthon family whose work is on a chair at Uppark, (Pl. 239) and another well-known Soho tapestry maker in the person of William Bradshaw (d.1775). They were uncertain of the usefulness of Hogarth's painting to Morris, but agreed with him, naturally enough, that the design 'was not finished in a workmanlike manner and that it was impossible for them to work tapestry by it'.

Morris moved from Frith Street in 1728 and his workshops were taken over by Bradshaw, who in 1730 was joined by the artist Tobias Stranover (1684–1756), seemingly as his partner.[93] The names have been formally linked since they were noted on a tapestry-covered settee (with six chairs *en suite*) formerly at Belton House, Lincolnshire and sold from there by Lord Brownlow in 1929: 'A suite of Queen Anne walnut Furniture, on cabriole legs and club feet, the seats and backs stuffed, and covered with Soho tapestry, woven

92 Stuart (1994) pp.8–11.
93 Thorpe (1946) pp.530–1; *Survey of London*, XXXIV (1966) p.517.

with vases of flowers, groups of flowers and fruit, and on the settee a medallion of poultry with parrots at the sides, and a medallion of Venus and Cupids in strapwork borders . . .'[94] The suite then 'disappeared', but has finally been traced, to be illustrated again in this book, with a detail too of the important names of Stranover/ Bradshaw (Pls 176–7). In 1914 W. G. Thomson had noted[95] Bradshaw's signature 'with the cross of St George' on a tapestry of a hunting scene, and those in the Cabal Room at Ham House are also signed by him. The provision of tapestries to hang or as chair covers was an activity which suited Bradshaw's primary role as an upholsterer. At the same time he was skilled enough in the service of his principal patron, the second Earl Stanhope, at Chevening in Kent to erect the great geometrical staircase there, seemingly designed by the French Huguenot architect, Nicholas Dubois.[96]

In 1732 Bradshaw and Stranover separated and the upholsterer moved to 27 Soho Square, where at some time before June 1735 a Paul Dominique assigned the thirty-five year lease to him. The back premises extended southwards down the west side of Greek Street to include the sites of nos 59 and 60. It is probable that Bradshaw had workshops here, although he gave up the house in Soho Square in 1748 and retained the back premises only. He was assessed for rates at No.60 from 1748 to 1751 and at No.59 from 1752 to 1754.

The furniture Bradshaw supplied to Chevening in 1736 (Appendix A31) is still more or less intact at the house. Principally, it included two suites, a mahogany one, originally of twelve armchairs and two sofas (of which eleven chairs and one sofa survive), covered with Soho tapestry (Pl. 198) and a carved and gilt set of chairs and a 'love seat'.[97] The backs and slats of the tapestry covered chairs seem devised in a rectilinear way to show it off to advantage. A number of other chairs have been attributed to Bradshaw and Stranover, mainly on the evidence of the 'signed' Brownlow settee; principally, a set of upholstery panels for four armchairs (Pl. 203) and two settees.[98] Bradshaw also completed an unfinished series of tapestries by John Vanderbank at Holkham. In the second edition of the elder Matthew Brettingham's book *The Plans and Elevations of the late Earl of Leicester's House at Holkham* (1761) which his son, Matthew junior, issued in 1773 it was claimed that Mr Coke's bedchamber was hung with tapestry by Vanderbank after designs by Francesco Albani, 'excepting the two Door-Pieces (Venus, Vulcan and Cupids) which additions were manufactured by the late Mr Bradshaw'. This is a little puzzling because both William Bradshaw and his relative George Smith Bradshaw were still alive. However, William had retired, and as he was then out of the younger Brettingham's circle he may have thought him dead. George Smith Bradshaw is unlikely to have been the intended 'Mr Bradshaw', as he lived on till 1812. His partnership with Paul Saunders, which continued the Soho tapestry tradition, is mentioned below (p.160). They took over William Bradshaw's workshops at 59 Greek Street in 1755.[99] One final aspect of William's active career was the support he seems to have given in the 1740s to Robert Gillow the elder. This enabled Gillow to set up in London, win the support of titled patrons and to lay a successful foundation to what became a renowned firm (p.222).

Bradshaw and Benjamin Goodison

The cabinet-maker Benjamin Goodison, who had trained under James Moore,[100] had succeeded his master in royal service in 1726–7. There is evidence in his many bills that whilst primarily a cabinet-maker he did supply upholstered furniture too. He seems to have been involved in this way with William Bradshaw and the important commission for furniture for Longford Castle, Wiltshire, ordered in particular by Sir Jacob Bouverie, who was created Viscount Folkestone in 1747. Unfortunately the Longford accounts note names and payments only:

94 Christie's. 14 March 1929, lot 78.
95 Thomson (1914) p.155, fig.51.
96 Colvin (1995) p.323.
97 Edwards and Jourdain (1955) pl. 52.

98 Beard (1994) pp.842–9.
99 *Survey of London*, XXXIV (1966) p.518.
100 Beard and Gilbert (1986) p.351.

1737	23 Dec. Mr Goodison – Cabinet-maker – a bill with some old goods	
	exchanged	£148
1740	21 Oct. Goodison furniture	£413
1741	1 Dec. Goodison	£71 11s
1742	21 May Goodison £100	
1743	28 May Goodison cabt. maker	£90
1743	15 Dec. Goodison	£342 5s
1745	22 Feb.	£21 3s 6d
Gallery at Longford		
Goodison		400

These payments amount to £1,585 19s 6d and allow attribution of the frames of the mahogany and gilt day-beds, stools, armchairs and chairs to be attributed to Goodison. Those in the long gallery and elsewhere, in either green damask, *en suite* to the 83 yards provided to hang the walls at 12s a yard, or (*en suite* to the wall hangings of the green drawing room Pl. 201) in Genoese cut-velvet, are likely to have been upholstered by Bradshaw or another London upholsterer, William Kilpin. Whatever the success of his career he was insolvent by November 1759 and died in 1762.[101] The chairs in the green drawing room are unusual in that the covering is taken behind a fretted rail (Pl. 202). The backs are fastened in by turn-buttons. Bradshaw also provided carpets and arranged the hanging of tapestry.[102]

The 1740 account entries read:

> Laid out on the Gallery at Longford.
> Mr Goodison, the Cabinet Makers bill   £400.0.0
> Kilpin, uph. £125 for Gallery
>   £42 for Chapel

There are further entries in 1741 and 1742:

> 28 November 1741 Bradshaw the upholsterer for the furniture of my chamber
> at Longford   £144 15s

and

> 17 December 1742 Mr Bradshaw the upholsterer for a great chair at Longford   £12 8s

Finally, it should be stated that the green velvet chairs at Longford Castle have been attributed to Giles Grendey,[103] but I do not agree with this. Payment is admittedly made in the Longford accounts of £68 in 1739 to 'Greenday, chair-maker', but as a prominent cabinet-maker and a member of the Joiners' Company (of which he was made a liveryman in 1729 and Master in 1766) he is unlikely to have been an active upholsterer.[104]

SOME LESSER NAMES

Any detailed research in archives throws up information about many upholsterers of whom all too little is, at present, known. William Dale (fl.1709–24) was obviously successful financially in that he had profited from speculation in the South Sea Company and purchased the Bolingbroke estate for £50,000 in 1720.[105] But Dale

101   *Ibid.*, p.513.
102   *Country Life*, 26 December 1931, p.716.
103   Edwards and Jourdain (1955) p.47, citing *Country Life*, 19 December 1931, p.698.
104   Beard and Gilbert (1986) p.372.
105   *York Mercury*, 12 December 1720: 'Mr Dale, an upholsterer of Covent Garden, has purchasd the estate which belonged to the late Viscount Bolingbroke for £50,000'.

seriously over-extended himself. The estate at Kenwood he had also acquired in 1720, from the Earls of Islay and Bute, reverted to the Earl of Islay in 1724.

The many French Huguenot members of the Deschamps family, stemming from James Deschamps of Curry in Poitou, included the London upholsterer Francis Deschamps (1715–93), whose sister-in-law had, in 1742, married the talented silversmith and Chelsea porcelain manufacturer, Nicholas Sprimont. Many members of the family occur in the records of the Upholders' Company.[106] The London upholsterer, John Howard (fl.1710, d.1742), active at West Smithfield, also dealt in tapestries and Oriental carpets. His trade card,[107] c.1728, stated that he:

> Makes and Sells all manner of Household Furniture, viz. Damask, Mohair, Workt and Stuff Beds, & Bedding, with Chairs and Glasses, all sorts of Silk Worsted Damask, Camblets & Water'd Cheneys, &c. by Wholesale or Retale. Where are also sold all Sorts of Persia, Muskat and Turkey Carpets, fine and ordinary Tapestry Hangings, at reasonable Rates. N.B. Fine Tapestry and Carpets are clean'd after the best manner.

The Upholders' Company records are useful at charting the start of many subsequently successful careers. In 1689 the upholsterer Henry Heasman, senior was made free and ten years later, in 1699, he was the company's steward.[108] Heasman traded from the Great Piazza at Covent Garden and his son, Henry, was apprenticed to him in 1710. Heasman lived in the house formerly occupied by the painter, Sir Godfrey Kneller. The Heasmans' main activity was spread over twenty years for the Hon. Wrey and Lady Mary Saunderson for their London house in Grosvenor Square and that in Lincolnshire. A considerable amount of furniture was obviously freshened with new covers: for example, on 10 December 1716 they charged for reupholstering two window seats with curled hair and green and gold coverings, and two large settees, re-covered with green silk, 'Flower'd with Gold' and trimmed with lace.[109]

The Colombine family in Norwich are known principally for their work in the 1730s at Holkham Hall, Norfolk. Paul Colombine was the son of a Norwich physician. He was apprenticed in 1714 to a London upholsterer, William Braithwaite, active in Cornhill, and became free of the Upholders' Company in 1721. He was not prompt in subsequent years in paying his quarterage to the company and was asked to send it 'to Town' in 1732.[110] He worked at Holkham in both 1743 and 1757.

In this brief selection of the less well known upholsterers, there must be mention of the London upholsterer, Remey George. He had been apprenticed to Thomas Dixon (who had worked at Felbrigg Hall, Norfolk in 1709–10)[111] in 1697 and was free of the Upholders' Company in August 1704. By 1712 he had received the company's livery.[112] His most important activity yet known was in supplying furniture in 1718 to Arthur Ingram, third Viscount Ingram, for use at his Yorkshire houses of Barrowby and Temple Newsam and for Hills Place, near Horsham, Sussex. George's bill of £471 8s 10d was submitted in May 1718 but was not settled in its entirety until 1726, partly due to the third Viscount's death in 1720 and problems arising from speculation in South Sea stock. I note from George's two published bills[113] for this commission an entry for 21 February 1718, from a total bill of £843 3s 2½d:

> A very Rich Crimson damask Bed all Compleat Trimmd wth Rich Crimson silk double figur'd Lace, 6 chairs, 2 Elbow Dressing Chairs, made of Damask, Trimm'd wth Silk Lace & false cases to them made of Crimson haratine, all Compleat and Fashionable   170.0.0.
> 108 yards of Fine Rich crimson Damask ye same wth ye Bed, to make 5 Large pieces of

106 Guildhall Library, MSS. 7141/1 and 2. Francis was apprenticed to Susanna, widow of Isaac Deschamps, in 1729 (MS. 7141/2, f.2).

107 There is a copy, Lincolnshire C.R.O., MS., 2 ANC 12/D/18.

108 Guildhall Library, MS., 7141/1, ff.121, 267.

109 Lincolnshire C.R.O., MS., Monson 101/A/16.

110 Guildhall Library, London, MS. 7141/2, f.19.

111 Norfolk C.R.O., MS., WKC 6/23.

112 Guildhall Library, London, MS., 7141/1, ff.114 and 334.

113 Gilbert (1967) pp.20–1.

hangings, for the Bed chamber and Drawing Room, a saffoy, 4 chaires, 2 square stools ye Backside of the Fire Skreen, & 3 Large window Cushions.   78.6.0

Finally, a consideration of the career of George Reynoldson (1695–1764), a York upholsterer active across most of the reigns of George I and George II. Reynoldson was a Catholic upholsterer and this partly dictated the commissions he obtained. The range of his business is best observed by the advertisement he inserted in the *York Courant* on 1 October 1734:

> George Reynoldson upholsterer, undertaker and sworn appraiser, in Stonegate, York. Makes all sorts of looking glasses and sconces, in gilt Mahogany or walnut frames and coach glasses . . . He also makes and sells all sorts of Beds, of Mohair, Silk and worsted Damasks, Camblets, Harrateens, cheneys and printed stuffs; Feather Beds, Mattresses, Blankets, Quilts, Rugs and Coverlets, *Flanders* and *English* Ticks, Paper Hangings, imbosed, damasked or plain, Tapestry Hangings, Silk, Worsted Bed-Lace, *Turkey*, *Muscate*, *Persian* and *French* carpets, List, Hair or Painted Floor Cloths, *Dutch* and Floor Matts . . . He also undertakes Funerals at reasonable rates and in decent manner will perform them to any part of *Great Britain*, when required.

He undertook the Catholic funerals of Lady Hungate and the Fairfax children, among others.

An upholsterer working in York could benefit from the neighbouring county gentry using the city for most of its material needs. There is correspondence between the Grimston family of Kilnwick Hall in both 1748 and 1752. On the first occasion Reynoldson had arranged a funeral, and on the second he had written to John Grimston to ask for instructions for making the curtains for principal rooms and for wall-papering.[114] Reynoldson had married Mary Brigham, daughter of a York woollen draper, shortly before 1733. She was a Catholic too and related to other papist families in Yorkshire, notably the Fairfaxes.[115] After her husband's death she carried on his business and I give brief details of that in later pages (p.220) and publish some documents in the appendix (A37).

THE GILBERTS AND WILLIAM REASON

I have mentioned (p.147) John Gilbert taking over the upholsterer's duties for the Crown at the death of Thomas Phill in 1728, and of his own death in 1729. The duties he had carried out then devolved over the next ten years or so on his (presumed) widow, Sarah Gilbert, who was latterly, 1736 to 1741, in partnership with William Reason. Sarah Gilbert was active in continuing the new fashion for festoon curtains made popular by Thomas Phill and was soon ripping things apart. In 1730 for the 'Duke's New Apartment at St James's' she charged £6 10s 'For Ripping to peices Some Yellow Mohair Window Curtains and Hangings and making them up into 4 Large Festoon Window Curtains, Yellow Serge to cover the Laths and for O's, Tape, Sewing Silk &c., and putting up the Same.'[116] In company with the joiner, Henry Williams, mercer, Henry Shelley and lace-man William Weeks, Sarah Gilbert seems to have specialized in making curtains and setting them on 'bright rodds with pulleys' on the pulley laths installed by Williams. She used brass O's, lead 'plumbetts', and trimmed all with lace. Her work in 1733 in the Chapel at St James's Palace for the marriage of the Princess Royal to the Prince of Orange must have looked rich and splendid:[117]

> for making 2 Crimson Taffeta Festoon Curtains to fix up to the Ceiling at each end of the Chappel with Vallance to them, trim'd with Gold Lace with large Gold Roses fixt over them to Answer the Roses in the Ceiling.   £30

114   Ingram (1951).
115   Hutchinson (1976) p.31.

116   P.R.O., LC9/288, No.14.
117   P.R.O., LC9/289, No.17.

Equally, there were both many humdrum tasks for her, such as, in 1735:[118] 'Making Taffeta Curtains for a Night Table, 7s 6d' and the grander ones of providing, in 1738, pulpit cloth, altar cloth and altar carpet for the chapel of the Earl of Albemarle as Governor of Virginia.[119] By this time Sarah had joined forces with William Reason, and at some point in 1742 she seems to have remarried, becoming Sarah Lowry.

Sarah's partner, William Reason, continued on alone after 1744 and was used frequently by the court of George II. He provided carpets, curtains and bedding and covered the king's chairs and footstools at several of the royal palaces. Yet there was a flaw in someone so well thought of: he was dismissed finally from his post on account of dishonest practices.[120]

WILLIAM MASTERS

A few London upholsterers are known mainly through commissions for Scottish patrons. Two such are William Masters (fl.1740–61) and James Cullen. Masters ran a flourishing business in London from the sign of The Golden Fleece in Coventry Street, near to Piccadilly. His only recorded commission is Blair Castle, Perthshire, where he supplied furniture, c.1746–60 to the second Duke of Atholl. Twenty bills[121] survive, totalling some £4,700, for furnishings and decoration of Blair Castle.[122] He was able, equally, to supply both grand and serviceable furniture. Interestingly, in February 1749 he provided a type of chair better known as a Chippendale production:

> 10 Mahogy Ribband back chairs with Carved Knees stuft in Canvas
> & Check cases   a) 32s. £16.0.0.

and in the same bill, for 15 May 1750:

> A wainscot Bedstd on Castors 5 ft wide 6 ft 6 long & 7.6 high. Mahogy feet Posts fluted on
> an Eagles Paw   £3.10.0.
> . . . To 129 yds of yellow silk Worsted Damask for ye Bed, two Peices of Hangings, 18
> Chairs & 2 Settees   a) 6s. £43.10.9
> To 10 Doz 6 yds of the best Silk figure Covd Lace for ye Bed & Hangings   £1.11.6

The settees and mahogany back chairs 'Stuft over the Rail' were covered *en suite* in the yellow damask, and had smart yellow and white check case covers.

So much furniture for a destination hundreds of miles from London necessitated careful packing. In 1758, for example, Masters charged for:

> 13 Packing Cases Containing 1017 feet at 3d including Battins, Nails & time in
> Packing   12.14. –
> To 2 Matts.   0.2. –
> To Coarse Paper to Line ye Packing Cases & fine Lawn Paper to putt ye Bed in . . .
> Do upon ye Side of ye Curtains
> Also on ye Vallins & Basses   0.14.0

There was also need to take additional care on fine furniture that rust from nail shanks did not spoil it. A minor expenditure, but necessary:

> 8000 Large Gilt Nails a) £2   16 – –
> 216 yd of Red silk ferret to put under the Nails   1.16 –

118 P.R.O., LC9/289, No.44.
119 *Ibid.*, No.23.
120 Beard and Gilbert (1986) pp.732–3.
121 Blair Castle, Perthshire.
122 Coleridge (1963).

Patrons were demanding furniture from makers such as William Masters with Gothic and rococo embellishments, and this ready market was encouraged by a growing number of pattern-books, pre-eminently by Thomas Chippendale's *The Gentleman and Cabinet-Maker's Director*, with a first edition in 1754 and two more in 1755 and 1762.

WRIGHT AND ELWICK

Richard Wright stated on the informative trade card (Pl. 234) he issued in the 1750s (along with his partner, Edward Elwick of York) that he had 'been in ye direction of ye Greatest Tapestry Manufactory in England for upwards of Twenty Years . . .' This probably referred to the important Soho tapestry workshops, which in their final phase were to come, about 1757, under the supervision of Paul Saunders (p.160). Wright had come from London in the mid-1740s and took up with Elwick, then a young man in his early twenties. They set up in Wakefield and were soon to become the pre-eminent firm of cabinet-makers and upholsterers in Yorkshire during the second half of the eighteenth century. Their many commissions have been listed[123] and fall mostly beyond the limits of this chapter. However, as early as 1746 they had started to work for the second Earl of Strafford at Wentworth Castle. This great house, vying for supremacy in length with its near neighbour, Wentworth Woodhouse, had been built for the first Earl of Strafford, *c*.1710–20, by the Prussian architect, John van Bodt (1670–1745). The first Earl had been Ambassador to Prussia from 1706 to 1711 and directed some of the building operation of his house from Berlin.[124] In her travel diary, Elizabeth, first Duchess of Northumberland, noted at Wentworth Castle in 1760 a suite of 'French chairs embd with flowers upon Brown by the famous Mr Wright'.[125] Five armchairs and a settee answering this description were sold from Wentworth Castle in 1919: two of the chairs, *c*.1746, are in the Victoria and Albert Museum, London (W36–1964), and others have been in and out of the hands of prominent furniture-dealers. My illustration (Pl. 210) shows how superb they are, adequate testimony to Wright and Elwick's considerable abilities.

THE FULHAM TAPESTRY FACTORY

Whilst there is still considerable doubt about all the details of the Fulham factory, it is clear that it was conducted in the early 1750s by a naturalized Frenchman, Peter Parisot. He had taken over the foundering enterprise from two French carpet weavers from the national manufactory at the Savonnerie who had emigrated to England and had endeavoured, *c*.1750, to make it all succeed. Parisot took them with him when he moved his own workshop from Paddington to Fulham. According to a pamphlet he issued he said that he practised tapestry weaving after the style of the Gobelins and his carpet-weaving was in the style in use at Chaillot. He tried to school his young artists in the arts of drawing, weaving and dyeing, and stated that he employed a hundred workmen. But despite good patronage from the Duke of Cumberland and others, the venture foundered and a catalogue was issued in 1755 announcing the sale of all the stock. Some items currently in the Metropolitan Museum of Art, New York[126] might be identified with those listed in the 1755 catalogue, and a panel for a fire-screen in that collection is illustrated here (Pl. 224).

Parisot's factory, which had moved to Exeter, was purchased in 1756 by a Swiss Huguenot, Claude Passavant, who continued the activity there. In the six years he flourished some superb woollen carpets were made. Only three are now known to survive: the one for the Earl of Dumfries (Pl. 240), woven with the inscription 'EXON 1758', another of 1757 in the Victoria and Albert Museum, London (T78–1946), and one at Petworth House, Sussex, dated, again, 'EXON 1758', and possibly the prize-winning entry for the Society of Arts competition in 1758. The Earl of Dumfries, an important early patron of Thomas Chippendale, had acquired his carpet in London in 1759, seemingly from the retailers Crompton and Spinnage of Charing

123 Beard and Gilbert (1986) pp.1006–8.
124 Colvin (1995) p.136.
125 Percy and Jackson-Stops (1974) p.251.
126 Standen, II (1985) Nos 132, 133.

Cross.[127] In March 1758 Passavant had been joint winner with Thomas Whitty of Axminster of the Society of Arts premium 'for the best Carpet in one Breadth after the Manner of Turkey Carpets'.[128] This had given a prominence to their activities but there was an English antipathy to tapestry carpets in favour of those woven at the French royal factory of the Savonnerie at Chaillot.[129] Passavant's factory functioned for only a short time and, despite his having in his employ the French weavers brought over from France by Parisot, and one from the Gobelins named J.-B. Grignon, it closed with his bankruptcy in 1761. What the spirited commercial interlude had done was to persuade weavers such as Thomas Moore of Moorfields[130] to take the lead with the production of carpets of neo-classical design to fit in with the decorative schemes of Robert Adam at Syon House, Osterley Park and elsewhere. Moore's competitor, Thomas Whitty, was also very active with his manufacture of carpets at Axminster in Devon. He provided fine examples to Adam designs at Saltram in Devon. That in the saloon (1770, £126), with another in the library (now dining room, Adam drawing for the ceiling 1768), echo the ceiling designs. More of Whitty's Axminster carpets were provided for other Adam patrons such as Edwin Lascelles of Harewood House and William Weddell of Newby Hall, both in Yorkshire.

PAUL SAUNDERS AND GEORGE SMITH BRADSHAW

On 5 December 1751 Paul Saunders was admitted as a freeman of the Upholders' Company.[131] He had been born in January 1722 to a London skinner, John Saunders and his wife Sarah. In 1738 he was bound to a seven year apprenticeship to a London upholsterer, Michael Bradshaw, who himself had been apprenticed in 1710 to Richard Bradshaw. Both Richard and Michael were presumably related to the important upholsterer, William Bradshaw (p.153). By 1747 the young apprentice had set up in Westminster and within three years had moved to a more advantageous address 'near Slaughter's Coffee house in St Martin-in-the-Fields'. It was at the coffee house at this time that a group of artists and craftsmen important to the spread of the rococo style gathered.[132]

About 1751 Saunders and the cabinet-maker, upholsterer and tapestry maker, George Smith Bradshaw (1717–1812) entered into a partnership as 'Smith Bradshaw and Saunders'. This may have included William Bradshaw too because they succeeded him in 1755 as rate-payers at 59 Greek Street. They also leased Carlisle House on the east side of Soho Square from 1753 and established workshops there. One of the ever-present fears to a furniture-maker was the threat of fire raging through a highly combustible stock. Whilst they might nervously insure against this, with the Sun or Hand-in-Hand companies (as the partnership had done with the Sun since 1750), the risks remained great. A notice in the *Public Advertiser* (6 February 1755) makes sombre reading: 'The late unhappy Fire at the Workshop of Mess. Smyth, Bradshaw & Saunders, Upholders and Cabinetmakers, Soho, having not only consumed the same, but also the Chests and Working tools of thirty-seven journeymen there employed . . .', whilst their landlord, the second Duke of Portland, tried to help by granting a reversionary lease of Carlisle House until 1853, with the usual fine remitted out of 'His Grace's regard for their loss by the late fire'.[133] For whatever reason, and it is not productive to search for one, Saunders ended the partnership in October 1756, with the announcement concluding, tersely: 'Business will continue to be carried on as usual, by Mr Bradshaw in Greek Street, Soho, and by Mr Saunders in Soho Square, the corner of Sutton Street.'[134] Saunders's stock and equipment was at least substantial enough to be insured, in the same month of 1756, at £3,000.[135]

Throughout his career Saunders seems to have had an important series of patrons supporting him, the Dukes of Cumberland, Norfolk, Northumberland, leading them, and to have been on terms familiar enough to ask, with a considerable literary style, about their health and families. In September 1757 this support had

127 Gilbert, Lomax and Wells-Cole (1987) p.54; Sherrill (1996) pp.152–70.
128 Jacobs (1970) p.25; Sherrill (1996) p.167.
129 Verlet (1982) pp.144–5.
130 Hefford (1977) pp.840–8; Sherrill (1996) pp.171–85.
131 Guildhall Library, London, MS., 7141/2, f.135.

132 Girouard (1966) pp.56–61.
133 Beard and Gilbert (1986) p.783.
134 *London Gazette*, 26–30 October, 1756.
135 Guildhall Library, London, Sun policy registers, Vol. 117, p.410.

been strengthened by Saunders' appointment as Tapestry Maker to His Majesty, thus succeeding John Ellys as Yeoman Arras-Worker to the Great Wardrobe. During their partnership Saunders and Bradshaw had supplied tapestries to both the first Earl of Leicester at Holkham Hall, Norfolk and the Duke of Somerset and the Earl and Countess of Egremont at Petworth House, Sussex. In May 1761 Saunders received a second position in the Great Wardrobe as Yeoman Tapestry Taylor. He arranged the 'upholstery details' of the funeral of the Duke of Cumberland in 1765,[136] but by this time, when he was forty-three years old, he had sold the lease of the Carlisle House site to the carver and gilder, Samuel Norman. He had already moved to the house in Great Queen Street formerly occupied by John Vanderbank and John Ellys, and the site of the Great Wardrobe's tapestry workshops until 1742. Norman agreed to buy the unwrought stock valued at a little over £2,270 and this detailed list has provided an important insight into the contents of an eighteenth century furniture maker's workshop.[137] A contract sharing out cabinet, upholstery and funeral orders for a year from June 1760 was entered into, but problems arose over Norman's repayment of his debt to Saunders, and in 1762 Paul Saunders's trustees filed a suit, to which Norman replied in 1764 with a Chancery bill.[138] This dispute and others were not settled when Norman went bankrupt. From the several examples of Saunders's work which have survived I have illustrated an armchair at Petworth of *c*.1764 (Pl. 276).

BOOKS OF DESIGNS, PARTNERS AND RIVALS

When Thomas Chippendale issued *The Gentleman and Cabinet-Maker's Director* in 1754, with its fulsome dedication to the Earl (later the first Duke) of Northumberland, he took a commanding lead with new designs for almost every kind of furniture – even in Europe there was nothing as comprehensive in a single folio volume. On the title-page it was announced that the book contained 'a large collection of the most Elegant and Useful Designs of Household Furniture in the Gothic, Chinese and Modern Tastes'. English craftsmen who were engaged in the furniture trade, including twenty-eight upholsterers, made up about two-thirds of the 308 subscribers, and most of them lived in London. Chippendale's former master in York, Richard Wood, ordered eight copies; twenty-eight noblemen also subscribed.

The *Director* contained many designs that were frivolously rococo, and sixty-four plates were devoted to Chinese-type furniture. Chippendale included all these exotic forms in his repertoire and I have illustrated (Pls 227–32) a selection of the many forms of bed he published. He exhibited a full mastery of the rococo style in the 1754 edition and was equally adept at the contrasting styles of the 1750s. It has been shown that sixty-four plates in the 1754 edition exhibited 'a marked Chinese character', but by the third, (1762) edition this had been reduced to forty-three; the 'Doom' Bed (Pl. 231), corrected to 'Dome' in the third edition, had also by then been 'deprived of its picturesque Chinoiserie head-board'.

Analysis of the 1762 edition (with plates dated from 1759) show the annual totals incorporating neoclassical motifs to be 2 (1759); 7 (1760); 7 (1761) and 2 (1762). Chippendale was thus early in that field, which was becoming rapidly desirable through the work of architects such as Robert Adam, and was able to invest it all in 'the same unrestrained spirit that he treated Gothic and Chinoserie themes'.[139]

The success of the *Director* encouraged Chippendale to move, in August 1754, into larger premises in St Martin's Lane, which he called 'The Cabinet and Upholstery Warehouse', adopting a chair for his sign. Fire ravaged two of his workshops on a windy Saturday night, 5 April 1755. It destroyed twenty-two chests of journeymen's tools – a significant part of his workforce. However, the damage was less than feared and the insurance money from the Sun office provided an opportunity to rebuild and enlarge the premises.

Apart from Chippendale's leading position there were many other able contenders for a patron's interest and purse, in particular William and John Linnell and John Mayhew and William Ince. William Linnell had served his apprenticeship as a joiner but specialized in carving. Becoming a freeman of the Joiners' Company

136   P.R.O., LC9/293
137   Kirkham (1969) pp.503–13.
138   *Ibid.*, pp.506–10.

139   These comments are based on the analysis by Gilbert (1978) I, pp.108–21.

in 1729, he set up his own general furniture workshop and married; his eldest son John was born in 1729. By the time of his death in 1763 he had formed a successful business with forty to fifty employees for his son John to inherit. John had assisted his father from the early 1750s and he became well known to influential clients such as the banker Robert Child, William Drake of Shardeloes, and Lord Scarsdale of Kedleston. All were to be busy in the 1760s with furnishing their houses. John Linnell headed the firm, based in Berkeley Square, until his own death in 1796 and became noted not only as a talented designer (Pls 225, 236–8) but as a competent businessman.

Most of the Linnells' upholstery was done in their own workshops, but seat furniture was often re-stuffed and re-covered at the patron's house. That they were successful may be attested by the fact that the names of over one thousand clients of the firm have been listed.[140] Two competitors of John Linnell and Chippendale were John Mayhew and William Ince. In 1759, with most of the money coming from Mayhew, they set up business together as Mayhew and Ince at the upper end of Broad Street, Soho. Ince was the designer – he had learned his trade as a cabinet-maker with John West (d.1758), while Mayhew acted as manager and dealt with the upholstery side of their activities; he seems to have been apprenticed to William Bradshaw.[141]

Once Ince and Mayhew had established the outline of a business, they decided, in 1759, to issue designs 'in weekly Numbers'. They imitated Chippendale's *Director* both in the intended number of plates (160) and in the use of Matthias Darly as engraver. Unfortunately they underestimated the amount of work required, and they had to compete with the build-up by Chippendale of issuing plates in parts towards their eventual gathering in a third edition (1762) of the *Director*; the venture foundered in the autumn of 1760, after the late appearance of Part 21. Robert Sayer, one of the most successful eighteenth century print-sellers, not averse to plagiarism when it suited him, then issued in 1760 sixty of the engravings in a volume entitled, in its original form, *Household Furniture in Genteel Taste for the Year 1760*[142] by A Society of Upholsterers, Cabinet-Makers, &c. The title was reissued in 1762 with forty additional plates and reprinted in 1763. In its final folio form Mayhew and Ince's book, titled *The Universal System of Household Furniture*, was dedicated to George Spencer, fourth Duke of Marlborough, for whom the firm was later to work at Blenheim Palace, under the supervision of the duke's architect, Sir William Chambers. Sayer helped in its distribution as he had done with the *Director* and publications by the carver, Thomas Johnson. Rococo, with Gothic and Chinese overtones, formed the main style of the designs. Some were unashamedly copied from the 1754 edition of the *Director*, and explanatory notes were printed in both English and French. At the end of the century Sheraton regarded the book as Ince's: the majority of the designs (Pls 261–73) were his, with Mayhew contributing just eleven plates; it has been observed that the 'inclusion of a small number of distinctive and original furniture types . . . goes some way to relieving the charge of plagiarism as does the accomplished re-interpretation of certain forms popularized by Chippendale.'[143]

In the notes it was stated that the state bed (Pl. XXXII in the edition and Pl. 266 here) was upholstered in blue damask 'and may be esteemed one of the best in England'. The preface indicated that 'the CABINET and UPHOLSTERY Branch is at present raised to a very high Pitch . . . ', an understandable attempt at asserting their position against that of the successful Chippendale, with three editions of the *Director* to his name.

Royal preferment on any scale eluded Chippendale, the Linnells, Mayhew and Ince, and only came late to their successful rivals, the partners William Vile and John Cobb. They had not purchased a copy of the *Director* (at least not by subscription) so as to avoid any charge that they copied (as many of lesser status did) its attractive designs. They had enough ability in any case to survive by their own merits.

Their senior partner, William Hallett the elder, is known to have been a London cabinet-maker from the mid-1730s, having established himself in Great Newport Street, Long Acre, by Christmas 1732. In 1745 he was able to buy the site of Cannons, the first Duke of Chandos's great house at Whitchurch, Middlesex, and to build himself a house on the centre vaults of the old one.

140   Hayward and Kirkham (1980).
141   Kirkham (1974) pp.56–60.
142   Heckscher (1974) pp.61–7; Gilbert (1978) I, p.89.
143   H. Roberts and C. Cator in Beard and Gilbert (1986) p.591.

At this time there was either apprenticed to him, or more likely acting as a journeyman, the young William Vile. He called Hallett 'my master' in 1748[144] and this is one reason why work formerly attributed to him – in the royal collections, at Chatsworth and elsewhere – must, more firmly, be regarded as the work of the older Benjamin Goodison, who had set up on his own by 1727, and preceded Vile in the royal favour. Vile's eventual partner, John Cobb, had been apprenticed as an upholsterer to Tim Money of Norwich in 1729, implying a birth date about 1715. The names of William Vile and John Cobb first appear together in the rate books in 1751, and by the following year they had four premises. On 5 June 1752 William Hallett left Newport Street and, according to the rate books, took a house in St Martin's Lane, next to the newly established 'Wm Vile & Co.' By June 1755 Cobb had taken over Hallett's premises, probably because there was no room for an extensive upholstery shop in the partners' St Martin's Lane premises. A Sun insurance policy records him in 1755 as having his 'Dwelling House . . . over a Gateway leading into the yard of Messrs Vile & Co in St Martin's Lane'.[145] I have noted elsewhere[146] that Hallett married a wealthy heiress in 1756. He seems to have given up active furniture-making, leaving some of this to be dealt with by his son, William, who also married advantageously. Hallett then seems to have acted as a 'sleeping partner' in the Vile and Cobb business, with his bank account showing regular payments in from his active colleagues, in amounts of £150 to £300, almost monthly. For example, the 1758 account has fifteen in-payments from Vile or Cobb, totalling £3,419. In 1761 he received an amazing £2,350 in only four payments.[147] As well as supporting Vile and Cobb, William Hallett had also been active in 1755 in supporting the wish of his nephew, Samuel Norman, to marry Anne Whittle, daughter of the successful carver James Whittle (d.1759). The amazing rococo bed (Pl. 241) by Whittle and Norman (*c*.1758) at Petworth House is testimony enough to the blending of their talents.

The furniture that Vile made in partnership with Cobb was done between about 1752 and 1764. However, as Vile and Cobb's royal service did not begun until 1761 I have considered the activity in chapter VI. In particular their work for George William, sixth Earl of Coventry at Croome Court, Worcestershire had reached a formative point by the time George II died in 1760. Careers which had been fashioned through apprenticeship in his reign saw most of their full flowering in the reign of George III. It was in chairs (Pls 253–4), provided by Vile and Cobb and upholstered by Katherine Naish that George III and Queen Charlotte sat on that momentous day of their coronation, 22 September 1761.

144 Beard (1975) p.114.
145 Westminster City Archives, Rate Books (New Street Ward, Castle Lane) MSS., F519, 527, 530 (1750–5); Guildhall Library, London, Sun policy registers, MS., 11936, 110 (1755) p.387.
146 Beard (1985) pp.220–5.
147 Accounts for Hallett, Vile and Cobb are at the Drummonds Branch, Royal Bank of Scotland, Charing Cross, London; see Beard and Gilbert (1986) p.924.

114.   Chair (*c.*1700) 52 × 20 × 26 in (131.8 × 50.9 × 66.4 cm) *Port Sunlight, Lady Lever Art Gallery*, Inv. LL4058.

En suite to the Dyrham state bed (Pl. 124). It is thought that the chairs and stools supplied to William Blathwayt were given new covers to match the bed when it was made for Queen Anne's state visit.

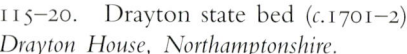

115–20.   Drayton state bed (*c.*1701–2) *Drayton House, Northamptonshire*.

Oak frame and upholstered interior attributed to Etienne (Stephen) Penson, with embroidered curtains documented as by Elizabeth Rickson and Rebekah Dufee. For a discussion of this important bed see pp.135–8. Details show the curtains, cornice, headboard, braid on the counterpoint, and a preserved fragment of the original covering of the *en suite* settee (now reupholstered). For a chair *en suite* see Pl. 111.

121.   Chair of state (1702) 41 × 26 in
(103.5 × 66 cm) *Hatfield House, Hertfordshire.*

Used at the coronation of Queen Anne
with a footstool *en suite.* Gilded frame by
Thomas Roberts, upholstery by Anthony
Ryland originally in blue and gold brocade
(now upholstered in red). The back is
surmounted by the royal arms.

122–3.   Sofa (*c.*1705) 39 × 55 × 25 in (99 ×
140 × 33 cm) *Drumlanrig Castle, Scotland.*

One of a pair. Upholstered in red velvet,
with coronets of a duke and duchess,
worked in silver wire embroidery above the
cypher of Anne, Duchess of Buccleuch. The
duchess lived in great style at Dalkeith
Palace. She bought furniture in London,
employed the cabinet-maker James Moore
and in 1706 Francis Lapiere and his second
wife, to whom I attribute the upholstery of
these sofas. Repaired *c.*1880; stamped hessian
on base of seats 'Fredk Muntzer' of Piccadilly, London.

124–5.   Dyrham state bed (*c.*1705) *on loan to
Dyrham Park, Avon* (The National Trust).

Made for William Blathwayt. Attributed to
Francis Lapiere. Crimson velvet and silk
upholstery. The bed is not mentioned in the
1703 inventory of the contents of Dyrham
Park but is there by 1710. Red and yellow
silk velvet, moulded headboard covered in
Chinese brocaded silk, modern case-
curtains. The detail shows the tester cloth.

References: Walton (1986) p.39.

128.   Armchair (*c*.1710) 48 × 31 in (121.5 × 79 cm) *Clandon Park, Surrey* (The National Trust).

Walnut and beech frame with a *gros* and *petit-point* needlework cover.

129–30.   Chair (1711) 35 × 19 in (89 × 48 cm) *Virginia, Colonial Williamsburg Foundation*, Inv. 1954-990.

Ash frame with 'Russia' leather back and seat. The date is worked into the tacking

pattern of the brass nail border on the lower back rail. The chair is upholstered with a stuffing of curled hair and marsh grass. An oval stitching pattern in the seat centre keeps this in place. The back has a thin layer of grass beneath the leather.

126–7. (*opposite, top row*)   Eight armchairs and a day-bed (*c.*1710) *Drumlanrig Castle, Scotland.*

The velvet coverings with *appliqué* panels (detail) may well be French, being similar to those on chairs at Penshurst. However, the framing and under-webbing is English. They may well have been part of the activity, *c.*1706, of the French upholsterer Francis Lapiere for Anne, Duchess of Buccleuch (see Pl. 122).

References: Thornton (1978) Pl. X.

131.   State bed (1711) *Hatfield House, Hertfordshire.*

Supplied by Thomas How in 1711 to James Cecil, nineteenth Earl of Salisbury. Upholstered in crimson damask to a design close to those of the Huguenot weaver, James Leman. Fabric supplied by Henry Strudwick (£458 7s 9d). How charged £289 13s 4d (see p.141). It was restored in 1982–3 under the supervision of Mrs Joan Kendall working in the old materials with matching new pieces.

132–6.   Queen Anne's bed (1714) *Hampton Court, Surrey.*

Ordered in 1714 for her bedchamber at Windsor Castle but delivered after her death. The wooden structure was by Richard Roberts (his father Thomas having died in 1714) and the upholstery was by Hamden Reeve. The silk velvet with a cream-coloured ground and a dull-red and yellow-brown pattern was supplied in May 1714 as part of an order of 321 1/8 yards 'of white, crimson and yellow figured velvet' at 42s a yard. Details show the, headboard, counterpoint, tester and a chair *en suite* to the bed.

References: Thornton (1977) p.141; Fowler and Cornforth (1974) Pl. XI; Appendix A26.

137–8. (*above and left*) State bed (1715). For the Prince of Wales (later George II). The bed has an elaborate tester (detail) and a fan-shaped motif over the headboard which may represent the prince's ostrich-plume device. *En suite* were two armchairs and eighteen square stools.
Upholstered by Thomas Phill and Jeremiah Fletcher (see p.145). This bed is sometimes mistakenly called Queen Caroline's Bed (Appendix A27).

139–40. (*opposite, bottom*) State bed (*c*.1715) *Calke Abbey, Derbyshire* (The National Trust).

Lady Caroline Manners, daughter of the second Duke of Rutland, had served as a maid of honour at the marriage of Princess Anne, daughter of George II, to the Prince of Orange in 1734. Lady Caroline married Sir Henry Harpur in that year and it is likely the Calke bed was a gift from the princess to mark the wedding of her maid of honour. The bed is a magnificent example of Baroque upholstery, probably made for George I about 1715. As it was not erected at Calke the colour of its Chinese silk hangings are still brilliant. The dark blue material is light in weight, like taffeta, and covered with exquisitely embroidered flowers and birds. The white hangings are heavier with a satin finish, decorated with processions of figures, warriors on horseback, mandarins and ladies in brightly coloured robes.

141. (*top*) Settee (1715) *Canons Ashby, Northamptonshire* (The National Trust).

One of a set including six chairs (Pl. 142) and a firescreen, supplied by Thomas Phill to Edward Dryden of Canons Ashby, Northamptonshire in 1715. The settee and

firescreen are not included in Phill's bill and this may mean they were made to match the chairs at a slightly later date. Indeed, the needlework (with pastoral scenes in *petit-point*) on the tall back of the settee is in quite a different style from the chairs. The needlework could have been produced by the ladies of Edward Dryden's household, led by his wife, Elizabeth Allen.

References: Jackson-Stops (1985) pp.217–19.

142. (*top right*) Chairs (1715) *Canons Ashby, Northamptonshire* (The National Trust).

A set of six with a settee (Pl. 141) and firescreen, supplied by Thomas Phill to Edward Dryden of Canons Ashby, Northamptonshire in 1715. The chairs were charged at £7 10s for '6 wallnuttree back chaires frames of ye newest fashion stufft up in Lynnen & ye seats coverd a 2nd time' with a further £1 13s 'for makeing ye needle worke covers & fixeing yn on ye Chaires & for sewing silk', and 5s 6d 'for green serge for ye backs of ye 6 chaires', with false or case covers for an extra 15s. This implies that Phill merely fixed existing needlework to the chairs.

References: Jackson-Stops (1985) pp.217–19.

143. (*below*) Chair (*c*.1715) $46\frac{1}{2} \times 19\frac{1}{2} \times 22$ (101.7 × 50.2 × 55.1 cm) *Port Sunlight, Lady Lever Art Gallery*, Inv. LL4102.

One of seven. Covered in leather, painted with flowers. In shape the chairs are similar to those provided by Thomas Phill to Canons Ashby (Pl. 142).

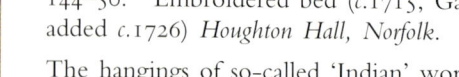

144–50.   Embroidered bed (*c.*1715, Garter added *c.*1726) *Houghton Hall, Norfolk.*

The hangings of so-called 'Indian' work are actually Indian and worked with flowers and birds on a white quilted ground. They imitate work on Chinese lacquers and silk (see also Pl. 140). The tester and headboard contain the Walpole coat-of-arms. The bed was almost old-fashioned by the time it was used in 1731 by the future Emperor of Austria, Francis I. In fact it would seem that the bed itself is *c.*1715 with the Garter added to the arms after Walpole had received the order in 1726. For this observation I am indebted to Annabel Westman. Details show the headboard and tester.

References: Jackson-Stops and Pipkin (1985) pp.166–8.

151–4.   Armchair (*c*.1715–20) 47¾ × 29½ × 29½ in (121.5 × 75 × 75 cm) *Houghton Hall, Norfolk.*

One from a suite of four armchairs and eight side chairs. Almost certainly made by James Moore for James Brydges, later first Duke of Chandos. Upholstered in original crimson Genoese velvet of Roman acanthus on a gold ground. The seat rail is centred at the front by an oval cartouche containing a double 'C' cypher commemorating either the elevation of James Brydges to Earl of Carnarvon in 1714 or for a Cholmondeley house in Cheshire or London. What is known is that they were not at Houghton in the eighteenth century. It has been suggested that Moore was working to a design by the architect James Gibbs. The details show the back of the chair, upholstered *à chassis* and released by loosing three turn buttons and the criss-cross tape. The underneath shows threads through the webbing fastened to the seat rail to retain the seat cover. No nails are used.

References: Cornforth (1994) p.vii; Christie's, Houghton catalogue, 8 December 1994, lot 135.

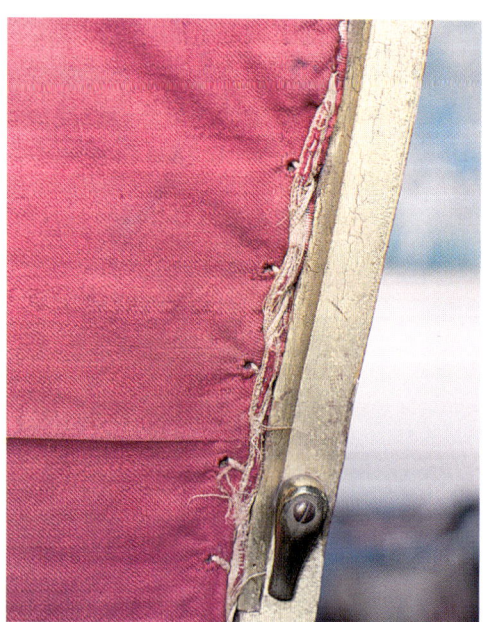

155. (*top left*)   Chair (1717) 48 × 24½in (122 × 62.25 cm) *London, Victoria and Albert Museum*, Inv. W62–1935.

Beechwood with carved and gilded gesso. Upholstered in red and gold cut velvet of the early eighteenth century. Cresting carved with the arms (sable, three nags's heads erased argent), granted in April 1717 to Sir William Humphreys, Lord Mayor of London,1714-15.

156. (*top right*)   Ticket to apply to bales of silk goods (1717) *Boston Athenaeum*.

Finished proof by Bernard Picart 'AD 1717'. This rare ticket shows the elements of importing and making fabric – the ships, looms and even attention from the mythological figure of Mercury (top right).

157.   State bedroom (1720–30) *Powis Castle, Wales* (The National Trust).

Surviving from the 1660s the state bedroom at Powis Castle is the only one in Britain where a balustrade rails off the bed alcove from the rest of the room. The furniture, a silver gesso set of *c.*1725, upholstered in crimson Spitalfields silk cut-velvet fringed with gold, is similar to a set at Erddig (Pl. 160). The state bed has a mahogany frame, partly gilded, covered in the same velvet. However, only the inside of the canopy appears to be contemporary with the rest.

158–9. (*opposite*)   State bed (1720) *Erdigg, Wales* (The National Trust).

The bed was probably the joint creation of the cabinet-maker John Belchier (for the carved and gilded gesso work) and the upholsterer Philip Hunt, working at 'Ye Looking Glass and Cabinet at the east end of St Paul's Church Yard'. The material covering the bed is composed of a number of Chinese coverlets and hangings. They may have been purchased in London or given to Erddig's owner, John Meller, by his neighbour, Elihu Yale, who had been in the service of the East India Company, *c.*1679–99. At the top of the headboard and at the centre of the tester (Pl. 159) there are carved cartouches sheltering a peacock and similar birds. Each is formed from a Chinese embroidered silk coverlet mounted on a block carved to a bird's shape. The bed was conserved by Sheila Landi and Charles Wright in 1968 and is now *in situ* at Erddig.

References: Hardy, Landi and Wright (1972).

160. (*opposite, bottom right*)   Chair (*c.*1720) $41\frac{1}{2} \times 23$ in (104 × 58.5 cm) *Erddig, Wales* (The National Trust).

Decorated with silvered gesso and upholstered in crimson Spitalfields cut silk-velvet of a pattern used also on those at Powis Castle (Pl. 157). From a set of eight with a settee *en suite*. Noted in the 1726 Erddig inventory as in the withdrawing-room.

References: Drury (1978) pp.46–55.

161.   Model of state bed (*c.*1720) *Port Sunlight, Lady Lever Art Gallery*, Inv. LL4782.

This fascinating and rare survival has the faded red velvet curtains and rope-laced webbing, gilded cartouches and pyramidal tester so often found in the originals.

162.   Tapestry settee cover (*c.*1725) *London, Victoria and Albert Museum*, Inv. T473-1970.

After designs by William Kent and John Wootton for John Gay's *Fables*. Left side 'The Painter', No.xviii.

163.   Wing armchair (*c.*1725) 49 × 33 × 32 (124.5 × 83 × 81.7 cm) *Virginia, Colonial Williamsburg Foundation*, Inv. 1956-449.

Oak frame, stripped of its needlework upholstery and showing back webbing and hessian infills. The seat has a loose cushion covered with stamped harrateen. The seams at its rear retain the original green silk finishing tapes.

164.   Trade card of Elkington Hall (*c.*1725) *London, British Museum* (*Heal Collection*).

A partner in Nash, Hall and Whitehorne at The Royal Bed on Holborn Bridge.

166.   Chair back (*c.*1725–30) chair, $42\frac{1}{2}$ × $24\frac{1}{2}$ × 27 in (109 × 62.25 × 69.5 cm) *Belgrave Hall* (Leicester Museums).

Mahogany frame, upholstered in fine wool and silk needlework. A man and woman in sixteenth-century dress are pruning a bush. One of a set of twelve chairs and a settee.

165.   Settee (*c.*1725) 49 × 48 in (124 × 122 cm) *Port Sunlight, Lady Lever Art Gallery*, Inv. LL4234.

Walnut, upholstered with needlework bearing the arms of Thomas Wyndham of Hawkchurch, Dorset and Elizabeth Helyas of Yately, Hampshire. They were presumably married about 1723 as their first child was christened in 1724.

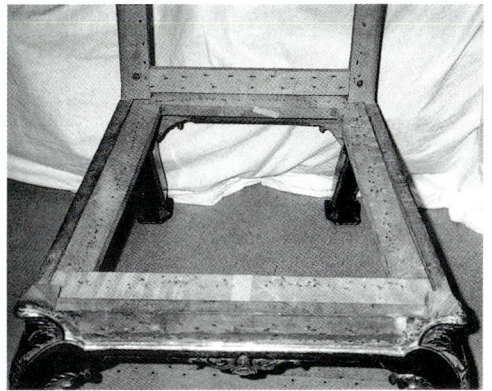

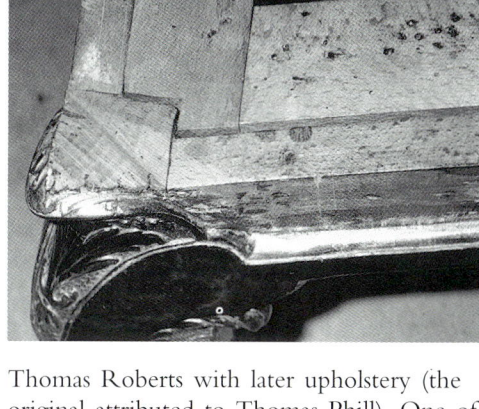

167–9. (*top row*) Side chair (*c*.1725–30) 41¾ × 25 × 29 in (106 × 63.5 × 74 cm) *Houghton Hall, Norfolk*.

Burr-walnut and parcel-gilt, upholstered in dark green silk-velvet, trimmed with silver galloon (originally gold). Supplied to Sir Robert Walpole as part of a large set of twenty-three chairs and two settees placed, originally, at Houghton Hall in the 'Cabinett' and 'Cov'd or Wrought Bedchamber'. Attributed to the Roberts family (see p.149), the chairs probably came from Sir Robert's earlier house at Houghton which he finally razed, to start building afresh in 1722. The two details show the unusual slip-in seat revealed when the chair was stripped prior to reupholstery.

References: For citation of an extensive literature see Christie's Houghton catalogue, 8 December 1994, lot 126.

170. (*below*)   Side chair (*c*.1725–30) 41½ × 23 × 22 in (105 × 59 × 56 cm) *Temple Newsam House, Leeds*, Inv. 16/60.

One of a set of six, presumed to have been made for Sir Robert Walpole at Houghton Hall, Norfolk. The frames and upholstery of this chair are identical to the large suite at Houghton, although there is no proof of it or the other five having come from that distinguished collection. The Houghton chairs (Pls 167–9) have a silver galloon trim instead of, as here, gilded nails.

References: Sotheby's, 29 January 1960, lot 117.

171. (*below, right*)   Open armchair (*c*.1727) 38½ × 32½ × 30¼ in (98 × 82.5 × 77 cm).

With a gilt-gesso frame. Attributed to

Thomas Roberts with later upholstery (the original attributed to Thomas Phill). One of the chairs used by Queen Caroline during the coronation ceremony of 1727. Such chairs can be seen in the engraving of the coronation setting for James II in 1685 (Pl. 62). The present coverings 'are the result of a second or third reupholstery', possibly using some of the green velvet in the state bedroom at Houghton (Pl. 188). The chair has an early association with the queen's coronation. It is not known when the chair came to Houghton. I am indebted to Dr Tessa Murdoch for sharing her notes on this chair which are at slight variance (correctly, I think) to the entry in Christie's Houghton catalogue, 8 December 1994, lot 129, when the chair was sold and subsequently exported.

172. (*far left*)   Side chair (1728) 41 × 23½ × 25 in (104 × 60 × 63.5 cm) *Houghton Hall, Norfolk.*

Walnut, upholstered in red and yellow floral silk damask. Part of a suite supplied on 24 November 1728 to Sir Robert Walpole for the yellow drawing-room at Houghton. Roberts's bill of 24 April 1729 mentioned '12 fine wallnuttree chair frames', a settee and couch frames covered 'with your own Crimson Damask strong ticken'. For a discussion of this chair and its upholstery see p.151.

References: Christie's Houghton catalogue, 8 December 1994, lot 128.

173. (*left*)   Armchair (*c.*1730) 38½ × 25 × 28 in (98 × 63.5 × 71 cm) *Houghton Hall, Norfolk.*

From a set of twelve and a settee. Supplied to Sir Robert Walpole for the marble parlour at Houghton. Attributed to William Bradshaw or Benjamin Goodison. Covered in green damask (of the pattern now known as 'Amberley') and brass-nailed. An armchair with related eagle arm terminals, is illustrated (Pl. 171).

174. (*left*)   Chair (*c.*1730).

Front and side elevation of a chair designed by William Kent. Illustrated by John Vardy in *Some Designs of Mr Inigo Jones and Mr William Kent* (1744) Pl. 43.

175. (*below*)   Close stool (*c.*1730) 18 × 16 in (46 × 40.5 cm) *Virginia, Colonial Williamsburg Foundation*, Inv. 1969-32.

The top is of black leather, showing horsehair stuffing (held in place by the original webbing); the leather nailed to the seat frame.

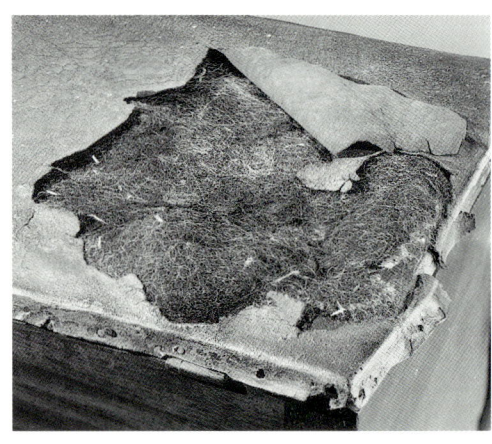

176–7.   Settee (*c*.1730) 43 × 65 × 22 in (109 × 165 × 56 cm) *Private Collection, England*.

Walnut frame, woven upholstery signed 'Stranover/Bradshaw' (detail, Pl. 176), with patterns probably based on engravings by Jean Baptiste Monnoyer. This important settee had been lost since its sale with six chairs at Christie's, 14 March 1929 and has come to light through research for this book (see pp.153–4).

178.   Part of a bed or window valance (*c*.1730) *Virginia, Colonial Williamsburg Foundation*, Inv. 1967-699.

Bright yellow silk satin with knotted red wool threads, worsted lining.

179.   Chair (*c*.1730) 40½ × 23 × 27¼ in (103 × 60.3 × 69.2 cm) *Ham House, London* (The National Trust).

Fruitwood, with red and green figured velvet upholstery, probably Spitalfields. One of a set of eighteen chairs, one settee and two 'love seats'. The cover is removable. Attributed to William Bradshaw. The Spitalfields silk workers produced furnishing velvets equal to those (but cheaper) from Genoa, which was a considerable advantage to English upholsterers.

References: Thornton and Tomlin (1980) p.181.

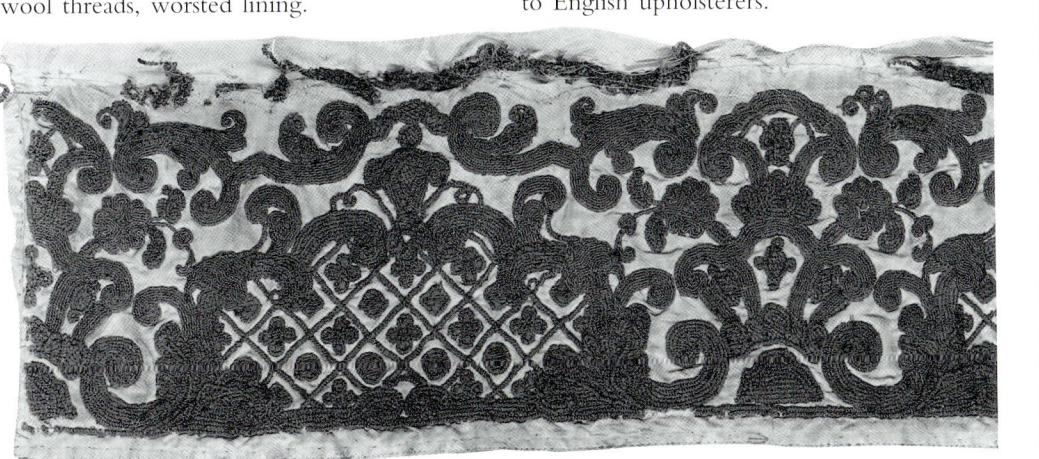

180. (*left*)   Armchair (*c*.1730) 45 × 27 × 25 in (114 × 69 × 63 cm) *Stoneleigh Abbey, Warwickshire.*

Walnut veneer with gilded gesso. The needlework depicts Venus approaching Vulcan, who is working at his anvil, a scene from Ovid's *Metamorphoses*. The covers were probably supplied ready-made, as is implied by the small notches woven into the back and seat of the side chair. These notches seem to have been provided to accommodate absent arms, an inference confirmed by their placement on this armchair. Attributed to the upholsterer Thomas How (see p.141).

181. (*right*)   Open armchair (*c*.1730) 43 × 32 × 25½ (108 × 81.3 × 67.4 cm) *Port Sunlight, Lady Lever Art Gallery*, Inv. LL4205.

Walnut, parcel gilt. Similar in style to those in the collection at Stoneleigh Abbey (Pl. 180). The needlework on the back depicts the sacrifice of Iphigenia.

182–4.   Side chair (*c*.1731) 39¼ × 25 × 25½ in (100 × 63.5 × 75 cm) Jon Gerstenfeld, Washington D.C.

Walnut, upholstered in dark green silk velvet with gold metal-thread border. Part of a large set (33 chairs, 2 settees and 4 stools) supplied to Sir Robert Walpole for use in the velvet drawing-room, green velvet bedchamber and the Van Dyck dressing-room at Houghton Hall, Norfolk. Their upholstery was meant to complement the hangings of the state bed (Pl. 188) and the wall coverings. The details show the fastenings on the outer cover and the embroidered numeral 13 to match the cover to the similarly numbered chair.

185–6.   Armchair (*c.*1731) 45 × 28 × 24 in (114.3 × 71 × 61 cm) *Houghton Hall, Norfolk.*

Designed by William Kent, made in mahogany with parcel-gilt and upholstered in crimson caffoy, part of that supplied in 1729 by Thomas Roberts. The chairs in this set were obviously made by a superb carver. This role could have been filled by James Richards who worked at Houghton and on the state barge designed by Kent (1732) for Frederick, Prince of Wales, Benjamin

Goodison, a consummate carver in mahogany and working in royal service, or William Bradshaw whose chairs at Chevening (Pl. 198) have similar profiles and measurements.

187.   The saloon (*c.*1731) *Houghton Hall, Norfolk.*

The saloon is dedicated to Apollo and Venus with allusive shells appearing in various parts of the decoration. The walls are covered with some of the crimson caffoy supplied in 1729 by Thomas Roberts, whilst the chairs (Pls 185–6) have been variously attributed to James Richards, Benjamin Goodison and William Bradshaw. They were originally in the drawing room.

References: Cornforth (1994) p.vi.

188–94.   Green velvet state bed (*c.*1732) *Houghton Hall, Norfolk.*

This bed with its scallop-shell dominated headboard, green silk velvet hangings and superb detailing, was supplied to Sir Robert Walpole (p.149). It is sufficient here to note it as one of William Kent's outstanding designs, upholstered perhaps *in situ* by Thomas Roberts. Details show the tester, headboard and galloon on the front curtains.

195.   Engraver's proof of the trade card of Christopher Gibson (*c.*1735) *London, Victoria and Albert Museum*, Inv. P&D14435-60.

Gibson was an upholsterer at the King's Arms, St Paul's churchyard, London. Whilst some elements are fanciful, the card gives an idea of an upholsterer's shop of the 1730s. The stock shown includes cane chairs, chairs and a stool with upholstered seats, an angel bed, mirror, funeral hatchments and numerous bales of cloth. Gibson's business was last recorded in 1745.

References: Beard and Gilbert (1986) p.337.

196–7.   Chair (*c.*1735) $42\frac{1}{2} \times 25 \times 23$ in (108 × 63.5 × 58.5 cm) *Temple Newsam House, Leeds*, Inv. 5/61.

One of a set of four from an original set of six and a sofa with walnut legs, beech seat, upholstered in needlework in red, white and purple (faded to tan), the canvas drawn over the rails and fastened with brass nails. The trifid feet suggest a Scottish origin and the suite was at Brahan Castle, Ross-shire until 1950. The detail of the underneath of the chair shows the English style of webbing with a thin web ($1\frac{1}{2}$ in; 3.8 cm) interlaced to form an open lattice through which is visible the hessian supporting a filling of curled hair.

198. Armchair (1736) 44 × 31½ × 30½ in (111.7 × 80 × 77.5 cm) *Chevening, Kent.*

Mahogany, upholstered in Soho tapestry. The original suite was of twelve armchairs and two sofas, of which eleven chairs and one sofa survive. It was supplied by William Bradshaw to the second Earl Stanhope of Chevening, Kent. The bill survives (Appendix A31), and shows that the twelve chairs cost £5 10s each with the cases at £5 8s 4d for each chair. The tapestry survives in remarkable condition and is placed on a chair designed (with its low and rectilinear shape) to show it to advantage.

199. Curtains and valances shown in an engraving *After* by William Hogarth (*c.*1736) *Virginia, Colonial Williamsburg Foundation*, Inv. 1967.568.2.

The bed curtains have fallen showing that the bed has inner and outer valances. The curtains are on sewn metal rings, sliding on a rod.

200. Genoa velvet (*c.*1738) *Ditchley Park, Oxfordshire.*

It has the pattern of the Hindu god Siva in crimson and golden yellow. Bought in Genoa in 1738 by the second Earl of Lichfield for the state bedroom (now velvet room) at Ditchley. The room was fitted up with a chimney piece by Sir Henry Cheere (May 1743). When the bed was removed in the nineteenth century the fabric may have been rearranged.

References: *Country Life*, 24 November 1988, p.84.

201–2.   Green drawing room (*c.*1740) *Longford Castle, Wiltshire.*

Showing the green cut-velvet of the wall-hangings carried through on to gilded armchairs, the frames of which are attributed to Benjamin Goodison with upholstery by William Bradshaw.

203.   (*left*) Armchair (*c.*1740) back, 28 × 23 in (71 × 58 cm); seat, 28 × 32 in (71 × 81 cm); armrest, 13 × 6 in (33 × 15 cm) *New York, Metropolitan Museum of Art, gift of Mrs Dannie Heineman, Inv.* 66. 71. 2.

One of a set of four. The back, seat and armrest are upholstered in Soho tapestry, probably designed by Tobias Stranover and woven by William Bradshaw. The vases of flowers on stands are based on an engraving by Jean Baptiste Monnoyer.

References: Standen (1985) II, No.130.

205. Toilette and draw curtains shown in *Mariage à la Mode* (Plate IV) by William Hogarth (1745) *Virginia, Colonial Williamsburg Foundation.*

206. Chair (*c.*1745) 39 × 21½ in (99.5 × 54.5 cm) *Private Collection, England.*

Carved walnut with contemporary needlework seat. The open work splat in the form of a shell occupies the whole of the back, with the seat upholstered over the rail. There are chairs of this form at Stourhead, Wiltshire and in the Victoria and Albert Museum, London.

207. Trade card of Ann Buck (*c.*1745) *London, Guildhall Library.*

Ann Buck was a London dealer in upholstered furniture at 'The Queen's Head' in Holborn. Her trade card bears a likeness of Queen Anne. Mrs Buck was the widow of Henry Buck, a cabinet- and chair-maker who traded from St Paul's churchyard.

204. Trade card of John Boothby (*c.*1740) *London, British Museum (Heal Collection).*

Boothby was an upholsterer and appraiser working from the Strand, London.

Richard Wright was in charge 'of ye Greatest Tapestry Manufactory in England for upwards of Twenty Years' as their trade card (Pl. 234) attested. This was probably a reference to Soho. He then moved to Wakefield and set up with the younger Elwick. Two chairs from this set are in the Victoria and Albert Museum, London.

208–9.   Green velvet bed (*c.*1745–50) *Hardwick Hall, Derbyshire* (The National Trust).

This was brought to Hardwick from Londesborough, Yorkshire by the sixth Duke of Devonshire. It was made presumably for the 'Architect Earl', Richard Boyle, third Earl of Burlington. He had married Dorothy Savile in 1721. Their possessions passed to the Cavendish family through their daughter Charlotte, who married the fourth Duke of Devonshire in 1748. With its gadrooned, undulating cornice the bed relates, stylistically, to Charlotte's marriage date. The two stools are attributed to Francis Lapiere (*c.*1697) and are *en suite* to the state bed fragments, formerly at Chatsworth and since the early nineteenth century in the long gallery at Hardwick (Pl. 92). The detail is of the cut-velvet covering the cornice and the bed.

210.   Armchair (*c.*1746) 43 × 26½ in (109.5 × 67.25 cm).

The armchair has a gilded frame with tapestry covers. One of a set of six attributed to Richard Wright and Edward Elwick and made for the second Earl of Strafford for Wentworth Castle, Yorkshire.

211–15. Settee, day bed and chair (1746); settee, 41 × 67 × 31 in (104 × 170 × 79 cm); day bed, 34 × 85 × 34 in (86 × 216 × 86 cm); chair, 36½ × 26½ × 23 in (92 × 67 × 59 cm) *Temple Newsam House, Leeds*, Inv. 16. 1–25/39.

From a suite of twenty chairs, four settees and a day bed. Gilt beech and walnut, upholstered in wool needlework in tent stitch, fastened by round-headed brass nails cast in one piece (see detail of nailing on a chair of this suite, Pl. 211). Provided by James Pascall of London for Henry, seventh Viscount Irwin for his long gallery at Temple Newsam, where it remains. The brightness of the wool needlework may be seen on a part of the day bed bolster protected form the light (Pl. 215). Details of the nailing on the front left leg and of the contemporary webbing are shown.

References: Gilbert (1978) I, pp.61–3.

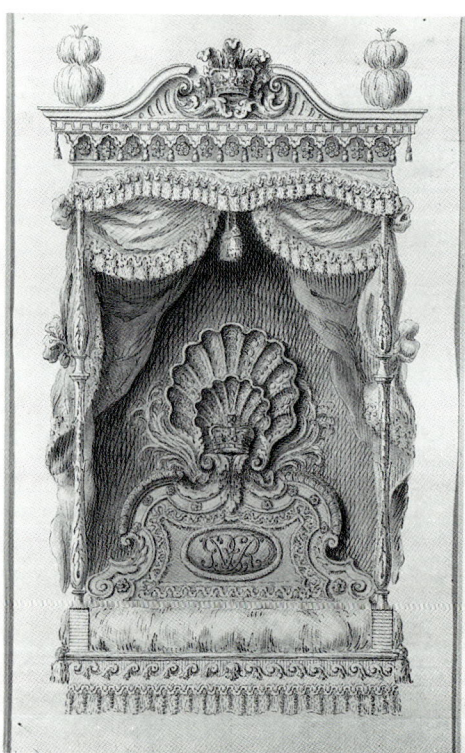

216–17.   State bed (*c.*1750) *Hardwick Hall, Derbyshire* (The National Trust).

It is upholstered in Genoa velvet (possibly woven in England). The bed was based on John Vardy's design of 1749 (Pl. 218). A variant to the drawing is the use of a ducal coronet and cypher of a Duke of Devonshire (possibly replacements) although it has been suggested that the bed was royal and acquired as a perquisite. It was seen at Chatsworth in 1766 by the first Duchess of Northumberland who recorded it in her travel diary as by 'Cobb & Vile'. They had entered into partnership in 1751 (p.162). The detail shows the headboard.

References: Thornton (1977) p.122; Percy and Jackson-Stops (1974) II, p.260.

218.   Design for a state bed (1749) *London, Victoria and Albert Museum*, Inv. E3143-1938.

The design is by John Vardy (1718–65). It is signed on the back 'J. Vardy Invent et delin 1749' and inscribed with the title. The drawing incorporates a royal crown and the cypher of George II. Note the similarity of this design to the state bed at Hardwick Hall, Derbyshire (Pl. 216).

References: Colvin (1995).

219. Furnishing chintz (*c.*1750) *London, Victoria and Albert Museum*, Inv. T243-1979.

The most active figure in textiles at this period was John Baptist Jackson who had trained abroad, setting up his own business in Battersea by 1752. His rococo style textiles owe much to French models and were used for dress and furnishing purposes.

220. Armchair (*c.*1750) *Virginia, Colonial Williamsburg Foundation*, Inv. 1955, 179-4.

Mahogany frame, upholstered in wool *gros* and *petit-point*. Formerly at Glemham Hall, Suffolk. (See Pl. 221).

221. Armchair (*c.*1750) 40 × 28 × 24 in (101.6 × 71 × 61 cm).

Mahogany frame, upholstered in wool *gros-point* needlework of the Fulham type with exotic birds in wool and silk *petit-point*. One of a set of twelve of which eight or nine survive, made for Lord North, Glemham, Suffolk. An article in *Old Furniture* says there were nine of the twelve chairs survivng at that date. One of the designs for the needlework (by tradition said to have been worked by Lady Barbara North, d.1755) is illustrated in Percy Macquoid, *A History of English Furniture: The Age of Mahogany* (1906) figs 188–90. The designs were destroyed by a fire in 1913 at Waldershare Park, Kent. Another chair from the set is illustrated in *D.E.F.* (1954) I, fig.197. The design of the frame is similar to that illustrated as 'French chairs' in Chippendale's *Director* (1762) Pl. XX.

References: *Old Furniture* October–December 1927, p.130ff.

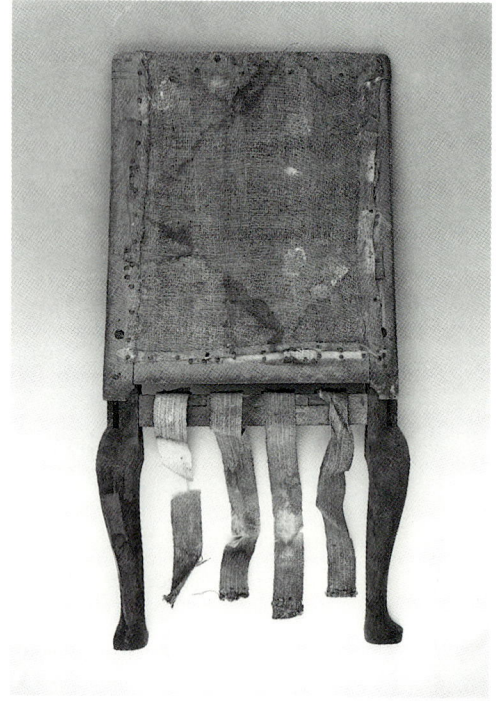

222.   Upholstery fragments on a backstool (*c.*1750) $37\frac{1}{4} \times 19\frac{1}{2}$ in (92 × 49.5 cm) *Virginia, Colonial Williamsburg Foundation*, Inv. 1983-254, 1.

The stool has a beech frame with the original linen webbing and a coarse linen bottom. Evidence of a red wool covering has been found under wrought nails on the back. Nailing patterns indicate that brass nails were not used, suggesting gimp as the original trim. The chair was broken early in the nineteenth century, and the fragments stored in an attic at Blandfield, Virginia, home of Robert Beverley II (1740–1800) who bought quantities of English furniture.

224.   Panel for a fire screen (*c.*1753) 36 × 29 in (91 × 74 cm) *New York, Metropolitan Museum of Art, gift of Irwin Untermyer, 1964.*

It shows a red parrot and squirrel in a landscape background, with an overturned basket of fruit in the foreground. This example was probably woven at the Fulham tapestry factory set up by Peter Parisot in 1751 (p.159). A related panel (1759) is illustrated in Gilbert (1978) I, Pl. 3.

References: Standen (1985) II, p.740, No.133.

223.   Wing armchair (*c.*1750) 47 × $32\frac{3}{4}$ × $25\frac{1}{2}$ in (119.5 × 83.5 × 64.75 cm) *Virginia, Colonial Williamsburg Foundation*, Inv. 1986-267.

Mahogany frame, original upholstery linen and horsehair remaining on sides and back. A linen weaver or seller's mark 'W. Lm' is inked on the linen at the back of the chair.

227. 'Chinese Sofa' from Thomas
Chippendale's *Director* (1754) Pl. XXVI.

Chippendale felt that his several designs 'in
the present Chinese manner' would
'improve that taste, or manner of work'.
This design was not repeated in the third
edition of the *Director* (1762) as by then its
exotic pagoda roof with bells would have
been considered outmoded. The depiction
of the sofa indicates a seat worked in
needlework with figures in a landscape.

225. (*opposite, bottom centre*)   Design for a
chair (1753–4) *London, Victoria and Albert
Museum*, Inv. E71-1929.

The design is by John Linnell. The actual
suite, consisting of a state bed and eight
chairs, was made for the fourth Duke
of Beaufort at Badminton House,
Gloucestershire, and remained there until
the sale of most of it in 1921 (Christie's, 17
February 1921). The watercolour drawing in
red, yellow and black suggests the japanned
decoration of an outstanding Chinoiserie
suite.

References: Hayward and Kirkham (1980)
p.132, n.34–5; Hayward (1969) p.85.

226. (*opposite, bottom right*)   Chamber horse
(*c.*1754) 54 × 34 in (138 × 87 cm) *Belton
House, Lincolnshire* (The National Trust).

This was a contrivance for exercising in the
second half of the eighteenth century.
The leather-covered seat had a concertina
movement and was formed of boards
supported on blocks, around which strong
wire was twisted. The weight of the sitter
served to compress the air, thus securing an
upward and downward movement. Henry
Marsh of Clement's Inn Passage claimed in
1739–40 in *The London Daily Post and
General Advertiser* that he had invented the
chamber horse. Sheraton gives a useful
description of them in the 1802 edition of
his *Drawing Book*. See also *The Times* 31
March 1962, p.11. This chair was made for
Lord Tyrconnel by his joiner Samuel Smith.

228.   Rococo style bed from Thomas
Chippendale's *Director* (1754) Pl. XXVII.

This design is interesting in that it also
shows the arrangement of the wheels in the
pulley board. Lines were passed over these
and through rings on the back of the
curtain arranged so that they could be
drawn up and aside to form a pleasing
appearance. The design was repeated as Pl.
XLIV in the 1762 edition. The height of
the bed is given as 7 ft 6 ins (229 cm); width
5 ft (152 cm); depth, 6 ft 4 in (193 cm).

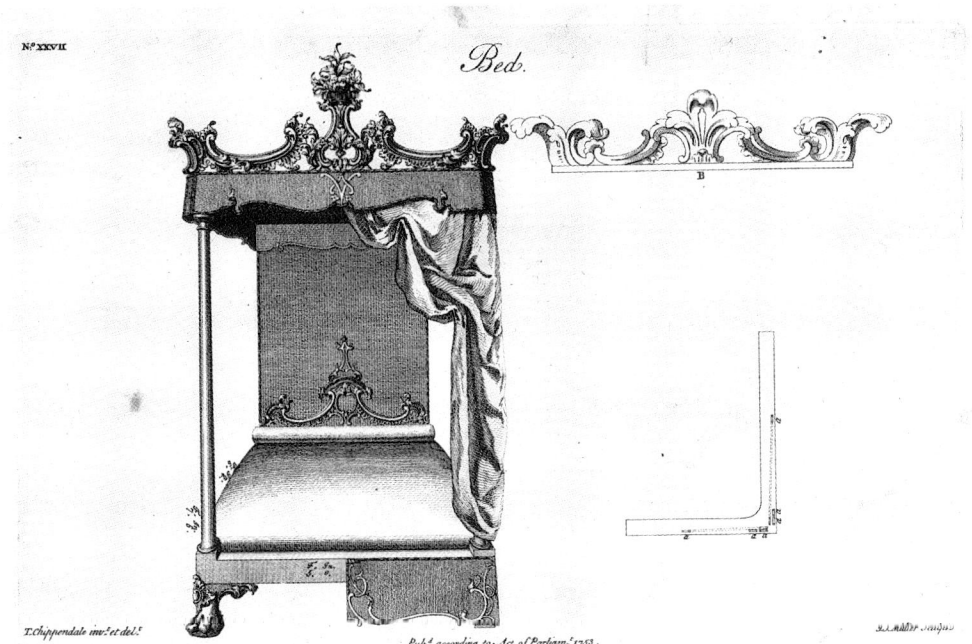

229.   'Gothick Bed' from Thomas Chippendale's *Director* (1754) Pl. XXIX.

This design was repeated in the 1762 edition (Pl. XLI) with a note saying 'A Design of a Bed, with the proper dimensions, and requires no Explanation. B is another Cornice, which may be covered with the same stuff as the Curtains, a a a , are the Lath, with pullies to draw up the Curtains'. Eight pullies are shown, obviously to be repeated at the left side, but no overall dimensions are given other than a foot and inch scale.

230.   'Canopy Bed' from Thomas Chippendale's *Director* (1754) Pl. XXX.

Repeated in the 1762 edition (Pl. XLII) with a note saying 'A Design of a Canopy-Bed with its Head-Board. Both the Curtains and Valances are to draw up in Drapery. The Dimensions are specified: 'a' is a fourth Part of the Tester; c is a small oval Dome in the inside; b, d, the outside Canopy; h, h, a Mosaic work in the Flat round the Dome; i is the Lath which goes round the Bed; f is the Bed-Pillars; k, k, the Places where the Pullies are fixed to draw up the Curtains'. The overall dimensions are given only for the depth, 6 ft 6 in (203 cm) although there is a yard scale with feet and inches.

231. 'Doom Bed' from Thomas Chippendale's *Director* (1754) Pl. XXXI.

The plate was modified for the 1762 edition (Pl. XLIII) with a different headboard for the Chinoiserie one, and 'Doom' corrected to 'Dome'. The note to Pl. XLIII is a long one indicating all the parts, giving a scale and the overall dimensions, height (without vase) 10 ft 4 in (315 cm); width 6 ft (182 cm); depth 6 ft 7 in (198 cm). The height of the bed from the floor was 1 ft (30 cm) and the height of the vase was 18 or 20 in (45.5/50.8 cm).

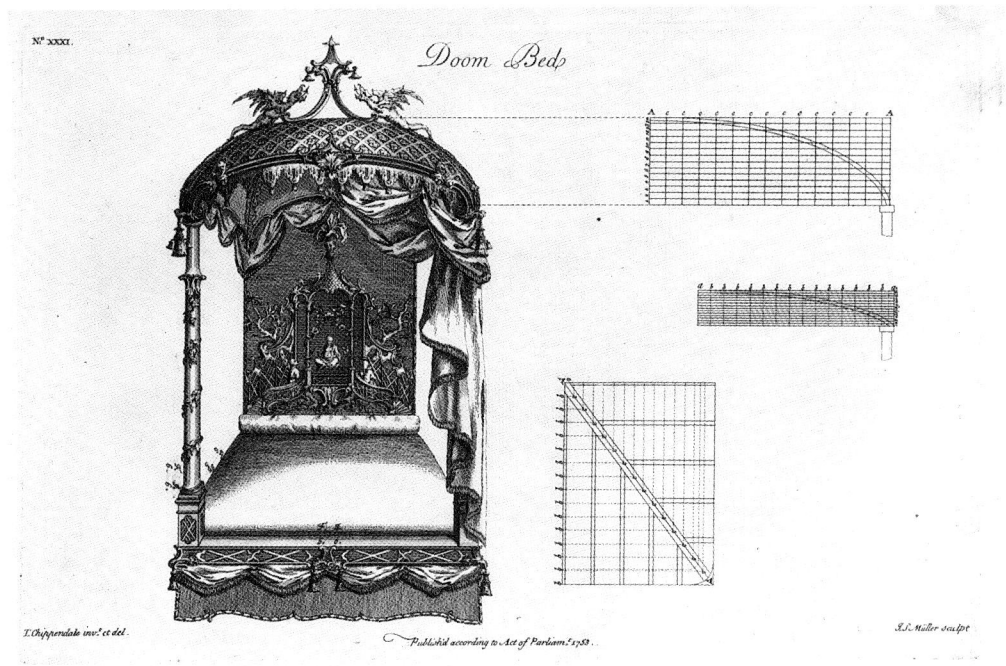

232. 'Chinese Bed' from Thomas Chippendale's *Director* (1754) Pl. XXXII.

The design was not repeated in the 1762 edition. The curtains are drawn up 'in drapery' as in the canopy bed (Pl. 230) a plan of the tester and section of the canopy is given with an indication of the fixing of the posts. No dimensions are given but there is a yard scale.

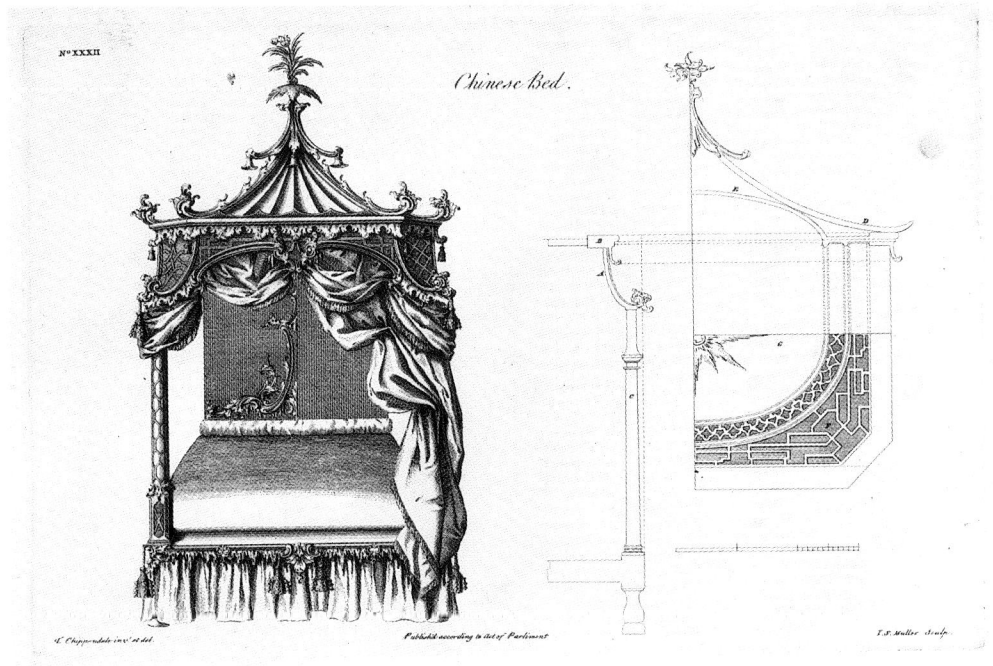

233.   The saloon (*c*.1755) *Holkham Hall, Norfolk.*

The walls are hung with crimson caffoy, from a large consignment provided by the London mercer, Robert Carr. The 244 yards cost £195 (*Country Life,* 4 August 1988, p.92). Mrs Lybbe Powys who visited Holkham in 1756 noted the room as 'just finished'. Thomas Coke, first Earl of Leicester, had worked on his house from 1735 and a great deal of furnishing and decoration was done after his death (1759) by his widow. The original pictures by Procaccini and Chiari were restored to the overmantels in 1988 after nearly 200 years in store.

234.   Trade card of Richard Wright and Edward Elwick of London and Wakefield (*c*.1755) *Leeds Archives Department.*

The text is useful in indicating a little of Wright's work before he came to Yorkshire (p 159) and also the sort of work he and his partner could undertake. They were two of the most successful Yorkshire furniture-makers and upholsterers.

235.   Chair (*c*.1755) $36 \times 23\frac{3}{4} \times 23$ in ($91.4 \times 60.3 \times 58.4$ cm) *Hardwick Hall, Derbyshire* (The National Trust).

One of a set of twelve. Made in mahogany. Traces of the original blue silk damask remain, backed with blue serge. The chair has its original webbing and curled hair stuffing under an upper layer of linen. A knotted thread on the back indicates that the back was originally tufted.

236.   Design for the side of a room (*c.*1755)
London, Victoria and Albert Museum, Inv.
E263-1929.

This attractive drawing by John Linnell may
have been intended for the owner of a
London town-house. The portrait may be a
fanciful one of Inigo Jones pointing to
a plan. The red damask of the settee is
repeated in the colour of the walls.

References: Hayward and Kirkham (1980)
pp.20, 61 and Pl. 3; Snodin (ed.) (1984)
No.M15.

237. (*top right*)   Design for a sofa
(*c.*1755–60) *London, Victoria and Albert
Museum*, Inv. E120-1929.

The design is by John Linnell who in the
mid- to late-1750s gave much thought to
these imposing designs. This culminated
eventually in a commission for four sofas
from Sir Nathaniel Curzon (Viscount
Scarsdale from 1761) for use at Kedleston
Hall, Derbyshire. The frame is yellow to
indicate gilding, and the upholstery is pink.
The sofas remain at Kedleston but have
been reupholstered.

References: Hayward V (1969) fig.20.

238. (*centre*)   Design for a sofa (*c.*1755–60)
London, Victoria and Albert Museum, Inv.
133-1929.

By John Linnell. The frame is yellow to
indicate gilding and the upholstery is blue.

References: Hayward (1969) V, fig.23.

239.   Armchair (1755–60) 42 × 29 × 26 in
(107 × 74 × 71 cm) *Uppark, Sussex* (The
National Trust).

Attributed to John Bladwell. The chair has a
gilt wood frame with tapestry upholstery,
representing (on the back) the Aesop fable
of the hare and the tortoise under starter's
orders from the fox. The tapestry was made
by the London workshop of the Danthon
family who were Huguenot weavers
working from before 1707, first in
Spitalfields and then in Soho. The armchair
is one of a set of eight, each representing a
different Aesop's fable, and a settee; the
cover of one of the chairs is signed
Danthon. The set was bought by Sir
Matthew Fetherstonhaugh in the mid- to
late-1750s for Uppark, his house in Sussex.

References: Hefford (1984) pp.103–12.

241.   Rococo headboard of the state bed (*c.*1758) *The Lord Egremont, Petworth.*

It was provided by James Whittle and his son-in-law Samuel Norman for the second Earl of Egremont. Except for the carved part of the headboard, the dome and two valances the bed needed new silk damask hangings. These were arranged in accordance with the evidence provided on the bed frame and the illustration of the 'Doom [Dome] Bed' in Thomas Chippendale's *Director,* 1754 (Pl. XXXI). This work was done in 1984 by Annabel Westman.

References: *Country Life,* 14 June 1984; Snodin (ed.) 1984, p.178.

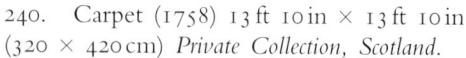

240.   Carpet (1758) 13 ft 10 in × 13 ft 10 in (320 × 420 cm) *Private Collection, Scotland.*

Woollen knotted pile, every tenth pair of warp threads blue-brown. It has a woven inscription, 'EXON 1758'. This fine carpet is one of three surviving examples made by the short-lived Exeter factory acquired by the Swiss Huguenot Claude Passavant in 1756. The carpet was exhibited at the Society of Arts in 1758 and 1760.

References: Gilbert, Lomax and Wells-Cole (1987) p.53; Sherrill (1996) p.163.

242–3.   Open armchair (*c.*1760) *London, Victoria and Albert Museum*, Inv. HH23-1948.

Mahogany, upholstered in a woollen cut velvet, with red, green and blue as predominant colours. The detail of the underneath of the chair shows the original webbing.

References: Thornton and Tomlin (1980) Pl. 172.

244–5.   Chair (*c.*1760) $41\frac{1}{2} \times 22 \times 22\frac{1}{2}$ in (105.4 × 56 × 57.5 cm) *Marble Hill House, Middlesex* (English Heritage).

One of a set of six and a settee. Upholstered in wool and silk needlework on canvas in tent and cross stitches. The backing is modern and the webbing has been renewed. Tradition implies that the needlework was worked by Anne Northey, *c.*1750. The central pictorial scenes are, however, somewhat akin to late seventeenth- or early eighteenth-century designs and Anne Northey may merely have worked floral surrounds to earlier panels. A detail shows the back of the chair.

246.   Open armchair (*c.*1760) $42\frac{1}{2} \times 29 \times 29$ in (107 × 74 × 74 cm) *New York, Metropolitan Museum of Art, gift of Irwin Untermyer.*

Mahogany, upholstered in a modern fabric shown here for the similarity of the frame to Pl. XXII in the 1762 edition of Chippendale's *Director*. The plate is dated 1759 (Pl. 258) and is described as a 'French' chair. Chippendale stated that there should be an open space between the lower rail of the chair-back and the seat in order to lighten the general effect. The carving is of a quality which suggests a provincial maker. The armchair is thought to have been supplied to William Plummer of Gilston Park, Hertfordshire. Another is in the Victoria and Albert Museum in London.

247.   State bed (*c.*1760) *Holkham Hall, Norfolk.*

248.   Design for a state bed by John Linnell (*c.*1760) *London, Victoria and Albert Museum,* Inv. E152-1929.

The headboard is a splendid example of carving in soft wood, then gilded, with the curtains held back by caryatid figures at either side. The bed has a fringed base valance raised at the centre foot with a rosette and tassel.

References: Hayward and Kirkham (1980) pp.21, 79, Pl. 7.

Designed for Thomas Coke, first Earl of Leicester. When Lord Leicester died in 1759 the state bedroom was not complete. The three-colour cut-velvet was available (part of a large consignment of over £3,166-worth provided by Robert Carr) and was also used on furniture *en suite.* The upholsterer Paul Saunders was paid in 1756 and 1757 for models for the bed and James Lillie put up a canopy in 1758. The carving of the canopy was paid for by Lady Leicester. The present bed is not old but the canopy originally covered a sofa which converted to a bed. Three tapestries of the Continents were acquired in France by Lord Leicester but were extended with woven slips by Saunders to designs by James Stuart and Francesco Zuccarelli. The decoration and dating in this room is, however, complex with some accounts missing.

References: *Country Life,* 14 February 1980, pp.428, 430.

249.   Design for a state bed (*c.*1760) *London, Victoria and Albert Museum,* Inv. E146-1929.

By John Linnell. The design is an alternative to that (Pl. 248) using caryatid figures to support the bed curtains. The carving is pre-eminent – on tester, headboard and front posts – but the tasselled curtains with their elaborate suspension enhance the whole.

References: Hayward and Kirkham (1980) pp.21, 79, Pl. 8.

VI

Visions and Revivals 1760–1790

GEORGE III AND THE FURNITURE MAKERS

At eleven o'clock on the morning of 22 September 1761, the coronation procession of George III and Charlotte of Mecklenburg-Strelitz set out from Westminster Hall to the abbey. The preparations had, as usual, been in hand for some time and the Great Wardrobe had been asked for a considerable number of state chairs and footstools. The Lord Chamberlain's Office had obtained these from the royal chair-maker, Katherine Naish (who had succeeded her father, the joiner Henry Williams, in 1758), and from the royal cabinet-makers and upholsterers, William Vile and John Cobb. Following the ceremony of crowning, the king, accompanied by his queen, was led to two splendid rococo state chairs, which had footstools *en suite*. Partly as a result of the later taking of such furniture as perquisites by the Lord Chamberlain, these still survive at Chatsworth, Derbyshire. George III's Lord Chamberlain was the fourth Duke of Devonshire.[1] Katherine Naish had charged £30 each for the two chair frames and £6 each for the two footstools. Vile and Cobb charged a further £8.18s for 'Stuffing up in Canvas 2 large State Chairs & Footstools, & covering them with rich Brocade Gold, Silver and Colours, & 2 Down Cusheons covered with ditto Brocade & trimmed with Gold fringe & Tassels at the corners.' They used the $16\frac{1}{2}$ yards of 'rich Brocade' provided by the successful London mercer, Thomas Hinchcliff, junior[2] at a cost of £6 16s 6d a yard (£112 12s 3d). This still survives (Pls 253–4), although the chairs and stools now lack the gold fringe obtained from the laceman Francis Plummer, listed as part of his bill for £121 8s 8d.

Vile and Cobb were also involved in the upholstering of throne and State chairs needed in 1761 for the House of Lords. The frames were again made by Katherine Naish, with footstools and high stools *en suite*. Whilst not as grand as the coronation chairs, Naish had carved the throne with 'Lions Paws & Lions faces on the knees, with 2 Boys at the Top supporting a Crown, & a Scepter . . .' (£46), and also carved the footstool (£7 10s) and two high stools (£16 10s each). It was placed under a 'Large State Canopy' (Pl. 255) provided by Naish (£52), upholstered with $118\frac{1}{2}$ yards of crimson Genoa velvet (29s 4d a yard), bearing embroidered royal arms (Richard Harrison, £110) and embellished with 'trebble gilt rich lace' and fringe supplied by Francis Plummer (£363 12s 4d). Vile and Cobb made up and erected the canopy (£74 10s 6d), and upholstered the chairs and stools (£10 16s). The giltwood throne is now at Grimsthorpe Castle, Lincolnshire as result of its owner, the Duke of Ancaster, being Lord Great Chamberlain, and thus entitled to perquisites. He also acquired the parcel gilt throne (Pl. 256), footstools and high stools from the prince's chamber in the House of Lords. Again these were made by Naish in 1761 (£24; footstool £4, two high stools £7 each) and upholstered by Vile and Cobb, using a rich flowered velvet supplied by Robert Carr (38s a yard). Whilst faded, this is still on the chair and stool. Attention has been drawn to the astute Katherine Naish charging £36 each for the two coronation thrones and footstools (albeit with more expensive fabric) and a more substantial sum, £53 10s, for the Lords throne and stools. Is it that she could achieve economy by the simultaneous production of parts for two chairs rather than one?

1 Roberts (1989) p.64.   2 Rothstein (1990) p.317.

A word of explanation about the taking of perquisites is sensible. The Duke of Devonshire, through his office as Lord Chamberlain, was able 'to claim the contents of the sovereign's apartments at the time of death'. A graphic, if belated, instance of this is revealed in a document at Chatsworth which reads:

> To be sent to Devonshire House this Evening
> 5 June 1761

Articles

1. His late Majesty's Crimson Damask Standing Bed & from above stairs, Hangings of the Room & Window Curtains of Crimson Damask.
2. One Easy, one Elbow chair & Six Square Stools covered with Crimson Silk Damask.
3. Four Mahogany Elbow Chairs covered with Crismon [sic.] silk Damask.
4. A Mahogany Card Table lined with green Velvet & Gold Lace.
5. A Walnut Tree Card Table lined with Do.
6. Two Walnut Tree Night Tables.

The bed is that now set up in the state bedroom at Chatsworth. The older office of Lord Great Chamberlain, conferred from 1133, had descended to the Duke of Ancaster in the 1760s. He was the 'effective viceroy of the Palace of Westminster' and was entitled to claim 'old or redundant furniture from within the Palace as soon as it ceased to have any use'. Such items are now at Grimsthorpe Castle, Lincolnshire, and three are illustrated here (Pls 255–6, 364).[3]

THE CROOME COURT COMMISSION

George William, sixth Earl of Coventry (1722–1809), succeeded to the title in March 1751 and a year later married Mary Gunning. To provide a fitting home for his new bride Lord Coventry had asked Lancelot 'Capability' Brown (who remained a life-long friend) to design Croome Court on the site of an older family house (and perhaps incorporating parts of it), some dozen miles or so south of Worcester. The house was being roofed by 1757 and a small group of talented craftsmen then concentrated on the interior. During the earl's long lifetime there was steady employment for them at both the Worcestershire house, its neighbouring church and for the London houses, principally 29 (now 106) Piccadilly. This interior work at Croome started in August 1760 under the overall architectural supervision of Robert Adam.

The Croome furniture archive[4] is an extensive one, with a large amount of work given in the early years of the commission to Vile and Cobb (Appendix A34) and to Mayhew and Ince. In all there are 130 bills for equipping the house, dating from 1757 to the earl's death in 1809. William Vile and John Cobb's first three bills submitted as partners covered the period from May 1757 to March 1759. They had been soon engaged in what they were excellent at – well upholstered carved mahogany furniture – and adding their usual services of making curtains, laying carpets and providing their fine furniture with case-covers. They had good contacts with the London mercers and, for example, covered twelve chairs in 1759 with damask which had been supplied by the 'Mercer, at the White Lyon against the church in Ludgate Street', Spencer Morris, '130 yards of Sky Blue Genoa Damask (13s 6d a yard, £87 15s)' with a further $56\frac{1}{2}$ yards at the same unit price.

THE CROOME TAPESTRY ROOM

Almost as soon as the Seven Years' War had ended – the Treaty of Paris was signed on 10 February 1763 – Lord Coventry visited Paris. French bills in the Croome archive show that he was there by April 1763 and

---

3 Roberts (1989), pp.61–6; Chatsworth MS, 247.7.
4 Beard (1953) pp.73–6; Beard (1993) pp.88–110. See also Parker and Standen (1959) pp.77–111 and Parker, Standen and Dauterman (1964).

there are several more bills for September–October of that year; in fact Lord Coventry's first visit to the Gobelins tapestry factory seems to have been a little before 20 April 1763. He would have met Jacques Neilson, head of the workshops from 1750 (and of Scottish origin), with the neoclassical architect, Jean-Germain Soufflot, as director and the painter François Boucher as artistic adviser. Soufflot had taken over at a difficult time, when the financial position at the Gobelins was severe, with large stocks of unsold tapestries. However, he turned matters around by working with Jacques Neilson at improving the quality of the low-warp (*basse-lisse*) looms and reducing the prices for finished work. Nevertheless, what had been in the active minds of the Gobelins directors was in accord with what Lord Coventry wanted: a tapestry room. In 1762 Maurice Jacques, one of the Gobelins artists who specialized in the designs of flower bouquets for seat covers, had made a drawing described (in translation) as 'a picture in colour, showing an apartment as it should be with the tapestry wall-hangings, the bed, the armchair and the settee.'[5] This picture was later sold to Lord Coventry for £400, and was probably the one billed by Robert Adam to Lord Coventry in January 1764: 'Altering the French designs of the Tapestry Room in Colours',[6] although no drawing that can be so identified now survives.

Lord Coventry's ideas for the structure of the tapestry room had been forming in 1762–3 with Adam's ceiling design for it dated in January 1763. In November Adam billed for a 'Section for the Tapestry Room' and in January 1764 a 'Design for finishing the side of the Tapestry Room'.[7] During the remainder of that year the ceiling was plastered by Joseph Rose, senior, (£48), and the pine panelling was made, embellished and erected by the carpenter John Hobcraft and the carver Sefferin Alken.[8] The room was re-erected at the Metropolitan Museum of Art, New York in 1964.

By 1764 the furniture maker William Vile had retired from his royal service and his partnership with the imperious John Cobb. The latter was capable of doing Lord Coventry's upholstery as formerly but was soon turning his attention more and more to elaborate marquetry furniture.

JOHN MAYHEW AND WILLIAM INCE

Vile and Cobb were succeeded in furnishing Lord Coventry's houses by several makers, including William France (Appendix A35) and John Mayhew and William Ince. The partnership of Mayhew and Ince had been set up in 1758–9 and, as it lasted until Ince's death in 1804, was 'one of the most significant and longest lived but, as far as identified furniture is concerned, the least well-documented of any of the major London cabinet-makers of the 18th century'.[9] I have made brief reference (p.162) to Mayhew and Ince's *Universal System of Household Furniture* (1762). In their preface they stated that the whole of 'above 300 Designs in the most elegant taste . . .' were made 'convenient to the Nobility and Gentry, in their choice, & comprehensive to the workman, by directions for executing the several Designs . . .' They indicated that their cabinet and upholstery branch was raised to a very high pitch and that 'Neatness through the whole House' should be joined with elegance. That is what they were to practise for Lord Coventry and others. There are twenty of their bills in the Croome archive, and three of them record the progress on its tapestry room.

Of the thirteen medallion tapestry suites woven in Paris between 1764 and 1789, six of them went to England[10] and all, except No.3, included furniture upholstery; they were:

1	Croome Court, Worcestershire	
	The Earl of Coventry	1766–71
2	Newby Hall, Yorkshire	
	William Weddell	1766–71

5   Parker, Standen and Dauterman (1964) p.17.
6   Beard (1953) pp.65–6; Beard (1993) pp.91–2.
7   Sir John Soane's Museum, London, Adam Drawings, Vol. 50, nos 12, 13.
8   Parker, Standen and Dauterman (1964) pp.30–1; Beard (1993) pp.92–3.
9   H. Roberts and C. Cator in Beard and Gilbert (1986) p.589.
10 E. Harris (1967) p.188, citing Fenaille (1907) IV, pp.299–300. See also Standen (1985) I, pp.385–401.

3	Weston Hall, Staffordshire	
	Sir Henry Bridgeman	1766–71
4	Moor Park, Hertfordshire	
	Sir Lawrence Dundas	1767–9
5	Osterley Park, Middlesex	
	Robert Child	1775–6
6	Welbeck Abbey, Nottinghamshire	
	The Duke of Portland	1783

Five of the patrons (with the Duke of Portland as the exception) were patrons of Robert Adam. All the suites remain *in situ* with the exception of the Dundas set for Moor Park. One of the chairs and a settee, which are at Osterley Park are illustrated here (Pls 330, 332).

Three of Mayhew and Ince's bills concerning the tapestry room have details, as follows; the numbers in parentheses refer to the relevant number of a bill in the Croome archive.[11] See also appendix (A38) and (A39).

(48)   April–December, 1768 (April 1768) 'Mounting Your Lordships own Tapestry Backs with Crimson Lustring on a Neat Redwood Claw and Varnish'd Compleat, £3 3s.'

(58)   March 1769–April 1770, '6 Large Antique Chairs . . . proper for Covering with Tapistry in the Country . . . £77 8s; 2 Settees . . . to match the Chairs, £56 10s.' (Pl. 313)

(61)   June 1771–June 1772 'Three Men's time at Croome putting up the Tapestry' – the men were Jones, Elwood and Bolton, at 44, 44 and 41 days each at 5s, 4s 6d and 3s 6d per day respectively, (£28 1s 6d, including 'Paper Case hangings, Stuffing & Covering, 2 Settees and 6 Chairs, fixing Gilt Border & Sundry other Jobbs').

The terse citations in the bills do little to prepare one for these brilliant displays of the tapestry weaver's art. They established Mayhew and Ince as regular and competent suppliers of furniture, who went on working, on and off, for Lord Coventry, until 1794.

SIR LAWRENCE DUNDAS AND THE GOBELINS

Sir Lawrence Dundas (*c.*1710–81), had acquired great wealth whilst acting as Commissary-General and Paymaster to the armies of George II, from 1748 to 1759. He fortunately used most of his money wisely and established his position as a discriminating patron, not only on his north Yorkshire estate at Aske Hall but also at Moor Park, Hertfordshire and his London town house at 19 Arlington Street. For the last two properties he engaged the architectural services of his fellow Scotsman, Robert Adam. Dundas had purchased Moor Park in 1763 but used Adam only sparingly, to work on his tapestry gallery, in the park, and at Arlington Street. This town house (illustrated in *Country Life*, 17 September 1921) survived until 1936, with the dispersal of its contents starting with a Christie's sale of 27 April 1934.[12] It remains well-known through Zoffany's painting (1769) showing Sir Lawrence with his grandson in the Library or pillar room at Arlington Street (Pl. 310).

Sir Lawrence and his agent, John Stewart, had been attracted to consider the productions of the Gobelins factory by being offered, in 1763, a one-third reduction on the price of its stock of tapestries. Nevertheless, as with Lord Coventry, they wanted the attractive medallion suite. The surviving documentation is full and has been related carefully but it needs to be remembered that there are 'no Adam designs and no bills for designs for any of the pieces of tapestry furniture either at Moor Park, or at Croome, Newby or Osterley'.[13] The significant surviving furniture bills related to the tapestry suite are from Lawrence Fell and

11   Beard (1993) pp.102–3, Nos 48, 58, 61.
12   J. Harris (1967) pp.171, 177.

13   E. Harris (1962) pp.100–16 and (1967) pp.181–2, 186.

William Turton. Other bills for furniture are from, principally, Thomas Chippendale, Samuel Norman, William France and his partner John Bradburn, and James Lawson.[14]

By 1770 Lawrence Fell, a London cabinet-maker, had entered into partnership with William Turton. Whilst little enough is known about them they were to receive over £5,000 from Sir Lawrence in the ten years from 1765 to 1775.[15] When the Moor Park suite was dispersed one sofa, six armchairs, two window stools and two firescreens went to the Philadelphia Museum of Art (1941.6.1–11); the four remaining armchairs and a sofa are now at Temple Newsam House, Leeds (Pls 316–17).

Fell and Turton's account[16] for the suite is dated to 1771; it records providing only two sofas, six chairs and two window stools. Four more chairs were obviously supplied at a slightly later date. The bill included:

> To 2 Sophas Carved and gilt in Burnished fold, stuffed with Best Curl'd hair and fine
> linnin . . .   £25   50.0.0
> To Covering do with your Tapestry, used Brass naills, sewing silk, fine Durant for the back
> Backs, tax &c.   1.10.0
> To 6 Elbow Chairs carv'd and gilt in Burnished gold stuffd in Best Curl'd hair and fine
> linnin . . .   £10   60.0.0
> To Covering do with your Tapestry used sewing silk, fine Durant for the Back, Backs tax
> &c.   2.8.0

CHIPPENDALE'S UPHOLSTERY BRANCH

It is necessary to record, for completeness, some details of Thomas Chippendale's upholstery work, based on the facts published in 1974 and 1978.[17] The Yorkshireman had set up efficient workshops in London at St Martin's Lane, including a two-storey upholsterer's shop, a carpet room, and two feather rooms. The upholsterer's shop contents accounted for nearly half the Sun Office's insurance valuation of the business premises – £2,600 in 1756. Chippendale kept a selection of carpets to show to his customers, and provided them to the size needed by laying out the plan of the intended room in a chalked outline on his carpet wareroom floor. Apart from the three fine carpets surviving from Passavant's *atelier*, one supplied to the Earl of Dumfries by Chippendale in 1759 (Pl. 240), the cabinet-maker and his contemporaries also used Axminster carpets made by Thomas Whitty.[18]

Chippendale was hindered in the specialized trade of upholstery by not having the knowledge or facilities for the complex task of dyeing cloth. In view of this he sub-contracted such jobs to professional dyers and was sometimes let down with their services. Sir Rowland Winn had asked Chippendale in August 1767 if a set of silk damask bed hangings could be dyed. Chippendale replied to him on 26 August[19] to indicate that he had received the 'furniture' of two beds:

> & have unript them and sent them to be dy'd, but am very sorry I unript the red Damask as
> I find it will not take a garter blue as the Ingenious Mr Elwick said it would, I trusted to his
> knowledge for which I am sorely vexd, it will take a dark blue and no other coloure therefore
> it stands as it was in the same Colour till I have your further orders . . .

The 'French chairs' which Chippendale illustrated (Pl. 258) in the 1762 edition of his *Director* could, as the accompanying note indicated, 'be covered with Tapestry or some other sort of Needlework'. Despite a long-held interest by patrons in covering their chairs in silk damask, which they sometimes provided, the chairs and settees at Newby Hall, Yorkshire made for William Weddell have their original Gobelins tapestry covers. They are mounted on the 'only known seat furniture by Chippendale which preserves its original upholstery'.

14 Coleridge (1967) I, pp.190–203; II, pp.214–25.
15 Beard and Gilbert (1986) pp.294–5.
16 North Yorkshire C.R.O., MS., ZNK X 1/7/11 cited by Gilbert (1978) I, p.63.
17 Walton and Gilbert (1974) pp.26–32; Gilbert (1978).
18 Sherrill (1996).
19 Gilbert (1978) I, p.176.

The furniture maker was involved too in hanging the walls in the Newby tapestry room with Neilson and Boucher's attractive tapestries (but in a different background colour of pale pink-grey) and for supplying '3 window Curtains of Green water'd Tabby lined & silk Fringe a sett of Cornices carv'd & Gilt in burnished Gold'.[20] These festoon curtains have needed to be replaced with replicas but a 1977 illustration of one of the original curtains (Pl. 322) which is now in storage at the house is shown here. It has its original line of brass rings sewn to the lining fabric, the circular lead weights to assist correct hanging, and its silk fringe.

CHIPPENDALE AND SIR LAWRENCE DUNDAS

Sir Lawrence Dundas had known from a law suit decision in the case of *Norman v. Dundas* that Chippendale, George Smith Bradshaw and Mayhew had examined bills for furniture intended for him from Samuel Norman, dating 1763 to 1766. With the gilding of the Moor Park gallery also by Norman, the total came to £2,410 1s. By 1766 Sir Lawrence, feeling that he had been overcharged, had ceased payment, and so Norman took him to court. The examiners agreed finally that Dundas was only entitled to the return of £290.[21] This apart, Dundas was a good patron of several furniture makers, and had known Chippendale from at least the early 1760s. When Lady Shelburne visited the Dundas's Arlington Street house in March 1768 she recorded in her diary[22] that she had seen 'Gilt chairs' in the great room ('now hung with red damask'), and the May 1768 Dundas inventory (which has, alas, been mislaid) mentioned further that there were '4 Sophas gilt, covered with Damask' and '8 Gilt chairs, covered with Do'. The long room next to the great room contained a further three sofas and ten armchairs. Chippendale invoiced on 9 July 1765 for the '8 large Arm Chairs . . . cover'd with your own Damask' and the '4 large Sofas Exceeding Rich to match the Chairs'. The superb quality was indicated by the considerable sums of £20 which he charged for the frame of each chair and their upholstering, with Sir Lawrence's own fabric, and £54 for each sofa. Robert Adam[23] had designed this splendid suite – his design for a sofa, signed and dated 1764, is illustrated (Pl. 277) – but the Dundas commission remains the only one known, to date, in which Chippendale executed an Adam furniture design. A chair, one of eight, with a sofa,[24] *en suite*, is shown here with its (crimson) floral damask, which had to be replaced on reupholstering (Pls 278–80).

JOHN BRADBURN AND WILLIAM FRANCE

The London cabinet maker, upholsterer, appraiser and undertaker, John Bradburn (or Bradburne; d.1781), had been employed in the 1750s by the Vile–Cobb partnership. In fact he may well have been responsible for some of the finely carved mahogany furniture produced in the 1750s by that successful partnership.

By 1764, Bradburn, who was established at Hemming's Row, off Long Acre, was in partnership himself with William France, who had, from 1759, also been working for Vile and Cobb. Both Bradburn and France's names appear in Vile and Cobb's bank accounts, and they signed frequently for money due to their masters. When Vile retired in 1764 from his post of royal cabinet-maker Bradburn succeeded him, and with his new partner continued, ably, what Vile and Cobb had done over the previous three years. Apart from their royal service they were soon working for William Murray, first Earl of Mansfield and for Sir Lawrence Dundas, both of whom were using the architectural services of the outstandingly successful Robert Adam. With plenty of work in hand Bradburn and France took on a number of apprentices and, particularly in 1766, William France's son, Edward.

20   Gilbert (1978) I, p.265.
21   Coleridge (1967) I, p.191.
22   I am indebted to the Earl of Shelburne for showing this to me at Bowood and to his archivist, Dr Kate Feilden, for the use of her transcript of the diary.

23   E. Harris (1963) pp.91–2; Beard (1978).
24   The location of Moor Park furniture following the Christie's sale, 26 April 1934, is noted by Gilbert (1978) I, p.157. Since that date pieces have been acquired for the Iveagh Bequest at Kenwood.

The Earl of Mansfield had been living at Kenwood House on Hampstead Heath for ten years before he turned, in 1764, for architectural help from Robert Adam. After the consideration of drawings the remodelling of Kenwood was put in hand and its fine surviving interiors are an eloquent reminder of why Adam was so much in demand. They show, as he put it later in *The Works in Architecture* he and his brother James issued (1773–9), the 'full liberty to make the proper deviations' in order that harmony could be achieved 'between the new and the old parts of the building'. A talented group of craftsmen[25] had been assembled across the years to carry out most of Adam's decorative work and, amongst their number, were Bradburn and France. Surprisingly France, in particular (who did most of the Kenwood work), sent his bills direct to Lord Mansfield and not through the architect. This arrangement had been varied by the careful lawyer patron when France was involved with Thomas Chippendale in supplying mirror plates for the two recesses flanking the saloon chimneypiece. The £170 due to Chippendale was paid to France in August 1769 to hold in case Chippendale did not deliver the glass within three months. The carved and gilt frames by France were set above two sofas he provided: '2 Sophas made to Mr Adams Design carv'd & gilt in burnish'd Gold the carving all finished in very Elaborate manner, £50 14s.'[26] The mirror and sofa are shown in the Adams's *The Works in Architecture* (1774, I, No.2, plate V). France also made in 1769 'three Scrole headed Sopha frames for the windows carved & Gilt in burnish'd Gold the carving all done on the same principal as the sophas, £48.'

Due to the wide dispersal and disappearance of furniture following the Kenwood sale in 1922, it has been necessary in recent years to search for both the originals and furniture of comparable standard. There have been notable successes in this quest,[27] including the purchase of a mahogany scroll stool designed by Adam in 1764 and one of a set supplied by France and carved by Sefferin Alken for the gallery at Croome Court. The design for it was made in 1766, firstly for Sir Lawrence Dundas for Moor Park and then, at his disinterest, it was passed on to Lord Coventry.[28]

James Lawson and William France

A cabinet-maker who did a few upholstery jobs for Sir Lawrence Dundas was James Lawson. He had premises in Chandos Street, Covent Garden, firstly (1763–5) with Peter Lawson but after 1767 solely in his name. However, his bills to Sir Lawrence from 1763 onwards[29] are in his own name too. On 26 May 1764 he charged for:

> Covering 6 Arm Chairs with Tapestry, best double burnish'd nails &c for Do   a 4/6d.   £1.7.0
> Covering a Sopha and 2 bolsters with Tapestry best burnish'd Nails, Morine for the back &c (£1 18s).

In October of the same year he charged £72 for '2 Carved & gilt sophas cover'd with blue Turkey leather.' They had three cushions and two bolsters to each and there were six armchairs (£75) (Pl. 281) and two scroll headed stools (£20 2s 6d each) *en suite*. At the same time the servants were not forgotten: 'A Porter's Chair on Casters cover'd with leather inside & out & brass nail'd & Cusheon for Do. (£7)' and: 'Enlarging the top of the Steward's Dining table, a new frame, 2 new legs (£1 11s 6d)'. In the three years of his activity, 1763 to 1766, Lawson received £668 18s 3d for his varied cabinet-maker's activity at Moor Park and Arlington Street. Most of the upholstery was done from 1764 by William France.

The extensive Dundas archive[30] is useful in showing details of the many tasks William France undertook. In April 1764 he had visited Moor Park to select places to hang pictures. In his account of April 16, 1764 France stated that these needed to be hung on brass headed nails 'with carved heads' of various sizes

25   Beard (1978) II, pp.181–93.
26   Harris (1963) p.79.
27   Bryant (1988) pp.192–5.
28   Sir John Soane's Museum, London, Adam drawings, Vol. 17, No.73; Harris (1963) p.91.
29   North Yorkshire C.R.O., MSS. ZNK X 1/7/26–30; 72.
30   *Ibid.*

'to suit the weights of the pictures'. Whilst the drawing room was 'new laying' hangings of cartridge paper had been put to cover the blue damask hangings and gilt border (£3 17s 6d). When eight large pictures were hung canvas and cartridge were put behind the frames to prevent 'the frames and Nails scratching the Damask' (£2 14s). The making of the 'Crimson Genoa Damask' hangings and fitting them to two rooms meant it was necessary to have 'Trussels & Scaffolding' in position for, as France indicated, with feeling: 'without which Assistance in Rooms so large & so high [they] could not be hung without the Greatest Difficulty & large expense' [£28 16s]. When the cartridge paper protecting the damask hangings was taken down finally, in January 1765, it was necessary to dust very well, and also to clean 'very well with Bread the damask hangings and all the Lines & Tossels &c' (£1 14s).

At Arlington Street in June 1764 there was a need to bring the decoration of some beds up to date:

> For undoing intirely, and altering the Plan & piecing out D° to fit the Bedsd above by gluing large Additions on each side of every Quarter, and new making over the whole to make the shape of the Dome agree, making out the Cornices, and making 4 Angle Ornaments 4 Centre Do & 8 other large Ornaments to fill up the flatt space which the inlargement unavoidably left all round the inside of the Dome, 4 new field Bed Pins, a Screw and Nutts.   £5.18 –

Sir Lawrence was paying France on a regular basis but about two and a half years late; for example, the bill finishing June 1764 was paid on 3 January 1767. In June and September 1764 France and Bradburn took inventories of the household furniture at Arlington Street and Moor Park, charging one guinea (Arlington Street) and £2 12s 6d (Moor Park). A further 16s and 18s was charged for copying the details into two books. By contrast to present-day living there seemed many changes of mind and a consequent constant upheaval in moving furniture. Even allowing for preparation of the house France and Bradburn had much to charge for. They were obviously competent and dealt with everything from new bell lines, tightening the sacking of the 'Garret Beds', covering wall hangings and window hangings to protect from dust, moving pictures as well as providing a variety of furniture, both carcase and upholstered, and lining a dog basket with a hair canvas cushion. A selection of these tasks is described in the appendix (A36).

The Linnell Enterprise

When William Linnell died intestate in 1763 his son John, who had been involved actively with the day-to-day running of the business since at least 1753, took over. An inventory of stock-in-trade and tools was taken.[31] There were three upholsterers' shops, a main one, with a 'Middle' and a 'Back' one. The middle shop seems to have mainly held the stock of Wilton, Turkey and Kidderminster carpets and the main upholsterer's shop everything from blankets, bed furniture, curtains, case covers, stocks of materials, fringes and line. The back shop had a miscellaneous array of furniture from a kitchen dresser, a wool carder, a large field hammock and various bedsteads. What was, however, of greater concern in the large premises at 28 Berkeley Square was 'Mr John Linnell's Drawing Room'. This was a room for the preparation of his fertile designs, of which over a thousand survive,[32] and included three tables, four mahogany drawing boards, T-squares, 'a deal Academy drawing board, a folding stool, a leather covered armchair and fireside implements'. One can imagine a neat productive area, warmed by a fire; the creative centre of the Linnell enterprise.

Linnell had learned to draw and acquire a knowledge of styles at the St Martin's Lane Academy, founded in 1735 by William Hogarth.[33] He was friendly with a leading landscape painter, George Barrett, and showed talent as a painter himself. When Linnell took over the firm he and his father had already done carving and upholstery for the sixth Earl of Coventry at Croome Court, William Drake of Shardeloes, Buckinghamshire, and at Lord Scarsdale's Derbyshire seat, Kedleston, all early Adam houses. At Croome they had worked

31 Hayward and Kirkham (1980) I, Appendix III, pp.168–80.   33 Girouard (1966).
32 Hayward (1969).

alongside Vile and Cobb from July 1758 doing such jobs as carving a chimney 'in the French taste with lions faces in the frieze', other chimneypieces, various window curtains in 'green morrine' and crimson silk damask, together with providing 57 yards of Wilton carpet.[34]

In January 1762 William Drake had moved into his London town house in Grosvenor Street. The Linnells had worked for him since 1749 and from 1751 Drake had regarded William Linnell as his regular upholsterer.[35] As I have noted in relation to William France's work for Sir Lawrence Dundas, the acquisition of a new house or remodelling of an old one gave plenty of work to craftsmen, although often paid for tardily. There was much remaking of curtains and adapting furniture to new positions as well as measuring up and then making many items with supplies of fabric made available by Drake.

It says much for the harmonious relations the firm created with its patrons that Sir Nathaniel Curzon (created first Baron Scarsdale in April 1761) used the Linnell firm over some forty years. John Linnell's designs for seat furniture for Kedleston are justly celebrated. Lord Scarsdale, under the pervasive influence of Robert Adam, had created a great palace in the Derbyshire countryside, and its magnificent state rooms needed furniture worthy of the settings. There are several Linnell sketches (Pls 237, 257) for the famous suite of four sofas, two of thirteen feet in length and two slighter shorter, of twelve feet, for the east and west walls. The carving and gilding of the free-standing merfolk at each end of the sofas is memorable. They took three years to make, *c*.1762–5. Lord Scarsdale's clerk of works, the architect Samuel Wyatt, reported to him in July 1765: 'the sofa arrived safe and it is certainly as elegant a piece of furniture as ever was made and as well executed. The gilding is by far the best done of any I ever saw, it suits the place in point of size very well.'[36] All four were in place by August and presumably accounted for a substantial part of the £800 paid to the firm in 1765 and 1766. They were upholstered in blue damask, *en suite* with the wall hangings, a material and colour which was continued in the adjacent state bedroom. It has been retained in the re-upholstering of the sofas and the bed furniture.

The early 1760s were an interesting and challenging time as architects such as Adam and Sir William Chambers, fresh back from years of training and observation in Italy, pushed back the heady swirls of the rococo style and its variants before their introduction of a precise 'new' classicism. Furniture makers and other craftsmen in the decorative trades needed to adapt to this to survive. Thomas Chippendale and Mayhew and Ince accomplished it and John Linnell too. He vied with them for jobs from the limited circle of patrons keen to be in the vanguard of taste. Two such were the bankers Francis and Robert Child, but Francis died in 1763 and work on Osterley Park, Middlesex came to a halt for a short time.[37] Sir William Chambers, who was interested in furniture design, may have drawn out a set of 'Twelve large Mahogany french Elbow Chairs', with four settees *en suite*, for the gallery at Osterley Park, and perhaps made by Linnell.[38] It has been pointed out[39] that the small finial of inverted lotus leaves capping the central front legs on the settees was also used by Linnell on the backs of the hall settees he designed and made for William Drake, and a similar feature appears on the front legs of the Osterley tapestry room chairs, *c*.1776 (Pl. 321). No bills survive to present a correct story.

There is a considerable amount of furniture at Osterley Park thus attributed to John Linnell. Nevertheless, he cannot be credited with that in the state bedroom. Dominating the room is the oak, beech and pine, painted and gilded bedstead. A Robert Adam design for this 'Temple of Venus' (Pl. 324) is dated 16 May 1776,[40] and the Osterley inventory description of 1782 shows how 'very Elegant' it was, and still is: 'A very Elegant State Bedstead with Eight painted & Japanned Columns . . . A rich Carved and dome Teaster . . . the furniture Velvet Drapery richly embroidered in Colours . . . the Dome fringed in festoons . . .' (Pls 325–9). The valance (Pl. 327) is decorated with alternating panels with an eagle holding an adder in its beak (the Child family crest), and a marigold, the symbol of the Child banking house. The inside of the dome (Pl. 326) is lined with silk, embroidered in colours. Round the outside of the dome are festoons of artificial flowers. These have

34 Beard (1993), Bill No.8.
35 Hayward and Kirkham (1980) I, p.98.
36 *Ibid.*, p.111.
37 E. Harris (1994) p.26.
38 Tomlin (1972) p.33.
39 Hayward (1969), fig.15.
40 Sir John Soane's Museum, London, Adam drawings, Vol. 17, No.157.

been restored (by Lucy Henderson in 1982), so that the observation by Horace Walpole on his visit to Osterley in 1778 can again ring true: 'like a modern head-dress, for round the outside of the dome are festoons of artificial flowers', with the added sharp comment: 'What would Vitruvius think of a dome decorated by a milliner'.[41]

Robert Child was also interested in the acquisition of one of the Gobelins tapestry rooms he would know of at Croome, Newby and Moor Park. It is, however, not known whether Linnell had a hand in setting up what arrived eventually, *c.*1776, at Osterley. The Linnell authorities indicate[42] that 'both the chairs and the settee [there are eight armchairs and one settee in the room, Pls 330–2] have stylistic and structural features characteristic of the Berkeley Square workshop'. There are, moreover, two Linnell designs,[43] one for a chair and one for a settee, which approximate closely to what was made. So, Osterley has a mixture of furniture held reliably to be by Linnell and some which is attributed firmly to him, overlaid by designs by Robert Adam. Continuing research (by Eileen Harris and others) is doing much to unravel the complexity of his involvement in many commissions which included the supply of furniture in neoclassical style.

UPHOLSTERERS AT CORSHAM COURT

In 1575 Sir Christopher Hatton sold off the derelict medieval house at Corsham, Wiltshire to a local man, Thomas Smythe. Smythe had made a successful career in London, becoming a collector of customs there, and soon had the money to rebuild, incorporating parts of the earlier house. In subsequent years the house had several owners including, for a short time (1706–16), Lord Thomas Thynne of Longleat. Then in 1745 it was acquired for Paul Methuen (1723–95), descended from a long line of powerful clothiers, who had been active in the Wiltshire woollen industry at Bradford-on-Avon. Numbered in the family was his cousin, another Paul Methuen (1672–1757), who had been appointed Comptroller of the Royal Household in 1720 and created a Knight of the Bath in 1725. Many of the paintings and architectural books he acquired on his extensive travels came to Corsham at his death and remain there. They needed a worthy setting, and particularly a picture gallery.

Paul Methuen's tenure at Corsham had started finally in March 1747 when he was twenty-three years old. He grew up in an atmosphere where his contemporaries were commissioning houses in the Gothic style but his own extensive travels turned him more to Palladian principles, but confusingly to several architects. The façades of Corsham today are a complex series of interlocking ideas: the Elizabethan house, the Palladian façade of the north front, Gothic influences, dabbling with designs by Henry Keene and finally Lancelot 'Capability' Brown. He offered the considerable advantage that he could both remodel the house and set out the park as he was doing for Lord Coventry at Croome Court, sixty miles to the north-west. The greatest problem was to incorporate the picture gallery so that it could take advantage of a north light: the result was a triple cube room (72 × 24 ft) with an ornate coffered ceiling by the Bristol stuccoist, Thomas Stocking, on which his normal spritely motifs are kept in severe check. The white marble chimneypiece by Peter Scheemakers (1763, £325)[44] observed the published dictums of the architect, Isaac Ware, in his *A Complete Body of Architecture* (1756): 'Instead of bestowing the richest coloured marbles upon these chimneypieces where he intended the greatest expense of ornament . . . he will adopt for these high sculptured pieces always a plain marble of one uninterrupted colour.' It stands well against the crimson damask on the walls, and the gallery and the other state rooms seem to have been ready to receive furniture by 1766–7.

There are some difficulties in being precise about who did what in the realization of the upholstered schemes at Corsham Court. Most of our knowledge[45] stems from a day book kept by Paul Methuen's son, Paul Cobb Methuen (1752–95), the second owner of the house.[46] From 1761 to 1774 the principal London

---

41 Lewis ed. vol. 29 (1955), Walpole to Rev. William Mason, 16 July 1778.
42 Hayward and Kirkham (1980) I, p.119.
43 Victoria and Albert Museum, E76-1929 (chair); E123-1929 (settee) Hayward and Kirkham (1980) figs 94, 260.

44 Ladd (1978) p.161.
45 Lord Methuen (1891–1975) took a considerable interest in the archives, carefully examining them and noting matters of interest to art historians.
46 Now at Wiltshire C.R.O., Methuen archive.

upholsterer mentioned was George Cole of Golden Square. There is little indication of the nature of the goods supplied and work done but the payments included some substantial sums:

1761	10 March		130.14.0
	16 September	on account	100.0.0
	25 November	on account	105.0.0
1763	21 April	on account	50.0.0
	30 April		101.8.0
1764	10 May		16.4.0
	27 October		98.14.0
1765	21 November		91.0.0
1766	26 April		19.7.0
	4 June	on account	95.0.0
	9 November		10.13.0
1768	17 April	Upholstery goods sent to Corsham House, being furniture for Great Room [i.e. Picture Gallery]	34.11.6

There are further big payments in 1773 and 1774 totalling over £600.

The suite of furniture at Corsham by Cole is a large one – thirty armchairs, four settees and eight window seats. The mercers were active in providing crimson silk damask, still *in situ* on the picture gallery walls, and the suite of furniture. In 1765 the London mercers Morris and Young sent 700 yards of eighteen inch width damask at 13s 6d a yard (£472 10s). This was used principally on the gallery walls (Pl. 308). Four years later another 478$\frac{1}{2}$ yards came from Robert Young alone (at 14s a yard) to be used by Cole senior on the furniture. It is interesting that in 1766 Morris and Young also supplied the sixth Earl of Coventry with crimson Genoa damask at 14s a yard.[47] Other small orders of flowered velvet for Corsham were fulfilled by a Mr Palmer (£36 6s, 11 December 1764) and Thomas Hinchcliff (£27, 19 December 1768). I have illustrated details of the fine Corsham suite (Pls 306–8) alongside a painting by Sir Joshua Reynolds (Pl. 294) dated to *c*.1765–6. The painter has depicted a similar nailing pattern and a flat profile to the seat, characteristic of upholstered furniture from good makers.

John Gordon and John Taitt

One cannot tell why a patron furnishing the rooms of a new house – and there were many indulging in this heady and expensive delight in the 1760s – turned to one upholsterer instead of another. Recommendation was obviously a factor, price yet another, but many of the reasons will always remain obscure. This is so with the partnership of John Gordon and John Taitt. By the late 1740s he was settled in London but had work in hand for the Duke of Atholl at Blair Castle, near Perth. And yet William Masters too was also making a considerable amount of furniture for the duke (p.158). At some time in the late 1750s or early 1760s, with a substantial enterprise at his call, Gordon entered into a partnership with John Taitt. His origins, as also the details of what Gordon was doing in the 1750s, remain obscure.[48] They submitted, jointly, their first bill to Lord Coventry covering furniture supplied in the period from 11 April 1767 to February 1768.[49] The bill is only a short one but its principal item concerned an important neoclassical suite 'in the Antique manner'. How grand it must have looked with the 'Grounds' picked out in green against crimson damask:

47 Croome Court Archive, Furniture Bill 27 (Beard, 1993) p.100.   49 Croome Court Archive, Furniture Bill 38 (Beard, 1993) p.101.
48 Beard and Gilbert (1986) p.356.

1768   Feby 11. To 8 Large Elbow Chairs Richly Carv'd in the Antique manner, and Gilt
in Burnish'd Gold the Grounds pick'd in green Covered with his Lordship's Crimson
Silk Damask & Naild with Gilt nails, with 3 Large Sophas to match Ditto   200.0.0
To making 8 Crimson & white Erminett Check Cases for Ditto with Thread, Tape
&c.   2.0.0
To 47 Yards of Check   a) 2/6   5.17.6
To making 3 Setts of Crimson & white Check Cases for the Sophas with Thread,
Tape &c.   2.5.0
To 53¾ yards of Check   a) 2/6   6.14.5
217.1.11

Recd 19th May 1768 the full Contents & all Demands for Mr Gordon & Self.   Jno
Taitt.   £217.

It is sensible to assume in partnerships that each partner had a specific responsibility, although the available evidence does not always allow the distinction to be made. John Cobb had trained as an upholsterer but was equally adept, with William Vile, at making carcase furniture. John Mayhew had been apprenticed to William Bradshaw but that versatile craftsman counted tapestry weaving, joinery and making carcase furniture as well as upholstery amongst his many accomplishments.

Gordon and Taitt's principal commission was the work they did (1771–3), for Sir John Griffin Griffin at Audley End, Essex. He had assumed the additional name of Griffin (instead of Whitwell) in 1762, as a condition of inheriting the estate from his aunt, Elizabeth, Countess of Portsmouth. As a distinguished soldier as well as a member of Parliament Sir John, together with his wife Katherine (Clayton), was often in London, and he asked Robert Adam, in the late 1760s, to design a new ground floor suite of reception rooms within the great Jacobean house at Audley End. Capability Brown, who was often to landscape the parks of houses designed by Adam, had already transformed the surrounding formal gardens and deer park into a picturesque landscape.

Robert Adam was involved at Audley End particularly with the design and decoration of the dining parlour, great drawing room, little drawing room and a library (destroyed, alas, in 1825, when a new one was created on the first floor). The main outlines of the restoration have been documented,[50] but more details of the upholsterers' work are included here.

On 2 March 1768 the London mercers Harris, King, Thompson and Padgett had submitted a bill[51] for 309 yards of 'Crimson & Green rich furniture' fabric (18s 3d a yard; £281 19s 3d). This was passed finally to the use of the upholsterers, Gordon and Taitt, but it was three years before the mercers were paid for it, with Thomas King receiving 'For Self & Co' £150 on account on 19 January 1771, a further £80 on 25 June and the final £51 19s on 31 December. Gordon and Taitt rendered their bill in 1771.[52] As at Croome Court they covered two carved and gilt sofas 'party green' with 'your own Damask' (£52 10s), eight cabriole elbow chairs to match (£58 16s), all with pea green and white striped linen cases (sofas 15s each; chairs 1s each), and then turned their attention to the great drawing room. The room had given Robert Adam the sort of problems he had faced earlier at Syon House, where the conversion of an older house gave different levels and heights to those needed. The proportions of the great room were adequate in length and breadth but not in height – it was but 11½ feet (3.5m). Nevertheless, the plasterers Joseph Rose and his nephew Joseph followed Adam's intricate patterning with a skill born of familiarity. It was painted by John Wateridge to harmonize with the silk hangings. Gilded woodcarving came from the chisels of John and William Robert Adair, and the chimney-piece on the north wall was by John Moore.[53] The upholsterers then gave the final grand touch (Pl. 318),

50   Williams (1966) based on Essex C.R.O., Braybrooke MSS., D/DBy. I am much indebted to Gareth Hughes (English Heritage) for the loan of many photocopies and for elucidating their contents.

51   Essex C.R.O., D/DBy A 29/12; see Rothstein (1990) pp.316, 321.

52   *Ibid.*, A31/3.

53   *Ibid.*, A32/8 (Adair); A28/3 (Moore).

charging £15 for '. . . hanging the Great Drawing Room with your own party coloured Damask' and a further £9 for '180 Yds Silk Lace, to go round the Hangings' (1s a yard). Three festoon window curtains were made, lined with tammy (£3 10s), needing '42 yards of best Silk Lace' (1s a yard), with a further 26½ yards of 'very fine deep Silk fringe with a Gimp head' (11s 6d a yard; £11 15s 9d). The silk line, six large silk tassels and the Oes, braid etc. added £6 11s more. For the bow window in the room Gordon and Taitt made four 'Scrole Stools' (£25 4s) with carved and gilt frames, stuffed with hair in canvas *en suite* to the two sofas and eight chairs. These were covered with more yards of Sir John's 'own Damask' and finished with gilt nails.

It has been suggested that 'the lines of the sofa backs were designed by Gordon and Taitt precisely to follow the silk pattern . . . The eight chairs were upholstered to suit the sofas. Thus each piece of furniture was tightly locked into the overall pattern'.[54] This precise placing is an attractive theory but I am not sure it holds up; in any case thoughts of the complex unity in Adam's work need to encompass the 1962 restoration, when the silk was rewoven to the original pattern (Pl. 318).

The little drawing room, which opens to the east out of the great drawing room, was intended as a sitting room for ladies while their male companions stayed on in the dining parlour. Adam had drawn a section of the room in October 1764, but his design was modified; the ceiling 'in the Taste of the Painting of the Ancients' was not carried out. Instead Sir John invited Biagio Rebecca to paint a mosaic ceiling and panels, based partly on Bernard de Montfaucon's *L'Antiquité Expliquée* (Paris, 1719–24). Again the ceiling was painted to reflect the colours in the wall paintings, and in the adjoining room. Gordon and Taitt then billed, in August 1771: 'To a very large double headed Couch richly carved after the manner of the Antique, & gilt in burnished Gold stuffed with hair in Canvas & covered with your own flowerd Sattin & gilt Nails &c. £30.' Their furniture was covered with either a set of blue and white striped silk cases or a set of white flannel cases (£1 11s), and two 'scrole Stools' (£35) and 'four small Stooles' (£22) were similarly covered. A damask leather cover (6s) was provided for the circular table (£10), which matched the couch. The screened sofa niche in the little drawing room was hung with more of 'your own flower'd Sattin'; this may have been made originally as a dress material.

One of the tasks at which upholsterers usually excelled was the making of curtains. The pair made in 1770 for the first room of Adam's great apartments, the great parlour, were of pea green lustring lined with tammy. In their lace-bedecked form they were drawn up on silk line over four brass pulleys with a careful counterbalance of balance weights helping the process. The three curtains for the great drawing room *en suite* with the room's hangings were also lined with tammy, trimmed with silk lace with a 'very fine deep silk fringe with a Gimp head' (11s 6d a yard; £11 15s 9d), and six large silk tassels (9s each). The two festoon curtains in the little drawing room were of the 'flower'd Sattin', lined with tammy, similarly ornamented with lace, two silk tassels (7s 6d each), and one yard of stuff to cover the pulley laths. In all, Gordon and Taitt charged Sir John £695 11s 3d.[55]

LEADERS IN TRADE

Sir John Griffin Griffin was typical of several patrons who used a good quality firm like Gordon and Taitt, yet turned to the leading men for other furnishings. Mayhew and Ince had supplied six painted green and white 'French cabriolets' in 1773[56] – Thomas Sheraton in his *The Cabinet Dictionary* (1803) described these as an 'arm-chair stuffed all over', or a 'French easy chair'. They cost Sir John a guinea each. A year later Thomas Chippendale provided a rosewood (cross-banded with tulip wood) hexagon claw-table (3 guineas).[57] However, both firms were involved with much more important commissions.

Mayhew and Ince had been paid almost £2,000 for their furnishings from 1767 (and on to 1779) for Brownlow Cecil, ninth Earl of Exeter at Burghley House, Cambridgeshire and at the London town house in

54   I. R. Gow in Apted and Allen (1984).
55   Essex C.R.O., D/D By A.365.
56   *Ibid.*, A32/2.
57   *Ibid.*, A32/9.

Lower Grosvenor Street. Of this sum, £1,245 3s 11½d was for work in 1767–8. A principal surviving piece of an antiquarian kind is the four-post bedstead (Pl. 309) in the blue and silver bedroom. The earl had determined to restore the existing seventeenth-century interiors, rich with mural paintings by Antonio Verrio and wood carvings by a team of craftsmen led by the joiner, Roger Davies. The earl took for his own use the bedroom occupied previously by his deceased countess. It was hung with blue and silver Soho tapestries by John Vanderbank which Mayhew and Ince repaired and cleaned. This done, they were ready with a new bed, with its hangings, blankets and quilted fine calico counterpane at a total cost of £164 4s 3d. The style of the bed suited the room and it was significantly cheaper than the one Thomas Chippendale provided for Edwin Lascelles of Harewood House, near Leeds in 1773. That state domed bedstead, admittedly with 'the whole Gilt in burnished Gold', cost £250.[58] The bill describes the bed as: 'A Large Antique Headboard, sunk with mouldings, a carved tester, with a Dome in the centre with all the Ornaments very richly finish'd in Deep Imboss's and Laid on. A sett of Cornices, to the outside, Richly Carv'd and very highly finisht with Large Centre Leaves very full and Corners to the Vallance (£54 10s)'. The bedstead had 'Large mahogany feet posts . . . the Cullumns fluted and Counterfluted', separately charged at £23 14s. The bed in its overall styling has been classed as looking 'back to the 17th century and consequently to a baroque interpretation of Classical motifs'.[59] The curtains for the bedroom, with a cornice, matched the bed. Two men were sent up to Burghley with their tools and materials. In the twenty-three days they lodged at the local inn they assembled the bed, fixed the cornice, restuffed and upholstered old chairs and even mended the house bells. Meanwhile, Mayhew and Ince were making more furniture, obtaining French glass plates (presumably for the two fine mirrors hanging in the Library (£348 9s)), supplying a 'spectacular rococo overmantel' for the red drawing room (£110), and various commodes and corner cupboards. Inlaid work dating from the late seventeenth century was made up into two superb commodes, which involved re-laying the motifs on to a lighter wood ground. In this Mayhew and Ince demonstrated that as well as being competent upholsterers they were cabinet makers of extraordinary skill, a fact that had already been recognized by the sixth Earl of Coventry, to whom they had supplied in 1765 two early neoclassical commodes. As noted, the 1767–8 Burghley bill had amounted to some £1,245; payments in a day book continue to 1779 and exceed by £382 the amount accounted for by the bill.

As Mayhew and Ince had dedicated their *The Universal System . . .* (1762) to George Spencer, fourth Duke of Marlborough, it was to be expected that they would be used not only at the duke's principal seat at Blenheim Palace, Oxfordshire but at his other properties. No bills survive but careful examination of a steward's daybook has shown continuous activity at Blenheim from about 1772 and for some twenty years.[60] The private apartments at Blenheim were inherited by the fourth Duke in 1758 and were somewhat old-fashioned. Charles, the third Duke, and Elizabeth his wife had 'enjoyed Blenheim without making a single major alteration';[61] so much had, in any case, been done during the long tenure of Sarah, the redoubtable first Duchess. George, 'a man of fashion and culture', was determined to spend out and bring it all up-to-date. To do this he enlisted the architectural services of Sir William Chambers and (in Chambers's view) the upstart and interloper landscapist, Capability Brown. Chambers, in an oft-repeated phrase fancied himself as 'a Very pretty Connoisseur' of furniture,[62] and may have resented that his ducal patrons had definite ideas of their own, and that Mayhew and Ince were established in their service prior to his arrival. Some of this may have surfaced in the furnishing of the south-facing state bedroom. The State Bed (Pls 295–6), now partially dismantled and in store, occupied a position facing the two windows. Its making, credited to Mayhew and Ince, included a carved and gilded frame, a head-cloth embroidered with 'their Grace's coat of Arms work'd in Sattin . . .', and a ducal coronet topping its fabric-covered dome. The bed was hung with 'blue Silk damask & Silk fringed border' and its curtains drew up in drapery festoons. However, its awkward design was certainly not by Chambers, who had garnered his extensive knowledge of neoclassicism at the French Academy in Rome, and

58 Hayward and Till (1973) pp.1604–7; Gilbert (1978) I, pp.206–7.
59 Hayward and Till (1973) p.1605.
60 Roberts (1994) pp.117–49.
61 Green (1951) p.183.
62 For a full discussion of Chambers see J. Harris (1970); the claim to be a furniture connoisseur is in B.L., Add. MS 41133, f.107.

the bed has been likened to three plates (XXIX, XXX, XXXII) in *The Universal Director*.[63] That with a dome (XXXII) is illustrated here (Pl. 266).

At this time the other leading cabinet-maker and upholsterer, Thomas Chippendale, was at the height of his activity with many commissions, including those for Sir Edward Knatchbull (Mersham Le Hatch, Kent), Edwin Lascelles (Harewood House, Yorkshire) and William Weddell (Newby Hall, Yorkshire). The details of Chippendale's varied activity have been recorded meticulously;[64] I note here his furnishings at Newby (*c.*1772–6) and at Petworth (1777–9).

In September 1772 Chippendale's foreman, William Reid, who was working at Harewood House on his master's behalf, spent three days away at Newby Hall, some twenty miles to the north. Its owner, William Weddell, who had acquired the seventeenth-century house *c.*1750, had visited Rome in about 1765 and on his return had called in Robert Adam to add a two-storey wing, including a sculpture gallery. The drawing[65] by Adam at Newby, dated about 1767, is titled: 'Section of a Room for the Reception of Antique Statues Bas reliefs Busts and Sarcophagi &c . . .'

Adam arranged the room as three chambers, the central one domed, and Weddell placed here, among the large collection of sculptures he had acquired in Italy, the Barberini *Venus*. It was, however, a room which needed no furniture – only six matted chairs are listed in 1792[66] – but Adam and Chippendale remedied that in the drawing (or tapestry) room by installing one of the sets of Boucher–Neilson tapestries woven in Paris at the Gobelins (p.207). Weddell had ordered it all when he visited Paris (as Lord Coventry did) in 1763. The seat furniture, to incorporate some of the flower bouquet tapestry, was provided by Chippendale, and there is little doubt that he also supplied the green watered silk curtains which hung in the room until 1980 or so.[67] They needed then to be replaced by exact replicas, and, as already noted (p.210) a complete set is in store at the house.[68] The Axminster carpet was designed by Adam[69] in 1775 and this perhaps indicates a date when the suite of twelve armchairs, two sofas and a firescreen arrived.[70] As an under-used room and with the Gobelins furniture protected from the time of its making by green serge covers (listed in the 1792 inventory),[71] it has all stayed bright and fresh.

There is a great deal of well-made but less important furniture at Newby Hall and some of it was probably supplied by Chippendale. The documentation is, however, lacking but the evidence has been examined for both Newby and Denton Hall nearby.[72]

SOME LESSER NAMES

One of the principal towns that supported the services of craftsmen of all trades was York. It had acted as the religious and administrative centre for a wide area of the north-east of England since Roman times, and enjoyed particular favour in the eighteenth century. The third Earl of Burlington had designed the Assembly Rooms in York (1732), and often journeyed from the south to his Yorkshire estates at Londesborough. The third and fourth Earls of Carlisle, building and decorating at Castle Howard, thirteen miles to the east, had used many York craftsmen, and extended a patronage typical of the informed circles of which they were, in turn, active leaders. All great families and many lesser ones had their town houses in York, to reside at when attending the races, routs in the Assembly Rooms, seeing their lawyers on estate business, or buying chocolate and tea for their burgeoning families back in the Ridings. One of them was the Roman Catholic peer Charles Gregory, the ninth and last Viscount Fairfax of Emley, whose only surviving child and heiress was his daughter, Anne. Together, father and daughter from the early 1760s retained the services of John Carr, the fashionable

63   Roberts (1994) p.123.
64   Gilbert (1978).
65   Beard (1978) pl.104.
66   Low (1986) p.155.
67   *Ibid.*, p.142.
68   I am indebted to Mrs Robin Compton and Mr Christopher

Gilbert for information on the Chippendale curtains at Newby.
69   Sir John Soane's Museum, London, Adam Drawings, Vol. 17, No. 194; Sherrill (1996) p.192.
70   Gilbert (1978) I, p.266.
71   Low (1986) p.155.
72   Gilbert (1971) pp.1446–51.

architect from York, with a wide northern practice, to remodel Fairfax House in Castlegate. He assembled his favoured team of craftsmen,[73] with the successful York (and Catholic) upholsterer George Reynoldson (1695–1764) not only providing most of the soft furnishings but acting as general agent when the family returned to Gilling Castle for the summer months. Reynoldson had been active in York since the 1720s, with many of the families he served being of the Catholic faith. In particular, his activities for John Grimston of Kilnwick have been well documented.[74] He took at least ten apprentices in the years between 1718 and 1762,[75] including (in 1722) Richard Farrer, who was to work with him at Burton Constable, 1762–3.

In 1762 the saloon, the principal room at Fairfax House, had been given a crimson colour scheme but four years later it was rehung in a 'Sky & Mixt' damask. Mary Reynoldson's bill of 16 February 1766[76] included a charge for 275 yards of this (7s a yard) to be used, not only for the hangings in the saloon but for three pairs of window curtains and covering eight chairs, two armchairs and one sofa.

Another Yorkshire patron for whom Reynoldson had worked was William Constable of Burton Constable. He had inherited his East Riding estate in 1747 and, as a man of 'wide sympathies and enquiring mind, interested in everything which was happening in the artistic, scientific and intellectual circles of the age of reason',[77] was soon travelling and building. He not only patronized the leading architects and furniture makers such as Robert Adam, James Wyatt and Thomas Chippendale but gave many commissions to local men like Edward Elwick (p.159), Reynoldson and Farrer and John Lowry[78] (Pls 312, 320).

Reynoldson died in 1764 and on 11 December it was announced in the *York Courant* that his widow Mary (daughter of a York wool draper) was to carry on his business with the help of her son, Joseph, and two servants, Thomas Lupton and Henry Smith. Two of her bills of 1765–6 to Viscount Fairfax are given here (Appendix A37) with that of 4 June 1765, including an interesting entry which throws light on what services were more effectively dealt with in London. She charged £4 5s 0d for 'Taking the crimson Damask bed curtins and vallens in pieces carrage up and down to London and dying ditto.' In view of the dominance of the Yorkshire woollen industry dyeing was surely available in York, but to dye damask to another colour (or even renew the existing faded crimson) was perhaps beyond the ability of the local facility.

Two Yorkshire upholsterers with active practices were William Brailsford of Sheffield, who was trading from c.1774 to 1837, and William Armitage of Leeds, active in the 1770s. Brailsford's principal commission was for the fifth Duke of Devonshire at Chatsworth. On 12 April 1774 the accounts[79] list his providing two wainscott four-post beds with hangings and bedding, Wilton and other carpets, chests of drawers, tables, backstools, mahogany swing-frame looking glasses, servants' furniture and bedding, 'verditer blue furniture paper and border', and '32 pieces of Rich pea green furniture paper' (£14 8s). In January 1775 Brailsford fitted up the Chatsworth dining room with Turkey and Persian carpets, festoon window curtains, '4 open cut & moulded cornices covered wth superfine green morine' (£4); thirty-six dining room chairs, having curved backs, moulded feet and 'compass seats stuffed over the rails with curly hair in two liners well quilted down to secure to seats afterwards covered with hair seating tyed down and finished with a double row of best burnished nails (£56 14s).' Comfort was assured in his provision of '4 Bergere Arm'd Chairs with Compass seats and oval – Richly Carved and moulded, Stuffed in the best manner with Curl'd hair and afterwards coverd with Green flowered Silk Mantua and finished with best Burnished nails complete (£5 10s)'.

Armitage, like Reynoldson, used a local newspaper to announce details of his activities. On 12 September 1769 he stated in the *Leeds Mercury* that he was moving his shop and that, from his new premises 'at the back of the Shambles' he could offer a large assortment of paper hangings, fabrics, carpets and bedding. On 29 May 1770, in the same newspaper, he stated that, being 'just returned from London' and in a new shop near the Town Hall, he had for sale a wide selection of paper hangings, carpets and furniture. By 1773 he had moved again (*Leeds Mercury*, 11 May), to the sign of the Chest of Drawers and Chair in Briggate. The stock

73 Brown (1989).
74 Ingram (1951).
75 Beard and Gilbert (1986) p.739.
76 N. Riding, Yorks. C.R.O., MS., ZDV(F) MT.4.

77 Hall (1970) p.3.
78 Hall (1970).
79 Chatsworth, Green Vellum Copy Book.

had been improved to include 'Italian and Spring Blinds for Windows, Pier Looking Glasses, Mahogany, Rose and Swing ditto, Green and Gold, Blue and Gold and Black and Gold ditto for Ladies Toilets; Paper Machee Ornaments for Rooms and Chimney Pieces etc and Girandoles in Gold and ornamented frames . . .'.

Apart from this cabinet-maker's stock of carcase furniture Armitage was an upholsterer and appraiser and as such worked during the 1770s for Edwin Lascelles at Harewood House. Lascelles was a patron well used to receiving, at the same time, fine furniture from Thomas Chippendale. Nevertheless, whilst many of the items Armitage supplied were utilized by Chippendale's workmen his business still fell into a sorry way, and in July 1779 he was declared bankrupt.[80]

THREE COMPETING LONDON FIRMS

Beckwith and France

The successful cabinet-maker and upholsterer William France died in 1773 and his son, Edward, then entered into partnership with Samuel Beckwith. The latter had been employed by Thomas Chippendale until 1774. Within four years the new partners had settled at 105 St Martin's Lane. Their principal private commission was for Lord Salisbury at Hatfield House and the London town house in Stratford Place. Their account,[81] January 1781 to March 1790, is a long one and included unusual items such as dining, sleeping and servants' tents for use at Danbury Camp.

At Hatfield itself the firm was capable of creating a grand effect. The dining room was furnished with '24 Mahogany chairs of Jamaica wood, seats covered with pea green leather quilted . . .' These, the sideboards and tables, stood on '139 sq yds of pea green India sprig mat floorcloth made of duck & painted in oil'. The pea green colour scheme was continued in the adjoining breakfast room with the use of 'Taberet paper hangings', chintz and pea green persian for window curtains and green japanned furniture. The succession of colours was continued – buff in the drawing room, pink and white paper hangings in the pink bedchamber and pink and white in Lady Salisbury's sitting room. Lord Salisbury was given a 'pea green sprig paper' in his sitting room. Many of the papers were supplied by the successful London manufacturer, Thomas Bromwich, with canvas hangings under the papers themselves. The sheer quantity of fabrics used was staggering: 284 yards of French grey damask in three large window curtains in King James's drawing room. In the three years of 1781–3 the account for 'Hatfield, Camp and Town' had risen to £8,227 18s 9d and a further £4,397 12s was spent in the next seven years.

Litchfield and Graham

Another London firm, active as competitors to Beckwith and France was Litchfield (or Lichfield) and Graham. Despite their prominence it has not been easy to establish the partners' names. The Croome Court archive includes a number of their bills: that for March–July 1780 is headed 'Litchfield & Graham' with the money received by 'Wm Lichfield'.[82] Graham was probably the John Graham who carried on the business alone from 1809. Their activity was careful but unexceptional. For example, they had two men and a woman at Croome in 1781, 'purfecting & fixing 3 window Curtains with new Lines in Dining Parlour', fixing cornices and repairing window blinds and other curtains. And yet the partners had claimed that they were the successors, from 1778, of John Cobb, who, with his late partner, William Vile (d.1767), had been active for Lord Coventry over some twenty years. They had even moved into Cobb's London business premises at the corner of St Martin's Lane and Long Acre and in 1779 their insurance cover was substantial – £5,000 with some £4,200 allocated to stock and utensils.[83] The firm specialized for the most part in providing good quality bedroom furniture, although they supplied other carcase furniture to Croome Court, some in zebra wood. They were a competent firm whose activity deserves to receive more attention when pieces by them are fully identified.

80   Beard and Gilbert (1986) p.18.
81   Hatfield House, MS., Accounts 151/23.
82   Beard (1993).

83   Guildhall Library, London, Sun policy registers, vol. 276, p.650; vol. 306, p.613.

Chipchase and Lambert

As with a number of other London firms, Robert Chipchase and Robert Lambert had Scottish customers. They had joined together as partners at some time prior to 1767 with premises near Golden Square. The third and fourth Dukes of Atholl at Blair Castle, near to Pitlochry, followed their predecessor, the second Duke, in turning to a London supplier for their important furniture. William Masters had served the second Duke (*c.*1747–60, p.158); now it was Chipchase and Lambert's job to take on the various tasks of repairing carpets and curtains, making a fine set of mahogany dining tables with twenty dining chairs, six of which still survive (28s each), and, in 1783 of working for the fourth Duke in a restrained neoclassical style to provide twelve giltwood chairs and a pair of sofas. These are still in the state drawing room at Blair Castle.[84]

In 1786 Chipchase and Lambert were retained by the fourth Lord Howard de Walden (the former Sir John Griffin Griffin) to design a state bed (Pl. 341). With its bedding this cost £398 and the bill is given in the appendix (A41). When finished it was obviously a source of some comment. Emilia Clayton, writing to her friend Mrs Port in 1787, said: 'the bed is grey & embroidered most beautifully and made up with the greatest taste I ever saw'.[85] Part of the embroidered hangings are believed to have come from a court dress belonging to Elizabeth, Countess of Portsmouth, who had purchased Audley End in 1751 from the Earl of Effingham. It is interesting to note that for a time she had 'entertained the idea of converting Audley End into a silk manufactory'.[86]

THE GILLOW ENTERPRISE

This active firm originated in Lancaster in the early eighteenth century but established a London branch, at 176 Oxford Street, in 1769. The responsibility of managing this new enterprise was entrusted to Robert II (*c.*1745–95), one of the two sons of the founder, Robert I (1704–72), who had retired in 1769. The other son, Richard (1734–1811), stayed on in Lancaster. From its opening the London branch seems to have acted as both a factory and a retail outlet for furniture made in Lancaster.[87] In fact they wrote to Sir George Strickland of Boynton on 11 November 1771 to point this out: 'We have established a Shop in London, No 176 Oxford Street, as afforesaid, where we send up all size Billd Tables & other Furniture in Quantities for sale & where are said Partners do likewise Carry on Cabenet & Upholsterers Buissiness in all its Branches.'[88]

The Lancaster branch of the firm had expanded to a sizable concern with the consistent demand for its billiard-tables. It meant that upholstery services in Lancaster needed reorganization; the London end of the business was already active in providing upholstery services as Gillows and Taylor, Cabinet Makers and Upholsterers. This was not accomplished at Lancaster until 1785, when Richard Gillow set up a veneer room, a feather room, a long ware room and an upholsterers' shop (consisting of several workrooms) on a property known as 'Gibsons Stables'.[89] It has been shown that prior to 1785 the upholstery business at Lancaster could and did supply upholstery work but this was done by outside upholsterers; they were unable to supply all the usual upholstery services required by an owner equipping a house.[90] It may well be that it was felt steps had to be taken to remedy this situation in order to stay on competitive terms with other northern makers. An upholstery service enabled the business to offer the refurbishing of a complete house. The firm wrote to Philip Saltmarsh of York in January 1786 advising him that they now carried on an upholstery business at Lancaster and 'it may be in our power to supply you with Articles in that as well as the Cabinet Branch, to your Satisfaction . . .' Further, they wrote to James Whalley in June 1786 to ask him '. . . if agreeable & Convenient

84 Coleridge (1966) pp.96–101.
85 Llanover ed., (1861) III, p.400.
86 Williams (1966) p.2.
87 I am indebted to Sarah Nichols for use of her Winterthur Master's thesis (1982), hereafter as Nichols (1982), and for other information on the firm of Gillow.

88 Nichols (1982) p.35, quoting Westminster City Library Archives Department (WCLAD) Gillow MSS., Letter Book 344/170, p.53.
89 Nichols (1982) p.36.
90 Nichols (1984) p.8.

to you to send the Bed Furniture to be mad up here. It may be done & shall be glad to do it in the neatest Manner by upholsterers we now employ here fm our Warehouse in London, who we think woud do it much to your Satisfaction . . .'[91]

The Gillows' archive,[92] dating from 1731, is the most complete to survive for any leading English furniture manufacturer. There is a full series of estimate sketch books from the 1760s onwards that show the range and detail of the firm's large output. The whole enterprise is in the course of detailed assessment and a welcome start has been made with the publication of many designs, up to 1800, taken from these sketch books.[93]

One of the firm's important patrons was John Christian Curwen with his wife, Isabella. They lived at Workington Hall on the west coast of Cumbria (the house remained in the family until 1932), and Gillow and Company refurbished it from 1788. Some of the furniture, comprising fourteen side chairs, a pair of window sofas, a sideboard table, a pair of pier tables, a pair of pedestals with urns, and a wine cooler, survives, and is now in the possession of the United States Department of State.

In 1785 J. Cooke, an upholsterer from the London branch, was moved to Lancaster and it was his slow task, with others, to equip the firm to be ready for such large commissions involving upholstery. The seating furniture for Workington Hall was upholstered in green morocco leather 'tied down with silk tufts and brass nails'. Each of the fourteen chairs (one is drawn in the estimate sketchbook)[94] for the dining room cost £1 6s 6d for the mahogany frame and 19s 6d for the upholstery. This was a shilling more than the upholstery (18s 6d) of the hall chairs on account of their having two rows of brass nails at the front and sides. The difference to profits which the employment of an upholsterer made is instanced in the costs of two bedsteads supplied to the Curwens:

> 1784   £4.7.3 'naked', minus cornice.
> 1788   £5.8.6 plus £28.18.0 for mattresses, blankets, pillows, feather bed, bolsters, the cornice and bed hangings.

In an analysis of the firm's turnover figures for 1778, 1783 and 1788[95] the point is reinforced: 1778 £3,314; 1783 £4,887; 1788 £9,671. By 1800 or so the Gillows were allowing their clients six months' credit but offered a 5 per cent discount 'for ready money'.[96]

The intermesh of ideas which the Gillow archive demonstrates is nowhere more apparent than in the anticipation of designs published by George Hepplewhite and those before or after Sheraton. As early as 1908 Percy Macquoid had noted (in his book *A History of English Furniture, IV, The Age of Satinwood, 1770–1820*) that 'much of the inlaid and satinwood furniture generally attributed to Hepplewhite, Shearer and Sheraton might be the work of Gillows'. This is regarded now as an accurate observation with it being 'more than likely that Gillows' London showrooms provided material for him [Sheraton] and for Hepplewhite'.[97] Two illustrations shown here reinforce the point with the alcove bed, bedsteps and carpet (Pl. 347) seemingly after plate XL in Sheraton's *Drawing Book* and the drawing room window curtains, alternative cornices &c. (Pl. 346) after plate LI. Which came first in the plagiarizing game will perhaps never be established; the bright colour schemes are of course those set out by Gillows's designers. Normally, these watercolour drawings 'were retained for use within the firm, with occasional outside use by the partners or their travellers'.[98] At a time when competition was acute the Gillow enterprise aimed at survival, with the provision of elegant furniture that did not hint to the purchaser of undue extravagance. They took care to stay up-to-date in choice of materials and worked carefully in, for example, lining silk damask coverings with flannel (Appendix A42).

91 Nichols (1982) p.38; Nichols (1984) p.9.
92 Westminster City Library, Archives Department (WCLAD). See Nichols (1986).
93 Boynton (1995).
94 Nichols (1985) pp.1352–9.
95 Nichols (1982) pp.37, 42.
96 Gillow Letter Book, 344/174, p.160 (WCLAD) cited in Goodison and Hardy (1970) p.3.
97 Boynton (1995) p.17.
98 Hall (1978) I, p.1614.

CHARLES ELLIOTT

Among the many successful cabinet-makers and upholsterers who found active employment in the court circles of George III Charles Elliott (1752–1832) has an assured place. A descendant of the Scottish Elliotts of Liddesdale, he was born in 1752 in Essex, a year before the death of his father. His start in life was not promising, arriving in London in 1770 with only a shilling in his pocket. But by 1774 he had joined as a partner a man named Davis and in 1775 he married a clergyman's daughter. The 1770s, with three good neoclassical architects, Adam, Chambers and James Wyatt all active, was a good time to prosper by hard work. Elliott did this and within four years (1775–9) the firm's insurance cover had advanced from £1,100 to £2,500. By 1781 it had increased to £3,200 and continued to rise steadily.[99]

In 1783 Elliott received his first appointment as royal upholsterer and cabinet-maker, receiving a fixed salary of £157 10s each quarter in addition to his submitted bills for work done. He was involved in the regular contract work of cleaning, washing and mending all manner of upholstered objects in both Houses of Parliament, and renewing where necessary.

In 1787 a dispute arose between Elliott and the Prince of Wales over a bill for £1,745 rendered for various articles of furniture and other furnishings. A committee of three upholsterers found (not surprisingly) in Elliott's favour and he continued to rise, almost unchecked, in royal service. He subscribed to the first edition of Sheraton's *Drawing Book* as 'Upholsterer to his Majesty and Cabinetmaker to the Duke of York'. Descriptions of furniture in the royal accounts[100] indicate the range of Elliott's work, with much of it concerned with upholstery. In 1783 he refurnished Swindley Lodge with 'mahogany cabriole chairs covered with crimson silk damask' and 'festoon window curtains' as well as providing a folding camp bedstead. In May 1784 Elliott's wife died, and eighteen months later he married Eling Venn, whose father, Rev. Henry Venn, was one of the most important figures in the evangelical movement in the Church of England.[101]

GEORGE HEPPLEWHITE

Hepplewhite's fame rests on the pattern-book *The Cabinet-maker and Upholsterer's Guide* which his widow, Alice, issued in 1788, two years after George Hepplewhite's death. In the preface it was stated that it was intended 'to produce a work which shall be useful to the mechanic and serviceable to the gentleman. With this view . . . our judgment was called forth in selecting such patterns as were most likely to be of general use . . . and convey a just idea of English taste in furniture for houses.'

The book enjoyed a success and by 1794 was in a third edition. The title-page categorized forty-nine types of furniture for which patterns were provided. In examining the thirty-one plates for chairs it is obvious that it was the intention – as with Thomas Chippendale's earlier *Director* – that they be copied. It was stated that:

> The general dimension and proportion of chairs are as follows: width in front 20 inches, depth of the seat 17 inches, height of the seat frame 17 inches; total height about 3 feet 1 inch . . .
>
> Mahogany chairs should have the seats of horse hair, plain, striped, checquered &c., at pleasure, or cane bottoms with cushions, the cases of which should be covered with the same as the curtains.

Of the new fashion for painted or japanned chairs (after noting that they allowed 'a frame-work less massy than is requisite for mahogany'), the account continued: 'Japanned chairs should have cane bottoms, with linen or cotton cases over cushions to accord with the general hue of the chair.' I have illustrated plate 4 of 1 September

99 Guildhall Library, London, Sun policy registers, vol.236, p.490; vol. 240, p.368; vol. 272, p.83; vol. 299, p.176; vol. 342, ref. 528260; vol. 419, ref. 706221.

100 P.R.O., LC9/331–9; 11/1–27.
101 Joy (1959) pp.34–9.

1787 which shows nailing patterns (Pl. 342). For several of the designs where the backs and seats were of leather Hepplewhite suggested that 'they should be tied down with tassels of silk or thread'.

The advantage of Hepplewhite's *Guide* is that it provides a record of household furniture dating from the mid–1780s in which (as the preface stated) it had been possible 'to unite elegance and utility, and blend the useful with the agreeable.' Inevitably they were designs which attracted criticism from the other pattern-book distributor of the early 1790s, Thomas Sheraton. He thought, in 1791, that those for chairs had 'already caught the decline', which caused Alice Hepplewhite to attempt some revision of them for the 1794 edition.[102] As no bills for furniture by 'Mr Hepplewhite, cabinet maker deceased' have ever come to light his reputation rests, a little uneasily, on what others did in his name.

102 Beard and Gilbert (1986) p.422.

250.   Design for the side of a room (*c*.1760–5) *London, Victoria and Albert Museum*, Inv. E308-1929.

By John Linnell. The woodwork is yellow to denote gilding, the curtains red and the mirror plate blue. Inscribed on the right '3 for eating parlour in paint' and on the left '5 of these B[urnished]gold'.

References: Hayward and Kirkham (1980) pp.23, 28, Pl. 222 and endpapers.

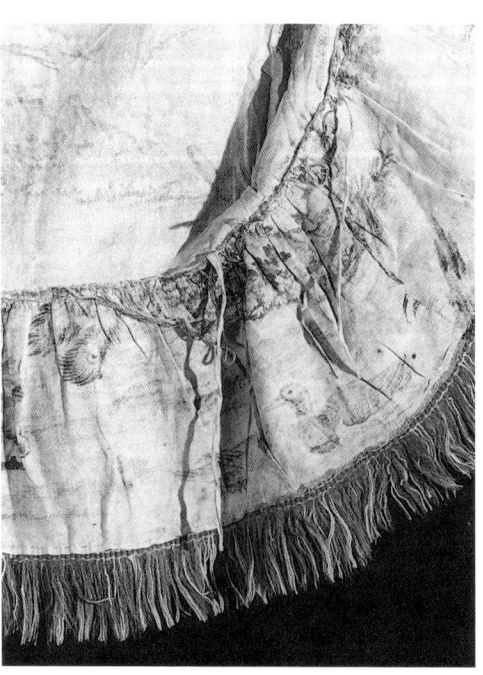

251.   Slip cover (1761) 32 × 34½ in (81.7 × 88 cm) *Virginia, Colonial Williamsburg Foundation*, Inv. 1963-36, 11 and 12.

For an easy chair cushion, *en suite* with slip covers for side chairs. Linen/cotton with red copperplate print. The tapes and fringes are original. The T-shaped cushion cover is bound with red and white linen and wool tape.

252.   Slip cover (1761) 26 × 38 in (66 × 97 cm) *Virginia, Colonial Williamsburg Foundation*.

For a side chair, one of a pair. The reverse side. The tapes for tying around the chair legs may be seen.

253.   Brocade (1761) *Chatsworth, Derbyshire.*

Provided by Thomas Hinchcliff, the London mercer in 1761: '16½ yds of rich Brocade, Gold Silver & Colours a[t] [£]6.16.6', costing £112 12s 3d. Used to cover the coronation thrones of George III and Queen Charlotte (see Pl. 254). Francis Plummer provided gold fringe (total bill of £121 8s 8d) but this is now missing.

References: Roberts (1989) p.64.

254.   Coronation thrones and footstools (1761) 60 × 27 in (174 × 68 cm); footstool width, 25 in (68 cm) *Chatsworth, Derbyshire.*

These were for George III and Queen Charlotte. They were carved and gilded by Katherine Naish and upholstered by Vile and Cobb. They were acquired as perquisites by the fourth Duke of Devonshire, Lord Chamberlain to George III. He took them to Chatsworth where they remain. Naish charged £30 for each chair frame and £6 for each footstool. The upholsterers charged £8 18s. The rich brocade covering them is shown in Pl. 253.

References: Roberts (1989) p.64.

255.   Backcloth (1761) *Grimsthorpe Castle, Lincolnshire.*

From the House of Lords throne canopy, embroidered by Richard Harrison. The canopy was provided by Katherine Naish, using crimson Genoa velvet supplied at 29s 4d a yard by Edward Ingram (£173 16s). Francis Plummer supplied rich gilt lace. Acquired as a perquisite by the Lord Great Chamberlain (the Duke of Ancaster) and taken to Grimsthorpe Castle where it remains although remade as a bed canopy.

256. *(below right)*   Throne and footstool (1761) *Grimsthorpe Castle, Lincolnshire.*

Parcel-gilt and walnut. From the Prince's chamber 'near the House of Lords'. Frame made by Katherine Naish (£46). The footstool to match cost £7 10s. This with two high stools was placed beneath the canopy (Pl. 255). Vile and Cobb carried out the upholstery in crimson Genoa velvet. Acquired as a perquisite by the Lord Great Chamberlain (Duke of Ancaster) and taken to Grimsthorpe Castle where they remain.

257.   Design for a sofa (*c.*1761–2) *London, Victoria and Albert Museum*, Inv. E129-1929.

By John Linnell. One of several designs for the large sofas still *in situ* at Kedleston, Derbyshire. The '13ft' measurement is given beneath the centre legs. The frames are yellow to denote gilding and the upholstery red.

References: Hayward (1969) pp.64, 88, fig.25; Hayward and Kirkham (1980) fig.240.

258.   'French' chairs from Thomas Chippendale's *Director* (1762) Pl. XXII.

The legs and splats show the overlapping influence of the French rococo style although 'Chippendale on the whole avoided the extreme flamboyance and distortions' common to that. This plate was the inspiration for the armchair *c.*1760, shown in Pl. 246.

259.   'Design of a Sofa for a Grand Apartment' from Thomas Chippendale's *Director* (1762) Pl. XXXI.

Chippendale noted that 'Pillows and Cushions must not be omitted, though they are not in the Design', and that a workman should 'make a model of it before he begins to execute it'. The length (without scrolls) was given as 108in (264cm) and height of seat (without castors) as 14in (35.6cm).

260. 'Design for a Bed' from Thomas Chippendale's *Director* (1762) Pl. XLV.

The accompanying note indicated that 'The Feet-Pillars and Cornices are different. The Head-Part of the Bed must be in the same Shape, all the way up to the Canopy, as the Foot-Rail and Foot-Cornice, and continued in the Canopy to the upper work, which goes round the top Part of it. The flat Part of the Canopy in the Inside must be pannelled, and a carved ornament go round it. The Pillars stand with the Angles forward, which give an Advantage for the better finishng of the Corners of the Cornice and the Ornaments which go up each Corner of the Canopy. The Lath of the Tester must have the same Shape as the Plan of the Pedestal-Part of the Bedstead. The Sides of the Bed run streight'.

261. 'A Bed to appear as a Soffa, with a fixt Canopy over it . . .' from Ince and Mayhew's *The Universal System of Household Furniture* (1762) Pl. XXVII.

The accompanying note continues: 'the Curtains draw on a Rod; the Cheeks and Seat takes off to open the Bedstead. A shews the Bedstead when folded up, and the Box under for putting the Bedding; at B is the Bedhead shewn as let down'.

262. 'A single headed Couch or field Bed' from Ince and Mayhew's *The Universal System of Household Furniture* (1762) Pl. XXVIII.

The tester was made to take off and was concealed in a recess under the seat. The 'furniture' of the bed was stored underneath at 'D'.

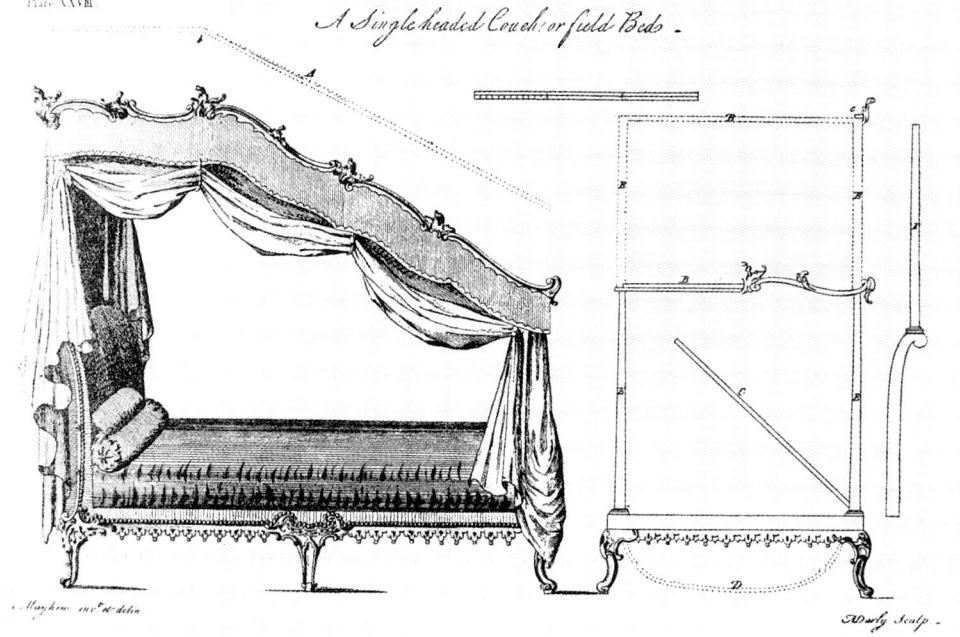

263. 'A Bed proper for an Alcove' from Ince and Mayhew's *The Universal System of Household Furniture* (1762) Pl. XXX.

The accompanying note indicated that 'the Ornaments may be either gilt or cover'd with Damask'. The formation of the tester was indicated in the plan.

265. Design by William Ince for a state bed with a dome tester (*c.*1762) *London, Victoria and Albert Museum*, Inv. D838-1906.

It was published as Pl. XXXII in Ince and Mayhew's *The Universal System of Household Furniture*, where it stated that the damask was blue, with the ornaments richly burnished in gold. The inside and outside of the tester were 'differently formed'. (See Pl. 266).

264. 'a French Bed with Fronts each way . . .' from Ince and Mayhew's *The Universal System of Household Furniture* (1762) Pl. XXXI.

An iron from the posts concealed by the carved ornament supported the canopy.

266. 'A State Bed with a Dome Teaster' from Ince and Mayhew's *The Universal System of Household Furniture* (1762) Pl. XXXII.

The note stated that the bed 'may be esteemed amongst the best in England; the furniture was Blue Damask, and all the ornaments in burnish'd Gold, and richly fringed; the inside and outside of the Teaster are differently formed; it is drawn to an Inch Scale'. See also Pl. 265.

267. 'Lady's Toilette' from Ince and Mayhew's *The Universal System of Household Furniture* (1762) Pl. XXXVI

This form of draping a dressing mirror with muslin is shown particularly in the paintings of the 1760s by Johan Zoffany (Pls 282, 303).

269. 'Designs of Stools for recesses of windows' from Ince and Mayhew's *The Universal System of Household Furniture* (1762) Pl. LXI.

The top example in the plate is shown tufted; leather was also often used as a covering.

268. 'Two Designs of Birjairs or half Couches . . .' from Ince and Mayhew's *The Universal System of Household Furniture* (1762) Pl. LX.

The accompanying note indicated that 'the back of the Lower One is made to fall down at pleasure by that and the Elbows going in a Centre, and a Pin to go through the Elbow in the Holes marked'.

270. 'Two Designs of Sofas' from Ince and Mayhew's *The Universal System of Household Furniture* (1762) Pl. LXII.

The lower example is heavily fringed and tasselled and is shown with the customary long pillows at each end.

271. 'A Grand Sofa' from Ince and Mayhew's *The Universal System of Household Furniture* (1762) Pl. LXIII.

The accompanying note indicates the alcove was ornamented in 'the Gothic Taste' and that, with the sofa, it was adapted to the whole side of a room.

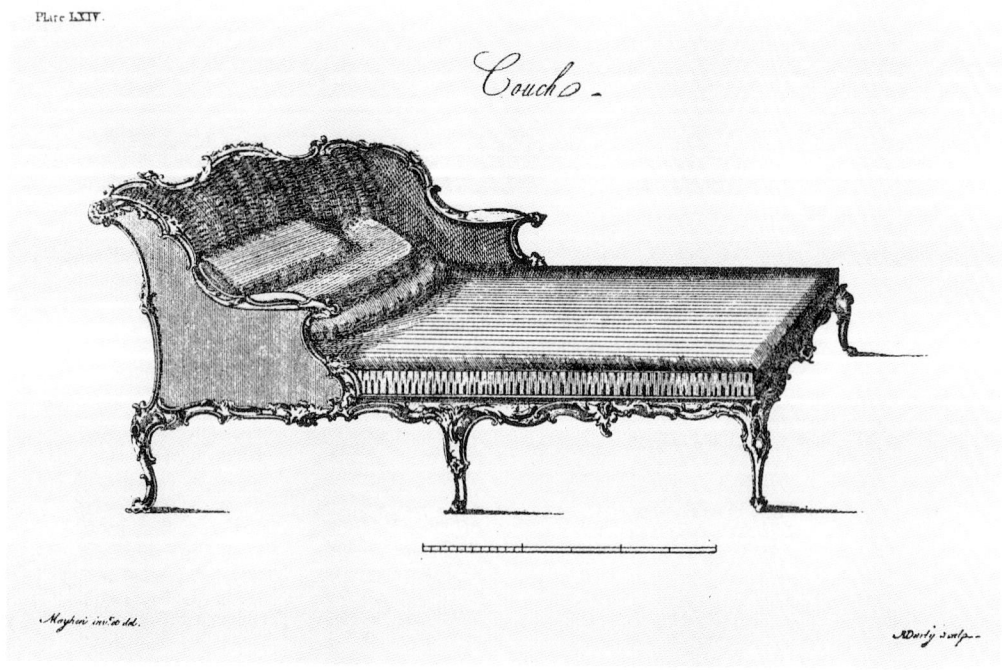

272. 'Couch' from Ince and Mayhew's *The Universal System of Household Furniture* (1762) Pl. LXIV.

It was shown as a 'single-headed Couch, which if the Ornaments of the Frame are well carved, will be very handsome'.

273. 'An Alcove with whole side of a Room described' from Ince and Mayhew's *The Universal System of Household Furniture* (1762) Pl. LXV.

The alcove was fitted with cushions in the form of a 'Turkish Soffa, a Drapery Curtain in Front, and Girandoles on each Side'.

274. Window cornice and curtains (*c.*1762/3) *Philadelphia Museum of Art.*

This cornice is *en suite* to the bed cornices on a bed possibly supplied by Thomas Chippendale to William, fifth Baron Craven of Combe Abbey, Warwickshire. The curtains have been renewed. The bed was sold Christie's, 11 April 1923, lot 99. The cornice was acquired from T. Crowther of London in 1930 and is presumably ex-Combe Abbey. No documentation survives for the Chippendale attribution; the bed was sold as that by Christie's (Monaco), 20 June 1994, lot 219, and is obviously the work of a competent maker.

275. Chair (*c.*1762–3) $39\frac{1}{2} \times 24 \times 25$ in (99 × 61 × 63.5 cm) *Burton Constable, Yorkshire.*

One of three, now covered in red velvet (*c.*1840) and originally with needlework, at a cost of £1 11s each. The chair was made by the partnership of Richard Farrer and George Reynoldson for Burton Constable.

276.   Open armchair (1763) 40 × 21 in (101 × 55 cm) *The Lord Egremont, Petworth.*

Attributed to Paul Saunders (d.1771). Possibly one of '14 French Elbow Chairs' supplied by Saunders in 1763 for £70. Saunders also supplied two sofas, *en suite* (£16 each) and '8 smaller French Elbow Chairs' (£40) and '2 Settees to Match them £23 10s 0d'. Whilst the sofas and settees

have gone there are still at Petworth 'armchairs of both sizes'.

References: Jackson-Stops (1977) p.365.

278–80.   Open armchair (1764) 42 × 30$\frac{1}{2}$ × 30$\frac{1}{2}$ in (106 × 77 × 77 cm) *London, Victoria and Albert Museum,* Inv. W1-1937.

One of a set of eight made for Sir Lawrence Dundas by Thomas Chippendale

to a design by Robert Adam (Pl. 277). The chairs, and four sofas *en suite* were covered with Sir Lawrence's own damask; reupholstered in the nineteenth century and again in 1966. The Chippendale bill (Gilbert, 1978, p.157) shows the chairs were supplied at £20 each, with leather cases and crimson check cases. Details show the top back and front seat.

277.   Drawing of a sofa (1764) *London, Sir John Soane's Museum,* Vol. 17, no.74.

The drawing is by Robert Adam and inscribed 'Sopha for Sir Lawrence Dundas, Baronet'; it is signed and dated 1764. The sofa, one of four with eight chairs (Pl. 278) *en suite*, was made for use at 19 Arlington Street, London. The set of furniture itself was dispersed at the Arlington Street sale, Christie's, 26 April 1934, with three sofas and four chairs being retained by Dundas's descendant, the Marquess of Zetland, and taken to Aske Hall, Richmond. The sofas cost £54 each.

References: Gilbert (1978) I, p.157, II, Pls 176, 356, 357.

281. Open armchair (1764) 36 × 39 × 30 in (91.4 × 99 × 76.2 cm) *Kenwood House, London* (English Heritage).

One of a suite of six with two sofas and two stools, made in beech by James Lawson for Sir Lawrence Dundas for Moor Park (£12 10s each). The chair was restored to its original appearance by Carole Thomerson in 1986, using a dark blue leather and reinstating the tufting. Every care was taken in preserving the original horsehair stuffing and scrim which formed the eighteenth-century silhouette.

References: *English Heritage Conservation Bulletin,* June 1988, pp.6–7.

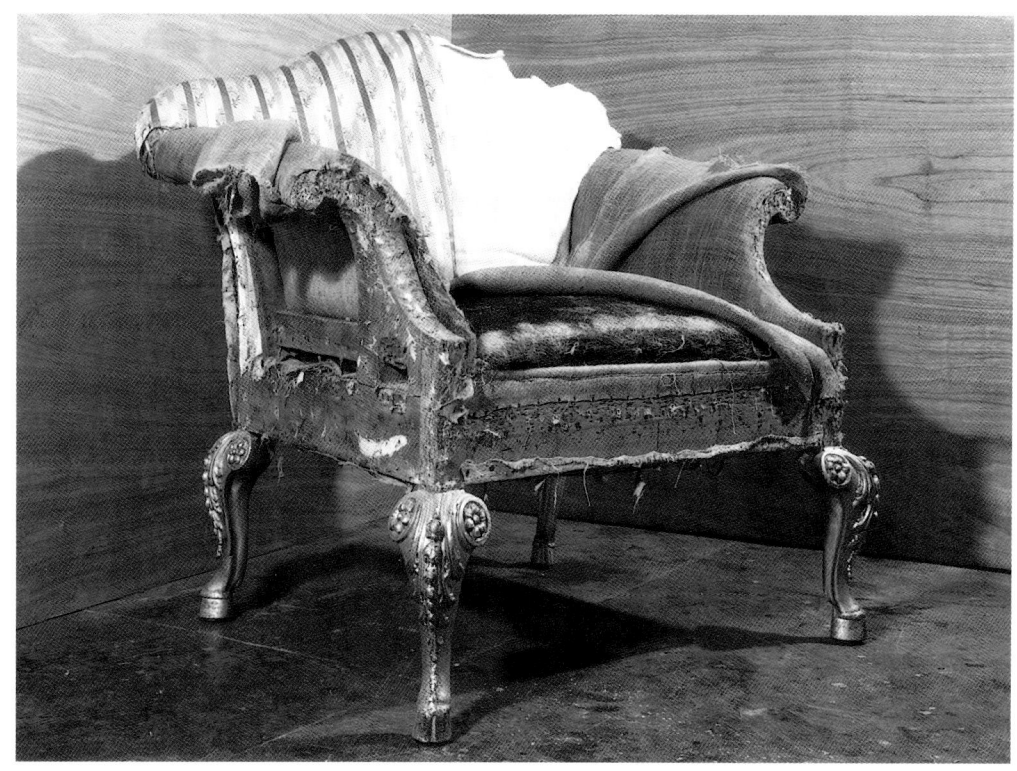

282. Festoon curtains and a 'toylette' seen in the painting of *Queen Charlotte with her two eldest sons* by Johan Zoffany (1764). *Royal Collection.*

The carcase was supplied by William Vile.

References: *Furniture History,* XI (1975) pp. 112–13.

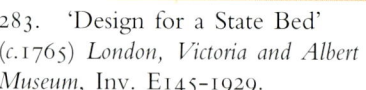

283.   'Design for a State Bed'
(*c.*1765) *London, Victoria and Albert
Museum*, Inv. E145-1929.

The design is by John Linnell. There
is an earl's coronet on the footboard.

References: Hayward and Kirkham
(1980) p.21, Pl. 9.

284.   Seat (*c.*1765) 22 × 29 in (56 × 74 cm)
*New York, Metropolitan Museum of Art, gift of
Marion E. Cohn, 1950.*

From a set of six, probably woven from
wool and silk in the Soho workshops of
Paul Saunders.

285.   Chair (*c.*1765) *Osterley Park, Middlesex*
(The National Trust).

One of a set of eight, made for the green
drawing room at Osterley Park. Attributed
to John Linnell on the basis of his drawing.
The chairs were upholstered originally in
pea green silk damask; reupholstered 1983
by Carole Thomerson.

References: Tomlin (1972) p.49; Hayward
and Kirkham (1980) Pl. 50.

286–9.   Chair (*c.*1765) 37 × 23 in (94.5 ×
58.5 cm) *Virginia, Colonial Williamsburg
Foundation*, Inv. 1982–188.

Made in mahogany. The original yellow
wool or silk-finish upholstery has been lost
but the chair retains its curled hair under a
linen foundation. Details are of the quilted
front and back, showing the retaining strings
for the tufts.

290–3.   Chair (*c.*1765) *Virginia, Colonial Williamsburg Foundation*, Inv. 1980-186.

Whilst the outer cover has gone, this mahogany chair retains much of its original upholstery materials. The details show close nailing, curled hair and grasses used as stuffing.

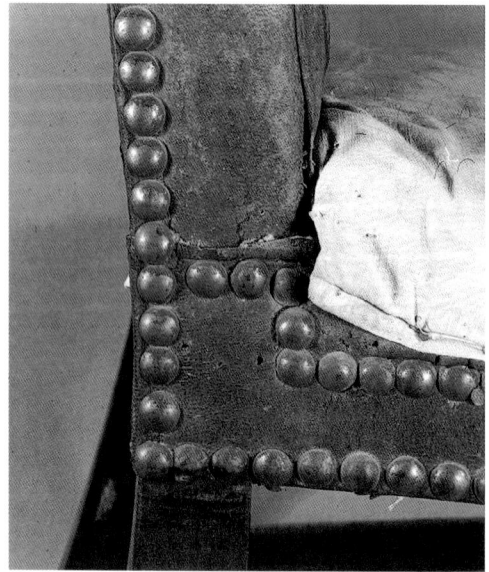

294. Chair seen in the painting of *Lord Rockingham and his secretary Edmund Burke* by Sir Joshua Reynolds (*c.*1765–6) *Cambridge, Fitzwilliam Museum.*

Note the gilded nailing on the seat and arm of the chair. The flat profile of the seat is followed closely in chairs such as those at Corsham Court (Pl. 306).

295–6. State bed (*c.*1765–70) *Blenheim Palace, Oxfordshire.*

The identity of the designer of the bed is an open question. It has been attributed to Sir William Chambers but is closer in spirit to designs in Ince and Mayhew's *The Universal System of Household Furniture* (1759–62) plates XXIX, XXX and XXXII (Pls 265–6). It was provided for George Spencer, fourth Duke of Marlborough. It was originally upholstered in blue silk damask. The detail shows the inside of the tester. It is now partly dismantled and in store at Blenheim.

References: Roberts (1994) p.123.

297–8.   Chair (1766) $41\frac{1}{2} \times 26\frac{1}{2} \times 28\frac{1}{2}$ (105.8 $\times$ 67.9 $\times$ 72.3 cm) *Port Sunlight, Lady Lever Art Gallery*, Inv. LL4068.

Mahogany, in a chinoiserie style. One of a set of seven with a settee. This pattern of chair was made by William Davidson for Ford Castle, Northumberland in 1766. The detail is of the back with the turn button which releases it.

References: Wood, *Furniture History*, XXXI (1995).

299.   Curtains seen in the painting of *John, 14th Lord Willoughby de Broke and his family in the breakfast room of Compton Verney, Warwickshire* (1766) *Los Angeles, J. Paul Getty Museum*.

The curtain would have been drawn diagonally up by a line on the back.

References: Westman (1990) p.1417.

300.   Drawing (*c*.1766) *London, Sir John Soane's Museum*, Vol. 17, no.166.

By Robert Adam, inscribed 'Carpet for Mrs Montagu'. As usual the carpet picked up the pattern of the ceiling except that the roundels at its corners have been replaced by ovals of Chinese figures and there are subtle variations in the borders.

301.   A length of fustian (*c.*1766) *London, Victoria and Albert Museum*, Inv. T75-1914.

Plate printed with the subject of 'Lethe, or Aesop in the Shades'. Fustian was 'a general term covering a large category of linen and cotton' and was in very wide use for furnishings and clothing.

References: Montgomery (1984) p.244.

302.   (*above, centre*) Chair (*c.*1767) *Osterley Park House, London* (The National Trust).

One of a set of twelve. Made in mahogany with the seat upholstered in crimson leather, faded to brown. Edged with a gilded metal band. The chairs are attributed to John Linnell, made for Robert Child's use at Osterley Park in his eating room. On his visit to Osterley in 1773 Horace Walpole noted 'the chairs are taken from antique lyres, and making charming harmony'. The design for these chairs is in the Soane Museum, London (Vol. 17, no.93).

303.   (*right*) 'Toylette' seen in the portrait of Mrs Abington in 'The Way to Keep Him' by Johan Zoffany (1768) *Petworth House, Sussex* (The National Trust)

See note to Pl. 267.

304.   Festoon curtain (1768) *Kenwood House, London* (English Heritage).

One of three (made in 1988 by Annabel Westman) for the library at Kenwood. The originals, also in crimson silk damask, were invoiced to William Murray, first Earl of Mansfield by William France, senior, in 1768 and were *en suite* to eight gilt elbow chairs reupholstered to match with Lord Mansfield's 'Own crimson silk India damask'. They are shown in the section of the south wall of the library by Robert Adam.

References: Westman (1990) pp.1406, 1411.

305.   (*above, left*) Brocatelle hanging (1768) *The Vyne, Hampshire* (The National Trust).

In the drawing room of John Chute's Hampshire house. Chosen by him and said to have been obtained in Italy at a cost of 18s 6d a yard in 1760. Hung by John Bradburne by 1768.

306–8.   Open armchair (*c.*1768) 47 × 24 × 22 (119.5 × 61 × 56 cm) *Corsham Court, Wiltshire*.

One of a set of thirty with four settees and one winged armchair. The frame is mahogany and upholstered in crimson silk damask. The set was ordered by Paul Methuen of Corsham Court for his new picture gallery (designed by Lancelot 'Capability' Brown). It was provided by George Cole of Golden Square, London who worked at the house from *c.*1761–74 although no details are given of what the many payments to him were for. The damask was supplied for walls and furniture in September 1765 by Morris and Young (700 yards at 13s 6d a yard: £472 10s). The nailing patterns on the chairs and settees conform to good practice and there are many areas of the long gallery and other walls with the fabric in good condition. (See p.214)

309.   (*opposite, top left*) State bed (*c.*1768) *Burghley House, Cambridgeshire*.

Supplied by Mayhew and Ince to Brownlow Cecil, ninth Earl of Exeter. The bed is of the 'antiquarian' kind in that it was intended to fit in with the late seventeenth-century decoration of a room hung with blue and silver Soho tapestries. The bed with its bedding cost £164 4s 3d but the domed bed itself 'Richly Carv'd and very highly finisht' cost £54 10s.

References: Hayward and Till (1973).

310.   (*opposite, top right*) Moreen curtains and a Turkey carpet seen in *Sir Lawrence Dundas and his grandson in the Pillar Room, 19 Arlington Street, London* by Johan Zoffany (1769) *Aske Hall, Yorkshire*.

311.   (*opposite, bottom left*) Drawing of a chair (*c.*1768–70) *London, Victoria and Albert Museum, Inv.* E109-1929.

By John Linnell. It has a yellow frame, denoting gilding, and blue upholstery. As a transitional design the drawing combines rococo features with classical motifs taken from Kent or Vardy. The shape of the front legs, festoons below the seat rail and the angular arm terminals derive from J.C. Delafosse (1734–89).

References: Hayward (1969) p.85, fig.10.

312.   (*opposite, bottom centre*) Chair (1769) $35\frac{3}{4}$ × 22 × 21 in (87.2 × 56 × 79 cm) *Burton Constable, Yorkshire*.

Formerly one of a set of at least four, supplied by John Lowry in 1769 to Burton Constable at a cost of £2 12s 6d each. The chair is a simplified version of plate XII in Chippendale's *Director* (1762).

313.   (*opposite, bottom right*) Open armchair (1769) $42\frac{1}{2}$ × $28\frac{1}{2}$ × 27 in (108 × 71 × 68.5 cm) *New York, Metropolitan Museum of Art, gift of the Samuel H. Kress Foundation, 1958*.

One of a set of six and two settees. Frames are by Mayhew and Ince covered with Gobelins tapestry supplied to George William, sixth Earl of Coventry by 1769.

314–15.   'Drawings for chair seats at Shelburne House' (*c.*1770) *Bowood House, Wiltshire.*

Shelburne, later Lansdowne, House, was designed by Robert Adam, 1762–5 and sold by Lord Bute to the second Earl of Shelburne, later Marquess of Lansdowne. There is a neoclassical emphasis in these seat designs by Adam. They were probably painted by Cipriani.

316.   Open armchair (1771) $38\frac{1}{2} \times 28 \times$ 25 in (97 × 71 × 64 cm) *Temple Newsam House, Leeds*, Inv. 66/75.

One of four and a sofa (Pl. 317) provided by William Fell and Lawrence Turton for Sir Lawrence Dundas at Moor Park, Hertfordhire. The chairs were part of the furnishings for the tapestry drawing-room and were covered with Sir Lawrence's own Gobelins tapestry at £10 each. Other items from the suite are at the Philadelphia Museum of Art.

References: Gilbert (1978) I, p.64.

317.   Sofa (1771) 43 × 83 × 29 in (109 × 211 × 74 cm) *Temple Newsam House, Leeds*, Inv. 66/75.

Carved, with a gilt frame. Provided by William Fell and Lawrence Turton for Sir Lawrence Dundas at Moor Park, Hertfordshire. The sofa (one of an original pair) was charged at £25 and then covered with Sir Lawrence's 'own' Gobelins tapestry for a further £1 10s. The other sofa, along with six armchairs, two window stools and two firescreens is at Philadelphia.

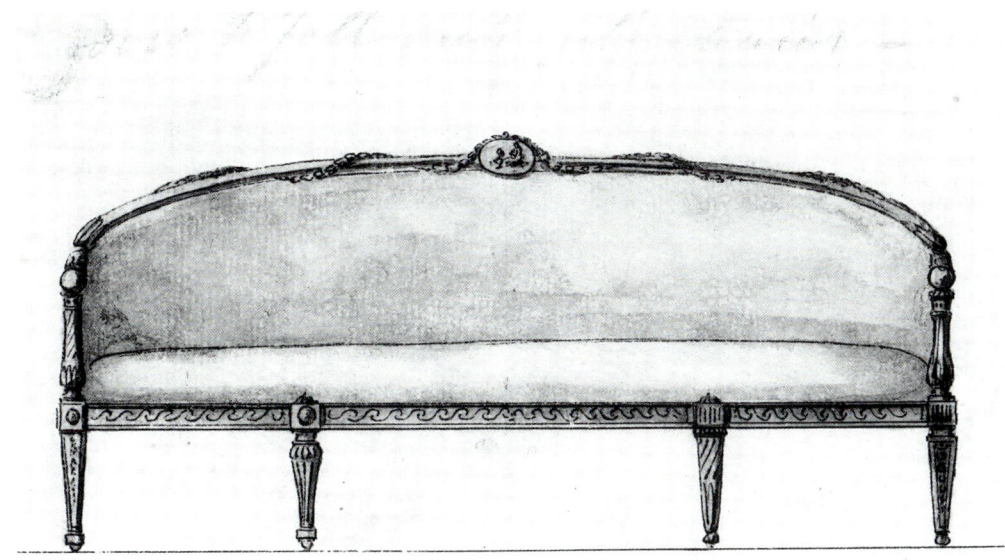

318.   Chair (1771) 35 × 23 in (89.2 × 58.5 cm) *Audley End, Essex* (English Heritage).

One of twelve with two sofas. Made by Gordon and Taitt for Sir John Griffin Griffin. Gilt frame, upholstered in crimson, green and white silk damask, which was also hung on the walls of the great drawing-room at Audley End. This was one of five rooms forming part of Robert Adam's work for Sir John. As the height of the room was below normal the furniture was made a little smaller and the dado rail lower. The chairs cost £50 8s for twelve, and the two sofas 13 guineas each. The total bill from Gordon and Taitt was £695 11s 3d. It was suggested some years ago that by placing the furniture in certain positions so that the top of the backs touched the wall, the pattern of the damask was repeated. The truth of this may be impossible to establish but it is true that Adam thought carefully about the arrangement of the rooms. The damask was rewoven to its eighteenth century form in 1962 but some of the unity of the original scheme was inevitably lost.

319.   Design for a sofa (1772) *London, Victoria and Albert Museum*, Inv. E123-1929.

The frame is coloured yellow to denote gilding. The drawing by John Linnell is probably the basis for his authorship of a gilt settee (*en suite* with eight armchairs, Pl. 321) made for Robert Child of Osterley Park, upholstered with Gobelins tapestry, *c.*1776 (see Pl. 332).

References: Hayward and Kirkham (1980) Pl. 260.

320.   State bed (1773) *Burton Constable, Yorkshire.*

Provided for William Constable by Edward Elwick in 1773 at a cost of £66 6s. The bed hangings were renewed in the nineteenth century.

321.   Tapestry room (*c*.1773) *Osterley Park,
Middlesex* (The National Trust).

Showing part of the Gobelins tapestry-
covered suite, with frames attributed to John
Linnell (see his design for a similar sofa, Pl.
319) supplied to Robert Child *c*.1773. The
wall hangings were created after cartoons by
François Boucher with the overall design of
the room by Robert Adam.

322.   Festoon curtains (*c.*1775) *Newby Hall, Yorkshire.*

One of an original set of three, supplied by Thomas Chippendale for the drawing- (now tapestry) room at Newby Hall. They were listed in the 1782 inventory as '3 window Curtains of Green watere'd Tabby lined & silk Fringe a sett of Cornices carv'd and Gilt in burnished Gold'. The curtains have been renewed with one original set retained, carefully in store.

References: Gilbert (1978) I, pp.225–6; Westman (1990) p.1415, n.20.

323.   Open armchair (*c.*1775–8) *Inveraray Castle, Scotland.*

Gilt frame. One of a set of six and two settees made for John, fifth Duke of Argyll at Inveraray Castle, Scotland by John Linnell. A design for the armchair survives in the Linnell archive but there are no bills to itemise what sums were charged and when.

References: Hayward and Kirkham (1980) Pl. 89.

324.   Drawing of a bed (1776) *London, Sir John Soane's Museum*, Vol. 17, no.157.

The drawing by Robert Adam is inscribed 'Design of a Bed for Robert Child Esq: Adelphi, 16th May 1776'. The surviving bed (Pls 325–9) follows the drawing closely.

325–9. State bed (*c.*1776–8) *Osterley Park, Middlesex* (The National Trust).

Closely corresponding to an Adam design of May 1776 (Pl. 324), made for Robert Child. The hangings are of olive green velvet and pale green silk, with embroidery in silver and silk of various colours; yellow fringe and tassels. The inside of the dome (Pl. 326) is also lined with green silk, embroidered with festoons and other ornaments. Horace Walpole thought the dome 'too theatric, and too like a modern head-dress'. Other details show the upper right of the bed; the valance decorated on alternate panels with an eagle holding an adder in its beak, the crest of the Child family, and a marigold, the symbol of the banking house of Child; the bed carpet designed by Robert Adam and woven by Thomas Moore.

References: Hefford (1977) p.848; Sherrill (1996) p.184.

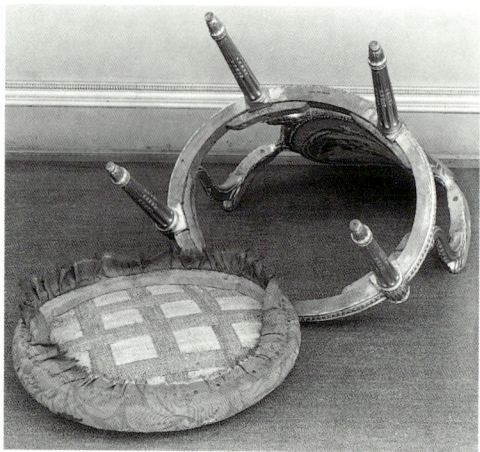

330–1.   Open armchair (*c.*1776) height, 37½ in (95 cm) *Osterley Park, Middlesex* (The National Trust).

One of a set of eight. Gilded beech, upholstered in Gobelins tapestry. The chair backs illustrate scenes form François Boucher's *Loves of the Gods*, whilst the seat covers are decorated with floral bouquets after designs by Maurice Jacques and Charles Tessier. The chairs are probably based on a French prototype. Made for the tapestry room at Osterley Park (see Pl. 321) and possibly by John Linnell. The detail is of the underneath of the chair.

332.   Settee (*c.*1776) height, 43¾ in (111 cm) *Osterley Park, Middlesex* (The National Trust).

En suite to eight armchairs (Pl. 330). Gilded beech upholstered in Gobelins tapestry, and related to a design by John Linnell (Pl. 319). Made for Robert Child's tapestry room at Osterley Park.

333–4. State bed (1778–9) *The Lord Egremont, Petworth.*

Carved and fluted mahogany posts by Thomas Chippendale with a 'furniture' of Spitalfields silk woven in 1764. The invoice for this from van Sommer, Triquet and van Sommer was dated 7 March 1764 (total £469) and included the 'Rich Shad'd flow'd velvet' of this bed, at £2 2s a yard.

335–6. Velvet *The Lord Egremont, Petworth.*

'Rich Green flow'd velvet' used on another of the five beds Chippendale supplied to the third Earl of Egremont. The details show the 'Rich Green flow'd Velvet' supplied at £1 12s a yard in 1764. Chippendale used the material in 1778 as hangings.

References: Gilbert (1978) I, pp.282–6, Pls 23–5.

337. Conversation picture, English school (*c.*1780) *Temple Newsam House, Leeds.*

The furnishing details of this interior show a check slip-cover on the chair at the left and on the floor the lattice pattern consistent in flat woven 'Scotch' carpets.

339. Bed curtain (*c.*1780) *Virginia, Colonial Williamsburg Foundation*, Inv. 1978-781-7.

Plate-printed cotton with linen tabs and brass rings. Attributed to the Bromley Hall fabric printing factory.

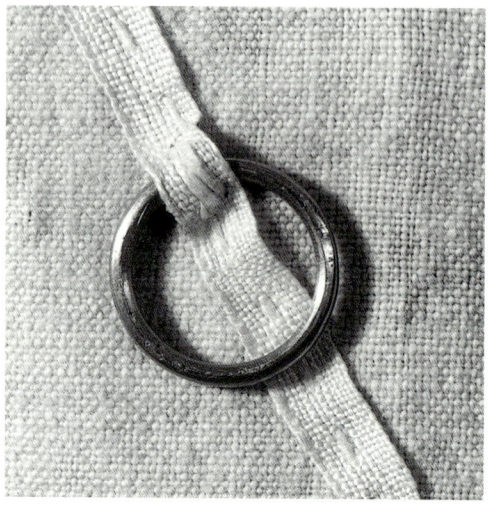

340. Brass ring (*c.*1780) *Virginia, Colonial Williamsburg Foundation*, Inv. 1974-403.

From the back of a plate-printed cotton curtain used for the threading of a cord to draw the curtain up. I use the words of Linda Baumgarten and Ronald Hurst, curators at the Colonial Williamsburg Department of Collections: 'The cord was first tied to the lower ring, then threaded through each ring, passed over a pulley at the top corner of the bed or window, and passed back down where the cord was tied off on a pair of cloak pins or knots' (See Pl. 344).

PLENTY.   L'ABONDANCE.

338. Slip-cover shown in a hand-coloured mezzotint engraving printed for Carrington Bowles, London (*c.*1780) *Virginia, Colonial Williamsburg Foundation*, Inv. 1980-332.

The young lady in the print is seated on a chair which has a typically loose and wrinkled eighteenth-century slip-cover.

341. State bed (1786) *Audley End, Essex* (English Heritage).

Supplied in 1786 by Chipchase and Lambert to Lord Howard de Walden (the former Sir John Griffin Griffin) for the state bedroom at Audley End. I have cited the relevant bill in the appendix (A41). The bed hangings are more or less consistent with the details of the bill and there seems little reason to assume a wholesale re-hang in the nineteenth century.

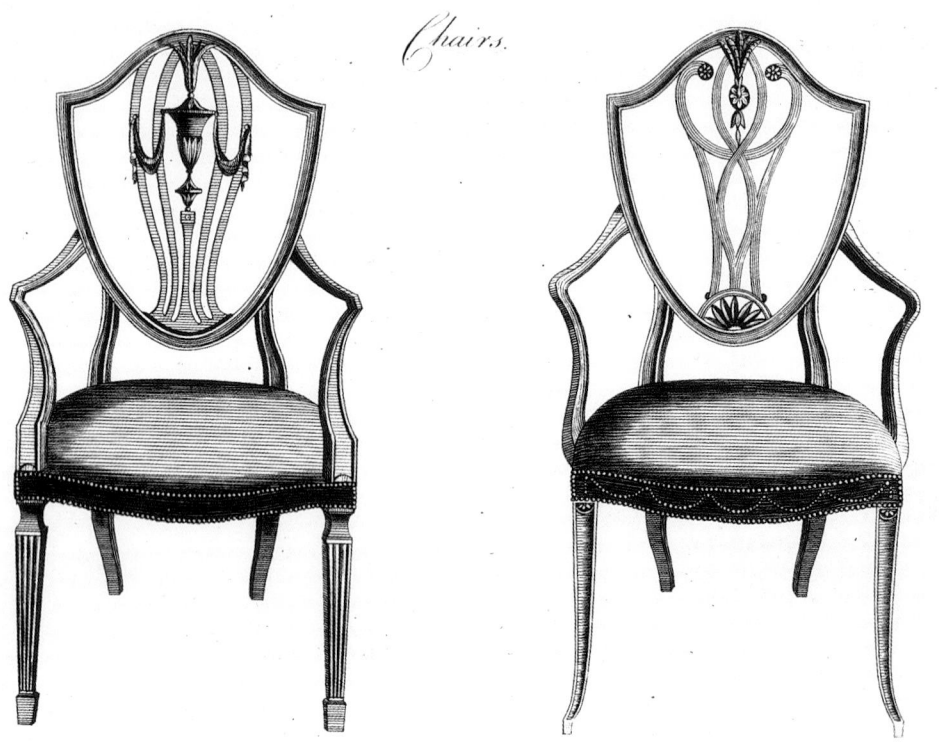

Chairs.

342.   Two chairs (*c.*1787).

Shown in George Hepplewhite's *The Cabinet-Maker and Upholsterers Guide* (1788, Pl. 4). The nailing patterns at the front seat edge show two popular styles.

Duchesse.

London, Published Octr 1.st 1787 by I. & J. Taylor N.º 56. High Holborn.

343.   Design for a Duchesse sofa (1788).

Shown in George Hepplewhite's *The Cabinet-Maker and Upholsterers Guide* (1788, Pl. 28). He noted that 'this piece of furniture also is derived form the French. Two Barjier chairs, of proper construction, with a stool in the middle, form the duchesse, which is allotted to large and spacious anti-rooms: the covering may be various, as also the frame-work, and made from 6 to 8 feet long'.

VII

Fluctuations in Taste 1791–1840

Thirty years into his reign George III had already endured several serious and misunderstood bouts of illness. A diagnosis of his insanity appealed to both Whigs and Tories; it was not until 1966[1] that it was established 'that the diagnosis of manic-depressive psychosis was untenable and that King George's illness was a classic case of porphyria' which, in its acute stages, leads to symptoms mistaken for mental illness. Across the Channel, France was locked into bloody revolution, but this had not altered the king's personal control here, and he had 'as much work after his illness as before'. He was deeply troubled domestically, not least by the bankruptcy of his rakish son, the Prince of Wales. He urgently insisted to him that his problems could be solved by sorting out his debts and giving up his mistress, Mrs Fitzherbert to marry his cousin, Princess Caroline of Brunswick. This he did in 1795, but her untidy style of life, which sank further into a deeper mire, turned the prince back to his mistresses, and so eventually, again, to Mrs Fitzherbert. In due time the king's illness had become such that, in 1811, his son took the oaths of office as regent. His mother died at Kew on 17 November 1818 and George III at Windsor on 29 January 1820.

The new king, as George IV, continued at a great pace the lavish spending which was an abiding characteristic throughout his life; by 1811 his debts stood at half a million pounds. His mania for building and decoration – Carlton House, the Pavilion at Brighton, the rebuilding of Buckingham Palace, the restoration of Windsor Castle – gave work to many craftsmen. They provided the settings and furnishings into which the acquisition of large and impressive collections of French furniture, silver and porcelain could be fitted. But it was all a conspicuous expenditure which angered the labouring poor and there was an attempt on the king's life in 1817. Even so his passion to build, at Windsor in particular, lasted until the end of his erratic life. He lived recklessly, without regard to normal rules, spent money constantly, enjoyed what the monarch's position allowed him to do and yet neatly avoided its onerous duties. Finally, in 1826 he decided to abandon Carlton House; this was done in 1827, and within three years, in as complete an eclipse as the falling stones created of the building, the king himself was dead.

CARLTON HOUSE

On a site in Pall Mall (now occupied in part by the Institute of Directors and the Athenaeum Club) the Prince of Wales, at his coming of age in 1783, started to transform Carlton House into his London residence.[2] It became a main focus of continuing alterations and improvements, but was always too small for such an avid collector and generous host. The prince was head of a small group of Francophiles (the Marquess of Hertford among them) who were the first to collect French works of art. It has been suggested of the prince[3] that 'it was to the courts of Versailles and the Tuileries that he must have turned for inspiration for his grander interior arrangements at Carlton House and for his more splendid fetes'. It is, however, with the Prince's patronage of

1 Brooke (1972), p.339.
2 Queen's Gallery (1991) p.9.
3 Queen's Gallery (1966) p.2.

English furniture makers that this account is concerned. The London cabinet-maker and upholsterer, Robert Campbell (who by the 1780s was advertising himself as 'Upholsterer to their Majesties' and 'Cabinet maker to the Prince of Wales'), was employed extensively at Carlton House. By 1791 he had supplied over £10,500-worth of furniture.

The work of Campbell and others (such as the French furniture maker in London, Francis Hervé) has been analysed for the furnishing of the Chinese drawing room at Carlton House.[4] Six 'Chinese' chairs, four armchairs, four *bergères* survive, being those supplied in 1790 by Hervé (frames and carving) with upholstery by Robert Campbell. He used a yellow brocaded satin and crimson braid supplied by Ibbetson, Barlow and Clarke, mercers on Ludgate Hill. The relevant sections of the analysis (whilst printed in 1967),[5] are repeated here for the conspicuous expenditure they denote:

> For the Chinese Room, Charlton [*sic*] House
> 40½ yds richest plain yellow Satten
> for the chairs   15/–   30.7.6
> 119 yds Middle border for Do   25/–   148.15.0
> 19½ yds Narrow border for Do   13/–   12.13.6
> 48 Shapes for Chairs richly Brocad.   105/–   252.0.0

Robert Campbell charged for the upholstering on 13 June 1792.

> To square stuffing the seats & backs of 6 single Chairs, covering Do with Irish linen &
> afterwards covering with Chinese shape brocaded Sattin Lined with White Cotton &
> bordered with Chinese border & welted over with Crimson Ingrain Silk   18.6.0
> To Square Stuffing 4 Feutelles & covering Do to correspond   15.14.0
> To Square Stuffing 4 Tete a Tetes & covering Do to match with a squab to each   27.10.0

Campbell also supplied curtains for the room and pink and green 'Clouded Cotton' loose covers for each of the chairs (£4 7s 0d) from material supplied (84 yds at 5/3; £22 1s 0d, lined with white calico 2s; £8 8s 0d) by Richard Ovey, a linen draper at 22 Tavistock Street. The final touch to the appearance of the upholstered seats, all gilded by Sefferin Nelson, was the tassels, supplied by 'John Helsa, Furniture Fringe and Tassell Manufacturer' of 35 Tavistock Street. He charged 12s for large tassels, 10s for medium size and 8s for small. He also provided tassels to bell pulls at 8s each. In subsequent years the suite has undergone several reupholsterings but the original satin covers were retained and reunited to Hervé's chairs in 1819.

Other furniture makers whom the prince used at Carlton House were Nicholas Morel (who may have been of French extraction) – later trading as Morel and Hughes – and Tatham, Bailey and Saunders, later as Elward and Marsh. Some of them were employed by the prince's architect, Henry Holland (1745–1806), who was also assisted in the interior decoration of Carlton House by two *marchands merciers*, Guillaume Gaubert and Dominique Daguerre. Gaubert had worked with Hervé at Chatsworth (1782–5), where, together, they supplied numerous suites of upholstered and caned seat furniture, much of which is still in the private apartments of the house.[6] Daguerre had worked for Holland at Althorp (1785), providing furniture for the second Earl Spencer,[7] and the prince was soon heavy in debt to him for furniture for Carlton House and Buckingham Palace.[8] They were years when others, less fortunate, had to take their designs from published patterns.

4   G. de Bellaigue (1967) p.520.
5   *Ibid.*, p.520.
6   Hall (1980) pp.400–14.

7   Stroud (1966) pp.145–6.
8   H. C. Smith (1931) Pls 169–70.

SHERATON AND ELEGANT TASTE

Hepplewhite's *Guide* had been followed by another important publication in 1788 – *The Cabinet-Maker's London Book of Prices*. Sponsored by the London Society of Cabinet-Makers, it appeared again in 1793 and in 1803, and at various dates in the nineteenth century.[9] The Society consisted of journeymen who had banded together as a collective organization to protect and improve wages and conditions – an early form of trade union activity. The *Book of Prices* was drawn up to present to the masters for approval. It set out piece-work rates for cabinet work – articles such as beds, chairs and settees were excluded – and contained twenty engraved plates, seventeen of which were contributed by Thomas Shearer. Upholsterers must have longed for something similar and the answer, in part only, was provided for them by Thomas Sheraton's *Drawing Book*.

Sheraton had been born at Stockton-on-Tees, Durham in 1751. He came of poor stock and described himself, at thirty-one, as 'a mechanic, and one who never received the advantages of a *collegial* or *academical* education'. He nevertheless progressed as a very competent draughtsman, undoubtedly trained in a furniture making capacity, but, like Hepplewhite, is not known (at least to our present knowledge) to have made a single piece of furniture. It was his books of design and instruction which ensured his lasting reputation, and, like Hepplewhite, the name Sheraton denotes a type of elegant furniture, usually in satinwood, and made after the dimensions in his engraved plates (Pls 347–351). In about 1790 Sheraton left the north of England, and was said, after 1793, to have 'supported himself, a wife and two children, by his exertions as an author'.[10] His trade-card[11] advertised that he taught: 'Perspective, Architecture and Ornaments' and made 'Designs for Cabinet-makers' and sold 'all kinds of Drawing Books'.

Sheraton's *The Cabinet-Maker and Upholsterer's Drawing Book* came out in parts between 1791 and 1794. Parts one and two concerned themselves with geometry and perspective and paraded Sheraton's fascination with both; part three, much the most valuable, stated the author's intention 'to exhibit the present taste of furniture, and at the same time to give the workman some assistance'. The intention was realized very successfully, and the work displayed the author's technical knowledge of the cabinet trades. The *Appendix*, which gave 'a variety of original designs for household furniture', was issued in 1793, and an *Accompaniment* in 1794 contained 'ornaments useful for learners to copy from, but particularly adapted to the cabinet and chair branches: exhibiting original and new designs of chair legs, bed pillars, window cornices, chair splats and other ornaments'.

The extent to which Sheraton was responsible for inventing his own designs is uncertain: he seems to have taken what was good and current in the London workshops, and he acknowledged his indebtedness to others. His sense of proportion and balance was that of an aesthete, but some of the designs reflect over-elaboration and an excessive use of drapery and upholstery. As in Hepplewhite's *Guide*, the most numerous designs in Sheraton's *Drawing Book* were for chairs and chair backs. Chairs of the newest taste were rectilinear in form, a near rectangle back composed of four or more carved bars arranged vertically above a caned or upholstered seat. Sheraton distinguished between chairs for the parlour and chairs for the drawing room. The Spanish or Cuban mahogany dining parlour chairs were to be 'substantial, useful things avoiding trifling ornaments and unnessary ornamentation'. The drawing room chairs, in contrast, were to be painted and gilt or japanned. They had rounded seats, turned, fluted or reeded legs tapering to the foot, and turning was also applied to the back uprights and arm supports. The parlour chairs had straight-fronted seats, square taper legs, and flat moulded uprights. Sheraton had favoured filling the backs of rectangular chairs with vertical bars, but many makers improved (or so they thought) on his recommendation. The diagonal lattice was popular, as were fillings which consisted of either a horizontal lattice between horizontal bars or one in which an oblong or oval panel was put into the back of a larger cane-work oblong or oval. The seat rails, legs and uprights would be

9 See facsimile in *Furniture History*, XVIII (1982).

10 Noted in his obituary, *Gentleman's Magazine*, November 1806.

11 B.L., Heal Collection.

japanned black with gold lining and painted floral motifs. In his *Drawing Book* (plate XXXII), Sheraton noted: 'The figures in the tablets above the front rails are on French pleated silk or satin, sewed on to the stuffing, as is the ornamented tablet at the top of the left hand chair. The top rail is pannelled out, and a small gold bead mitred round, and the printed silk is pasted on'. The settees he illustrated, of chair-back form, upholstered or caned, were handsome creations, severe in outline with usually a straight back centring on long oblong panels in the top rail. A variation was the *chaise-longue*, which Sheraton said was 'to rest or loll upon after dinner'. But events had moved ahead very fast and Sheraton, by 1800, seemed almost out-moded.

CHINOISERIE AT BRIGHTON

An interest in the Orient had persisted, and was revived, particularly in work for the Prince Regent at the Brighton Pavilion. This seaside residence had already gone through three building phases in fifteen years: Henry Holland's Marine Pavilion of 1787, an enlargement of this from 1795 onwards, and then a strong Chinoiserie phase from 1801. Holland's accounts for that year included charges for designs for Chinese decorations and using 'Works & Furniture by Messrs Saunders, Hale & Robson, Marsh & Tatham, Morell, Crace'. The prince's main agent in these decorations was Frederick Crace (1779–1859),[12] and his design for an alcove with a tented ceiling in calico, *c.*1801, shows his proficiency with upholstered surfaces, and knowledge of French interiors of the 1790s.[13] But the main furnishings came from others.

The Mount Street firm of Elward, Marsh and Tatham made a great deal of 'India' furniture for Brighton in japanned bamboo. The firm had a succession of names in its eighty or so years of known activity. William Marsh and George Elward had entered into partnership about 1785, and were joined by Edward Bailey in 1793, and Thomas Tatham in 1798. The firm was then known as Elward, Marsh and Tatham until 1803, when Elward's name disappears from trade directories.[14] Their activities overall were also bound up in a close but unclear way with Henry Holland and the talented team of craftsmen working for the Prince Regent. For example, the general form of the chairs they made for the Brighton Pavilion is similar to those they made for Carlton House, with their sweeping concave front legs. This characteristic was 'soon to become one of the most distinctive marks of Regency character'[15] in its furniture.

In February 1811 the Prince of Wales had become regent. Whilst he had waited for the position, without any of the training or the strength of character to endure his long exclusion from affairs of state, he had pursued his extravagant remodellings at Carlton House and at the Brighton Pavilion. The regent had many French friends, spoke the language fluently, and, as I have noted, collected fine works of art on an extensive scale. Many were on the market in France as a result of the French Revolution and the Napoleonic wars. These were available to the regent through friends and agents, or they were sent on approval to him. When peace came in 1814 there seemed every reason to brighten up the English court. And so, in 1815, John Nash began a further wide-ranging reorganization of the Brighton Pavilion buildings. Nash gave to the seaside palace a cosmopolitan set of interior spaces.[16] The banqueting room, with its exuberant decorations in carved, gilded and painted work was perhaps the most astonishing of all of them. Surmounted by a forty-five foot high dome, with a representation of a plantain tree wreathing from its centre, the room was equipped by 1817 with dining chairs to seat some thirty-six guests. Tatham, Bailey and Saunders provided a set of thirty-six chairs[17] and two armchairs in that year made of lacquered beech (£669 12s). The impressive rosewood sideboards with their overlaid ornament of carved and gilded dragons made the chairs and even the diners seem insignificant. At a cost of £4,129 3s they were among the firm's best achievements, at a time when they were well into such lavish provisions.

12 Aldrich, ed. (1990) p.21.
13 *Ibid.*, pp.22–3, Pl. 1.11.
14 Frances Collard in Beard and Gilbert (1986) p.277.
15 Musgrave (1961) p.32; see also Collard (1985) for an authoritative account of Regency furniture.

16 Morley (1984).
17 Collard (1985) Pl.198b.

The Influence of Thomas Hope

Nelson's victory at the Battle of the Nile, and the resulting preoccupation by many with the architectural wonders of Egypt and Greece was epitomized in the career of the eldest son of a rich Dutch banker, Thomas Hope (1769–1831).[18] His family had fled from Holland at its occupation in 1794 by the French but Hope had been away travelling for several years, studying and drawing in the Middle East and in Greece. In 1801 he had acquired all the second collection of vases, busts and bronzes assembled by Sir William Hamilton. In planning his Adam house in Portland Place as a setting for his collections Hope designed 'ancient furniture' for the rooms and set out these designs in 1807 in an important book, *Household Furniture and Interior Decoration Executed from Designs by Thomas Hope*. In the meantime, he had bought Deepdene in Surrey and moved his collections there. His book, however, remained as the record of the Portland Place settings and the suite of his apartments there included an Egyptian or black room 'with ornaments from scrolls of papyrus and mummy-cases' – the furniture was pale yellow, blue-green, and black and gold. Surrounded by his 200 Greek vases, tables, pedestals and 'the mantlepiece of an Egyptian portico', people were admitted by 'application signed by some persons of known character and taste'. Only Horace Walpole at Strawberry Hill, thirty years before, had taken such trouble to single out the discerning from the merely curious.

In the preface to his own book, Hope characterized what he looked for in contemporary furniture: 'breadth and response of surface, that distinction and contrast of outline, that opposition of plain and upholstered parts, that harmony and significance of accessories . . . which are calculated to afford the eye and mind the . . . most unfailing enjoyment'. It was a noble aim if imperfectly realized.

In 1808, George Smith, a cabinet-maker and upholsterer then living in London off Cavendish Square, published *A Collection of Designs for Household Furniture and Interior Decoration*. He had seized upon much of what Hope had done (although the plates are dated 1804–7), and had presumably visited the former's London house when, on occasion, it was opened to the general public. Smith was, however, less concerned with classical purity – he wanted to provide practical designs, many of them Gothic, for the wide range of carcase and upholstered furniture needed to fill many entire houses. Hope's furniture, he thought, was for an educated minority who knew their pattern-books, Hamilton's *Antiquities* (1766), D'Hancarville's drawings of Hamilton's Greek vases (1766–7) or Vivant Denon's classic work *Voyages dans la Basse et la Haute Egypte* (1802). Smith showed designs like Hope's of tables with animal monopodia, but he did include two Chinese designs for cornices and window drapery. Almost twenty years later, in 1826, he announced in his last book, *Cabinet-Maker's and Upholsterer's Guide, Drawing Book and Repository*, that it was now 'wholly obsolete and inapplicable'. He also announced himself as 'Upholsterer and Drawing Master to His Majesty'.

Some of the Grecian chairs designed by Hope had deep arc-backs, ebonized and gilded, with satin or damask upholstery only on the seat. Other armchairs had iron monopodia front legs, and an upholstered back gently scrolled from half-way up the back rails, or had arms carved with rams' heads and an outswept arc-back in shiny leather set over a curved frame. But the preoccupation of Smith and other Regency chair-makers, in contrast, was to satisfy the near-insatiable demand for cheap, painted chairs. Rudolph Ackermann's invaluable *The Repository of Arts* . . . (August 1814) recorded that such chairs were intended for use in 'best bed chambers, for secondary drawing rooms, and occasionally to serve for routs' at assembly rooms and other social venues. The best kind were those supplied by the firm of Morgan and Sanders, from their Trafalgar House premises in Catherine Street, London (Pl. 355).

18 Watkin (1968).

Morgan and Sanders

Much is known about this firm because of its involvement with Rudolph Ackermann, to whose monthly *The Repository of Arts . . .* they supplied, between 1809 and 1815, a succession of furniture designs.[19] They had also provided Lord Nelson with furniture in 1805 for his house at Merton in Surrey, and carried the name of 'Trafalgar' chairs forward in their extensive provision of a popular form of chair having 'scimitar' or 'sabre' shaped front legs, a rope-moulded top rail (a reference to the victories of Nelson's fleet), and back supports. They were made in beech, with caned seats and remained in popular use in parlours long after 1815. The upholsterers provided them with loose cushions in many coloured materials to contrast with the painted black frames, or, those in dark green which simulated bronze. The firm had good upholsterers whose work was costed accordingly. For two armchairs they supplied in 1811 for the new County Hall at Lewes the chairs were charged at £21 each with the remainder of the account, amounting to £71 10s, being for upholstery materials. Both Morgan and Sanders had been employed at the start of their careers by Thomas Butler, a London upholsterer and cabinet-maker who had established a business in 1787 supplying patent furniture.[20] They were thus aware of the important part upholstery played in a varied output. In fact, if one consults the many upholstery patents granted in the nineteenth century it is apparent that anyone involved with patent furniture needed to know of new ideas, of Charles de Berenger's substitute for horse hair stuffing (1806), and John Clark's air-tight cushions (1813).

Morgan and Sanders issued an elaborate trade card,[21] which showed a number of their portable chairs, four post bedsteads, tables and 'Army and Navy Equipage'. They were specialists in the provision of patent camp and tent bedsteads and advertised that their 'Patent Brass Bedsteads' were in 'Every Respect Superior to all others'. The furniture was made 'with good taste and craftsmanship', a popular concept encouraged by Sheraton's publication which had included ingenious arrangements and mechanical gadgets. Comfort and utility were at last closely related to compact and portable items.

George IV at Windsor

By the time the Prince of Wales became king in 1820 his building activities at Carlton House and the Brighton Pavilion had been well charted. Thomas Sheraton had published three designs of the drawing room and Chinese drawing room at Carlton House in his *Drawing Book* (1793, plates XXX–XXXII). The leading watercolour artist, W. H. Pyne (1769–1843), had been working for some time in publishing copies of watercolours by Charles Wild and James Stephanoff (Pls 359–61), of the interiors of royal residences.[22] Then, between 1820 and 1824, John Nash published his aquatint views of Brighton Pavilion.[23] As a compulsive builder the king then turned in the 1820s to the private apartments at Windsor Castle, and to the skills of his furniture makers, Morel and Seddon.[24]

Some seventy drawings of interiors, elevations and items of furniture at Windsor were auctioned[25] in 1970 and a number were acquired for the Royal Collection. I reproduce some of the elaborate curtain designs (Pls 370, 372). At Carlton House and at Windsor the architect Sir Jeffry Wyatville and Morel and Seddon were answerable directly to the king. This allowed him a direct intervention and even an ignoring of expenditure at certain times. The king, for example, questioned Morel and Seddon on certain colour schemes, changed one, and also personally selected the pattern of the principal carpets. Nicholas Morel did, however, enjoy the king's confidence since being awarded the contract in 1826 to furnish the royal apartments at Windsor. He had

19 Agius and Jones (1984).
20 Joy (1962); Austen (1974).
21 Joy (1962) p.14, Pl. 9.
22 Watkin (1984).
23 Jackson-Stops (1991).
24 G. de Bellaigue and Kirkham (1972) pp.1–34.
25 Sotheby's, 9 April 1970.

entered into a partnership with Robert Hughes about (Pl. 358) 1805, and when by the mid-1820s this had slowed down entered, the following year, into a second partnership with George Seddon, specifically to cater for the Windsor commission. Morel was granted his warrant as 'Upholsterer in Ordinary to George IV' in July 1828.[26] By this time Morel and Hughes had laid the foundations and assiduously built up a good firm. Their patronage by the first Earl of Bradford at Weston Park, Staffordshire (1802–6), at a cost of over £4,714, had been outstandingly successful, and a good deal of furniture by them survives at the house.[27] They had also worked for Lord Mansfield, at Lord Harewood's London house, for the Dukes of Bedford, Buccleuch and Northumberland, and at Longleat for the Marquess of Bath.

The partnership with Seddon brought to Morel the resources of the largest furniture-making firm in London. It was at their commodious Aldersgate Street workshops that the furniture was made for Windsor. They had an excellent command of using high quality fabrics to match their furnishings; Morel also visited Paris in 1826 and, armed with ideas saw to it that the goods made or supplied by various weavers, mercers, printers and glaziers were sent to them direct. 'They upholstered the furniture, made the curtains and hung the materials on the walls'. Other artists provided designs including Jacob-Desmalter, the second son of the famous menuisier Georges Jacob. After 'retiring' in 1825 he came to England to work on the Windsor furnishings.[28]

DRAPERY IN GENERAL

In 1823 Rudolph Ackermann re-issued a serious of forty-four coloured engravings of fashionable furniture. In his introduction[29] he stated: 'the difficult and important branch of the upholstery art, drapery in general, requires the talents of the draughtsman, combined with professional experience and taste.' The engravings had been taken from the second series of his *The Repository of Arts . . .* issued between January 1816 and December 1822.[30] French style was an important consideration in view of designers such as Percier and Fontaine seeking to achieve the same kind of synthesis undertaken in England by Robert Adam – to harmonize architecture, decoration and furniture, and to strive for an effect of dignified simplicity. Additionally, Ackermann's work was rivalled by the plates of *Meubles et objets de goût* issued in Paris (irregularly between 1802 and 1835 by Pierre de la Mesangère (1761–1831)).[31]

By the time Sheraton issued the parts forming his *Drawing Book* (1791–3) he was taking note of French drapery patterns. His plate 'Cornices, Curtains & Drapery for Drawing Room Windows' (anticipated, or followed by the Gillow firm, Pl. 346),[32] dated 11 June 1792, was accompanied by the note: '. . . It is, however, necessary to observe, that the French strapping and tassels in the right-hand design is no part of the cornice, as some cabinet-makers have already mistaken it to be. It is the upholsterer's work, and is sewed on within the valance or ground of the drapery.' Designs were also used lavishly by George Smith in the first and second editions (1808; 1826) of his *Household Furniture*, in Ackermann's *The Repository of Arts*, John Taylor's *The Upholsterers' and Cabinet Makers' Pocket Assistant* (c.1825), and in the splendid early nineteenth-century drawings by Morel and Seddon and the Gillow furniture-making enterprises (Pls 362, 372). The comment from Ackermann on his illustration of 1809 (Plate 26) of 'A French Window Curtain and Grecian Settee' (Pl. 356), shows a preoccupation with French styles and classically-inspired furniture: 'An elegant French window-curtain, most tastefully ornamented with beautiful borders, rich Parisian fringe . . . A Grecian settee, or window-seat . . . fringed *en suite* . . .' Such curtains were hung from and draped around a rod or French pole usually of mahogany, or metal richly embellished with ormolu or brass rosettes and plaquettes. Sheraton again is explicit about his 1792 plate, 'of the Drapery':

> These curtains are drawn on French rods. When the cords are drawn the curtains meet in the
> center at the same time, but are no way raised from the floor. When the same cord is drawn

26 Frances Collard in Beard and Gilbert (1986) p.624.
27 Rogers (1987) pp.11–34.
28 G. de Bellaigue and Kirkham (1972) pp.5–6.
29 Ackermann (1823) p.2.

30 Agius and Jones (1984) p.200.
31 Dornsife (1975) p.70; Winkler (1994).
32 Boynton (1995) p.180, note to his col. Pl. 20.

the reverse way, each curtain flies open, and comes to their place on each side, as they are now represented. The cord passes on a side pulley fixed on the right-hand. To effect this, the rod is made in a particular manner, having two pulleys at one end, and a single one at the other . . .

Ackermann in describing his plate 64 of May 1814, a design by Morgan and Sanders, noted further on a French source: 'The whole design and colouring of the drapery are correct and appropriate. The azure and white, which may be sprinkled with lilies, are the colours of the legitimate dynasty of France . . .'

Both he and George Smith illustrated a 'French Bed' in which the silk drapery was thrown over a sceptre-rod projecting from the wall (Pl. 369). Ackermann noted further, of his plate 84 of 'A French Bed' (1816), that it was 'a design lately imported from Paris . . . decorated agreeably to Parisian fancy'.

One of the talented designers and furniture-makers of whose activities Ackermann published eight plates in *The Repository of Arts* . . . (1816–24) was George Bullock (*c.*1777–1818).[33] Admittedly these had probably been provided by Bullock himself and they were still being used after his death. That of 'A French Bed' noted above, was probably from one of the designs submitted by Bullock. Only his early death, aged about forty, prevented much of what he designed being carried out. His use of both exotic and native British woods in his furniture allowed an assertiveness which, with finely modelled metal mounts, was enhanced, as *The Times* had it, on 1 July 1819, 'to a degree of perfection'.

OAKLEY AND SHACKLETON

George Oakley (*c.*1759–*c.*1841) had trained as an upholsterer under William Elliott from 1773 to 1780 or so.[34] He was admitted to the freedom of the Upholsterers' Company in 1782. His trade card announced him as an 'upholder' working from 'the south side of St Paul's Churchyard' and indicated that he appraised goods and furnished funerals.[35] He also stocked a great variety of fabric patterns for purchase wholesale. Oakley's first partner had been Henry Kettle, a competent cabinet-maker and upholsterer but the liaison was a short-lived one. In 1798 he acquired a new partner in the person of Thomas Shackleton, son-in-law of the successful George Seddon.

Oakley's printed furniture fabrics were a very remunerative part of his activities. He came, in this respect, to the notice of the royal family (several members of which visited his premises in 1799), and by the following year he was able to announce that 'Geo. Oakley & Co' were 'Furniture Printers to her Majesty'. Additionally they had, at 8 Old Bond Street, a 'Magazine of General and Superb Cabinet Furniture'. It is interesting that one of their designers was John Taylor, who in 1825 issued his own book on upholstery (Pl. 367). The firm gained a wide reputation, a German writer stating, in 1807, that Oakley, Gillows and Charles Elliott were the chief makers and sellers of furniture and upholstery in London.[36] An advertisement the firm placed in the *Morning Chronicle* (4 July 1788) stated that they stocked patent chairs for drawing and eating rooms and that they could also supply '. . . French and Polonese Beds, with elegant draperies, and Beds of all other kinds: Window Curtains, and every other article of elegance, of the newest invention and most tasteful design . . . adapted both to the superb mansion and the cottage ornee . . .'

The firm maintained that, from an extensive stock always kept ready for delivery, they could 'completely furnish capital Houses in a few days'. Rooms could be arranged to the taste of the owners, although it was the primary concern of Oakley and Shackleton to see that this was done by uniting 'elegance and convenience'. Fine words, but they accomplished both successfully.

33   Wainwright, Wood and Levy (1988) pp.118–25.
34   Mary Stirling in Beard and Gilbert (1986) p.658.
35   B. L., Heal and Banks collections.
36   Joy (1972) p.112.

A LESSER COMPANY

One of the patrons to whom Oakley and Shackleton supplied furniture in 1813 was James Henry Leigh of Stoneleigh Abbey, Warwickshire. The extensive Leigh archive[37] contains several bills from lesser London and provincial firms. John Johnstone of 67 New Bond Street were assiduous in their attentions. On 20 August 1816 they wrote to Mrs Leigh about the provision of ottomans, with two sketches to help along the discussion.[38] One had a raised middle to act as a 'rest' for those seated on all four sides. They continued:

> Pillows that we make for Soffas & Ottomans are generally filled with Goose Feathers, they answer the purpose quite as well as downe – the Squab or seat should be stuffed with Curled hair – Indeed for Ottomans we frequently make the back Cushions of Hair also . . . The 6 Cushions for the backs of the 2 Ottomans will take about 18 or 20 lbs [of feathers Mrs Leigh possessed] – the Hair Cushions Sit neater than the feather ones.

They promised covering in her crimson silk, with a lace trim, but for the square ottomans they did not advise a fringe – 'Tassels at the Corners and the Silk round the frame I propose to be fluted will look pretty'. The firm's bill, 1816 to 1818,[39] shows that they charged sixteen guineas for making the square ottoman and £3 16s 8d for covering it in silk, and the same price each for two further square ottomans (Appendix A44).

The Leigh family also patronized other London makers and suppliers such as George Woolley's 'Cabinet Upholstry & Carpet Warehouse' at 196 Piccadilly in 1813 (£611 16s 7d),[40] and, in the same year, the firm of Chipchase and Proctor in Albemarle Street. This was a continuation of the firm of Chipchase and Lambert I have noted as working at Audley End, Essex, in the mid-1780s (Pl. 341). Chipchase and Proctor were active at providing much japanned furniture with cane seats, japanned window cornices 'in imitation of bamboo', or of 'ebony inlayed with Ivory', rosewood tables, folding firescreens, lined with scarlet tammy, and all the requirements for numerous bedrooms and servants' quarters.[41] For 'Mr Leigh Junr's room they provided 'A Four post Bedstead with handsome carved Mahogany posts, plated compass rod, lath bottoms & French Castors, for £11 15s.' This had a set of 'sweep top moulding Cornices neatly japanned and varnished'. It must have made a handsome sight, with its thirty-four yards of 'Handsome green & salmon Trellis fringe' and its furniture of 'your Tea ground Chintz lined with white Calico, bound & fringed'. The window curtains were *en suite*, in the 'tea ground Chintz lined with white Calico', set under the japanned cornices. The lines for drawing the curtains together passed over brass pulleys and then fastened on to 'handsome Curtain pins'.

Not all patrons could use London upholsterers and there were plenty of competent men and women able to visit a house. In 1828 Ann Turner of Chester announced that, as the widow of Samuel Turner, she was carrying on the business and for upholstery had engaged someone formerly with Gillows. She guaranteed to give satisfaction to those who found their own material and would execute the work in the most fashionable style, 'for which purpose they will be waited upon either in town or country'.[42] As well as this convenience of *in situ* work (to which upholsterers had always needed to give considerable attention), there were many warehouses and specialist wholesalers who could supply to the casual or discerning purchaser. Joseph and Samuel Harper of Ludlow, active from 1822 to 1835, announced on their trade card[43] that they were 'bed, window cornice and pier glass makers' and it showed elaborately draped curtains, a Regency chair, a folding bed, secretaire and a classical sofa with drapery hanging over the ends to underline the point of their versatility. Many upholsterers advised that they travelled to London to select stock, and several in London that they would wait on families 'in any part of the United Kingdom'. One such was Henry Cooper of Bishopsgate Street in

37   Shakespeare's Birthplace Trust, Stratford-upon-Avon.
38   *Ibid.*, MS., DR 18/12/41.
39   *Ibid.*, MS., DR 18/5/7156.
40   *Ibid.*, MS., DR 18/5/7032.
41   *Ibid.*, MSS., DR 18/5/6999; 7100.
42   Beard and Gilbert (1986) p.911.
43   B.L., Heal collection.

London. He advertised widely in the late 1820s[44] and his stock and skills seem to have embraced every field of house furnishing. His upholstery department featured 'the improved Elastic Steel Stuffing for Carriage Cushions, Chairs, Sofas, Mattresses &c'; and he had in stock 'a handsome assortment of Bedstead Furniture, Window Cornices, Curtains &c.' Carpets, looking-glasses, carving and gilding, paper-hanging, painting, fitting-up cabins of ships all came into his busy activity. He also furnished funerals, conducted sales and appraisals, collected rents and stored furniture. Fringes could be obtained easily in London, or directly from agents, such as John Dean of Macclesfield,[45] where many were made. There were also makers of specific kinds of furniture. James Gouldie's trade card[46] showed him, *c*.1810, as a 'Cabinet, Grecian Couch and Chair Manufacturer' in Liverpool, whilst George Fraser of Clerkenwell was, in the years 1802 to 1813 a 'fancy chair and sofa manufacturer'. John Hall of London made bed pillars and music stools, as well as chairs and sofas. Henry Goff of Brighton supplied 'Hotel, Tavern and Lodging House Keepers & families' with featherbeds, mattresses, carpets and rugs. Feathers were now purified by steam but some stockists, G. Watson of Liverpool for example, stated that silk flocks, 'at 6d a pound', were superior and 'far more essential to health'. Into this category came 'beds for overseas use, and mosquito nets as soldiers and others travelled further afield'. Steam had also cheapened the making of window blinds,[47] a trade which had blossomed since the (unlikely) claim in 1769 of William Deering of Long Acre to be the 'original maker of Venetian blinds'.[48]

THE WAY FORWARD

In March 1827 Augustus Welby Pugin wrote in Ackermann's *The Repository of Arts . . .* of the Gothic style: 'No style can be better adapted for its decoration [the Library] than that of the middle ages, which possess a sedate and grave character, that invites the mind to study and reflection . . .'. The romantic novels of Sir Walter Scott had brought it forward again and the great early nineteenth-century castles of Eastnor and Lowther by Sir Robert Smirke were the soaring settings for its apotheosis. In 1827 the *Repository* noted that there were then so many skilful workers in Gothic 'that very elaborate pieces of furniture may be made at a moderate price, compared with what it was a few years ago.' In contrast to its text, the *Repository* continued, obstinately, to publish classical items of furniture. They were, of course, ignored by Pugin, who was preparing for publication, by the entrepreneurial Ackermann (who turned whichever way was profitable), the first of four volumes of his illustrations, *Gothic Furniture in the Style of the 15th Century*. This appeared finally in 1835,[49] with simpler pieces, including chairs, adapted for commercial production.

By the early years of Queen Victoria's reign the main styles of design were still those described in 1833 by J. C. Loudon in his valuable *Encyclopedia of Cottage, Farm and Villa Architecture and Furniture*.[50] He firstly described the fashionable styles, which he reduced to four:

> the Grecian or modern style, which is by far the most prevalent; the Gothic or perpendicular style which imitates the lines and angles of the Tudor Gothic Architecture; the Elizabethan style, which combines the Gothic with the Roman or Italian manner; and the style of the age of Louis XIV, or the florid Italian, which is characterised by curved lines and excess of curvilinear ornaments.

Loudon's analysis of the four styles betrayed a lack of knowledge of their historical origins. He expressed dislike of the Louis quatorze revival as 'unsuitable to the present advancing state of the public taste'. He preferred the 'Grecian style', although he was critical of the interpretation of it by furniture makers. Gothic

44   *Liverpool Mercury*, 17 October 1828.
45   Beard and Gilbert (1986) p.237.
46   Metropolitan Museum of Art, New York, Landauer Collection.
47   Beard and Gilbert (1986) pp.212 (Croskell); 348 (Goff); 949 (Watson).

48   *Ibid.*, p.356. Vile and Cobb invoiced Lord Coventry for Venetian blinds in the 1760s (Beard, 1993, no. 12).
49   Wainwright (1976) pp.3–11.
50   Gilbert (1970); Gloag (1970).

earned his full praise, and iron bedsteads in that, or any other fashion, he considered 'hygienic'. Furniture, he argued, with upholsterers probably casting their eyes upwards, was to be designed so that it did not harbour dirt or dust. The Louis quatorze style manifested an influence from France which the Anglo-French wars of 1793–1815 had not entirely overturned. With the favourable Francophile atmosphere at George IV's court it was possible for an architect such as Benjamin Dean Wyatt to introduce the style in London in the late 1820s at such important town houses as York (now Lancaster) House, Londonderry House, Crockford's Club and, magisterially, at Apsley House for the first Duke of Wellington.

The 'Elizabethan style' had been given a push forward by the popular historical novels of Sir Walter Scott, and by two books, T. F. Hunt's *Exemplars of Ancient Furniture* (1830) and Henry Shaw's *Specimens of Ancient Furniture* (1836). The style was given further approval by the Queen's decorators, H. W. & A. Arrowsmith. In their *House Decorator and Painter's Guide* (1840), they stated that of the four fashionable styles 'none are in themselves more picturesque or so well suited to the manners and customs of the English people than the Elizabethan'.

The chaste purity of the 'Grecian style' encouraged by the publication of Thomas Hope's *Household Furniture and Interior Decoration* (1807) had, within a few months, become tainted by the commercial designer, George Smith's book on household furniture and interior decoration, issued in 1808. Smith had, of course, adopted the style without having the benefit of Hope's scholarly background. Others succeeded in part where Smith, perhaps, failed, and there are many competent classical, Greek-inspired designs evident in Peter and Michael Angelo Nicholson's *The Practical Cabinet-Maker, Upholsterer and Complete Decorator* (1826–7). It became a favourite style for dining-room furniture in the new London clubs, and there are well-known pieces, of 1834, designed by the architect Philip Hardwick for Goldsmiths' Hall. As for the many 'innovations' of the Victorian years, it is clear that most of them had been long anticipated.

In the quest for status and comfort there was, nevertheless, for a time, little else new to make, copy, or even invent, but there were enough who tried. Design was not, admittedly, in the forefront of their minds but some technical developments were. There was an increasing use of the Jacquard loom after 1830 and the general improvements in power-loom weaving increased both the quality and quantity of woven textiles. This trend was concurrent with similar increases made possible when machine printing of fabric superseded the older, laborious method of hand-block printing. New aniline-based dyes provided a wider range of more vibrant colours.

Many of the efforts of nineteenth-century house planners were devoted to achieving domestic comfort, even if some of the buildings they created also contained soaring and draughty spaces. John Arkwright, who in 1834 was rebuilding the seventeenth-century Hampton Court, Herefordshire, defined the priorities for his class: 'Comfort is the only consideration which had induced me to make any alteration whatever, and that obtained, I care as far as my own taste is concerned, but little for the rest.'[51] The 'rest', for those who wanted comfort, might consist of little more that waxed oak-panelled walls reflected in a cheerful fire, surrounded by deep-buttoned armchairs, crafted with a fine skill. Indeed, most quality Victorian furniture was fashioned from excellent materials by hand-work, reliant on long established methods.

There were many furniture makers in royal employment during Queen Victoria's long reign – 160 have been noted[52] – with some enterprises more significant than others. The firm set up by Thomas Dowbiggin (1788–1854) was one of the most prominent. It made the state throne for the queen's coronation in 1837, at a cost of £1,187,[53] and shared (with Holland & Sons, a name under which it later traded) the responsibility for the Duke of Wellington's funeral in 1852. It is possible to chart the very considerable activity of Holland & Sons in exhaustive detail through the survival of 150 volumes of their day books.[54] One of their principal commissions was furnishing Osborne House on the Isle of Wight, which the queen had purchased in 1845, and to which she virtually retired after Prince Albert's death in 1861. The funeral arrangements for the prince were

51 *Country Life*, 28 July 1973, p.582.
52 Joy (1969) pp.683–4.
53 H. C. Smith (1931) p.147.
54 National Art Library, Victoria and Albert Museum, London.

of course made by Holland & Sons, who turned aside to the precise trappings of morbidity from their fashionable clinetele and activity in furnishing the *salons* of London clubs and official residences.

There had been, of course, an extension in the range of working even if there was no radical change in organization. The market for furniture and the work of upholsterers was encouraged by a rapid growth in population. Pattern books proliferated; there were at least a dozen in the ten years from 1830 to 1840.[55] An active proponent was Thomas King, with one of his publications, *The Upholsterer's Accelerator* (?1833), indicating that he had forty-five years experience as an upholsterer. Cheapness of production was his recurring theme and matched with a general availability of materials and deep-sprung upholstery (the earliest patent for a coiled spring had been taken out in 1828) could incorporate many refinements in comfort. It was an attribute with a wide following. At the time of the Great Exhibition of 1851 the official catalogue could point out that the entire furniture class betokened a high degree of national prosperity and noted 'no less distinctly the wealth and domestic refinement of those for whom the articles were intended'. In the early Victorian interior considerations of comfort took first place; only after 1860 was it subordinate to theoretical considerations.

No one could dispute the status of the queen, and the Bath furniture maker Henry Eyles displayed in the exhibition an 'English pollard oak table supported by 4 dolphins entwined with foliage of oak and ornamented with various other English devices. In the centre of the top is a porcelain star with Prince of Wales plume, garter etc., the china manufactured by Messrs Chamberlain & Co., of Worcester.' This is now in the Victoria and Albert Museum, London, with two 'walnut-tree easy chairs', decorated with marquetry and displaying in the back splat position an oval porcelain plaque with portraits respectively of Queen Victoria (Pl. 376) and Prince Albert.

Sir Henry Cole wrote in 1849 that he thought that the 'one great advantage of exhibitions is that it teaches the public and people who are not otherwise taught at all'. Whatever the truth of this there were many exhibitions before the end of the queen's long reign, with that of 1862 perhaps having a greater importance for the history of furniture than its well-known exemplar of ten years or so earlier. The newly established firm of Morris, Marshall, Faulkner and Company then showed its wares, explaining that 'a company of historical artists had banded themselves together to execute work in a thoroughly artistic and inexpensive manner; and that they determined to devote their spare time to designing for all kinds of manufacture of an artistic nature.' But living up to Morrisean standards needed a long purse. There were not so many who could still depend on the uncomplaining service of rows of baize- and cotton-clad servants hurrying along dark corridors and up back staircases at the insistent tolling of the nodding service bells. They filled their employers' baths, heaped more coal on an already glowing fire, and pushed a favourite upholstered, Morris fabric-covered chair into its welcoming heat. The ultimate in status and comfort had perhaps at last been achieved.

55   Cooper (1972) pp.115–23.

344. A pair of cloak pins (*c.*1790) $2\frac{5}{8} \times 1\frac{7}{8}$in (6.5 × 4.9 cm) *Virginia, Colonial Williamsburg Foundation*, Inv. 35, 1–2.

The lines of drawn curtains were secured by wrapping round the cloak pin.

345. (*top right*)   Design for a Bergère armchair (*c.*1790–5) *London, Victoria and Albert Museum*, Inv. E117-1929.

By John Linnell. The frame is shown yellow to denote gilding, with pink upholstery, scooped and fringed below the seat-rails. Ince and Mayhew characterized the 'Birjair', as they called it, in their *The Universal System of Household Furniture* (1759–62) plate LX, as 'half-couches'. See also Pl. 268.

References: Hayward (1969) p.86, fig.19.

346. (*bottom right*)   Window curtains (*c.*1792) *Westminster City Archives.*

Curtains in a drawing-room showing alternate cornices and a pier-glass and table. Sheraton's Drawing Book has a plate (LI) dated 1792 which is similar apart from minor differences in the carpet. The colour scheme was that of Gillows of Lancaster and London and is in their *Estimate Sketch Book* (f.125/6).

References: Boynton (ed.) (1995) Pl. 20.

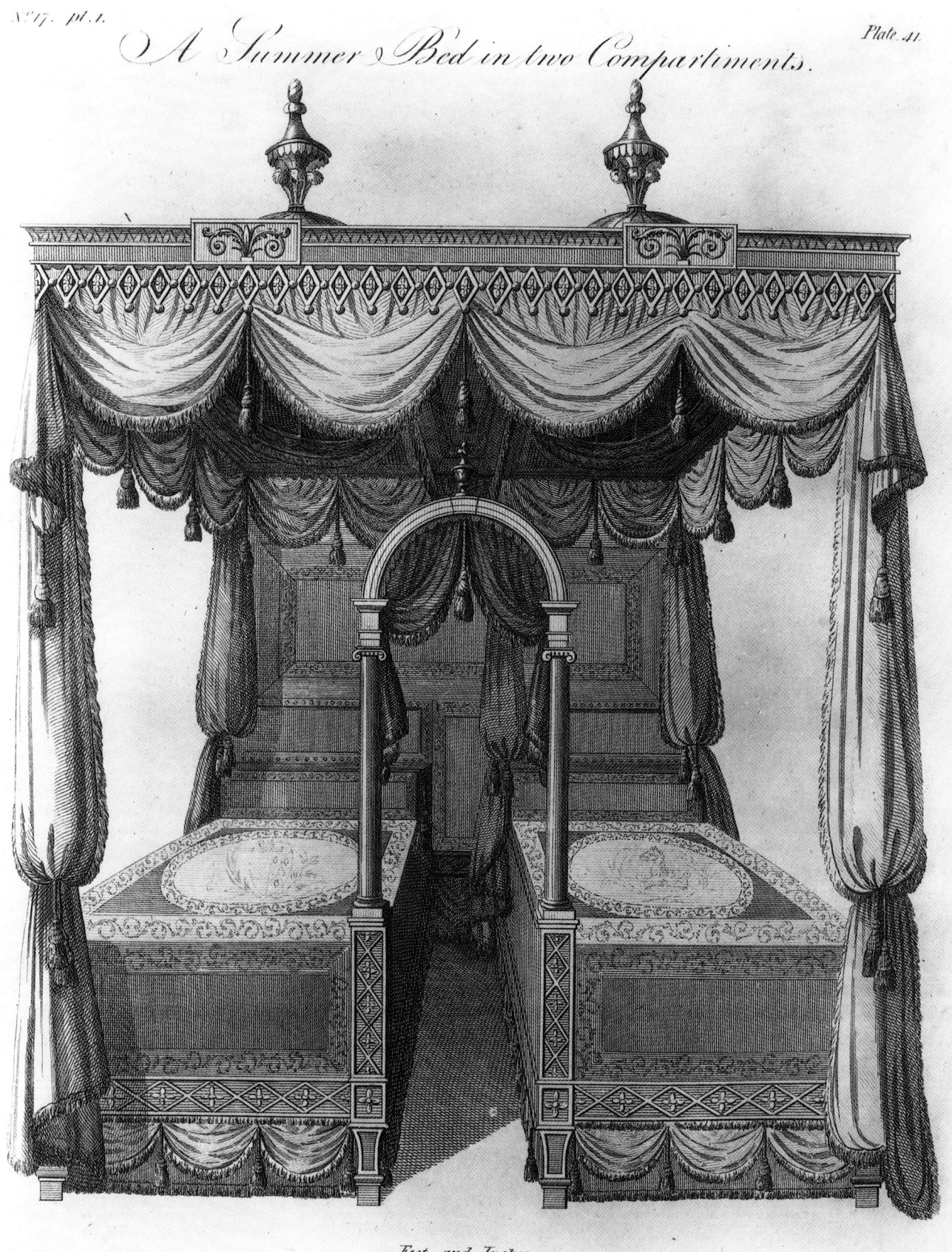

A Summer Bed in two Compartiments.

347. (*opposite*) 'A Summer Bed in two Compartiments' (1792).

Shown in Thomas Sheraton's *Drawing Book* (1791–4) plate XLI. The author notes: 'these beds are intended for a nobleman or gentleman and his lady to sleep in separately in hot weather. Passage in the middle which is about twenty-two inches in width, gives room for the circulation of air, and likewise affords easy access to the sevants when they make the beds'.

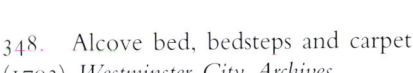

348. Alcove bed, bedsteps and carpet (1793) *Westminster City Archives*.

After plate XL in Sheraton's *Drawing Book*. This however is a colour scheme by Gillows who may have plagiarized Sheraton or vice versa. The carpet pattern has been used recently in a re-weaving for Temple Newsam House, Leeds. Gillows *Estimate Sketch Book* (f.117).

References: Boynton (ed) (1995) Pl. 19.

349. A pair of cloak pins (*c.*1800) *Virginia, Colonial Williamsburg Foundation*, Inv. 1979-48, 1–2.

In gilded brass and with iron screws. For a note on the use of cloak pins see that to Pl. 344.

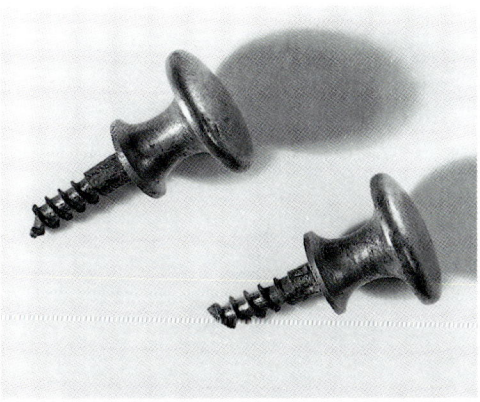

352.   Curtains at three windows (*c.*1806) *London, Victoria and Albert Museum*, Inv. E31-1952.

Shown in a drawing by Gillow on paper watermarked in 1806. Elaborate curtain designs, many French, were a feature of early nineteenth-century interiors.
References: Dornsife (1975); Winkler (1994).

350.   Curtain (*c.*1800) *Virginia, Colonial Williamsburg Foundation*, Inv. 1966–7, 10.

This is for a field or camp bed. It has an arched tester (see Pl. 351). Cotton dimity tied back by a loop from the back slipped over a button.

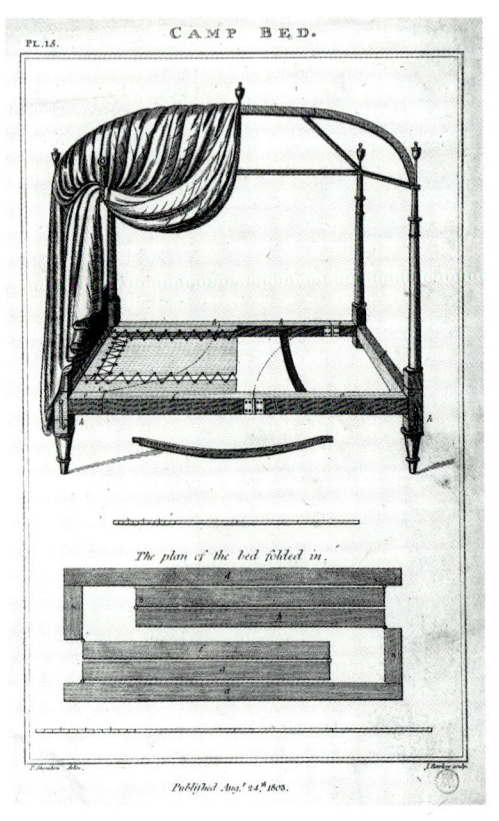

351.   Camp or field bed (1803).

Shown in Thomas Sheraton's *The Cabinet Dictionary* plate 15. The plan shows that the frame of the bed was hinged to allow folding into a small space. For a curtain suitable to such a bed see Pl. 350.

353.   Trade card of George Smith (*c.*1807) *Oxford, Bodleian Library* (*Johnson Collection*).

George Smith was a cabinet-maker and 'upholder' to the Prince of Wales (later George IV). See p.257.

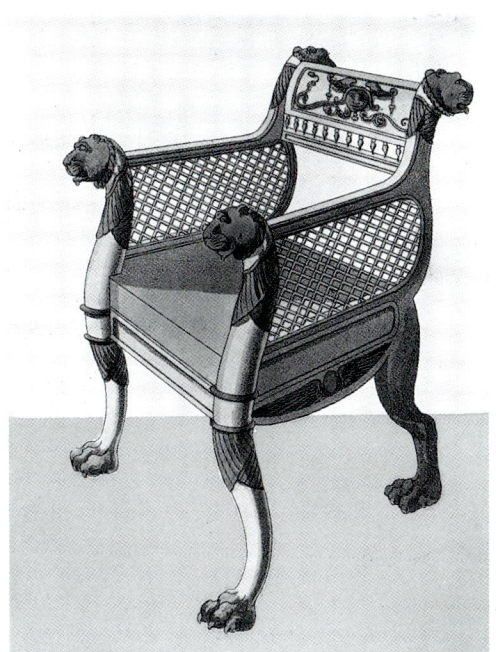

354.   Design for a Bergère (*c.*1807).

Engraved as plate 56 in George Smith's *Household Furniture* (1808). The two chairs on Smith's plate were described by him as 'Drawing Room' chairs. One similar was sold Christie's, 16 November 1995.

355.   The interior of Morgan and Sanders's furniture shop in Oxford Street, London seen in Rudolph Ackermann's *The Repository of Arts* (1809).

This fashionable firm obviously found it advantageous to display its wares in suitably grand and comfortable surroundings swathed in curtain arrangements; they were well able to provide to discerning customers.

356.   'French' window curtain and Grecian settee (1809).

Shown in Ackermann's *The Repository of Arts* series I, Vol. 2, Pl. 26.

References: Agius and Jones (1984) p.48.

357.   Trade card for J. & A. Semple (*c.*1809) *Temple Newsam House, Leeds*, Inv. 25/62.

The card was designed by Thomas Sheraton and portrays the Semples' upholstery warehouse at 2 Berners Street, London. The card appears on a sofa-table supplied in March 1809 to William and Charles Shadbolt and now at Temple Newsam.

358.   Armchair (*c.*1812) *Royal Collection.*

One of a set of six. Probably to be identified with those supplied in 1812 by Morel and Hughes for use at Carlton House (£951 12s). This very successful firm, producing furniture of the highest quality, became, on changes in partnership, Morel and Seddon, and supplied a great deal of

furniture for George IV at Windsor Castle. See pp.260–1.

359.   Crimson drawing room at Carlton House, London seen in a watercolour by Charles Wild reproduced from W.H. Pyne, *The History of Royal Residences* (1819) III. *Royal Collection.*

This large room at the north-west corner of the house acted originally as a dining-room and was given a wall decoration in scagliola and paint. The crimson satin damask was introduced in 1806 and was formed on stretched panels, as curtains with elaborate looped swags, and on the handsome seat furniture, supplied by Tatham, Bailey and Sanders.

References: *Furniture History,* XXVI (1990) pp.10–19; Queen's Gallery (1991) pp.207, 223.

DRAWING ROOM WINDOW CURTAIN.

360.   Curtains for a drawing room window (1816).

Illustrated in Ackermann's *The Repository of Arts*, series II, Vol. I Pl. 8. The curtains embracing both windows have elaborate cords and tassels and are suspended on a French rod with central rosette and Thyrsis's ends.

References: Agius and Jones (1984) p.105.

361. Rose satin drawing-room (or bow room) looking south-west, Carlton House, London (*c.*1817) seen in a watercolour by Charles Wild reproduced from W. H. Pyne *The History of Royal Residences* (1819) III *Royal Collection*.

There were many changes of mind over the wall fabrics and upholstery in this room. As Wild depicts it, the seat furniture is *en suite* to the elaborate swagged curtains with secondary ones in white taffeta. The swagged arrangement continued around the whole room.

References: Queen's Gallery (1991) pp.213–14.

362. Curtains at three windows (1819) *London, Victoria and Albert Museum*, Inv. E17-1952.

Shown in a drawing by Gillows. The fashion for 'enclosing' all three windows as one at their head gave rooms a greater importance. The Gillow firm often provided such 'room views' to their clients so that the whole arrangement could be envisaged.

363. Giltwood throne and footstool from the House of Lords (1820) 75 × 43 × 35 in (190.5 × 109 × 89.3 cm) *Chatsworth, Derbyshire.*

Made for George IV but later used by Queen Adelaide at the coronation of William IV in 1831. This throne and footstool were made by Russell, Valance and Evans for the coronation of George IV in 1821. When William IV acceded he decided to reuse existing thrones and this was used 'most improperly' as Queen Adelaide's coronation throne at Westminster Abbey. The firm charged £175 10s for the throne and £23 10s for the footstool. They were covered by Elliott and Francis to correspond with the canopy. The Duke of Devonshire, as Lord Chamberlain, claimed the coronation thrones as his perquisite and they arrived, finally, at Chatsworth.

References: Roberts (1989) pp.68–71.

364. Throne (1820) 87 × 46 in (221 × 116.8 cm) *Grimsthorpe Castle, Lincolnshire.*

Giltwood and composition. The throne was used by George IV in Westminster Hall during the celebration of his coronation in 1821. Made by Russell, Vallance and Evans for £117 14s with £17 18s for the footstool. The upholstery was carried out by Bailey and Sanders in crimson velvet supplied by William King and gold lace and fringe from Thomas Charlton. The Deputy Great Chamberlain claimed the throne and canopy as perquisites and they were taken to Grimsthorpe.

References: Roberts (1989) pp.68–9.

365. Library chair (*c.*1820) *Stratfield Saye, Hampshire.*

Cane seat and sides, leather squab cushions, feet extension and reading lectern. The convenience of such chairs owed not a little to the ingenuity of the patent furniture manufacturers who were active in the Regency period.

366.   Cushion (*c.*1820) *London, Victoria and Albert Museum*, Inv. OPH1-1979.

Used by King George IV at his coronation in 1821. Made of floral silk.

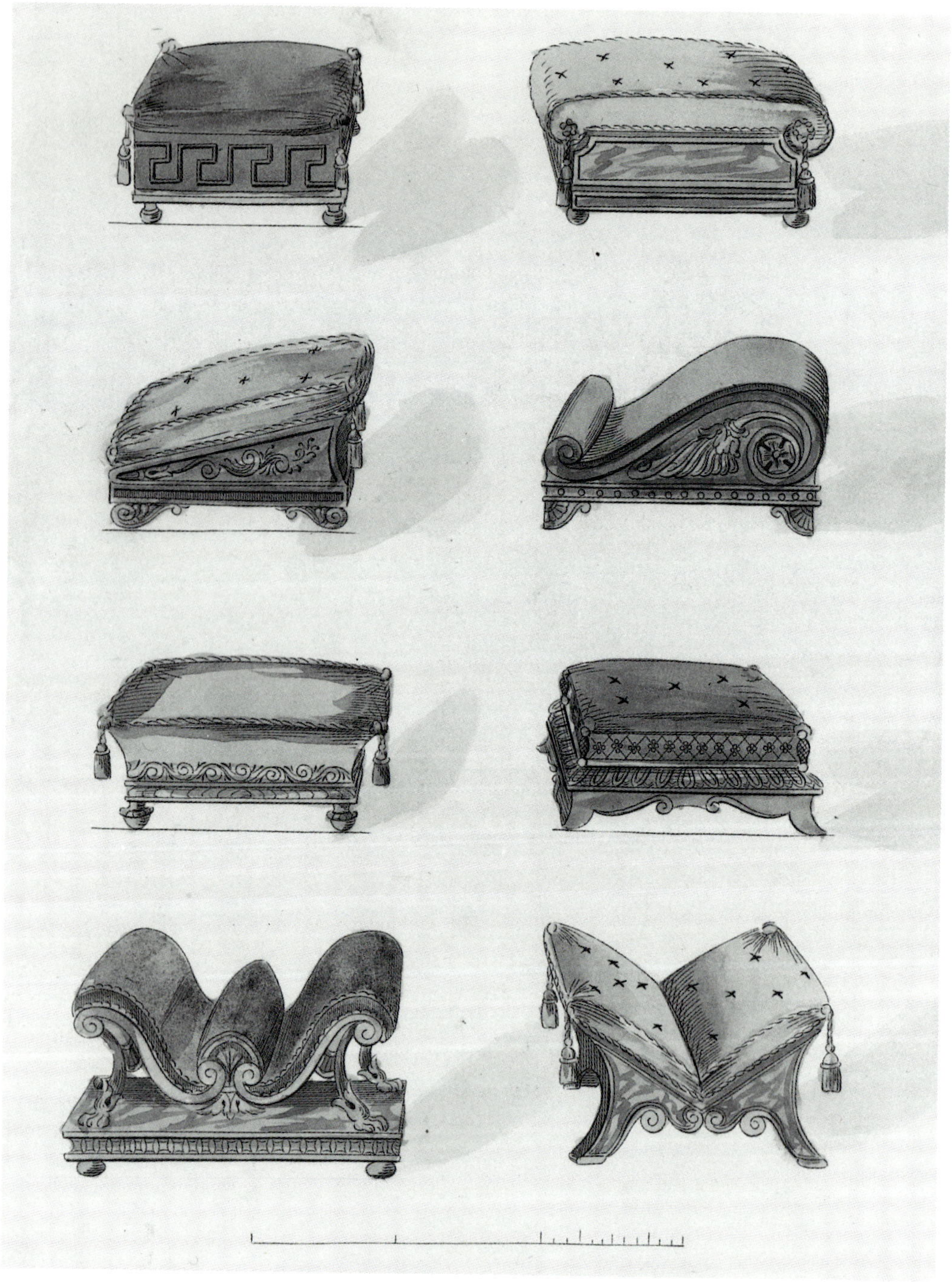

367.   Footstools (*c.*1825).

Illustrated by John Taylor in his *The Upholsterer's and Cabinet-Maker's Pocket Assistant*, plate 21. Ackermann had remarked in his *The Repository of Arts* in October 1813 that footstools had been neglected and he therefore included them in several plates. Taylor obviously moved on to a fashion which persisted, with that at the bottom right suitable for the display of a book.

References: Agius and Jones (1984) p.33.

368. Camp bedstead (1825).

Illustrated by Rudolph Ackermann in his *The Repository of Arts* series II, vol. 6, plate 5. A camp-bed made in mahogany and of such lavishness was destined obviously for an officer's permanent quarters. The blue hangings are held aloft by military trophies and inverted mortars. A statuette of Victory surmounts the tester. The base valances are elaborately swagged.

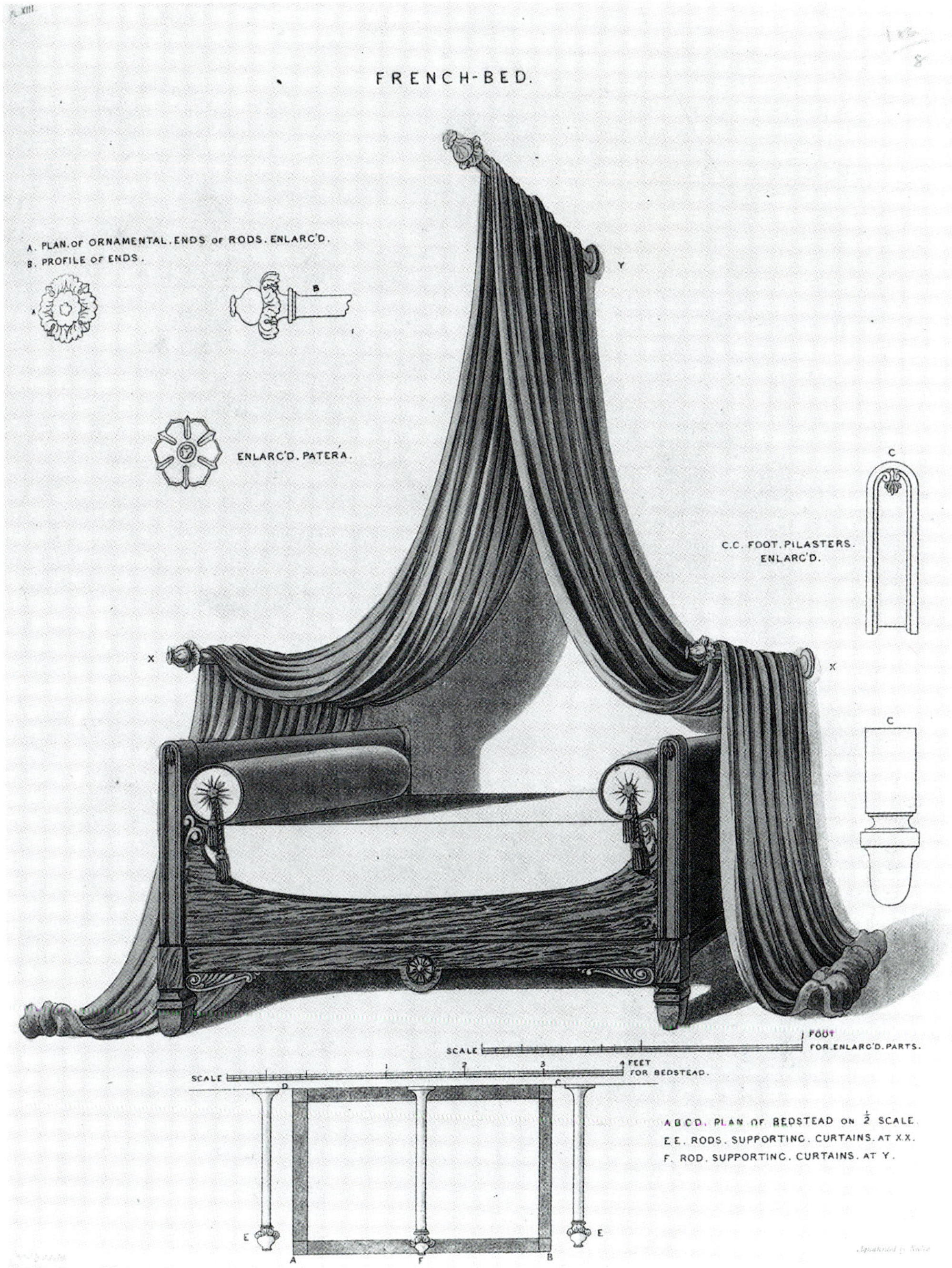

369. French bed (*c.*1826).

Illustrated by George Smith in his *The Cabinet-Makers and Upholsterers Guide*, plate XIII. Smith was an entrepreneur providing his clients with what they wanted – fashionable French-style furniture. He also illustrated the sceptre-rod over which the curtain is draped and an elaborate rose-wood frame.

370. Design for the window side of the George IV closet at Windsor Castle (*c.*1826) *London, Victoria and Albert Museum*, Inv. E739-1970.

The design, by Sir Jeffry Wyatville shows a stylized double pelmet at the centre and curtains gathered with ties.

371. 'A Gothic Window' (1826).

Illustrated by Rudolph Ackermann in his *The Repository of Arts* series III, Vol. 7, Pl. 11. Ackermann makes a long statement about the origin of the oriel window 'which takes the whole width of the room . . . and in order to admit the whole of the light, the curtains are placed at a little distance from it . . .'.

References: Agius and Jones (1984) pp.165–6.

372. Windows and curtain (*c.*1826) *Royal Collection.*

On the east wall of the great drawing-room of Windsor Castle, created for George IV by Morel and Seddon. Approved and initialled by the king.

References: G. de Bellaigue and Kirkham (1972) p.29, Pl. 14B.

374. (*below*) Throne (*c.*1827) 96 × 45 × 43 in (243.8 × 114.3 × 109 cm) *Chatsworth, Derbyshire.*

Giltwood, made for George IV, probably at St James's Palace and used at the coronation of William IV in 1831. Possibly by Bailey and Saunders. Taken as a perquisite by the Lord Chamberlain, the Duke of Devonshire, to Chatsworth.

References: Roberts (1989) p.70, Pl. 17.

373. Inner frame of a chair (1827) *Temple Newsam House, Leeds.*

Enclosing ten coiled upholstery springs. The padded top is covered with linen; canvas bottom reinforced with a cross of broad webbing. Endorsed in ink 'Mr Wilkie, 1827'. John Wilkie owned a large chair-making business in London.

References: Beard and Gilbert (1986) p.975.

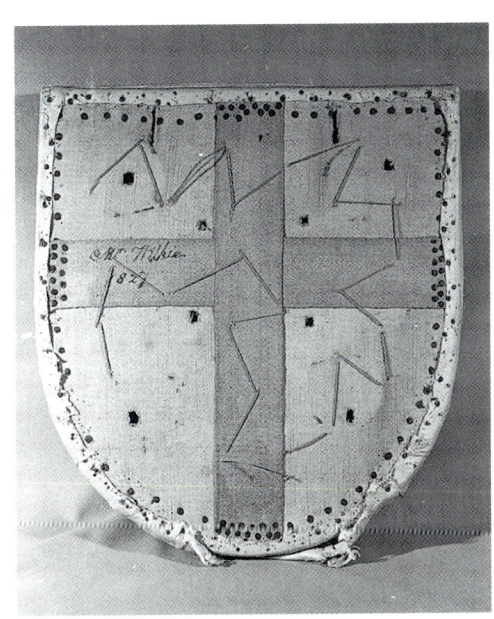

375. Inside of the tester of a state bed (*c.*1830) *Port Sunlight, Lady Lever Art Gallery,* Inv. LL4207.

The bed itself was designed in the late 1750s by Giovanni Battista Borra for the state bedchamber at Stowe, Buckinghamshire and it was put together and gilded by 1759. It was reupholstered *c.*1830. The tester of the bed was altered in the early nineteenth century and the bed furniture was entirely renewed in the Victorian period and again in the early twentieth century. Sold from Stowe in 1922.

376. Chair (1851) $36 \times 20 \times 19\frac{1}{2}$ in (91.5 $\times$ 50.7 $\times$ 49.5 cm) *London, Victoria and Albert Museum,* Inv. W31–1953.

Carved and inlaid walnut with a porcelain plaque of Queen Victoria (Messrs Chamberlain of Worcester). Exhibited at the Great Exhibition in 1851. Presented to the Museum by W. S. Eyles grandson of the maker Henry Eyles. The Museum also has an armchair with a porcelain plaque inset of Prince Albert.

APPENDIX A

This appendix brings together a selection of passages from documents which are considered important statements of contemporary furnishing. They illustrate points made in the body of the text and also show the importance of royal and other patrons. The source of each quotation is given at the start of each entry and expanded as a full title in the references and abbreviations. A short commentary precedes each passage. Unfamiliar terms are noted in the glossary and prices are converted to £ s d. Superior letters are ignored and printed as being on the same line. (e.g. Maties for Majesty's). Imprimis and item are omitted. The way the passages are displayed does not always follow that of the original document. For convenience a table of contents is given below. The extracts are also referred to in the text as, e.g. (Appendix A6).

No.	Date	Name	Description
1	1509	Edmund Dudley	Great chamber
2	1537	Catherine of Aragon	Beds
3	1556	Sir John Gage	Beds and testers
4	1559	Elizabeth I	Coronation chair
5	1565	Temple Newsam House, Leeds	Great chamber
6	1581	Dame Elizabeth Blount	Mapledurham, Oxon.
7	1582	Elizabeth I	Beds
8	1582	Edward Baker	Cushions
9	1588	Robert Dudley, Earl of Leicester	Chairs, stools, cushions
10	1611	Robert Singleton	Salisbury House, London
11	1611	Hatfield Inventory	Hatfield, Herts.
12	1614	Henry Howard, Earl of Northampton	Northampton House, London
13	1618	Anne of Denmark	Hangings at Oatlands
14	1630	Great Wardrobe Orders	
15	1637	Ralph Grynder	For Henrietta Maria
16	1638	Anne, Viscountess Dorchester	Gosfield Hall, Essex
–	1645	Edward Sackville (see No.21)	
17	1651	Colonel Edward Phelips	Montacute, Somerset
18	1677	John Casbert	Part of an account
19	1686	Jean Poictevin	For James II
20	1688	Jean Poictevin	For the Duke of Hamilton
21	To 1696	Knole, Kent	Extracts, Sackville Archives
22	To 1698	Francis Lapiere	For Barbara, Duchess of Cleveland
23	1699	Hampton Court	Estimate for furniture
24	1701–2	Stephen Penson	For the Duchess of Norfolk
25	1710	Jean Poictevin	Inventory of his effects
26	1714	Windsor Castle	Queen Anne's bed
27	1715	Windsor Castle	State bed for the Prince and Princess of Wales
28	1727	Kensington Palace	Work by Thomas Phill
29	1730–1	Hampton Court	New furniture
30	1735	Stephen Langley	Furniture at Chiswick House
31	1736	William Bradshaw	For the Earl of Stanhope
32	1738–45	Longford Castle	Archive extracts
33	1752	Lady Leicester	Holkham House, Norfolk
34	1757	Vile and Cobb	Croome Court, Worcs.
35	1763	France and Bradburn	Croome Court
36	1764–5	France	Moor Park, Herts.
37	1765–6	Mary Reynoldson	Fairfax House, York
38	1767	Mayhew and Ince	Croome Court
39	1771–2	Mayhew and Ince	Croome Court
40	1774–5	Mayhew and Ince	Croome Court
41	1786	Chipchase and Lambert	Audley End, Essex
42	1793	Robt. & Geo. Gillows & Co.	Croome Court
43	1793	Eyre and Large	Arundel, Sussex
44	1816–18	Jno. Johnston	Stoneleigh Abbey, Warwicks.

1.   1509 London
      Inventory of Edmund Dudley: The Great Chamber

Dudley Inv., p.40

Both in clothes and upholstered furniture the Dudley Inventory presents a picture of a richly coloured scene. The furniture mentioned includes sparvers or canopies, coffers, joined forms, stools and various sizes of cushions.

. . . In THE GRET CHAMBRE: a selar: a testar of bawidken enbrodrid: a ffederbed: a bolster: a payr of fustiaunce: a counterpoynt of verders: a hangyng of vij paynes of course tapstree werk: ij courteyns of grene say hangyng in the wynddowes: ij short carpettes: a long carpett: a cupbourd: a round borde: a table: a payr of trestelles: a long joyned fourme: iij short joyned fourmes: a stolle and a aundyron: a Sprewis Coffer, wherin is a carpet, ij doublettes of blak tynsell sathan, ij doblettes of crymeson saten, a doblytt of black sathen, a doblytt of grene tynsell sathen, a doblytt of crymeson velvyt, a doblytt of purpull saten, iiij quarters of a gown of old black damaske, a jakett of crymeson saten furred with sable pollys, a jaket of blake velvyt lyned with tawny saten, a gowne of blake saten lyned with tawny velvytt, a gown of blake saten furred with buge, a gowne of blake velvyt furred with boge, a gown of blak velvytt furred with marturns, a gown of ffrensh bak lyned with blake velvett, a gown of crymeson velvytt vnlynyd, a gown of black velvyt lyned with black sarsinett, a gown of black chamlett lynyd with black sarsnett, a syngle old gown of crymeson velvytt, a rydyng gown of blak velvytt lynyd with blak saten, ij gownes of blak cloth lyned with sarsnett, a gown of ffrensh blak furred with martryns. A gret coffer with ij lyddes; wherin ys a sparver of purpull velvytt with curteyns of blewe sarsenett. A sparuer of blewe sarsenett. A counterpoynt of blewe sarsenett lyned with blewe buckeram. A sparver of rede sarsenett with a canape of rede sylke knyt, enbrodrid about the skyrttes of the capape with sleydes. A sperver of crymeson cloth of gold and grene and crymeson saten, fugrie palie. A selar and tester of blak and yelowe damaske; iij curteyns to the same of blak and yelowe sarsenett. Also a seler, a tester, courteyns, a counterpoynt of popynjaye and blonkett, palie, for a trussyng bed. iij Whit curteyns of sarsenett. A counterpoynt of bawdkyn, embrodrid, for the bed in the Gret Chambre. iij quyltes; one of blonket sarsenett of diaper werk, and the other of rede sarsnett and yelowe palye, and the thyrde of rede sarsnett. A pece of Ray staynell with dyvers coloures. A long cussion and ij short cussions of crymeson and blewe velvytt. A cussion of purpull velvytt. ij Cussions, the on syde of crymeson damaske and the oder syde blak saten. vij peces of ymagerie, enbrodrid for the monethes of the yere, to set upon a cloth. A coffer with on lydd: wherin ys a payr of fustiaunce, a nold seler and tester with ij curteyns of whit lynnen cloth, vj payr of shettes, v litell stayned clothes, iiij table clothes of diaper, viij towelles, a xj napkyns of diapur . . .

2.   1537 Baynard's Castle, London
      View of the Wardrobe Stuff of Katharine of Aragon:
      Beds, Canopies, &c.

Camden Misc (1855)

This extract from a 1537 inventory is concerned with the section on beds, canopies, cloths of estate and curtains. There is a considerable use of cloth of gold, various tissues and coloured velvets, with curtains in damask, taffeta and silk.

. . . BEDDIS, THAT IS TO WITE AS WELLE CEELOURS AND TESTOURS, AS ALSO SQUARE BEDDIS AND SPARVARS, WITHE THEIR COUNTERPOYNTES.

A square bedde of blewe velvette enbrowdered Fyrste, a square bedde of blewe velvette, enbrowdered as welle with Rooses as also withe lettres crowned, lyned with blewe bokerhame, and fringed with red silke and golde, havinge a counterpoynte of the saide stuffe likewise enbrowdered and lyned, and the curteynes be lacking.

Sparvers Item, a sparvar of Damaske golde Turkey making paned crymsene and blewe, lyned withe blewe bokerhame, havinge single valaunce fringed withe purple silke and Venysse golde, withe a counterpoynte of the saide stuffe, and mantille and curteynes of purple sarcenette.

Item, a sparver paned of yalowe clothe of golde, clothe of silver withe workys, and russette velvette lyned withe blewe bokerham, havinge single valaunce, fringid as welle withe silke of white, yalowe, and russette colours, as also withe Venysse golde, withe mantille and curteynes of russette sarcenette.

Ceelours and Testours Item, a ceelour, testour, and counterpoynte, of white damaske, withe loosingies of yalowe clothe of golde, lyned with red bokerham, havinge single valaunce fringide withe white and red silke, withe two curteynes of white sarcenette, either of theme cont' iiij. bredis of the saide sarcenette, and in depthe iiij. yardes qrt.

Item, a ceelour, testour, and counterpoynte for a cradille paned of yalowe clothe of golde, and crymsene velvette lyned withe grene bokerhame, havinge single valaunce fringid with blewe and red silke myxid withe Venysse golde, withe iiij. curteynes paned of red and blewe sarcenette, everye of theme cont' in depthe one yarde iij. quarters, and in bredithe one yarde quarter.

A large canapie of clothe of golde and velvette paned A large canapie paned as welle of yalowe clothe of golde, as also of grene and blewe velvette enbrowdered withe rooses, every of theme crowned withe a crowne imperialle, lyned withe purple sarcenette, and fringid withe grene silke and Venysse golde.

A clothe of astate of riche clothe of tissue Item, a riche clothe of astate of crymsene clothe of tissue enbrowered withe tharmes of Englande and Spayne, as welle in the ceelour and testour, as also in the valaunce, lyned withe grene bokerhame, havinge doble valaunce fringid withe crymsene silke and Venysse golde, the ceelour cont' in lengthe iij. yardis, and in bredithe iiij. yardis quarter, the valaunce in depthe di. yarde, and the testour cont' in depthe iiij. yardes di. di. quarter, and in bredithe iiij. yardis di.

Frustrate pecis of clothe of tyssue Item, one pece of the saide clothe of tissue withe a large scochione of tharmes of Spayne in the myddis, lyned withe grene bokerham, cont' in depthe iiij yardis quarter, and in bredithe iiij. yardis di. di. quarter, whiche belongid to the saide clothe of astate whatte tyme it was a bedde.

Item, two pecis of the saide clothe of tissue unlyned, the one cont' in lengthe ij. yardis di. quarter, and in bredithe one yarde quarter, and the other pece cont' in lengthe ij. yardis quarter and in bredithe di. yarde di. quarter, whiche was parcelle of the saide clothe of astate whatte tyme it was a bedde.

Curteynes of clothe of gold Item, three curteynes of red clothe of golde withe workys, everye of theme lyned withe Damaske white and grene, cont' in the hoole xij. bredis of the saide clothe of golde, and in depthe the pece ij. yardis skante.

Curteynes of taffata Item, two curteynes of taffata paned white and red, cont' boothe vij. bredis of the saide taffata, and either of theme in depthe iiij. yardis quarter, perisshid with rattis.

Curteynes of damaske Item, two curteynes of Damaske paned white and purple, cont' boothe vj. bredis of the saide Damaske, and either of theme cont' in depthe iiij. yardis quarter.

Curteynes of silke chamlette Item, two curteynes of silke chamlette, paned red, grene, russette, yalowe, and tawneye, cont' boothe viij. bredis of the saide stuffe unlyned . . .

3.   1556 The Household Goods etc., of Sir John Gage of West Firle, Co. Sussex, K.G., 1556.
Beds and Testers.

Firle Inv., 1556

The inventory of Sir John Gage's effects is a long one. This extract shows, as with most Tudor inventories, the presence of highly colourful interiors made warm and cheerful by the use of textiles of various kinds.

. . . A TESTER of a bedd of crymson velvat and clothe of golde paned, wt a frynge of crymson silke and gold with iij curtens to the same of chaungable sarcenet, with a standinge bedsted of waynescot to the same. Item a tester of murrey velvat and clothe of gold paned, wth a frynge of murrey silk with three curtens of chaungable sarcenet, and a standing bedsted of walnuttree. Item a tester of blacke velvat and clothe of gold paned, and frenged wth yellowe and purple silk with iij curtens of purple sarcenet, and a trussing bedsted of walnuttree. Item a tester of black velvat and yellow damaske paned, with a frenge of blacke and yellow silke with iij curtens of blacke and yellow sarcenet. Item a tester of black velvat and yellow satten of Bridges, with a frendge of blacke and yellow silk, with iij curtens of blacke and yellowe sarcenet old, with a bedsted of waynescot. Item a tester of black and yellow damaske paned, wth a frendge of black and yelloo silke, with v curtens of black and yellow sarsenet old, wth a trussing bedsted for the feld to the same. Item a tester of crymsen and yelloo sarcenet paned, wt a frendge of crymsen and yellow silk, with iij curtens of crymson and yelloo sarcenet, wth a smale bedsted of waynscot to the same. Item an old tester of tholde faction of clothe of bawdkyn and white damaske paned, with iij curtens of chaungable sarcenet old, with a square bedsted wth cordes to the same. Item a tester for a trussing bedd of dor'ixe, wth curtens of the same, with a trussing bedsted of waynscott therto. Item a tester for a trussing bedd of blewe and yellow saye, with curtens of the same therto, with a trussing feld bedsted of walnut tree. Item an old tester of redd and grene saye with curtens of the same. Item an old tester for a standing bed, withoute curtens, over the owter gate. Item, an old spaver of dornixe, in the nurcery. Item a white sparver of lyncn clothe . . .

4.   1559 Coronation Chair, Elizabeth I

P.R.O., LC9/53

Within the abbey the coffer-maker, John Grene, had dressed both St Edward's Chair and the dais on which it stood. He used seven assistants for the task.

. . . for coveringe of the same Chaire with clothe of Tisshewe with gilt nailes ffor the garnishinge of the same xxxiij s. iij d. Itm. ffor 2,000 gilt nailes for the garnishinge of the same Chaire, price the Thowsande . . . xxiij s. viij d.
Off the quenes Maties Store at his Palace West xv yardes ij qrt satten Crimsin wroughte with gold for garnishinge and Coveringe Parte of the Mounte [i.e. dais] at xij s the yarde   £9.9s
Of the same Store of Westm 91 5/8 yardes Satten crimsin Raied with threds of golde for coveringe the Steppes of the mount goinge uppe to Sainct Edwardes chaire at xij s.,   £54 19s 6d

5.   1565 Leeds
'A Temple Newsam Inventory, 1565': 'in the Greate Chambre'

Temple Newsam Inv., 1565

A tester of cloth of gold, curtains of sarsenet, satin and damask, chairs covered with velvet, often paned with a contrasting colour, show the Leeds house of the Duke of Lennox, cousin of

James I to have been well furnished. The duke's subsequent extravagance made it necessary in 1622 to sell Temple Newsam to the able and unscrupulous financier, Sir Arthur Ingram, for the large sum of £12,000.

. . . IN THE GREATE CHAMBRE. One olde cloke and hoode lynyd with sarcenett, xls, one cloke unlyned, xxx, a Frenche gowne of clothe of tisshew, 1£, a parre of wide sleves of clothe of golde, iiij£, a bearinge clothe for a childe of cremysyn velvett lyned wth powdred armynze and two parchementt laces, vj£ xiijs iiijd, a bearinge clothe of cremysyn satan edged wth powdred armynz, xls, a credle clothe of redd velvett lyned wth powdred armynze, xls, a waste coote of white sattan, vs, a caparison of clothe of golde and purple velvett for a greate horse, xx£, a quyltt of redd sarcenett imbrodered, vij£, another of redd and white sarcenett imbrodered, vij£, one of yellowe and white sarcenett inbrodered, vij£, a tester of clothe of silver and cremysyn sattan & curtens of cremysyn taffata, xij£, a tester of clothe of golde and silver wth the armes of Therle & his wife imbrodered & curtens of yellowe and white sarcenett, 1£, a tester of redd damaske wth curtens of cremysyn taffata, vij£, two beddes of downe, two bolsters and five pillowes, xij£, sixe fetherbeddes & sixe bolsters, xij£ a chaire couered wth redd damaske, xs, a chaire couered with grene taffata, xiijs iiijd, a chaire of olde clothe of golde, xs, one of olde clothe of silver and sattan, xiijs iiijd, one of russett sattan, vjs viijd, one of wallenuttree & wroughte, xiijs iiijd, two longe quysshens of olde clothe of siluer & redd sarcenett, xxs, two of olde clothe of golde, xxs, two of russett sattan, xs, one of grene sattan imbrodered, xs, two of cremysyn sattan, xxvjs viijd, one of olde clothe of silver, two benkers stayned wth armes, xvs, two sewed quyshens of silke, xxxs, one of black velvett & damaske, vjs viijd, one verie olde, panyd, xvjd, two panyd wth tawney sattan, xs, one of verie olde tissue garded, vjs viijd, two of crewlez nedle worke, iiijs viijd, two panyd wth yellowe velvett and sattan, xijd, a ioyned stoole couered wth grene taffata, iiijs, one withe grene velvett, ijs, one wth redd velvett, ijs, one wth black velvett & redd sattan, iiijs, one wth redd velvett panyd, iiijs, one wth olde blacke velvett, ijs, two stooles & two foote stooles uncouered, viijd, eight grene clothes . . .

6.   1581 Mapledurham, Oxfordshire.
Inventory in the Will of Dame Elizabeth Blount

P.R.O., Prob. 11/651

It is unusual to have an inventory within the text of a will but this extract from Dame Elizabeth Blount's shows a lavish provision of tapestry and painted hangings.

. . . *Parlour* two joynedd tables of wallnut tree twoe short joyned formes, six joyned stooles, one longe joyned forme, a standinge cupborde of walnuttree joyned, one joyned chist, the picture of the Queen's maiestie, the picture of Lucretia, the picture of a little boye . . . *In the hall* . . . the Kinge's armes, fower pictures, twoe longe dining tables, fower tressells, fower formes, a standinge cupborde, a benche, a settle and a paire of great anndirons . . . *In the midle chamber over the lower Plot*, Item, fyve peeces of tapestrie wherewithe the chamber is hanged, the standinge bedsteede, the boulster, the featherbedd, twoe pillowes, one paire of blanketts, the coverlett, the tester and the corteynes therto belonginge, and the lyverie cupbode in the same chamber. *In the ynner chamber to the same midle chamber*, Item the bedsteede, the bedd, the boulster, the blankett and coverlet in the same ynner chamber. *In the chamber over my sonne Richarde Blounte his chamber* Item, the paynted hanginges of blewe and yellow, the standing bedstede, the tester, the curtens, the bedde, the boulster, the matteris, the blanketts and coverlett thereunto belonginge, the joyned cupborde, the square borde, the chaire of red fustian in apes, the paire of tonge and the fyer panne in the same chamber. *In the ynner chamber to it*, Item, the hangings of redd and yellow, the bedsted, the bedd, the boulster, the blankett, the coverlett, the longe table with tressells in the same chamber . . .

7.   1582 A bed for Queen Elizabeth
P.R.O., LC9/73

The collaboration of various craftsmen on an important piece of furniture, the queen's bed (or at least one in some use by her), is well shown. The Greene family of coffermakers, the serjeant painter, with ironwork and lace trimmings from Montague and Ellewick respectively combined on this and many other occasions.

A bed, walnut, carved, painted, gilt. With a ceeler, tester and vallances of black velvet embroidered with various devices: *of the Queen's store*: the vallances fringed with a long fringe of venice gold and silver, and silk, one pair of the curtains of silver cloth with works of the said work threaded through with black colours by George Gower sergeant painter with the making of silver cloth plain drawn and threaded through with similar works of the said Gower, the said ceeler, testor, vallances and curtains lined with white satin or chamblet striped with gold on silver, the laths covered with similar stuff, the curtains laced on the seams and fringed on the edges with gold and silver and long loups of similar lace of gold and silver, brass rings, silk ribbon, silk for sewing the hoops and staples of wire for the said bedstead. Price of timberwork [by Wm Jasper]   £16.

To Geo Gower for ptg & gilding bedst with "good gold and silver with beasts and flowers embossed in colour, well gilt, the ground silvered and worked through with good biss'   £20.
Thos Grene. bottoming double girth webb & work, 1.68.
Gilbert Polson ironwork 4.13.4
Roger Montague 5 lb. 4½ oz.
long fringe of venice gold and silver
for the vallances   £4 16s 1b (8/– oz)   £25.16 –
To same for 2 lbs. 15 1/8 oz. of long fringe of Spanish silk for the same purpose 48/– lb (3s per oz).   £7.1.4½
To George Gower for drawing and threading through the aforesaid cloth of silver with works.   £4.7.6
Roger Montague 4 lb 6 1/8 oz of lace of gold & silver used on the seams and edges   £5.8s lb (9/– oz)   24.7.1½
To James Ellewicke for 46 1/8 yards of white satin for lining ceeler, tester, vallance and curtain 12/6   28.16.6¾

8.   1582 Cushions made by Edward Baker
P.R.O., LC9/73

The provision of cushions, in varying sizes, was always an important part of the upholsterer's and embroiderer's commission. They are shown in many paintings (Pls 8, 47) and as well as helping to provide comfort, also demonstrated status.

To Edward Baker for making of 30 cushions of similar cloth of gold tissue, cloth of gold and velvet and satin of diverse colours, part embroidered with cloth of gold cloth of silver and satin of diverse colours, venice gold and silver, silver and silk spangles in colour lined with satin of diverse coloures, lined with lace [?] on the seams with gold and silver lace, fringed, buttoned and tasseled with venice gold, silver and silk with the cushions of fustian filled with down and the cases of cotton to the same, part of the said tissue, cloth of gold, velvet and satin received from the said [Thomas] Knevett and Hope of the separate store aforesaid, the whole thing of the Queen's Great Wardrobe silk for sewing nicely and sweetly and all other necessaries to the same pertaining the price for making each piece 6/8   £10

9.   1588 Robert Dudley, Earl of Leicester
Halliwell (1854)

Elizabeth I's favourite, Lord Leicester, gathered everything suitable to comfort in his great houses, and particularly at Kenilworth Castle, Warwickshire, often visited by the queen.

Chayres, Stooles, and Cushens.

A chaier of crimson velvet, the seate and backe partlie embrothered with R. L. in clothe of goulde, the beare and ragged staffe in clothe of silver, garnished with lace and fringe of goulde, silver, and crimson silke; the frame covered with velvet, bounde abowte the edge with goulde lace, and studded with gilte nailes.

A square stoole and a foote stoole of crimson velvet, fringed and garnished suteable.

A long cushen of crimson velvet, embr. with the ragged staffe in a wreathe of goulde, with my lo. posie, '*Droyte et Loyale*', written in the same, and the letters R. L. in clothe of goulde, being garnished with lace and fringe; buttons and tasseles of golde, silver, and crimson silck; lyned with crimson taff.; being in length 1 yard quarter.

A square cushen of the like velvet, embr. suteable to the long cushen.

A chaier of wallnuttree, carved with the cinque-foile and the ragged staffe, covered with crimson velvet, the back richlie embrothered with cinque-foiles of clothe of silver, with two beares and ragged staves standing on the topp; the seate all lozenged with silver twiste, trimed with fringe of crimson silck and silver; the back of the chaier lyned with crimson sattin. A case of buckerom to the same.

A square stoole and a foote stoole suteable to the same.

A long cushin of crimson velvet, embr. with cinquefoiles, with tassells of crimson silck and silver, lyned with crimson sattin suteable.

Two chaiers of crimson velvet, embr. with black clothe of goulde, lyned with purple taffata, and fringed with redd silck and goulde. Two square stooles suteable.

Two long cushins of the same sorte suteable, lyned with purple taffata, buttoned and tasselled with crimson silck and goulde, in length 1 yard, in breadth 1 yard.

Two chaiers of black velvet, embr. with clothe of gould, lyned on the backe with purple taffata; two square stooles suteable. Two long cushins of black velvet, embr. with clothe of goulde, suteable to the sayd chayers, with buttons and tassells at the corners of blacke silck and goulde; in lenght and breadth, 1 yard.

A chaier of purple velvet, embr. with my lo. armes in the quarter, and letters, &c., fringed with purple silck and silver; the back lyned with purple sattin, with ragged staves, and a white lyon on the backe.

A chaier of crimson velvet, embr. with a broade wreathe of goulde, lyned on the backe with purple taffata.

10.   1611 Part of a bill from Robert Singleton, upholsterer, to Robert Cecil, Earl of Salisbury (see also A11)
Hatfield MSS., Bills 67b

. . . In the newe Rome at London
5 peeces of bulrosh mats, 20 yd peece, in all 100 yards at 2d½ p.yard   1.0.10
1 pound of pack thread   0.0.8
half a thousand of 2d neales   0.0.10
1 dayes work for 2 men to lay mattes   0.4.0
1 bed stoule & a pane   0.7.0

2 bed stoules & 2 panes	0.14.0
1 8 qter 2 seale tik & boulster	1.4.0
for macking	0.2.0
4 stone & a half of fethers	2.5.0
3 pair of midell blankets at 14s pair	2.2.0
13 peeces of bulrish mattes 20yd a peece in all 260 yards at 2d½ a yard	2.14.2
2lb of pack thread	0.1.4
1 thousand & a half of 2d neales	0.2.6
1 dayes work & a halfe for 4 men at 2s a peece a daye	0.12.0
5yd of holmes fustian for 3 pillowes at 1s.4d yard	0.7.0
19lb of fine whit flockes 9d pound	0.7.6
for macking 3 pillowes	0.1.0
for altering 3 square quissiones, one of velvett & the other of cloth of gold & silver	0.2.0
for sack cloth & girth web for a Cheare	0.1.0
for black & yellowe neales	0.1.0
for altering a foulding Cheare and puting in one Reall	0.2.6
for 1 Closse stoule & a pane	0.9.0

. . .

for 1 Cheare frame of walnute with winges & Iron work	1.5.0
for sack cloth & girth web for the Seat & the winges	0.1.6
for buckram to cover both sides & the winges	0.1.6
2yds of tik for a bagge	0.2.8
9lb of fethers in ye bagg	0.9.0
2 littell pillowes for ye Elboyes of flockes	0.1.0
for Red lether, canvas & pasting the back of the chair	0.2.0
1 filed Iron stay	0.2.6
for black & yellow neales great & small for ye cheare & elboyes & winges	0.2.6
for macking the Chear of Red Cloth wth borders, winges & covered Elboyes	0.8.0
for Iron work & covered wth wood 3 pair of Restes for his arme pittes & for altering one paire of Restes	0.13.4
for Canvas, buckrame & flockes to cover the 3 pair of Restes for the Armpittes & altering one pair	0.5.0

. . .

11. 1611 The Hatfield Inventory of September 1611.

This is important in that it shows the furnishing of Hatfield House, Hertfordshire at the conclusion of its building for Robert Cecil, Earl of Salisbury.

Hatfield House MSS

. . . in the greate Parlor
1 Longe Norwitch Carpitt lyned with buckrom
1 Cupbord Carpett sutable to it
1 greate Chaire of grene velvett
19 Stooles sutable to it
1 longe Quishon sutable to them
much gilt leather. Pertian & Turkie carpett.
In your Lo. bedchamber
Five peeces of Tapestrie hangings of
Imagerie theronne wainscoted.
1 bedsteed of walnuttree
The Tester vallance and headepeece of
Crimson velvet with your honors Armes
imbrothered on the heade peece
lyned with a stripp stuffe.
1 paire of inward taffata vallance
5 Curtains of Crimson taffata lyned
1 Crimson taffata Quilte
1 Featherbeed and boulster

1 paire of downe pillows
1 paire of woollen blankets
1 Canvass matteres
1 window Curtaine of changeable taffata
lyned with grene saye
2 Curtaine rodds
1 heighe Chaire of Crimson velvett
1 lowe Stoole of the same
2 longe Quishons sutable to the same
1 little square table of wainescotte
1 Cupbord of winescotte
2 shorte Turkie Carpitts
1 picture of your Lo. mother
In the Pallett Chamber to your Lo. bedchamber
Two Fether Beeds and Boulsters
2 paire of wollen Blanketts
2 Tapestrie Coverings
1 Canvas matteres
1 Close stoule covered with leather with a pann
2 Chamber potts
In the great Chamber
Six peeces of deepe Tapestrie hangings
of the storie of Haniball & Cipio
Eighte windowe Curtinges of grene taffata lyned
with grene bayes, and foure Curtinn rodes.
Two heighe Chaires of grene wrought
velvett trimed with grene fringe.
Fower Backchares of the same.
Twelve heighe Stooles sutable to the same.
Six longe quishons and one square sutable.
One shorte Percian Carpitt
One Faire greate Organn
. . . In the King's bed chamber
Six peeces of Fyne Tapestrie hangings of the storie of Josephe
One Faire gilded Bedsteed
Tester and vallance headcloth & Curtaines of grene velvett
imbrothered with Collored sattaine
One Counterpointe of the same sutable
One Cupbordcloth sutable
One Quilte of grene taffata
One square Carpitt of grene velvet with gould and silke fringe lyned
with satten abridges.

One lowe Chaire ⎫
One Backe Chaire ⎪
Two heighe Stooles ⎬ of grene velvett with
One lowe stoole ⎪ silk and silver fringe
Three longe Quishons ⎭

One Fether Bed and Boulster
Two downe pillows
One white quilte
One paire of blankets
One course Matteres
Three windowe Curtins of changeable taffata
One square Table and Courte Cupbord
One paire of Brasse Andirons
. . .
The inventory also arranges the holdings by type, as follows:
. . . In the Wardrobe upper Sto.
Five peeces of shallowe Tapestrie hangings of Antickworke.
One fyne square peece of Tapestrie hanging for a Chimney peece.
Two peeces of shallow Tapestrie hangings of Forest worke.
Three peeces of Coarse Tapestrie hangings for borders over wainscot
unlyned.

One large peece of Tapestrie hangings with flowers & branches.

Hangings viz. Two shallowe peeces of Tapestrie for borders over the wainscotte.

One greate peece of hangings of Arras worke with your honours Armes.

Fower peeces of shallowe Tapestrie hangings of Forrest worke lyned throughe with Canvase.

Three peeces of shallowe Tappestrie hangings of Imagerie.

Fower pieces of shallow Tappestrie hangings of Forrest worke.

One olde peece of Forrest work unlyned.

One old border of networke to hange over the wainscott.

Fower peeces of gilt leather hangings.

Carpitts viz. Three shorte Turkie Carpitts.

One grene velvet Carpitt lyned with satten with silke & silver fringe.

One grene wroughte velvet Carpitt lyned with grene taffata with grene fringe.

One ritch needle worke Carpitt wrought with silke and silver lyned, with grene taffata with silke & silver fringe.

One square Pertian Carpitt.

Twoe shorte Turkie Carpitts.

One longe grene Cloth Carpitt 9 yards longe.

One olde Turkie Carpitt.

Quishions viz. Three longe Quishions of blacke velvet imbrothered all over with goulde silke and silver.

Twoe longe Quishions of watchet Cloth of silver lyned with blew satten.

One longe Quishion rich imbrothered the grounds of yellow satten and imbrothered with goulde & silver.

One longe Quishion of Crimson velvet imbrothered with goulde and lyned with Changeable taffata.

One longe Quishion of Crimson velvett wrought with beasts in silkes of diverse Colors.

One longe Quishion of Crimson velvett imbrothered with Your honours Armes in the Midle lyned with watchett taffata.

One longe Quishion of Needleworke bottomed with Changeable taffata.

Twoe verie ritch longe Quishions of Taune velvett imbrothered and imboste with goulde and lyned with blew satten.

Twoe square quishions of Tapestrie lyned with leather.

One longe Quishion of Needleworke bottomed with Changeable taffata.

One olde longe Quishion of blacke velvett imbrothered.

One other longe Quishion of blacke velvett imbrothered.

Six square Quishions of Needleworke lyned with leather.

Twoe square Quishions of Tapestrie.

One longe needleworke Quishion of silke of the Cittie of Antewarpe.

One longe Quishion of Tapestree lyned with leather.

One olde blacke velvett Quishion cut uppon white.

One redd Needleworke Quishion silke and goulde.

Two longe Quishions of Crimson satten imbrothered with twist.

One olde Quishion of russett velvet lyned with damaske satten.

Fower longe Quishions of redd taffata tuffted and twisted.

Thre square Quishions of the same.

Chaires viz. Two Chaires of Crimson sattin imbrothered with silke twists.

One lowe Chare of redd taffata tufted and twisted.

One back Chare of olde Cloth of silver.

One olde Chare of yallowe Cloth.

One olde Chare of Cloth of silver.

One olde Chaire of Russett velvett.

One olde Chare of blacke velvett.

One Chare of olde redd Cloth.

Stooles viz. Twoe low stooles of Crimson satten imbrothered with silke twiste.

Three lowe stoles of redd taffata tufted and twisted.

One olde stole of needleworke.

One lowe stole of Cloth of silver.

One lowe stoole of russett vellvet.

Two litle olde stoule(s) of Cloth of goulde.

Bedsteeds viz. Five liverie Bedsteeds.

One other liverie Bedsted.

Feather-beds and boulsters Thirten Feather beds and boulsters.

Two other Feather bedds.

Two other Feather beds and boulsters.

Blancketts Thirten blancketts.

Two pare of another sort.

Nyne fustion blanckets belonginge to the best bedds in the middle storie.

Ruggs, Coverlitts and Coverings for bedds viz. One Course Coveringe of Tapestrie of Imagerie.

Fow(r) peces of Tapestrie for Coverings.

Thirten Coverlitts and Ruggs.

One yallow rugge.

One gray rugge.

Five olde liverie rugs for servants.

One gray rugge.

One white rugge.

Quilts One olde Turkie Quilte of Crimson silke.

Mattresses viz. Five Canvas mattresses.

Matts, viz. One matt for a bedd.

Cannapies and cloth bedds with testers vallances and heade clothes viz. One fyne Chena Cannapie of Nedleworke with Tester vallanc & headcloth with a trame sutable to it.

One other Cannapie the tester and vallance of Cloth of tishow with Crimson silke & goulde fringe.

The trame of Changeable taffata with silke & goulde fringe.

One Cannapie heade with vallance of olde Carnation velvet imbrothered with silver without anie other thinge sutable to it.

One furniture for a bed viz Tester vallance and headcloth of redd cloth with blew and yallow lace.

One other furniture viz: tester vallaunce and headcloth of redd Cloth with grene statute lace.

One other furniture viz: tester vallaunce and headepeece of blew Cloth laced with Carnation silke lace.

One olde yallow Cloth bedd with tester and vallaunce.

One old grene cloth bed with tester and vallaunce.

One Tester and vallance of sackecloth.

Curtins for bedds viz. One sute of Curtins of red Cloth with blew & yallow lace.

One other sute of Curtins of redd Cloth with grene statute lace.

One other sute of blew Cloth laced with Carnation silke lace.

One other olde sute of grene Cloth.

One other sute of yallowe Cloth.

One other sute of olde gren cloth.

One other sute of orenge Colored Cloth.

Counter-points One Counterpointe of white Chena with Needleworke.

One Counterpointe of Swans downe of diverse Colors.

One Counterpointe of old Tapestrie.

One Counterpointe of red Cloth with blew & yallow lace.

Windowe clothes and windowe curtins viz. Fower longe windowe Clothes of blacke and grene fugered Satten with blacke and grene silke fringe.

Three window Clothes of Arras worke wrought with silke & lyned with satten abridges.

One window Curtine of grene taffata lyned with grene saye.
Eight window Curtins of blew Cloth.
Fowerten shallow Curtins of sackcloth.
Fower olde Curtins of redd cloth.
　Cupbords viz. One Cupbord
　Tables viz. One Table longe
One drawinge table with a Carved frame.
　Virginalls One paire of virginalls Covered with grene velvet.
One harp virginall.

12.　1614 Northampton House, London.
Henry Howard, Earl of Northampton
(1869) Howard Inv.

One of the greatest gatherings of riches was assembled in the early seventeenth century at Northampton House in London. The contents of tapestries, carpets, velvet chairs and pillows, inlaid cabinets and so on are described further on pp.53–4.

. . . Howshold-stuffe at London
　Greate Chamber fower pieces of buskedge verdure with the armes in a losendge　£xxviii xvⁱs
sixe greene stooles embrodered with velvett and greene twist upon clothe and a little backe chaire suteable to the same　£iii
a greene velvett chaire and a longe cushin, and fower greene velvett stooles　£iii xs
a foote carpett cross billetted in coulors, contayninge 6 yardes　l [50] s
a cupboard and Turkie carpet　xvs
a greate paire of brasse Norenburgh Andirons　£iii vs
　Dininge Chamber five pieces of buskedge hanginges of huntinge worke, conteyninge 132 elles at dim at iiis. viiid the sticke　£xxiiii iiiis
a longe Turkie carpett of Englishe worke with the Earle of Northampton his armes being 5 yeardes and 3 quarters longe　£xiii
a high chaire, a lowe chaire, a short cushin two high stooles, and one lowe stoole of clothe of golde, the ground maidenheare with frindge and tarsels of golde lined with damaske watchett and maidenheare　£xiiii
6 highe stooles of russet velvett frindged　£iii
a longe table of walnuttree　xlvs
a cupboard of walnuttree with a Turkie carpett, the grounde redd　xls
two small creepers with brazen toppes　iis vid
a foote carpett of Turky worke, the grounde redd and yelowe £iii
　Withdrawinge Chamber fowre pieces of busted hanginges of the storie of *Sawle and David*, conteyninge 105 elles at iiiis iid the sticke　£xxi xvⁱs vid
one highe Chaire with a longe cushin, two scrowle chaires, two highe stooles of braunched clothe of silver, the grounde blacke frindged and tassled with blacke silke and silver, all suteable　£xi
a large foote carpett of Turkie worke　£v
a walnuttree cupboarde with a Turkie Cupboarde clothe　xxxs
6 highe stooles of russett velvett frindged with silke of the same coulour　l [50] s
　Studio Chamber three pieces of hanginges whereof two are of the former storie of *Sawle and David*, the third of men in Armes, conteyninge 80 elles at iiiis iid the sticke　£xvi xiiis iiiid
a large chaire with too low stooles of stuffe Taffata striped black & yelowe tarseled with blacke silke and golde frindge　xxxs
a *China* quilte cabonett upon a frame　xxxs
a *Dansque* cabonett inlaid with coloured wood the fore front three stories of colombes　£v

two longe windowe curtanes of striped buffin, red white and greene, lined with green saye　xxiiiis
two Andirons topped with copper　iiis
three highe stooles and a carpett of Turky worke　xxxs
. . .

13.　1618 Oatlands Palace, Surrey
Queen Anne of Denmark
Oatlands Inv., (1618) East Sussex County Records GLY 318, (reproduced by permission of the County Archivist, copyright reserved).

The queen used Oatlands Palace a great deal and saw that it was lavishly furnished, including some of the tapestries and carpets from Henry VIII's great collection. Inventories were taken in 1618 when the queen. then seriously ill, moved to Hampton Court, where she died in 1619.

Hangings
1 suite　A suite of branch sattin hangings in her bedchamber paned viz one pane of watered white & yellow, the other of red white and yellow laced downe right in evry seame, with lace of greene silke gold & silver, bordered about wth a fringe of gold & silv greene & red silke, embrodhered in ye border wth her Mats letters & Crowne in one pane & her Mats Molta in ye other & lyned with Canvas.
　The first peece consisting of 4 panes
　The second of 13 panes
　The third of 11 panes
　The fourth of 11 panes
　The fifth peece being a Chimney peece of 4 short panes & 2 long panes
　The sixth a window peece of 3 panes
　The seaventh a window peece of 5 panes
2　An other Suite of hangings in ye next WthDrawing Chamber of like Stuffe, laceing, embrothery, fringe and lineing
　The first peece of 7 panes
　the Scond of 10 panes
　the third of 4 short panes for a chimney peece
　the fourth of 5 panes
　the fifth of 5 panes
　the sixth of 5 panes
　the seaventh of 6 panes
　the eigthe of 2 panes
　the nynth a window peece of 4 panes
　the tenth a window peece 3 panes
An other suite in ye outer Wthdrawing Chamber of fine new tapistry of ye story of . . . [blank] consisting of 8 peeces.
[List of carpets, including two sent as a New Year's gift by Edward Somerset, Earl of Worcester, together with Turkey foot and table carpets, Persia and embroidered carpets.]
1 suite　In ye Bechamber a field bedsted painted red & gold wth a Canopy & Curtaines of Carnaton & Yellow damaske & a counterpaine of ye same, lyned wth changeable Taffita, laced wth pchment lace of gold & Silver spangled & double vallanded above, a Single vallance belowe under ye bed, laced & fringed sutably, & 5 plumes of feathers sutable
[The bed had a down bed of fustian to it with a pair of fustian blankets, a wool bed in white canvas, a quilt in canvas, three down pillows, a bolster, an embroidered sweet bag, and there was an *en-suite* chair, two high stools, one foot stool, a square cushion and a close stool, with cases of red cotton to them all.]
2 suite　In ye next wthdrawing Chamber a suite of darke Tammy Satten stript & chequered wth gold, laced wth gold spangled lace,

& ye cushions lyned wth a chequered stitcht Taffita of greene white & tammy, &

a bige Chaire one foote Stoole 2 high stooles 2 lowe stooles 7 long Cushions one square cushion	with cases of Tammy Cotten

3 suite   In ye outer wthdrawing chamber an other suite of greene velvet or Tuft taffita wrought into cut flowers betwixt a paned border, ye frames painted on a greene ground with flowers of gold, laced with a gold spangled lace, fringed wth gold fringe above, & belowe with greene silke & gold, & embrothered wth ye Queenes lres [letters] & Crowne
ye pticulars are

A bige Chaire one foote stoole 8 high stooles 2 long cushions One square cushion	all wth cases of greene Cotten

A canopy of the same laced, fringed and embrothered sutably wth Curtaines of greene Damaske laced & buttoned sutably, with tenn plumes of feathers, wth cuppes painted gold & greene

4 suite   In ye South gallery next ye vineyard one suite whereof ye frames are painted white & gold, spotted with flowers, covered with white & red Tuftaffita, laced wth gold spangled lace, and fringed below wth crimson & gold & above wth gold onely, embrothered with her Mats lttes & crowne, ye pticulars are
A canopy wth curtaines of red & wighte Damaske so laced & fringed wth ten plumes of feathers with cuppes sutable

One great Chaire 2 stooles with backes 8 high stooles one foote stoole 7 long cushions one square cushion	wth red cotten cases

5 suite   In ye booke chamber a suite of silver Chamlet branched wth greene flowers fringed wth greene silke, and silver, ye frames painted sutably, the pticulars are

A high chaire 2 high stooles 2 low stooles a foote stoole 4 long cushions one square cushion	wthout cases

6 suite   In ye North gallery a suite of silver & carnaton velvet, laced wth silver pchment spangled lace, & curtaines of Carnacon sattin, lyned with carnacon damaske, laced sutably, & layed wth long silver buttons, ye pticulars are
A Canopy wth vallens, 2 curtaines, ten cuppes & plumes

a Cooch 4 long cushions 2 square cushions 2 low stooles	wth cases of red cotten for all, but ye 2 square cushions

7 suite   In ye same gallery an other suite, ye frames painted wth carnaton ground & garnished wth flowers, covded wth carnatton sattin, stript wth white & betwixt wth flowers of silver, & colded silke, fringed wth silver, ye pticulars are

A chaire 2 long cushions one square cushion 4 high stooles 2 low stooles a foote stoole	wth cases of red cotten to them all, but ye chaire

8 suite   In ye same gallery a suite of silver chamlet, caysed wth watchett & tammy velvet flowers, lyned wth changeable stuffe, stript with gold, tasselled wth silver blue & tammy silke & fringed sutably, ye pticulars are onely
7 long cushions wth red Cotten cases.

9 suite   In ye Cabbinett a suite of cloath of silver branched wth flowers of gold & other flowers of severall collored silkes, ye pticulars are

a low Chaire a square cushion 2 long cushions 2 low stooles	wth cases of yellow cotten

10 suite   In ye privy chamber on ye kings side a cloath of state in panes, one of crimson cloath of gold, ye other of rose cold velvet, embrothered wth flowers of silver purle & trailed wth twist & Ols of gold, wth her Mats armes largly embrothered & embost on ye backe, & on head wth double vallances sutable, wth a deepe call fringe of gold & silver, bound all about wth an uncut narrow fringe of gold & silver & ye pticulars ensuing sutable to it

a high chaire a square cushion a long cushion a foote stoole	wth cases of red cotten

11 suite   In ye K bedchamber unset up, a canopy of saime cold silver velvet, laced wth a silver spangled lace, wth vallance of ye same, lyned wth white & same colded Damaske, laced fringed & set, wth long buttons of silver 2 curtaines laced, buttoned & lyned sutably, wth a backe of ye same lyned wth white fustian, & one plume of feathers, wth a cup of same colde white but wthout any chaire, stoole, cushion or any thingelse to suite ye Canopy but one long cushion.

12 suite   In ye privy Chamber on ye Queenes side 7 high stooles of ash Colored cloath of silver, spotted with red Carnaton flames, fringed with silver, and ye frames painted sutably, all cased wth red Cotten.

. . .

14.   1630 Articles for the better ordering of the Great Wardrobe.
    National Library of Scotland, MS 191, ff.1–4v.

After the impeachment of Lionel Cranfield, Master of the Great Wardrobe, in 1624 there were moves, early in the reign of Charles I, to instil a new order into an old institution. It was hardly successful and became even more ill-organized during the Civil War which severely limited activity and control.

. . . That the Master of the Greate Wardrobe shall have an Assignment of Sixteene Thousand Pounds per Annum by way of imprest upon Accompt towards the defrayinge of the gennerall and yearely expense of the sayde Wardrobe.
£3,000 was payable for Robes
1.   Details about who may draw warrants.
2.   His Majesty's Linen.
3.   Warrants for 'all other necessaryes'.
4.   That there shalbe Creditors and Artifficers of all sortes belonginge to the Great Wardrobe as have been heretofore

accustomed to deliver in Wares and necessaryes for his Maties service, And for such thinge as they shall delyver in for the furnishinge of his Mats Robes, Wardrobes of Bedds, his Mats Howses and for Ambassdors or the like They shall ymediatly with the Stuffe & Worke done or very suddenly after, bringe in their Bills of the pticulars thereof to the Clarke of his Mats Wardrobe to be examined and avouched by him, and then to be delivered to the Mr of the Great Wardrobe, whoe by himselfe or his sufficient Deputie, together with the Clerke of the Greate Wardrobe and the sayde Clerkes of His Mtre Wardrobes, shall prize the same. And all their handes beinge inscribed thereunto the Clerke of the Wardrobe shall engrosse the sayde Bills with their prizes into a Warrante for his Mats Signature to be directed to the Mr of the Greate Wardrobe to make payment thereof . . .

5. . . . That the sayde Clerk of his Mats Wardrobes or his sufficient Deputie shalbe alwayes presente att the delyvery of all such Stuffe, golde, silver or silke laces and fringes, Clothe, fustian, Lynnen, or any other necessaryes whatsover as shalbe delyvered to any Artifficer from the Great Wardrobe or any Tradesman for the garnishinge, trymminge and makeinge upp or repayreinge of any thinge whatsover for the Kinge and Queens Service or for Ambassadors . . . And that the sayde Clerke shall make recorde of the quallity and quantity thereof in a Booke to be kepte by him And after the sayde Artifficer shall sett downe in his Bill what he receaveth for the same accordingly.

6. No allowances or payments to be made for repairing and mending hangings and other stuff unless certified by the Clerk of the Wardrobes in whose custody 'the same stuffe remayneth . . . and the sayde workemen be payde their Wages Quarterly or every half yeare . . . And for as much as their hath been heretofore abuses comitted by some of his Mats Wardrobes in takeinge and Tearinge out of the lyneings of his Mats Arrace and Tapestry hanginge, and soe sendinge them to the Great Wardrobe without any Lyneings in them, whereby they must be new lyned quite through to his Mats great charge and expense whereas if the lyneings were lefte in them the same might be repayred and made useful and serviceable with farre less cost & charge to the Kinge . . . That from henceforth all hangings or other Wardrobe stuffe that shalbe brought from his Mats Houses or Wardrobes to the sayde Great Wardrobe to be repayred shall come with the Lyneings in them and a Labell of Parchment sewed to the same with the Clerk of his Mats Wardrobes hande subscribed thereunto signifying the charge . . .

7. Liveries and payments for them.

8. That the Clerk of the Wardrobes shall draw all Warrants dormant for Liveryes payable out of the sayd Great Wardrobe to such his Mats servants as are sworne under the Lorde Chemberlaine . . . The same for those employed at the Stables . . .

15. 1637 Ralph Grynder: Work for Queen Henrietta Maria

P.R.O., LR5/66

The fascinating story of the queen's Catholic household at Greenwich and elsewhere is well documented in the LR5 series of documents at the Public Record Office, London. It is possible to chart almost every object acquired during certain years.

'Ralph Grynder Uphoulster Craveth Allowance for Wares Deld. & Worke Done for her Ma.tie from our. Lady day to Michaellmas 1637'

April 2die 1637

Foe a dayes Work for my selfe & 3 of my Servants to take downe her Ma.tis Rich Bedd & Canopie att St James & putting other in the Roome — 00-10-00

Foe Twist Tasseling and new making 2 Thick french fustian Quilts — 01-00-00

Foe 20 yards of fine fustian for an upper Quilt for her Ma.ti att 2s 6d a yard — 02-10-00

Foe 34 lbs. of fine Shauers [sic] to fill them att. 14d a pound — 01-14-00

Foe Twist Tasseling & making it — 00-10-00

Foe 6 Close Stoole panns for her Ma.ts use — 01-10-00

More foe her Ma.tis Suite of figured Velvett with a Cloth of Tissew ground May 13th 1637

Foe 10 yards of fustian & 3 yards of Rone [sic] buckram to lyne Tester headcloth & Vallance of The Canopie — 01-10-00

Foe hookes & staples for the lathes and vallan — 00-03-06

Foe 1 Lardge payre of Cortinge Rodds being Tynned with 4 lardg Staples — 00-15-00

Foe 4 french Cupps to Cov. — 00-03-00

Foe fine Silke Ribband to Ring the Cortinges — 00-04-00

Foe Lardg burnish Ringes for the Cortinges — 00-04-00

Foe 3 lbs of fine Strong Layre to hange upp the Canopie — 01-01-00

Foe Workmanshipp in making a Rich furniture of figuredd Velvett the Curts. being 3 yards Deepe, with Tester headcloth vallance and Cupps being lyned quite through with Cloth of Tissew & fringed one both sides with Silvr. Fringes — 04-00-00

Foe doble Sackcloth girth & bustia [sic] for the seates of 2 french Chayers 6 foulding Stooles & 2 heades of a Couch — 01-00-00

Foe 8 Baggs of Tyke for the 2 Chayres & 6 Stooles — 01-04-00

Foe 1 lardge Bagg of fine Stript Tyke for the Seate of a Couch bedd — 00-12-00

Foe 70 pounds of fine Burgis feaths. to fill them att 14d a pound — 03-10-00

Foe 4 Baggs of flox for the backe of 2 french Chayres & 2 Couch heades & for doble Sackcloth & girth for them — 00-12-00

Foe 2 Iron stayes with Staples for the 2 backs being silvered — 00-06-00

Foe 2,000 of Silvered Burnish nayles foe to garnish the Couch & 2 french Chayres all ovr. — 01-00-00

Foe 350 of lardge bullen nayles for the Couch Cheares & Stooles att 9s. a hundred — 01-08-00

Foe black Tacks foe all of them & Staples to fitt one the Bagg — 00-05-00

Foe 25 yards of fine broad bayse to Case 2 Chayres 6 foulding stooles & a Couch being Cased down to the ground att 2s 8d — 03-02-06

Foe making 2 french Chayres being Covered all ovr. with figured Velvett & garnisht Round with silvr. fringes — 02-00-00

Foe making 6 foulding stooles suteable — 01-10-00

Foe making a Lardge Couch bedd of figured Velvett with 2 heades the seate being fitted on with Staples & garnished Round with fringes & covered all ovr. Styles and feete — 03-00-00

Foe Tape & making Cases foe all the Cheares Stooles & Couch — 00-08-00

Foe a Couch Cheare foe her Majs. Suteable

Foe double Sackcloth & girth for the Seate — 00-08-00

Foe 3 Baggs of Tyke for the seate & 2 Winges of the Couch — 00-15-00

Foe 46 pounds of fine Burgis feathrs. to fill the seate and Winges — 02-06-08

Foe Stuffeing of felt & lyning of buckeram for the back & Elbowes of the Couch — 00-06-00

Foe 500 of Silvered Bullen nayles for the Couch — 02-00-00

Foe 1,000 of burnish Silvered [nails] — 00-10-00

Foe Black Tacks for it — 00-02-06

Foe 11 yards of bayse to Case it all ovr. att 2s 8d — 01-07-06

Foe Workmanship in making a Lardge Couch Chayre of brancht Velvett being Covered all ovr. on Rayles, Styles and feete with 2 Cushion winges garnished with Silvr. Fringes   04-00-00

For Tape & making Cases for it   00-03-00

Foe 20 Baggs of Strong Tyke foe 20 Cushions att 4s a pece   03-00-00

Foe 162 pounds of fine burgis feathrs. to fill them   08-02-00

Foe 48 yards of fine Scarlett Collor Penistone to Case 20 Cushio. att 3s a yard   07-04-00

Foe making 20 Lardg Cushions of figured Velvett being garnished with Tassells fringes & with baggs of feaths. att 4s a peece   03-10-00

For 2 dozen of Ribbands & making Cases of bayse for them   0-10-00

Foe 6 yards of fustion to lyne a Screene Cloth att. 18d a yard   00-09-00

Foe making a french-fashioned Screene being lyned and fringed   00-08-00

Foe Carriage of those thinges to Summerst. house   00-03-06
Foe her Mats. Barge
May 25th 1637

Foe 3 Baggs of Tyke for 3 Cushions for the barge   00-12-00

Foe 26 pounds of fine Burgis feathrs. to fill them [ask.]   01-10-04
          [paid]   01-06-00

Foe making a Bardgcloth for her Mat.ie of greene Taffety being fitted Round with Stringes   01-10-00

Foe 7 yards of grene bayse to Case 3 Cushions att 2s 8d p. yard   00-17-06

Foe making 3 Longe Cushions of greene damask fringed Round & with baggs of feathrs.   00-12-00

Foe 1 yellow ground Turkey Carpett   01-06-00

Foe making upp a Greene Cloth carpet delivered to the Robes   00-03-04

Foe the office of the Robes
For doble Sackcloth & girth for 3 Chayres and 3 foulding stooles   00-06-08

For 6 baggs of Tyk for them   00-15-00

For 18 pounds of Burgis feaths. to fill them att 14d a pound   00-18-00

For 7 [changed to '6'] Cushions of Turkey work of Rose & pansa [or 'pausa'; of Rose and pansies?] with Styles   01-10-00

For 3 backs   00-08-00

For Stuffeing of felt for the backs   00-01-00

for 12 oz. of fine mockado fring for them att 7d an ounce 00-07-00

For 300 of bullen nayles for them & for black Tacks & burnish nayles   00-08-00

For making 3 back stooles & 3 foulding stooles of Turkey work garnished with fringes   00-10-00
More for Greenwich
June 7th 1637

Foe two ells of Clouded Taffety to Repayre her Ma.tis Pavillion   01-10-00

Foe 5 oz. of gould & Silvr. Fringe used about the Chayres and Stooles at 6s. an oz.   01-10-00

Foe 3 yards of fustian for the bottomes of the Cheares & Stooles   00-04-06

Foe 3 new Stayes foe the Chayre Backs   00-09-00

Foe guilt burnish & Bullen nayles foe them & foe black Tacks   00-10-00

Foe 8 great Wall hookes to hang her Ma.tis Pavillion with   00-03-00

Foe 12 yards of Stronge threid Leyre to hange it upp with   00-18-00

Foe workmanshipp in mending & Repayring her Ma.tis Pavillion   01-05-00

For new making 6 foulding stooles   01-10-00

For altering and Repayring 3 french Chayres in divers plases   00-15-00

Foe making up 2 Clouded Taffety Carpetts being fringed round and lyned   00-10-00

For my owne labor & my Sr.vants & for charges in going and coming by water to fitt up the pavillion   00-15-00

For Carriage of these thinges from Summersett house & by watr. to Greenwich   00-06-08
Jun. 19 1637

For 2 days Labor for 2 men to goe to Oatlands & for Charges and Expences for my Selfe in going toe & froe by watr. to fitt upp her Mats. Pavillion   01-10-00
Augst. 28th 1637

Foe 1 12/4 Superfine Bedd Tycke Flanders Garnished with Silk Roundes   05-00-00

Foe 32 pounds of fine Swans downe to fill it att 4s a pound   05-06-08

Foe Carriage of it to Denmark House   00-01-00

Foe 2 dayes Work for 2 men to putt up her Majs. Bedd & hanging up hangings & Takinge down   00-10-00
Foe her Mats. Grene Bedd Sent to Hampto. Court

Foe lardge Burnish Ringes used about the Curtaynes   00-02-06

Foe altering & Inlarging a Grene Velvett Bedd being garnished with gould Lase & Lyned with Damask & Lased Round on the Inside & making 1 New Coeting [curtain?]   01-10-00

Foe Charges and Expenses for my Selfe & foe hors hyer to goe to Hampton Corte by her Majs. Command & for Carriage of these things to Hampton Court   01-10-00

[paid, in effect,   107-16-04]

16. 1638 Gosfield Hall, Essex
The Inventory of Anne, Viscountess Dorchester.
Notes & Queries, March 1953 and January 1954

Within Lady Dorchester's will the following items relevant to upholstery are noted. The names of the recipients are not given here.

. . . halfe my carnation flowred satten for a bedd being three peeces and in measure ninety yards, all my silver tissue imbrodered with nett to lyne the bedd, my fugure satten bedd, and furniture to it with the feather bedd and canopie, tenn featherbedds whereof fower to bee good ones and the six residue for servants bedds . . . my white suite of hangings being eight peeces of it, fower white Turkey carpets, and the long one that John Frithe wrought, twelve back chaires to it with the unicorne [Lord Dorchester's crest], my purple velvett saddle . . . my white satten flowered peece of stuffe, and cloake of the same for vallance and cantoones for a bedd and thirtie pounds in money to buy her damaske for curtaines to it, my crimson velvett bedd with the featherbedd, blanketts, furniture and all thinges belonging to it, tenn featherbedds whereof fower to bee of the best sorte and the six residue for servants bedds, my best suite of hangings with the beasts beinge eleaven peeces, my best Persian carpett with a white ground that was my Lord of Dorchester's, three ordinarie square Turkey carpets . . . my tawny satten furniture for a bedd imbrodered with silver with the peece of tawney and white damaske for curtaines with a faire featherbedd and blanketts to it, my Irish stitched furniture for a bedd with the silk fringe which was made for it, my hangings which I used to hang in my dyninge roome at Westminster being eight or tenn peeces, my Turkie carpett usuallie used in that dyning roome . . . my canopie, couch stooles and chaires which did stand in my gallerie att Westminster, my great tawney velvett cabinett, which was in my chamber att Westminster . . . the other halfe of the carnation flowered satten, the gold fringe to it, my tawney imbrodered cloth bedd which was wrought in my house with the carpets, sideboard, clothes, stooles, and all thinges belonging to it, together with a faire featherbedd and blanketts to it, my new suite of hangings which I bought att second hand, and cost me two hundred pounds, fower of my best Turkey worke carpetts . . . my purple plushe couch canopie which did stand att my house att Westminster with the carpets stooles and chairs thereunto belonging . . .

[1645 – Edward Sackville – see Appendix A21]

17.   1651 Montacute, Somerset
Somerset C.R.O.,
MSS DD/PH, 226/8

An Inventory of the goods sold by John Whitehead and Samuel Wall the second day of October 1651 by virtue of a sequestration issued out of ye Chancery . . . in the sume of £500 (see pp.65–6).

Goods in the lying down chamber
1 high bed stead, flocke bed; and bowlsters   3 white blanketts   2 feather pillows   2 white carpetts wrought with greene   4 curtaines & vallens of ye same worke lined wth white belladine   1 white tester   1 trundle bed   1 featherbed and bowlsters   1 paire of white blanketts   1 greene coverlid   3 greene curtaines   1 greene skreene   1 red chaire   2 wrought chaires   9 wrought stooles   3 greene velvett stooles . . .

In ye hall chamber
1 bed stead, feather bed & bowlster   3 white blanketts   1 blew rugg   4 blew grosgraine curtaines wth vallins   1 blew callicoe tester   2 feather pillows   2 orange tammy stuff Caffatae chaires   4 large stooles of ye same   2 old cushions of ye same   2 tenn stitch old cushions   2 greene velvett chaires   4 lowe velvett stooles of ye same   4 high stooles of ye same   2 side cubbards   2 Arras carpetts   6 paire of fine Arras hangings   2 callico window curtaines . . .

In ye yellow bedchamber
5 paires of darnix hangings   1 bed stead, feather bed & bowlster   1 feather pillow   5 yellow curtaines wth yellow fringe & vallins   A tester of ye same   2 cubbards   2 greene stooles

In ye dineing roome
1 longe boarde   2 side cubbards   1 greate chaire of her stitch worke   2 little stooles of ye same

In ye greate chamber
3 high greene stooles   1 bed steed   1 downe bed & bowlster

18.   1677 John Casbert
Part of a Great Wardrobe Account.
P.R.O, LC5/41, ff.121–8

The French upholsterer, John Casbert, was active (with his son, John) in the crown's service from the coronation of Charles II in 1661. It has been established (p.82) that he provided chairs of estate for that ceremony, one of which survives (Pls 40–2); he continued to serve, as this bill made in 1677, the year of his death indicates.

. . . Tacks, Tape and white nayles, used about the formes and Seates, four dayes worke for six men and for carriage of the Packs [Hay and wool-filled cushions] to Westminster Hall against the Arraignement of the Earle of Pembroke (£28 8s); makeing Cases of Serge for a Chair of Estate, Two High Stooles, a footstoole, and two Cusheons for the Privy Chamber of our dearest Consort the Queene (10s); forty yards and a halfe of greene Oyled Cloth to make four Curtaines and a Tester for the Queene's Volary, and for Ringes, Tape and Makeing them (£4 5s); makeing an Altar Cloth, Pulpit Cloth and three Cusheons of Crimson damaske fringed with Crimson fringes, Dyed Linnen fustian and feathers for them for the Earle of Carlisle, Governour of Jamaica (£50 18s); makeing Two window Curtaines of white Taffata; Cases for one Elbow Chaire, Two Stooles and a footstoole of the same, Taffata, Tape and Burnished ringes for the Curtaines for the Queene's little Bedchamber (£2 2s 6d); Two Cloth Carpets for the Queene (13s 4d); large Ringes, Tape and makeing three Crimson window Curtaines for Our withdrawing Roome and mending the Cases of Chaires and Stooles there and in our Bedd Chamber (53s); A fine Musketto Carpet for our Seate in Our Chappell (£3 10s); Six Paire of Great Blankets, Six Paire of downe Pillowes and makeing seven fustian Blankets for the Gentlemen Groomes and Pages of Our Bed Chamber (£14 10s); makeing thirteene paire of rich Embroidered Banners for Twelve Trumpetors (£3 5s); Altering and makeing a Crimson Damaske Bed into a new fashion and the Covers of the Chaires to it, Cleaning the fringe, Dyed Linnen to it, stuffing and all the furniture to six stooles and Two Armed Chaires and for washing, Carding and new makeing up two wooll Quilts, which Beds &c remaine in Our Standing Wardrobe at Whitehall (£28 4s); Altering and makeing a Travelling Bed into a new fashion and the Covers of the Chaires, cleaning the fringe, Tenn yards of dyed Linnen, Stuffing and furniture for an Armed Chaire and four Stooles, new Carding of five Thick woollen Quilts and washing a Holland Quilt and makeing them up for Our Removeing Wardobe (£28); altering and makeing a Crimson velvet Bed into a new fasheon and Covers of the Chaires and Stooles, cleaning all the fringes, fifteen yards of Dyed Linnen, nine yards of Crimson velvet for covers for the Chaires, a Set of Cupps, stuffing and furniture for two Armed Chaires and four stooles (£36 14s); for One hundred and fifty yards of dyed Linnen and Buckram to line the Bed and Hangings, makeing a Crimson Damaske Bed (Vizt) double Vallance with Cuts and Scollops, Six Curtaines, Cantoones, Basis, Testor, head Cloth, head board post Cases, Counterpoynt, Covers for Chaires and Stooles, All fringed with silke fringe, makeing two Armed Chaires and four Stooles, Stuffing and all furniture for them, Embroidering the inside of the Bed, Tape and Ringes, Sixty Copper Pulleys, Two fine fustian Quilts of washt wooll, a holland quilt, a haire quilt, a fine Bedtick, sixty pounds of Swans downe, Two paire of fine Spanish Blankets, makeing, lineing and fringeing the Hangings to the Roome and Curtaines for the doores, and makeing a Taffata Case fringed about, with Small Ringes, Tape and Leaden Plummets all for Our Bed Chamber in the new Lodgeings at Whitehall (£94 8s); makeing and quilting Two haire Quilts for Our Dogs (£3); varnishing Two Armed Chaires and Six Stooles with Black and Silver, stuffing and all furniture and makeing Velvet and Taffata Cases for them, All for the withdrawing Roome of our dearest Consort the Queene (£23 12s) . . . makeing a Canopy of Estate of white and greene velvet, with a riseing Testor, head Cloth, and double Vallance lined with Silke and Silver fringes, fifteene yards of Buckram, fifty yards of dyed Linnen, Sackcloth, Girth web and Tackes, for the Chaire of Estate, three Stooles and lineing the Back (£9 4s 9d) . . .

19.   1686 Jean Poictevin
       Work for James II and Mary of Modena
              P.R.O, LC9/287.f.56

The upholsterer charged a travelling rate of 15s a day for himself, 6s 8d for each of his men, and coach-hire. He was one of the most successful of the French upholsterers working in England, and more details of his activities, particularly in the provision of state beds, are likely to appear as research continues (see also A20).

May 10 1686
In the Bed chamber For making of the blew and gold Colour & White Damask Bed with Chaires and Stooles and the case of the bed of blew Taffata & false Covers for the Chaires and stooles Silk tape Rings hoocks & eyes   020.00.00
For Embroydering the bed & Counterpoint with gold & Silver
                                                            150.00.00
For 18 yardes of Taboy at 14s p yard   012.12.00
For a Bedstead with a riseing testor headboard Cornishes with 16 Skrews   006.00.00
For a Sett of polished rods gilt   007.00.00
For a downe bed and bolster weighing 70 lb   014.00.00
Swanns downe at 4s
For 28 yardes of pillow fustian at 2s p yd   002.16.00
    For her Mats Bed chamber For a thick Sattin quilt   006.00.00
For a thick fustian quilt   004.00.00
For a fine Holland quilt   004.00.00
For 2 pair of fine 13/4 blancketts   006.00.00
For a Sett of Carved Cupps   005.00.00
For a Sett of Carved feet gilt very fine   006.00.00
for 2 chaires & 6 Stooles Carved & gilt £8 each Chair & £6 a Stoole
                                                            052.00.00
For 120 yardes of Linnen & Buckram to line the bed Chaires & Stooles at 12d   006.00.00
For 4 yards of white sattin to cover the Pillowes at 8s p yard
                                                            001.12.00
For making three white damask window Curtains with tape & rings
                                                            001.10.00

20.   1688 Jean Poictevin
       A bill to the first Duke of Hamilton.
       The total bill of £329 4s 9d was settled finally at £270.
              Scottish Record Office, MS., NRA(S), 2177–F2/501 (By courtesy of the Duke of Hamilton)

A Bill for His Grace the Duke of Hambillton, commansee le 15 May, 1688.

for a Crimson mohare bed lynd with greene Satin, Frenge, with Silk Frenge & quilted mohare Cushing a Sille, bedsted, the base, alle complet for agrement   35.00.00
for working 12 Stript of nill work 3/4 of a yde lounger ech stript
                                                            15.00.00
for 80 yde of greene morela mohare for ye bed.
Cases of Chayres at 5s 6p the yd.   22.00.00
for 123 yd of white florance Satting for the lynein of ye bed at 6s a yd.   36.18.00
For Imbroydring the Strept openne the Mohare   04.00.00
For Imbrothern &c Satin with Scarlet Silk   15.00.00
For a bedsteed tester, hed bord & Cornich   04.00.00
For 4 carved Fette varnished black   00.16.00

For 738 ounces of Scarlett Silk Frenge at 12s & 2 pence the ounces
                                                            79.19.10
For 70 yd of dyde lining the . . . [?] the bed and casse of chayeres at 10p the yd.   02.18.8
For a bernished Case rod for the bed   01.15.0
For 71 yd of fine grene Salone [shalloon?] for the case of the bed and chayres at 2s 6p   08.17.00
For making the bed Case of the chayere &c cover of serge, silk, tape & ring   08.00.0
For a sett of Cups for ye bed covred with greene Mohaire   01.10.0
For arme Chayres Canes ter baks, varnished black &c stuffed with Curl haire at 1 lb 10s   12.00.0
For a thick Lustieng quilt &c a checkered lining quilt & a fine holand quilt & a Fustienne quilt to put betwene the other 10.05.0
For 2 pare of fine 12/4 blanquette   05.00.0
For 9 ell of Stroung Canevas for Rapp the quilt at 1s 1p   00.09.11
For a foulding lether   01.00.0
For a Eassee Chayer of wallnut tree Stuff with curl haire with a downe Cushing   02.00.0
For 9 yd of s. strep p. Cush, the cover the Eassee chayer at 6s 6p
                                                            02.14.0
For 25 ounces of gould coleur and white Silk Frenge at 1s 2
                                                            01.07.4
For 8 arme chayres of wallnot tree stuft with curle herre at 1 lb 5 apecce   10.00.0
For 18 yd of Cremeson Cofa [caffoy?] for the cover, the cayse at 12s a yd.   10.16.0
For 176 ounces of Silk Frenge at 1s 2   10.05.4
For 45 yd of Cremeson Serge for the cover at 2s 2 pence   04.17.10
For a large Easee chayer of walnot stufed whit curle hare & a downe Cushing   02.05.0
For 8 yd of Cremeson Cofa tho cover the Chaire at 12s   04.16.0
For 35 ounces of Silk Frenge for the Ese chayrres at 1s 2d 02.00.0
For 9 yd of Cremeson Serge at 2s 2p for the false cover   00.19.6
For making the Esee chayre & quilned   00.10.0
For a large Couch of walnot tree saking bottam & a cutte hed bord
                                                            02.00.0
For a quilt & bolster for the Couh   02.00.0
For 39 ounces of Silk Frenge at 1s 2   02.06.6
For leining & Making the Couh   00.12.0
For 4 large Casses top of ye Furnitur   01.05.0
For matt & cord   01.00.0

                                   In all   326.04.9

For a sette of washed fether for the bed   03.00.0

                                   In all   329.4.9

[Endorsed] Mr Potivin has received only in money . . .   50
           and my Lord has given his note for   220
                                                                270

London 6 November 1688
   Received of his grace The Duke of Hamilton by the hands of Mr Cranford the Soume of two hundred and seventy Pound; In full of the wthin written account and all others, Preceiding this day, I being oblidged to Ship Safely all the particulars, in any Ship his Gr. shall order me going to Scotland
270 . . .   [Signed]   Jean Poictevin
Remember my Lord gave his note for £220 and so David Cranford payed only £50 in money, and which is only to be allowed in his accounts.

                                   Mr Potivins account.

21. To 1696 Some items in the Sackville archives relating to upholstery

Kent C.R.O. MSS. U269

The provision of furniture by commission, or by the taking of perquisites, is well exemplified by the splendid, and in many cases unique, items still at the great Sackville house of Knole. For this reason I have given extracts from the full archive, ranging here in date from 1624 to 1696. I am indebted to John Chesshyre and to the late Gervase Jackson-Stops for facilitating this by reference to photocopies at the regional office of The National Trust at Scotney Castle.

1624   8 July   [U269 E1 (60 and 85)]
An Inventory of such things as were sent to Knoll the 8th of July 1624 by Symonds the Waggoner . . . A note of household stuff sent by Symonds to Knoll the 28th of July 1624 . . . sent to Knoll from Dorset House
[includes] A crimson velvet bedde, wth double valeins, test (:) & tester embroidered wth my Lords Armes, five crimson taffita curtins wth gold lace & lyned wth greene taffita a counterpoint of crimson taffita embrodered wth gold twist, & a gold edging fringe made aboute itt, a wrought velvett table carpett, & a wyndowe carpett of ye same of crimson trimmed wth gold lace & fringe – table. A Chyna blew silke damask pavillion for a bedde, wth a woodden rounde block on toppe gilt wth golde, a deepe silke & gold fringe about itt, ye pavillion edged wth a silk & gold fringe rounde [. . .]

1642   14 August   [U269 E15 (74)]
The Hurt done at Knole House the 14th day of August 1642 by the Company of Horsemen brought by Colonel Sands . . . and there is of Gold branches belonging to the Coach, in the rich Gallery as much cut away as will not be made good for – £40
And in my Lord Chamber 12 Long Cushion cases embroider'd with satin and Gold & the plumes upon the bed tester to the value of £30 . . .

Sir Edward, an ardent Royalist, suffered great losses in goods and furniture at the hands of the Parliamentarians. Everything listed had an appraisal and sale price, together with the name of the purchaser. I have ignored these and select only some of the items from a fifty-page listing. The full text is given by Phillips (1929) II, pp.319–70.

1645   [U269 010/1]
The Right Honoble Edward Earle of Dorsett
Inventory of his goods taken ye 30th of September Ano 1645.
[This appears to be a sale catalogue of twenty-two pages giving prices realised and names of purchasers and includes:]
    . . . *In ye wth Draweing Chambr*
The Roome hanged with Guilt Leather
One large Canopie of Crimson Damaske wth a Deepe fringe wth large embroydered lace, 4 Curtaines Sutable, 1 Guilt Couch, bedstead, 4 pillowes of Damaske laced Knobby Sutable to them, 2 large cheyers, 6 high backstooles, 4 lowe Stools all Damaske, 1 Damask Cover for the Couch 2 Quilts, some pte of the ffringe Silver and some Copper, the bases Sutable.
    In ye Queenes Chambr
One Standeinge bedstead 4 Guilt Knobs
3 Curtaine Rodds
Two high Stooles, 1 cheyer, 2 lowe stooles of Grene Cloath of gold Collr. wth Covers of Green bayes . . .
    In ye Servants Lodgeing wth in yt
A little pece of ould Dornix, 1 bedsted, Cord & Matt, 1 little table, a Closetoole & pann.

In ye Purple bed Chambr
One guilt standeing bedstead 4 guilt knobs wth feathers & silver ffringe, 1 round bolster 1 paire of blanckets, 1 Elbow cheyer & 2 Stooles wth Silke & Silver ffringe Covered wth green bayes 3 Curtaine Rodds . . . one Counterpaine of blew Damaske wth Coper lace lyned wth bayes, 2 sarcenett Curtaines . . .
    In ye Damaske Bed Chamber
One Standing bed stead, 3 Curtaine Rodds, 2 ffuston Mattresses & 1 of Canvas & a ffustion bolster.
One Couch bedsted, 2 ould Mattresses, 4 long Damaske Cushions 18 Cups of Damaske for the bed & for the Couch wth Silver lace, 2 elbowe cheyers, 2 backstooles, 4 lowe Stooles of Dour Coulored Damaske laced wth Silver bone lace . . . ffower windowe Curtaines of white sarcenet lyned wth yellow Bayes.
    In Leicester Gallery
A Rich guilt Couch bedstead, 1 flock bed, a case for the bedd, 2 pillowes of greene Velvett & 2 Stooles all of the Same wth silke & silver lace, the pillows Cases greene bayes & a Buckrom Cover . . .
Twelve high backstooles of yellowd Stuffe, laced & the frames painted, wth some yellowe covers.
One cheyer, 2 high stooles wth Silke & Silver fringe the fframes being painted with gould.
Two elbowe cheyers, 2 high stooles & 2 lowe stooles all Covers exept on the frames being guilt wth Crimson & gould wth silke and silver ffring 3 long Cushions sutable.
One elbowe cheyer, 2 high stooles, 2 long Chusions: the fframes being Crimson gould wth Cloath of Tissin & Covers of bayes, the woorke raysed in Branches.
One elbowe cheyer, 2 lowe stooles & a foote stoole of gould Coulor & white; 3 long Cushions of the same wth Silke & silver ffring Some Branched being Raysed.
Thirty pictures in the same Roome & 2 in the passag Comeing in, 7 of them wth Curtaines.
    In Leycester Chambr
The roome hanged wth guilt Leather.
One guilt high Standeinge bedstead, 1 ould woodmeale Cover for the Tester, 3 greene Sarsenett Curtaines lyned wth bayes & a Taffety Curtaine for the windowes.
One great elbowe Cheyer 2 high Stooles & 2 lowe Stooles, 1 long Cushion gould Colored laced wth Silke & Silver relaced Covered wth redd bayes.
    In ye Rich Gallery
A Rich Canopie of watchett Velvett & the Curtaines of Watchett Damaske one great cheyer, 2 high stooles & a foote Stoole, 1 Case for a long Cushion, The Tester & Vallance being embroydered with gould & silver & cheyers & stooles embroydred with silver & gold, the Curtaines laced with gould Lace some of them Cased wth yellowe bayes 6 elbowe cheyers & 6 high backstooles of blewe watchett Velvett embroydered with gold & silver, there Covers blewe bayes.
    In my Lords Chambr
Six peeces of Tapestry hangeings.
One guilt ffrench bedstead wth Tester & head Cloath & Duble Vallance of Crimson velvett embroydred with Silver & gold & Silke & gold ffringe, ffive Crimson Taffetty Curtaines lined with greene Sarsenet laced with silver & gold Lace 2 elbowe cheyers 2 high Stooles 2 Cases for 2 long Cushions of Sattin embroydred with gold & silver & silke ffringe.
Two windowe Curtaines of red Cloath very ould.
. . . A ffustian Mattress & a Canvas Mattress a small Turkey Carpet & a small greene Cloath Carpett
    . . . *In ye Outer Chambr to ye Matted Chambr in ye Outer Gallery*
A Sloope bedstead wth 5 Curtaines, Vallance, tester & Head Cloath

of Greene Carsey.

In ye Chambr by that

One halfe-headed Bedstead, one Court cupboard, two ould torne Stooles, one table & one joyned stoole.

In a listing of bed hangings &c., the most expensive items, appraised at £75, were:

> The ffurniture ffor A bedd of damaske wachett and white, 5 curtaines, dubble vallance, tester & head peece, Cases for 2 pillers and Cownterpane, 2 little Carpetts of the same all trimed with silver bone lace and silke & silver fringe underneath, the ffurniture for a canopie sutable to the bedd beinge fouer curtanes duble vallance tester & head cloath and cases & cover for the Couch 2 windowe cloaths all sutable to the bedd trimed with silver bone lace & silver & silke fringe underneath marked with the figur 18.

1664   [U269 E79/3 (85)]

Goods sent to Knoll by Baker 20th Octr 1664: for Bexhill

A piece of 10 yds stuffe bought of Mr. Phillipps, upholsterer, consisting of 24 yards:

The Greene bed & furniture late in my chamber att Dorset House with a bedstead to itt, feather bed, bolster & 2 quilts to itt, One greene counterpaine. One rugg, 2 blanckets, One mattresse: Flocke bed & cord: allso & pillow Allso ffoure back greene high chaires & two low ones. An old greene window curtain 6ft. A close stoole pan, A pewter bason; A chamber pott, A paire of candlesticks An yron chasing dish; A paire of bellowes, A pr. of snuffers; A close stoole case, a set of curtain rings. A warming pan, A brass candlestick . . .

1674   An Inventory of Copt Hall   [U269 E118/2]

[Fullest of a number of Inventories of Copt Hall for the period 1625–91 though none of them seems to be specific enough to relate items to any now at Knole.]

1675   June 19th   [U269 A183/1]

Bill to Edward Sackville from Pat Barrett for hangings, beds and installation, total: £75.13.9

For one Sute of Hangings of ffrench yellow Parrogon for your Dyneing Roome Printed with Roman Statuaries and other Ornament containing 46 yds of Parragon at 4s p.yd   09.04.0

For shashes for the same Rome, excellently well painted, and for their fframes and cutting up (very troublesome)   12.00.0

For one Sute of Hangings on Persian Taffetie Printed wth Roman Statuaries, and Sattin Pillers and Borders and Lined with Callicoe. Containing 34 yds ½ Square at 7s p.yd   12.01.6

A Sattin Bed Lined with Sattin Flowered, and a Quilt with headpeece and tester of sattin and Painted with Imagery in Gold and for Fringes and Bell buttons with many other things to it, at with a Sett of Gold Cupps at £1.6s and gold Clawes at 14s.   02.00.0

With a Bedstead and Sacking bottome &c.   01.18.0

With 5,000 Nailes and tape for yt.

Really Cost   00.08.11

For a Sute of Hangings for [torn] Roome of Watered Callicoe and bordered with French yallow

. . . Containing 38 yds square at 2s p.yd.   3.16.0

For a Closett very neatly hung with Stained Callicoe containing 25 yds at 16d. p.yd.   01.16.4

For making and cutting up the Hangings of all yor Roomes with Five dayes tedious Journeys

Yor Valluable Consideration

for yor Servant Pat Barrett   £75.13.9

Received in parte of this bill

fifty pounds

Octobr the 11' 75

Thomas Penson for ye use of my Mr, Pat Barrett.

1679   [U269 A218]

The Upholsters Bill ffor ye Rt. Honoble The Earle of Dorset 1679 . . .

[Bill for repairs, bedding, covers etc including £85.0.0 for a Greene damaske bed – Total bill £394.16.6 some work done at Copthall and Whitehall]

1682   November 30th   [U269 T71/3]

An Inventory of the Countesse of Dorsets goods mentioned to be assigned by Indenture dated the last day of November 1682

[Gives full inventory of Knole room by room]

1686   July 24th   [U269 A193/4]

[Bill for upholstery paid to John Reynolds   £15.19.4 (see p.93)]

1687   [U269 A194/4]

Bought of Thom:s Alchowe [Alchorne] & Part. [ner]

9 April, 1687: velvets, brocade, total: £339.9.9 [see p.93]

1687   17th May   [U269 E2/3 (85)]

An Inventory of ye goods in particular Rooms or Chambers hereafter named

[Room by room inventory of Knole]

1687   [U269 E2/3]

My Ldys chamber: 1 velvet bed & bedstead . . . 6 pieces of tapestry, 6 gilt chairs, 1 table & a stand, 1 great looking glass & 2 little ones. 1 cabinet, 2 other stands 19 pictures 2 jarrs 23 pieces of China . . . 2 pair of andirons, 2 little tables 1 great skreen . . . a hangng shelfe, 1 jepan boy . . . dining rooms: hangd wth gilt leather

below stairs:

old parlour: 46 pieces of China

Leicester Gallery: 12 pictures 6 chaires 12 stooles 1 table 1 gilt chest, 1 paire of andirons . . .

Room at ye end of Leicester Gallery: 1 velvet bed & bedstead . . . 2 stands 6 chair 2 stools same wth bed

Matted gallery: 10 pieces of hangings 1 couch 4 squa – 4 cushions 14 chaires brass and irons . . .

King's Chamber: 1 blew damask bed & bedstead 7 peices of hangings 10 chaires same with ye bed 1 table 2 stands, 1 looking glass, brass andirons . . .

The Inner roome: 1 bed & bedstead, 4 chaires

My Ldys closett: field bed & bedstand & silk hangings 19 pictures 2 meddalls 1 little glass 2 sconces 1 glass sconce 10 chaires . . .

1689   September 20th   [U269 A193/8]

[Bill for upholstery paid to Sam Richardson   £68.2.11]

1689–97   [U269 069/1]

[Lists & inventories of furnishings, plate etc. from Whitehall, Windsor, Hampton Court & Kensington – papers of the sixth Earl of Dorset, Lord Chamberlain, viz:]

– Delivered to Mr Askew for my Lord's use . . .

– A Note of what goods Mr Child had . . . (in Dorsett's hand) . . .

– A Note of what Goods was delivered to the Lord Chamberlaine (in Dorsett's hand) . . .

– Goods from ye Standing Wardrobe at Wtehall Jany 1693/4

– Goods in ye wardrobe and ye 2 pare of staires Rooms that came from wtHall and Windsor in my Custody . . .

– Goods that are in ye Rooms beyond ye great Dyning roome that came out of the Wardrobes are in, June ye 3rd 1697 in Mr Henry's Custody . . .

– Goods from ye standing Wardrobe in September 1695 . . . [includes goods marked for Knowle and Copt Hall]

– March the 26 1696 delivered to Mr Askew Sert. to my Lord Chamberlane . . .

– A Noate of what goods were delivered to Mr Askew for my Lord

Chamberlaines use out of ye Wardrobe att Hampton Court June ye 22nd 1693 . . .

– A List of his Ma:ties Goods in the Standing Wardrobe of White-hall 16: Febr. 1694 . . .   [8 pages]

– Kensington . . .

– Brought from Kensington May ye 22: 1696 . . .

Brought from Wthall June ye 4:5 & 6 1696 . . .

– An Inventory of Goods Brought from Kensington May ye 29 1695 . . .

– An Inventory of the Kitchin goods Decr ye 15th 91 Cockpitt . . .

– An Inventory of ye goods at Hampton Court as they were left Saturday Ffebry ye 22d 1689 . . .   [2 parts]

– A Generall Inventory of the Plate Taken this 20th Day of December 1690 . . .   [9 pages]

– Aprill ye 17 1694 Recd from Mr Hall Wardrobe keeper at Windsor Castle . . .

– Janrry ye 4 1694/5 Recd. then from Mr Child Keeper of ye Standing Wardrobe ye furniture of the Chapell Closett at Wthall to ye Cockpit . . .

– An Inventory of ye Goods in ye late Queens Apartment at Whitehall 6th March 1694/5 . . .   [3 pages, room by room]

– Brought from ye Standing Wardrobe May ye 17 1695 . . .

– Accomp of Pewter Augst ye 30th 1694 . . .

– July ye 14 1696 Recd. then from ye Moving Wardrobe . . .

1691   Accounts   [U269 A7/24]

2 Feb. Pd. Mrs. Reeves embroiderer for stars . . . £3.16.00

1692   July 9   [U269 193/4]

Bill of John Reynolds

used to the 12 green velvett Cheres 2,458½ of green twisted silk fringe att 16d p. ounce – £16.7.4

Paid for Gilding the fore Rayles and the Carved worke att 3s 6d A pece – £2.2.0

for two new Irons to the frames – £0.2.0

for new straying the Bottums – £0.3.0

for new fileing 300 and ½ of the old nailes at 2s & 6d p. hundred and varnishing them – £0.8.9

etc.

July ye 9th: 1692. Recd: of ye Earl of Dorsett by ye hands of Richd. Downing ye some of Thirty seven pounds in full of this bill . . .
                              £37.0.0

1692   Accounts   [U 269 A193/8]

8 Nov. Given ye man yt brought goods from ye Wardrobe a 2d time   £1.01.09

8 Nov. Pd. ye Carts wch brought ye beds from ye Wardrobe
                              £0.10.06

1693   June   KNOLE [U 269 0.69/1]

Delivered to Mr Askew for my Lords use
                              [from Hampton Court]

[includes:]

too elbow chaires

six stooles all with yellow silk cases

to the bed of state/2 double Curtains/2 single . . . /

12 large pieces of vallins & 14 little ones and all the tasells

(+2 stands, Chair of state & footstool) [no colours mentioned]

2 persion carpitts & a fine turkey work

1 Couch – blue Indian sattin flowered with gold [+ chain]

1 Couch – Crimson & green sattin stript with gold . . .

2 Easy Chairs . . . Indian stuff with a gold ground & blue leaves trimmed with white silk fring   etc.

(ditto June 22, 1693 Hampton)

2 chaires of state one velvett, ye other Crimson cloath of Tishew wth high stooles, & ffoote stooles,

1693   Francis Lapiere   [U269 A195/3]

5 July 'For an easey chare frame of wall nutte stufed wth hare couerd wth Lyning   £2.00.00'

'For making of a case of green serge   0.03.03'

'For 5 yds a ½ of serge   0.13.09'

'For a Round Stoole carved & Japand black stufd wth hare couerd wth Lyning   0.16.00'

'For 3 qrs of a yard of stript indian velvet to blew velvet to couer ye stoole   0.09.00'

'For making ye stoole   0.02.00'

'For a yd & ½ of blew parragon to mak a case for ve cushing
                              0.03.00'

'For Leather to make ye Cushing   0.03.00'

'For 2 & a ½ of green & goold seaming & Lace to go round ye stoold 0.06.00'

'For gilt nayles   0.06.00'

'For 2 Kane chares Japand black wth Bannister backs   0.18.00'

'For an Easey chare frame of wallnut tree wth eaves & Arme to it stufed wth hare couerd wth Lyning   £2.15.00'

'For making a case of blew parrogon   0.04.00'

'For 7 yds of parrogon at 28 pr yd   0.14.00

'For souing silk hooks & eyes   0.01.00'

'For making of a satting counterpan fild wth Eidder down 1.00.00'

'For 3 pd of Eidder down   3.00.00'

'For 26 yds of white sattin at 38 pr yd   3.00.00'

'For alltering of a chare that was stufd wth hare & making a cushing to it   0.02.06'

'For 5 pd of down to fill it at 28 bd p   0.12.06'

                    Total: £17.03.09

                [For Lapiere see p.93]

1694   Bill of Particulars   [U269 A194/11]

10 Feb. Pd. for a paire of Curtaine Rods for ye Gold & Crimson Damaske Bed   £0.06.06

1694   KNOLE [U269 0.69/1]

Goods from ye Standing wardrobe at Wthall Jan 9, 1694 A furniture for a Closet Crimson black and gould being 3 peces of Hangings a Couch with 2 guilted Squabbs 1 bolster 2 Elbow Chaires 4 Stoles 2 Window Curtanes of Wt Indian Damask 5 peces of balck velvet Imbroydered being Covers tor Chair 3 stoles 1 Crimson Damask furniture for a Canopy wth gould & silk fring 1 looking glass Table and Stands inlaye

1694   [U269 0.69/1]

Febby ye 16 1694 Recd from ye Wardrobe at Wthall

1 Cloth of Silver Bedd as followeth

6 Curtanes ⎫ with Cupps outer vallance 3 bases 2 arme
2 Cantoones ⎬ Chaires and 6 Stooles of Cloth of Silver flowered
            ⎭ with gould

Teaster headcloth   ⎫ Crimson satin
Inner vallance Counterpaine ⎬ Richly
bedpost cases and all ye inside ⎭ Embroydererd

4 Read Taffaty Case curtanes with silver fringe and a guilded Case Curtane Rodd

1 Cover for a head board ye same with ye Lyning

1 sute of Read and White plumbes of feathers

4 Spriggs to ye feathers

ye bedstead with all materialls to it

1694   Febby ye 22   [U269 0.69/1]

an accompt both of the last goods that came from ye standing wardrobe & an accompt of ye bed Prince Lewis lay in.

1694   8 June   [A7/28]

Accounts, including: 'Pd. Mr La Peire upholdsterer'   £17

1694   24 Oct.   [U269 A194/10]

Bill of Mich. Aiskew, including:

'for fetching a field Bed stead from St Jameses   £0.02.00'
'for nayles and studds vsed about ye field bedsted   0.02.06'
'. . . 18 porters Burthens from ye Standing Wardrobe in WtHall to ye Cockpitt   0.04.06'
'. . . Unloading ye Wagon when it Came from Copthall and went back ye Same Day for ye bed   0.01.00'
'for vnloading ye Wagon ye next Day at ye Cockpitt with ye bed and furniture   0.01.00'
'for my Expense goeing and Coming to and from Copt Hall being 2 dayes about ye bed   0.05.00'

1695   [U269 0.69/1]
Askew: recd from Child from Chapell Closett & Little Oratory, Whitehall.

January 4 & 9, 1695.

2 Large Elbow Chaires ⎫ Crimson velvett
2 fote Stools   ⎪ fringed with gold & silver
2 Large arme Chaires   ⎬ new blue Damaske
5 Fote Stools   ⎪ with blue silke
6 fourmes   ⎭ fringe . . .

1695   [U269 A194/11]
Bill of Mich. Aiskew From Novembr ye: 10 1694 to Febry the 22 1695

3 Jan. 'To porters for bringing ye Crimson veluett furnitur being Hangings Chaires fourmes stooles Chshons and Carpetts out of White hall'   £0.03.00
9 Jan. 'For Bringing ye blue Damaske furniture out of ye Litle orrectory by ye Water Side at Wte hall being 10 pece of Hangings Long fourms Chaires stools Carpets etc.'   £0.04.06
17 Jan. 'My Jurney to Copt hall when I brought the bed before me on Horsback'   £0.05.00
17 Jan. 'given by my Lds order to ye vpholdsters men at ye blew Lyen for brining an Easy Chair out of ye pall mall'   £0.02.06
28 Jan. 'For Carying a Bedstead with all bed furniture at 6 Load to my Lady orrary'   £0.03.06
15 Feb. 'For bringing a Rich gould and Sky Coloured Damaske furniture out of ye mouing Wardrobe with all furnitur for a Roome'   £0.04.00
18 Feb. 'For bringing a figured veluet Bed with all furniture for a Rome out of ye Standing Wardrobe'   £0.05.06
'Febbry ye 22d: 1695 Recd then ye Contents of this Bill of Mr Richd Downing, Steward to ye Rt Honr ye Earle of Dorsett'
                                                             £1.17.08

1695   Febb ye 26   [U269 A196/3]
Groom of the chambers Bill
March ye 5   'for 3 Chamberpotts ye day ye Quene was buried
                                                             1/8
         10   for fetching 36 Blue Damask Cushons from Whitehall
                                                             1/-
May ye 17   Porteridge from Whitehall with ye furniture Bed and Beding Cabinett looking Glasses Stands and Everything belonging to that Roome   6/-
      ye 20   for Porteridge out of ye Prince of Bayden's Lodgings with all the furniture that Lyes now in my Ldys old bedchamber at ye Cockpitt   5/-
             [. . .]
May ye 29   For 2 Carts to Kingsington to fetch ye goods that now Lyes in my Lds withdrawing roome above   10/-
             For 2 chairmen to fetch ye Rich glas Skrene and 2 more glases on a Cariage from Kingsington   8/-

1695   April 5th   [U269 A196/1]
[Bill for upholstery and pictures paid to Francis Lapiere £47.10.00 & £20.0.0]

1695   April 5   [U269 A196/1]
'for 3 Pictures' francis d lapiere   £20
April 5 pd Mr La Peire ffrench upholdsterer   £47.10.0
[detailed bill incl.] '3 peices of Skoch plad   £11.14.0
'For a Easey Chear freame japand Black stufed with corled hear & coverd with Lynen & Making ye Chear & gilt Naigls all round & a Coshing   £3.12.0
For 8 Large torkey Skins . . . to cover ye chear   £3.12.0
For making of ye cas For ye Blue lether Chear   £0.3.0
[another similar but in Skoch plad . . .]
For a traviling fild Bedsted folding together with hooks   £10.0.0
For a Walnotre Engreaved teable ovell   £2.10.0
                (total bill = £47.10.0)

1695   July 30   [U269 A196/4]
Given ye french upholdstersman   10/-
1695   May 17   [U269 0.69/1]
(Goods) Brought from ye Standing Wardrobe
Bed of checquered Indian Damask + 2 armchairs
[presumably from Queen's little Bedchamber Whitehall]
6 stools, 2 Indian Screens, fine Indian Chest etc.
+ mourning furniture Black Velvett
+1 large Cabinet of an ollive Colour
2 Larg Looking glasses and ⎫ ye one Japand and
2 pare of stands   ⎬ the other inlaide
1 Large Clock & pendilum

1695   May 29   [U269 0.69/1]
From Kensington incl. white & red damask bed & furniture w. green & white fringe.

1695   July 24   [U269 A196/4]
Accts./Richard Downing
Receipt Philippe Guibert   £9
Sgd.
endorsed 'pd ye ffrench upholsterers pacqts'

1695   2 August   [U269 A198/9]
A Bill for the Right honble Lord Dorset by P. Guibert
For 12 holland chaires at 7s 6d a piece   4.10.0
For mending ye bed 2 paires of staires   1.15.0
For 2 haire Quiltz coverd with holland cloath fine quilt at 3tt 10s apiece   7.0.0
                                                          ─────────
                                                            13.5.0

. . . Rec'd P. Guibet
[endorsed on verso 'ffrench upholsterer']
1695   2 Aug.   [U269 A198/9]
Bill from P. Guibert, French upholsterer [bill pd. 25 Dec. 1697]
For 12 holland chaires at 7s 6d apiece   £4.10.00
For mending ye bed 2 paire of staires   1.15.00
For 2 haire Quilts covered with holland cloath fine quilt at 3£ 10s a piece   7.00.00
plus un petit matte las de Coille dollande de Crejn et de Laine de
                                                           1.12.05
                                                         £14.17.05

1695   September   [U269 069/1]
'Goods from ye Standing Wardrobe in Septembr 1695
Carried to Knole 1 Large fine old Carpet
1 Silk shagg Carpett
the greene Mix'd furniture for a bed
1 Satin quilt and bolster
1 fustian quilt and Hangings of indian Sattin

To Copt hall   2 Wyer skreens
2 Cushons of blue and Muske Coloured figured velvet
To Knowle all but ye Cushons 3 of them to Knowle and 2 to Ldy Orrary   (2 Chaires) of greene white and Crimson figured

(2 Cushons) velvet with white knoted fringe

(6 Stooles)

13 white Damaske Curtaines with silk fringe to Knowle and 2 to Lady Orrary

2 white Damask Curtaines with Cover fringe & to Mr Henry and me.

4 Crimson and gould Coloured Damask Curtanes

To Knowle   A sky Damask Quilt and bolster for a Couch

1 Crimson sattin quilt and 2 bolsters for a Couch

1 Balack Jappan Scrutore

1 Canopy of Crimson Damaske

ye Blankets to Knowle 2 quilts and one white Blanket with a topp blanket of Calico quilted

1 weather glass

Given to Mr Child

4 peces of sad coloured mohair hangings

1 Chair and 6 stools of Black and blue figured velvet

2 pare of White Linen Curtanes'

> 1695   [U269 o.69/1]

Goods from ye Standing Wardrobe in September 1695

Caried to Knowle [presumably from Whitehall since same gifts on same paper to Mr Child]   1 Large fine old carpet

1 silke shagg Carpett

the grene Mix'd furniture for a bed . . .

to Copt Hall   2 Wyer Skreens

to Knowle all but ye Cushons   (2 Chares) of grene white and Crimson

(2 Cushions) figured velvet with white

(6 Stooles) Knoted fringe

[Knowle]   1 Black Jappan Scrutore

        1 Canopy of Crimson Damask

        1 weather glass   [and lots of textiles]

> 1695   [U269 E79/2]

Carried to Knowle September ye 24 1695.

The great blue Damaske bed from Windsor

The grene . . . silk furniture for a bed

. . . 2 arme Chaires and 6 Stoles with covers of green white & crimson figured velvet

1 blue Damask Couch with 2 squabbs from the Cockpitt

Caried to Knowle September ye 24 1695

The great blue Damaske bed from Windsor

1 feather bed and bolster

The grene mixt silke furniture for a bed

1 White Satin Quilt and bolster

1 fustian Quilt

1 blanket

4 feathers

2 arme Charies and 6 stoles with Covers of grene white and Crimson figured veluet

5 White Damask window Curtanes

1 Large persian Carpet

1 Silke shagg Carpet

2 Large Branchd veluet Easey Chaires ye one blue ye other Read and grene

2 Large Black Looking glases

2 tables

2 pare of Stands

1 Larg Skrene

1 blue Damask Couch with 2 squabs & 1 bolster

> 1695   October 10   [U269 A195/10]

Michael Aiskew

for porteridge from Whitechall to ye Cockpitt with ye Timber and teaster and furniture of the Quenes Bed of State   5/-

Sept. 11   for carying a Couch and 2 squabbs to my Lady

Lainsborowes and some goods to my Lady Orrerys   1/6

> 1695   [U269 A196/12]

Bill Begining Dec 24 1695 [Michael Askew]

to porters at Windsor bringing Downe to ye Cart   2/-

for a Cart to Cary ye Goods from ye Castle to Eaton Bridge being Christmas Day   2/6

. . . from Darby Staires with ye Goods on Christmas Day when scarce any helpe could be gott   6/-

to ye Windsor coach for bringing another pece of the hangings a weke after . . .   1/-

> 1696   [U269 o.69/1]

Brought from Wt.hall Jan. 4, 5, 6 1696

   out of ye King's side ye purple bed etc . . .

   out of ye Quenes Closett

1 speckled Deske and ye Cupboards with glass Doores and ye Glasses in ye wanescot all suteable out of that furthes [sic] Closett

1 Couch and 3 Litle Round Stooles with purple silk cases

23 Dutch pictures

1 Large Cabinet with glas Doores

1 princes wod Cabinet

1 Deske Coverd with grene velvet . . .

> 1696   March 26   [U269 o.69/1]

delivered to Mr Askew servt. to my Lord Chamberlane

a bedstead the furniture of Scarlett cloth stript with black and lined with white damask + 2 chaires

6 stools

delivered before

Winsor Castle cutt in glass wt a guilt frame and 23 mays [?maps] from the Queen's apartment Whitehall – 'one looking-glasse engraved with Windsor Castle'

> 1696   26 March
>
> [including:]   [A193/3]

[Bill of Mr Aiskew] to porters for bringing Bedsted bed beding and furniture for a Rome from Whitehall to ye Cockpitt the furniture was ye Read and back Stripd cloth   £0.04.00

> 1696   20, 26 May
>
> [including:]   [U269 A197/3]

[Bill of Mich. Aiskew] For taking a Desk and a Cabinett and a Litle Cabinett Lite a table from Wthall   £0.01.06

For a Cart from Kingsington with ye purple State bed and furniture   0.06.00

For fetching 21 Lookinglasses   1.00.00

To a porter for Carying an Easy Chair to Ld Ensiquenes   0.00.06

> 1696   30 June   [U269 A197/7]

[Mich. Aiskew's bill, including:] for fetching ye Crimson velvet Canopy and Chaires from Whitehall   00.01.00

> ?1696   [U269 E79/2]

. . . Saturday, December ye 21:

peces of Hangings out of ye 2 Chapells

1 arme Chair and fote stoles

2 Stools – of purple veluet siluer fringe

2 Cushons

3 Embroyderd Cushons

1 old grene Embroyderd veluet Carpet out of ye Chapell

a Couch with 2 Heads

1 Crimson veluet Chair of state and fote stol & fringe

1 Large arme Chair

2 Stools   Cloth of siluer

2 Cushons

1 Large grene flowerd satin bagg to knele on

1 Large persian Carpet out of ye Quens Chamber my Ldy Norhamton had it

2 pare of Iron Dogs

1 pare of tongs

1 fire shoule

1 skrene being grene Geuves flowerd with jeuld on one side and Indian paper work on ye other

2 arme Chaires of Crimson Damask Stools – fringd wth gould

The Quene's bed and beding being bedstead Curtanes valence teaster and head cloth of purple Cloth Laced with whitish silke Lace

1 feather bed tester and pillow 2 . . . [?] and a Lead Colourd Rugg

?1696   [no date, no title]   [U269 E79/2]

[includes:]

6 Large fine old Carpits 2 of them Lined

1 Large Shag silk Carpet lined wth blew lineing

4 Green Mixt silk furniture for a Bed

. . .

2 Chaires 3 stooles & 3 Cushions of Crimson & Musk collerd figured vellvet

2 Chaires 2 Cushions & 6 Stooles of green, white & Crimson figur'd velvet, trim'd wth wt knoted fringe

1 Chaire & 6 stooles of black & Blew figur'd vellvet

. . .

A sky Damaske Quilt & Blouster for a Couch

A Crimson sattin Quilt & 2 Boulsters for a Couch

A Black Japan Scratore wth shevs in it

A Canopy of Crimson Damaske

1697   4 Feb.   [U269 A198/11]

Bill of Particulars, including:

Given Mr LaPeire ye french upholsterers man   £0.05.00

22. To 1698 Chancery suit brought by Francis Lapiere against Barbara, Duchess of Cleveland. Goods supplied 1687–97.

P.R.O C5/138/No.19 July 8 1698

Whilst the French Catholic upholsterer, Francis Lapiere, had a good and remunerative profession, he was not afraid to go to law against tardy payers or those who defaulted against him in some way. See pp.96–7.

. . . for altering a yellow damask bed (vizt) peiceng the Curtains longer & altering them & the head, cloth & vallance of the new fashion & altering the cornish & furnishing rings tape thread & silke & taking down the bed & setting it up again complete at £3 10s –; for imbrodering the cornishes head cloth & head bord £2; for a sett of cups for the bed £1 10s; – for a bedstead scrowles (?); & Tester & a sett of cornishe;

for ye gold & silver bedd £5; for six scrowle Charis, varnished black & stuffed with curled hair & covered with gold colored Linnen at 35s apiece £ten, ten shillings; for 63 yds of dyed linnen for the lining of the bedd & cases of the Chairs at 12p p. yard £3.3s; for making up the beds & ye Cases of ye Charies complete £7; for a Leather Carpett, 8s; November the 10 1695.

for new stuffing & covering of a Chair with Needlework & Nayles 8s; for one pound of downe to help to fill the cushion 3s; for two yards of green Paragon 5s; for putting up two beddes & taking down one 7s/6d; April 25 1696, for new stuffing up another chair & covering it with needlework 8s; for two yards of black serge for the Box 5s; for two yards of linnen to cover the chiar 2s; . . . [?] up two cases of Beng..!! L [?] & sowing silke & tape 4s; May the 8, 1697; for taking downe a flowered Callicoe pavilion & putting up of a blue damask bed in ye same place & Nayles 10s; for taking down eight window curtains & vallances, cleaning them & folding them up, 3s for taking down an oyle & gold coloured damask bedd 5s; July 11 1697 for altering of the damaske bedds (vizt) taking out of the breadths that was torne at the foot & putting it to the head & sowing

on the fringe & rings where they were ript in severall placis & now gageing the vallance & bases & covering the new set of cornishes & thread tape & silke £4 10s; for a new set of cornishes to it & two new half rounds for the Tester £1; & amounting in ye whole to ye sume of £41 11s & six pence. And Yr Orator further sheweth that after he had sold to the Ds such goods & done business to the value aforesaid he sent her a Bill to which she made no objection or scruple . . .

[At last the Duchess sent: 'a damaske bedd with ye furniture & things thereunto worth between £20–30 in part satisfaction of the debt'.

The Duchess refused to pay and had raised an Action to be brought against Lapiere in the Court of King's Bench in the name of Roger, Earl of Castlemaine; declared for £200 damages.

Lapiere asked the court that his accusers be present to answer his charges.]

23. 1699 Estimate for Furniture, Hampton Court.
National Art Library, Victoria & Albert Museum, MS.
RC U 6   (One of nine estimates)

Beds were one of the most important provisions to great palaces and houses. Hampton Court, which William III eventually returned to after his beloved queen's death in 1694, still has the king's state bed and those of Queen Anne and others (Pls 87, 136, 137).

For the Gentlemen and Groomes of His Majestys Bedchamber in wayting at Hampton court for their present service:

For the loane of a Damask Bed & Bedding, Chairs and Cushions, Curtains and all appurtenances to the same – Also a Camblett Bed & Bedding and all appurtenances to the same att 4d p month from October 20th 1699.

An Estimate of a new Damask Bed & a new Camblett Bed with all furniture to be provid'd for the above said service. The prices for ready money:

For a Bestead and carv'd Tester, headboard and cornices suitable and curtain Rodds to the same	£12
For two Elbow Chairs and 4 back chair frames	£5
For 140 yds of Damask to make the Beds and Chairs	£98
For fringe for Bed and Chairs	£50 5d
For lineings for Tester, head cloth, Trimmer, Vallence, out Vallence, Bases, and headboard cloth	£2
For searg lineing for ye counterpoint	£1 10s
For rings, tap, sewing, silk thread and severall small materials used about the Bed	£1
For making the Damask Bed compleate	£10
For bottoming, backing, stuffing and lynnen to stuff in all the six chairs and cured hair to stuff them with	£4 10s
For gilt nayles and tacks used about them	£1 15s
For making all the chairs cover'd with damaske fring'd and made fine	15s
For a chequer'd matress quilt	£2
For a fine feather bedd and bolster	£6
For a fine dimety quilt	£2 10s
For a large stain'd callico quilt	£1 18s
For four larg fine blanketts	£3
For a Case, rod and Parragon or Serg Case curtains and Cases for the Chairs	£8 10s
For 2 Cornice pulley laths carv'd	£2 10s
For 40 yds of white flowered Damaske in Curtains	£34 10s
For fring, strings and silk tasells for them	£5 15s
For making the curtains and covering cornices	£2
For plumetts, Os, sowing, silk and small materials	12s

For a large looking Glass, Table & Stands of Walnuttree £15

For a bedstead, rising tester, head board, cornices and curtain rodds £7 5s

For 50 yds camblett to make the Bed and 6 cushions £7 10s

For 50 yds of Persian Taffaty to line the Bedd and make a quilt £12 10s

For lining for Tester, head cloth, outer Vallence, inner Vallance and Bases £1 8s

For Bays to line Quilts and head board cloth 16s

For quilting them £1 10s

For silk fring for the Bed weight 240 oz £28 2s

For making the bedd and all materials to the same £4

For rings, tap, silk thread and severall small materials 15s

For making 6 chushions and materials £1 10s

For 2 bed quilts £3 15s

For a feather bed & bolster £5 10s

For a stain'd callico quilt £1 10s

For 4 Blanketts £2 15s

For 2 Elbow and 4 back fine cane chairs £3

For searg window curtains & rodds for 2 windows and making them and all materials £4 10s

For a large looking glass, table and stands, Japan'd £13

_____

£369 19s 5d

For the Groom of the Bedchamber in close waiting:

A Handsome looking glass, table and stands £15

Great Wardrobe, 7 December 1699.

An Estimate of the charge of the Furniture for His Majestys Horse Guards at Hampton Court.

For 3 Officers Rooms:

For 3 Beddsteades £6

For 3 setts of stuffe curtaines made compleat with double Vallence bases and cornishes fringed with woasted £34 10s

For 6 Matresse Quilts £12

For 3 Feather Boulsters £3

For 3 stained Callicoe Quilts £4 4s

For 2 dozen of Turky Work chairs £14 8s

For 3 pair of Blancketts £4 4s

For 3 looking glasses £12

For 6 brasse candlestickes £1 10s

For 3 pewter chamberpotts 9s

_____

£92 5s

24. 1701–2 Bill of December 1700–1, to 'Her Grace ye Duches of Norfolk' unsigned, but assumed to relate to Etienne (Stephen) Penson's work. (See pp.135–8)

Drayton House, Northamptonshire MS.2475

1700 Decembr

ye 17 ffor ye Covering of all ye Carv'd worke belonging to gray Cloath bed and putting on all ye Case   05.10.00

ffor 15 Doz of twill for ye inside of ye bed att 12d p doz   00.15.00

ffor 8 doz of Scarlet twill for ye outside of ye bed   00.12.00

ffor ye putting up of ye sd bed and unlynging yt great curtines & fixing yn a new wt silke thread & tape   01.05.00

ff 2 wood screws 4 spicks wt ropes to put up ye tester   00.04.00

ffor ye laying of ye matt under ye bed   00.02.06

ffor gallom & wyre nails to put round ye matt   00.05.00

June ye 4th for ye taking asunder 2 door Curtings to make biger wt that vallne all lynd wt green sarge & border'd wt silke gallom all round   00.12.00

ffor 5 yds of green sarge to make out ye lyning of ye sd Curtings & ye vallne att 2 sh & 2d p yd   00.10.10

ffor 2 laths & 4 holdfasts for ye sd Curtings   00.02.00

ffor 20 yds of green Silke gallom att. 3d p.yd.   00.05.00

ffor thread silke tapes & rings   00.02.00

ffor ye making & putting up 2 window Curtings & ther vallne of crimson taffity lynd wt shallon   00.14.00

ffor ye making & putting up 2 Indian Callico window Curtings & ye vallne lynd wt Callico, trim'd wt Crimson Silke gallone   00.14.00

ffor 2 pullee laths   00.05.00

ffor silke thread, tape & ows wt plumets & holdfasts   00.05.00

ffor 36 yds of silke Casing line for ye sd Curtings   00.12.00

May ye 1st 1701 ffor ye Cutting out ye black Cloath hangings and pntg. ffor 4 nails   00.10.00

ffor ye making & putting up 2 black window Curtins & there vallns trim'd wit blake silke, gallome all round   00.12.00

ffor all ye Silke gallom, wt thread, silke tape, rings and great black line to draw them   00.18.00

ffor a oacken bedstead, taster, Cornishes, base moldings & head board for ye yellow damaske bed   12.10.00

ffor ye Carving of all ye sd bed to wit ye head board, taster, Cornishes & base mouldings   13.10.00

Septbr ye 2nd 1701 ffor 35 yds & ½ of yeallow lining that lynes ye head board ye head Cloath ye taster & Counterpane att 12d p yd.   01.15.06

ffor 9 yds of Buckraham that lynes ye outt Side Vallances, ye Inside Vallance & Bases at 1 sh & 4d p yd   00.12.00

ffor a polisht rod 2 wood screws 2 chains & 4 spicks   02.05.00

ffor silke Thread, tape, rings for ye sd bed   01.10.00

ffor all ye upholsterers worke now done to ye sd bed and for Covering att ye wd worke   14.00.00

ye 20th ffor a oaken bed stead head board tester, Cornishes and base moldings for ye white Indian Imbroidered bed   09.10.00

ffor all ye Carved worke to ye sd bed viz head board & taster   04.05.00

ffor a polisht rod 2 chains, 2 wood screws & 4 spiks   02.00.00

ffor 51 yds of blue linen to lyne ye head board head Cloath roman Curtings taster inside Vallne out side vallance and bases att 12d p.yd.   02.11.00

ffor silke thred, tapes, rings, round ows, and other furniture for ye sd bed   01.10.00

ffor 8 yds of blew Buckraham yr lynes ye vallns bases and drapes att 1s p yd.   00.08.00

ffor all ye workemanship bellong ye Sd bed trim'd wt gold gallom all over   12.00.00

ye 22d ffor a ocken bedstead headboard, taster, Cornishes and base moldings for ye wrought bed lynd wt yeallow   09.00.00

ffor all ye Carved worke belonging to ye sd bed which is head board & taster   03.10.00

ffor a polisht road, 2 chains, 2 wood screws & 4 spicks   02.00.00

ffor 48 yds of lying that lynes ye head board head cloath taste inside vallne out side vallne and bases att 12d p yd.   02.08.00

ffor 7 yds buckraham yt lynes ye outsyde vallance and ye bases att 1 sh. 2d p yd.   00.08.02

ffor silke threed, tapes, rings, round ows and other small thgs   01.10.00

ffor all ye workemanship belonging to ye sd bed trim'd wt fringe of ye lyning   11.00.00

Novembr ye 12th payd to bring ye white Sattin bed from my Lord Peterborow's to your Grace's house   00.03.00

22d ffor making & delivering of wallnuttree Saffoy stuff wt hare and lether bags filled wt Swan feathers covered wt gold & silver imbroidery trim'd wt gold gallom wt ye Sarge & other Small furniture   06.15.00

December ye 11th 1701 ffor ye wallnutree Elbow Charet Stuff wt

Curle hare Cover'd wt gold Coular'd lining ye Cases lyned wt ye Same and Buckraham all under ye gold galloom and all ye Sarge for ye Backs and all other small furniture, threed, tapes, silke, hooks & O's att 50s.

p. Chare   10.00.00

                                                             ──────────

                        Sume in hole   138.06.02
                        Receded in part   30.00.00

                                                             ──────────

                        Rests Dew   128.06.02

Decembr ye 13th 1701

25. 1710 'A True and Just Accompt of all and Singular the Goods, Chattells and Credits of John Poictevin, late of the parish of St James in the liberty of Westminster, but in the Kingdome of France widower . . . deceased, which have come to the hands or possession of Stephen Penson, the Nephew of the Sister and administrator of the goods of the said deceased.' [Signed 22 January 1710]

                        P.R.O., *Prob. 30/54 ff.28–35*

Etienne (Stephen) Penson, Poictevin's nephew, may well have taken up contacts in England made by his uncle for his own work as an upholsterer (see pp.135–8). This accounting shows the large amount of money due to the estate from the deposed James II.

[Summary]

£149 17s, to be deposited in Penson's hands, 'and to be received by him, the said Accomptant', of Esquire Norton, the late Dutchess of Buckingham and the Lord Cholmondley and the value of the yellow worsted damask bed also mentioned in the said Inventary'.

1698 2 guineas lent by Penson to Poictevin; 12s for one thousand gilt nails 'sent by the deceaseds order to him at Mr Conyers house'. £4 'payd by him this Accomptant to Mr Toulouse, Embroiderer by the deceased's Order'. [This may be a reference to Stephen Toulouse, an embroiderer (P.R.O., LC9/144, 1713–14)].

£3 10s 'for an Easy Chair . . . sold to the Dutchess of Norfolk'. £3 18s 'lent by him to the said deceased at severall times when he was in trouble with my Lord Ranelegh'.

December 1700 3. 15s paid to Mr Haisman by the said deceased's order. [This may be a reference to Henry Heasman, a London upholsterer in a considerable way, who, with his son, also Henry, traded 1687–1750. See Beard and Gilbert (1986) p.418.]

£6 'to redeem a Yellow Damaske Bed'.

£8 8s 'for the discharge of the said deceased's son, John Poctivin . . . out of a Regiment of Dragoons'.

31 January 1707 £17 5s 10d. Paid to Mr Dottin, junior the Attorney for Law Charges of the Suits between the deceased and the Lord Cholmondley and the Dutchess of Buckingham and others.

£119 2s 6d 'a debt due from the said deceased to Peter Poictevin . . . and assigned by the said Peter Poictevin to this Accomptant.

Appended is a document:

'A True and Perfect Inventory . . . of John Pocitevin' which mentions four sums of money 'received in the deceased's lifetime by vertue of a Letter of Attorney' – £36 10s from General Chomley; £38 7s 6d from 'Esq Norton'; £30 'of the late Dutchess of Buckingham'; £35 from 'the Lord Cholmondley' and 'a yellow worsted damask bed now in this Estate's possession worth about £10'.

From Charles Chevalier, due £18

Her present Majestie Queen Ann when princesse of Denmark   £70

The Lord Ranelagh   £72
Mr Poulteney   £3 7s
The Lady Fretwell   £4 3s
The late King James the Second   £2,377 16s
                [Total]   £2,544 7s

Signed by Stephen Penson, 22 January 1710.

26. 1714 **Queen Anne's Bed**
        Royal Archives, Windsor
        R.A., 81105, nos 10, 15, 17
                and 20

This splendid bed is at Hampton Court (Pls 132–6)

10th August 1714 The Bedchamber, Windsor
Richard Roberts, Joyner

For a large carved molding Teastor and headboard wth large molding Cornishes and Base moldings   26 – –
For a Sett of large cups turned all Hollow   2 – –
For a Sett of strong smooth filed Curtain Rods & platoons to the said Bedd   2 – –
For 3 large molding wind° Cornishes and fixing them up wth Iron Work   5 5 –
For 8 handsome Wallnuttree square stool fframes pollished
For an Elbow Chair fframe Suitable   2 15 –
For 3 large packing cases & packing them up   2 10 –
For 12 days work helping to fix up all the said ffurniture   3 6 –
For 5 Dayes work at Severall times, used 4 Deals ½ wth Nailes and holdfasts   1 8 6

[R.A., 81106, no.15.]

John Johnson and Comp: Mercers For 321 yds. 1/8 of white, Crimson & yellow figur'd Velvet for a Standing Bedd Compleate, three pair of large wind° Currtains, Vallance and Cornishes, a large Arm Chair and 8 square Stools at 425 p. yard   674 7 3
For 81 yds: of white Sattin to line ye said Bedd & Curtains at 10s   40 10 –
For 125 yds ½ of white Mantua silk to line the sd: window Curtains and Vallance at 7/6   47 1 3

[R.A., 81107, no.17.]

Hamden Reeve, Upholsterer

For dyed linnen and Buckram to line the double Vallance, Bases, Testor & headcloth   2 5 –
For smooth filed Brass rings and fferrit Ribbons for the Curtains
                                                1 13 –
For making the ffigured Velvet Bedd covering and laceing the Teastor, headboard and Cornishes, the Curtains and Counter point lined wth. silk and the whole Bedd richly trimed: with silk Lace
                                                25 – –
For Sewing Silk, thread, tape &c: used   1 15 –
for Bottoming Backing and rolling Armchair and 8 Stools   – 18 –
For dyed linnen and hair to cover the Stools, and Stuff the Back of the Chair   1 – –
For Ticken Bagge filled wth. fine Goose feathers for yᵐ   7 10 –
For making up and covering wth. ffigured Velvet the Stools and Chair laced wth. Silk lace   2 2 0
For Making 3 pair of large figured Velvet window Curtaines lined with silk and covering and laceing the Vallance and Corniches
                                                12 – –
For three large smooth filed Rodds wth. double brass pullys in them and Spring Hooks   3 10 –
For smooth filed brass rings and ferrit Ribbons for the said Curtaines
                                                2 – –
For Buckram to line the wind° vallance   – 10 –
For Sewing Silk, thread, tape &c: used   – 17 6

For a very large fine Burnisht case Rodd double gilt with gold
15 – –

For 4 Men 7 Dayes to take down the old furniture and affix up the
new
8 8 –

[R.A. 81109–81110, no.20.]

William Weeks, Laceman

A Standing Bed complete 3 pair of large wind° Curtains Vallance and Cornishes a large Armchair and 8 square Stools for the Bed-chamber there.

For 336 Yards $\frac{1}{2}$ of broad mix'd Lace upon an Arras ground at 3s/4d p. yard
56 1 8

For 402 Yards of narrow Ditto at 2s/9d p. yd
55 5 6

For 81 Yds: of D° line weight 40 ou: $\frac{1}{2}$ at 2s/6d
5 1 –

For 3 large tassells wth. lead and pully's suitable at 10s each 1 10 –

For Making severall patterns to shew her Matie
5 – –

27.   1715 State Bed for the Prince and Princess of Wales
Royal Archives, Windsor, Great Wardrobe Accounts.

This Bed is also at Hampton Court (Pls 137–8, sometimes called Queen Caroline's Bed).

Furniture 1. State Bed
Lord Chamberlain's Warrant 28 March 1715
. . . a Crimson Damask Bed with Bedding . . . with case curtains for ye Bed of Taffaty . . .
[R.A., 81160, no.47.]
Sept. 1715
Supplied by Richard Roberts, joiner – a large Bedstead all Oak, the bottom to hang low with Iron work, a very large handsome carved Teastor and Cornishes, a very rich carved headboard and Base mouldings
– a Sett of large Cups turned all Hollow and carved
– a Sett of large Smooth filed Curtain Rods and Platoons etc for the said Bedd
[R.A., 81163, no.52.]
Supplied by Richard Chamberlayne & Co – 282 yds of rich Crimson genoa Damask, 480 yds of Crimson Taffata
– 116 yds of white florence Sattin to cover 2 Down Beds (P & P of Wales's Aparts)
[R.A., 81166–81167, no.62.]
Supplied by Thomas Phill & Jerem Fletcher Upholsterers – Buckram to line the Outside and inside Vallance and Bases, and dyed linnen to line the head Board
– very large pollished Rings and ferril Ribbon for ye Curtains
– embroidering very richly the Crimson silk Lace with raised work on the Outside and inside Vallance, Bases, headcloth and Coun-terpoint
– covering and laceing a very large carved Teastor and headboard, a Sett of large carved Cornishes, Base mouldings, and Carved Cupps for the corners.
Making up the Crimson Damask Bedd all compleate the Vallance and Counterpoint lined with Crimson taffata
– Crimson ingrain Silk and other Materials used about the said Bedd
– a very large Strong case Curtain Rodd double gilt and gold and Standards to it
– large pollished Rings and ferril Ribbons for the Case Curtains
Supplied by Thomas Phill & Jerem Fletcher Upholsterers – Making 4 very large case Curtains of Crim: taffata
– Crimson ingrain Sewing Silk used about the same
– a very large Down Bedd and Bolster with Demity case
– 3 large thick ffustian Mattress's, one of y°° covered w°° White Sattin
– holland Quilt covered w°° White Sattin

– Quilting and Making a pair of large white sarcenett Blanketts
– a pair of fine large fflannel Blankets bound w°° Ribbon
[R.A., 81165]
Supplied by William Weeks Laceman – 617 yds: $\frac{1}{2}$ of very broad rich Crim. ingr. silk arras lace . . .
– 2,740 yds of narrower Ditto . . .
– 399 yards $\frac{1}{2}$ of naileing Ditto . . .
– 90 Doz and 6 yds of breed Ditto . . .
(These items for bed and other items as well)
Receipt of Yeoman of his Majesty's Removing Wardrobe 12 May 1716 for . . . a standing bed of State all compleat, the furniture of a Crimson Damask and a counterpaine of the same . . . all trimmed with a rich arras silk lace suitable and a case curtain to the bed of crimson taffaty . . . also Bedding, a large down bed and satting bol-ster and 2 satting pillows, 2 fustian mattresses, one thick satting quilt, one thin satting quilt, one pair of flaning blankets, one pair of sarsnett blankets . . .

28.   1727 Kensington Palace
Work by Thomas Phill
P.R.O., LC9/384 Pt.II
(unpaginated bills)

Thomas Phill was one of the most innovative of the upholster-ers who worked for the crown. In this account, a year before his death, he was providing curtains to the new festoon fashion and providing comfortable chairs.

9 January 1727
For the Great Gallery at Kensington

– For fine dyed Linnen to line the Crimson Damask Hangings
25.10.00

– For making the Crimson Damask Hangings lined with linen and trimd with crimson Arras lace   26.00.00

– For putting up ye sd Hangings and for Sewing Silk and nailes used
5.2.00

– For 9 very strong pollisht pully rods and hooks   5.8.00

– For fine large pollisht brass rings and ferrit for 9 pair of crimson Damask window Curtains, Buckram to line the Vallance and brass pully's for the side lines   5.8.00
For making up 9 pair of crimson Damask Window curtains, the Lace richly Embroider'd upon ye Vallance with large carved Cornishes   18.00.00

– For putting up the 9 pair of Crimson Damask Window Curtains and Vallance   18.00.00

– For Sewing Silk, Nails and Glew us'd abt ye Sd Curtains, Vallance & Cornishes   1.18.00

– For O's stay tape, Leaden plumbets, sewing silk and making 9 festoon false curtains of crimson shalloon and for 9 wire Rods sew'd to the bottoms to make them draw straight   5.8.00

– For nails and putting up the false curtains and for 18 brass screw pinns for the lines   1.8.00

– For Girtwebb, bottoming rolling [?] curled hair linnen and stuffing 20 square stools   12.00.00

– For Stuffing 2 Easy Elbow Chairs Do   5.16.00

– For making crimson Damask covers for the 20 square stools and fixing on the same   9.00.00

– For making crimson damask covers for the 2 Elbow Chairs and fixing them on   1.16.00

– For making false cases of crimson taffety for the 20 square stools
4.00.00

– For making false cases Do for the 2 Elbow Chairs   16.00.00

29. *c.*1730–1 A Particular of New Furniture Order'd for His Majesty at HAMPTON COURT

P.R.O., LC5/89, f.143

There was not a great deal of activity at Hampton Court for some years after William III's death in 1702, but by the date of this bill, three years into the reign of George II, the upholsterers were busy again.

The King's Side

Presence Chamber Four long forms to be new cover'd with crimson Serge; four Crimson taffaty window curtains to draw up, with new cornishes and vallce; one large hanging Pier Glass in a walnuttree frame and a table and pair of Stands; Two large Glass Sconces in Gilt frames with two arms each; one pair of wrought brass Arms to the Chimney.

A Room called Kg William's Eating Room Three pair of crimson taffaty window curtains to draw up wth new cornishes and vallce; two long forms to be new coverd wth crimson Damask; 1 pr of wrought brass arms to ye Chimney; and a gilt branch wth a Silk lyor to carry twelve candles.

Privy Chamber Three pair of crimson taffaty window curtains to draw up, with cornish and vallence.

Withdrawing Room Three crimson taffaty window curtains to draw up, wth new cornish's & vallce to be trimd wth lace of ye Same Colour.

State Bedchamber Two pair of new crimson taffaty window curtains.

Back Stairsroom Six Strong wallnt matted bottom chairs.

First room in his Mats low Appts next ye Iron Gate One large mohogony table, 14 handsome wallnt matted bottom chairs with India backs, hanging peer Glass in a glass in a carved and gilt frame. A table and pr of Stands do.; 1 draw up crimson Silk window Curtain & Vallce; One Green cloth carpet for ye play table, 1 pr of wrought brass arms to ye Chimney & two cane blinds for ye windows.

The Bedchamber One pr of wrought Arms to ye Chimney; 1 pr of Stands and a table to match, the Glass & leather covers to do. and one wallnt night table.

A Waiting room Two wallnut card tables covered wth Green velvett trimd wth gold lace and Gilt nails; 1 pr of Wallnt Stands; 1 Dozn of new wallnt matted bottom chairs.

A Withdrawing room below ye Closett & waiting room Two crimson taffaty window curts to draw up wth vallce & trim lace to match ye goods in ye room. A hanging peer glass in a wallnt frame; a table and pr of Stands do. with leather cover.

Corner closett Three crimson taffaty window curts & vallce, lines etc; a hanging glass in a wallnt frame.

Closett next ye Greenhouse A hanging glass to match with ye bureau.

Chappell Closett One Arm chair for her Maty coverd wth velvet & trimd to match one here; 4 square Stools coverd wth ditto & footstool do.; 2 hassocks for their Mats coverd do.

Ld Bedchamber dressing room One large wainscot flap table.

Groom Bedch close wait Two pr of Camblett window curts to match ye yellow camblett Bed; a wallnut matted bottom chairs; a Wainscot flap table; wainscot close Stool & pewter pann.

Do. in by wait. A 4 post field bed upon casters, green Camblett furniture and counterpne do.; a hanging Glass in a wallnt frame; do. table wth Drawers; 1 wainscot flap table; 1 wainscot Close Stool & pewter pann.

A passage room A wainscot flap table.

Servts room A new table Bedstead.

Gold Staff Officer Two pr of yellow taffaty draw up window curts & Six matted bottom Chairs.

Silver Staffs servt A wainscot close Stool & pewter pann.

Mr Brinkman Senr A 4 post field bed upon casters, green harrateen furniture; 2 pr of window curts do.; a small hanging glass in a wallnut frame; a wainscot flap table; a Wainscot oval dining table, six wallnuttree matt'd bottom Chairs; a wainscot close Stool & pewter pann & deal table. . . .

Her Majesty's Side

Presence Chamber Two long & 2 short forms coverd wth crimson Serge.

Private Oratory Two long forms and Six Square Stools to be coverd wth crimson Serge; one wallnuttree reading desk; two plain crimson velvet carpets for ye Duke and lined with crimson Serge.

Pg Bed wait room now a Side Board room Four mattd bottom chairs.

Woman Bed chr her Bed cha A 4 post field bed upon Casters, green mohair furniture and counterpn trimd wth lace of ye Same colour, a dressing Chair Stuffed & coverd Do., 6 wallnuttree matted bottom chairs. A hanging Glass in a wallnut frame and a table wth drawer Do.; a Small wainscot breakfast table.

Lady bed chr room An oval wainscot dining table; 1 peer glass in a wallntt frame; a table Do.; 3 callico window curtains.

Dos. dressing room One pr of crimson taffaty windw curts to draw up & a wainscot flap table.

Dos. Bed chr Two crimson taffaty windw curtns to draw up.

A Closett for Do. Two crimson taffaty draw up window curts; a dressing glass in a wallntt frame; 1 wainscot flap table & wainscot breakfast do.

Her woman A Square deal table wth a drawer.

Wom Bed chr in Close wait a Closet 1 pr crimson harratn window curts, with a Small Wainscot dress table & a Dressing glass; 3 matted bottom Chairs.

A room lately a Bedr but now to see company in Two pr of crimson harateen draw up window curts; a hanging Glass in a wallnut frame; a table & pr of Stands; 6 matted bottom Chairs wth India Back; a wainscot flap table; a wainscot Close Stool & pewter pann.

Her woman A 4 post field bed upon Castors, green parragon furniture, & a deal table wth a drawer.

Mrs Howard two rooms & a closett One peer glass in a walnut frame, gilt Edge; a pr of Stands Do. a wallnutt Cabinet; a mohogony breakfast table; 1 wainscot do., with a green cloth carpet; a pr of wrought arms to ye Chimney.

Her Woman's room A 4 post field Bed upon Casters, green parragon furniture, 4 matted bottom chairs; a Square deal table wth a drawer.

A maid's room A press Bedsteady with Green Stuff furniture.

For the room lately the Countess of Sussex Four pair of harrateen window curtains; 2 field Beds of the same; 2 hanging peer glasses in Wallnt frames; 2 tables & 2 stands Do. with leather covers; 3 wainscot flap tables; 24 wallnt matted chairs; a night stool & pann.

Mrs Ireland a necessary woman An oval wainscot dining table; 6 matted bottom chairs.

Another room for do. 3 Strong wooden Chairs; a small Wainscot breakfast table.

Mrs Malibone & Mrs Hamling Two 4 post field Beds upon Casters, green harrateen furniture, a small Glass; Six matted bottom Chairs; 2 square deal tables with drawers; 2 draw up window curts ye same as ye Beds; a small wainscot ovall table; a wainscot close stool & pewter pann.

Servant to Do. A table Bedstead & 2 ordny matted bottom Chairs.

. . .

30. 1735 Chiswick House, Middlesex
Stephen Langley to the third Countess of Burlington,
11 April 1735

Chatsworth, MS., 247.0

As Langley died in 1735, the £218 was paid to his wife. The armchairs by Langley survive at Chatsworth, Derbyshire (state music room), but are now upholstered in crimson cut-velvet.

For tenn Large Elbow chair frames made wt fine Carved feet, Elbows & Stumps in the Wood, whiting wt Keywork flowers, Oak leaves, Acorns and other Ornaments very richly gilt in Burnish'd gold after the most curious and compleated manner at 8£ 5s each

82. 10 –

For Girts, bottoming, fine curld hair, white linnen to lyne, other materials requisite, work in Stuffing up backs and Seats to tenn Elbow Chairs   10 – –

For 5,200 of Charriot Bullion nailes double gilt wt gold used to the ten Chairs, two Saffoys, to trim yr Damask hangings at 18s p hund.

46. 16 –

For 170 Ounces $\frac{1}{2}$ of the best fine green Baladine Silk fring cut, made wt a broad head to it used to ye 10 Chairs, 2 Saffoys and hangings

22. 14. 8

For makeing 30 yards of fring out of her Ladyps knotted silk, providing silk for the head   1 – –

For 3 ounces $\frac{3}{4}$ of Knotted silk fring wanting to make good the trimming to the Window Curtas   – 13. 1$\frac{1}{2}$

For work covering the back Seats of ye Tenn chairs wt green Damask ornamented wt Silk fring and gilt nails   4 – –

For Two Large Saffoy frames wt Carved feet, Elbows and other Ornaments richly gilt in gold made suiteable to the Chairs at £11.15

23. 10 –

For gerts, bottoming, fine curld hair, white Linnen to lyne, other materials requisit, Stuffing up 2 Saffoys at £2.12.6 each   5. 5 –

For Work covering the backs and Seats suiteable to the Chairs at 17/6 Each   1. 15 –

For 9 yds of fine green waterd haratine used to ye back part of 10 Chairs and 2 Saffoys   – 18 –

For 20 Ouns of green Silk lyne used to ye windo curts. a) 18d

1. 15 –

For 64 yards of Strong Linnen to lyne & Sewing the same together to interlyne the Damask Hangs in the Room at Chiswick 3. 17. 6
For Sewing Silk other materials needful and makeing up the hangings redy to be fixt up in the Room   2. 15. –
For work makeing up 3 large draw up Window Curtains neatly trimm'd wt Silk knotted fring   2. 5 –
For Oes, tape, plumets, Sewing Silk, 3 large window boards wt boxholes, 6 brass hooks, long hooks and other materials 1. 12. 6
For work at Chiswick in putting up the hangings in the Room trimm'd wt Silk fring ornamented with large Bullion nailes, fixing up ye Window Curtains in the new House, Sewing on rings and plumets & reparing all ye window-curtains in the Old & new Houss, sewing on the Oes of the velvet Bed curtains, ye counterpane and crimson Silk cases takeing down 4 Pcs of Tapestry hangings at Sutton Court, mending ye 4 Pcs of Tapestry hangings & putting up, takeing down ye green camlet Bedcurtains, Sewing on the rings, mending ye curtains, mending 2 Damask leather carpets, Silk, rings, other materials   5. 10 –
Paid Board wages for 2 Men 24 Dayes Each, one Man 9 Dayes 57 Dayes   2. 17 –
For an Extraordinary large lead Mould weight Boxpipe, Strong Iron Staple & Turn'd handsome wood mould, made compleat, trimmed wt fine green knotted Balladine silk fring used in covering the large

lead and wooden moulds   6. 17. 6
For a very strong green silk Raine lyne to the Sconce compleat

2. 15. –
_____
£229. 6. 3$\frac{1}{2}$

deducting out of the £5 10s charged for worke &c as above what relates to ye Velvet Bed Tapestry hangins &c being since charged to his Lordp accot & out of board £2 6. And the Executors on Account of p sent pay admit to above the Sume of 09 – 3$\frac{1}{2}$

11 6 3$\frac{1}{2}$
_____

Reduceth this bill to   218 0 0

31. 1736 William Bradshaw to the Earl of Stanhope
Kent C.R.O., MS., U 1590, A20a

This account includes details of the two sets of Bradshaw's chairs which survive at Chevening. One of the tapestry chairs is illustrated here (Pl. 198).

. . .

Camblett Room
A Wainscott Bedstead, Sacken &c   2 – –
A Teaster, Cornish & Case Lath   1 15 –
A Strong Compass Rod and hooks   – 15 6
128 yds fine green Camblett in a Bed. 3 Pr of window Curtains and Chairs   a 2/6   16 – –
14 Dozen & 2$\frac{1}{2}$ yds of Lace to Do   2 9 8$\frac{1}{2}$
6$\frac{1}{2}$ yds of Stuff to Line the Vallens and Window Laths   – 6 6
7 yds Buckrum 10$\frac{1}{2}$ yds, wide Canvas   – 17 6
Making the Bed, Rings, Tape and brass Hooks   3 – –
A Large flanders bordered feather Bed and bolster filled with 60 lb of the best Swan Feathers   8 – –
2 down Pillows   1 4 –
3 Blanketts   2 11 –
A white Callico Quilt   3 12 –
A white holland mattrass   2 5 –
Making 3 draw up Curtains, Rings, Silk, tape, lace   1 11 6
3 Laths box holes and bracketts   – 7 6
28 yds green silk breed   – 4 8
9 Leads & 48 yds green silk Line   1 5 6
6 Cloak Pinns   – 3 –
6 Mahogany Chairs stufft & Cover'd Compleat   a 35s   10 10 –
A Easy Chair   3 8 10
15 yds fine Check in Cases to all the Chairs   a 2/6d   1 17 6
96 yds green Caffoy Paper to hang the Room   a 8/-   3 4 –
60 yds Bordering to the Paper   – 5 –
34 yds . . . [?] to Line the Paper a 6d   – 17 –
Pd for Cleaning 76 yds painted Serge that Came out of this Room

1 11 6

2 Spring Umbrellows and Rod   2 10 –
Drawing Room
135$\frac{1}{2}$ yds green mohair   cost   47 8 6
89 yds Linnen to Line the Hangings   a 10d   3 14 2
Making the Hangings, Silk, thread &c.   5 10 –
170 Sheets Cartridge Paper glewed together to putt behind the Hangings   4 1 3
7,800 gilt Nails   7 16 –
14$\frac{1}{2}$ yds green Silk, Nailing   – 18 –
11,500 Tax to this & other work   – 11 6
52 yds green Lutestring in 3 pr of Curtains   a 6/6d   16 18 –
52$\frac{1}{2}$ yds fine Stuff to Line Ditto   a 16d   3 10 –
35 yds Lace   a 3d   – 8 9

38 yds green silk breed a 1½d		– 4 9
3 Carved and gilt Cornishes, Bracketts &c.		4 10 –
61 yds green Silk Line to Ditto		1 10 6
9 Leads & 6 Cloak Pinns		– 3 6
Making the Curtains & Cover'd the Cornishes, Rings, Tape, Silk &c.		2 5 –
8 chairs a £2.3.7		17 8 8
20½ yds of Check in the Cases a 2/6d		2 10 –
Making the Cases, Tape &c.		1 3 –
2 Settees like the Chairs Compleat		8 17 –

. . .

Tapestry Room

12 Ells and 2/8 of Tapestry in 3 borders and two Additions a 3.3		37 16 –
Joyning D° and fitting the Peices to the dimentions		5 5 –
127 yds strong Linnen to line Do a 10d		5 5 –
101 yds Girt webb to bind		– 16 11
1,515 Eyes and Studds &c.		1 10 –
Lining Do, Silk, Thread &c.		9 10 –
50 yds green Lutestring in the 3 Windows		16 5 –
43¾ yds fine Yard wide Stuff to Line Do with		3 5 –
34 yds Lace a 3d		– 8 6
36 yds Breed to D° & Cornishes		– 4 6
3 Rich Carv'd gilt Cornishes		11 – 6
61 yds green Silk Line		1 10 6
9 Leads & 6 Cloak Pinns		– 3 6
Making the Curtains and Covering the Cornishes, Rings, Tape, Silk &c.		3 – –
14½ yds green Lutestring to back & make Scarves to the 8 Chairs & 2 Settees		3 16 8
8 Rich carv'd and gilt Chair frames a £3s 15s		41 12 –
Stuffing Do a £1 9s		
2 Settees Do. a £11 11s		23 2 –
29 yds fine green Genoa Velvett a 24s		34 16 –
20 yds fine Check in Cases to the Chairs		2 10 –
Making the Cases, thread &c.		1 13 4

The Carved Room

12 Large mahogany Elbow Chairs on Castors, finish'd with gilt Nails and fringe & holland Check Cases a £5.8.4 p.Chair [see Pl. 198]		65 – –
2 Large Saffoys Do & Cases & mohair to the cheeks		29 13 10
12 yds Lutestring in Scarves a 6/6		3 18 –
5 Ells of Tapestry to the Elbows a 42s		10 10 –
A Large mahogany Screen mounted		5 10 –

. . .

32.   1738–45 Longford Castle, Wiltshire. Accounts of furniture-making interest.

Longford Castle Archives

The importance of the furniture at Longford Castle, Wiltshire has been long known. The bills are not too helpful in determining exact authorship but there is no denying the quality (Pls 201–2).

1738 Feb. 4 Mr Bradshaw for a Tapestry Carpet	26. 5. 0
April 22 Mr Killpin the upholsterer, a bill	219. 15. 0
Dec. 14 Mr Hallet the cabinet maker, a bill	42. 0. 0
1739 Grenday the chair maker a bill with an allowance of £8.8.0 for a side board table he had from Red Lyon Street	68. 0. 0
1740 March 18 Mr Deschaux for 83 yards of green damask at 12s – for Longford Gallery	49. 16. 0
April 5 Mr Deschaux for 200 yds more of green damask at 12s for the Longford Gallery	120. 0. 0

November 21 Mr Goodison a bill for furniture at Longford	413. 0. 0
November 28 Mr Kilpin, the upholsterer, a bill, wherein there is £125 for the Gallery, £42 for the furniture of the Chappell at Longford & rest for gt pew etc in Conduit Street Chappell	179. 0. 0
1741 1 December Mr Goodison Cabinet maker a bill to ye 9 Sept. last	71. 11. 0
1742 May 21 Mr Goodison the cabinet maker a bill to this day	100. 0. 0
Dec. 17 Mr Bradshaw upholsterer a bill for a great chair at Longford	12. 8. 0
1743 March 31 Mr Philips on acct of green flowered velvet for Longford agreed at £1.4.0 a yard	150. 0. 0
May 28 Mr Hallett the cabinet maker on acct	15. 15. 0
May 28 Mr Kilpin the upholsterer on acct.	42. 0. 0
Mr Goodison the cabinet maker on acct	90. 0. 0
1744 Jan. 3 Mr Kilpin the remainder of his bill (NB paid 28 May £42 on acct).	240. 0. 0
1745 Jan. 5 Mr Kilpin ye upholsterer a bill (& some things to be sold)	89. 14. 6
Feb. 22 Mr Goodison ye cabinet maker a bill & he is to put a spring to the chimney blind	21. 3. 6
Feb. 25 Mr Kilpin a bill for Jakeys funerall	85. 17. 0

Layed out on the Gallery at Longford

For planning the Gallery, architrave round the doors, ornaments to the chimney, etc. at least	25. 0. 0
Painting to Gallery, at least	10. 0. 0
(Stucco, marble slabs and pedestals)	35. 0. 0
A carpet £14, – cleaning, mending and binding £3	17. 0. 0
83 yards of green damask at 12/-	49. 16. 0
Two hundred do.	120. 0. 0
Mr Goodison the Cabinet makers bill	400. 0. 0
Mr Kilpin the upholsterers bill	125. 0. 0
Carriage of the Chimneypiece & furniture	25. 0. 0
	1,296. 0. 0

33.   1752 Extract from Lady Leicester's 'An Account of Furniture for Holkham House, begun in 1752'.

Holkham MSS., Norfolk

The great Palladian house built for Lord Leicester still contains a fine array of upholstered rooms and furniture of the period 1750–70.

Saunders, Upholsterers Bill

For 1 set of Tapestry Hangings by Walton, 5 Pieces made by him	366 02 06
Part of Velvet Bed made up Chairs & 2 setts of leather chairs &c.	373 03 04

Carr   [Richard Carr, mercer]

164 yards white Damask	61 08 06
259 of velvet	899 10 00
349 Crimson Velvet	668 06 00
280 Crimson Damask	210 00 00
39 Crimson Damask	19 08 06
434 Crimson lutestring	190 06 00
62 of Armurine	34 02 00
[Addition is incorrect = £2,083 1s 0d]	2,094 05 06
244 Yards of Coffoy	195 1 00
318 of Belemine	199 00 00

419 of Ditto   251 00 00
193½ of Blue Damask   135 09 00

    780 10 00
Other Silks &c.   291 18 06

Total Carrs Bills   3,166 13 00
Deduct for Silks returnd   158 08 00

    3,008 05 00

Furniture Bought (& made up at Holkham) by Lady Leicester
Window Blinds   − 15 00
3 Tables   05 11 00
Blankets   03 19 00
Lanthorn   01 04 00
Quilts & tickings   02 15 00
Paper. 18 Peices for Lady Leicesters B Chamber   06 06 00
Ditto. Counting Room   03 09 00
Brown role   04 00 00
A Grate   05 17 00
A Stove   06 00 00
Lines
Nettley, Upholdster for Furnishing Lady Leicester Apartment &
Blue Paper   42 14 00
Jo Miller for 5 Picture Frames   11 09 06
Carr for Blue Lutestring   08 04 00
Cloth & Hair   04.08 06
Nettley   03 05 00
Pappe Mashe   03 17 09
Linings for Hangings & Tassells   08 08 03
Nettley making up the red Velvet furniture   38 12 08
... Furniture Bought to November 1765 by Lady Leicester
    2,480 07 10
In this list the architect Matthew Brettingham is noted as 'carving 35
Chairs, 4 Sophas, 4 Settees, 4 Picture Frames   86 12 10

34.   **1757 Croome Court, Worcestershire**
    Vile and Cobb to the sixth Earl of Coventry.
    Croome Court Archive, Furniture Bill 1 (Beard, 1993)

The Croome Court furniture bills, which I edited in 1993 are
among the most important that survive. Frequent reference is
made to them in discussing the careers of such leading makers
as Vile and Cobb and Mayhew and Ince (pp.206–8; see also
A35).

1757 May 13. For 2 Good 4 Post Bedsteads on Castors with
Mahogy foot Posts, Lath Bottom, Compass Rods & Cornishes to
Ditto   11 10 −
For 52½ yards of Silesia to Line your Cotton for a Furniture to the
2 Bedsteads   ½d yd   3 1 3
For Cloath to Line Head Cloath & Teaster   − 17 −
For Ditto to Line the Vallens & Cornishes   − 14 −
For Ditto to Line the Bases & Strapes   − 9 −
For 163 Yards of Binding   1 13 11½
For Rings, Thread, Tape, Studs &c.   1 − −
For Makeing the 2 Cotton Furnitures Lin'd Compleat   3 10 −
To 2 Garden Matts, Cord &c to Pack the 2 Beds   − 3 −
For 8 Good Mahogy Backstools Stuff'd and Quilted in Linen
    8 8 −
For 19½ yards of Silesia to Line your Cotton for Cases & Back
backes   ½d yd   1 2 9
For 34 yards of Binding   a 2½d   − 7 1
For Thread, Tape, Studs, Tax &c Makeing your Cotton into Cases
& Lin'd Compleat   1 4 −

For 4 Matts, Cord &c to Pack the 8 Chairs   − 6 −
For a Case &c to Pack ye 2 bed Furnitures & Cases &c.   − 9 −
Paid Cartage with Ditto to the Inn   − 4 6
May 28 For 2 Good Beds & Bolsters fill'd with sweet feathers & 4
white Fustian down Pillows   16 16 −
For 2 Good Thick Check Under Mattrasses   5 8 −
For 2 White Upper Ditto   4 4 −
For 6 Good Blankettes   4 13 −
For 2 Good Cotton Counterpaines   4 4 −
For 12 Matts 6 Paper Covers &c to Back Ditto   1 1 −
For 2 Good Mahogy Sopheys on Castors Stuffed & Quilted in
Linen, one Cover'd with your Damask & Nail'd with the Best Brass
Nails, the Other not Cover'd   18 − −
For a Case to Pack one of the Sopheys   1 10 −
For 3 Matts, Battens, Nailes, Cord &c to pack the other   − 10 6
Paid Cartage with Ditto to the Inn   − 9 −
July 9 For 6 Good Mahogy Sopheys on Casters for the Round
Summer House, Stuffed & Quilted in Linen   23 10 −
For Making your Cotton into Cases for Ditto   2 10 −
For 12 Matts, Battens, Nailes &c to Pack Ditto   1 14 −
For a Garden Matt Cord &c to Pack 22 Peices of Paper & Border
Came from Mr Bromwiches   − 2 −
   [Thomas Bromwich, fl.1740–87, see Beard (1981) p.248]
For 2 Pulley Laths & Bracketts   − 6 −
For 31 yds of Solesia to Line your Cotton for 2 Festoone Curtains
  ½d   1 16 2
For 32 yds of Lace   − 6 8
For Braides, Oes, Leades, Thread, Tape &c   − 5 −
For 12 yards of Line, 2 Tossells & 4 wrought hookes   − 12 −
For Makeing your Cotton into 2 Festoon Curtaines Compleat
    − 16 −
For a Case &c to Pack Ditto   − 1 6
...
For 7 Good Mahogy Arm'd Chaires on Castors Stuffd and Quilted
with your Damask and finish'd Compleat with a double Rowe of
Burnish'd Nailes   20 6 −
For 7 Check Cases to Ditto & 2 to ye 2 Sopheys & Carterage Paper
Cases, Strong thred with Cloth & 2 Ditto to ye Sopheys, Tape,
thread &c   9 15 −
For an Addition of 11 yds of Damask to Make out the Hangings
a 14s   7 14 −
For 10½ yds of Cloth to Line Ditto   3 18 −
For Silk, Thread, Tape &c   − 10 −
For Makeing the Hangings Compleat   2 10 −
...
For Itallion window Blinds Painted Green for your drawing roome
at Croome   9 15 −
   [Venetian blinds]
...
For 2 pulley Laths & Bracketts   − 6 −
For 35 yds of Blue Tammy to Line your blue damask for 2 Festoone
Curtains at 15d   1 17 9
For 24 yds of Fringe   at 10s   12 − −
For 49 yds of Lace   at 4d   − 16 4
For Braids, Oes, Leades, Silk, Thread, Tape &c.   − 8 −
For Makeing your Blue damask into 2 Festoone Curtenes, Lin'd &
fring'd Compleat   1 6 −
For a Case &c to Pack ditto   − 4 6
For a man 39 days repairing & Puttin up Furniture at Croome
at 3s 6d   6 16 6
Paid Coach hire & Expences   2 10 −
For a Man Laying Carpitts down & mending Cases to a Peir frame
&c.

Tax, Paste &c.   − 9 −
Jan 7 1758. Recd for self & Co.
Wm Vile

35. 1763 William France and John Bradburn to the sixth Earl of Coventry December 1763–September 1764
Croome Court Archive, Bill 22 (Beard, 1993)

Upholstery items only

1764 July 26. For a very good 4 post large Wainscott Bedsd on large Casters, double screw'd with a wainscott Lath Bottom, and double Wainscott headboard and stout Mahogy Foot posts neatly fluted with a Stave and Plinths at Bottom and a Sett of gadroon Cornices to Ditto and also an inside Cove Teaster and a pollish'd Compass Rod and Hooks.   9 6 −
For 79¾yd of fine yellow Silk Mohair   a 9/6   37 17 7½
For 122yd of Silk Binding to do   a 3½   1 15 7
For 62yd of Tamy to line the Vallens and Basis at 21d   − 11 4½
For 19½yds of fine dy'd Linnen to back line the head & Teaster and Vallens and Basis   a) 15d   1 4 4½
For pollish'd Rings, Silk and Thread, Glue, Paste &c.   − 11 −
For Making the Yellow Mohair Furniture to the above large Beds and Covering the Gadroon Cornices and Coves &c.   2 18 −
For a very good Feather Bed and Bolster Case filld with good and sweet Feathers   8 15 −
For a pr of large Fustian Pillow Cases fill'd with fine sweet Down   1 7 −
For a Check under Mattrass and a white upper Ditto to the Bedsd above with fine Scour'd Wool   5 14 −
For 2 very fine large upper Blanketts and Under, Do   3 18 −
For a large white Counterpane to Ditto   3 8 −
For a Man taking down a 4 post Bedsd and Furniture and putting up Ditto in the Nursery, Tacks &c.   − 1 6
For 46¼yd of yellow Silk Mohair   a 9/6d   27 19 4½
For 39yd of Silk binding to Ditto   a 3½d   − 11 4½
For Silk, Braid and brass Oes, Leads, Silk and Thread, Tax &c.

     − 9 −
For 53 yds of yellow Line   a 2½d   − 11 −
. . .
To a large Wainscott double Screw'd Bedsd very stout with a Wainscott Lath Bottom, and 2 Beares supported with strong Iron Shoulders and Foot Posts out of fine Mahogy 6 Inches Square worked very Correctly in a waving flute, and the Wave terminating with a Corinthian Capital, very well carv'd and neatly finish'd and a Carv'd pedestal to Ditto   16 4 −
For a Sollid Dome to take in Part with a Cove at the Bottom in the Inside and a Vitruvian Scrole all round the Top of the Cove and a Carv'd Ornament in the Centre of the inside, the outside of the Bottom Part work'd in fluted Shapes to fit over the opening of the Ornaments in the Cornice, & the Bottom Part divided from the Top by a Molding Carv'd with a Ovilo round where it is worked hollow in the Bottom Part below the Molding, the whole outside a Dome finish'd with a large Centre Vauze   18 9 −
For a Sett of Cornices the Bottom Part Cov'd and fluted all round and an Ornament in the Centre of each and an Ovilo put round above the Cove and a busy carv'd Ornament above the Ovilo and a Wainscott frame cut in a Shape for a stuft headboard, and Iron Plates to fix the Cornices to the Dome   15 8 −
For 10½yd of Buckram to interline Vallens and Basis   a) 14d

     − 12 2
For 21¼yds of Tamy to back line the Vallens and Basis. Cover the head part of the Dome and the Bottoms behind Cornices and Laths, and to line the falls of the Counterpane   a 21d   1 17 2¼

For 15¼yds of fine green dyed Linnen to line the headcloth and Top of the Counterpane and Stuff the headboard   a 15d

     − 19 1¾
For 117yd of Silk Binding   a 4d   1 19 −
For best Curl'd hair and Bottoming &c for the headboard frame

     − 11 6
For 22yds of finest green Silk Lace at 8d   − 14 8
For 67yds of green Silk Bellendine Fringe 3 Inches deep with a double Gimp Head   a 6/6d   21 15 6
For 56yds of green Silk Bellendine Bow fringe   a 3/6   9 16 −
For 24yds of green Silk Vauze Fringe   a 15d   1 10 −
For 73yds of green Silk Line   a 4½d   1 7 4½
For 10 green Silk Tossells   a 3/6d   1 15 −
For 8 brass hooks to Ditto   a 9d   − 6 −
For 12 brass Screw pulleys   a 9d   − 8 −
For Buckram Heads and Paper for Vauze, and Serge for Base Bags

     − 6 −
For Silk Braids, Oes, Sewing Silk and thread to make the whole furniture and sew on the different fringes   − 14 −
For Glew, Paste and nails to Cover the whole Dome inside and out and all the Ornaments, the Cornices and all the flutes in Do and all the Wood work entirely − and Cord to make a large with Tacks, nalls &c to do the stuff'd headboard   − 16 −
For Making a furniture of Green Silk Damask to the large Bedsd above made to draw up in the inside of the Mahogy Footposts Fring'd every Part with broad & narrow fringes, and Covering the Dome inside & out and the outside fluted, and molding to Divide Ditto, Cornices and fluted all the other ornaments entirely − and stuffing and Covering the headboard, the headboard frame, and Making a Counterpane Lin'd all through and fring'd with a deep and a bow fringe and every other part Compleat.   13 4 −
. . .
For 3 Rowler Curtains of brown Holland gudgeons &c. Staples and made to draw up with Silk Line and brass Sliding Pullys for the 3 Windows in the Bedchamber and Dressing Room   a 24s

     3 12 −
For 6 Mahogy arm'd Chairs on good Strong Castors with a mahogy molding all round the Seat, and the arms neatly fluted and finish'd with a rich fluted Rose. Stuff'd in fine Linnen   a 46s   13 16 −
For 4½yds of Stuff for the back backs of 6 Chairs and Strong Cloth first nail'd under Ditto   − 9 6
For best burnish'd nails to the above 6 Chairs   2 − −
For green Silk Twist Silk and thread, Tacks &c and welting Cord

     − 9 −
For Covering with Green Silk Damask the 6 Arm'd Chairs above border'd, welted and Quilted, and finish'd with burnish'd nails, and double Sow'd   a 7/6d   2 6 −
For a large Mahogy Sofa, on Strong Casters, with a molding work'd all round the Seat and Mahogy arms fluted and finish'd with a rich flut'd Rose at Top, Stuff'd in fine Linnen and Cording, with a bolster at each end   6 4 −
For best burnish'd nails to the Sofa   13 6
For Stuff and Strong Canvas for back Backs & Tacks   − 6 6
To Silk Twist Silk and thread, welting Cord tacks &c.   − 2 6
For Covering with green Silk Damask the Sofa and Bolsters above and finishing Ditto with a double Row of burnish'd nails   − 13 6
For 6 Cases of green ½ Inch worsted check to the Chairs above

     2 14 −
For a Case of Ditto check to the Sofa and Bolsters   1 14 6
For a Carpet and Border/Moors uncut sort/to go round the Large Bed above
     Cost of Moor   8/6d p yd   6 5 4
[This is a reference to the carpet maker, Thomas Moore (see

p.160, and Hefford (1977))]
For 9 Matts, 3 large Paper Covers and Cord to pack the Beding &c.
         − 18 −
For 8 packing Cases to pack the Dome, Cornice and pillars, Chairs, Sofa and furniture &c., containing 571ft at 3d   7 2 9
1764 Sept 15   For 6 Mahogy french armd Chairs on Casters with a Bead on the feet and arms neatly carv'd to a drawing, Stuff'd and Cover'd with black Spanish Leather bordered, welted, quilted and Tuffted and finish'd with burnish'd nails   a 3.13.6   22 1 −
For 3 Cases, Battens, Screws, nails &c. 187ft a 3d   2 6 9
For 25 yd of green silk Line to a pattern sent from Croome   a 8d
         − 16 8

     Rec'd Jany 4th 1765 . . .
     (£343 13s 2d)   Signed
                    Wm France

36.   **1764–5 Moor Park, Hertfordshire**
      William France working for Sir Lawrence Dundas
        North Yorkshire C.R.O., MSS., ZNK X/1/26–30

Sir Lawrence Dundas was one of the most important patrons of Robert Adam and the neo-classical furniture-makers. Work was done in particular for his houses at 19 Arlington Street, London and Moor Park, Hertfordshire (see pp.211–12).

Upholstery items only
May 1976
For a Wilton Carpitt, and Border of the roman Pavement Pattern for the blue Damask Dressing Room   13 14 6
For a Wilton Roman Pavement Carpitt to fill all round the Bed with a Boarder on the outside of Do, Tape, thread, tacks &c. 13½yds   4 1 −
June 1764
For 95½yds of large fine blue silk Line & very strong   a 2/8d
         12 14 8
For 40 large Tossels of fine Blue Bellindine silk a 4/10d to hang the Girandoles, and all the Pictures in long room, and making Ornaments over Do.   9 13 4
July 1764
For 2 Mens Time, taking down all the Curtains and Cornices in the House, and cleaning Ditto very well, and papering up the Cornices, paper, tacks &c, and taking up the Carpets, that cover all over the floors, in Lady Dundas's and Lady Charlotte's Dressing Rooms   1 2 −
For the use, & porteridge of 2 Trussels & a Board and making Hangings of Cateridge paper to cover the blue Damask hangings in the drawing Room & gilt border while the floor is new laying
         3 17 6
For putting up the paper hangings over Ditto, Damask Tacks & long white Nails &c us'd   − 18 6
September 1764
Taking Down the Cateridge paper hangings from the blue Damask hangings in the drawing Room, & putting up in the long Room, over the blue Damask Drawing Room, to preserve the Crimson Damask Hangings from the Dust, &c., while the floor is taking up & new laying. 5 Quire of new paper, glue Cloth & Tax & long white nails &c.   − 16 6
October 1764
Taking down the Cateridge paper Hangings from the Crimson Damask hangings in the long Room, 1 Pr stairs, & laying by in a Box.   − 4 −
For 2 Mahogony French arm'd Chairs on Casters, stuff'd and cover'd with Haircloth finished with a double Row of the best burnished Nails and Welted & quilted.   7 − −

For 42½yds of strong stout Tick to assist in straining the hangings the Rooms being so large and high   a 2/4d yd   4 19 2
For 19yds of stout brown Cloth to assist as the Tick above
    a 16d yd.   1 5 4
For making hangings of your own Crimson Genoa Damask, to fit the 2 large Rooms Compleat, & puting up the whole, & moving Trussels & scaffolding, as the Business required without which Assistance Rooms so large & so high, cou'd not be hung without the greatest Difficulty & large Expence.   28 16 −
November 1764
For hanging a China Closet in my Ladies dressing Room, with crimson plain paper, on Canvas back & sides & scraping the paint from the shelves, and then covering with the above Crimson plain paper . . .   3 8 −
Laying down the Carpet to cover all over the floor in the dressing Room . . .   − 2 −
December 1764
For making curtains of the above blue Morine [24¾ at 2/3d a yard] &c to the 2 windows in the Blue Room, in the Attick, and puting up Do Compleat, long Nails, Tax &c.   − 11 6
For 7 Yds of blue fringe for Bottoms silk hangers a 2s yd.
         − 14 −
For a blue & white Inch & Inch Check furniture to a 4 Post Bedstead head & Teaster Cloth lin'd and all bound, a paper Cover to Do, with 4 Olives to Tye Back the Curtains   3 17 −
For 3 Ticken sand Bags covered with Blue morine for the blue Drawing Room windows   − 6 6
[as draught excluders?]
For 3 Spring Barrels in Frames with Catches, green lutstring Curtains ferreted with silk Ferret and every other Particular; as the 3 in the Blue drawing Room on the ground floor, Silk, &c.
         9 10 −
January 1765
For a brown Leather Spot, for the gilt Table, lin'd with Flannel & bound all round with gilt Leather   − 1 6
March 1765
For a Carpet of the green Pattern, with border all round Do, to go round the Crimson Damask Bed. 15½ Yds of Carpet & Border
         4 13 −
For a Brass Rod, with projecting brass hooks & pulleys, & a Curtain to Do of full Lutstring bound with crimson silk Quality Lines, Tossels and Brass hooks compleat to Draw before the Picture of Sleeping Cupid in the fore Room   6 13 −
July 1765
Cleaning very well with bread & bran, all the large Damask Curtains & Cornices & papering up all carefully   − 11 −
August 1765
For lining of your Dogs Basket, with a hair Canvas Cushon all round covered with a crimson Serge Cushon, for the bottom thicker than the other & a Cover for Do, Serge for the Outside of the Top, Silk, & Thread, Tax &c.   − 11 −
December 1765
For a Brown Leather Cover [to a marble topped table carved with rams' heads and husks at £37 10s] lin'd with flannel with a fall to hang quite to the floor, welted & bound with Gilt Leather 1 15 −
For Scowering & Dying a Crimson Ingrain Silk India Damask, furniture of a Bed & Window Curtain &c. 262 oz a 13d p oz.
         14 5 4
For Scowering & new dipping 34 yds of full ¾ Crimson Lutestring a 8½d p yd   1 2 8

37. 1765–6 Fairfax House, York
Two bills from Mary Reynoldson (4 June 1765; 16 February 1766)

North Riding, Yorkshire C.R.O. MSS., ZDV(F), MIC 1128–9, 1131–2.

The Fairfax town house in York has been well restored and it is possible to feel something of the settings created for Viscount Fairfax and his family. Mary Reynoldson continued the successful business of her Catholic upholsterer husband, George Reynoldson, after his death in 1764.

4th June 1765   The Rigt Honble Lo Viscount Fairfax
To Mary Reynoldson Uph^r

14 yds green check all 21d per yd	1 4 6
6 yds yellow check all 21d per yd	0 10 6
4 Dozen large curtin rings	0 1 0
500	
24 "	0 1 0
26 June paid for unriping the chince curtin, fringe and Lining and making and fixing up ditto again	0 12 6
8 July 1½ yds check one brass latch and screws	0 3 11½
10th paid for news due 5 July as	2 10 0
paid Land Tax and window money	2 9 3
30 Augt. One quarters poor assessment	0 7 4
paid for repairing and mending furniture Desks Tables Drawers Chairs nails sprigs glue &c	2 18 9
Strong bedstead mahogone pillars upon casters bottom Laths bolster	6 5 0
Taking the crimson Damask bed curtins and vallens in pieces carrage up and down to London and dying ditto	4 5 0
Buckeram for the vallens and bases	0 9 0
Silk thread glue and paste used for the bed	0 8 9
Compass rod screw'd and altered	0 7 0
6 Dozen 6 yds crimson binding att 3:6 Dozen	1 2 9
3 Dozen 4 yds nailing	0 11 0
paid for new brass handle and jobs to White Smith	0 6 6
9th Oct. Land Tax and Windows paid	2 10 0
2 Novr. Serge used to cover two bed posts	0 5 0
one Rubber	0 2 0
Serge to cover screen and mending ditto	0 4 6
4 yds buckeram	0 4 6
7 yds Garter blew att 7^s:6	2 12 6
6 yds white persian att 2^s:9 yd	0 16 6
10 yds broad ariss binding – 21d yd	0 17 6
12 yds narrow Lace	0 12 0
7 yds ¾ of Ribon	0 2 7
Silk thread and making	1 6 0
13 Jan. 12 pounds wax thread	1 16 0
for carraing and fetching chairs tables &c – paid	0 5 6
24 Jan. cartrage paper India 2 yds Lining and covering) chimney stop in Drawing Room	0 12 0
	£37 01 8½

11th Feb 1766 Rec^d The Contents Full payment for Mary Reynoldson By Thos Lupton

The Right Honble Lord Viscount Fairfax
16 Feb. 1766 . . . Mary R..Noldson Uph^r Dr.

For 275 yds of Sky & Mixt Damask used for the Hangings of the Drawing Room, 3 pair Window Curtins 8 small and 2 Armed Chairs and one Large Soffa ATT 7/– yd	96 5 0
152 yds of Gold Burnished Border ATT 6/– yd	45 12 0
70 yds Tamy to line Window Curtins, Backs of Chairs and Soffa	
ATT 16d yd	4 13 4
8 dozen 2 yds Covered Binding used for Curtins 3/– doz.	1 4 6
3 Laths with Pulleys and Brakets used	0 12 0
Rings Tape Silk Thread, Leads used for Window Curtins	1 15 0
For 80 ounces of Fringe used for Window Curtins ATT 2/4 d p ounce	9 6 8
6 dozen Mixt Line and 12 Tassils and 4 Cloak Pins	1 18 0
Buckeram for the Heads and 84 Brass Hooks	5 0
For making up 3 pair Drapery Window Curtins, Tacks and Fixing up the same	2 14 0
8 Mahogone Chairs Fluted Feet Stufft Backs and Seats To Fine Linnen, Bordering and Wellting the Damask Covers, Gilt Nails Tacks Fringe and Finishing Ditto ATT 36/– Chair	14 8 0
2 Mahogone Armed Chairs upon Casters Stufft to Fine Linen. Back Seats and Armes Stufft and Carved [Covered?] and Wellting the Damask Covers, Gilt Nails Frings Tacks and Finishing Ditto	7 0 0
For Silk and Twist used for the Chairs and Soffa	8 0
For Sowing the Damask for the Hangings of the Room and Silk used	1 15 6
For 6 yds of Strong Linnen for . . . the Hangins 15d yd	8 1½
Tin Twopeny Nails, Tacks, 16 ounces Brass Pins used for Hanging the Drawing Room and Fixing on The Gold Bords	5 0 0
Worked Tassill and Line for the Bell	1 6
44 yds Blew and White Check used for 2 Armed Chairs and 8 small Chairs and Large Soffa ATT 22d yd.	4 0 8
Thread Tape and Making Cases for all	1 0 6
For Large Soffa Mahogoney Frame Upon Casters Carved Scroles & Stufft to Fine Linnen Welting and Bordering The Damask	
Gilt Nails Frings Tacks and Finishing ditto	14 14 0
	214 11 9½

21 March 1766   Recd: of the Right Honble Ld Viscount Fairfax two hundred and fourteen pounds

38. 1767 Mayhew and Ince to the sixth Earl of Coventry, 1767–8

Croome Court Archive, Bill 48 (Beard, 1993)

See note to A34

1767 June 16 Repairing a French Chiffonier, Wood Glue Wax &c.	– 10 3
1768 April Mounting Your Lordships own Tapestry, Backs with Crimson Lustring on a Neat Redwood Claw and Varnish'd Compleat	3 3 –
Making a Crimson Lustring Cover to do Borderd and Neatly Welted, Sewing Silk, Wealting Cord &c	– 2 6
1⅞ yds of full ¾ fine Crimson Lustring	– 16 10
	– 19 4

(April) 14 A Mahogy Round Study Chair Cover'd with Leather	3 8 –
June Loss by Carving Patterns for Stool to Closett, and Altering the four (when made) wider and making out the Ornament Prime Cost	2 2 –
Sept 1st An Upholsters time at Croome 6 Days	1 10 –
To My going to Croome about the Tapestry, & for Carriage and Expences for Self and the Man	10 10 –
3 lb Rusia Leather	– 3 –
A very neat Carved Stand for Bason & Ewer of Redwood and Varnish'd	14 17 –
Decr 16 yds of Green Druggett Carpett for the Octagon Room 1½ yards wide a 5/–	4.00
Thread Tapes Making to Compleat fitting & fixing	4 8 6
	– 8 – 6

39. 1771–2 Mayhew and Ince to the sixth Earl of Coventry

Croome Court Archive, Bill 61 (Beard, 1993)

See Note to A34

1771   July

Two Fine Brown Holland spring Blinds with brass Racks & Rowlers   3 12 –

Three Men's Time at Croome putting up the Tapestry, Making Paper Case hangings for ditto Stuffing & Covering 2 Settees & 6 Chairs, fixing Gilt Border & sundry other Jobbs and going & Coming. viz.   28 1 6

Jones 44 Days at	6/–	11.0.0
Elwood 44 "	4/6	9.18.0
Bolton 41 "	3/6	7.3.6

Paid the 3 Mens Coach hire, there and back   6.18.0

Ditto, their Expences	2.14.0	
Ditto, Carriage of Tools &c.	– 9 –	
Paid their Lodging	2.10.0	2 11 0

10,000 Jovial Tacks 2000 Clout Nails   1.12.0

6 yards of fine Linnen for over the Doors, yard wide   – 6. –

6 Yards of Girth Webb, 18 Yards of strong
Boote tape, One Ounce of Sewing Silk,   2 13 6

4 Ounzes of Yellow thread & 24 1½ Inch Screws   – 15.6

104 yards of Linnen, Yard wide, for Taper Case hangings   4.6.8

14 Quire of large Cartridge Paper   0.17.6

                                                                                  5 9 2

2000 Tinn'd Tacks   0.5.0

With repairs to two Japan Lamps, a mahogany combtray, a gilt lantern, a mahogany frame for winding silk, and a mahogany claw table, done from February to April 1772, the firm was paid £71.6s in all on 10 June 1772.

40. 1774–5 Mayhew and Ince to the sixth Earl of Coventry

Croome Court Archive, Bill 70 (Beard 1993)

The almost daily attention of a leading firm to the minutiae of dealing with curtains, blinds and beds is well in evidence in this bill. Only the upholstery items are shown here for the London town house.

1774   *June 22* A Man fixing up a rolling Blind in Drawing Room, Us'd 2 Iron Plates and Screws   – 2. 9

24th 2 upholsterers taking down 11 Window Curtains & Cornices in the first Floor and Dining Parlor & 2 Window Curtains in your Lordships dressing Room   – 6. 8

1775   *Jany 14th.* 2 Upholsterers fixing up 3 Window Curtains & Cornices in Parlor 3 Do in Drawing Room, 2 in Anti Room, 2 in Lady's dressing Room, 2 in Lords dressing Room, one in Octagon Room, the Paper Teaster to my Ladys Bed & laying down the Drugget in Octagon Room.   3 Days   – 12. 0

Usd 500 Tacks & Nails and other Materials   – 2. 3

24th. 3 rolling Blinds of brown Holland with white silk Line, lackering your Lordships own . . . [?] Racks, Screws & fixing up Do.

                                                                                  3. 0. 0

Scraping & cleaning down & making good the Walls in your Lordships Closet & putting up 36 yards of thick brown Paper on the front & side Walls to keep out the Damp, Paste & 63 yards of fine stampt Paper included   – 10. 8

Elephant Paper put up with a thick interling Paper under it in your Lordship's closet & colair'd fine green in Verditure at 20d a

yard   5. 5. 0

31st An Upholsterer taking down a Window Curtain in Bed-chamber   – – 9

Feby 2d An Upholsterer fixing up a Window Curtain, Time & Nails   – 1. 0

An Upholsterer & a Cabinet maker fixing the Pulley Racks lower & rectifying the rolling Blinds in Drawing Room   – 2. 8

May 10 An Upholsterer taking down a 4 Post Bedstead and Furniture in the back Room, 2 pair Stairs fixing it up in the Nursery & removing a Crib Bed from the Nursery into the back Room Tacks and Nails usd.   – 2. 6

May 11 2 Men taking down a Bedstead fixing it up again for the Honble Mr Coventry
        Time and Materials   – 2. 9

18th An Upholsterer and a Cabinetmaker taking down 2 Bedsteads in the Middle Room, 2 pair Stairs fixing them in the left hand Room, fixing it in the middle Room, 2 pair Stairs & moving a Chest of Drawers

. . . Us'd 200 of white Tacks and 2 dropping Hooks   – 5. 0

June 3 2 Upholsterers taking down 2 Beds in the 2 pair Stairs moving and fixing them up in different Rooms
        Time and Materials   – 2. 8

(Part of a bill of £37.14.2, settled with discount at £36 and paid 23 June, 1775.)

41. 1786 Audley End, Essex
Chipchase and Lambert. A state bed for Sir John Griffin Griffin.

Essex C.R.O. MS., D/DBY A45/3

Chipchase and Lambert were a successful London firm whose activities are discussed on pp.222.

A very large Wainscot Bedsd. for a State Bed 7 foet long 6 foot wide with lath bottoms, side rails & proper fastonings to support the Counterpane, wainscot base & slips, the bedstead double screwed and bracketed   £6.15.0

A pair of very rich carved foet posts, twisted & reeded columns, loose panels to hide the screws, the Ornaments party gilt, the ground Japan'd French grey and Varnish'd   £19.0.0

A set of very strong three wheel brass Casters with screws & fixing   £0.12.0

A large Doom Tester, wainscot Ribs lined with deal, cover'd with blue paper, broad tester laths and slips compleat   £9.9.0

Japaned mouldings & Center for inside of Doom   £6.0.0

A very strong polished curtain rod   £2.10.0

2 Irons to support the corners of the Valance and 4 Iron pins for the parts   £0.11.0

A set of very Rich carved Cornices with Crest, Coronets, order of the Garter &c party gilt in Gold, French grey Varnished Gr.d
                                                                                  £42.10.0

4 Rich carved Trophies for the cornices party gilt French grey Varnished ground   £27.0.0

A large stuffed head board   £1.8.0

13 Iron fastenings and screws   £0.9.0

4 Gold Embroider'd tassels & knots for and of the outside valance
                                                                                  £2.15.0

Buckram for the Valance   £0.12.0

32 yds of fine white Tammy to line the Counterpane outside & inside valance bases and head board   £2.13.4

6 yds of glazed linen to line the Head cloth   £0.7.0

12 yds of Canvas to line the Doom & head board   £0.9.0

100 yds of rich silk lace French grey and white   £3.6.8

17½ yds of very deep silk fringe richly ornamented with Gold and

fancy silk festoon hangers and broad gimp head, for the outside valance, bottom of counterpane and top of the headboard
@ 60/– £52.10.0
$10\frac{1}{2}$ of deep French grey silk fringe with gold and fancy hangers for the bottoms of the Curtains @ 50/– £26.5.0
$9\frac{1}{2}$ yds of deep fringe with plain gold head, gold and coloured silk hangers for the inside valance @ 35/– £16.12.6
44 yds of rich party colour and gold Gimp used in different parts of the Bed @ 24/– £52.16.0
21 yds of narrow silk fringe with coloured faggots @ 6/6 £6.16.6
2 Gold and coloured Bows and festoons for the corners of the Valance £2.0.0
Sewing silk, Thread, tape, rings Tacks &c £1.0.0
Japanning and making good the flowers of the inside of the Doom £0.15.0
Placeing and fixing the Embroidery and gimp of the top of the Counterpane £2.10.0
Contriving and placeing the Work of the whole Bed upon the Silk for the Embroiderer making the Bed compleat, fixing at Audley End with expences on the Journey £45.0.0 [(Total) £332.12.0]
[This is the continuation of the state bed bill detailing the bedding]
A best seasoned Swan Down Bed and bolster in a fine border'd & welted Tick with a pair of white pillows £20.0.0
a thick border'd hair & flock mattress £6.10.0
a white Holland do £4.15.0
a pair of very large superfine Blankets £4.2.0
a pair of under do £1.18.0
a very large Marsailles Quilt £8.12.0
An outside polished Curtain rod, make to fold on the Doom, with a set of white Irish cloth Curtains to draw round the Bed £10.15.0
391 feet of $\frac{3}{4}$ Inch packing case £6.10.4
8 large packing Mats, Carterage paper, screws, nails, packthread, packing the Bed & Bedding £1.16.6
Cartage to the Inn £0.9s 6d [Final Cost] £398.0.0

42. October 1793 'Robt & Geo Gillows & Co' to the sixth Earl of Coventry

Croome Court Archive, Bill 116 (Beard, 1993)

Satin wood, japanned or painted, is taking over from mahogany in the repertoire of many cabinet makers and upholsterers. Care is also taken by them in lining the yellow damask outer coverings with flannel.

To Eight very Elegant sattin wood Chairs all Japd in Imitation of inlaid work highly Varnished & finished seat & Back stuffed with best curled hair into fine Canvas border'd & french stuffed, a large french Cushion for ea seat all ready for the sattin $3\frac{1}{2}$ yds 29. 8. 0

To Covering the Eight Chairs with rich Yellow Damask all lined with flannel Border'd round a rich silk Gimp to Do to go all round with silk & Morine for bottoms of Cushions Tamy &c. 22 yds. 8. 16. 0

To 2 large & Elegant Sofas to match the Chairs all sattin wood & Japaned in Imitation of Inlaid work ends made with loose Ends also the Back Stuff'd, all in the french stile into a Rabbit also large thick french squabs for the seats double stuffed & made all ready for St Covering, £11.15.0 23. 10. 0

To Covering the 2 Sofas with rich Elegant Yellow Damask all lined with flannel Border'd & highly finished with rich silk Gimp &c Complete £3.2.0 6. 4. 0

70. 10. 6

To a large & Elegant french Windows Curt. Vizt.

To $31\frac{1}{4}$ yards of rich Yellow Tammy	18d		2. 6. $10\frac{1}{2}$
$39\frac{1}{4}$ yds of rich silk Lace	$4\frac{1}{2}$d		0. 14. 8
$7\frac{3}{4}$ yds of rich silk fringe	7/6		2. 18. $1\frac{1}{2}$
4 large & handsome silk Tassell		9/–	1. 16. 0
2 Smaller Do Do.	6/9		0. 13. 6
4 yds of rich Platted Line	3/3		0. 13. 0
2 Olives 3/– Rack Pully	1/9		0. 4. 9
$15\frac{1}{4}$ yds of silk Curtain Line	6d		0. 7. $7\frac{1}{2}$
Brass Rings, Tape silk thread &c.			0. 6. 6
Cutting out & making up Do Complete			1. 7. 0
			11. 2. 1

To a large & Elegant Window Curtn exactly same as do. 11. 2. 1
To 2 Pully Rods with brass Pullies 8/6 0. 17. 0
To 2 Laths & Iron bracketts 2/– 0. 4. 0
To 2 very neat Cornices Japaned in Colour to suit the Chairs 19/6 1. 19. 0
To a Cotton outside Cover for one of the Chairs, viz.
5 yards of Printed Cottton 2/3 0. 11. 3
5 yds of Callico to line Do 1/5 0. 7. 1
Tape thread &c also Cutting out & making up Do Complete 3/6 1. 1. 10
To 7 Covers Exactly same as Do. £1.1.10 7. 12. 10
. . .
104. 9. 4

43. 1793 Eyre and Large to Charles, eleventh Duke of Norfolk.

Arundel Castle, Sussex MS., Account 13/2

The eleventh Duke was an active builder for whom the present Arundel Castle was created on a site in continuous occupation since 1086. The family also owned Norfolk House in London. This bill is for a small amount but is of interest in showing the daily activity of upholsterers.

Fixing up 2 Silk damask Window Curtains and 1 Curtain over the door and laying down a Carpet to close fitt the Ball Room 0. 6. 0
Apl. 20 Laying down a large Brussels Carpet in Drawing Room and moving sundrey furniture, taking down a large 4 Post Bedstead & furniture moving & fixing up Do. in another Room, moving a Couch Bedst[d]. and Bedding from the 1st to the 2nd Floor us'd tacks, Nails &c. 5. 2
May 1 Taking down a 4 Post Bedstead & furniture 1. 0
4 2 Cartridge Paper testers lin'd with Canvass 7. 0
14 A 5ft Bedstead with Mahogy. Carv'd and Reeded feet Pillars, best Sacking, filed Rod Iron Castors & Brass Caps 4. 16. 0
$4\frac{1}{4}$ Yds of Green Harrateen furniture 2/– 8. 6
Making a New tester Cloth, cutting and Piecing part of a 4 post furniture 9. 8
Taking down a 4 Post Bedstead & furniture fixing the furniture on the New Bedstead Removing & fixing the Old Bedstead over the Stable & moving a Couch Bedstead, use'd 1 Bedcord & 2 Hooks 11. 0
May 27 A Sett of 5ft 3 Tester Laths 3. 0
June 6 Taking down 18 Window Curtains in diff[t]. Rooms, taking up 3 Close Carpets & 2 Square Do. brushing, cleaning & folding up Window Curtains & Carpets 13. 6
15 $6\frac{1}{4}$ doz[n]. of Green Silk Cover'd Lace 3/– 18. 9
$4\frac{1}{4}$ yds of Green tammy @17 6. 0
$1\frac{3}{4}$ yds of Hessian @12 1. 9
Silk, thread, paper &c. to a 4 Post Bedfurnit[e]. 5. 0

Ripping a large 4 Post Green Worstead damask Bedfurniture, altering, squaring & making up Do. with, Head, tester & Valence lin'd &c. Complete   1. 16. 0
Scowering, cleaning & pressing the Green Worstead damask furniture   1. 8. 0
Nov. 12   Fixing up 16 Window Curtains in diffrent Rooms, taking down 2 Window Curtains in the Library, Laying down 3 Carpets to fitt Rooms & fixing up two 4 post furniture, Us'd tacks &c. 19. 6
Nov. 19   2 Cartridge Paper testers lin'd with Canvass   7. 0

                                                            £.14. 2. 10

44.   1816–18 Jno Johnstone, 67 New Bond Street, London
      to James Henry Leigh, Stoneleigh Abbey,
      Warwickshire and Portman Square, London.
      *Shakespeare Birthplace Trust, MS., D18/5/7156 (by courtesy of the
      Stoneleigh Preservation Trust)*

This account shows the continuation of tasks upholsterers were often involved in, particularly the covering of walls with hessian (or other materials such as cartridge paper) prior to covering with finer fabrics, and remaking items such as curtains to different styles, some as 'french hang down'.

Acct. for Stoneleigh Abbey
1816, Sept–Octbr.   Paid Wharfage of Boxes from Coventry   3. 6
A large square ottoman double stuffed & covered with fine brown linen, best Feather Pillows in white fustian Cases & wedge Cushions of Hair for Pillows to lay in, for the middle Drawing room. Covering do with rich crimson silk, fluted & ornamented with gold coloured silk Lace & Silk Tassells &c.   16. 16. 0
                                                            3. 16. 8
25 yds rich Crimson silk Lutestring,   9s   11. 5. 0
5 yds Suprfine Crimson Callico   2/9   13. 9
Swissing Do.   2   10
33½ yds rich Gold Color Silk Lace   3/6   5. 17. 3
34 yds Gold color Silk Cord   10   1. 8. 4
4 large handsome ornamented Silk Tassells & Rosettes
                                           15/6   3. 2. 0
16 Smaller do.   7/—   5. 12. 0
6½ yds Flannell   1/9   11. 5
Silk, Thread & Tacks &c.   10. 10
2 square Ottomans with thick squab seats & Feather Pillows & wedge Cushions &c for large Drawing room   33. 12. 0
Covering do. with your Crimson silk velvet richly ornamented with Silk Gymp & Cord &c.   6. 19. 8
9 yds Suprill Crimson Callicoe   2/9   1. 4. 9
Swissing Do.   2   1. 6
36 yds large handsome French Silk Gymp   7/6   13. 10. 0
8 large ornamented Silk Tassells & Rosettes 15/6   6. 4. 0
32 smaller do.   7/—   11. 4. 0
66 yds Gold color Silk Cord   10   2. 15. 0
8½ yds of Flannell   1/9   14. 11

Silk, Tacks & Brads &c.   15. 8
8 Canvas curled Hair Cushions for Ceylon wood Chairs in the middle Drawing Room   14/—   5. 12. 0
Acct. for Portman Square
1817 Nov.   Upholsterers time covering up the Walls of Bed Room on drawing room floor with Hessian, carrying up 2 Bedsteads to bed Room, . . .   19. 5
. . . Cutting & making 1 Pr French hang down Callico Window Curtains with Draperies lined with Blue, bound & fringed for Back Parlor   2. 2. 0
32 yds Callico   6/—   9. 12. 0
32 yds Blue Callico Lining   2/4   3. 14. 8
9 yds ornamented Parisian Fringe   6/6   2. 18. 6
3 yds Drapery Rope to correspond   2/—   6.0
38 yds silk Binding   6d   19. 0
Silk, Tape, Rings, drawline, side Pullies, Bracketrs &c. 1. 3. 2
4 handsome Brass Curtain Pins   7/—   1. 8. 0
2 brass Pully rods & Hooks for Do.   1. 2. 0
. . .
Cutting & Making a neat printed Callico case to a Chair Bed in Mr L [eigh] Junr Room, lined & bound &c.   1. 9. 8
13 yds Callico   6/—   3. 18. 0
Swissing do.   2   2. 2
16½ yds White Callico Lining   1/6   1. 4. 9
Glazing Do.   1   1. 4
40 yds Silk Binding   6   1. 0. 0
Silk, Thread &c.   3. 1
Cutting & making a neat printed Callico furniture to Do when used as a Bed, lined & bound &c.   1. 0. 10
. . . Taking to pieces the Curtains belonging to Dining Room
                                                        9. 11
Redying the Morine a fine bright Scarlet & Watering, 72 yds
   1/6   5. 8. 0
Upholsterers time making up do into 2 Pr french hang down window Curtains & Draperies for Dining room   5. 19. 8
60 yds wide black Velvet Border   .8   2. 0. 0
58 yds narrower do.   .6   1. 9. 0
14 yds neat ornamented Parisian Fringe   6/—   4. 4. 0
6 yds Drapery Rope to match   2/—   12. 0
Tape, Rings, Silk, Thread &c.   1. 3. 8
Upholsterer's time fixing up 2 french Window Curtains & Draperies in Dining Room, fixing up 1 Pr french Window Curtains & draperies with laths, rods & Curtain pins &c, fixing 4 Bell Pulls in drawing Room, Tacks &c.   9. 7
. . . Taking to pieces the stuffing of 4 Chair Cushions in Library, opening the Hair & Remaking Do.   9. 3
1818 May   Cutting & making 4 Pr of Muslin Curtains for the Front Drawing Room. 36 yds fine White Muslin   2/— 3. 12. 0
Tape, Thread, Rings, Pullies, Hooks, 44 yds Line &c.   18. 10
Altering your brass Pully rods for Do. cleaning up, Lacquerg as new
                                                       16. 0

Upholsterers time fixing up Do.   3. 0

APPENDIX B

Extracts from R. Campbell's *The London Tradesman* (1747), relating (Ch.XXXII) to the Upholder and the Trades employed by him; the Mercer; the Gold and Silver Lace-Man (Ch. XXX), including the Silver-Spinner, Orrice-Weaver, Bone-Lace Maker, Button-Maker, and Embroiderer.

THE UPHOLDER AND THE TRADES EMPLOYED BY HIM

Sect.1 Of the Upholder's proper Business I Have just finished my House, and must now think of the furnishing it with fashionable Furniture. The Upholder is chief Agent in this Case: He is the Man upon whose Judgment I rely in the Choice of Goods; and I suppose he has not only Judgment in the Materials, but Taste in the Fashions, and Skill in the Workmanship. This Tradesman's Genius must be universal in every Branch of Furniture; though his proper Craft is to fit up Beds, Window-Curtains, Hangings, and to cover Chairs that have stuffed Bottoms: He was originally a Species of the Taylor; but, by degrees, has crept over his Head and set up as a Connoisieur in every Article that belongs to a House. He employs Journeymen in his own proper Calling, Cabinet-Makers, Glass-Grinders, Looking-Glass Frame-Carvers, Carvers for Chairs, Testers, and Posts of Bed, the Woolen-Draper, the Mercer, the Linen-Draper, several Species of Smiths, and vast many Tradesmen of the other mechanic Branches.

The Upholder, according to this Description of his Business, must be no Fool; and have a considerable Stock to set up with: However, a young Man who has a Mind only to be a mere Upholder, and has no Prospect of setting up in the Undertaking Way, does not require such an universal Genius as I have been speaking of: He must handle the Needle so alertly as to sew a plain Seam, and sew on the Lace without Puckers; and he must use his Sheers so dextrously as to cut a Valence or Counterpain with a genteel Sweep, according to a Pattern he has before him. All this Part of the Work is performed by Women, who never served an Apprenticeship to the Mystery, as well as Men. The stuffing and covering a Chair or Settee-Bed is indeed the nicest Part of this Branch; but it may be acquired without any remarkable Genius. All the Wooden-work they use is done by the Joiner, Cabinet-Maker, and Carver. *His Wages* A Tradesman who is a good Hand in the Upholder's own Branch is paid Twelve or Fifteen Shillings a Week; and the Women, if good for any thing, get a Shilling a Day.

Thus far we have seen what the Upholder originally was, what he ought to be, and what he is now, let us take him as we find him, and make a Tour through the Tradesmen he employs.

Sect.2 The Cabinet-Maker The Cabinet-Maker is his right-hand Man; he furnishes him with Mahogony and Wallnuttree Posts for his Beds, Settees of the same Materials, Chairs of all Sorts and Prices, carved, plain and inlaid, Chests of Drawers, Book-Cases, Cabinets, Desks, Scrutores, Buroes, Dining, Dressing, and Card Tables, Tea-Boards, and an innumerable Variety of Articles of this Sort. *His Business and Genius* The Cabinet-Maker is by much the most curious Workman in the Wood Way, except the Carver; and requires a nice mechanic Genius, and a tolerable Degree of Strength, though not so much as the Carpenter; he must have a much lighter Hand and a

quicker Eye than the Joiner, as he is employed in Work much more minute and elegant. *His Education* A Youth who designs to make a Figure in this Branch must learn to Draw; for upon this depends the Invention of new Fashions, and on that the Success of his Business: He who first hits upon any new Whim is sure to make by the Invention before it becomes common in the Trade; but he that must always wait for a new Fashion till it comes from *Paris*, or is hit upon by his Neighbour, is never likely to grow rich or eminent in his Way. *Wages* A Master Cabinet-Maker is a very profitable Trade; especially, if he works for and serves the Quality himself; but if he must serve them through the Chanel of the Upholder, his Profits are not very considerable. A Journeyman who knows his Business may have a Guinea a Week; and if he works Piece-Work, and applies with tolerable Diligence, may earn Thirty Shillings and some Weeks Two Guineas.

Sect.3 The Chair-Carver The Cabinet-Maker and Upholder employ a Species of Carvers peculiar to themselves; who are employed in carving Chairs, Posts and Testers of Beds, or any other Furniture whereon Carving is used. Their Work is slight, and requires no great Ingenuity to perform it; I mean, he needs no elegant Taste in the general Art of Carving who performs that used at present upon Furniture. *Wages* They are generally paid by the Piece, according to the Pattern of the Work, and may earn Thirty or Forty Shillings a Week. As this Taste in Furniture has prevailed for some Time past, Tradesmen in this Way are much wanted, and are never out of Business. *His Education* Drawing is absolutely necessary for this as well as all other Classes of Carvers, and the rest of their Education may be as mean as they please.

Sect.4 Glass-Grinder The Glass-Grinder is the next Person in the Upholder's Books: He furnishes him with Looking-Glasses and Sconces. The first article belonging to Looking-Glass is casting the Plates at the Glass-House; the particular Manner of which is pretended to be a Secret; nor could I find any Person who pretends to know it that could give a rational Account of the Matter: However, as we have mentioned Glass, and may afterwards speak of it as a Commodity, we shall in this Place relate the Method of making Glass in general.

The Manner of making Glass The Materials of which it is made is Sand and Salt of Vegetables. Flint-Glass is made of Flint pounded into an impalpable Powder, and mixed with a Proportion of Kelp, Sea-Salt, or Ashes of Vegetables: These are mixed together with the powdered Flint, and allowed to lie for two or three Months. It is then put into a Furnace where it vitrifies by the constant and intense Heat of the Furnace; when it is sufficiently boiled, and fit for Use, the Workmen take it out in Ladles and throw it into Moulds, out of which it is yet malable, and blown, if it is to be made into Bottles or Glasses, &c.

The Manner of grinding Glass The Plate-Glass is made of the same Materials; but the Secret consists in casting it into these Plates. The Glass-Grinder buys them from the Glass-House rough, and it is his Business to grind them even and then polish them, which is done by Sand and Water. The Plate of Glass is fixed horizontally in a weighty

Frame, and is rubbed backwards and forwards upon another Plain, on which Sand and Water is constantly running. It requires nothing but Strength to perform this Part of the Work: Any common Labourer may execute it; and such as are so employed have Twelve or Fifteen Shillings a Week. *The Manner of silvering Mirrors* After the Glass has been ground to a true Plain, it is then polished with Emery and Putty. The next Operation to form the Looking-Glass is, to silver it; which is done with Plates of Lead and Quicksilver: The Plate of Glass is laid upon an horizontal Plain, with a Ledge round it; it is then covered with a thin Sheet of Leaf Lead, which is to be had of all Dimensions fit for this Use; over this is poured Quicksilver till the Lead is compleatly covered, then Weights laid upon the whole. This lies some Days, after which the Weights are taken off, and the Lead and Quicksilver stick firmly to the Glass. If the least Speck or Crack is in the Silvering, there is no mending it, but by silvering it a-new all over.

Sect.5 The Glass Frame-Maker We have prepared the Looking-Glass, we must send for the Frame-Maker, Carver, and Gilder, before it is fit for Use. There are a Set of Joiners who make nothing but Frames for Looking-Glasses and Pictures, and prepare them for the Carvers. This requires but little Ingenuity or Neatness, as they only join the Deals roughly plained, in the Shape and Dimensions in which they are required: If the Pattern chosen for the Frame is to have any large Holes in it, these they cut out in their proper Places, or, if it is to have Mouldings raised in the Wood, they plain them on; but they leave the Carver to plant on the rest of the Figures. But we have said enough of this Trade, who is no more than a cobbling Carpenter or Joiner.

Sect.6 The Glass Frame-Carver The Frame-Maker sends the Frame thus prepared to the Carver: For there are a Class of Carvers who do nothing else but carve Frames for Looking-Glasses. There are two Sorts of Carving upon these kind of Frames: One Sort of them is carved in the Wood entirely, and is designed to be painted or gilded with Burnish-Gold: In the other, the Figures are first roughly cut out in the Wood, then the whole is covered with two or three Coats of Whiting, to the Thickness of a Quarter of an Inch; when this is dry, the Carver wets the Whiting with a Brush, then finishes his Figures, by making such Flourishes in the Whiting as is agreeable to his Pattern. When he has done his Part to it, he sends it to the Gilder, who puts on the Leaf in the Manner mentioned in the Chapter of Gilders upon Wood, Page 107. Neither those Frames that are finished in the Wood, nor those in the Whiting are cut out of the Solid: All Figures that rise above the Plain of the Frame are glued on; that is, suppose a Figure is to rise two Inches above the Plain of the Frame, in that Case a Piece of Wood of that Height, and of the Bulk of the Figure designed, is glued on: All such Pieces are glued upon the Frame before the Carver begins to Work; which he does with Chissel and Mallet, but uses a Number of Instruments of different Figures and Bulk.

The Youth designed for this Branch of the Carving Business ought to have a good Invention to find out new Patterns, and ought to be early taught Drawing; without which it is impossible for him to succeed in his Business. It is a very profitable Branch: If they work as Journeymen they may earn a Guinea a Week, if good Workmen; and if they work by the Piece, as they generally do, they may clear considerably more. It requires some Strength; therefore the Boy ought to be about fifteen Years of Age before he is bound.

Sect.7 Of the Appraiser The Appraising Business is generally joined to that of the Upholder, and as such he makes Estimates of Goods upon all Occasions, when that is necessary: But, for the most part, the Business is carried on by Brokers of Houshold Goods. They are called Sworn-Appraisers, because they take an Oath to do Justice between Parties who employ them; but they generally value Things

very low, not out of Respect to any of the Parties, but because they are obliged to take the Goods if it is insisted on at their own Appraisement.

I do not find that Appraisers, who are Brokers of Old Goods, ever take an Apprentice. The Trade is learned by Experience, and taken up without any regular Servitude; though it requires an universal Knowledge in the Nature of all Houshold Utensils, and a pretty large Stock to deal to any Extent.

Sect.8 Of the Screen-Maker The Screen-Maker deals in Leather, of which their Gilt-Leather-Screens are made, and are of Kin to the Joiner, as they make their own Frames to mount their Screens on. There are a great Variety of this Piece of Furniture, serving both for Ornament and Use, and all of them have their Share of Ingenuity. The Business is clean, reputable, and profitable to the Masters, who are mostly Shopkeepers, and some of them are little inferior to Upholders, as they frequently sell other Goods besides Screens. A Journeyman earns but a Dozen or Thirteen Shillings a Week, and the Hands employed in the whole Branch are but few.

Sect.9 Of the Buckram-Marker The Upholder, besides the Trades above-mentioned, employs the Buckram-Maker. The Cloth of which this Commodity is made comes chiefly from *Scotland*: It is coarse and thin, wrought on purpose for them; when it comes here, it is stiffened with Paste and pressed. It requires but little Ingenuity to learn the Art; nor is there much made of it when acquired.

Sect.10 The Spring-Curtain-Marker, Bell-Hanger, and Narrow-Weaver He likewise employs the Smith for Castors, Hinges, and Locks, to his Beds, Tables, Cabinets, &c. in making Curtain-Rods, and Springs for Spring-Curtains. There are particular Smiths who profess this late Invention as well as that of Bell-hanging. He employs the Narrow-Weaver, for making Laces; a Trade of little Profit, and as little Ingenuity. He buys his Woolen-Stuffs from the Woolen-Draper, his Silks from the Mercer, his Linen and Ticks from the Linen-Draper, and his Leather from the Leather-Merchant; but of the four last we shall treat under another Head.

THE MERCER

Sect.3 Of the Mercer The Mercer is the Twin Brother of the Woollen-Draper, they are as like one another as two Eggs, only the Woollen-Draper deals chiefly with the Men, and is the graver animal of the two, and the Mercer traficks most with the Ladies, and has a small Dash of their Effeminacy in his Constitution.

His Talents The Mercer deals in Silks, Velvets, Brocades, and an innumerable Train of expensive Trifles, for the Ornament of the Fair Sex: He must be a very polite Man, and skilled in all the Punctilio's of City-good-breeding; he ought, by no Means to be an aukward clumsey Fellow, such a Creature would turn the Lady's Stomach in a Morning, when they go their Rounds, to tumble Silks they have no mind to buy. He must dress neatly, and affect a Court Air, however far distant he may live from St *James*'s. I know none so fit for that Branch of Business, as that nimble, dancing, talkative Nation the *French*: Our Mercer must have a great deal of the *Frenchman* in his Manners, as well as a large Parcel of *French* Goods in his Shop; he ought to keep close Intelligence with the Fashion-Office at *Paris*, and supply himself with the newest Patterns from that changeable People. Nothing that is mere *English* goes down with our modern Ladies; from their Shift to their Topknots they must be equipped from Dear *Paris*.

The Mercer who intends to succeed in his Business ought to humour the Ladies, and accommodate himself to their Taste and Understanding, as much as a Rational Creature can; but I would have him Master of so much natural good Sense, as to mind the main Chance of getting Money, which requires that he should now and then lay aside his mercurial Airs and act with Gravity.

The Business of a Mercer requires a very considerable Stock; Ten

Thousand Pounds, without a great deal of prudent Management, makes but a small Figure in their Way; nor will the Profits, though reasonable, admit of the Expence of a Nobleman: A City and Country-House, a Pack of Hounds in the Country, and a Doxy in a Corner of the Town, Coaches, Horses, Gaming, and the polite Vices of St *James's*, cannot be afforded out of the Profits of Silk and Velvet. The Wife ought not to be ashamed of her Compter, nor affect the Airs, Dress and Equipage of a Lady of Quality; Oeconomy and living within Bounds are the only Methods to make a Tradesman thrive; and whenever he, or Madam his Wife, are pleased to be any thing else than the mere Tradesman, Ruin and Destruction are not far off.

THE GOLD AND SILVER LACE-MAN

Sect.1 His Business, and the Furniture in his Shop The Gold and Silver Lace-Man may be esteemed of Kin to the Dealers in Metal, as the greatest Value of his Commodity is Metal, and that of the most precious Sort. The Lace Shop is furnished with all Sorts of Gold and Silver Lace, Gold and Silver Buttons, Shapes for Waistcoats, Lace and Network for Robeings and Women's Petticoats, Fringes, Bugles, Spangles, Plates for Embroidery and Orrice, and Bone-Lace Weavers, Gold and Silver Wire, Purle, Slesy, Twist, &c. A Lace-Man must have a well lined Pocket to furnish his Shop; but his Garrets may be as meanly equipped as he pleases. *His Qualifications* His chief Talent ought to lie in a nice Taste in Patterns of Lace, &c. He ought to speak fluently, though not elegantly, to entertain the Ladies; and to be Master of a handsome Bow and Cringe; should be able to hand a Lady to and from her Coach politely, without being seized with the Palpitation of the Heart at the Touch of a delicate Hand, a well-turned and much exposed Limb, or a handsome Face: But, above all, he must have Confidence to refuse his Goods in a handsome Manner to the extravagant Beau who never pays, and Patience as well as Stock to bear the Delays of the sharping Peer, who pays but seldom. With these natural Qualifications, five Thousand Pounds in his Pocket, and a Set of good Customers in view, a young Man may commence Lace-Man: If he trusts moderately, and with Discretion, lives with Oeconomy, and minds his Business more than his Mistress, he may live to increase his Stock; but otherwise I know no readier Road to a Jail, and Destruction, than a Lace-Man's Business.

Sect.2 Of the Wire-Drawer The Original of his Commodity is Silk; but we shall leave that Branch of his Dependants to its proper Place. The first Person in his Employ is the Wire-Drawer: He furnishes him with Wire of all Dimensions for Spinning, for Purle, making Spangles, &c. *The Manner drawing Wire* The Business of a Wire-Drawer is performed thus: If it is Gold Wire is to be drawn, an Ingot of Silver is double gilt, and by the Help of a Mill is drawn into Wire; the Mill consists of a Steel Plate, perforated with Holes of various Dimensions, and a Wheel which turns the Spindles. The Ingot, which at first is but small, is passed through the largest Hole, and then through one a Degree smaller, and so continued till it is drawn to the Fineness it is wanted, and still remains gilded if drawn to the Fineness of a Hair. Silver Wire is drawn in the same Manner, only it is not gilded. The Wire-Drawer makes Purle, which is Silver or Gold Wire twisted upon a small Needle in a Wheel for that purpose: When the Needle is full, the Wire is pulled and remains twisted in Rounds, like the Windings of a very small Worm. This is used by Button-Makers and Embroiderers. The Business of a Wire-Drawer is purely mechanical; a Hobby-Horse is capable to execute their Business, since the whole of their Work is performed by the Engine, which they have nothing to do but turn round; nor are their Engines costly; their chief Care is in preserving the Colour of the Metal, to which a moist Hand is a very great Enemy. They are paid so much an Ounce for their Labour by the Lace-Man, who furnishes them with the Plate. They employ but few Hands, and give but small Wages.

The Wire being once drawn to a proper Fineness, is sent to the Flatting-Mills, where it is made flat by passing between two Rollers.

Sect.3 Flatting-Mill The Silver by being flatted is made ready for Spinning, which is performed by Spinners brought up to that Business: *Sect.4 Of Silver Thread Spinners* It is done in a long Room; at the one End of which stands their Wheel, made of Steel; the Spindles are placed on this Wheel in the same manner as those used in Rope-Walks, or for spinning Thread for Sail-Cloth; a Thread of Silk is fastened to the End of one of the Spindles; one Person turns the Wheel, while another holding the Thread of Silk in one Hand, and the flatted Silver in the other, allows the Silver to wind gently about the Silk as it is turned round by the Wheel: In this Manner the whole Thread of Silk is covered, which is rolled upon a Bottom, and is now called Silver or Gold Sleysy. A moist Hand cannot be employed in this Work; and it requires much Care to preserve it from tarnishing, and much Experience to compleat the Workman. Women are employed in this as well as Men, and may earn Twelve or Fifteen Shillings a week honestly; but they are much given to pilfering the Stuff, and have a Trick of moistening the Silk to make up the Deficiency of Weight. The Master is paid by the Lace-Man at so much an Ounce, who generally furnishes him with the Materials.

Sect.5 Of the Orrice-Weaver We have now prepared this rich Thread, let us pursue its Progress till we have gratified the Lady's Pride with Lace or Robeings composed of it: To this purpose the Lace-Man employs the Orrice-Weaver, who is an ingenious Tradesman: He understands Drawing so much as to design upon Paper his own Patterns, wherein are described the Figure and Number of Threads to be moved, in order to raise it on the Lace. There are some Workmen of this Trade who can neither draw their own Patterns, nor put the Work into the Loom, though they can work it after it has been put in for them; but these are esteemed but half Tradesmen. Their Figures are raised by the same Principles that the Damask or Silk Weavers work, and their Looms are constructed much in the same Manner, making Allowance for the Largeness and Smallness of the Work; and both are so perplexed, that the Reader would reap but little Benefit from a Description without a Plate or Model, which is inconsistent with the Design of our Undertaking. The Master Orrice-Weaver weighs out his Silk and Silver to his Men, who are obliged to return the same Weight in Work or Cuttings: If a Master is cautious, they have but little Opportunity of stealing from him; but they may from one another: yet I have always heard, that there is scarce such a Thing to be heard of in the Trade as a Pilferer. *Their Wages* They are paid at so much a Yard according to the Pattern, and generally earn Fifteen or Eighteen Shillings a Week, if they have an easy Job, and refrain the Alehouse, the Bane of most *London* Workmen. It requires a lively Apprehension, to make a compleat Workman in this Trade, and he must not be of a weakly Constitution; for the Weight they are obliged to move with the Treadles, require a greater Degree of Strength than Weavers employed in the Manufacture of coarser Materials; a dry cold Hand, free from Sweat, is likewise absolutely necessary; because if they tarnish their Work, so as to put it past Sale, they are obliged to pay for the Stuff and lose their Labour: The cleanest Hand that is, tarnishes, in some measure; but they have a Method of restoring the Gloss, if it is not too much spoiled.

Sect.6 Of the Bone-Lace Maker The Bone-Lace Maker is another Servant of the Lace-Man. Their Work is not performed in the Loom, but wrought by Hand in different Parts, and put together on a Pillow, in the Manner that Thread-Lace is made. The Ground Work of some of their Patterns are made by Orrice-Weavers, and afterwards ornamented by the Bone-Lace Maker. He ought to be a good Pattern-Draughts-Man, as the Beauty of his Work depends upon the Richness and Variety of the Figures. We are but Bunglers in this Art in *England*; the *French Point de Espagn* beats all our Performances in that Way. They not only excel us in this, but in Orrice-Lace: They have a Method of giving a lively rich Look to mere Trifles: Our *English* Lace is much richer in Metal, but still the *French* Lace has a richer Aspect till you come to weigh it. They exceed us in Colour; but this I take to be owing to our Climate, which is moister than theirs, and consequently finely polished Metals or Goods of that Fabric must tarnish here sooner than in *France*, though the Workman's Skill should be equal.

Sect.7 The Silver and Gold Button-Marker The Button-Maker, I mean the Silver and Gold Button-Maker, is the next humble Servant of the Lace-Man; the Lace-Man furnishes him with all Materials for his Buttons, except Moulds, and buys them of him when done. The Silver and Gold Button-Maker is a pretty ingenious Business: He must have a Fancy and Genius for inventing new Fashions; a good Eye, as his Business is poreing, and a clean dry Hand. It requires no great Strength, and is followed by Women as well as Men, which has reduced the Trade to small Profits, and a small Share of Reputation; the Women are generally Gin-Drinkers, and, consequently, bad Wives; this makes them poor, and, to get something to keep Soul and Body together, work for a mere Trifle, and hawk their Work about to the Trade at an Under-Price, after they have cheated the Lace-Man of his Stuffs. This has reduced the Craft to a very low Ebb; however, a good Workman, if he can get Employ among the Crowd, may earn Twelve or Fifteen Shillings a Week.

Sect.8 The Spangle, Bugle and Button-Maker The Lace-Man employs, besides the Craft abovementioned in the Metal Way, the Spangle, Bugle, and Button-ring Maker. The Spangles and Plate Figures in Embroidery are made of Gold or Silver Wire, first twisted round a Stick of the Bigness they want the Spangles, &c. to be made of; then they are cut off in Rings and flatted upon an Anvil, with a Punch and the Stroke of a heavy Hammer. The Anvil is made of Iron, fixed in a large Block of Wood bound round with Iron Hoops; the Face of it is of case-hardened Steel, nicely polished and perfectly flat, the Punch is nine inches long, and about an Inch over in the Face, which is likewise of case-hardened Steel, flat and curiously

polished; a Frame of Iron is raised from the Block over the Anvil, which supports the Punch: When the Workman is to make Spangles, Rings for Buttons, or other Plate Figures, he places the Rings above described, upon the Anvil under the Punch; then, with both Hands, gives a smart and sudden Blow with the Hammer, which flats the Wire Rings into the Shape of Spangles, &c. If the Anvil or Punch is not hardened to an equal Temper, either of them gives way to the Metal the Work is spoiled; or if they are not truly polished, the Spangles want their proper Gloss, in which their chief Beauty consists. Note, When we speak of Gold Wire in all these Branches, we mean only Silver double gilt, and drawn after the Manner described in the Section of Wire-Drawers.

Sect.9 The Fringe, Frog, and Tassel Maker The Fringe, Frog, and Tassel Maker is likewise employed by the Lace-Man. Some of the Button-Makers perform the Work; but it is chiefly done by Women, upon the Hand, who make a very handsome Livelihood of it, if they are not initiated into the Mystery of Gin-Drinking.

Sect.10 Of Embroidery Embroiderers may be reckoned among the Dependants of the Lace-Man; as in his Shop the greatest Part of their rich Work is vended, and he furnishes them with all Materials for their Business. It is chiefly performed by Women; is an ingenious Art, requires a nice Taste in Drawing, a bold Fancy to invent new Patterns, and a clean Hand to save their Work from tarnishing. – Few of the Workers at present can Draw, they have their Patterns from the Pattern-Drawer, who must likewise draw the Work itself, which they only fill up, with Gold and Silver, Silks or Worsteds, according to its Use and Nature. We are far from excelling in this Branch of Business in *England*: The Nuns in Foreign Countries far exceed any thing we can perform. We make some good Work; but fall short of the bold Fancy in *French* and *Italian* Embroidery: This I take to be chiefly owing to the Want of a Taste for Drawing in the Performers; they may go on in a dull beaten Tract, or servily imitate a Foreign Pattern, but know not how to advance the Beauty of the old or strike out any new Invention worth Notice. An Embroiderer ought to have a Taste for Designing, and a just Notion of the Principles of Light and Shade, to know how to range their Colours in a natural Order, make them reflect upon one another, and the whole to represent the Figure in its proper Shade.

At the conclusion of his book Campbell gives 'A General Table of the several Trades' in which he sets out the premiums paid for apprenticeship, those required to set up as a master and the hours of working. Those relevant to this study have been extracted.

Name of Trade	Sums given with an Apprentice £'s	Sums necessary to set up as Master £'s	Hours of working (A.M. to P.M.)
Appraiser	–	50 to 2,000	–
Bone Lace Maker	5 to 10	50 to 200	
Button Maker – of Mohair, Silver and Gold	5 to 10	to 50	6 to 8
Buckram Maker	5 to 10	50 to 200	6 to 8
Cabinet Maker	10 to 20	200 to 2,000	6 to 6
Carver of Chairs	10 to 20	50 to 200	6 to 6
Carver of Frames	5 to 10	50 to 100	6 to 8
Dyers of all sorts	10 to 20	100 to 500	6 to 8
Embroiderer	5 to 10	50 to 200	6 to 8
Frame Maker	5 to 10	50 to 100	6 to 8
Fringe and Tassel Maker	–	–	6 to 8
Glass Grinder	to 5	50 to 100	6 to 8
Lace Man	50 to 100	1,000 to 10,000	7 to 8
Mercer	50 to 200	1,000 to 10,000	8 to 8
Orrice Weaver	5 to 20	100 to 1,000	6 to 8
Screen Maker	5 to 20	50 to 500	6 to 8
Silk Man	20 to 100	unlimited	–
Silk Throwster	to 5	400 to 3,000	6 to 9
Upholder	20 to 50	100 to 1,000	6 to 8
Weavers in general	5 to 20	100 to 500	6 to 8
Wire Drawer	5 to 20	100 to 200	6 to 8
Woollen Draper	50 to 200	1,000 to 5,000	8 to dark

GLOSSARY

I have quoted freely from Thomas Sheraton's *The Cabinet Dictionary* (1803) abbreviated as Sheraton, C. D. (1803).

It is usually possible to establish the meaning of a term by reference to one of several dictionaries:

Randle Cotgrave, *A Dictionarie of the French and English Tongues*, London, 1611 (facsimile edn., Amsterdam and New York, 1971).
Ephraim Chambers, *Cyclopaedia; or, An Universal Dictionary of Arts and Sciences*, London, 1741.
Malacy Postlethwait, *The Universal Dictionary of Trade and Commerce Translated* 2 vols, London, 1751–5.
Samuel Johnson, *A Dictionary of the English Language*, London, 1755 and later edns, (6th, 1785).
S. W. Beck, The Draper's Dictionary: A Manual of Textile Fabrics, London, 1882.

My short entries on types of fabrics are taken mostly from the full descriptions in Montgomery (1984). Good modern glossaries are to be found in Arnold (1988: largely Elizabethan terms); Gilbert (1978) and (1991); and Hayward and Kirkham (1980). The various references in Thornton (1978) are invaluable for seventeenth-century terminology.

A CHASSIS *See* CHASSIS

AIGRETTE French. A tuft of feathers, usually of the egret, osprey or ostrich, used as a finial on four post beds, springing from the cups (q.v.) at each corner.

ANTIQUE An eighteenth-century term, often written 'antick' in contemporary documents, to describe ancient Greek or Roman art or design.

ARRAS A kind of tapestry, named after a town in Artois famed for its making. There are many Shakespearean allusions to being hidden behind the *arras*. The name became a generic term in England for all woven wall hangings.

ASH COLOUR The colour of ash, that is, white/grey. Noted in Tudor inventories.

AXMINSTER Carpets Pile carpets made at the Axminster, Devon factory established in 1755 by Thomas Whitty. Whitty won three Society of Arts competitions in 1757, 1758 and 1759 and often wove carpets (e.g. Saltram, Devon) to designs by Robert Adam. He published an autobiography in 1790 (see Jacobs, 1970).

BACK STOOL A side chair, often having an upholstered back.

BAIZE A heavy woollen cloth, raised and napped on both sides. In use for covering tables (especially those for billiards) and doors to servants' quarters. Differed from bays (q.v.) which is light, whereas baize is thick and heavy. Dr Johnson (*Dictionary*, 1755) defined it as 'A kind of coarse open cloth stuff, having a long nap; sometimes frized on one side.' See also Baumgarten (1990), p.161.

BAUDEKIN (Baudkin, Bawdekyn) A rich silk woven with gold, now called brocade (q.v.). It was first woven with a warp of gold thread, but the name came to be applied to rich shot silks.

Mentioned in connection with medieval bed-hangings. Name said to have derived from Baldacco, the Italian form of Baghdad.

BAYES (Bays, Baies) Coarse open woollen stuff having a long nap, woven in England from the sixteenth century, of worsted warp and woollen weft. A MS. of 1592 defined the best Bayes as '80 Bayes', the second 60 and the worst 40, or 'ordynary Bayes' (Arnold, 1988, p.360). Used for lining and stiffening.

BEARE (Bear, Bere) *See* PILLOWBEARE.

BED A framework with mattress and coverings (Furniture, q.v.) to sleep on. There were many types; for example, angel (without foot-posts, French: *lit à la duchesse*); canopied, or domed (Pl. 296); for use on campaigns (Pls 262, 351), French beds to be placed against a wall (Pl. 37); those having a headboard (half-headed), or with a half or hanging tester, various kinds of sofa-bed (Pl. 38), and pre-eminently state beds, particularly lavish in the late-seventeenth century (Pls 87–96). Sheraton, *C.D.* (1803), illustrated and listed many types common in the late eighteenth century, including special forms such as the 'Summer Bed in two Compartments' (Pl. 347). There are also good examples of press bedsteads which were built into cabinets to outwardly resemble a chest of drawers or clothes press. A 'feather bed', however, was a mattress filled with feathers.

BED CARPET/MAT A carpet fitted around three sides from the base of a bed. There are splendid neoclassical examples (e.g. at Osterley, Middx., Pl. 328).

BED CORD Rope used to secure the canvas bottom of a bed, through eyelets, to the frame sides.

BED TICK A case containing feathers, stuffed to form a bed.

BELLADINE A coarse raw silk, which Levant and Turkey merchants called white silk. Used as a sewing silk.

BERGAMO (Bergamot) A coarse tapestry or wall hanging, perhaps first produced at Bergamo, Italy. Made with several sorts of spun thread in a great variety and mixtures of colours. See Thornton (1960).

BERGERE (Burjair) An armchair with canework sides, back and seat, with either the seat upholstered or using a loose cushion. The French word *bergère* describes an easy-chair. They were illustrated by Mayhew and Ince in *The Universal System* (1762, Pl. LX) and here as Pl. 268. Gillows provided 'bergiers' in 1784–7 and Sheraton, C. D. (1803) noted the *bergère* with a caned back and arms and a seat having loose cushions.

BERLIN WORK Canvas embroidery worked in worsted yarns by copying patterns printed on squared paper. A popular German production, exported widely in the 1840s.

BINDING Sheraton noted: 'Amongst upholsterers is applied to the various kinds of narrow laces used to strengthen and ornament the edges of any sort of curtain, drapery, or bed furniture. Bindings for tickings are about three-fourths of an inch broad, of white and blue stripe of cotton and linen, others a little broader, of a diamond pattern, of worsted and linen.

The principal bindings are as follows:
Bindings of silk ribbonds, various Silk and worsted ditto.
Silk covered laces, of various colours, 1 inch and upwards broad.
Silk guard lace, a silk quality.
And at present there is introduced from France, very recently, a sort of black velvet binding, which having not yet seen, I can give no account of it; but may on some future occasion'.
Sheraton, C. D. (1803) I, p.51.

BLANKET   A white woollen cloth used for bed covers and heavy clothing. Many of superior quality were imported from Spain, from the sixteenth century onwards. Blankets are often noted in accounts by their size, measured in quarters, e.g. 8/4. (See also Irish Rugg, RUGGS (q.v.) and Thornton, 1978, p.112.)

Sheraton noted: 'The most famous place for their manufacture is Witney, in Oxfordshire. The wool of which blankets are made is called felt wool, or that which comes off sheep skins . . . they make blankets of 12, 11 and 10 quarters broad; of the ordinary and middle sort, blankets of 8 and 7 quarters broad; of the best tail wool, blankets of 6 quarters wide.' Sheraton C. D. (1803) I, pp.55–6.

BLINDS   A fabric, usually, on rollers, to be set at windows and raised or lowered, by cords, as needed, as a protection against the sun. Slatted blinds (Venetian blinds) were used by Thomas Chippendale, fitted with a spring mechanism (which frequently went wrong: see Gilbert, *Chippendale*, 1978, I, p.59). Blinds were sometimes also fitted to needlework or tapestry firescreens. They could be also made in a folding form to close, like shutters.

Sheraton noted: Window blinds for internal use, either with spring barrels made of tin, or turning on a plain oak stick of $1\frac{1}{4}$ inch diameter. Those without springs 'have either a wood or brass pulley at each end, one with a channel to receive a line, the other without any, to guard the canvas as it rolls up, which is effected by a line passing round the above channel, fixed to a brass rack which contains a small pulley that receives the line, which, by being tight drawn down, the line draws up the blind to any height'. Sheraton, C. D. (1803) I, pp.57–8. He described those with springs as follows: window blinds 'charged by a worm spring made of wire, extending the whole length of the tin barrel or cylinder; but when the blind is drawn up to the top close to the cylinder, the spring is relieved, and the above-mentioned worm spring contracts in, but increases in diameter. Hence, if the power of this spring be not properly adjusted to the length of the canvas, or in other words, to the height of the window, they are liable to go wrong, and be spoiled . . .' *ibid*., I, p.57.

BOLSTER   A long, round bed pillow. They were often waxed to give a denseness through which feathers could not pierce. Also used in this form as cushions at the ends of eighteenth-century sofa seats. Sheraton noted that 'Bolsters stuffed with hair is, in my opinion, the best . . .' Sheraton C. D. (1803) I, p.64.

BOMBAZINE   A cloth made of silk warp and worsted weft in a twill weave. Made in Norwich from the late sixteenth century onwards, and later at Spitalfields. Woven grey the bombazine was dyed to various colours. There were 'white bumbasine' curtains in 1677 at Ham House, Surrey (Thornton and Tomlin, 1980).

BONEGRACE (French, *bonnegraces*)   The narrow curtains at the back corners of a bed closing gaps between the main curtains and enclosing the posts or headboard. The *bonnegraces* were normally at the back and *cantonnières* (q.v.) at the front (Thornton 1978, p.165).

BONE LACE   Made by twisting bobbins of gold, silver, silk and linen threads above a pattern marked with pins. The bobbins were origi-nally made of bone, hence bone lace.

BOOK PILLOW   A padded pillow to support and protect a book binding when the book was being read.

BRAID   A woven band, used to edge fabric, or to contrast it against another piece.

BRANCHED   A pattern in the pile of, particularly, velvet. Also used to describe the use of branches of a plant or tree as motifs for embroidery.

BROADCLOTH   Made of carded wool in plain weave and fulled, after weaving on a wide loom (54 to 63 inches).

BROCADE   Made of gold, silver or silk, raised and enriched with flowers, foliage and other ornaments.

BROCATELLE   Made, particularly in Italy (Venice) with a linen weft strengthening silk; in imitation of furniture damask, with large foliate patterns, and much used for wall-hangings (Pl. 305).

BUCKRAM   A coarse cloth made of hemp, gummed, calendered, and dyed several colours. It was used in those linings which required stiffness, e.g. valances (q.v.).

BUTTONS and LOOPS   Found at the corners of bed valances and used to join the sides to the ends (see Pl. 44). A braid loop was passed over a button but by the eighteenth century this had become decorative, disguising hook and eye fastenings (q.v.).

CABRIOLE CHAIR   A chair having an oval or cartouche-shaped back, popular in the late eighteenth century.

CADDOW (Cadow)   A rough woollen covering.

CAFFA (Capha)   Coarse taffeta, of silk which may have been origi-nally woven in Caffa, a town on the Crimea coast, so taking its name therefrom.

CAFFART DAMASK   French, 'in imitation of the real, having woof of hair, coarse silk, thread, wool or cotton. Some have the warp of silk and the woof of thread; others are all thread or all wool'. Sheraton, C. D. (1803) I, p.91.

CAFFOY   A type of woollen velvet, originally a rich silk, but subse-quently made in India, and at Norwich, of cotton and worsted wool respectively.

CALICO   Cotton cloth of varying grades first made in India. Sheraton, *Encyclopedia* (1804–7), defined it as 'a sort of cloth resem-bling linens made of cotton. The name is taken from that of Calicut, the first place at which the Portugese landed when they discovered the Indian Trade . . .' (*see also* SWISSED).

CALIMANCO (Calamanco)   A worsted stuff with a fine gloss, woven on the loom of various patterns and an endless range of colours. Manufactured, particularly, in Norwich. Sheraton noted: '. . . it has a fine gloss and is checquered in the warp, whence the checks only appear on the right side. Some calamancos are quite plain, others have broad stripes, adorned with flowers, some with broad stripes quite plain and others watered'. Sheraton, C. D. (1803) I, p.121.

CAMBRIC   A fine white linen of a plain weave, often used, in dyed form, for curtain linings.

CAMLET (Camblet)   Woven in many widths, lengths, qualities and colours from wool, silk, linen, and goat's hair and, given different finishes, appeared as 'figured', 'water' and 'waved'. Used for bed hangings, cushions, etc.

CAMP (or FIELD) BEDS   A great variety. Sheraton noted: 'they have all folding tester laths, either hexagonal or elliptical shaped, and hinged so as to fold close together. In size they run about 6 feet long and 3 feet 6 or 9 inches in width, and between 5 feet 6 inches to 6 feet high, to the crown of the tester. They may be considered for domestic use, and suit for low room, either for servants or children to sleep upon'. Sheraton, C. D. (1803) II, pp.123–4. (See Pl. 351)

CAMP CHAIRS   Sheraton noted: '. . . made to fold up, the backs and bottom of which are formed of girth-webbing.' 'There are camp chairs made of mahogany, with the back framed to some simple pattern, but having the side rails so hinged as to admit the front to lay close to the back frame. The seats are formed of webbing, and when used, may have a cushion laid over it.' Sheraton, C. D. (1803) I, p.20; II, p.125.

CANOPY   An architectural term for a projection. Canopies were frequently part of medieval furniture (see Eames, 1971). They were usually formed from rich textile hangings and were hung above chairs of estate, couches etc. (See Pl. 14)

CANTOONS (French, *cantonnières*)   A narrow curtain at the front corners of a bed closing gaps between the main curtains and enclosing the posts or headboard. The *cantonnières* were normally at the front, and *bonnegraces* (bonegraces) at the back (Thornton, 1978, p.165).

CANVAS   A clear unbleached cloth of hemp or flax used for working needlepoint tapestry, and in coarse form for ship sails. Used for window blinds, when usually dyed green, and for various clothing and upholstery linings and bases.

CARDING   The process of combing out imperfections in used stuffings so that they could be reused, with a proportion of new material added (see Appendix A19).

CARTRIDGE PAPER   A strong lining paper (often referred to as 'Whatman' paper after a celebrated maker) used to make covers for furniture, and line walls under fabric. It was also used as a wallpaper and coloured with distemper.

CASE COVER   *See* SLIP COVER.

CASE-CURTAINS   The outer curtains of a bed, which when fully drawn protected hangings in more expensive fabrics from light and dust. They were hung from a case-rod (q.v.). See Pl. 87.

CASE-ROD (Compass Rod)   An iron, polished steel or brass rod fixed to the top of a bed tester to support protective case-curtains (see Pl. 87). Many are described in accounts as 'bright polished', being rubbed to a shine with a fine abrasive powder. Others were 'bright filed' by abrading to a finish with fine files.

Sheraton noted: 'Rods, for beds, are made to circumscribe the foot pillars, and the sides of the rod screw off about 8 inches from the pillars towards the head end, where the side rods slip on to a screw hook.

The rod of a tester for a canopy bed is made in two parts, which lap past each other, and admit the curtains to come close in the centre or to draw back to each other behind. These rods are made with a long plate at each end bent down about an inch, with two or three screw holes, with which to fix them to the under side of the rail.' Sheraton, C. D. (1803) II, p.298.

CELURE   The term, as mentioned in inventories and accounts, denoted a part of the bed hangings. It was generally applied to the back above the pillows, and was usually of some kind of textile. Celure and Tester (q.v.) are often mentioned together. There is reason to believe in early usage that 'celure' related to the canopy only, and 'tester' to the back.

CHAIR BEDS   Sheraton noted: 'The design shews a trunk below the seat, which is intended for the bed clothes. When the frame is folded quite down, within the seat, the cushion is placed upon it, and the back cushion being loose, is laid upon the frame when opened out, so that both of them make up nearly the whole length of the frame . . . When the whole is folded in, there is a case of cotton &c to hide the whole.' Sheraton, C. D. (1803) I, p.19.

CHAISE LONGUE   'A kind of sofa' is the description given in 1826 in George Smith's *The Cabinet-Maker and Upholsterer's Guide*. A form of chair with an elongated seat, with one end left open (see Pl. 272).

CHALONS   From an Italian (Renaissance) term, 'celone', but also a medieval name for woollen coverlets or blankets, referred to in Chaucer's *The Canterbury Tales* (lines 4139–40). As an upholstery material it was related to Dornix (q.v.) And could be rich, incorporating silk, even gold. It was figured on a draw-loom.

CHAMBER HORSE   An exercising chair in which a deep leather seat has a spring concertina movement to allow an active occupant to simulate horse riding. (See Pl. 226)

CHANGEABLE (Chaungeable)   An obsolete term applied to taffeta, where the warp and weft in different colours change the appearance, giving a 'changeable' effect.

CHASSIS (*à chassis*: French)   A removable seat (or back), upholstered over its frame (see Pl. 152).

CHENEY   A worsted furnishing material which may derive from the French *chaîne*, meaning warp. Related to harrateen and moreen (q.v.). Often dyed red, green, blue, yellow or purple, and sometimes watered.

CHIFFONIER BED   As with a press bed (q.v.), a folding bedstead is concealed in a carcase that resembles a chiffonier or sideboard.

CHIMNEY BLIND/BOARD   Alternatively a canvas roller blind or a painted, fabric covered board to close up a chimney opening in summer. The most celebrated examples of such boards are the two provided for Robert Child at Osterley, Middx. by Robert Adam. (See Beard 1978, Pls 74, 75, col. Pl. 6).

CHINTZ   A word derived from *chitta*, meaning 'spotted cloth'. Often a glazed cotton printed in vegetable colours with wood or other blocks, produced originally in India and then in France and England.

CLOAK PIN   A brass, threaded pin, often gilt, around which the draw lines of window curtains were fastened. (See Pl. 344)

CLOSE STOOL (Necessary Stool)   A chamber pot enclosed in a stool or box. This was frequently covered with velvet and leather and sometimes made by coffer-makers. The close stool was placed in a small 'closet', or cabinet, opening from a bedroom. Pans were specified in early inventories as made of pewter; later of a glazed ceramic body. (See Pl. 39)

CLOTH OF ESTATE   A cloth of estate consisted of a roof piece, called a ceeler (variants include celure, selour etc.), with valances around it, and a back piece called a tester. Some cloths of estate had a matching chair, footstool, stools and cushions. Often made of silk with armorial embroidery (see King, 1989, pp.314–15), the cloth of estate projected from the wall above the sovereign (see Pl. 14).

CLOTH OF GOLD/SILVER   A tissue of gold or silver threads interwoven with silk or wool. Used for fine bed hangings and clothes and denoting status and luxury. Silver-gilt and silver thread were imported to England from Venice and are referred to in accounts as 'Venice Gold' and 'Venice Silver'. For their use in the Wardrobe of Robes see Arnold (1988) p.375.

CLOTH, STAINED Hanging of linen, hemp or wool, decorated with biblical or mythological figure subjects by use of water-colours, distemper etc. In 1502 the crafts of painters and stainers amalgamated as one Company (D.E.F. II, p.106).

COMPANION CHAIR Three conjoined upholstered double seats. One was shown at the Great Exhibition of 1851.

CONFIDANTE A term used sometimes to describe a small sofa.

CONVERSATION CHAIR A single chair with a padded top rail. One is illustrated in Sheraton, C. D. (1803) Pl. 29.

CORDWAIN (Cordovan) Leather prepared from goatskin, named after Cordova in Spain. A cordwainer worked in Cordovan leather, being, usually, a member of the Cordwainers' Company.

COTT Sheraton noted: 'A sort of bed used at sea, and formed of canvas, sewed together in the shape of a chest, and is about 6 feet long, 2 feet broad, and 1 foot deep. The bottom is made of a wood frame, and strained with canvas; the whole is suspended by cords to some beams of the ship; it swings, and gives way to the motion of the sea. From these sea Cotts we have derived the notion of swinging cribs or cradles for children.' Sheraton, C. D. (1803) I, p.180.

COTTON The white fibrous substance which covers the seeds of the cotton plant, used for making cloth and thread. Confusingly, the term was used from the sixteenth century onwards for a woollen fabric manufactured in Westmorland, Lancashire (Manchester) and Wales, and to also denote the forming of a down or nap.

COUCH A long upholstered seat with a back and one or two ends. Evelyn in his *Diary* (8 May 1654) mentions 'the couch and seats were carved *à l'antique*.' (See Pl. 101)

COUCH BED A couch with a canopy and curtains, convertible to a bed (see Pl. 262). Sheraton noted: 'made sometimes with fixed and sometimes with loose testers, the pillars screw off from each corner of the couch, and the tester lath folds together, so that the whole may be enclosed within the seat of the couch, which is made hollow for that purpose.' 'To give more breadth to the bedding, they are sometimes made with a Board, hinged to fold in or out. When out, there are a couple of feet to support it; made either to screw off of fold in with the Board; and the whole being covered with a cotton case, it appears simply a couch or sofa.' Sheraton, C. D. (1803) II, p.182.

COUCH CHAIR An upholstered couch with hinged arm-rests, adjustable by moving iron stays on a toothed iron ratchet. There is a celebrated seventeenth century example at Knole, Kent (Pl. 38), which gave rise to many later, Edwardian, copies. In Henrietta Maria's accounts (See Appendix A15), a distinction is made between 'couch chair' and 'couch bed'.

COUCHING Stitching a thick thread to the surface of material by means of a fine thread.

COUNTERPOINT (Counterpane; French *courtepointe*) A decorative bed covering, frequently incorporating motifs present on other parts of the bed. Sheraton noted: 'the utmost of the bed clothes; that under which all the rest are concealed. The counterpane is a coverlet woven in squares . . . White cotton counterpanes of different quali- ties measure from 7 to 16 quarters. Coverlets . . . measure from 5 to 9 quarters, various stripes. From 6 to 10 quarters black weft diapers. Worsted red weft ditto of the same size . . . there are also double black and red weft diapers. Also there are silk coverlets, bordered and fringed . . .'. (See Pl. 134).

Diamond or Brussils coverlets . . . together with quilts, blankets &c of various sizes, may be purchased at Mr Carpenter's, Iron-

monger-Lane, Cheapside, who was kind enough to furnish me with this account of Counterpanes.' Sheraton, C. D. (1803) II, pp.182–3.

CRANKEY (Cranky) A mattress with a checked linen ticking, filled with horsehair.

CRETONNE Originally woven with a hempen warp and a linen weft, this strong plain-weave cotton cloth was produced in many colours and printed by various processes.

CREWEL A two-ply worsted yarn suitable for embroidery and knit- ting and used particularly in the creation of curtains in the seven- teenth and late nineteenth centuries.

CUP A finial on top of bed posts; cup-shaped, often covered with fabric, and from which feathers might be displayed.

CUPBOARD CLOTH When dressing a cupboard with plate or *objets* it was customary to place them on a cupboard cloth (see Pl. 1). Also known as a frieze cloth.

CURRICLES Sheraton noted: Arm chairs so named 'from their being shaped like a kind of carriage. These may claim entire originality, and are well adapted for dining parlours, being of a strong form, easy and conveniently low, affording easier access to a dining table than the common kind.' Sheraton, C. D. (1803) I, p.18.

CURTAIN Suspended cloth used as a screen round beds, at windows, occasionally in front of paintings, etc.

For window curtains the evolution by type was involved but progressed from a single curtain hanging from a rod, to those divided into two. By the end of the seventeenth century, the 'pull-up' or 'festoon' curtain had been introduced. This form was raised verti- cally in one piece to the window head by pulling on lines threaded through rings and passing over pulleys (see Pl. 304). It continued to be popular during the eighteenth century, in addition to the 'draw up' or 'drapery' curtains from the 1750s which divided into two when pulled up diagonally to drape at each side of the window (see Pl. 310). The use of the various terms in archives is contradictory. In summary it may be re-stated that in this study 'festoon' implies a curtain drawn up vertically and 'draw-up' or 'drapery' those dividing and hanging in a swag or 'fall' at each side. It is usually possible to ascertain the type by noting the details of pulleys and cloak pins but caution is necessary with the archival references. However, both these styles were replaced by the end of the 1780s by various forms of draw curtain, many inspired by French prototypes, with elaborate valances or drapery over wooden or gilded metal poles. They hung down straight from the rod. Designs of such, by Morel and Seddon, survive in the Royal Collection (Pl. 372) and many were illustrated in Ackermann's *Repository* (Pl. 360). See Baumgarten (1990) p.173 and Westman (1990). Sheraton noted: 'At present the most approved way of managing window curtains is to make them draw from the centre to each side of the window, by drawing a line which is fixed to a pully rack, and communicates to the rod fixed to the under side of the window lath with hooks; and that the curtains may lap over each other in the centre, the rod is made in two parts, shooting past each other about two or three inches . . .' Sheraton, C. D. (1803) II, pp.185, 269.

CURTAIN ROD A wood or metal rod upon which curtain rings are threaded. Sheraton noted: 'The common curtain rod is merely a piece of straight worked iron with a hole at each end to slip on to screw hooks. The French window rod is made of brass about three quarters of an inch diameter, having a pulley at the left end, and two at the right, one of which is fixed in a pin perpendicular to the rod.

At present they frequently make the French rods of satin wood, two to a window, to lap past each other about 3 inches in the centre. These rods have the same pulleys as those made in brass, which are morticed through the satin wood rod, and are fixed in with wire, and the hanging-pulley at the right hand is all of brass and screwed into the rod. To keep the ends of the rod secure they are hooped with brass, let on to the ends, which are filed level with the wood.'

CUSHION (Quisshion)   A fabric bag or case of varying shape filled with feathers or other soft material. Accounts refer to long, square and window cushions. Sheraton noted: 'A pillow for a seat, a soft pad placed upon a chair.' For sofa seats made 'in one length, some for the backs of sofas and couches in two or three lengths and for the ends. Cushions . . . much in use for the seats of cane chairs. Cushions are stuffed with hair in a canvass case, and are then quilted or tied down, and have loose cases into which they slip.' Sheraton, C. D. (1803) I, p.186.

DAIS   A raised platform. The French word *dais* means a canopy (Pl. 19).

DAMASK   A silk figured fabric, with its name derived from Damascus. From there its manufacture spread throughout Europe. Used for bed-hangings and furniture coverings and woven in England at Norwich and at Spitalfields. However, many patrons preferred Italian damasks for embellishing State Beds, chairs, curtains etc. Sheraton noted: 'It is a sort of silken stuff, having some parts raised above the ground, representing flowers or other figures. Damask should be made of dressed silks, both in warp and woof.

Damask is also a kind of wrought linen, made in Flanders, and in some parts of England; so called because of its large flowers, which resembles those of real damask. This kind is chiefly used for table service, but the Syrian damask, for all kinds of dress, and various hangings.' Sheraton, C. D. (1803) I, 191.

Inventory references to 'Watchet Damask' relate to its colour of light blue.

For Spitalfields silk dress damasks see Rothstein (1990).

DAMASK LEATHER   A stamped glazed leather, often used as a table cover, and as a protective case for, e.g. library tables. Used frequently by cabinet makers such as Thomas Chippendale, e.g. 12 November 1773 (Harewood House):

A large Commode . . .

A Damask leather Cover to do 15s

7 June 1774 (Paxton House)

2 Damask leather Covers lind and Bound with Gilt leather for the round Top of your Dining Tables. £1 8s 0d Gilbert (1978) I, pp.206, 274.

DAYBED   A long seat with an end so that it could be lowered to form a bed. Many, however, have an angled back which does not lower. Loose squab cushions were set on wicker panels forming a framed seat and back (see Pl. 100).

DIMITY   A stout cotton cloth, woven with raised stripes and fancy figures; used undyed for beds and hangings and sometimes for garments.

DOME BED   A bed with a canopy or tester in the form of a dome (see Pl. 296). Sheraton noted it as 'a spherical roof. This term amongst upholsterers is used without regard to the differences of the plan, when they apply it to the figure of a tester or roof of a bed . . . a hip-dome, signifies one raised from a square tester lath; an octagonal dome, from a tester lath of a regular octagon; a poligonal dome may signify . . . that it is raised from a tester of more or less sites than eight but not from four; a spherical dome, whose plan is a circle.' Sheraton, C. D. (1803) I, pp.197–8.

DORCER (Dorsal)   Medieval term for a hanging suspended upon the lower part of a wall to protect the backs of those seated from the coldness of the wall.

DORNIX (Darnex, Dornick, Dornix)   A cloth of linen warp and woollen weft, brought to Norwich in the sixteenth century by Flemish weavers. The range and patterns varied considerably (Thornton (1978) p.109). Not often mentioned in documentary sources after 1700.

DOWLAS (Doulas)   A kind of strong coarse calico.

DRAB   An undyed cloth of grey-beige colour.

DRAPERY   Sheraton noted: 'the dressy part of beds and window curtains, and is suspended to the tester of the former, and the lath of the latter . . . in upholstery work there seems to be no article in that branch more eagerly sought after. It has already been turned into so many shapes, that it is become quite a difficult task to produce anything novel.' Sheraton, C. D. (1803) I, p.200.

DROP TESTER   The part of a press bed (q.v.) acting as a tester.

DRUGGET   A stuff, all of wool, or half wool, half silk or linen, used originally for wearing apparel. Now implies a material protecting carpets or table surfaces, made from wool and linen.

DUCAPE   A stout silk fabric which is often corded and watered. There are samples in the P.R.O. (LC9/267) dated 1754–9. However, the material is said to have been introduced to England by French Huguenots and it is mentioned in 1687 in Thomas Alchorne's bill (Kent C. R. O., MSS., U269, M68/3).

DUCHESS(E)   Sheraton noted: 'a kind of bed, composed of three parts, or a chair at each end and a stool between them. They are only intended for a single lady, and are therefore not more than about 30 inches wide. The chair-ends, when apart, have the appearance of large arm or fauteuil chairs, and the middle part may be used as a stool. (See Pl. 343).

The pillars are made short, that they may be either inclosed within the stool chairs, for which reason the tester is also made to fold.' Sheraton, C. D. (1803) II, p.337.

DURANCE (Durant)   A glazed worsted cloth of plain weave, finer than tammy (q.v.). It was used to back the chairs (Pl. 316) supplied in 1771 by William Fell and Lawrence Turton to Sir Lawrence Dundas.

DUTCH CHAIR   One having a ladder back and a rush or 'matted' seat, often with a walnut frame. In the 1714 inventory of the effects of the French upholsterer resident in London, Francis Lapiere, descriptions suggest that on occasion such a chair was upholstered. Westman (1994) p.13.

EASY CHAIR   An upholstered winged arm-chair (see Pl. 128).

ELBOW   Described by Chippendale in the 3rd edn of his *Director* (1762) as the open, padded arms of 'French' chairs.

ELBOW CHAIR   An armchair, usually having open arms and padded rests. (See Pl. 246).

ELL   Measure of length (now obsolete), varying in different countries. The English ell measured 45 in. (112.5 cm).

EMBOSSING   A raised pattern on leather, cloth or metal which stood out in relief.

EMBROIDERY   The application of decorative needlework to the surface of a textile fabric, usually with needle and thread by hand work, but also by machine.

FALSE COVER   *See* SLIP-COVER.

FARTHINGALE CHAIR   A romantic Victorian term for a side chair or back stool, with a broad seat, popular in Elizabethan and Stuart England.

FAUTEUIL   'From the French, signifies a large chair.' Sheraton, C. D. (1803) II, p.337.

FEATHER BED   An early form of bed with the luxury of using whole feathers to impart softness and comfort.

FEATHERS   Taken from the skins of various birds such as swans, geese, eider (an Arctic species of duck), egrets, ostriches and hens. Used as a stuffing for pillows, cushions etc. Many pounds were imported to England from Dantzig in Poland, being known, in accounts, as 'Dantzic feathers'. Eider feathers were often known in accounts as 'Hudson's Bay feathers'.

Upholsterers had rooms for storing and drying feathers, and in the 1830s purified them by steam. They were frequently in dispute with the searchers of their livery company for using cheaper substitutes. Methods included *dressing*: airing and curing them, especially when reusing old material; and *driving*: beating in bags to loosen dirt.

FERRET   A tape, ribbon or binding made of cotton or silk. See its use by William France in December, 1764 (Appendix A36).

FIELD BED   *See* CAMP BED.

FILLING   The material used for stuffing upholstered furniture, such as hair or flock.

FINIAL   The terminal ornament on chairs, settees, beds. See also pomell (q.v.).

FIRE SCREEN   A panel of tapestry or needlework, or of painted wood, mounted into a frame and made to slide vertically on a pole, supported by a tripod (pole screen) or with two feet (Pl. 224).

FLANNEL   A loose textured woollen stuff used to line leather chair covers. It was bleached in sulphur fumes to improve its whiteness.

FLEDGE   A material with a herringbone effect in the weave. Mentioned in the Hardwick Inv. 1601 as being placed on beds, or on the floor around beds, Thornton (1978) p.113.

FLOCK   Tufts and sprigs of wool or cotton waste used to stuff mattresses. Also used in powdered form, sprinkled on an adhesive ground, to form flock wallpaper.

Sheraton noted it as: 'a kind of wool, used by upholsterers for mattresses'. Sheraton, C. D. (1803) II, p.216.

FLOOR CLOTH   A canvas floor covering, painted with formal or abstract patterns to represent tiles, marble etc. Several authors such as Batty Langley and John Carwitham published patterns in the 1730s. See *Country House Floors* (1987) p.21.

FLORENTINE STITCH   Also called bargello, Hungarian point, Irish stitch and flame stitch. The upright stitches work wool in rows on canvas to resemble a shaded zig-zag pattern. The tablecloth in Pl. 32 was so worked, *c*.1620.

FOOTBOARD   The panelled or upholstered end of a bedstead, rising above the level of the mattress.

FOOTSTOOL   A low stool, often *en suite* to a high chair. During the eighteenth and nineteenth centuries they became more elaborate in form (see Pl. 367) and often incorporated storage space beneath an upholstered, hinged lid.

FRENCH BED   The wooden framework supported hangings 'so as to form a plain, rectangular box' (Thornton, 1978, p.160 and pl. 135), with the framework completely hidden (See Pl. 37). However, from

c.1660 onwards the term also denoted a bed having a tester 'rising' in a coved form. Sheraton in 1803 described it as 'a form having an arched tester as in a tent or field bedstead', Sheraton C. D. (1803) II, p.24. At this time it may also be regarded as a couch bed with a head and footboard with a curtain draped over a pole projecting from the wall. (See Pl. 369).

FRENCH CORNER CHAIR   Illustrated by Ince and Mayhew in their *The Universal System* (1762, Pl. LVII), having a broad seat with a back and curved side, similar to a short sofa.

FRENCH ELBOW CHAIR   An armchair with upholstered back and seat popular in the 1750s and illustrated in Chippendale's *Director* (see Pls 246, 258).

FRENCH MATTRESS   Made from a mixture of wool and hair, in equal amounts.

FRENCH STOOL   Illustrated by Ince and Mayhew in their *The Universal System* (1762, Pl. LXI) as a seat with curved ends on four, or six, legs, with or without a back. Sometimes called window seats.

FRINGE   An ornamental bordering of threads of silk, cotton, etc., either loose or formed into tassels or twists. The pendants from the head of a fringe are called hangers. Knotted fringes were made as a pastime by ladies, but the quantity needed by upholsterers saw to their commercial availability. (See Pl. 82).

Sheraton noted it as: 'an ornament of worked silk or worsted, much in use amongst upholsterers, who introduce it occasionally to bed furniture, and window curtains. The French have begun to use fringe at the bottom of their chair backs. There is a kind of net fringe made in France, which looks well, somewhat like that in the French bed.' Sheraton, C. D. (1803) II, pp.214–15. See also Jackson (1987).

FULLING   Scouring and pressing of woollen goods to rid them of grease and form into a felted mass.

FURNITURE   In the upholstery sense coverings, usually in fabric, *en suite* to the bed.

FUSTIAN   A coarse twilled cotton cloth used for bed-hangings and clothing. From the fourteenth to the sixteenth century it was made in England, principally at Norwich. Fustian was also imported from Milan and Naples, Ulm (called Holmes) and Holland (Thornton, 1978, p.356, fn.60).

GALLOON (Galon, Gallon)   A tape or ribbon, frequently woven of thick gold or silver threads, and used to form patterns on bed valances, furniture, servants' liveries, etc. (See Pl. 89)

GERMAN STOVE   Used in workshops for heating and drying.

GINGHAM   A cloth of pure cotton woven with dyed yarns in stripes and checks. Often used for making slip-covers (q.v.).

GIRTH WEB   Strips of woven flax or hemp used to support the stuffing of upholstered chairs.

GOBELINS   A family of French dyers, who in the sixteenth century added tapestry-weaving to their activities. In 1662 Colbert bought the works on behalf of Louis XIV and established a manufactory for general upholstery. Robert Adam designed several 'Gobelins' rooms in the 1760–70 period, containing tapestry and furniture coverings made in Paris (see Pls 321–2). Also, an embroidery stitch invented to imitate tapestry.

GREAT WARDROBE   A section of the Royal household dealing with furnishing and textile provision, clothing (Wardrobe of Robes) and with various Standing Wardrobes in royal palaces (see Ch. I).

GROSGRAIN   A plain weave textile wherein the weft yarns are heavier than the warps to give a corded effect.

GROS-POINT   A form of cross stitch embroidery carried out in wool on squared canvas.

HALF-TESTER BEDSTEAD   A bedstead having a canopy bracketed forward from posts at the head.

HARATEEN (Harrateen)   A worsted furnishing fabric made, particularly, at Norwich and used extensively for furnishing and upholstery prior to *c*.1750. It could be patterned between hot copper rollers and was usually dyed green, red, yellow, crimson or blue. Closely related to Moreen (q.v.).

HEAD-BOARD (French: *champtourné*)   A board of shaped outline covered with material and placed behind the pillows and in front of a head-cloth on a bed. Many elaborate designs were proposed in the late seventeenth century by Daniel Marot (see Pls 95, 99).

HEAD-CLOTH (Backpiece: French, *fond-de-lit*)   The fabric at the back of a bed, held at the top by the tester and at its lower end by the shaped headboard. A place for armorial or other embroidery.

'HERCULANIUM CHAIR'   An early nineteenth century upholstered armchair reproducing classical motifs uncovered in the excavations of the 1750s at Herculaneum and Pompeii. Illustrated by Sheraton, C. D. (1803) Plate 7.

HESSIAN   A coarse hempen cloth, used for packing and for upholstery linings.

HOLLAND   A linen fabric, used for bed linen and linings, first made, as its name implies, in Holland.

HOOKS AND EYES   Small varnished metal fastenings to join fabric panels together. Used often on slip-covers, bed valances etc.

In 1771 Thomas Chippendale charged Edwin Lascelles of Harewood House for thirty-two hours' work 'Setting on hooks & eyes on the bases to beds on the Attic Floor & altering Counterpaines', Gilbert (1978) I, p.214.

HORSE HAIR   A form of covering for furniture woven from the mane and tail hairs of horses, with a linen or cotton warp. Could be made in plain, striped, chequered and coloured varieties. Used in making haircloth for covering dining and library chairs, and loose, in curled form, as a stuffing. (See Pl. 175).

INDIAN GOODS   The Anglo-Indian commerce in textiles from *c*.1600 onwards, at which English weavers protested frequently. See Irwin and Schwartz (1966).

INGRAIN CARPET   A non-pile reversible carpet made at Kidderminster, Worcestershire, in Cumbria and in Scotland. The carpet was woven in narrow strips, ranging from 18 to 36 inches wide, from a wool that was dyed with fast colours. They appeared about the middle of the eighteenth century and were produced to about the time of World War I (1914). See *Country House Floors* (1987).

IRISH STITCH   *See* FLORENTINE STITCH

JAPANNING   The method of imitating Oriental lacquer by applying a resin dissolved in spirits of wine in successive thin layers. John Stalker and George Parker issued *A Treatise of Japanning and Varnishing* from Oxford in 1688 which described ways of imitating Japanese lacquer. Compilers of inventories were usually unable to distinguish between Oriental and European lacquered wares.

KENDAL   A north-west English town in Cumbria known for Kendal cottons (Kendal greens) made, particularly, in the sixteenth century.

KERSEY   A cheap, coarse woollen cloth of twill weave. It was good at resisting water and was in demand for clothing.

KIDDERMINSTER CARPET   *See* INGRAIN CARPET

KIDDERMINSTER STUFFS   Diamond and chevron patterned worsted cloths made at Kidderminster, Worcestershire.

LAMBREQUIN   French. A valance or pelmet.

LAMPAS   Indian painted and resist-dyed textiles. In the west the term was applied to many patterned fabrics made, usually of silk, with metallic threads.

LATH BOTTOM BEDSTEAD   Wooden cross laths supported the mattress, rather than canvas supported by cords.

LAWN   A kind of fine linen resembling CAMBRIC (q.v.). Often used in dress for sleeves of e.g., a bishop's robes.

LEATHER   An animal skin, prepared for use by tanning (that is, soaking in various liquids rich in tannin, a group of astringent vegetable-substances). Used frequently in embossed and gilded form as wall-hangings and for durable chair seats. Holland and Spain were the principal suppliers.

   See also CORDWAIN, DAMASK, MOROCCO and RUSSIA LEATHER.

LIBRARY (or Reading) CHAIR   Sheraton noted: 'These are intended to make the exercise easy, and for the convenience of taking down a note or quotation from any subject. The reader places himself with his back to the front of the chair, and rests his arms on the top yoke. The desk is moveable to any point in the circumference of the yoke or top rail, by means of a groove cut in the wood and plates of iron screwed on. To the underside of the moveable piece is sometimes fixed a long and narrow drawer for ink and pens. To the underside of this same piece is tenoned a rail of mahogany half an inch thick, which is cut in notches to receive a foot, by which the reading flap is supported to any position.' Sheraton, C. D. (1803) I, pp.17–18.

LINE   A twisted cord, usually of silk, used over pulleys to draw up or part curtains, threaded through rings sewn to the back of the fabric and then tensioned by fastening to a cloak pin (q.v.).

LINEN   A cloth of many grades and weaves made from flax fibres.

LINSEY-WOOLSEY   A coarse cloth of linen warp and woollen weft, first made at Linsey in Suffolk. Cheap, and often used in servants' rooms for bed hangings.

LIT 'à la Duchesse' (French)   It is generally considered that beds *à la duchesse* (or 'angel' bed) differ from other sixteenth- and seventeenth-century beds in their lack of supporting foot posts. The State Bed at Erddig (Pl. 158) may be regarded as a late example of the form.

LIVERY   Clothing, or uniform used on ceremonial occasions, and by servants in royal or noble service. Staff of the Great Wardrobe were allowed their livery, on appointment, by issue of a warrant.

LOOSE COVER   *See* SLIP COVER

LOOSE SEAT   A slip seat, upholstered, and usually Roman letter numbered, to fit into the matching numbered frame of a chair or stool. A detail of one without upholstery is shown (Pl. 168).

LUSTRING (Lutestring)   A light crisp plain silk having a high lustre. (See Thornton, 1965, p.27.) Noted in Samuel Pepys's *Diary*, 18 February 1661, when a lady bought a 'suit of Lutestring'. Its manufacturers incorporated in the 1680s as The Royal Lustring Company.

Imported in the eighteenth century from France and Italy and much used for curtains and for linings.

LYON   The most important silk-weaving centre in France in the eighteenth century. The silk industry had been established in France under the protection and sponsorship of Louis XIV and enjoyed considerable success at Lyon and elsewhere in France in the period 1667–1791. Thornton (1965).

MADDER   A red vegetable dye used for dyeing wool, silk and cotton. Obtained from *Rubia tinctorum*, a plant found in Asia Minor.

MANCHESTER VELVET   A cotton velvet (including velveret and corduroy) made in all colours in Manchester and its environs in the eighteenth century. Thornton (1978) p.356, fn.61.

MANTUA   A silk of plain weave, heavier than taffeta. It is mentioned in Thomas Alchorne's 1687 bill (Kent C. R. O., MSS. U.269.168.3) at 9s a yard.

MAT   As a 'Garden mat' a chequered weave matting used as a packing material. Cornish, 'Portugal mats', 'Indian mats', 'Tangier mats', 'Barbary mats' and 'Dutch mats' are all encountered in English archives, particularly in the seventeenth century. They were used in less important rooms as a floor covering. See *Country House Floors* (1987) pp.96–100.

MATTED SEAT   Formed from rushes. In frequent use in Colonial American homes (see Forman, 1988). Matted chairs are often mentioned in English probate inventories which list country or 'vernacular' furniture.

MATTRESS   A case of canvas or other coarse material stuffed with hair, flocks, straw or the like. Used as a bed or a support for one.

MERCER   A dealer in fabrics ranging from costly silks and velvets to those of simple style, e.g. black fabric used in dressing rooms for mourning. Details of many eighteenth century mercers are given by Rothstein (1990). Most were members of the London livery company which regulated their trade.

MOCKADO (Moquette, moucade)   A wool velvet derived from French *mosquets* and English 'Musquetta carpets' (Thornton, 1978, p.109). Imported from Anatolia and mentioned, frequently, in inventories. The warp and weft were of linen with the pile formed by an extra weft of wool. Moquettes could be figured or plain or stamped with patterns after their weaving.

MOHAIR   Cloth made from the hair of the Angora goat. Alexander Pope referred to it (*Moral Essays*, Epistle 11, lines 169–70):

And when she sees her friend in deep despair,

Observes how much a chintz exceeds mohair.

MOIRÉ   Cloth with a lustrous surface finish to give a watered figure.

MOREEN (Morine)   A woollen material, sometimes mixed with cotton. Used as an upholstery material in the late seventeenth and eighteenth centuries.

MOROCCO LEATHER   Originally applied to a red goatskin leather produced in North Africa. Later a similar leather was made in the Levant (whence came the name of a distinctive grain), Turkey and countries bordering the Mediterranean; 'a sumach-tanned goatskin'. Crushed morocco had the grain flattened by plating to produce a mosaic of polished high parts and dull veinings, sometimes called 'Turkey leather'.

MURREY   A dull purple red colour often used to describe velvet – 'murrey velvet'.

MUSLIN   A fine cotton textile imported originally from India.

When the mule-jenny was invented in 1779 a fine cotton yarn suitable for weaving muslin was processed in England and Scotland.

NAILS   Used in various forms and sizes to fasten upholstered coverings to a wooden frame. They ranged from large copper ones, gilded, known as bullion nails (Pl. 23), to decorative patterns in smaller ones on eighteenth-century chairs (Pl. 342). This was known as 'close nailing', with the nails having gilded heads.

Nails were described by weight or price (or both) in accounts, e.g. '1 lb. of twopenny nails', and were often tinned or varnished to prevent staining. Small tacks (tax) held braids and laces in a similar way. Dutch nails are mentioned in accounts. I assume these differ from English nails in having a distinctive shaped head. Many eighteenth century accounts mention items being 'brass naild', a reference to nails with an iron spike and a decorative brass head, sometimes gilded.

NEEDLEWORK   A general term for patterns worked by hand with silk and a needle.

NORWICH STUFFS   Worsted goods made in East Anglia and marketed at Norwich.

OLIVE   An oval fabric-covered button, shaped as an olive, used for fastening upholstery. See their use in 1764 by William France (Appendix A36).

OS, OES   Curtain rings of varying size, usually of brass (but also found made of horn and wood); sometimes gilded. 'Os, Oes' take their name from their form. They are mentioned in archives as such, and more rarely as rings.

OSTRICH FEATHERS   Used particularly for the plumes on state beds, and, as a motif, in Elizabethan embroidery.

OTTOMAN   Described by Sheraton, D. B. (1791–4) as a fashionable novelty 'in imitation of the Turkish mode of sitting'. George Smith in his *Household Furniture* (1808) defined it as 'a form of long couch', usually without a back. It took many forms: circular, for corners, and for seating back to back. An 'Ottoman Footstool' was illustrated by Loudon (1833).

PALL   Cloth, usually of black, purple or white velvet, spread over a coffin, hearse or tomb. (See Pl. 22).

PALLIASE   A small mattress, usually stuffed with straw.

PANEL (Panes; Pantes)   Strips of fabric applied over other fabrics, usually of a contrasting colour, e.g., yellow panes on black.

On a bed the upper inside panels (French, *pentes de dedans*), upper outside panels (*pentes de dehors*) and lower panels (*soubassements*) formed an integral part of the overall decoration. The Hardwick Inv. (1601) mentions 'Pantes to goe about the sides of the bed at the bottome, of cloth of gold and crimson velvet, fringed with black and yellow silk frenge'.

PARAGON   A coarse worsted cloth, sometimes watered, used often for window curtains. Resembled chintz but was stated in 1605 to be a double camlet (q.v.) (D.E.F. III, p.15). Mentioned in Pat Barrett's bill of 1675 (Kent C. R. O., MSS. U.269 A183/1).

PARLOUR CHAIR   A chair with upholstered seat and sometimes a padded upper rail. Shown by Mayhew and Ince in *The Universal System . . .* (1762, Pl. IX) and by Sheraton, C. D. (1803) Pl. 31.

PASSEMENTERIE (Passement, Passamaine)   Narrow braids, formed by twisting threads, and including as a class laces, fringes, galloon, gimp. Elizabethan inventories often mention 'passamaine lace of golde'.

PAVILION   In France a circular canopy suspended above a bed, but in English use probably a tent with posts and pulleys, used for special entertainments. Many were circular, with a canopy and curtains (see Jervis, 1989, p.293).

PÉCHÉ-MORTEL   A French term for a couch. Mentioned by Horace Walpole in a letter to Horace Mann, 3 October, 1743: 'that I am only sitting in a common arm-chair, when I would be lolling on a *péché-mortel.'* Chippendale, *Director* 3rd edn (1762) Pl. XXXII, described two couches as 'what the French call peche-mortel'.

PELMET   (French, *lambrequin*.) A three-sided textile 'case' fixed at the head of a window to hide rods, rings and the tops of curtains. Often mounted on buckram and trimmed with fringes.

PELMET (Pulley) BOARD   A long rectangular board with various box-wood pulleys inserted. Draw lines would pass over these to raise or lower curtains, and be tensioned on cloak pins (q.v.) when the curtain was raised.

PENNYSTONE (Penistone)   A coarse woollen cloth made firstly at Penistone in the West Riding of Yorkshire. Ralph Grynder used it in 'scarlett collor', in 1637, a very early use of a dyed 'Penistone'. (See Appendix A15.)

PERFUME BAG   Ambergris, musk, civet and other powders were used in bags among clothes and fabrics, or as perfume used to impart an attractive odour to fustian, leather, etc. Also known as a 'sweetbag'.

PERPETUANA   A woollen fabric, made by combing and carding wool mixed in a twill weave. Its popularity was threatened in the late seventeenth century by the use of imported calicoes.

PERSIAN   A thin plain silk imported in the late seventeenth century by the East India Company. Mentioned in Thomas Alchorne's 1687 bill (Kent C. R. O., MSS. U.269.168.3) at 5s 6d and 6s a yard.

PETIT-POINT   A form of embroidery worked, usually, in tent stitch on a fine squared canvas.

PETTICOAT   *See* TOYLET

PILLOW   A support for the head in reclining or sleeping. A case made of linen, etc. was stuffed with feathers or other soft material.

PILLOWBEARE (Pillowbear, Pillowbere)   A pillow case, usually of white cotton or linen.

PINTADO   Originally block-printed cotton cloth but akin to chintz (q.v.). Imported into England in great quantity from the mid-seventeenth century as quilts, curtains, cupboard cloths &c. Mentioned in John Evelyn's *Diary*, 30 December 1665, 'I supp'd at my Lady Mordaunt's at Ashsted, where was a roome hung with *Pintado*, full of figures greate and small . . .'

PLAID   A plain woven twill with a pattern of intersecting strips in both warp and weft. 'Scotch plaid' is mentioned in inventories and used for blankets, hangings, ribbons, clothing etc.

PLEAT   Forming a shape in material by stitching and folding. Common forms are the 'box pleat' (a fold is made, with the material stitched down the length of the crease, and opened flat. The pleat is creased again on each side, forming the 'box', and stitched) and the 'organ pleat' (sometimes known as cartridge pleat. A long 'tube' is formed by stitching the fabric and filling with tight wadding). This often appears on the headcloth of state beds (Pl. 117).

PLUMBETS   Small lead weights incorporated in the linings of curtains to assist their correct hang.

PLUSH   A wool velvet made in several colours, and used in furnishing, altar frontals etc., as well as for clothing.

POMELL   A finial of ovoid form on the uprights of upholstered furniture (Pl. 6). Usually of gilt wood or copper, or covered with the velvet or damask used on the chair itself.

PORTIÈRE   A door curtain, used to ward off draughts and made *en suite* to other curtains in a room. Splendid late seventeenth century examples were provided at Hampton Court and have been renewed in the 1993/4 restoration (see Westman, 1994, p.45).

PORTUGAL MAT   A distinctive form of rush matting often used in the seventeenth century in bed-chambers. State beds often stood on them, as depicted in an engraving, *c*.1690, by Daniel Marot. Thornton (1978) p.100.

POUCH TABLE   Described as a 'Table with a Bag used by ladies to work at, in which bag they deposit their fancy needle work.

'The work bags of both tables are suspended to a frame which draws forward, in which frame is a lock which shuts its bolt up into the under edge of the rail of the top . . .

'. . . are also used as chess tables'. Sheraton, C. D. (1803) II, p.292.

PRESS BEDSTEAD   A folding bedstead which was built into a cabinet to outwardly resemble a chest of drawers or clothes press. The most splendid example was that provided for David Garrick by Thomas Chippendale, *c*.1775. Gilbert (1978) II, Pl. 62.

QUILT   A bed coverlet with soft material (wool, feathers) between two pieces of cloth. *Quilting* was a method of keeping this wadding in place by stitching through and through the layers to form a pattern in diamond, chequered or other geometric or naturalistic patterns.

A 'Marseilles Quilt' was one 'quilted in the loom in imitation of Marseilles and Italian quilting' and of linen, wool, silk or cotton. Common in the 1780s. One was provided for the Yellow Bed-chamber at Osterley Park, Middx., as noted in the 1782 inventory. *Furniture History*, XXII (1986) p.113.

RATTINET   A thin woollen stuff, similar to shalloon (q.v.) used for lining curtains. Appears frequently in Chippendale's accounts, e.g., March 1778, Sir Edward Knatchbull: '67 yds fine buff Rattinet to line [Drapery window curtains].' Gilbert (1978) I, p.233.

RAYNES Cloth of   A linen of fine quality used in the sixteenth century for sheets. Took its name from Rennes, where it was originally made (D.E.F., III, p.40).

RIPPING   Tearing apart or unseaming of upholstery, done frequently to form curtains into a new fashion by using the available fabric.

RUGG (Rug)   A coarse woollen coverlet for beds. 'Irish ruggs' are mentioned in inventories. They seem to have been similar to Spanish blankets (BLANKET, q.v.) and have been noted, in 1585, as a 'checkly' Irish rug and in 1591 as one from Waterford (Thornton 1978, p.355, n.46, 48).

RUSSET   A coarse woollen cloth; also a brown colour.

RUSSIA LEATHER   A distinctive leather of calf or cowhide, originating in Russia. Very resistant to water and not affected by humidity; resistant also to insects. Has a diced grain produced with a plaque of copper or wood whilst the leather is damp. Much used by upholsterers on dining room and library chairs (see Pl. 129).

SAD   Denoting a dull or neutral colour, e.g., 'For a set of sad culler Searge curtains . . .'

SARCENET (Sarsnet)   A thin, transparent silk. Its name derives from *Saracenus* (Latin) 'from first having been woven by Saracens, probably in Spain.' Listed in many inventories, being used for curtains, case-covers, sun-blinds (see Thornton and Tomlin (1980) pp.21, 52).

SATIN   A smooth, shiny silk made with the warp threads much finer and more numerous to the square inch so as to conceal the weft. Many brocaded satins are really two-colour damasks (q.v.). 'Thred' satin had a silk warp and linen weft. Westman (1994) p.14.

SAY   A thin woollen stuff of twill weave, akin to serge (q.v.). Much used for linings and for clothes.

SCOTCH CARPET   *See* INGRAIN CARPET

SCREEN/SCREEN CLOTH (French, *Paravent*)   A large frame of several hinged folds, covered with cloth or tapestry and used to keep off draughts. Some screens had protective, but detachable, 'screen cloths'. Thornton (1978) p.385, fn.42.

SCRIM   A thin canvas used for lining and covering the wooden frame of a chair, etc. prior to upholstery (Pl. 223).

SELVAGE   The edge of a piece of material so woven that the weft threads do not unravel.

SERGE   A twilled cloth having a worsted warp and a woollen weft. It was cheap and hard-wearing. Used for clothing, curtains, valances. Chippendale supplied Sir Edward Knatchbull in March 1778 with '48 yds Buff Serge in Bags to the window Curtains', obviously as a protective covering (Gilbert, *Chippendale* (1978) I, p.233).

SETTEE   A long seat, with a back and arms, for two or more people. The seat was usually upholstered but the back often took the form of two conjoined chair backs. Became fashionable from the 1660s onwards. (See Pl. 101).

SHAG (Shagg)   A cloth having a velvet nap on one side, usually of worsted, but sometimes of silk.

SHAGREEN   Untanned leather, often dyed green and used to cover small receptacles. First introduced to Europe from China and Japan in the seventeenth century. Whilst referred to as a sharkskin, it is really the skin of small tropical sharks such as rays and dogfish. Durable and resistant to scratching.

SHALLOON   A twilled worsted cloth, often glazed or hotpressed. Much used for curtains and linings.

SHAM BOOKS   Simulated book spines fashioned as tooled leather reliefs on panels, to be affixed to library doors so as to suggest continuous shelving.

SILK   Cloth woven from filaments reeled from the cocoons of, especially, the silk worm. See Beck (1882); Thornton (1965) and Rothstein (1990).

SILKWOMAN   A specialist in spinning and dyeing silk.

SLIP-COVER (Slip-over; Slip-on; Case; False)   A covering for furniture, particularly tables and chairs, made of leather, gingham or serge, as appropriate, to protect from light and dusk (see Pl. 337). Fastened by ties, or hooks and eyes, or made to fit loosely (see Baumgarten, 1993).

SLEEVE   A fabric covering to protect bed-posts and enhance the appearance of chandelier and picture chains.

SOFA   A long upholstered seat with a back and two ends.

SOFA BED   A sofa by day, a bed at night. Sheraton published a design for one, C.D. (1803) Pl.17.

SPARVER   A bed curtain (French, *Espervier*). Horman in *Vulgaria* (1519), p.167, says: 'Some have curteynes; some sparvers aboute the

bedde to kepe away gnattes'. Later it developed as a hanging or canopy to suspend over a bed. As such it is shown, in conical form, on the armorial bearings of The Worshipful Company of Upholders.

SPIKES (Spicks)   Used in particular at the top of bedposts in order that the tester could be located thereon, and occasionally as wall supports for chains/cords supporting a flying-tester or 'angel'.

SPITALFIELDS   The centre of the London silk weaving industry. Many Huguenot weavers settled there in the early eighteenth century. See Rothstein (1990).

SPRING UPHOLSTERY   Coiled metal springing to support upholstery came into use from 1828 (Patent No.5668 to Samuel Pratt). Loudon (1833) refers to springs and illustrates one in the form of a double cone. The metal springs were made usually at Birmingham (see Edwards, 1993).

SQUAB   A removable stuffed cushion. The 1710 Dyrham Park inventory, *Furniture History*, XXII (1986), p.59 mentions 'A Canopy Bed & Squab with Clouded Silk' in the Gilded Room. In December 1775 Chippendale supplied to Harewood House 'a full bordered Hair Squab', Gilbert (1978) I, p.209.

STANDING BEDSTEAD   This form of bedstead usually had a high panelled head and foot. A tester in the form of a rectangular frame connected these and sometimes had a light tester cloth stretched across. This was not a bed to be moved (as with the low Trundle Bed, q.v.) and may, as a term, refer to any substantially framed bed (Thornton, 1978, p.157).

STATE BED   An imposing bed used by royal personages or visitors of considerable rank. A state bed had head and foot curtains, an elaborate tester, a back cloth and head board with valances at front, sides and base. Carved wood was usually covered with silk damask to form elaborate scrolls. (See Pls 132–3, 134).

STAY (Staple)   A metal rod attached to a wood frame and working over a toothed ratchet to allow the back of the chair or settee to be raised or lowered. The rod was usually fabric-covered, or silvered (see Appendix A15 and Pl. 58).

STUFF   A general term for worsted cloths, but also used in inventories to describe textiles of all kinds.

STUFF-OVER   Used when the wooden frame of a chair or settee is completely covered by upholstery.

STUMP BEDSTEAD   In use by servants, this simple form of bedstead was without posts, tester and footboard. It had a simple headboard and was supported by four short wooden legs.

STUMPWORK   A form of embroidery, padded so as to be in relief. Popular in the last half of the seventeenth century as a covering for boxes, looking glass frames, etc. The crown of a royal duke, James Duke of York, on the King's bed at Knole, Kent, *c.*1673, is in stumpwork.

SUMMER BED   Two four-post single beds, separated by a narrow entry aisle, with the testers joined by a surmounting cornice. Designed in the late 1780s by Thomas Sheraton (see Pl. 347).

SWAG DRAPERY   A draping of fabric across the top of a window in place of a valance or pelmet. Usually cut and shaped to form a shallow scallop shell.

SWISSED   A term used in relation to calico and presumably implying some process, 'calico swissed', that rendered it more flexible.

TABBY   A plain silk, often with a watered or waved finish. Patterns were embossed from rollers. For those by Anna Maria Garthwaite at Spitalfields, *c.*1752, see Rothstein (1990).

TAFFETA A plain woven silk with the weft threads thicker than the warp ones. Made in all colours, checked, flowered or with patterns. Much used for bed canopies, window curtains etc. Related to lustring, sarcenet and tabby (q.v.).

TABLE BEDSTEAD A dual purpose piece of furniture, popular in the late eighteenth century. A folding bedstead was incorporated in a cupboard. (See also 'Press Bed'.)

TABLE CARPET/CLOTH Used as a protective covering for inlaid or marble table tops. A prominent example of its use, in 1604, is illustrated (Pl. 18). Tables were also covered with table cloths, often embroidered with elaborate patterns (Pl. 26).

TAMMY A lightweight worsted fabric, of an 'open' weave; often glazed. Derives from the French word *Etamine*, meaning a worsted yarn and a warp. Coloured tammy was much used for bed and window hangings. Chippendale's bills to Sir Edward Knatchbull in the 1770s included mentions of tammy for spring curtains, window curtains and linings (Gilbert, *Chippendale* (1978) I, pp.227–34).

TAPESTRY A thick, hand-woven fabric, usually of wool with pictorial or ornamental designs formed by the weft-threads. These are carried back and forth only across those parts where their respective colours are needed and not from selvage to selvage.

TASSEL Cut cords or threads gathered into a tight bunch at the top by a decorative braid. Alternatively they can be passed through a pierced wooden ball, covered with the same material forming the threads. Used as an ornament on cushions, curtain tie-backs, etc.

Sheraton noted: 'A kind of pendant ornament used in upholstery work. The drawing lines of festoon curtains have tassels at their ends. And opposite to this side, there should be a false line and a tassel to it, to match the right side of the window.

Balance tassels are those which are used in fire screens to keep the mount up.' Sheraton, C. D. (1803) II, p.317.

TAWNEY (Tawny) A colour, compounded of red and yellow.

TENT BED A bed with four posts supporting a fabric covered and curved canopy. Deep valances and curtains hide the framework. Sheraton designed a camp (or tent) bed which he illustrated in the *Cabinet Dictionary* (1803) and there is a further design (1827) in George Smith's 1826 edition of his *Cabinet Maker and Upholsterer's Guide* (see Pl. 351).

TESTER (French *ciel-de-lit*; *impériale*) In the late medieval period the tester was the upright piece at the head of a bed with the 'celure' as the roof-like projection. By the seventeenth century the use of a 'celure' had declined, and what had formerly been the 'tester' became the 'head-cloth' or 'head-board'. For the most part, modern usage regards the tester as the 'roof' of a bed. A half-tester bed had a 'roof' which only projected half-way over a bed. The *lit d'ange* (angel or flying tester bed) had its roof suspended by cords or chains. (See Eames (1971); Thornton (1978) p.365 and Ch. VII.)

TICKING A linen twill. The best came from Flanders and is often mentioned in bills and inventories for the making of bags, to enclose feathers, in use as mattresses, bolsters and pillows.

TISSUE A rich fabric having two sets of warp threads much used, with silver and gold threads, as bed hangings; and for coronation robes.

TOILET (Toylet; French, *toilette*) TABLE A dressing table, sometimes with drawers, kneehole recess and an adjustable looking glass above. Alternatively examples were common from the mid-eighteenth century onwards in having elaborate draperies below the top (see Pls 267, 282); also called a 'petticoat'.

The toilet was also provided with a veil (or scarf) to drape over the dressing-glass. This can be seen in the Zoffany portrait of Mrs Abington (Pl. 303).

TRAVERSE CURTAIN Used to divide parts of a room or screen alcoves, etc.

TRUNDLE (Truckel) BEDSTEAD A low bed on castors which could be wheeled away under a Standing Bedstead. Used by servants, in medieval times, when they slept in the same room as their masters and mistresses. Also used by children.

TUFTED The stitched and (later) buttoning techniques used by upholsterers to stabilize the fillings of chairs, couches etc (see Pl. 286).

TURKEY LEATHER *See* MOROCCO LEATHER

TURKEY WORK A woollen pile fabric made to imitate Turkish carpets and used for upholstery seats, and as floor and table carpets. Worked on a loom, mounted with hemp warp threads, to which the coloured yarns were tied by hand (see Pl. 61).

TWILL Textile fabrics in which weft threads pass alternately over one warp thread, and under two or more, to produce diagonal lines.

UTRECHT VELVET A stout velvet with a linen warp and weft with pile of goat's hair. Made in solid colours or striped. Seems to have had no manufacturing connection with Utrecht, but to be named by its weaving on a draw-loom (*velours de trek*, i.e., *à la tire*, drawn; Thornton, 1978, p.112).

UMBRELLO A sun shade fixed above a window. Much in use in the neoclassical years of the 1760–90 period and provided frequently by upholsterers such as Vile and Cobb and Mayhew and Ince.

VALANCE (Valence) A drapery hanging at the tester or base of a bed, hiding, between an outer and inner valance, the curtain head, draw-lines etc. Often stiffened with buckram (q.v.). The French term for the upper outside valances is *pentes de dehors*.

VASE (Vauze) *See* CUP

VELVET A pile fabric of silk, wool or cotton fibres. The best was imported from Genoa (see Pl. 103). The pile is produced by adding to the usual warp and weft threads an additional row of warp yarns. These are woven into the surface of the cloth and passed over wires on the surface. For a loop pile these wires are drawn out. For velvet or other cut pile a knife is passed along a groove at the top of each wire to cut the pile before the wire is withdrawn (see Chambers, 1741).

VOLARY An aviary. (O.E.D.). See Appendix A19 for a mention of one provided by John Casbert in 1677.

WALLPAPER A stout paper, usually patterned, pasted to the interior walls of rooms. Flock paper (powdered wool applied to an adhesive) was popular in the late seventeenth century as an alternative to velvet. Wallpaper followed fashion with Chinese paper imported from the Orient popular in the mid-eighteenth century.

Sheraton noted: 'Paper Hangings are a considerable article in the upholstery branch, and being occasionally used for rooms of much elegance it requires taste and skill rightly to conduct this branch of the business'. Sheraton, C. D. (1803) II, p.281. See also Sugden and Edmondson (1925); Entwisle (1960); Oman and Hamilton (1982); Wells-Cole (1983); Rosoman (1992).

WALLPAPER PASTE Sheraton noted: 'Used among upholsterers, is a preparation of wheaten flour, boiled up and incorporated with water. The flour should be mixed with cold water so as to leave no lumps, which should be little thicker than milk before boiling it; and if the paste be wanted of a very tenacious quality, gum arabic should be dissolved and mixed with it. When the mixture is boiling, it should be constantly stirred about, till it thicken and become like a strong jelly, which then, after this degree of boiling, is fit for use.' Sheraton, C. D. (1803) II, p.281.

WARP   Threads which are stretched lengthwise, or vertically, in a loom, to be crossed, horizontally, by the weft (q.v.).

WATERING   A waved or watered effect on fabric, achieved by means of a press having heated metal rollers.

WEBBING   Narrow bands of hemp or jute. These were interlaced and secured by tacks to the underside of a chair frame (see Pl. 243). They formed a strong base for supporting springs or stuffing (see Milnes, 1983).

WEFT   Threads which are stretched from side to side, or horizontally, in a loom, to be crossed vertically by the warp (q.v.).

WILTON   A small town in Wiltshire adjacent to the seat of the Earls of Pembroke and Montgomery, known from the sixteenth century for carpet weaving. Wilton was the first maker of a carpet with a short thick pile: 'Wilton' carpets are now made like this in other centres.

WINDOW CLOTH   An absorbent cloth fitted into window embrasures in the winter to absorb moisture and protect from draughts through ill-fitting frames.

WINDOW SEAT   An upholstered seat with two curved ends, made to fit into a deep window recess (see also 'French Stool'). There are splendid neoclassical examples at, for example, Corsham Court, Wiltshire (D.E.F., III, Pl. 59) and Ickworth Park, Suffolk (*ibid.*, Pl. 62).

WORSTED   A woollen fabric or stuff made from well-twisted yarn spun from long staple wool combed so that its fibres lie parallel.

X-FRAMED CHAIR   A popular form of chair from Egyptian times onwards, originally made to fold and therefore to travel with the household. It was highly regarded as a chair of state, and as such appears in many Elizabethan and seventeenth century portraits (Pls 7, 24). There are examples (at Knole, Kent, Pls 29, 31) but so upholstered and covered as to render 'folding' impossible. Also known as cross-framed chairs.

BIBLIOGRAPHICAL REFERENCES AND ABBREVIATIONS

Place of publication is London unless otherwise stated.

ACKERMANN, *Repository* Rudolph Ackermann, *The Repository of Arts, Literature, Commerce, Manufactures . . .* (1809–28).

ACKERMANN (1823) Rudolph Ackermann, *A Series Containing Forty-Four Engravings in Colours, of Fashionable Furniture* (1823).

AGIUS AND JONES (1984) Pauline Agius and Stephen Jones, *Ackermann's Regency Furniture and Interiors*, Crowood Press, Marlborough (1984).

ALDRICH, ed. (1990) Megan Aldrich, ed. *The Craces: Royal Decorators 1768–1899* (1990).

APTED AND ALLEN (1984) M. R. Apted and Juliet Allen, eds *Audley End, Essex* (1984).

ARNOLD (1978) Janet Arnold, 'The "Coronation" Portrait of Queen Elizabeth I', *The Burlington Magazine*, CXX (November 1978) pp.727–41.

ARNOLD (1988) Janet Arnold, *Queen Elizabeth's Wardrobe Unlock'd*, Leeds (1988). An impressive commentary on the Inventories of the Wardrobe of Robes prepared in July 1600, with an edition of Stowe MS 557, British Library; MS, LR2/121, Public Record Office and MS., V.b.72. Folger Shakespeare Library, Washington, D.C.

ARNOLD (1992) Janet Arnold, 'The Kirtle, or Surcoat, and Mantle of the Most Noble Order of the Garter worn by Christian IV, King of Denmark and Norway', *The Antiquaries Journal*, LXXII (1992) pp.141–67.

AUSTEN (1974) Brian Austen, 'Morgan & Sanders and the Patent Furniture Makers of Catherine Street', *The Connoisseur*, 187, No.753 (November 1974) pp.180–91.

AYLMER (1961) G. E. Aylmer, *The King's Servants: The Civil Service of Charles I, 1625–42* (1961).

B.L. British Library, London.

BAUMGARTEN (1990) Linda Baumgarten, 'Curtains, Covers and Cases: Upholstery Documents at Colonial Williamsburg', in Williams et al. (1990), pp.160–85.

BAUMGARTEN (1993) Linda Baumgarten, 'Protective Covers for Furniture and its Contents', in *American Furniture* (Hanover USA and London, 1993) I, pp.3–14.

BEARD (1953) Geoffrey Beard, 'Robert Adam at Croome Court', *The Connoisseur*, 132, (October 1953) pp.73–6.

BEARD (1955) Geoffrey Beard, 'Weston Hall, Staffordshire, Home of the Earl of Bradford', *Connoisseur Yearbook* (1955) pp.22–32.

BEARD (1970) Geoffrey Beard, 'William Kent and the Royal Barge', *The Burlington Magazine*, CXII, No.809 (August 1970) pp.488–94.

BEARD (1975) Geoffrey Beard, 'William Vile Again', *Furniture History*, XI (1975) pp.113–15.

BEARD (1978) Geoffrey Beard, *The Work of Robert Adam*, Edinburgh (1978).

BEARD (1978) II Geoffrey Beard, 'Robert Adam and his Crafts-men', *The Connoisseur*, 198, No.797 (July 1978) pp.181–93.

BEARD (1981) Geoffrey Beard, *Craftsmen and Interior Decoration in England 1660–1820*, Edinburgh (1981).

BEARD (1985) Geoffrey Beard, 'The Quest for William Hallett', *Furniture History*, XXI (1985) pp.220–5.

BEARD (1989) Geoffrey Beard, *The Work Of Grinling Gibbons* (1989).

BEARD (1993) Geoffrey Beard, 'Decorators and Furniture Makers at Croome Court', *Furniture History*, XXIX (1993) pp.88–110.

BEARD (1994) Geoffrey Beard, 'Some Eighteenth-Century English Seats and Covers Re-examined', *The Magazine Antiques* (New York, June 1994) pp.842–9.

BEARD AND GILBERT (1986) Geoffrey Beard and Christopher Gilbert, eds *Dictionary of English Furniture-Makers 1660–1840*, Leeds (1986).

BEARD AND WESTMAN (1993) Geoffrey Beard and Annabel Westman, 'A French Upholsterer in England, Francis Lapiere, 1653–1714', *The Burlington Magazine*, CXXXV, No.1085, August 1993, pp.515–24.

BECK (1882) S. W. Beck, *The Draper's Dictionary: A Manual of Textile Fabrics* (1882).

G. DE BELLAIGUE (1967) Geoffrey de Bellaigue, 'The Furnishings of the Chinese Drawing Room, Carlton House', *The Burlington Magazine*, CIX, No.774 (September 1967) pp.518–28.

G. DE BELLAIGUE AND KIRKHAM (1972) Geoffrey de Bellaigue and Pat Kirkham, 'George IV and the Furnishing of Windsor Castle', *Furniture History*, VIII (1972) pp.1–34.

BEN-AMOS (1991) I. K. Ben-Amos, 'Failure to become freemen: Urban apprentices in early modern England', *Social History*, 16, No.2 (May 1991).

BEN-AMOS (1994) I. K. Ben-Amos, *Adolescence and Youth in Early Modern England* (1994).

BETTEY (1977) J. H. Bettey, 'Cultivation of Woad', *Textile History*, IX (1978).

BLUNT (1970) Anthony Blunt, *Art and Architecture in France 1500 to 1700*, 2nd ed. (1970).

BOWDEN (1962) P. J. Bowden, *The Wool Trade in Tudor and Stuart England* (1962).

BOYNTON (1980) L. O. J. Boynton, 'William Gomm', *The Burlington Magazine*, CXXII, (June 1980), pp.395–402.

BOYNTON, ed. (1995) L. O. J. Boynton, *Gillow Furniture Designs 1760–1800*, Royston, Herts (1995).

BROOKE (1972) John Brooke, *King George III* (1972).

BROOKS (1943) E. St.-J. Brooks, *Sir Christopher Hatton* (1943).

BROWN (1989) Peter Brown, *Fairfax House, York*, York Civic Trust (1989).

BROWSHOLME INV. (1986) Simon Jervis, ed. 'Five Early Inventories of Browsholme Hall', *Furniture History*, XXII (1986) pp.1–24.

BRYANT (1988)   Julius Bryant, 'Back as Adam Intended', *Country Life*, 3 November 1988, pp.192–5.

BRYANT (1993)   Julius Bryant, *London's Country House Collections* (1993).

BURGON (1839)   J. W. Burgon, *Life and Times of Sir Thomas Gresham* (1839).

BURNHAM (1980)   D. K. Burnham, *Warp and Weft – A Dictionary of Textile Terms*, New York (1980).

CALDWELL (1986)   Ian Caldwell, 'James Moore, Queen Anne and the Duchess of Marlborough', *Antique Collector* (May 1986) pp.41–7.

CALDWELL (1987)   Ian Caldwell, 'John Gumley, James Moore and King George I', *Antique Collector* (April 1987) pp.66–71.

CAL. S. P. CALENDAR OF STATE PAPERS   Cal. S.P. Dom., State Papers Domestic, various years.

Edward VI, 1547–53, ed. C. S. Knighton, revd edn (1992). Treasury Books, 1699–1700.

CAL. S.P. Venetian, 1534–54, ed. R. Brown (1873).

CAMDEN MISC. (1855)   'Inventories of Henry Fitzroy, Duke of Richmond and of Wardrobe Stuff of Katharine, Prince Dowager at Baynard's Castle'. *Camden Miscellany*, III (1855).

CAMPBELL (1994)   Thomas Campbell, 'William III and the "Triumph of Lust"; The tapestries hung in the King's State Apartments in 1699', *Apollo*, CXL, No.390 (August 1994) pp.22–31.

CECIL (1973)   David Cecil, *The Cecils of Hatfield House: A Portrait of an English Ruling Family* (1973).

CHILD (1668)   Sir Josiah Child, *Brief Observations concerning Trade and Interest of Money, By J.C.* (1668).

CHAMBERS (1741)   Ephraim Chambers, *Cyclopedia; or, An Universal Dictionary of Arts and Sciences*, 2 vols (1741).

CLARK (1981)   Jane Clark, 'The Buildings and Art Collection of Robert Dudley, Earl of Leicester'. University of London, Courtauld Institute, M.A., Report (1981).

CLAY (1984)   C. G. A. Clay, *Economic Expansion and Social Change: England 1500–1700*, 2 vols, Cambridge (1984).

CLINTON (1979)   Lisa Clinton, 'The State Bed from Melville House', Victoria and Albert Museum, Masterpieces, Sheet 21 (1979).

COLERIDGE (1963)   Anthony Coleridge, 'William Masters and some Early Eighteenth Century Furniture at Blair Castle', *The Connoisseur*, October 1963, pp.77–83.

COLERIDGE (1966)   Anthony Coleridge, 'The 3rd and 4th Dukes of Atholl and the firm of Chipchase', *The Connoisseur*, February 1966, pp.96–101.

COLERIDGE (1967) I   Anthony Coleridge, 'Sir Lawrence Dundas and Chippendale', *Apollo*, LXXXVI, No.67 (September 1967) pp.190–203.

COLERIDGE (1967) II   Anthony Coleridge, 'Some Rococo Cabinet-Makers and Sir Lawrence Dundas', *Apollo*, LXXXVI, No.67 (September 1967) pp.214–25.

COLERIDGE (1968)   Anthony Coleridge, *Chippendale Furniture: The Work of Thomas Chippendale and his Contemporaries in the Rococo Style* (1968).

COLVIN (1995)   H. M. Colvin, *A Biographical Dictionary of British Architects 1600–1840*, 3rd revd edn (1995). The first and second editions were 1954 (1660–1840) and 1978 (1600–1840).

COLLARD (1985)   Frances Collard, *Regency Furniture*, Woodbridge (1985); re-issued 1995. Her comments and illustrations (pp.274–

314) on upholstery are invaluable.

CONSITT (1933)   Francis Consitt, *The London Weavers' Company*, Oxford (1933).

COOKE, ed. (1987)   Edward S. Cooke, ed., *Upholstery in America and Europe from the Seventeenth Century to World War I*, New York and London (1987).

COOPER (1972)   Jeremy Cooper, 'Victorian Furniture, An Introduction to the Sources', *Apollo*, XCV (February 1972) pp.115–23.

CORNFORTH (1965)   John Cornforth, 'Drayton House, Northamptonshire III', *Country Life*, 27 May 1965, pp.1286–9.

CORNFORTH (1986)   John Cornforth, 'British State Beds', *The Magazine Antiques* (New York, February 1986) pp.392–401.

CORNFORTH (1987)   John Cornforth, 'Houghton Hall, Norfolk II', *Country Life*, 7 May 1987, pp.104–8.

CORNFORTH (1987)   John Cornforth, 'Glow of Gold Brocade' (The King's Bed at Knole, Kent), *Country Life*, 6 August 1987, pp.64–5.

CORNFORTH (1988)   John Cornforth, 'Ditchley Park, Oxfordshire II', *Country Life*, 24 November 1988, pp.82–5.

CORNFORTH (1989)   John Cornforth, 'A Georgian Patchwork', in G. Jackson-Stops, G. J. Schochet, L. C. Orlin and E. B. MacDougall, eds, *The Fashioning and Functioning of the British Country House*, 1989, pp.155–74.

CORNFORTH (1994)   John Cornforth, 'The Creation of Houghton', Christie's Houghton Sale Catalogue, 8 December 1994, pp.iv–x. See also Fowler and Cornforth.

C.L.R.O. ORPHANS' INVS.   Corporation of London Record Office, Orphans' Court Inventories.

COUNTRY HOUSE FLOORS (1987)   C. Gilbert, J. Lomax and A. Wells-Cole, *Country House Floors, 1660–1850* (Temple Newsam House, Leeds, Catalogue, 1987).

C.R.O. County Record Office.

COURT (1938)   W. H. B. Court, *The Rise of Midland Industries, 1660–1838*, Oxford (1938).

COVENTRY INV. (1987)   Mary Hulton and Jean Shuttleworth, *Ten Tudor Families: Coventry Wills and Inventories*, Coventry (1987).

COWPER (1888)   Historical Manuscripts Commission, 12th Report. MSS. of Earl Cowper (1888).

CRATHORNE (1995)   James Crathorne, *Cliveden: The Place and the People* (1995).

CROFT-MURRAY (1970)   Edward Croft-Murray, *Decorative Painting in England, 1537–1837*, 2 vols; 1962 (I) and 1970 (II).

CUMMINGS (1994)   Abbott Lowell Cummings, *Bed Hangings: A Treatise on Fabrics and Styles in the Curtaining of Beds, 1650–1850*, 2nd edn, Boston (1994).

CUNNINGHAM (1897)   W. Cunningham, *Alien Immigrants to England* (1897).

CURL (1982)   J. Stevens Curl, *The Egyptian Revival* (1982).

DAVIES (1955)   Godfrey Davies, *The Restoration of Charles II* (1955).

DAVIS (1962)   Ralph Davis, *The Rise of the English Shipping Industry in the Seventeenth and Eighteenth Centuries* (1962).

DE-GRAAF (1983)   J. H. Hofenk De-Graaf, 'The Chemistry of Red Dyestuffs in Medieval and Early Modern Europe', in N. B. Harte and K. Ponting, eds, *Cloth and Clothing in Medieval Europe: Essays in memory of Professor E. M. Carus-Wilson* (1983).

DE'MARINIS (1994)   F. De'Marinis, *Velvet, History, Techniques, Fashions* (1994).

DENT (1962)   John Dent, *The Quest for Nonsuch* (1962).

DERRY (1931–2)   T. K. Derry, 'The Repeal of the Apprenticeship

Clauses of the Statute of Apprentices', *Economic History Review*, 3 (1931–2) pp.67–87.

D.E.F. (1954)   Ralph Edwards, ed., *The Dictionary of English Furniture*, 2nd edn, 3 vols (1954) superseding 1st edn of Percy McQuoid and Ralph Edwards, D.E.F., 3 vols (1927).

D.N.B.   *The Dictionary of National Biography*, ed. Sir Leslie Stephen and Sir Sidney Lee, 22 vols (1885–1900).

B. DIETZ (1972)   Brian Dietz, ed. *The Port and Trade of Early Elizabethan London: Documents.* London Record Society (1972).

F. DIETZ (1932)   F. Dietz, *English Public Finance, 1558–1641*, New York (1932).

DODD (1843)   George Dodd, *Days at the Factories or the Manufacturing Industries in Great Britain* (1843).

DONZEL AND MARCHAL (1992)   Catherine Donzel and Sabine Marchal, *L'Art de la Passementerie et sa Contribution a l'Histoire de la Mode et de la Decoration*, Paris (1992).

DORNSIFE (1975)   Samuel J. Dornsife, 'Design Sources for Nineteenth-Century Window Hangings', *Winterthur Portfolio*, 10, Univ. Press of Virginia (1975) pp.69–99.

DRURY (1978)   Martin Drury, 'Early Eighteenth Century Furniture at Erddig', *Apollo*, CXII (July 1978) pp.46–55.

DUDLEY INV.   'Inventory of the Goods of Edmund Dudley, 1509', *Archaeologia*, LXXI, 1921, pp.39–42.

DUNLOP AND DENMAN (1912)   O. J. Dunlop and R. D. Denman, *English Apprenticeship and Child Labour, A History*, New York (1912).

EAMES (1971)   Penelope Eames, 'Documentary evidence concerning the character and use of domestic furnishings in England in the fourteenth and fifteenth centuries', *Furniture History*, VII (1971).

EAMES (1973)   Penelope Eames, 'Inventories as Sources of Evidence for Domestic Furnishings in the Fourteenth and Fifteenth Centuries', *Furniture History*, IX, 1973, pp.32–40.

EAMES (1977)   Penelope Eames, 'Furniture in England, France and the Netherlands from the Twelfth to the Fifteenth century', *Furniture History*, XIII (1977).

EARLE (1989)   Peter Earle, *The Making of the English Middle Class: Business, Society and Family Life in London, 1660–1730* (1989).

EDWARDS (1993)   Clive D. Edwards, *Victorian Furniture: Technology and Design*, Manchester and New York (1993).

EDWARDS (1996)   Clive D. Edwards, *Eighteenth-Century Furniture: Materials, Manufacture and Markets*, Manchester and New York (1996).

EDWARDS (1937)   Ralph Edwards, 'The Last Phase of "Regency" Design', *The Burlington Magazine*, LXXXI (1937) p.272.

EDWARDS (1960)   Ralph Edwards, 'A Set of Carved and Gilt Furniture at Knole and its Restoration'. *The Connoisseur*, CXLV (April 1960) pp.164–7. Edwards, ed. (1960).

EDWARDS (ed.) 1960   Ralph Edwards, ed. *The Universal System of Household Furniture . . . by Ince and Mayhew*, facsimile edn. (1960).

EDWARDS (1968)   Ralph Edwards 'A Set of Royal Furniture restored at Knole', *The Connoisseur*, CLXVIII (June 1968) pp.69–71.

EDWARDS AND JOURDAIN (1955)   Ralph Edwards and Margaret Jourdain, *Georgian Cabinet-Makers*, 3rd edn (1955).

ELLIS (1861)   Sir Henry Ellis, 'Inventories of Goods &c., in the Manor of Cheseworth . . . taken 1549', *Sussex Archaeological Collections*, XIII (1861) pp.118–24.

ELLIS (1947)   L. B. Ellis, 'Wardrobe Place and the Great Wardrobe', *Trans., London & Middx. Archaeol. Soc.*, N.S.IX, Pt.III (1947) pp.247–61.

EMMISON (1976)   F. G. Emmison, *Elizabethan Life: Home, Work & Land, from Essex Wills and Sessions and Manorial Records*, Chelmsford (1976).

ENTWISLE (1960)   E. A. Entwisle, *A Literary History of Wallpaper* (1960).

FAIRFAX INV. (1624)   Edward Peacock, ed., 'Inventories made for Sir William and Sir Thomas Fairfax, Knights, of Walton, and of Gilling Castle, Yorkshire in the Sixteenth and Seventeenth Centuries', *Archaeologia*, 48, Pt.I (1884) pp.121–56.

FENAILLE (1907)   Maurice Fenaille, *Etat général des tapisseries de la manufacture des Gobelins*, 5 vols (1903–23). Vol. 4 (1907) pp.226–304 describes all sets.

FIRLE INV. (1556)   R. Garraway Rice, ed. 'The Household Goods etc., of Sir John Gage of West Firle, Co. Sussex, K.G., 1556'. *Sussex Archaeological Collections*, XLV (1902) pp.114–27.

FORMAN (1971)   Benno M. Forman, 'Continental Furniture Craftsmen in London: 1511 to 1625', *Furniture History*, VII (1971) pp.94–120.

FORMAN (1988)   Benno M. Forman, *American Seating Furniture, 1630–1730*, New York and London (1988).

FOWLER AND CORNFORTH (1974)   John Fowler and John Cornforth, *English Decoration in the 18th Century* (1974).

FRASER (1979)   Antonia Fraser, *King Charles II* (1979).

FRIIS (1927)   Astrid Friis, *Alderman Cockayne's Project and the Cloth Trade* (1927).

FURNIVALL (1890)   F. J. Furnivall, *Kenilworth Festivities*, New Shakespeare Society (1890).

GAUNT (1987)   Peter Gaunt, *Hampton Court Palace, The Private Apartments of Fountain Court, 1689–1986*, unpublished typescript, Historic Royal Palaces Agency (1987).

GAUNT (1988)   Peter Gaunt, *Kensington Palace* (1988), especially Chapter 3, 'The Palace; 1689–1714, Furniture and other Contents' unpublished typescript, Historic Royal Palaces Agency (1988).

GERE (1989)   Charlotte Gere, *Nineteenth-Century Decoration, The Art of the Interior* (1989).

GIEDION (1955)   S. Giedion, *Mechanization takes Command* (1955).

GILBERT (1967)   Christopher Gilbert, 'The Temple Newsam Furniture Bills', *Furniture History*, III (1967) pp.16–28.

GILBERT (1971)   Christopher Gilbert, 'Chippendale at Denton and Newby', *Country Life*, 10 June 1971, pp.1446–51.

GILBERT (1970)   Christopher Gilbert, introd., *Loudon Furniture Designs from the Encyclopedia of Cottage, Farmhouse and Villa Architecture & Furniture* (1839 edn) S. R. Publishers, and *The Connoisseur*, East Ardsley (1970).

GILBERT (1978)   Christopher Gilbert, *The Life and Work of Thomas Chippendale* 2 vols (1978).

GILBERT (1978)   Christopher Gilbert, *Catalogue of the Furniture at Temple Newsam House and Lotherton Hall, Leeds* 2 vols (1978).

GILBERT (1986), ed.   See Beard and Gilbert (1986).

GILBERT (1991)   Christopher Gilbert, *English Vernacular Furniture, 1750–1900* (1991).

GILBERT, LOMAX AND WELLS-COLE (1987)   Christopher Gilbert, James Lomax and Anthony Wells-Cole, *Country House Floors, 1660–1850*, Temple Newsam House, Leeds, Catalogue (1987).

GIROUARD (1966)   Mark Girouard, 'English Art and the Rococo', I. 'Coffee at Slaughters', *Country Life*, 13 January 1966, pp.58–61. Two further articles on 27 January and 3 February 1966 on

'Hogarth and his Friends' and 'The Two Worlds of St Martin's Lane'.

GLEISSNER (1994)   Stephen Gleissner, 'Reassembling a Royal Art Collection for the Restored King of Great Britain', *Journal of the History of Collections*, 6, No.1 (1994) pp.103–15.

GLOAG (1970)   John Gloag, *Mr Loudon's England* (1970).

GOODISON AND HARDY (1970)   Nicholas Goodison and John Hardy, 'Gillows at Tatton Park', *Furniture History*, VI (1970) pp.1–39.

GRAHAM (1994)   Clare Graham, *Ceremonial and Commemorative Chairs in Great Britain* (1994).

GRASSBY (1980)   Richard Grassby, 'The personal wealth of the business community in seventeenth-century England', *Economic History Review*, 2nd series, 23 (1980) pp.16–22.

GREEN (1951)   David Green, *Blenheim Palace* (1951).

GREEN (1967)   David Green, *Sarah, Duchess of Marlborough* (1967).

GRIER (1988)   Katherine C. Grier, *Culture and Comfort, People, Parlors and Upholstery, 1850–1930*, New York (1988).

GUIFFREY (1881–1901)   Jules Guiffrey, *Comptes des Bâtiments du Roi . . .*, 5 vols Paris (1881–1901).

GUIFFREY (1886)   Jules Guiffrey, *Inventaire Général du Mobilier de la Couronne*, 2 vols Paris (1886).

GUILDHALL LIBRARY, LONDON   Sun Insurance Office Policy Registers from 1710; Hand-in-Hand Policy Registers from 1696. Extracted for entries in Beard and Gilbert (1986).
Worshipful Company of Upholders' Court Books, etc. MSS., 7141/1–6.

GUSLER, GRAVES AND ANDERSON (1987)   Wallace Gusler, Leroy Graves and Mark Anderson, 'The Technique of 18th-century Over-the-Rail Upholstery', in Cooke, ed. (1987) pp.90–6.

HACKENBROCH (1958)   Yvonne Hackenbroch, *English Furniture . . . Irwin Untermyer Collection* (1958).

HALL (1970)   Ivan Hall, *William Constable as Patron, 1721–1791*, Ferens Art Gallery, Kingston Upon Hull, January–February 1970.

HALL (1978)   Ivan Hall, 'Patterns of Elegance. The Gillows' Furniture Designs, I', *Country Life*, 8 June 1978, pp.1612–15; – 'Models with a Choice of Leg: The Gillows' Furniture Designs, II', *ibid.*, 15 June 1978, pp.1740–2.

HALL (1980)   Ivan Hall, 'A neo-classical episode at Chatsworth', *The Burlington Magazine*, CXXII, No.927 (June 1980) pp.400–14.

HALLIWELL (1846–8)   J. O. Halliwell, *Letters of the Kings of England* 2 vols (1846–8).

HALLIWELL (1854)   J. O. Halliwell, *Ancient Inventories of Furniture, Pictures, Tapestry, Place &c., illustrative of the Domestic Manners of the English in the Sixteenth and Seventeenth Centuries* (1854).

HALSBAND (1973)   Robert Halsband, *Lord Hervey, Eighteenth-Century Courtier* (1973).

HAMILTON (1976)   Elizabeth Hamilton, *Henrietta Maria* (1976).

HARDY, LANDI AND WRIGHT (1972)   John Hardy, Sheila Landi and Charles Wright, 'A State Bed from Erthig', Victoria and Albert Museum, Brochure (1972).

HARDWICK INV. (1601)   L. O. J. Boynton, ed. 'The Hardwick Hall Inventories of 1601', *Furniture History*, VII (1971) pp.1–40.

E. HARRIS (1962)   Eileen Harris, 'Robert Adam and the Gobelins', *Apollo*, XXVI (April 1962) pp.100–16.

E. HARRIS (1963)   Eileen Harris, *The Furniture of Robert Adam* (1963).

E. HARRIS (1967)   Eileen Harris, 'The Moor Park Tapestries', *Apollo*, LXXXVI, No.67 (September 1967) pp.180–9.

E. HARRIS (1994)   Eileen Harris, *Osterley Park, Middlesex*, The National Trust Guidebook (1994).

HARRIS, 1912   F. R. Harris, *The Life of Edward Montagu, First Earl of Sandwich, 1625–72*, 2 vols (1912).

J. HARRIS (1967)   John Harris, 'The Dundas Empire', *Apollo*, LXXXVI, No.67 (September 1967) pp.170–9.

J. HARRIS (1970)   John Harris, *Sir William Chambers, Knight of the Polar Star* (1970).

HARRIS AND HIGGOTT (1989)   John Harris and Gordon Higgott, *Inigo Jones: Complete Architectural Drawings* (1989).

HARRIS, ORGEL AND STRONG (1973)   John Harris, Stephen Orgel and Roy Strong, *The King's Arcadia, Inigo Jones and the Stuart Court*, Arts Council of Great Britain, Exhibition (1973).

HARRISON (1968)   William Harrison, *The Description of England*, ed. Georges Edelen, New York (1968).

HARVEY (1984)   John Harvey, *English Medieval Architects, A Biographical Dictionary down to 1540*, Gloucester, 2nd revd edn (1984).

HARVEY AND MORTIMER (1994)   *The Funeral Effigies of Westminster Abbey*, Woodbridge (1994).

HATTON (1978)   Ragnhild Hatton, *George I, Elector and King* (1978).

HAVARD (1887–1890)   Henry Havard, *Dictionnaire de l'ameublement et de la decoration. Depuis le XIIIe siècle jusqu'a nos jours*, 4 vols (Paris, 1887–90).

HAYDN (1851)   Joseph Haydn, *Book of Dignities* (1851).

HAYWARD (1969)   Helena Hayward, 'The Drawings of John Linnell in the Victoria and Albert Museum', *Furniture History*, V (1969).

HAYWARD AND KIRKHAM (1980)   Helena Hayward and Pat Kirkham, *William and John Linnell: Eighteenth Century London Furniture Makers* (1980).

HAYWARD AND TILL (1973)   Helena Hayward and Eric Till, 'A Furniture Discovery at Burghley' [work by Mayhew and Ince], *Country Life*, CLIII, 7 June 1973, pp.1604–7.

HAYWARD, J. F. (1969)   J. F. Hayward, *Huguenot Silver in England, 1688–1727* (1969).

HEAL (1953)   Sir Ambrose Heal, *The London Furniture Makers, 1660–1840* (1953).

HECKSCHER (1974)   Morrison Heckscher, 'Ince and Mayhew: Bibliographical Notes from New York', *Furniture History*, X (1974) pp.61–7.

HEFFORD (1977)   Wendy Hefford, 'Thomas Moore of Moorfields', *The Burlington Magazine*, CXIX (December 1977) pp.840–8.

HEFFORD (1984)   Wendy Hefford, 'Huguenot tapestry weavers in and around London, 1680–1780', *Proceedings of the Huguenot Society of London*, 24, No.2 (1984) pp.103–12.

HINTON (1959)   R. W. K. Hinton, *The Eastland Trade and the Commonweal*, Cambridge (1959).

H.K.W.   H. M. Colvin, ed., *The History of the King's Works*, 6 vols, 1963–1982, viz. Vols I and II, *The Middle Ages* (1963); Vol. III, 1485–1660 Pt.I (1975); Vol. IV, 1485–1660 Pt.II (1982); Vol. V, 1660–1782 (1977); Vol. VI, 1782–1851 (1973).

HOPE (1807)   Thomas Hope, *Household Furniture and Interior Decoration* (1807); reprint, Tiranti, London (1970).

HOUSTON (1993)   J. F. Houston, *Featherbedds and Flock Bedds: Notes on the History of The Worshipful Company of Upholders of the City of London*, Three Tents Press (15 Cambridge Road, Sandy, Bedfordshire), privately printed (1993).

HOWARD INV. (1869)   E. P. Shirley, ed., 'An Inventory of the Effects of Henry Howard, K. G., Earl of Northampton, taken on his death in 1614 . . .' *Archaeologia*, 42, Pt.2 (1869) pp.347–78.

HOWARD (1987)   Maurice Howard, *The Early Tudor Country House: Architecture and Politics, 1490–1550* (1987).

HUTCHINSON   (1976)   Christopher   Hutchinson,   'George Reynoldson, Upholsterer of York, fl.1716–64', *Furniture History*, XII (1976) pp.29–33.

HUTTON (1985)   Ronald Hutton, *The Restoration: A Political and Religious History of England and Wales, 1658–1667* (1985).

INGRAM (1951)   Edward Ingram, *Leaves from a Family Tree* (1951).

IRWIN AND SCHWARTZ (1966)   John Irwin and P. R. Schwartz, *Studies in Indo-European Textile History* India, Calico Museum (1966).

JACKSON (1987)   Linda W. Jackson, 'Beyond the Fringe: Ornamental Trimmings in the 17th, 18th and Early 19th Centuries', in Cooke, ed. (1987) pp.131–47.

JACKSON-STOPS (1974)   See Percy and Jackson-Stops (1974).

JACKSON-STOPS (1977)   Gervase Jackson-Stops, 'The Building of Petworth', *Apollo*, 105 (May 1977) pp.324–33.

JACKSON-STOPS (1977)   Gervase Jackson-Stops, 'A Courtier's Collection: The 6th Earl of Dorset's Furniture at Knole' I & II *Country Life*, 2 June 1977, pp.1495–7; 9 June 1977, pp.1620–2.

JACKSON-STOPS (1978)   Gervase Jackson-Stops, *Drayton House, Northamptonshire* (1978).

JACKSON-STOPS (1981)   Gervase Jackson-Stops, 'Daniel Marot and the 1st Duke of Montagu', *Nederlands Kunsthistorisch Jaarboek* (1981) pp.244–62.

JACKSON-STOPS (1985)   Gervase Jackson-Stops, 'A Set of Furniture by Thomas Phill at Canons Ashby', *Furniture History*, XXI (1985) pp.217–18.

JACKSON-STOPS, ed. (1985)   Gervase Jackson-Stops, ed. *The Treasure Houses of Britain*, National Gallery of Art, Washington D.C., Exhibition Catalogue (1985).

JACKSON-STOPS (1991)   Gervase Jackson-Stops, *John Nash, Views of the Royal Pavilion* (1991).

JACOBS (1970)   B. J. Jacobs, *Axminster Carpets (Hand-Made), 1755–1957*, Leigh-on-Sea (1970).

JAMESON (1987)   Clare Jameson, *The Potterton pictorial treasury of drapery and curtain designs*, Sessay (1987).

JERVIS (1975)   Simon Jervis, *Printed Furniture Designs Pre-1650*, Furniture History Society, Leeds (1975).

JERVIS (1989)   Simon Jervis, 'Furniture in the Commonwealth Inventories', in Arthur MacGregor, ed., *The Late King's Goods . . .* (1989) pp.277–306.

JOHNSON (1952)   B. L. C. Johnson, 'The Foley Partnerships: The Iron Industry at the End of the Charcoal Era', *Economic History Review*, 2nd series, IV, No.3 (1952) pp.322–38.

JOHNSON (1974)   Paul Johnson, *Elizabeth I*, New York (1974).

JOURDAIN (1933)   Margaret Jourdain, 'Furniture at Ditchley Park', *Country Life*, lxxiii, 20 May 1933, pp.490–2.

JOURDAIN (1934)   Margaret Jourdain, *Regency Furniture, 1795–1820* (1934); 2nd edn (1949).

JOURDAIN (1952)   Margaret Jourdain, *Stuart Furniture at Knole* (1952).

JOY (1959)   Edward Joy, 'Charles Elliott, Royal Cabinetmaker', *The Connoisseur* (June 1959) pp.34–9.

JOY (1962)   Edward T. Joy, 'Georgian Patent Furniture', *The Connoisseur Year Book* 1962, pp.9–15.

JOY (1969)   Edward T. Joy, 'The Royal Victorian Furniture-Makers, 1837–87', *The Burlington Magazine*, CXI, November 1969, pp.677–84.

JOY (1972)   Edward T. Joy, *English Furniture, 1800–1851* (1972).

JOY (1989)   Edward T. Joy, introd. *Pictorial Dictionary of British 19th Century Furniture Designs*, Woodbridge (1989).

KAHL (1957)   William F. Kahl, 'Apprenticeship and the freedom of the London livery companies, 1690–1750', *Guildhall Miscellany*, London, 1957, No.7.

KAHL (1960)   William F. Kahl, *The Development of London Livery Companies*, Kress Library of Business and Economics, Boston (1960).

KELLETT (1957–8)   J. R. Kellett, 'The Breakdown of Gild and Corporation Control over the Handicraft and Retail Trades in London', *Economic History Review*, 2nd series, 10 (1957–8) pp.381–94.

KING (1989)   Donald King, 'Textile Furnishings', in Arthur MacGregor, ed. *The Late King's Goods . . .* (1989) pp.307–21.

KIRKHAM (1969)   Pat Kirkham, 'Samuel Norman, a study of an eighteenth-century craftsman', *The Burlington Magazine*, CXI, August 1969, pp.503–13.

KIRKHAM (1974)   Pat Kirkham, 'The partnership of William Ince and John Mayhew, 1759–1804', *Furniture History*, X (1974) pp.56–60.

KIRKHAM (1988)   Pat Kirkham, 'The London Furniture Trade, 1700–1870', *Furniture History*, 1988, XXIV.

KRAMER (1927)   *The English Craft Gilds: Studies in their Progress and Decline*, New York (1927).

LACOCK ABBEY (1575)   Thelma E. Vernon, ed. 'Inventory of Sir Henry Sharington: Contents of Lacock House, 1575', *Wiltshire Arch. and Nat. Hist. Magazine*, 63 (1968) pp.72–82.

LADD (1978)   Frederick J. Ladd, *Architects at Corsham Court, A Study of Revival Style Architecture and Landscaping, 1749–1849*, Bradford-on-Avon (1978).

LANDI (1992)   Sheila Landi, *Textile Conservators' Handbook*, 2nd edn, (1992).

LANGLEY   Batty and Thomas Langley, *The City and Country Builder's and Workman's Treasury of Designs* (1740).

LATHAM AND MATTHEWS (eds) (1970–1976)   R. C. Latham and W. Matthews, eds, *The Diary of Samuel Pepys*. The Diary was published in nine volumes, with full index (1970–6).

LATOUR (1953)   A. Latour, 'Velvet – Technical Features; Ceremonial; Historical Aspects of Production', *C.I.B.A. Review*, Basel, No.96, February 1953, pp.3441–63.

LEEDS (1973)   *The Golden Age of English Furniture Upholstery, 1660–1840*, Temple Newsam House, Leeds, Exhibition Catalogue (1973).

LEWIS, ed. *Horace Walpole's Correspondence*, 48 vols, New Haven and London (1937–85).

LIPSON (1921)   E. Lipson, *The History of the Woollen and Worsted Industries* (1921).

LITTEN (1991)   Julian Litten, *The English Way of Death: The Common Funeral Since 1450* (1991).

LLANOVER, ed. (1861)   Lady Llanover, *Autobiography and Correspondence of Mrs Delany*, 3 vols (1861–2).

LLOYD (1977)   T. H. Lloyd, *The English Wool Trade* (1977).

LOADES   David Loades, *The Tudor Court* (1986).

LOUDON (1833)   J. C. Loudon, *An Encyclopedia of Cottage, Farm and Villa Architecture and Furniture* (1833).

LOW (1986)   Jill Low, 'Newby Hall: Two Late Eighteenth-Century Inventories', *Furniture History*, XXII (1986) pp.135–75.

LUMLEY INV. (1590: 1609)   A) Lionel Cust, 'The Lumley Inventories' *The Walpole Society*, VI (1918) pp.14–50. B) Mary Hervey, 'A Lumley Inventory of 1609', *ibid.*, pp.36–45.

LUTTRELL (1857) Narcissus Luttrell, *A Brief Historical Relation of State Affairs, from September 1678 to April 1714*, 6 vols, Oxford (1857).

MACGREGOR (1989) Arthur MacGregor, ed. 'The Late King's Goods: Collections, Possessions and Patronage of Charles I in the Light of the Commonwealth Sale Inventories' (1989). See also Millar.

MERCER (1962) Eric Mercer, *English Art, 1553–1625*, Oxford (1962).

MILLAR (1972) Oliver Millar, ed. 'The Inventories and Valuations of the King's Goods, 1649–1651', *The Walpole Society 1970–2*, vol. XLIII (1972). See also MacGregor.

MILLER (1989) John Miller, *James II, a study in Kingship* (revd edn, 1989).

MILNER AND BENHAM Edith Milner and Edith Benham, *Records of the Lumleys of Lumley Castle* (1904). The text of the 1590 Inventory is printed in an appendix. See also Lumley Inventory.

MILNES (1983) E. C. Milnes, *History of the Development of Furniture Webbing*, unpublished typescript (copy at Temple Newsam House, Leeds).

MITCHELL (1995) David Mitchell, ed. *Goldsmiths, Silversmiths and Bankers: Innovation and the Transfer of Skill, 1550 to 1750* (1995).

MONTGOMERY (1984) Florence Montgomery, *Textiles in America, 1650–1870, A Dictionary*, New York (1984).

MOORE, ed. (1996) Andrew Moore, ed., *Houghton Hall, the Prime Minister, the Empress and the Heritage* (1996).

MORLEY (1984) John Morley, *The Making of the Royal Pavilion, Brighton* (1984).

MORLEY (1992) John Morley, *Regency Design, 1790–1840; Gardens, Buildings, Interiors, Furniture* (1992).

MOWL and EARNSHAW (1995) Timothy Mowl and Brian Earnshaw, *Architecture Without Kings: The rise of Puritan classicism under Cromwell*, Manchester (1995).

MURDOCH (1985) Tessa Murdoch, *The Quiet Conquest, The Huguenots 1685 to 1985*, Museum of London, exhibition catalogue, May–October 1985.

MURDOCH, ed. (1992) Tessa Murdoch, ed., *Boughton House* (1992).

MUSGRAVE (1961) Clifford Musgrave, *Regency Furniture: 1800 to 1830* (1961).

NEALE (1950) J. E. Neale, 'Sir Nicholas Throckmorton's Advice to Queen Elizabeth', *English Historical Review*, LXV (1950) pp.91–8.

NEVINSON (1973) John Nevinson, 'An Elizabethan Herbarium: Embroideries of Bess of Hardwick after the Woodcuts of Mattioli', *The National Trust Year Book* (1975–6) pp.65–9.

NEVINSON (1973) John Nevinson, 'Embroideries at Hardwick Hall', *Country Life*, 29 November 1973.

NICHOLAS N. H. Nicholas, *The Privy Purse Expenses of Elizabeth of York and the Wardrobe Accounts of Edward IV* (1830).

NICHOLS, *Progresses* (1823)/(1828) John Nichols, *The Progresses of Queen Elizabeth . . .* (1823) 3 vols; *The Progresses . . . of King James the First* (1828) 4 vols.

NICHOLS (1982) Sarah Nichols, 'Gillow and Company of Lancaster, England. An Eighteenth-Century Business History'. Winterthur M.A. thesis (Univ. of Delaware) 1982.

NICHOLS (1984) Sarah Nichols, 'Gillows of Lancaster: The Role of the Upholsterer', Abbot Hall Art Gallery, Kendal, *Quarto*, XXI, No.4, January 1984, pp.7–11.

NICHOLS (1985) Sarah Nichols, 'Furniture made by Gillow and Company for Workington Hall', *The Magazine Antiques* (New York) Vol. 127, No.6 (June 1985) pp.1352–9.

NICHOLS (1986) Sarah Nichols, 'A Journey through the Gillow Records', *Antique Collecting*, 20, No.9 (February 1986).

NOTTS. INV. (1516–1562) P. A. Kennedy, ed. 'Nottinghamshire Household Inventories, 1516–1562', *Thoroton Society, Record Series*, XXII (1962).

OATLANDS INV. (1618) East Sussex County Record Office, Oatlands Inventory, October 1618. MS. GLY, 320. Two other inventories of 1616 (GLY 315) and 1618 (GLY 319) also survive.

O.E.D. *The Oxford English Dictionary*.

OMAN and HAMILTON (1982) Charles Oman and J. Hamilton, *Wallpapers: A History and Illustrated Catalogue of the Collection in the Victoria and Albert Museum* (1982).

ORGEL AND STRONG (1973) Stephen Orgel and Roy Strong, *Inigo Jones: The Theatre of the Stuart Court*, 2 vols, London and Berkeley (1973).

OSWALD (1934) Arthur Oswald, 'Ditchley Park, Oxfordshire', *Country Life*, LXXV, 9 & 16 June 1934, pp.590–5; 622–8.

OVERTON (1983) Mark Overton, *A Bibliography of British Probate Inventories*, Newcastle-upon-Tyne (1983).

OXFORDS. INV. (1550–1590) M. A. Havinden, 'Household and Farm Inventories in Oxfordshire, 1550–1590', *Oxfordshire Record Society, Publications*, No.44 (1965).

PARIS (1973) *Des Dorelotiers aux Passementiers*, Catalogue of exhibition, Musée des Arts Decoratifs, Paris, January–March, 1973. Musée Inv. No.6687 is similar to that shown here in Pl. 59.

PARISSIEN (1992) A & B. Steven Parissien, A) *Adam Style* (1992); B) *Regency Style* (1992).

PARKER, STANDEN AND DAUTERMAN James Parker, Edith A. Standen and Carl Dauterman, *Decorative Art from the Samuel H. Kress Collection at the Metropolitan Museum of Art* (1964). Includes the Croome Court Tapestry Room, pp.1–57.

PARKER AND STANDEN (1959) 'The Tapestry Room from Croome Court, The Architecture and Furniture (James Parker); The Tapestries (Edith A. Standen)', Metropolitan Museum of Art, New York, *Bulletin*, XVIII, No.3, November 1959.

PECK (1779) Francis Peck, *Desiderata Curiosa* (1779 ed.).

PECK (1982) Linda L. Peck, *Northampton: Patronage and Policy at the Court of James I* (1982).

PERCY AND JACKSON-STOPS (1974) Victoria Percy and Gervase Jackson-Stops, 'The Travel Journals of the 1st Duchess of Northumberland', *Country Life* (I) 31 January 1974, pp.192–5; (II) 7 February 1974, pp.250–2.

PETTEGREE (1986) A. Pettegree, *Foreign Protestant Communities in 16th Century London*, Oxford (1986).

PEVSNER, *Oxfordshire* Jennifer Sherwood and Nikolaus Pevsner, *Oxfordshire* (The Buildings of England, 1974).

PHILLIPS (1929) Charles Phillips, *History of the Sackville Family*, 2 vols (1929).

PIPER (1957) David Piper, 'The 1590 Lumley Inventory: Hilliard, Segar and the Earl of Essex', *The Burlington Magazine*, XCIX (1957).

PLUMB (1965) Sir John Plumb, *Introduction to Calendar of the Cholmondeley (Houghton) Manuscripts*, Cambridge University Library (1965).

PLUMMER (1972) Alfred Plummer, *The London Weavers' Company, 1600–1970* (1972).

PRESTWICH (1966) Menna Prestwich, *Cranfield, Politics and Profits under the Early Stuarts: The Career of Lionel Cranfield, Earl of Middlesex*, Oxford (1966).

P.R.O. PUBLIC RECORD OFFICE, LONDON. C107/109 Order Books of James Brown, 1782–91.

LC Lord Chamberlain's Accounts for the Great Wardrobe: various references in LC2, LC5, LC9 as cited.

Prob.6 Various Inventories, as cited.

Prob.11 Various Wills or Administrations, as cited.

QUEEN'S GALLERY (1966) The Queen's Gallery, Buckingham Palace, Exhibition catalogue, *George IV and the Arts of France* (1966).

QUEEN'S GALLERY (1991) The Queen's Gallery, Buckingham Palace, Exhibition catalogue, *Carlton House: The Past Glories of George IV's Palace* (1991).

RAMSAY (1982) G. D. Ramsay, *The English Woollen Industry, 1500–1700* (1982).

RATZKI-KRAATZ (1986) Anne Ratzki-Kraatz, 'A French Lit de Parade *À la Duchesse*, 1690–1715', The J. Paul Getty Museum, *Journal*, vol.14, Malibu (1986) pp.81–104.

READ (1955) Conyers Read, *Mr Secretary Cecil and Queen Elizabeth* (1955).

READ (1960) Conyers Read, *Lord Burghley and Queen Elizabeth* (1960).

RIEDER (1977) William Rieder, *Highlights of the Untermyer Collection*, Metropolitan Museum of Art, New York (1977).

ROBERTS (1989) Hugh Roberts, 'Royal thrones, 1760–1840', *Furniture History*, XXV (1989) pp.61–77.

ROBERTS (1994) Hugh Roberts, '"Nicely fitted up"; Furniture for the 4th Duke of Marlborough', *Furniture History*, XXX (1994) pp.117–49.

ROBINSON (1983) John Martin Robinson, *The Dukes of Norfolk* (1983).

ROETHLISBERGER (1972) Marcel Roethlisberger, 'The Ulysses Tapestries at Hardwick Hall', *Gazette des Beaux Arts*, Paris (February 1972).

ROGERS (1933) J. Rogers, 'The Manor and Houses of Gorhambury', *St Albans and Herts. Archaeological Soc.*, IV (1933) pp.35–112.

ROGERS (1994) K. W. Rogers, '*The Art and Mystery of the Upholder': The London Upholstery Trade, 1667 to 1721*, Victoria and Albert Museum and Royal College of Art History of Design M.A. Course: Thesis (V & A Library, 94/DW/16/39).

ROGERS (1987) Phillis Rogers, 'The Remodelling of Weston Park', *Furniture History*, XXIII (1987) pp.11–34.

RORSCHACH (1991) Kimerly Rorschach, 'Frederick, Prince of Wales – taste, politics and power', *Apollo*, CXXXI, October 1991, pp.239–45.

RORSCHACH (1993) Kimerly Rorschach, 'Frederick, Prince of Wales as Collector and Patron', *The Walpole Society*, LV (1993).

ROSOMAN (1986) T. S. Rosoman, 'The Chiswick House Inventory of 1770', *Furniture History*, XXII (1986) pp.81–106.

ROSOMAN (1992) Treve Rosoman, *London Wallpapers: Their Manufacture and Use 1690–1840* (1992).

ROTHSTEIN (1989) Natalie Rothstein, 'Canterbury and London, the silk industry in the late 17th century', *Textile History*, vol. 20, No.1 (1989).

ROTHSTEIN (1990) Natalie Rothstein, *Silk Designs of the Eighteenth Century: In the Collection of the Victoria and Albert Museum, London, with a Complete Catalogue* (1990).

ROWLANDS (1985) John Rowlands, *Holbein: The Paintings of Hans Holbein the Younger* (1985).

ROWSE (1953) A. L. Rowse, 'Elizabeth's Coronation', *History Today*, III (1953), pp.301–10.

RUTHERFORD (1927) F. J. Rutherford, 'The Furnishing of Hampton Court Palace, 1715–1727', *Old Furniture* (November 1927).

SCHEURLEER T. H. L. Scheurleer (ed.) 'Documents on the Furnishing of Kensington House', *The Walpole Society*, 38, Oxford (1960–2).

SCHOESER AND RUFEY (1989) Mary Schoeser and Celia Rufey, *English and American Textiles from 1760 to the Present* (1989).

SCHOESER AND DEJARDIN (1991) Mary Schoeser and Kathleen Dejardin, *French Textiles from 1760 to the Present* (1991).

SCHREUS AND BRAUN-RONSDORF (1955) Theo Schreus and Margarete Braun-Ronsdorf, 'Damask', *C.I.B.A.*, Review, Basel, No.110, June 1955, pp.3966–94.

SEDDON (1970) P. R. Seddon, 'Robert Carr, Earl of Somerset', *Renaissance and Modern Studies*, XIV (1970), pp.48–68.

SHARPE (1992) Kevin Sharpe, *The Personal Rule of Charles I* (1992).

SHERATON, D. B. (1791–3) Thomas Sheraton, *Cabinet-Maker and Upholsterer's Drawing Book* (1791–3, 2nd edn 1794); in facsimile ed. L. O. J. Boynton, New York (1970).

SHERATON, C. D. (1803) Thomas Sheraton, *The Cabinet Dictionary* (1803); in facsimile ed. W. P. Cole and C. F. Montgomery, New York (1970).

SHERRILL (1996) Sarah B. Sherrill, *Carpets and Rugs of Europe and America*, New York (1996).

C. S. SMITH (1993) Charles Saumarez Smith, *Eighteenth-Century Decoration, Design and the Domestic Interior in England* (1993).

H. C. SMITH (1931) H. Clifford Smith, *Buckingham Palace . . .* (1931).

R. S. SMITH (1961) R. S. Smith, 'A Woad Growing Project at Wollaton in the 1580s', *Transactions of the Thoroton Society*, 65 (1961), pp.24–34.

S. R. SMITH (1973) S. R. Smith, 'The social and geographical origins of the London apprentices 1630–1660', *Guildhall Miscellany*, IV (1973).

SMOLLETT (1765) Tobias Smollett, *The History of England from the Revolution in 1688 to the Death of George the Second* (1765 edn) 6 vols.

SNODIN, ed. (1984) Michael Snodin, ed., *Rococo. Art and Design in Hogarth's England*, Victoria and Albert Museum, London (1984).

SOPHIE IN LONDON (1933) Clare Williams (trans.) *Sophie in London, 1786: being the Diary of Sophie v. la Roche* (1933).

SPEKE INV. (1945) 'A Speke Inventory of 1624', *Trans. Hist. Soc. of Lancs. and Cheshire*, 97 (1945) pp.112–43.

SPRATT (1667) Thomas Spratt, *History of the Royal Society*, facsimile edn ed. J. I. Cope and H. W. Jones (1959) pp.391–2.

STANDEN (1985) Edith A. Standen, *European Post-Medieval Tapestries and Related Hangings in the Metropolitan Museum of Art*, 2 vols, New York (1985).

Stemmata Shirleiana (1873) *Stemmata Shirleiana: or the Annals of the Shirley Family*, 2nd revd edn (1873).

STEPHENS (1969) W. B. Stephens, 'The Exchequer Port Books as a source for the history of the English Cloth Trade', *Textile History*, Vol. 1, No.2 (December 1969).

STEPHENSON (1923) John W. Stephenson, *Modern furniture upholstering. A practical handbook for the upholsterer*, New York (1923); facsimile edn n.d. (? c.1985).

STONE (1955) Lawrence Stone, 'The Building of Hatfield House', *The Archaeological Journal*, CXII (1955) pp.98–128.

STRAKER (1931)   E. Straker, *Wealden Iron* (1931).

STRONG (1969) Roy Strong, *The English Icon: Elizabethan and Jacobean Portraiture* (1969).

STRONG (1986)   Roy Strong, *Henry, Prince of Wales, and England's Lost Renaissance* (1986).

STROUD (1966)   Dorothy Stroud, *Henry Holland: His Life and Architecture* (1966).

STRYPE, SURVEY (1720)   John Strype, *A Survey of the Cities of London and Westminster Corrected, Improved & very much Enlarged . . . from the Year 1633 to the Present Time* (1720).

STRYPE   John Strype, *Ecclesiastical Memorials Relating Chiefly to Religion and the Reformation of It* (1721).

STUART (1994)   Susan Stuart, 'Was Squire Bradshaw of Halton Hall Robert Gillow's First London Connection?', *Quarto* (Abbot Hall Art Gallery, Kendal) Vol. 32, No.2 (July 1994) pp.8–11.

SUGDEN AND EDMONDSON (1925) A. V. Sugden and J. Edmondson, *A History of English Wallpaper, 1509–1914* (1925).

SUMMERSON (1959)   John Summerson, 'The Building of Theobalds, 1564–1585', *Archaeologia*, 97 (1959) pp.107–26.

SUMMERSON (1963)   John Summerson, *Architecture in Britain 1530–1830*, 4th edn, (1963).

Survey of London   F. H. W. Sheppard, ed. *Survey of London*, vol.34, *The Parish of St Anne, Soho* (1966).

SYMONDS (1934)   R. W. Symonds, 'Turkey Work, Beech and Japanned Chairs', quoting a petition to Parliament, *c.*1698, *The Connoisseur*, 93 (April 1934) pp.221–2.

SYMONDS (1937)   R. W. Symonds, 'The Royal X chair: its development from the XVth to XVIth centuries', *Apollo*, XXV, No.149 (May 1937) pp.263–8.

SYMONDS (1942)   R. W. Symonds, 'Domestic Furnishings in the Time of Charles II', *The Burlington Magazine*, September 1942, pp.218–22.

SYMONDS (1943)   R. W. Symonds, 'The Bed Through the Centuries', *The Connoisseur*, III, No.487 (March 1943) pp.34–43.

SYMONDS (1943)   R. W. Symonds, 'New Light on Tudor Furniture', I. 'William Grene, coffer-maker to Henry VIII', *Country Life*, 28 May 1943, pp.966–7; II, 'Queen Elizabeth's coffer-makers, John and Thomas Grene', *Country Life*, 11 June 1943, pp.1054–5.

SYMONDS (1945)   R. W. Symonds, 'The Upholstered Furniture at Knole', *The Burlington Magazine*, I, May 1945, pp.110–15; II, July 1945, pp.164–8.

TEMPLE NEWSAM INV. (1565)   'A Temple Newsam Inventory, 1565', *Yorkshire Archaeological Society Journal*, 25 (1920) pp.91–103.

THIEME–BECKER   Ulrich Thieme and Felix Becker, *Allegemeines Lexikon des bildenken Kunstler.*, 37 vols (1907–50). Supplement (1953–62) continues.

THOMAS (1861)   William Thomas, *The Pilgrim: A Dialogue on the Life and Actions of King Henry the Eighth*, ed. J. A. Froude (1861).

THOMSON (1937)   Gladys Scott Thomson, *Life in a Noble Household, 1641–1700* (1937).

THOMSON (1949)   Gladys Scott Thomson, *Family Background* (1949).

THOMSON (1914)   W. G. Thomson, *Tapestry Weaving in England* (1914).

THORNTON (1960)   Peter Thornton, 'Tapisseries de Bergame', *Pantheon*, 18 (1960) pp.85–91.

THORNTON (1965)   Peter Thornton, *Baroque and Rococo Silks* (1965).

THORNTON (1971)   Peter Thornton, 'Room Arrangements in the Mid-Eighteenth Century', *The Magazine Antiques*, New York, 99 (1971) pp.556–61.

THORNTON (1974)   Peter Thornton, 'Back-Stools and Chaises à Demoiselles', *The Connoisseur*, 815 (February 1974) pp.98–105.

THORNTON (1974, 2)   Peter Thornton, 'French Beds', *Apollo*, vol. 99 (March 1974) pp.182–7.

THORNTON (1974, 3)   Peter Thornton, 'Canopies, couches and chairs of state', *Apollo*, 100 (October 1974) pp.292–9.

THORNTON (1977)   Peter Thornton, 'The Royal State Bed', *The Connoisseur*, 195 (1977) pp.136–47.

THORNTON (1978)   Peter Thornton, *Seventeenth-Century Interior Decoration in England, France and Holland* (1978).

THORNTON (1984)   Peter Thornton, *Authentic Decor, The Domestic Interior 1620–1920* (1984); paperback edn (1993).

THORNTON AND TOMLIN (1980)   Peter Thornton and Maurice Tomlin, 'The Ham House Inventories', *Furniture History*, 16 (1980) pp.1–194.

THORNTON AND TOMLIN, II (1980)   Peter Thornton and Maurice Tomlin, 'Franz Cleyn at Ham House', *National Trust Studies* (1980).

THORNTON AND WATKIN (1987)   Peter Thornton and David Watkin, 'New Light on the Hope Mansion in Duchess Street, London', *Apollo*, vol. 126 (September 1987) pp.162–77.

THURLEY (1993)   Simon Thurley, *The Royal Palaces of Tudor England* (1993).

THURLEY (1994)   Simon Thurley, 'The Building of the King's Apartments', *Apollo*, CXL, No.390 (August 1994) pp.10–20.

THORPE (1946)   W. A. Thorpe, 'Bradshaws and their Connection', *Country Life*, I, September 20, II, September 27 (1946).

TOMLIN (1972)   Maurice Tomlin, *Catalogue of Adam Period Furniture*, Victoria and Albert Museum, London (1972).

TOMLIN (1986)   Maurice Tomlin, 'The 1782 Inventory of Osterley Park', *Furniture History*, XXII (1986) pp.107–34.

TOMLIN (1980), I and II   See Thornton and Tomlin.

TOUT (1920–33)   T. F. Tout, *Chapters in the Administrative History of Medieval England*, Manchester, 6 vols 1920–33. Vols 4 (1928) and 5 (1930) are useful for the early history of the Great Wardrobe.

UNWIN   George Unwin, *The Gilds and Companies of London* (reprinted, 1966).

UNWIN (1902)   George Unwin, *Industrial Organization in the Sixteenth and Seventeenth Centuries* (1902).

VAN DER ZEE (1973)   Henri and Barbara Van der Zee, *William and Mary* (1973).

VEALE (1966)   Elspeth Veale, *The English Fur Trade in the Later Middle Ages* (1966).

VERLET (1982)   Pierre Verlet, *The James A. de Rothschild Collection at Waddesdon Manor: The Savonnerie* (1982).

VICTORIA AND ALBERT MUSEUM'S TEXTILE COLLECTION   Donald King and Santina Levey, *Embroidery in Britain 1200 to 1750* (1989). Wendy Hefford, *Designs for Printed Textiles in England from 1750–1850* (1992).
Natalie Rothstein, *Woven Textile Design in Britain to 1750* (1994); *Woven Textile Design in Britain from 1750 to 1850* (1994).

WAINWRIGHT (1976)   Clive Wainwright, 'A. W. N. Pugin's early furniture', *The Connoisseur*, vol. 191, no.767 (January 1976) pp.3–11.

WAINWRIGHT (1989)   Clive Wainwright, *The Romantic Interior; The British Collector at Home, 1750–1850* (1989).

WAINWRIGHT, WOOD AND LEVY (1988)   Clive Wainwright, Lucy Wood and Martin Levy, *George Bullock, Cabinet-Maker* (1988).

WALTON (1973)   Karin-Marina Walton, 'The Worshipful Company of Upholders of the City of London', *Furniture History*, IX (1973) pp.41–79.

WALTON (1973)   Karin-Marina Walton, 'The Golden Age of English Furniture Upholstery, 1660–1840', Temple Newsam House, Leeds, exhibition catalogue, August–September, 1973.

WALTON (1980)   Karin-Marina Walton, *Eighteenth-Century Upholstery in England: The Work and Status of the Upholsterer (with particular emphasis on the period 1754–1803)*, Leeds University, M.Phil. thesis, 1980.

WALTON (1986)   Karin-Marina Walton, 'An Inventory of 1710 from Dyrham Park', *Furniture History*, XXII (1986) pp.25–80.

WALTON AND GILBERT (1974)   Karin-Marina Walton and Christopher Gilbert, 'Chippendale's Upholstery Branch', *Leeds Arts Calendar*, No.74 (1974) pp.26–32.

WALTON (1977)   Penelope Walton, 'Textiles', in John Blair and Nigel Ramsay, eds *English Medieval Industries: Craftsmen, Techniques, Products* (1991) pp.319–54.

WARD-JACKSON (1958)   Peter Ward-Jackson, *English Furniture Designs of the Eighteenth Century* (1958).

WATKIN (1968)   David Watkin, *Thomas Hope 1769–1831, and the Neo-Classical Idea* (1968).

WATKIN (1984)   David Watkin, *The Royal Interiors of Regency England* (1984).

WATKIN (1987)   See Thornton and Watkin (1987).

WEDGWOOD (1935)   C. V. Wedgwood, *Strafford* (1935).

H. VAN DER WEE (1963)   H. van der Wee, *Growth of the Antwerp Market and the European Economy*, 3 vols, The Hague (1963).

WELLS-COLE (1983)   Anthony Wells-Cole, *Historic Paper Hangings*, Leeds, Temple Newsam Country House Studies, No.1 (1983).

WELLS-COLE (1997)   Anthony Wells-Cole, *Art and Decoration in Elizabethan and Jacobean England: The Influence of Continental Prints, 1558–1625* (1997).

WESTMAN (1990)   Annabel Westman, 'English Window Curtains in the Eighteenth Century', *The Magazine Antiques* (New York) CXXXVII, No.6 (June 1990) pp.1406–17.

WESTMAN (1994)   Annabel Westman, 'The Textile Furnishings of the King's Apartments' (Hampton Court) *Apollo*, CXL, No.390, August 1994, pp.39–45.

WESTMAN (1994)   Annabel Westman, 'Francis Lapiere's Household Inventory of 1715', *Furniture History*, XXX (1994) pp.1–14.

WHINNEY (1988)   Margaret Whinney, *Sculpture in Britain, 1530–1830*, 2nd edn, revd by John Physick (1988).

WHITE (1982)   Elizabeth White, 'Two English State Beds in the Metropolitan Museum of Art', *Apollo*, CXV (August 1982) pp.84–8.

WHITE (1990)   Elizabeth White, *Pictorial Dictionary of British 18th Century Furniture Designs: The Printed Sources*, Woodbridge (1990).

WHITING (1945)   C. E. Whiting, ed. 'Durham Civic Memorials', *Surtees Society*, CLX (1945).

WILLAN (1976)   T. S. Willan, 'Provincial shops in the seventeenth century', in *The Inland Trade: Studies in English Internal Trade in the Sixteenth and Seventeenth Centuries*, Manchester (1976).

WILLIAMS (1970)   E. Carleton Williams, *Anne of Denmark, Wife . . . James I of England* (1970).

WILLIAMS (1966)   J. D. Williams, *Audley End, The Restoration of 1762–1797*, Chelmsford (1966).

WILLIAMS AND OTHERS (1990)   Marc A. Williams, ed., *Upholstery Conservation* (preprints of a symposium held at Colonial Williamsburg, February 1990). East Kingston, N.H. (1990).

WILLIAMS (1953)   Neville Williams, 'The Coronation of Queen Elizabeth', *Quarterly Review*, 597 (1953) pp.397–411.

WILLIAMS (1964)   Neville Williams, *A Tudor Tragedy: Thomas Howard, Fourth Duke of Norfolk* (1964).

WILLIAMS (1971)   Neville Williams, *Henry VIII and his Court* (1971).

WILLSON (1956)   D. Harris Willson, *King James VI and I* (1956).

WILSON (1653)   Arthur Wilson, *The History of Great Britain, being the Life and Reign of King James the First . . .* (1653).

WINGFIELD-DIGBY (1963)   George Wingfield-Digby, *Elizabethan Embroidery* (1963).

WINKLER (1994)   Gail Caskey Winkler, 'Capricious fancy – Curtains and drapery, 1790–1930', *The Magazine Antiques* (New York) CXLV, No.1 (January 1994) pp.154–65.
Related to an exhibition at the Athenaeum of Philadelphia, January to April, 1994, of the Dornsife Collection, of which Winkler was author of the catalogue. See also Dornsife (1975).

WOOD (1935)   A. C. Wood, *A History of the Levant Company*, Oxford (1935).

WOOD (1995)   Lucy Wood, 'William Davidson of Berwick-upon-Tweed', *Furniture History*, XXXI (1995) pp.29–46.

WREN SOCIETY   *The Wren Society*, ed. A. T. Bolton and H. D. Hendry, vols 1–20 (1924–43).

YEOMANS (1990)   Wendy Yeomans, 'Documentation of *c*.1737 stools at Hampton Court Palace', in Williams and others (1990) pp.55–62.

YORKS. INV. (1542–1689)   Peter C. D. Brears, ed. 'Yorkshire Probate Inventories, 1542–1689', *Yorkshire Archaeol. Soc., Record Series*, CXXXIV, (1972).

INDEX

PHOTOGRAPHIC ACKNOWLEDGMENTS

© Her Majesty, Queen Elizabeth II: 47, 282, 358, 359, 361, 372; Agecroft Association, Richmond, VA: 23; L'Antiquaire & The Connoisseur Inc., New York: 45, 46, 97; The Duke of Argyll: 323; The author: 17, 28, 29, 48, 75, 76, 80–2, 92–4, 98, 108, 115–19, 122, 123, 126, 127, 144–9, 168, 169, 176, 177, 180, 183, 184, 186, 188–93, 208, 209, 217, 241, 259–64, 266–73, 276, 306–8, 334–6, 342, 343, 347, 351, 354, 369; Bruce Bailey: 111, 112; Bodleian Library, Oxford: 353; Boston Athenaeum, USA: 156; Bridgeman Art Library, London: 355, 356, 360, 368 (Private Collection), 371 (Stapleton Collection); British Museum, London: 2, 19, 164, 204; The Duke of Buccleuch and Queensberry, KT: 60, 75–7, 79, 122, 123, 126, 127; Burton Constable Foundation: 273, 312, 320; Trustees of the Chatsworth Settlement: 254, 363, 374; Christie's, London: 151, 167, 171–3, 183, 221; The Marquess of Cholmondeley: 144–50, 151, 167–9, 172, 173, 188–94; College of Arms, London: 5; The Colonial Williamsburg Foundation, USA: end-papers, 110, 129, 130, 163, 175, 178, 199, 205, 220, 222, 223, 227–32, 251, 252, 286–93, 338–40, 344, 349, 350; Cooper-Hewitt Museum, New York: 99; Country Life Picture Library, London: 27, 29, 201, 202, 309; Courtauld Institute of Art, University of London: 21; The Ditchley Foundation: 200; The Master and Fellows, Emmanuel College, Cambridge: 14; English Heritage Photographic Library, London: 24, 25, 281, 304, 318, 341; The Syndics of the Fitzwilliam Museum, Cambridge: 294; Isabella Stewart Gardner Museum, Boston, USA: 4; The J. Paul Getty Museum, Los Angeles, USA: 299; Christopher Gilbert: 197, 258; Glasgow Museums, The Burrell Collection: 9, 10; Grimsthorpe and Drummond Castle Trust: 255, 256, 364; The Guildhall Library, London: 53, 207; John Hardy: 314, 315; Jonathan Harris Antiques, London: 85; Historic Royal Palaces Photographic Library (Hampton Court): 83, 84, 87–91, 132–8; Angelo Hornak Library: 198; The Hon. Simon Howard: 105; Christopher Hutchinson: 170, 196, 317, 322, 333; Jarrold Publishing, Norwich (Neil Jinkerson): 150, 185, 187, 194; Lady Lever Art Gallery, Port Sunlight (National Museums and Galleries on Merseyside): 74, 114, 143, 161, 165, 181, 297, 298, 375; Leeds Museums and Galleries, Temple Newsam House: 61, 86, 100–3, 109, 166, 211–15, 235, 240, 244, 245, 337, 357, 373; Leeds, West Yorkshire Archive Service: 234; The Earl of Leicester: 233, 247; Magdalene College, Cambridge, The Pepys Library: 37; Mallett & Sons Ltd, London: 141, 142, 210; The Duke of Marlborough: 295, 296; James Methuen-Campbell: 306–8; Metropolitan Museum of Art, New York: 203, 224, 246, 284, 313; J.R. More-Molyneux: 21; National Gallery, London: 1; National Portrait Gallery, London: 18, 22; National Trust Photographic Library, London: 28, 34, 38, 39, 43, 51, 66–8, 107, 113, 124, 125, 157, 159, 216, 302, 303, John Bethell 15, 16, 31, 128, 158, 160, Andreas von Einsiedel 27, 30, 49, 57, Mark Fiennes 139, 140, 226, Angelo Hornak 44, 104, 239, Horst Kolo 69, James Mortimer 305; The Earl of Pembroke and Montgomery: 7; Philadelphia Museum of Art: 73 (gift of Mrs John T. Dorrance); 274; Arthur Pickett: 120; Hugh Roberts: 255, 256, 295, 363, 364, 374; Rijksprentenkabinet, Rijksmuseum, Amsterdam: 70; The Marquess of Salisbury: 6, 11, 35, 129, 131; The Earl of Shelburne: 314, 315; The Master, Fellows and Scholars, Sidney Sussex College, Cambridge: 8; The Trustees of Sir John Soane's Museum, London: 277, 300, 324; Statens Museum for Kunst, Copenhagen: title-page illustration, 26; L.G. Stopford Sackville: 111, 112, 115–20; Board of Trustees of the Victoria and Albert Museum, London: vi, x, 12, 13, 20, 33, 36, 40–2, 52, 54–6, 58, 59, 62, 71, 72, 78, 95, 96, 155, 162, 179, 195, 218, 219, 225, 236, 238, 242, 243, 248–50, 257, 265, 278–80, 283, 285, 301, 311, 319, 321, 325–9, 330–2, 345, 352, 362, 366, 370, 376; The Duke of Wellington, KG: 365; Annabel Westman: 252; Westminster City Archives/Geremy Butler: 346, 348; The Dean and Chapter, Winchester Cathedral/Michael Jones: 3; Annabel Wylie: 50, 152–4; The Marquess of Zetland: 310.